D1559959

THE WELCOME CLAIMANTS
PROVED, DISPROVED AND DOUBTFUL

PENN'S COLONY:

**Genealogical and Historical Materials Relating
to the Settlement of Pennsylvania**

VOLUME II

The Welcome Claimants
Proved, Disproved And Doubtful

WITH AN ACCOUNT OF
SOME OF THEIR DESCENDANTS

By

GEORGE E. McCRACKEN
Ph.D., F.A.S.G., F.A.A.R.
Professor, Drake University
Editor, *The American Genealogist*

With a Foreword by
WALTER LEE SHEPPARD, JR.
President, The Welcome Society of Pennsylvania

Publications of the Welcome Society of Pennsylvania
Number 2

1985

THE WELCOME SOCIETY OF PENNSYLVANIA

A Facsimile Reprint
Published 1996 by

HERITAGE BOOKS, INC.
1540E Pointer Ridge Place
Bowie, Maryland 20716
1-800-398-7709

ISBN 0-7884-0397-4

A Complete Catalog Listing Hundreds of Titles
On History, Genealogy, and Americana
Available Free Upon Request

CONTENTS

ILLUSTRATIONS

ILLUSTRATION OF WELCOME II

Welcome II is a modern ship to be built in England and sailed to Philadelphia by 1975 by Alan Villers who sailed the *Mayflower II*. The cut has been supplied by the Pennsylvania Historical and Museum Commission which kindly grants permission to print an artist's conception of what the vessel will look like.

FOREWORD

In 1967 the Council of the Welcome Society decided to sponsor the publication of material related to the founding of Pennsylvania and the early years of "Penn's Noble Experiment." The first volume of the Publications included reprints of Mrs. John Balderston's articles on the ships that brought passengers to the Province in the years 1682 and 1683, together with reprints of articles on two families related to this early immigration, and previously unpublished material on the shipping to the New Jersey bank of the Delaware in the preceding years. Also offered were new material on the First Purchasers and new transcriptions of the Bucks and Philadelphia so-called Books of Arrival, and the *Submission* Log.

The second volume of our Publications is a study of all the individuals or families for whom passage on the ship *Welcome*, with William Penn, has ever to our knowledge been claimed, together with an assessment of the claim as proven, disproven, probable or improbable. In the thirties our President Henry Paul Busch suggested as a project that we produce a volume containing the first three generations of descent from all *Welcome* passengers, and the present work largely fulfills this scope. In keeping with our policy, adopted with Volume One, we have not sought to edit either content or conclusions of the authors whose work we offer. Nor do we accept responsibility in any sense for its accuracy. It is our belief that the quality of the works and the subject covered are of sufficient importance and interest that they should be made available to the public, and that the authors should be permitted to speak for themselves, and stand or fall on their own constructions, citing their sources so that the reader may form his own interpretation on the value of the work referenced and the validity of the conclusions.

Dr. George E. McCracken, the author of this work, has been my friend and correspondent for many years. He was born 6 Feb. 1904 in Dunmore, Pa., to Samuel and Phebe (Englert) McCracken. He received the degree of A.B. from Princeton in 1926, A.M. from Lafayette in 1928 and again in 1932 from Princeton, followed in 1933 by his Ph.D. from the same insti-

tution. He is a Fellow of the American Academy in
Rome and of the American Society of Genealogists,
and a lieutenant colonel in the Honorary Reserve,
United States Army. He has taught at Lafayette,
Grove City and Otterbein Colleges, and at Susquehanna and Drake Universities, and has been Visiting
Professor at the University of Texas. He is the
editor of *The American Genealogist*, and has written
articles and reviews too numerous to mention, as
well as five books, of which four are in the field
of patristics and one in ancient history. He has
edited a biography for publication and contributed
articles to the current editions of the *Encyclopaedia Britannica* and several similar publications.

Dr. McCracken became interested in the *Welcome*
and its passengers a number of years ago and has
been collecting and compiling information related
to it ever since. While some of what he says may
seem to be controversial, he has invariably supplied
the evidences on which his conclusions are based,
so that the reader may be aware of the extent of
source material available to him as he wrote. If
in the future new material shall come to light that
may modify some of his conclusions here stated, it
is our hope that such information will be supplied
to the Society so that it may be included by the
author in future editions.

                    WALTER LEE SHEPPARD, JR.

               President, The Welcome Society

The Welcome Society was incorporated at Philadelphia on 21 April 1906. Its purposes include the
"collection and preservation of historic data relative to the settlement of the State of Pennsylvania
and the founding of Philadelphia." Membership in
the Society is limited to the descendants, male or
female, of those persons who came to Pennsylvania
on the ship *Welcome* with William Penn, or any other
ship engaged in the transportation of passengers or
goods primarily to the Colony of Pennsylvania, arriving between 1 July 1682 and 2 November 1682, in-
clusive.

PREFACE

For more than a decade and a half much of my attention has been directed to the fascinating story of the *Welcome* and its passengers. Serious investigation began with the relatively simple problem of finding proof that the Buckman family, from four of whom I descend, was on the *Welcome*, but soon the scope was widened to include all the passengers. My interest was heightened by discovering in a Des Moines book store a copy of the 1864 reprint of the *Memoirs of the Historical Society of Pennsylvania*, vol. 1, in which Edward Armstrong printed the first hypothetical passenger list I had seen.

As a by-product of this undertaking a considerable body of information pertaining to the alleged passengers was gathered, often as bulky for the disproved and doubtful cases as for the proved.

Early in my search it was suggested by Walter Lee Sheppard, not yet President of the Welcome Society, that it would be well to present the evidence pro and con, together with a genealogical account to the third generation, in a book which the Society might sponsor, and after that his enthusiasm for the project was successful in winning consent of the Society to provide for the publication of this volume. For this valued assistance I am deeply grateful, as, without it, the book would probably never have come to light.

The result is a multiple-family genealogy in which, with not many exceptions, the accounts here included are the fullest yet published and in a number of instances the only one. The original goal of continuing the story to the third generation has been achieved except in a few cases where search for the necessary data has failed. In a number of cases the story has been carried further because it was easily possible to do so and seemed desirable.

Though published under the auspices of The Welcome Society, this book is in no sense an "official" document and the list of proved passengers in no way commits the Society. The verdicts given in each case are purely personal. The manuscript has been read, of course, in more than one draft, by Mr. Sheppard, but it has not been subjected to the page-by-page scrutiny of an editorial committee. Many statements in it are likely to be regarded by some as controversial but responsibility for these judgments rests on me alone.

Though every effort has been made to produce a definitive work, the fact that it can only be regarded as tentative has been borne upon me by two recent events. After the final typing of the model for the cameras was two-thirds finished, my attention was called to two additional hypothetical passenger lists, and even after page 599 was completed, names of seven additional claimants were discovered. It has been possible to insert the two lists in the proper place; the seven claimants, however, had to be satisfied with a somewhat hasty and brief treatment in the Addenda on page 600, though they are included in the Recapitulation on pages 25-29 and in the Index.

Now remains the pleasant duty of acknowledging valuable assistance from many friends. Of these, Mr. Sheppard deserves first place, having done most of the preliminary research for a number of sketches and having frequently checked points for me in the archives of the Philadelphia area between my annual visits. The sketches on the Claytons and on the Delaware Cowgills owe much to George Valentine Massey II; similarly, the Croasdale and Dimsdale sketches have been improved by the scrutiny of Milton Rubincam. Miss Helen Stark has supplied some data on the Fitzwaters of New York State. The first draft of the Heaton sketch was written by John Insley Coddington. Henry Hollingsworth's vast knowledge of the family which bears his name has been drawn upon, and the deep debt which I owe to Brigadier O. F. G. Hogg is mentioned last simply because the Penn family, of which he is a member, is alphabetically last. Mrs. Marion Balderston and Mrs. Hannah Benner Roach both answered many a question. My attention has been directed to important evidence by Henry Hollingsworth, Larry F. Mikesell, George Ely Russell and Dr. Elmer G. Van Name. Timothy Field Beard has furnished photographs of books in the New York Public Library and Raymond B. Clarke has searched for a document in Sussex County, Delaware. Mrs. Isaac H. Shelly, when secretary of the Welcome Society, consulted its archives on Joshua Clayton, the only instance in which this source has been exploited. The will of Richard Ingelo was supplied by Meredith B. Colket and other information came from Francis J. Dallett, but my debt to these last-named gentlemen is principally to their writings.

My examination of the Albert Cook Myers Papers

was made possible by Professor Frederick B. Tolles
and Bart Anderson of the Chester County Historical
Society, and a like service was performed in regard
to Mr. Colket's manuscript by George Vaux, then president of the Welcome Society and later by Mr. Sheppard.

I have had the advantage of a grant from the Drake
University Research Fund which made possible a trip
by air to Philadelphia during a spring recess, and
has also relieved me of the drudgery of making car-
bon copies by paying for xerox copies of the manuscript.

Important assistance in the proofreading has been
given me by my wife. She has caught many a slip
which I had missed.

Finally, I hope that the reader will derive as
much enjoyment from the reading of this book as I
have had in its writing.

Des Moines
6 February 1969   George E. McCracken

FREQUENT ABBREVIATIONS

This is in no sense a bibliography of works consulted. Abbreviations of British titles of honor, here omitted, will be found in BPBK. The superscript numerals refer to notes at the end of each sketch and never denote generation numbers.

*	The line from this person is extinct, but the sign is used only with claimants' names and only when certain. Other lines may also be extinct.
†	This person died at sea during the crossing.
BA	Bucks County Administrations, Register of Wills Office, Court House, Doylestown, Pa.
BD	Bucks County Deeds, Recorder's Office, Court House, Doylestown, Pa.
BHBC	J. H. Battle, *History of Bucks County, Pennsylvania* (Philadelphia 1887).
BPBK	*Burke's Peerage, Baronetage and Knightage,* 107th ed. (London 1967), unless other editions are specified.
BW	Bucks County Wills, Register of Wills Office, Court House, Doylestown, Pa.
CA	Chester County Administrations, Register of Wills Office, Court House, West Chester, Pa.
CD	Chester County Deeds, Recorder's Office, Court House, West Chester, Pa.
CW	Chester County Wills, Register's Office, Court House, West Chester, Pa.
DAB	*Dictionary of American Biography.*
DHBC	W. W. H. Davis, *History of Bucks County, Pennsylvania* (Doylestown, Pa., 1st ed., 1876). The second edition (1905) is cited only once.
DNB	*Dictionary of National Biography.* Both editions are identical except for volume and page numbers.
GM	Thomas Allen Glenn, *Merion in the Welsh Tract* (Norristown 1896).
GMNJ	*Genealogical Magazine of New Jersey.*
GWF	Thomas Allen Glenn, *The Welsh Founders of Pennsylvania* (Oxford 1911), vol. 1 (all published).
HEAQG	W. W. Hinshaw and Thomas Worth Marshall, *Encyclopaedia of American Quaker Genealogy* (Ann Arbor 1938), all citations to vol. 2.

JCRFP   John W. Jordan, ed. *Colonial and Revolu-*
          tionary Families of Pennsylvania (New
          York, 3 vols., 1911). Occasionally a ci-
          tation is to a later volume with slight-
          ly different title.

Jen-   Howard M. Jenkins, *The Family of William*
  kins   *Penn, Founder of Pennsylvania, Ancestry*
          and Descendants (Philadelphia 1899), all
          citations to the second printing.

KC   Leon de Valinger, ed., *Calendar of Kent*
          County, Delaware, Probate Records 1680-
          1800 (Dover 1940).

KPC   Charles Penrose Keith, *Provincial Council-*
          lors of Pennsylvania (Philadelphia 1883).

MHSP   *Memoirs of the Historical Society of Penn-*
          sylvania.

MIQ   Albert Cook Myers, *Immigration of the I-*
          rish Quakers into Pennsylvania 1682-1750
          (Swarthmore 1902).

MQA   Albert Cook Myers, *Quaker Arrivals at Phil-*
          ladelphia 1682-1750 (Philadelphia 1902).

NC   Colonial Dames of Delaware, *A Calendar of*
          Delaware Wills, New Castle County, 1682-
          1800 (New York 1911).

NEHGR   *New England Historical and Genealogical*
          Register.

NJA   *New Jersey Archives.*

NJW   *New Jersey Wills* (part of NJA).

NYW   *New York Wills* (in *Collections of the New-*
          York Historical Society).

NYGBR   *New York Genealogical and Biographical*
          Record.

PA   *Pennsylvania Archives.*

PCC   Prerogative Court of Canterbury.

PGM   *Pennsylvania Genealogical Magazine.*

PGSP   *Publications of the Genealogical Society*
          of Pennsylvania.

PhA   Philadelphia County Administrations, Reg-
          ister of Wills Office, City Hall, Phil-
          adelphia, Pa.

PhD   Philadelphia County Deeds, Recorder's Of-
          fice, City Hall, Philadelphia, Pa.

PhW   Philadelphia County Wills, Register's Of-
          fice, City Hall, Philadelphia, Pa.

PHMB   *Pennsylvania Magazine of History and Bio-*
          graphy.

SC   Leon de Valinger, ed., *Calendar of Sussex*
          County, Delaware, Probate Records, 1680-

1800 (Dover 1964).

TAG   *The American Genealogist.*

W&S   Warrants and Surveys, Province of Pennsylvania 1682-1759, Philadelphia City Archives, 7th Floor, City Hall, Philadelphia, Pa.

A NOTE ON DATES

Except when quoting directly, this book expresses
all dates in the order of day, month and year, thus
proceeding from the smallest to the largest and ob-
viating the need for a comma, e.g. "28 Oct. 1682."
When the source uses article, preposition or ordinal,
these are silently omitted, e.g. "the 28th of Oct.
1682" becomes "28 Oct. 1682."

The month is invariably given in letters unless
the source uses the Quaker system which employs digits for the more commonly used month names, e.g.
"28 8th mo. 1682." The month number is then uniformly an ordinal followed by "mo." so as to make clear
which is the day and which the month without need to
consult this note.

As is well known, the Julian calendar was replaced
in England and its possessions by the Gregorian in
September 1752, at which time two changes were made:
(1) a period of eleven days was omitted; (2) New
Year's Day was changed from 25 March to 1 January.
The first of these changes causes no difficulty as
these eleven days are ignored, and all days appear as
in the source, Old Style. The second, however, re-
quires some explanation. In the Julian calendar as
used in this country before 1752, the entire month
of March was designated the first month, April, the
second, and so on, January being the eleventh and
February the twelfth month. Thus, when dealing with
any year before 1752, it is necessary to make clear
which Style is being followed, and the best way to
do this is to use a double year. Thus, "22 Feb.
1731/2" or "22 12th mo. 1731/2" means that the year
was that which those who lived through it called
1731 but which we would now call 1732. In a few instances, the double year will not appear though it
should. This is because it has not always been possible to determine which year is meant. Beginning with
25 March, Old Style and New Style are the same but
sometimes records will be found with a double-year
for a day after 25 March.

THE WELCOME CLAIMANTS
PROVED, DISPROVED AND DOUBTFUL

THE WELCOME CLAIMANTS
PROVED, DISPROVED AND DOUBTFUL
INTRODUCTION
A. THE VOYAGE

Voyages have often been memorable from priority
of date but the *Welcome* in 1682 had been preceded
by other vessels bringing Englishmen to what is now
the United States three quarters of a century earlier;
other Europeans to the Delaware Valley in particular more than forty years before, while Quakers had
begun to arrive in the region during the preceding
decade. Even in the eventful year itself, the *Welcome* was only the eighteenth of twenty-three ships
to reach the infant port of Philadelphia. No important discoveries were made, the North Atlantic run
having by then become routine, if still not without
daring and danger. Furthermore, no document of high
historic import was composed and signed on board,
as had been the case with the *Mayflower* in 1620--
Friends produced many such landmarks of human liberty but not on the *Welcome*. This ship owes its
great fame solely to the fact that among its passengers was the Governor and Proprietor of Pennsylvania, William Penn himself, now arriving in his
American possessions for the first time.

Early in the month of July 1682 Robert Greenway,
master of the *Welcome*, began to load his vessel intending to sail to Pennsylvania,[1] and preparations
for the voyage were reported in various English
newspapers of the time.[2] *The True Protestant Mercury*
No. 168, covering the period 12-16 August 1682,[3]
carried the following:

> Yesterday Mr Penn the Quaker having a Patent
> for the Colony of Pensilvania took his farewell
> of his Friends in London and tomorrow goes on
> board the ship Welcome, and in Order for that Voy-
> [sic] in company of 5 Ships more of the people of
> that perswasion, some of great Estates, and tis
> the most improved Plantation for so short a time
> as one year as has been known, and there is al-
> ready settled 4000 Souls.

On 26 August 1682 the *Loyal Protestant* No. 200 said
this:

> This day William Pen Esq., took his leave of
> his Friends, and departed the Town, in order to
> his Voyage to Pensilvania of which place he is
> Proprietor, having taken along with him many Fam-
> ilies and others, who are gone to settle them-
> selves in that Colony, it being in all probabili-
> ty likely to prove a most plentiful & pleasant
> place to live in.

In the *Epitome of the Weekly News* No. 2 a dispatch
from Deal bearing date of 29 Aug. 1682 appeared:

> Being Wednesday, the Wind East North East,
> William Penn Esq., Sole Proprietor and Governour
> of Pennsilvania, went on Board the *Welcome*, in
> order to his Voyage for that Province, Accompan-
> ied with his Wife and others to Dover Road, where
> they parted: There are Ships from several ports
> preparing to go; and likewise another Ship from
> London, on the Account of the Society of Traders
> in Pennsylvania, which is already fallen down to
> Gravesend, and is to follow after the 10th In-
> stant.

Another dispatch from Deal was given to the public
in the *London Gazette* No. 1753 on 2 September:

> Two days since sailed out of the Downs three
> ships bound for Pensilvania, on board of which
> was Mr. Pen with a great many Quakers, who go to
> settle there.

The ship was of 284 tons burden[4] but the exact
number of passengers which it carried is unknown,
as no contemporary passenger list has survived.[5]
Often the number of "passengers," whatever this im-
precise term may mean, has been alleged to have been
about a hundred but we have seen no contemporary
document which supports this claim, and it appears
to have been first stated in print by Robert Proud,
History of Pennsylvania in North America (Philadelphia 1797), 1:205, where we read:

> The number of passengers in this ship was a-
> bout one hundred, mostly Quakers, the major part
> of them from Sussex, the Proprietary's place of
> residence.

The rest of this statement is quite correct and it

may be that Proud had seen some document reporting
a hundred as the number of the passengers.[6]
During the voyage many of the passengers were
attacked by smallpox. In a letter from James Claypoole in London to Robert Turner in Dublin dated
9 11th mo. 1682/3 and found on page 313 of his letter book preserved at the Historical Society of Pennsylvania,[7] appear these words:

> I suppose thou heard long since of 31 friends
> that dyed in William Pens ship of the smallpox.

The number given is precise and was recorded soon
after the event by one who probably had intelligence from Penn himself--Claypoole and his wife
had attended Penn's first wedding--and there is no
reason to doubt his accuracy, but we have also the
testimony of an eye-witness to the smallpox epidemic, the *Welcome* passenger Richard Townsend who, in
his autobiographical memoir quoted in the sketch
below,[8] speaking of Penn on the voyage, says:

> His singular care was manifested in contribu-
> ting to the necessities of many who were sick on
> board, of small pox, of whom as many as thirty
> died.

Townsend was an old man when he composed these
words, and his memory may not then have been perfect, but thirty or thirty-one is a small difference. Of the dead we can name some: John Barber,
Thomas Heriott, Isaac Ingram and William Wade, all
executed wills on the *Welcome* and presumably died
aboard shortly afterwards; Mary Fitzwater and her
children Josiah and Mary; Grace and Mary, daughters
of Dennis Rochford; three Buckmans, the Widow Joan,
her two sons Edward and Thomas; and John Snashfold,
making a proved total of thirteen, but John Burchel
may also have died on the voyage, and, though less
certainly, Miriam Short the elder, and there may
even have been another Thomas Buckman, eldest son
of William, though he may have died in England.
There is also the rather mysterious William Lushington whose bold and beautiful signature appears as
witness to one of the *Welcome* wills but who has
never been found subsequently in any Pennsylvania
record. If the doubtful cases be included, we have
the names of seventeen dead; if they are excluded,
we have thirteen. As for the rest of the casualties, we shall never know their names, and it is

quite possible that whole families were wiped out.

As will be seen, the ship took a fairly long time to cross the Atlantic, which fact led Henry Darrach[9] to suggest it may have stopped in the A-zores or Canary Islands for repairs. However that may be, it is possible that it stopped earlier at one or another of the Channel ports like Bright-helmston [now Brighton] to take on some of the Sussex passengers--Rochford was living at that port and others lived near, though the Buckmans from Bil-lingshurst had packed their luggage in July, long enough to ship it to London for loading.

It is also possible that in mid-ocean, but after 20 September, the *Welcome* encountered an east-bound vessel on which Penn was able to send letters home. Ships did meet at sea and have communication with each other. For example, the *Submission* spoke with a New England ship bound for Lisbon, on 11 Oct. 1682 as is clear from the log. The basis for thinking that the *Welcome* had a similar experience is the fact that William Wade made a second will on the *Welcome* on the 20th. He had, however, left an ear-lier will in London and this was offered for probate at the Prerogative Court of Canterbury on 28 Octo-ber 1682, the day on which the *Welcome* arrived at Upland, now Chester, Pa. How else could the news that Wade was dead have reached England so soon? If these stops were made and the east-bound vessel was encountered, Townsend did not see fit to recall them in his memoir.

The precise date of arrival also presents some difficulties. One of the passengers, Dennis Roch-ford, afterwards gave the date of his landing as 24 Oct. 1682,[10] and so does Penn in a letter to the Lords of Trade and Plantations.[11] It may well be that Rochford was giving the actual date for arriv-ing the Delaware River. His statement was doubt-less set down not earlier than 1684 and he may have been a bit hazy. In any case, it is certain that the *Welcome* arrived at New Castle, now in Delaware, on 27 Oct. 1682, for under the date of the 28th, we find in Book B, page 437, of the *Records of the Court of New Castle on Delaware* (Meadville, Pa., 1935), 2:21, the following:

On the 27th day of october 1682; arrived be-fore ye Towne of New Castle in Delowar from Eng-land William Penn Esqr Proprietry: of Penlivania . . .ye sd William Penn Received possession of

ye Towne of New Castle ye 28th of octob^r 1682.
This is a contemporary record and can be trusted.
   Having disembarked its passengers at New Castle,
Upland and Philadelphia, the *Welcome* was rather
soon headed out for the Atlantic on the return trip
but still under the command of Robert Greenway. A
letter of Penn to his Cousin [William] Markham under date of 28 9br 1682, about a month after the
arrival, says: "If Robert Greenway be not past that
sd port, I would willingly bespeak with him, having
received a letter out of Maryland yt concerns
Freight of a ship."[12] The subsequent history of the
ship is, however, clouded in mystery. There had been
a *Welcome* of Boston, in England, of course, of 300
tons, which John Winthrop's *Journal* in 1648[13] mentions: "The *Welcome* of Boston about 300 tons, riding
before Charlestown, having in her eighty horses and
120 tons of ballast," and it is discussed in such a
way that we must conclude it was on its way to Barbadoes. This ship's size is curiously close to that
of ours but it is probable that the two were not
identical. In the *Calendar of State Papers Domestic*
in 1678 we read that "Even now arrived from Majorca
the Welcome of London." This might have been Penn's
ship. Two vessels, one a *Welcome* and the other a
Unity, were sold to the English government for use
as hospital ships in 1683,[14] and we should probably
have thought this Penn's ship, were it not for the
fact that this vessel is recorded as of only 78 tons
burden. Moreover, it would hardly seem appropriate
to make a hospital ship out of a vessel which had a
smallpox epidemic aboard the year before! The remark
may be anachronistic in assuming that contagion was
well understood in the 17th century. The *Welcome*
of London is mentioned in 1684 in the *Calendar of
Treasury Books 1681-1685*, vol. 7, pt. 2, p. 1402.
This may also have been our *Welcome* but there is no
proof, and, in any case, this is the last we hear
of it. Greenway had, meanwhile, left the ship and
returned to America where he died.[15]
   A model of the *Welcome*, so entitled, made by the
late Gustavus Wynne Cook, a descendant of the passenger Dr. Thomas Wynne, is in the Maritime Museum,
427 Chestnut Street, Philadelphia, and was shown in
a photograph printed in the Philadelphia *Evening
Bulletin*, Saturday, 19 June 1965, p. G8. We have
heard of another such model but have no details, and
however ingenious the craftsmanship in such models,

important factors must be analogy and guesswork.

B. PENN'S FLEET 1682

In a letter to an unknown person dated 29 Dec. 1682, William Penn wrote of twenty-three ships which had crossed the Atlantic in 1682,[16] and to Lord Keeper North[17] he wrote: "I thank God I am safely arrived, and twenty-two sail more." No special research has been undertaken in connection with this book on the subject of Penn's fleet in 1682 but the following list is taken from Mrs. Marion Balderston's fundamental article on the subject, revised in the light of certain corrections which we understand are to appear in a reprint of these articles which will form part of Welcome Society Publications, Vol. 1. The present list is included here solely for purposes of ready reference.[18]

1. BRISTOL FACTOR, Roger Drew, master, first trip, stopped loading 6 Oct. 1681, left at end of October, arrived at Upland, 15 Dec. 1681. Though this vessel crossed in 1681, it was probably counted in the 23 ships.
2. JOHN AND SARAH, 100 tons, Henry Smith, master, stopped loading 24 Oct. 1681, cleared 11 Nov. 1681, had certainly arrived in the Chesapeake at least by 11 March 1681/2.[19]
3. AMITY, Richard Dymond or Diamond, master, loaded 21 Feb.-15 April 1682, left 23 April 1682, arrived at Upland, 8 Aug. 1682.
4. FREEMAN of Liverpool, George Southern, master, loaded 24 May-7 June 1682, arrived 5-6 Aug. 1682.
5. HESTER AND HANNAH, William East, master,[20] loaded 14 Feb.7 March 1682, left London after 3 March 1682, arrived 6-9 Aug. 1682.
6. LYON, 90 tons, John Compton, master, loaded 22 April-19 May 1682, left Liverpool in May, arrived 13 Aug. 1682.
7. FRIENDSHIP, Robert Crossman, master, loaded 22-30 May 1682, left Liverpool, arrived 14 Aug. 1682.
8. MARY [or MERCY] of Fowey, William Lugger, master, a very small ship, arrived 15 Aug. 1682.
9. SOCIETY of Bristol, Thomas Jordan, master, loaded 12 April-3 May 1682, arrived Aug. 1682.
10. GOLDEN HINDE, Edward Reade, master, arrived by 18 Sept. 1682.

11. SAMUEL, John Adey, master, loaded 12 April-19 May 1682, was at Falmouth, 10 June 1682, arrived by 18 Sept. 1682.

12. FRIENDS' ADVENTURE, Thomas Wall, master, loaded 3 June-4 July 1682, left Liverpool, arrived by 18 Sept. 1682.

13. PROVIDENCE, under 50 tons, Robert Hooper, master, loaded at Scarborough 13 July 1682, was at Falmouth 8 Aug. 1682, arrived 29 Sept. 1682 in the Delaware.

14. ISABELLA ANN KATHERINE, also called ELIZABETH ANN KATHERINE or ELIZABETH or ANN, Thomas Hudson always the master, loaded 1-31 July 1682, at London 4 Aug. 1682, arrived 29 Sept. 1682.

15. HOPEWELL, Michael Yoakley, master, loaded in early July, probably arrived early in October 1682.

16. LAMB of Liverpool, 130 tons, John Tench [or French], master, loaded 26 June 1682, arrived 22 Oct. 1682.

17. BRISTOL FACTOR, Roger Drew, master, second trip, loaded 26 July-26 Aug. 1682, arrived 28 Oct. 1682; came up the Bay with the WELCOME. It was on this ship that Seaborn Oliver was born 24 Oct. 1682, within sight of the Virginia Capes.

18. WELCOME, 284 tons, Robert Greenway, master, loaded 7 July-21 Aug. 1682, arrived 28 Oct. 1682.

19. JEFFREY, about 500 tons, Thomas Arnold, master, loaded 29 August, in the Thames 12 September, left London after 23 September, probably arrived by end of October 1682.

20. ANTELOPE, from Belfast, Edward Coole, master, arrived at Upland, 1 Dec. 1682 or 9-10 Dec. 1682.

21. UNICORN of Bristol, 300 tons, Thomas Cooper, master, loaded 25 Aug.-9 Sept. 1682, ready 5 Oct. 1682, arrived at Upland by 29 Dec. 1682.

22. SUBMISSION, James Settle, master, left Liverpool, 6 7th mo 1682, arrived in the Chesapeake 2 Nov. 1682, landed passengers at Choptank, Md. This voyge of the SUBMISSION is remarkable in that its log has been preserved and contains a complete passenger list, list of the crew, the only such lists preserved for any of the vessels which came to Pennsylvania in early days. Besides the master, the crew were: Sam-

uel Rich, mate; Brian Fleetwood, carpenter;
Anthony Busshell, cook; Elijah Cobham, Thomas
Bullock, Peter Graves, John Royle and Thomas
Haleby, "servants," i.e. seamen; Henry Blevin,
Michael Colon, apprentices.[21]

23. ADVENTURE, Moses Locke, master, loaded for Pennsylvania at London, 16 Sept. 1682; apparently
not registered from London but was in the
Thames for cargo sent by James Cox, a London
merchant; no known passengers.

C. RECONSTRUCTED PASSENGER LISTS

Long before the founding of the Welcome Society
in 1906, great interest was shown in discovering
just who had been on the *Welcome* with William Penn.
The first attempt to reconstruct such a list was by
Edward Armstrong, a prominent nineteenth-century
member of the Historical Society of Pennsylvania,
who, in 1852, published the earliest of many such
attempts. By the time the Society was founded, eight
such lists were in print, and since then many others
have followed. A total of 26 lists of this kind
have been located and examined. They contain serious
discrepancies, as well as numerous errors ranging
from the merely annoying to the supremely astound-
ing. Some compilers have thought it sufficient
merely to list heads of families; others nod to the
wives and children with a phrase like "and family."
On many lists persons are missing whose presence on
the *Welcome* is clearly attested, and persons whose
presence on the vessel can be demonstrated to be at
least highly illusory regularly appear. At least
seven mythical persons are on one or more, sometimes
several, lists. This situation has provided the
fons et origo for this study.

The following is a list of those reconstructions
which have thus far been seen, together with the abbreviations by which the several compilations will
be cited in the text.

A = List by Edward Armstrong, published by him with
the text of his printed address delivered at
Chester, Pa., on 8 Nov. 1851 (Philadelphia 1852).
A total of 94 persons is indicated, of whom ten
are printed out of alphabetical order at the end;
fourteen others are counted but not named; and
two families of unspecified size are listed but
not counted in the ninety-four.

B = List by the same Edward Armstrong, published in
    the Appendix (pages 467-471) of the 1864 reprint
    of the first volume of the *Memoirs of the Histor-
    ical Society of Pennsylvania* (original edition
    1826), Mr. Armstrong being the editor of the re-
    print which contains some material not in the
    1826 edition. This list forms Note I to page 32
    of the reprint which is in the inaugural address
    of William Rawle as president of the Society. Mr.
    Armstrong appears to have forgotten List A which
    he printed twelve years before: "We are not aware
    even of an attempt to collect the scattered in-
    formation on the subject . . ." He speaks of the
    ship as having a hundred passengers, claims in
    his introduction to have found 97 names, but he
    actually prints 99 names and numbers them, and
    these do not include either the master of the
    ship or William Penn, or two groups of children
    of unspecified number. An attempt is made to
    state the evidence for each name but the compiler
    was not critical enough.
C = List printed by Samuel M. Janney, *The Life of
    William Penn with Selections from his Correspon-
    dence and Autobiography* (Philadelphia, 2nd ed.
    rev., 1853), pp. 573 f. This has 73 passengers,
    of whom twelve are unnamed children, and there
    is an unnamed wife and two groups of unnamed and
    unspecified children.
D = List printed by J. Smith Futhey and Gilbert Cope,
    History of Chester County, Pennsylvania (Phila-
    delphia 1881), pp. 21 f. This list has 73 names,
    12 unnamed children, three unnamed wives and one
    unspecified family.
E = List printed by J. Thomas Scharf and Thompson
    Westcott, *History of Philadelphia* (Philadelphia
    1884) 1:99f. Evidence is not stated but there is
    a long negative note on one name. A total of 91
    persons are accounted for, of whom 74 are named,
    and the two families of unspecified size are al-
    luded to. Immediately after this list appears
    another containing the names of 35 men who are
    said to have come "probably about the time of
    William Penn, some before and others immediately
    afterwards, and before the end of 1682," which
    was compiled, but not copied, from Dr. George
    Smith's *History of Delaware County, Pennsylvania*
    (Philadelphia 1862). Of these names only two
    have ever been claimed as *Welcome* passengers,

both falsely, and one demonstrated long ago to
be false.

F = List printed by William J. Buck, *William Penn
in America* (Philadelphia 1888), pp. 62 f. Buck
acknowledges assistance from the then deceased
William F. Corbett and from Dr. E. D. Buckman.
Seventy persons are named, plus three unnamed
wives, two unnamed sisters and 27 unnamed children. Of all the early lists this shows the most
independence and the most critical judgment, but
like almost all the others, it contains some bad
errors.

G = List compiled by Howard M. Jenkins, printed by
John Russell Young, *Memorial History of Philadelphia* (New York 1895), 1:75-80. This list accounts
for 88 persons plus the two families of unspecified size, and names a total of 72 persons. Except for a note on page 42, which describes the
criteria for compilation, evidence is not cited.
Mr. Jenkins was capable of first class historical
research as his book on the Penn family shows.

H = List in Charles Burr Ogden, *The Quaker Ogdens*
(Philadelphia 1898), pp. 30-32. This lists 82
persons, plus 12 unnamed children, two unnamed
wives and two families of unspecified size.

I = List printed by T. B. Deem, *The Wynnes: a Genealogical Summary of the Ancestry of the Welsh
Wynnes, who Emigrated to Pennsylvania with William Penn* (Knightstown, Indiana, 1907), pp. 215f.
Besides the two families of unspecified size,
this accounts for 82 persons of whom 68 are
named. This book is far from satisfactory and
should not be used without verification of every
statement.

J = List printed anonymously on a single sheet of
paper, apparently the first official list put out
by the Welcome Society of Pennsylvania after the
founding, since it contains a plea for members.
An exemplar of this printing was seen in 1961 in
the Papers of the late May Atherton Leach in the
Genealogical Society of Pennsylvania. What was
probably another exemplar was seen in 1959 in
the Papers of the late Albert Cook Myers at the
Chester County Historical Society but was not
copied. This list contains forty names, to which
are added six unnamed wives and seven families
of unspecified size.

K = This list is available in two nearly identical

forms: (a) a single sheet printed by the Welcome
Society bearing date of Philadelphia, 14 Jan.
1907, in the form of a report of the Committee
on Ancestral Eligibility appointed 22 Oct. 1906,
the names being in upper and lower case letters,
followed by commas; (b) a reprint of the same,
completely reset, however, with a misprint corrected but otherwise identical, made somewhat
after 1910. To the first printing Joshua Clayton's name has been added by rubber stamp; in
the second, in printed form. Copies of both
forms were seen in the Albert Cook Myers Papers.
There are forty names in the list, with five unnamed wives and five unspecified families. Though
the tabulation comes out the same as for List N,
the names are not identical.

L = List by an unknown writer, published in the Philadelphia *Evening Bulletin*, 23 May 1932, clipping
seen at the Genealogical Society of Pennsylvania.
This list contains 41 names, plus six unnamed
wives and eight unspecified families.

M = List printed by Joseph Jackson, *Encyclopaedia of
Philadelphia* (Harrisburg 1933) 4:1181-1184. This
contains 74 names, plus three unnamed wives, 14
unnamed children and three unspecified families.
Though not quite the worst list of all, it surely
is the runner up and shows no knowledge later
than Armstrong's time.

N = List printed in Henry Paul Busch, ed., *The Welcome Society of Pennsylvania, Records and Activities* (Philadelphia 1940), pp. 85f., List of Ancestors. This has forty names, five of them with
unnamed wives and five with unspecified families,
but is not identical with List K which has the
same totals. Sixteen of the "passengers" then had
descendants among the members of the Society.
Though it is known that Mr. Busch was in communication with the compiler of List O, there is no
evidence to show it.

O = List compiled by Meredith B. Colket Jr. in a report which he made to Henry Paul Busch in 1940
and never published. Mr. Colket put 56 names on
his list but added three more about whom he was
doubtful, and rejected twelve heads of families
found among his predecessors' lists. He also
called attention to a number of claims for persons for whom he could present no evidence either
way, most, if not all, of whom had been on no

list. A copy of this report was shown me in 1963
by the then President of The Welcome Society, Mr.
George Vaux, and at that time I made notes on the
list. In 1966 a copy of the report was made a-
vailable to me for protracted study. This is the
ablest study of the problem thus far seen, but
it should be pointed out that it did not come into my hands until my own study was largely complete. Even so, the number of occasions when Mr.
Colket and I reached independently the same unor-
thodox conclusion is large.
P = List found in an offprint from the Welcome Soc-
    iety Year Book for 1944. This list has 41 names,
    five unnamed wives and seven unspecified families.
Q = This list is a work sheet found at the beginning
    of the Welcome Papers of the late Albert Cook
    Myers now in the Chester County Historical Soci-
    ety, West Chester, Pa. In 1959 I had a hurried
    glimpse of the list and copied it, and in 1963
    I had sufficient time for careful study of the
    two volumes of scrapbook type in which Mr. Myers
    had for many years collected information bearing
    on the problem. The list referred to was from
    time to time increased or decreased in accordance
    with Mr. Myers' changing opinions. Two groups of
    names were crossed out and the word 'no' put in
    the margin opposite two other groups. The list,
    as separate from the Papers themselves, contains
    47 names, with the names of 13 wives and twenty
    children. In addition, one unnamed wife and 19
    unnamed children are accounted for. A total of
    22 persons are either cancelled or marked 'no.'
    In the Papers as a whole there is nowhere any
    discussion of the validity of any claim. Mr.
    Myers was for many years an able and informed
    genealogist specializing in the Philadelphia
    area. He was still living when I did my earlier
    work on the problem but was aged and infirm and
    no contact was ever made with him personally. My
    knowledge of the Papers was not obtained until a
    very advanced stage of my own research. One who
    knew Mr. Myers well for a long period has stated
    that Mr. Myers was fond of claiming that he had
    a true list of the *Welcome* passengers, by which
    my informant understood him to mean an authentic
    document of contemporary date. No such list was
    found in the Papers and it is obvious that had
    Mr. Myers possessed one, he would hardly have

continued interest in a hypothetical reconstruction.

R = A list signed by "V.M." and printed in the Philadelphia *Evening Bulletin* ca. 1951, clipping seen
at the Genealogical Society of Pennsylvania. This
has a total of 39 heads of families but no wives
nor children are shown. Four other names are here
called controversial and one of the 39 names is
questioned.

S = A list in the Welcome Society Year Book for 1956,
pp. 52f. A total of 44 heads of families appear,
plus five wives and seven unspecified families.

T = A list in the Welcome Society Year Book for 1960,
pp. 58f. This also has 44 heads of families, five
unnamed wives and seven unspecified families.

U = A list compiled by me from data in Marion Balderston's article, "The Real *Welcome* Passengers"
(*The Huntington Library Quarterly* 26 [1962] 31-
56). This article is a valuable contribution to
our knowledge, since it contains evidence from
the English Port Books of the Port of London. A
total of 90 names are discussed but of these 43
are rejected and doubt is expressed by others. I
knew nothing of Mrs. Balderston's work until it
was in proof stage. In some instances I am in
disagreement with her conclusions but only where
she leaves the solid ground of the Port Books and
uses secondary sources for passengers not recorded
in the Port Books. Note also should be made of
her later articles, "William Penn's Twenty-Three
Ships, with Notes on Some of their Passengers"
(PGM 23:27-67), and "Pennsylvania's 1683 Ships
and Some of their Passengers" (PGM 24:69-114),
As these pages are being typed for the press, it
is expected that there will be a reprinting of
her articles, doubtless with some revisions, and
also a new article on earlier ships in the Welcome
Society Publications 1. Unfortunately, I have not
had the text of the volume in question in my hands.

V = List in the Welcome Society Year Book for 1964,
pp. 65-68. This list contains the names of 59 passengers as officially accepted by the Society in
1964, plus 71 other persons who came over on other
ships, most of whom were formerly believed to

have come on the *Welcome*. Even this list was not
quite perfect, since Ezra Croasdale was wrongly
placed under the children of Thomas Croasdale,
an error for which I was myself largely responsible, since it was copied from a list I had made
before I had thoroughly studied the Croasdales.
Mr. Sheppard, however, informs me that this error
was corrected in subsequent printings.
W = List printed in *The Pennsylvania Traveller*, Vol.
3, No. 1, Nov. 1966, edited by Richard T, and
Mildred C. Williams, of Hialeha, Florida, which
was kindly called to my attention by Mr. George
Ely Russell. It has 41 names, plus seven families shown as "and family," five as "and wife,"
and one as "children." It has obviously been copied from List L. That these "are the passengers
which have been accepted by the Welcome Society
of Philadelphia" is a statement that has not been
true for many years.
X = A list printed by H. Stanley Craig, *Salem County,
New Jersey, Genealogical Data* (Merchantville, N.J.,
no date but pre World War I). This list was first
called to my attention by Mr. Henry Hollingsworth.
This extraordinary document is the longest list,
having 121 names, one unnamed wife, one unspecified family and 22 unnamed children, a total of
144 persons without counting the unspecified
family [that of Cuthbert Hayhurst for whom we must
add a wife and five children], a grand total of
150 souls. It is also the worst. Of these 150
persons, 43 appear here for the first and only
time, and except for one possible instance (Robert
Saylor), the claimant can be shown by documentary
evidence of unimpeachable validity to have come
on another ship. For many of these shanghaied
names, there is no evidence of the very existence
of the person except the document that proves the
presence on another ship. As a sample of this
list at its very worst, consider the Robert Turner
family. Robert had a wife and daughter, both named
Martha. The wife died in Ireland in 1682 and her
husband came on the *Lion* in 1683, but Craig puts
the dead wife on that vessel and the husband and
daughter on the *Welcome*.

More than four hundred pages of this book were already ready for the printer when the following

two lists were first discovered, necessitating much
work to insert them here in their proper place and
to refer to them in the several sketches wherever
required.

Y = A list which appears on page 358 of a work which
    was printed in New York in 1934 under the title
    of *White's Conspectus of American Biography* but
    which is sometimes referred to as *A Conspectus
    of American Biography*. The volume forms part
    of *The National Encyclopaedia of American Bio-
    graphy* as a supplement, and sometimes in libra-
    ries is shelved with it, sometimes not. There
    are 77 names, two unnamed wives, two unspecified
    families and nine unnamed children. No source
    for the list is cited but I am inclined to think
    that it was copied from List L, which had been
    printed two years earlier, but with some items
    drawn from some other source.

Z = A list which appeared in partial form in Clark
    Kinnaird's syndicated feature called "Your Ame-
    rica" which was printed in *The Des Moines Regis-
    ter* on 10 Sept. 1968. This column was devoted
    to the *Welcome* and says, among other things,
    that among the passengers were persons bearing
    certain specified names, thirteen in all, of
    which nine are of *bona fide* passengers accepted
    in this book, one doubtful and three disproved.
    The article offered to send, for a stamped,
    self-addressed envelope, a leaflet with complete
    list of passengers, and a copy of the leaflet
    was obtained and it is this list which we de-
    signate as List Z. The leaflet is No. 29 Sup-
    plement to United States History Series. It
    states that this list was derived from *A Con-
    spectus of American Biography*, a work which
    was then unknown to me and which I had diffi-
    culty in locating, though I frequent three
    libraries which have it. Courteous and interes-
    ted correspondence has been had with Mr. Kin-
    naird himself, which I gratefully acknowledge.
    List Z, however, is not identical with List Y,
    having only 74 names, as against 77 in List Y,
    plus two unspecified families, three unnamed
    wives and nine unidentified children.

These twenty-six lists have, of course, no probative value but every name in each of them has had to
be scrutinized for clues.

D. THE SOURCES

While the sources used in this study have been
many and varied, "scattered," as, indeed, Edward
Armstrong said long ago, a few generalizations can
be made.

First of all, the four wills executed aboard the
Welcome provide us with the names of testators, witnesses, and a few beneficiaries, all of whom may be
presumed to have been present when the wills were
made. In addition, one Friends certificate of removal must have been in possession of the owner on
board since he obtained from William Penn an indorsement bearing date when the ship was at sea.

Secondly, in the year 1684 the Provincial Legis-
lature enacted a statute requiring residents to record their names, the name of the vessel on which
they had crossed the Atlantic and the names of the
servants brought with them together with their terms
of service. This statute ought to have provided us
with what would be tantamount to a census, but unfortunately only a relatively few residents complied
with it.

As a result, however, we have three important
documents available for our purpose. The first of
these is a Register of Arrivals made in Philadelphia
County, largely in a hand identified by some as that
of James Claypoole but certainly in other hands as
well. This document was presented to the Historical
Society of Pennsylvania in 1852 by Joshua Francis
Fisher. Its text has been printed in J. Smith Futhey and Gilbert Cope, *History of Chester County, Pennsylvania* (Philadelphia 1881), pp. 22-24, and again
in *Pennsylvania Magazine of History and Biography*
8:328-340. These printed versions leave much to be
desired and whenever the document is cited in our
text, it is the original document which has been
used, even though for the benefit of those who may
not have access to the original, reference to the
printed versions is given. The text is also to be
reprinted in a much improved transcription by Mrs.
Hannah Benner Roach in the Welcome Society Publications, vol. 1, but we have not seen this transcription.

The second document is a similar Register of Arrivals made in Bucks County and is entirely in the
handwriting of Phineas Pemberton, first Clerk of
Courts in that county. It exists in two contemporary

copies, both in Pemberton's hand, and they are
largely, if not entirely, identical in text. The
first form is now preserved in the Historical Society of Pennsylvania, though how it came to be there
is unknown to me. This may be the report of Phineas
Pemberton to Christopher Taylor, the Register General of the Province of Pennsylvania. Pemberton,
however, also kept his own records which he did not
forward to Taylor. They remained in his possession
when he ceased to be Clerk of Courts, though they
ought to have been turned over to his successor. After his death, they were preserved by the Pemberton
family and in the year 1843 were discovered to be
then in the keeping of James Pemberton Park, Esq.
The fact that Mr. Park had them was made known to
the judges of the Bucks County Courts who directed
that efforts be made to have the records themselves
returned to the county, and through the good offices
of Charles Roberts, Esq., Mr. Park graciously consented to return them to the custody of Bucks County.
At this time copies were made in a beautiful hand,
one for Mr. Park, the other for Mr. Roberts. One of
these copies was in 1938 bequeathed by Miss Elizabeth Ely of Lambertville, New Jersey, to the Bucks
County Historical Society in Doylestown, Pennsylvania
where it now is. The copy is fairly close to the
original though not perfect. The story of how the
papers were found and returned is contained in a
report to the Bucks County Court signed by Wm Carr,
dated at Doylestown, 6 Feb. 1843, appended to the
Ely copy. The original papers ought then to be in
the custody of the Clerk of Courts of Bucks County,
but they are not. They, too, are now in the Bucks
County Historical Society, beautifully laminated so
that they can be examined with ease and without danger to the papers. The paper, however, is now so
brown that photographs are impossible.

What these papers consist of is a small book of
Pemberton's early records, containing "A register
of the Wills and Letters of Administration 1684-
1693--First Minute Book of the Court of Common Pleas
and Quarter Sessions," with other memoranda including
a number of Quaker marriage certificates, copied
verbatim, even with the witnesses' names; two or
three wills and, of course, the Register of Arrivals.

This version of the Bucks Register of Arrivals was
followed in printing the text in *Pennsylvania Magazine of History and Biography* 9:223-232, and not, as

claimed in that printing, the version now preserved
in the Historical Society of Pennsylvania. In the
Collections of the Genealogical Society of Pennsylvania is a manuscript volume bound as "Bucks County,
Pennsylvania, Arrivals, Marriages &c, 1677-1686."
This is a copy of the Doylestown records, though a
note in the book signed "C.H.C" again claims that
it was copied from the original in the Historical
Society of Pennsylvania. It agrees most often with
the Doylestown version, not with the Philadelphia.

The three documents just described provide us with
some positive evidence: two families on the *Welcome*
are recorded in the Claypoole Register; several others in the Pemberton register, and, of course, there
is a good deal of negative evidence in both, e.g.
records that given persons crossed on other ships.

Another document giving valuable evidence of a
negative kind is the Log of the *Submission*, the
original of which is also in the Historical Society
of Pennsylvania, and the text printed as the first
article in the first volume of the *Publications of
the Genealogical Society of Pennsylvania*, which provides proof of the presence on that ship of those it
names. A new and improved transcript is expected in
the Welcome Society Publications, vol. 1.

In the third place, there is now available a certain body of evidence, great in extent for all ships
but rather limited in the case of the *Welcome*, which
until lately was hidden in the English Port Books
now published by Mrs. Marion Balderston. In no case
do these records give a complete passenger list of
any ship, but only of such persons as shipped goods
for trade, whether passengers or not. As a matter of
fact, many such shippers never came to America at
all. It may, however, be inferred that, if a man
shipped goods on a given ship, and he can later be
found in Pennsylvania at the right time, with no
conflicting evidence, he also crossed on that ship.
In the Port Books also, there is again much negative
evidence. As for positive evidence in the case of
the *Welcome*, the Port Books provide the names of two
persons we should not otherwise have suspected.

Finally, the Warrants and Surveys of the Province
of Pennsylvania 1682-1759, now in the Philadelphia
City Archives on the seventh floor of City Hall,
provide much information concerning the sale of land
by William Penn and his officials, and in some instances the information is pertinent to our purpose.

The same is true for the Minutes of the Board of
Property printed in the *Pennsylvania Archives,* Second Series, vol. 19. While these never provide the
name of the ship, they frequently state the original
residence in England of the purchaser. When land
rights were sold by Penn before he came to America,
the buyer is termed a "First Purchaser" and the
names of such people are printed by Samuel Hazard
in *Pennsylvania Archives,* First Series, vol. 1, and
in his *Annals of Pennsylvania* (Philadelphia 1850),
pp. 637-642. What appears in *Pennsylvania Archives,*
Third Series, vols. 1-3, seems to be an inferior
rehash of the same records. It should be remembered
that what was purchased in this way was not actual
tracts of land described with metes and bounds, but
simply rights to a given number of acres which had
later to be located, surveyed and recorded in the
land office.

Catherine Owens Peare, whose *William Penn a Biography* is otherwise an admirable work, has manufactured her own definition of "First Purchaser," namely, one who settled in Pennsylvania from the time of
the colony's founding through 1685, but this is not
the commonly accepted meaning of the term. She
prints information concerning the proportion of the
city lot which was given to all purchasers of farm
land, i.e. 10 acres for every 500 acres. Purchasers
of 5000 could have a township. Every purchaser had
to plant his land within three years or forfeit. The
cost of a propriety of 5000 acres was £100, and for
each servant the master would get 50 acres at 4/-
yearly quit rent, and the servant would himself get
50 acres at 2/- yearly quit rent.

E.   THE SETTLE CERTIFICATE

A considerable number of *Welcome* claims rest on
the authority of a document known as "the Settle
Certificate," a Friends certificate of removal issued on 7 4th mo. 1682 by the Settle Monthly Meeting
in Yorkshire to a group about to go to America. Efforts to locate the original paper brought to Pennsylvania in 1682 have thus far failed. This particular certificate is remarkable in that it covers by
far the largest number of persons of any we have
seen, namely, seven families in eight households,
comprising at least forty individuals, and possibly
one or two more, since there are some doubtful cases.
It is to be presumed that all the persons named or

implied in the certificate were intending to cross
the Atlantic on the same ship, since if they did
not, it would be entirely possible for the ship on
which the certificate was carried to be lost, and
those who had travelled on another ship would arrive
without the necessary document in their possession.
It may thus be inferred that if one of the persons
named can be shown not to have been aboard the *Welcome*, none of the others was. As a result, we must
here discuss the Settle certificate as a unit in order to avoid repetition of the same information at
least seven times.

So far as is known, the document was first mentioned in print by Isaac Comly in his "Sketches of
the History of Byberry" (*Memoirs of the Historical
Society of Pennsylvania* 2 [1827], pp. 182 f.). He
there stated that the original was then in the possession of Robert Waln, Esq., a man whom we identify
as the merchant, manufacturer and politician, the
Hon. Robert Waln, born 22 Feb. 1765, died 25 Jan.
1836, son of Robert and Rebecca (Coffin) Waln, the
father being son of Richard and grandson of Nicholas
Waln, both of whom were covered in the certificate,
to say nothing of collateral ancestors also so covered.[22] Comly asserts "on the authority of the above
named gentleman [the younger Robert] that this party
of Friends came to this country in the ship Welcome,
with William Penn." No other testimony has been adduced to support the claim, though it was long accepted as the Law and the Gospel.

Now Robert Waln was born only 83 years after the
voyage of the *Welcome*, and might have talked personally in his childhood with some of those who had
been children on the *Welcome*, and he could easily
have talked with grandchildren of the adult passengers. His testimony is therefore not inherently
impossible, and it is an undoubted fact that this
group from Settle did cross the ocean in 1682 and
about the time of the *Welcome's* voyage.

In addition to Comly's text, the certificate has
been printed, to our knowledge, at least four times.
The text, without any of the names, is in James Bow-
den's *History of the Society of Friends in America*
(London 1854), 2:15f. According to William John
Potts of Camden, New Jersey, "Brief Extracts from
Wills, etc., of Bucks County, Penn., in the County
Offices at Doylestown" (*New York Genealogical and
Biographical Record* 24:81-84), the late Dr. Edward

D. Buckman transcribed the text in his "Abstracts
of the Records of the Friends Meeting of the Middletown Bucks County, Penna," a manuscript said to be
in the Historical Society of Pennsylvania. I have
examined what I take to be the cited manuscript,
though it does not bear Dr. Buckman's name. The text
of the certificate printed by Mr. Potts presumably
derives from the Buckman transcript. Another text
was printed by Dr. John W. Jordan, *Colonial and Revolutionary Families of Pennsylvania* (New York 1911),
1:297, and this I now think was also derived from
the Buckman transcript. Still another text, probably
derived from Comly's version, ostensibly being followed, though with variations and deletions, appears
in Clarence Vernon Roberts' *Ancestry of Clarence
Vernon Roberts and Francis A. (Walton) Roberts* (Philadelphia, privately printed, 1940), pp. 282-284.

It would seem that the only person who can have
studied the original since Comly's day is Dr. Buckman, and I am inclined to think that even he saw only the Middletown copy. This was for many years in
the custody of the Meeting, but is now in the Department of Records, Third and Arch Streets, Philadelphia, where I have examined it. This text is the
form used throughout this study as the most nearly
primary form of the certificate now available. It
is clearly a contemporary copy of the original paper
which crossed the Atlantic, and it is worthy of trust
until some one discovers the original text written
in Yorkshire which, if extant, probably is owned by
some member of the Waln family. Attempts to make
contact with known Waln descendants have not located
the document.

Unfortunately, the printed versions are not identical. Some of the differences may be due to hap-
hazard handling of spelling and punctuation, but
there are serious divergences even as to the names
covered and in the signatures of the document. Some
names are omitted in certain of the versions, and
the Roberts text does not even pretend to be complete but runs only to the point where the names of
Mr. Roberts' ancestors are given and then stops.
The name of William Hayhurst, for example, comes
last but appears only in the Middletown, the Buckman-Potts and the Jordan versions. Apparently
William was omitted in the others on the mistaken
belief that he was Cuthbert Hayhurst's son, which he
was not.

Inquiries have been made to see whether the Minutes of the Settle Monthly Meeting might contain a
reference to the certificate, if not a copy of it.
The actual minutes were located by Mr. R. V. Perry-
man of 35, Vesper Lane, Leeds, in the Strong Room,
Carlton Hill Meeting, Leeds, but in the minutes for
7 4th mo. 1682, which are extant, no granting of a
certificate to a Friend going to America is shown,
nor any in a subsequent meeting before 1685. This
fact means, of course, not that there is anything
spurious about the certificate but simply that the
clerk thought it unnecessary to record issuance of
such a certificate.
On page 1 of Certificates [the volume has several
series of page numbers for various types of record]
in the Middletown [Bucks County] Minutes, now at the
Department of Records, Third and Arch Streets, Philadelphia, the names of the persons covered in the
certificate were read by me as follows:

> Cuthbert Hayhurst (his wife and family)
> Nicholas Waln his wife and three children
> Thom Wriglesworth and Alice his wife
> Thom walmesley Elizabeth his wife and [six]
>   children
> Tho: Croasdill Agnes his wife and Six children
> Tho: Stackhouse [and] his wife
> Ellin Cowgill widdow and her children
> William Hayhurst

The reason for the separation of William Hayhurst
from his brother Cuthbert is the fact that William
was a childless widower. The party consisted of six
couples, two of them childless, one widow with children and one widower without. Immediately below this
certificate, on the same page and from the same Settle Meeting and on the same date, is shown another
certificate for a man named Heaton and wife Alice,
children not mentioned, the man's name being no
longer legible but it must have been Robert. The
fact that two separate certificates were issued by
Settle Meeting on the same day lends further support
to the view that the seven families named in the
first certificate were a strongly united group, intending to travel together, but the Heatons, all of
whose unmentioned children are known to have been
born in Yorkshire, did not belong to this group, and
so got a separate certificate.
The eight households were largely related to each

other, only the Croasdales not being clearly indicated by evidence to be related to the others, though
they may have been. Cuthbert Hayhurst and his brother William had married sisters; another sister was
the mother of Nicholas Waln; and a cousin of the
three sisters was Elizabeth Walmesley, wife of Thomas, while Alice Wriglesworth was a sister of Cuthbert and William Hayhurst. Ellen Cowgill was perhaps
a sister of Thomas Stackhouse. These relationships
say nothing of the intermarriages within this group
which were destined to take place in Bucks County,
of which several will be discovered in the respective sketches.

If this were all the evidence uncovered, the Settle group would have been entitled to a verdict of
"probably on the *Welcome*," despite the fact that to
put them aboard would have necessitated a long and
perhaps dangerous journey by land from Yorkshire to
the Thames. A northern port would have been the most
natural point of departure for a Yorkshire group.

There is, however, more evidence and this entirely
negative. List Q, prepared by the late Albert Cook
Myers, includes all the persons named in the certificate except the William Hayhurst mentioned at the
end, but the entry for the Croasdales is crossed out
and there is a 'no' in the margin against the names
of the Hayhursts and Walns--there is no such qualification against any of the other Settle names. Undoubtedly, Mr. Myers at one time accepted the testimony of Robert Waln but later, in some cases, at any
rate, came to doubt it. What led him to that doubt
is unknown but it is possible to give some inkling
of what may have caused the skepticism, not for all
the list, but at least for the Croasdales.

Somewhat more than thirty years ago Mr. Myers informed Walter Lee Sheppard Jr. that he knew that the
Croasdales were not on the *Welcome* because "Eleanor
Pownall had the stomach ache," or words to that effect. This cryptic remark was interpreted to mean
that Mr. Myers had discovered some account of the
voyage by a member of the Croasdale family in which
allusion was made to Eleanor Pownall's indisposition,
a fact presumably known only to her fellow passengers. If this information were genuine and significant, this would suggest that the Settle group, at
least the Croasdales, had crossed on the *Friends'
Adventure* for George Pownall had recorded in "Bucks
Arrivals"[23] that he and his family had crossed on

that ship, Thomas Wall, master, arriving 28 7th mo.
1682. It was therefore expected that when Mr. Myers'
Papers could be examined at the Chester County Historical Society, we should discover the document to
which Mr. Myers had referred, but when the Papers
were examined by me in 1963 and independently by
Mr. Sheppard, no such document was found, not only
with reference to the Croasdales but in the entire
collection.

Another family covered by the Settle certificate
was headed by the Widow Ellen Cowgill and included
her children, names and number not specified. Dr.
Jordan, who never doubted that the Settle party came
on the *Welcome*, nevertheless pointed out that the
widow's eldest son Ralph had come as a servant on
the *Friends' Adventure*, though it seems not to have
occurred to him that the widow and her other children might have come on that same ship. That this is
what happened is not demonstrated, however, since
Ralph's passage on this ship was doubtless arranged
by his master, Randulph Blackshaw, who, with his
family, came on the *Submission*. Yet it was at least
worth noting that in the case of both Croasdales and
the Cowgills, the negative evidence, such as it was,
pointed to a single ship, not to two different ones.
The late Alfred R. Justice[24] believed that the Settle group did come on the *Friends' Adventure*, and
the same view was held by George Norwood Comly in his
Comly Genealogy.[25]

What evidence Mr. Myers had for his skepticism as
to the Hayhursts and Walns is unknown. Apparently,
he never rejected all the Settle group, simply because he was forced to reject some of them, since
no negative mark appears in List Q against the name
of the Stackhouses, the Walmsleys and the Wigglesworths.

These considerations tended to make me, and I suppose most of the better informed students of Pennsylvania genealogy, extremely skeptical of *Welcome*
claims for the whole Settle group, and this was the
state of my thinking when Mrs. Marion Balderston
published her epochal article, "The Real *Welcome*
passengers,"[26] in which she gave to the world a hint
of what would soon after appear in fuller form in
her "William Penn's Twenty-Three Ships,"[27] namely,
the evidence from the English Port Books showing
that four of the families named in the Settle certificate had loaded merchandise on the *Lamb* of Liver-

pool. Moreover, it was long known that James Dilworth had crossed on that ship, as he himself had recorded, and when the Waln family was studied, it was discovered that Dilworth's wife was a sister of Nicholas Waln, though the Dilworths, as Lancashire people, did not appear in the Settle certificate.

It therefore seems inescapable that the Settle Friends crossed the Atlantic on the *Lamb*, a ship from a northern port, and not, as long suspected, on the *Friends' Adventure*, or, as much longer believed, on the *Welcome*. The *Friends' Adventure*, to be sure, also sailed from a northern port, even the same port and about the same time as the *Lamb*, but the critical fact is that no member of the Settle party loaded on the *Friends' Adventure*, whereas some did on the *Lamb*.

The explanation of Mr. Myers' cryptic remark about the indisposition of Eleanor Pownall remains to be found. No document of this kind has been preserved among Croasdale descendants.

F. THE CLAIMANTS

This study has not been limited to persons whose presence on the *Welcome* can be proved but includes all who have been so claimed whether truthfully or falsely, and a few others now listed for the first time who might have been passengers. The word 'passenger' should here be understood to include those who were born or died during the voyage, and no distinction can be made between passengers and crew, since in this case the name of only one member of the crew is known, namely, the master, Robert Greenway.

In order to facilitate use of the book, a single series has been adopted, rather than several series separated according to the verdict reached after careful study of the evidence in each case. Cross references have been added to persons in each family who bore different surnames. In each case I have expressed my own opinion as to the validity of the evidence. Though some of the cases have been discussed with persons mentioned in the preface. each of the verdicts is mine and mine alone and commits no one else. It is hoped that the discussion will be convincing but there is no surety of this.

To recapitulate these verdicts we print now the names of all the claimants, classified according to the respective verdicts, as follows:

A. *PROVED*

John Barber   Isaac Ingram
Elizabeth Songhurst Barber   Thomas Jones
Joan Bagham Buckman   William Lushington
Edward Buckman   Jeane Matthews
Thomas Buckman   Hannah Mogeridge
William Buckman   Joshua Morris
Sarah Buckman   David Ogden
Sarah Buckman   John Ottey
Mary Buckman   Eleonor Pain
Ruth Buckman   William Penn
Thomas Fitzwater   James Portiff
Mary Cheney Fitzwater   Dennis Rochford
Thomas Fitzwater   Mary Heriott Rochford
George Fitzwater   Mary Rochford
Josiah Fitzwater   Grace Rochford
Mary Fitzwater   John Rowland
Thomas Gillett   Priscilla Sheppard Rowland
Bartholomew Green   Thomas Rowland
Robert Greenway   William Smith
Nathaniel Harrison   John Snashfold
Jeffrey Hawkins   John Songhurst
Dorothy Hawkins   George Thompson
Roger Hawkins   Richard Townsend
James Hawkins   Ann Hutchins Townsend
Daniel Hawkins   Hannah Townsend
Jeffrey Hawkins   James Townsend
Susanna Hawkins   William Wade
Elizabeth Hawkins   Zachariah Whitpaine
Thomas Heriott   Joseph Woodrooffe
Richard Ingelo   Thomas Wynne

B. *HIGHLY PROBABLE*

Jane Batchelor   Robert Smith
Benjamin Chambers   Mary Songhurst
Philip Theodor Lehnmann   Sarah Songhurst
Adam Short   John Songhurst
Miriam Short   John West
Ann Short   Elizabeth Chorley Wynne

C. *POSSIBLE*

John Burchel   Ann Stone Pusey
Benjamin Duffield   Ann Pusey
Roger Hawkins   Miriam Ingram Short
Sarah Hawkins   John Whitpaine
Hannah Ogden   Ann Whitpaine
Sarah Ogden   Francis Worley
Caleb Pusey   Henry Worley

D. *POSSIBLE BUT RATHER IMPROBABLE*

Thomas Buckman   Elizabeth Chambers
John Carver   Anne Gibbon
Mary Lane Carver   John Gilbert
John Chambers   John Houlston
                 Margaret Scott

E. *IMPROBABLE*

Samuel Barker   Mary Dutton
John Dutton   Mary Haworth

F. *HIGHLY IMPROBABLE*

William Bradford   Robert Hall
Elizabeth Towle Bradford   Elizabeth Hall
Henry Comly   George Hall
Joan Tyler Comly   Elizabeth Hall
Henry Comly   Thomas Ingals
Hugh David   Thomas Mann
Anthony Duché   Benjamin Mendenhall
----- Duché   George Mendenhall
George Emlen   John Mendenhall
John Fisher   Lancelot Strawn
Margaret Fisher   William Townsend
John Fisher   Daniel Wharely
Thomas Fisher   John Wynne

G. *DISPROVED*

Benjamin Acton   Agnes Hathownthwaite
Mary Ashmead   Croasdale
John Ashmead   William Croasdale
Mary Currier Ashmead   John Croasdale
Randall Blackshaw   Elizabeth Croasdale
Lemuel Bradshaw   Mary Croasdale
John Brearly   Bridget Croasdale
Alice Cales   Alice Croasdale
James Claypoole   Ezra Croasdale
Joshua Clayton   Richard Curtis
Benjamin Clift   Edmund Cutler
Margaret Colvert   Isabel Cutler
William Conduit   Elizabeth Cutler
Ellen Cowgill   Thomas Cutler
Jane Cowgill   William Cutler
Jennet Cowgill   Jacob Davis or Dawes
John Cowgill   Ann Ashmead Davis or Dawes
Edmund Cowgill   Robert Dimsdale
Ralph Cowgill   Lucy Robinson Dimsdale
Mary Cowgill   John Dimsdale
Thomas Croasdale   William Dimsdale

Mary Dimsdale
Ed Doyle
Benjamin Duffield
Joseph English
Joseph Fisher
Elizabeth Fisher
Martha Fisher
Moses Fisher
Mary Fisher
Henry Furnace
Joseph Furnace
Rachel Furnace
John Hallowell
Rowland Hambidge
Cuthbert Hayhurst
Mary Rudd Hayhurst
Elizabeth Hayhurst
William Hayhurst
Margery Hayhurst
John Hayhurst
Cuthbert Hayhurst
Alice Hayhurst
Mary Hayhurst
William Hayhurst
Andrew Heath
Robert Heaton
Alice Heaton
Grace Heaton
Robert Heaton
James Heaton
Agnes Heaton
Ephraim Heaton
Valentine Hollingsworth
Henry Hollingsworth
John Hoskins
Mary Hoskins
John Hoskins
Thomas Howell
Daniel Howell
Mordecai Howell
Miriam Howell
Priscilla Howell
Katharine Howell
Elizabeth Johnson
Robert Kilcarth
Humphrey Killingbeck
Joseph Kirkbride
Giles Knight

Mary Knight
Joseph Knight
Edward Lancaster
Robert Leister
Tobias Leach
Esther Ashmead Leach
Robert Lloyd
Peter Long
William Long
Thomas Maddock
Henry Maddock
Jane Maude
Margery Maude
Samuel Miles
Margaret James Miles
Christopher Newlin
Evan Oliver
Jean Oliver
David Oliver
Elizabeth Oliver
John Oliver
Hannah Oliver
Mary Oliver
Evan Oliver
Seaborn Oliver
Griffith Owen
Philip Packer
Richard Parker
John Parsons
Thomas Paschal
George Pownall
Eleonor Pownall
Reuben Pownall
Elizabeth Pownall
Sarah Pownall
Rachel Pownall
Abigail Pownall
John Reeves
William Robertson
William Rodney
Robert Salford
John Sharples
Jane Sharples
Phebe Sharples
John Sharples
James Sharples
Caleb Sharples
James Sharples

Joseph Sharples
Thomas Sharples
Thomas Stackhouse
Margery Hayhurst
  Stackhouse
John Stackhouse
Thomas Stackhouse
Thomas Tearewood
Robert Threwecks
Robert Threwecks
Mary Toole
Robert Turner
Martha Turner
Robert Wade
Thomas Walmsley
Elizabeth Rudd Walmsley
Margaret Walmsley
Mary Walmsley

Henry Walmsley
Thomas Walmsley
Elizabeth Walmsley
Rosamond Walmsley
Nicholas Waln
Jane Waln
Jane Waln
Richard Waln
Margaret Waln
Thomas Wigglesworth
Alice Hayhurst
  Wigglesworth
Martha Worrall
William Yardley
Jane Heath Yardley
Enoch Yardley
Thomas Yardley
William Yardley

H. MYTHICAL

John Buckman
Arthur Hayhurst
John Hey
John Key

----- Pearson
John Stackhouse
Ann Townsend
Robert Walton

TABULATION

Proved 60
Highly Probable 12
Possible 14
Possible but Rather Improbable 9
Improbable 4
Highly Improbable 26
Disproved 171
Mythical 8
Total number of claimants 304

NOTES TO INTRODUCTION

[1]See Marion Balderston (PGM 23:56-59). The earliest loading was on 7 July 1682, the last on 21 August. Only seven persons are recorded as having shipped goods on the *Welcome* for trade in Pennsylvania. This does not mean, of course, that these were all the passengers, since a passenger might take any amount of baggage for his own personal use.

Export goods were, however, dutiable, and the seven names represent persons who shipped merchandise for trade. The seven were: Daniel Wharley, Dennis Rochford, Thomas Fitzwater, Robert Smith, John West, Philip Ford and John Wilmer, of whom two, Rochford and Fitzwater, were passengers; two others, Smith and West, probably passengers; another pair, Wharley and Ford, never came to America, while nothing is known of Wilmer.

[2]The following quotations were printed, with some others, by Henry Joel Cadbury (PMHB 75:152-155).

[3]The date of this item is as given in the text, yet the statements seem to describe events later in the month. Dr. Cadbury's dates have been confirmed by Prof. James A. Hitt of the University of Texas who has kindly examined a copy of the newspaper, not a photograph, in the University of Texas Library.

[4]The tonnage is proved by Public Record Office, C.O. 13/14, cited in PGM 23:56f. According to George Vaux, 'The Embarkation, Voyage and Arrival of the Ship "Welcome," 1682,' a paper read at Chester, 21 5th mo. 1932, at a meeting of the Friends Historical Association (*Bull. Friends Hist. Assoc.* 21:59-62), the *Welcome* was of 300 tons, 108 feet long, had a 70 foot keel, was 27½ feet wide, 13 feet deep, had a draught of 10½ feet; the masts were square rigged except a lateen sail on the mizzen, and this was much larger than the *Mayflower*. Mr. Vaux does not cite his source for this very precise account, and I do not know where he got the information.

[5]See what is said concerning List Q in Section C, below.

[6]Proud seems not to have been related to Mary Proude, mother of the first wife of William Penn. He was born 10 May 1728, at Low Foxton, Yorkshire; died 7 July 1813. See Charles West Thomson (MHSP 1 [1864] 417-425; also "Autobiography of Robert Proud the Historian [Commentariolum De Vita R. Proudi written by self in 78th year]" (PMHB 13:430-440).

[7]See Marion Balderston, ed., *James Claypoole's Letter Book, London and Philadelphia 1681-1684* (San Marino, Calif., Huntington Library, 1967).

[8]See below, p.497.

[9]See Henry Darrach's lecture at the Annual Meeting of the Welcome Society, Ritz-Carlton Hotel, Philadelphia, 24 Feb. 1917, who suggests this.

[10]See below, p. 433.

[11]Penn to the Lords of Trade and Plantations, quoted by Catherine Owens Peare, *William Penn, A Biography* (Ann Arbor, 2nd ed., 1966), p. 245.

[12]W. J. Buck, *William Penn in America* (Philadelphia 1888), p. 76.

[13]John Winthrop's *Journal* (Hosmer's ed., 1908), 2:345 f., 28 June 1648.

[14]*Mariner's Mirror* 22:426. No copy has been seen.

[15]See below, p.

[16]Printed by Proud, *op. cit.*, 1:209; by Janney, *Life of William Penn* (Philadelphia 1852), p. 213.

[17]Penn to Lord Keeper North, Philadelphia, 24 5th mo. July 1683 (MHSP 1 [1864] 439-441); Peare, *op. cit.*, 267.

[18]PGM 23:27-67. A far from satisfactory set of "Early Passenger Lists" appears in H. Stanley Craig, *Salem County, New Jersey, Genealogical Data* (Merchantville, N.J., no date), 1:293-307.

[19]At this point in the original printing of Mrs. Balderston's list appeared an unknown ship from New England which arrived in the Delaware, 19 May 1682. Evidence for this ship is apparently the registration of Richard Lundy of Axminster in the County of Dorset, son of Silvester Lundy of the same, who came in a Catch from Bristol, the master Wm Browne, for Boston in New England, 6th mo. 1676, and from there 19 3rd mo. 1682. It would seem improbable that Penn would count such a ship, and we now have 23 ships without counting it. Mr. Colket states (p. 57 of the report described as List O) that a ship named *Unity* sailed for Pennsylvania in August 1682 and later says that it, John Knut, master, was receiving supplies for Pennsylvania on 7 Aug. 1682, and he then cites PRO E/190/113, one of the London Port Books. Mrs. Balderston's lists have no such vessel and she has kindly checked the reference given and finds that John Nott or Nutt was master of a ship of this name which was intending to sail to Tangiers, not Pennsylvania.

[20]See below, p. 525.

[21]That there was also a ship called the *William Penn* has often been claimed but the ship is mythical. The claim is based on a letter (GM 40-44; Myers, *Narratives*, 451-459) written by one John Jones who was son of Thomas Sion [John] Evans, about 1725, in which he says that his father had crossed on a ship of this name in a voyage that lasted thirty

weeks, and that he learned to speak English during
the voyage! It is improbable that Penn would have
allowed his name to be given to a vessel, and there
is no confirming document. We may also use this
space to note that James F. Shunk, editor of the
Argus, a newspaper published at Easton, Pa., perpe-
trated in his issue of 28 April 1870 the celebrated
Cotton Mather hoax. This was a letter supposedly
written 15 Sept. 1682, while the *Welcome* was at sea,
and pretending to be by Cotton Mather [then a youth
of nineteen!], referring in nasty terms to Penn's
voyage on the *Welcome*. The hoax was exposed by William F. Poole, editor of *Poole's Indexes*. See also
Friends Intelligencer and Journal 54 (1897) 295;
Boston Evening Transcript, 1 June 1870; Samuel A.
Green, M.D., *Proceedings of the Massachusetts Historical Society,* June 1870, pp. 328 f. This hoax
was, however, completely swallowed by Dr. Arthur Edwin Bye, *A Friendly Heritage along the Delaware*
(New York 1959), 224-228, and also in *The Historian*
(organ of the Bucks County Historical Society) 3:67.
We should also note that Peare (*op. cit.* 220) states
that the fares for master or mistress on Penn's
fleet were £6 a head; for servants, £5; 50/- for
each child under ten but a suckling child was free.
Freight cost 40/- a ton but one chest was free for
each person.
        22On Robert Waln see H. S. Perry (DAB 19:387);
on his son Robert Jr., b. 20 Ovt. 1794, d. 4 July
1825, satirist and historian, see J. C. Mendenhall
(*ibid.*) and W. S. Hastings (PMHB 76:71-80).
        23PMHB 9:223.
        24In his Hayhurst sketch, cited below.
        25George Norwood Comly, *The Comly Family in Amer-
ica* (Philadelphia 1939), p. 885, a superb work. Even
so, elsewhere he puts the Walmsleys on the *Welcome*.
The Settle certificate is handled uncritically by Dr.
Arthur Edwin Bye (*The Historian* 3 [1965] 67) who accepts as *Welcome* passengers the Croasdales, the Walmsleys, the Walns, the Hayworths [sic], the Cowgills
and the Stackhouses, who included, probably, he says,
Thomas Stackhouse's two nephews, John and Thomas Jr.,
but he omits the Wigglesworths, doubtless uninten-
tionally.
        26*Huntington Library Quarterly* 21:31-56.
        27PGM 23:27-67.

THE WELCOME CLAIMANTS

ACTON, BENJAMIN   *disproved*

This name appears only on List X, with the surname there misspelled "Aeton." Cushing and Sheppard[1] placed him on the *Kent* but the truth is that he came on the *Lion* of Liverpool, John Crumpton, master, arriving 14 8th mo. 1683, as servant to Robert Turner, to serve four years, loose on 14 8th mo. 1687, then to receive £3 and the usual fifty acres.[2]

He managed to get free, however, before the end of this term, for he bought property at New Salem, New Jersey, on 2 March 1685/6 from William Surridge[3] and he married under the care of Philadelphia Monthly Meeting, 27 6th mo. 1686, Christian England. There are records of people with her surname in early Philadelphia but her parents cannot be identified among them and it is probable that she came to this country without them, as she is shown as a renter on Blackwell's Rent Roll of 1689, a 48-foot lot on the north side of Chestnut Street going east from Broad, 5/- yearly for four years.[4] The fact that three years after her marriage to Acton she is still shown with her maiden name presents no difficulty, since Blackwell doubtless made up his roll from records and not from personal acquaintance.

Benjamin Acton is called a surveyor,[5] a weaver,[6] a carpenter,[7] miller, yeoman[8], and ordinary-keeper.[9] He became the town recorder of Salem in 1695 but died at an unknown date without probate.

Issue:[10] surname Acton

i. Elizabeth, b. 26 2nd mo. 1690, m. 1712 Francis Reynolds.

ii. Mary, b. 17 10th mo. 1692, m. 1715 William Wills.

iii. Benjamin, b. 19 8th mo. 1695, d. ca. 1749, a merchant, Esq.; will dated 18 Nov. 1749, calling him of Salem, Salem Co., tanner.[11] mentions "last wife's" three daughters by former husband William Shields, they under 18 and unm.; sons John and Joseph, heirs and executors; signed with seal; witnesses: John Whittall, Samuel Parker, Josiah Kay, inventory £1178/17/0. His late wife is referred to in the probate as Rachel. He m. (1) at Burlington, 9 1st mo. 1718/9, Mary Satterthwaite, daughter of James Satterthwaite, late of Burlington; (2) 1 10th mo. 1727, Elizabeth -----, widow of Thomas Hill; (3) ca. 1740-5, Rachel ---- widow of William Shields whose estate was in court 16 May 1741,[12] calling him of Salem Town and County, carpenter. In the papers is the affirmation of Rachel Acton, late Rachel Shields.

Issue:
1. John, b. 31 8th mo. 1728, d. 1774; m. Mary -----.
2. Joseph, b. 3 9th mo. 1730; m. Sarah Hall.
3. Benjamin, b. 15 9th mo. 1733, d.y.
4. Benjamin, b. 28 12th mo. 1735/6, prob. d. y.
5. Samuel, b. 31 6th mo. 1738, prob. d.y.
iv. Lydia, b. 24 11th mo. 1697.
v. Joshua, b. 9 7th mo. 1700.

NOTES

[1]Thomas Cushing and Charles E. Sheppard, *Hist. of Gloucester, Salem and Cumberland Counties* (1883), 16 f.
[2]Philadelphia Arrivals.
[3]1 NJA 21:581.
[4]PGM 23:83.
[5]1 NJA 21:639.
[6]1 NJA 21:344, 596, 610, 623f, 628-30, 632, 534f, 640.
[7]1 NJA 21:552.
[8]Ibid.
[9]Ibid. 594.
[10]HEAQG 19. See also GMNJ 10:59f.; 12:10.
[11]NJW 2:10.
[12]NJW 2:431.

ASHMEAD, MARY, widow[1]	*disproved*
ASHMEAD, JOHN, her son	*disproved*
ASHMEAD, MARY CURRIER, his wife	*disproved*

These Ashmeads have appeared on no list but the claim that they were on the *Welcome* was twice made

by the late Josiah Granville Leach,[2]specifically for
the widow and for her daughter Esther and the latter's husband Tobias Leach, and by inference for the
others of the family who included daughter Ann and
her husband Jacob Davis or Dawes.

The disproof of the claim is to be found in the
fact that Tobias Leach, and doubtless the rest of
the Ashmead family, came rather on the *Bristol Factor*. [3]

Frank Willing Leach's excellent sketch[4] of this
family makes no claim of their presence on the *Welcome*, nor does a small book based on it, *The Ashmead
Family, One of the Series of Sketches by Frank Willing Leach for the Philadelphia North American 1907-
1913, and Brought Down to Date* (Philadelphia: Historical Publication Society, copyright 1933). From
this book we learn that John Ashmead, born 1620 at
Cheltenham, Gloucestershire, England, died in England, date unknown but before 1682, "in which year,
so far as can be determined, his widow, Mary Ashmead,
with three children, two sons-in-law, one daughter-
in-law, and several friends, neighbors of hers in
Cheltenham, England, arrived in Penn's new province,
either shortly before or shortly after the advent of
the Founder himself." Mary Ashmead died 23 10th mo.
1688, perhaps as the result of the shock of the pas-
sing of her son John. According to this account,
she had at least the following

Issue:
i.   John, b. Cheltenham, Gloucestershire, 14
      Oct. 1648, d. 21 Dec. 1688; m. 1 Oct. 1677
      on his 29th birthday [dates given do not
      confirm this] Mary Currier (daughter of
      William Currier) who d. 1718 aet. 73,
      having m. (2) 6 12th mo. 1689/90 Edward
      White. John Ashmead of Cheltenham left a
      will dated 9 13th mo. 1688, in which he
      names his now wife Mary executrix; eldest
      son John £20; daughter Mary £10; youngest
      son Nicholas £20; trustees Tobias Leach,
      Edward Bolton, Chas. Gardner; witnesses:
      Edward Bolton, Toby Leach, Mary Bradwell;
      admin. c.t.a. to Leach and Bolton 30 Nov.
      1689, the widow having renounced. The
      said Bolton's first name was Everard but
      this is often misread by clerks.
      Issue:
   1. John, b. Cheltenham, England,21 5th mo.

1679, d. Germantown, Pa., 7 Oct. 1742;
m. Darby 12 Oct. 1703, Sarah Sellers,
b. 13 3rd mo. 1685, d. 1766, daughter
of Samuel and Ann (Gibbons) Sellers,
her mother a *Welcome* claimant. John and
Sarah were bapt. as Baptists at Penne-
pack Church, 3 May 1707. His will made
Aug. 1712, cod. 29 Sept. 1742, probated
18 Oct. 1742, names wife Sarah and son
Samuel executors; children: John, Samuel, Sarah, Hannah, grandchildren:John
and William. Sarah also left a will
dated 24 July 1766, probated 25 Nov.
1766, naming son Samuel and grandson
William Ashmead.
  Issue:
a. John, b. 12 May 1706, d. 30 July 1750;
   m. 23 Aug. 1734 Anna Rush who m.(2)
   13 Oct. 1751 Samuel Potts.
b. Anna/Hannah, b. 9 Feb. 1707/8, m. 1
   Sept. 1723 George Bringhurst.
c. Samuel, b. 4 March 1710, d. 19 March
   1794, m. 17 Aug. 1730 Esther -----,
   widow of David Morgan.
d. Sarah, b. 7 July 1712, m. 2 Oct. 1733
   (1) Samuel Marshall, (2) John Cor-
   den.
e. Mary, b. 12 Sept. 1719. m. ---- Louden
   of New Castle, Del.
2.William, b. England, 21 2nd mo. 1681, d.
  inf.
3.Mary, b. 24 1st mo. 1683, d. 1723, m.
  1707 Thomas White.
4.Nicholas, b. 8 4th mo. 1685, d. 1749, m.
  Sarah ----. All four children d. inf.

NOTES

[1]See also under LEACH AND DAVIS.
[2]*The Penrose Family of Philadelphia* (Philadelphia 1903), p. 15; also his *Chronicle of the Yerkes
Family With Notes on the Leach and Potter Families*
(Philadelphia 1904), p. 206.
[3]PGM 23:54 f.
[4]Philadelphia *North American,* Sunday, 3 Jan.
1909.

BACHELOR, JANE[1]   *highly probable*

This name appeared for the first time on any *Welcome* passenger list on List O and was repeated on List V. Mr. Myers did not include the name on List Q but thought Jane might have been a passenger and kept in his Papers a sheet for data on Richard Tucker, Jane's husband.

The evidence is circumstantial but impressive: (a) Jane Batchelor received a legacy of £5 in the will of Isaac Ingram, the first named of five persons who received special legacies of this kind in that will, and all the others were also on board. (b) William Penn's letter of 18 5th mo. 1685 to Thomas Lloyd[2] contains a paragraph referring to the settlement, too long delayed, of the estate of John Snashfold who had died on the *Welcome* and says that "Tucker's wife" could help John Songhurst with the problem of the settlement. As will appear, Jane was Tucker's wife when Penn wrote and the couple had been married during Penn's stay in America, so that Penn may even have attended the wedding. If Jane was party to information about Snashfold's estate, she could have become so only from her presence on the ship. (c) After the sailing of the *Welcome*, Jane's name is no longer found in the minutes of the Women's Meeting at Dorking, as Mrs. Balderston kindly informs me, and she also says that Jane had been a member of Penn's household at Warminghurst.

Jane was herself a First Purchaser of 250 acres in Group 57, the last name on the list.[3] This minimum investment was not large but shows that if she was a Warminghurst "servant," she was not a menial.

On 1 11th mo. 1683 Jane Batchelor and Richard Tucker were presented to the Philadelphia Monthly Meeting for marriage by Elizabeth Wynn and Mary Songhurst; second intentions, 1 2nd mo. 1684.[4] The marriage certainly took place for Richard Tucker with wife John was buried in Philadelphia on 22 March 1708/9, and Jane Tucker was buried on 11 2nd mo. 1716, both records on Hudson's list of non-Quaker burials.[5] It is probable that they had become Keithians.

The will of Richard Tucker of Philadelphia, yeoman, was signed by mark, 24 3rd mo. 1708, probated 27 May 1708,[5] and wife Jane is named executrix; son Nathaniel, daughter Mary Wildren; overseers and trustees: William Forrest, cordwainer; Thomas Las-

sell, glazier; witnesses: John Brown, Richard Abull
and John Cadwallader; inventory by Robert Burrow,
John Browne, came to £48/3/10.

Warrants and Surveys 4:33 show Richard Tucker,
28 3rd mo. 1700, 500 acres in right of unnamed
wife's purchase of 250 acres plus other land given
back to the Proprietor by Richard Tucker, return
dated 4 4th mo. 1701. Blackwell's Rent Roll of 1689
shows Jane Bachelor as owner of a 49½ lot on Front
Street, 1/- for 6 years to end 1 March 1689/90
"returned J By," which probably means that J.By,
whoever he was, noted that the land had been sur-
rendered. This city lot was on the northeast corner
of Third and Sassafras, now Race, Streets, Philadelphia.

Both Minshall Painter and Dr. George Smith[8] say
that Richard Tucker came perhaps from Warminster,
Wilts, but on what evidence I do not know. He can
not have been the Richard Tucker who purchased land
in West New Jersey in 1664, as that man was from
Weymouth and Melcomb Regis, a merchant.[9]

We have looked in vain for further information
concerning the daughter, Mary Tucker Wildren, and
of the son Nathaniel, we have found only that a man
with this name married Ann Broon on 15 Jan. 1705/6
at St. Paul's Episcopal Church, Chester, Pa.

                              NOTES
[1]See TAG 38:152; 41:40.
[2]See below under SNASHFOLD. There is no need to
interpret Penn's words to mean that Richard Tucker
and an earlier wife were aboard the *Welcome,* when
Jane Batchelor is available to be the "Tucker's
wife" of the letter.
[3]1 PA 1:46.
[4]PGSP 1:263, 265.
[5]HEAQG 448. The same list also records the burial of James Tucker, 28 11th mo. 1729/30, but he
can hardly have been a son of Richard and Jane, as
he is not mentioned in Richard's will. He also can
hardly have been their grandson, for a James Tucker
witnessed the will of Thomas Tebbie of Philadelphia,
carpenter, 10 6th mo. 1714, probated 6 Jan. 1714,
and also the will of John Harper of Philadelphia,
mariner, 30 Sept. 1713, probated 6 Nov. 1714. In
1713 Richard and Jane had been married only thirty
years, unlikely to have then had an adult grandson.
[6]Described from a photograph of the original;
abstract in PMHB 15:204 from PhW C, #87, 1708.

[7]Painter in PGSP 4:302; George Smith, *History of Delaware County, Pennsylvania* (Philadelphia 1862), p. 508.
[8]NYGBR 30:175.

*†BARBER, JOHN[1]   *proved*
BARBER, ELIZABETH SONGHURST, his wife   *proved*

John Barber appears on all lists; Elizabeth Barber appears on Lists A, B, C, D, E, F, G, H, I [here she is called daughter of "John Longhurst"], M, O, Q, U, V, X, Y and Z; Lists J, K, L, N, P, S, T and W call here merely the wife of John Barber.

The proof is that John Barber of Shipley, Sussex, executed his will aboard the *Welcome* on 20 7th mo. 1682, though it is not quite certainthat he also died on board; if he did land, then he died soon, and we have therefore marked him above as one of the casualties. The will, as we shall see, mentions his wife Elizabeth and identifies her as eldest daughter of John Songhurst, also known to have been a *Welcome* passenger, as was also Zachariah Whitpaine who later married the other daughter, Sarah Songhurst. Since it is highly probable that John Songhurst's wife Mary and his son John were also aboard, the Songhurst-Barber party thus numbered six, or, if we count Whitpaine in anticipation, seven.

The marriage of John Barber to Elizabeth Songhurst took place in England, first intentions 8 12th mo. 1681/2, second intentions 12 2nd mo. 1682, at Horsham Monthly Meeting. His mother, the widow Mary Barber, consented "that they should marry when they come beyond the seas; the Friends Meeting, however, think it would be more convenient that their marriage should be finished here before they goe." With him John Barber had two men servants and one woman servant, names unknown.[2]

On this Barber family in England, see Norman Penney, *My Ancestors* (London 1920), pp. 57 f., from which we draw most of what is said about John Barber's ancestors John Barber the elder, who was of Henfield, Susse.. in 1651, suffered much persecution as a Friend and died in Horsham jail on 11 1st mo. 1671/2, later buried in his own ground. By his wife Mary, who died 28 3rd mo. 1712 and was buried in the same ground, he had six children as follows:

i.   Mary, b. 13 9th mo. 1651; m. 14 1st mo.
     1675/6 William Gearing of Wickham near
     Steyning; she is mentioned in her brother
     John's will, 1682.

ii. Sarah, b. 18 5th mo. 1653; m. 24 7th mo.
     1678, at Thomas Parsons' house in Covold,
     Benjamin Coggin of Crewkerne, Somerset;
     also mentioned in her brother John's will,
     1682. This may be the Benjamin Cogan who
     was fined at Ilchester in Feb. 1661/2 as
     a Quaker (NEHGR 110:275).

iii. John, b. 1 2nd mo. 1654, the *Welcome* passen-
     ger; wrongly said by Mr. Penney to have
     come to America unmarried.

iv. Hannah, b. 25 10th mo. 1655; m. Jeremiah
     Prin [?] of Goringlea in Shipley; also
     mentioned in her brother John's will.

v.   Elizabeth, d. unm., not in brother John's
     will, so d. before 1682.

vi. Edward, b. 28 5th mo. 1661, d. 2 1st mo.
     1707; m. 27 Dec. 1697 Elizabeth Beard of
     Rottingdean near Brighton, daughter of
     Nicholas Beard, and she m. (2) Thomas
     Steele of Chichester, and d. 7 11th mo.
     1729/30.

The line from John Barber has certainly been extinct since 1682, as no evidence has been seen that
the unborn child mentioned in his will survived.
By her second husband, Robert Webb, Elizabeth had a
daughter who died unmarried; whether she had other
Webb children is uncertain, but she had none by her
third husband, Samuel Richardson. It is therefore
also almost certain that the line from Elizabeth
Songhurst also became extinct at her death in Philadelphia, 8 11th mo. 1726.

John Barber was a First Purchaser of 2500 acres
in Group 19,[3] and he also subscribed £50 to the
Society of Free Traders.[4]   There is a record of a
another John Barber who was First Purchaser of 250
acres in Group 3,[5] and our John is not to be confused with a John Barber of London, brewer.[6]   The
Blackwell Rent Roll of 1689 shows John Barber's
lot now John Songhurst's, an old purchase, 51 feet,
2/6 for 3 years, on Sassafras Street.[7]

The will reads as follows:

     The twenteyth of the Seventh Month one thou-
     sand Six hundred | eightey two: I John Barber

Late of Shipley in the Countey of Susex | yeoman
being weak of bodey but of good and parfect mind
and memorey | dou make and ordain this my Last will
and testament in maner and forme | folowing: and as
tuching sutch temparall estate as it hath plesed |
god too bestow upon mee I giue and bequeth thereof
as foloweth--| Item I giue unto my Dere Mother one
broad pees of gould: and too my | Brother Edward
Barber and my sisters Marey Sarah and Hanah Barber[8]
| eatch of them one giney a peese: and all the Rest
and Resedeu of my Reall and | parsonall estate boath
in England or pensilluania or one Bord this uesell
| the wellcom now gouing for pensilluania I giue and
bequeth to my Louing | wife Elizabeth the eldet [sic]
Doughter of John Songhurst and har Chilld that |
shee now gous by whether mall or femall: but my will
and mening is that | my Wife should have the dis-
posall of my whole estate both Reall and | Parsonall:
for the bring[ing] up of my Chilld untill it shall
Cum too the aige | of one and twentey years or daye
of mariage: and then to haue and Inioy | all my
Reall estate boath in England and Pensiluania: far-
ther my will | and mening is If it should hapen
that my Chilld should dey before the | it Cums to
the aige of one and twenty years or day | of maraige:
as afore | sayd: that then my wife Should haue and
Inioy all my whole estat both | Reall and Parsonall
| to har and har Hayers for euer: I apoynt my Louing
wife Elizabeth to bee my full and Sole execketricks
of this my Last will | and testament: In Witness
whereof I haue here unto set my hand | and Seall
this day and yeare a boue written.
Sealled and Deliuered in
the presence of us
Geo: Thompson   John Barber   [seal]
Joseph Woodrooffe
Thomas Gillett
    Thomas Wynne and Geo Thompson attest Jos
      Woodroffes [signature]

The reason for the attestation of Woodrooffe's signature is doubtless the fact that he had gone to his family in New Jersey. It seems certain that this will is
not in the handwriting of any of the witnesses unless
it be in Woodrooffe's. For the will itself, see page
42.

The twentyeth of the seventh Month one thousand sixhundred
Eightey two: I John Barber Late of Shepley in the County of Hereford
yeoman being weak of body but of good and perfect minde and memory
doe make and ordain this my Last will and testament in maner and
forme following: and as touching such temporall estate as it hath pleased
god to bestow upon mee I giue and bequeth thereof as followeth
Item: I giue unto my Dere Mother one broad peec of gould: and too my
Brother Edward barber and my sisters Mary Sarah and Hanah bar=
eath of them one giney a peece and all the rest and residew of my Reall and
Parsonall estate both in England and Pensilvania or one box this vessell
the Hollen now going for Pensilvania I giue and bequeth to my louing
wife Elizabeth the eldest Daughter of John Sengn: wife and her Child: that
shee now goes by i whether wiall or formall: but my will and meaning is that
my wife should haue the disposall of my whole estate both Reall and
Parsonall for the bring upp of my Child: until it shall com to the age
of one and twentey yeare or day of mariage: and then to haue and Injoy
all my Reall estate both in England and Pensilvania: fartherr my will
and mening is if it should hapen that my Child should dey before
it cums to the age of one and twentey yeare or day of mariage: as afore
sayd: that then my wife should haue and Injoy all my whole estat both
Reall and Parsonall to her and hers Proper for euer: I acoynt my
wife Elizabeth to bee my full and sole excorketrixks of this my Last will
and testamont In Witness whereof I haue here unto set my hand
and seall this dey and yeare a bouen written

Sealled and Deliuered in
this presence of us –

Geo: Thompson
Joseph Woodroffe   John Barber
Thomas Gillett

As stated above, no evidence has been found for
the birth of the unborn child mentioned in the will
but Charles Burr Ogden asserts[9] that a Robert Barber, cordwainer, son of John Barber of the *Welcome*
by Elizabeth Songhurst, married Hannah Ogden, sister of David Ogden, the *Welcome* passenger. Though
this marriage is genuine, it is impossible for this
Robert to have been son of John and Elizabeth, for
the first intention, 13 8th mo. 1690, second intention, 3 9th mo. 1690, show that the marriage
took place when any child of John and Elizabeth
would have been less than eight years old. Mr. Ogden further claims that the said Hannah (Ogden)
Barber married, secondly, first intention 30 11th
mo. 1709/10, William Hudson, later mayor of Philadelphia who was, as we shall see, stepson-in-law
of Elizabeth (Songhurst)(Barber)(Webb) Richardson.
This is correct but a somewhat better account appears in Edwin AtLee Barber's *Genealogy of the Barber Family* (Philadelphia 1890), p. 11, which says
that the cordwainer, supposedly from Yorkshire, arrived in 1687, died without issue in 1709, after
which his widow married, secondly, William Hudson
of Chester. Whether he supposed that William Hudson of Chester differed from William Hudson of Philadelphia is not clear, but it is certain that Hannah (Ogden) Barber did marry, secondly, William Hudson, sometime mayor of Philadelphia.

Mrs. Balderston informs me that William Penn referred to our Elizabeth as "Betty," and that she
returned to England where on 15 10th mo. 1684 she
attended a quarterly meeting at Steyning. While in
England she married, secondly, at an unknown time
and place, Robert Webb, who was buried in Philadelphia, 17 1st mo. 1700/1, recorded in William Hudson's list of non-Quaker burials. Robert Webb has
been found clearly recorded as of London, of Talbot
County, Maryland, and of Philadelphia, at different
times, and Mr. Colket appears to have seen evidence
that Webb was also at some time of Amsterdam. In
1686 he wrote a pamphlet on Pennsylvania which was
translated into Dutch.[10] This would seem to indicate that he had already been in Pennsylvania before that year but if he had married the Widow Barber, she might have supplied him with the necessary
data. In 1698 he was Marshal of the Court of Admiralty in Pennsylvania.[11]

Robert and Elizabeth Webb had a daughter Mary

buried in Philadelphia, 26 4th mo. 1714. Whether
there was other issue of the second marriage, we
cannot say, but at Burlington Monthly Meeting an
Elizabeth Webb married on 7 3rd mo. 1711 Daniel
Light, and a Robert Webb married on 1 3rd mo. 1713
Mary Gaunt. No Burlington records show births of
children of either couple and nothing shows them in
New Jersey wills or other sources consulted. A Robert Webb, the same or another, was dismissed by
Burlington Meeting for disunity on 1 2nd mo. 1751.
These Burlington Webbs married at just such a time
as one would expect children of Robert and Elizabeth
(Songhurst) Webb to be able to take that step.   An
attempt to find traces of Robert Webb at Third Haven
Meeting, Talbot County, Maryland, has turned up Webbs
but not our Robert or Elizabeth.   There were between
1713 and 1718 four marriages of Webbs in Philadelphia
but the names suggest no connection with our Robert
and in 1700 Philadelphia Monthly Meeting received
two families named Webb, John Webb from the City of
Gloucester and Richard Webb, also of the City of
Gloucester.[12]

Though we cannot date precisely this marriage,
it must have been as early as 1689, for a power of
attorney was granted 31 Dec. 1689[13] to Patrick Robinson of Philadelphia by Robert Webb of London gen't
and Elizabeth Webb his wife, to collect sums due the
Webbs from the estate of her former husband John
Barber and from others including [her brother] John
Longhurst [so printed] and [her brother-in-law and
sister] Zachariah and Sarah Whitpaine; witnesses:
Richard Morris, John Day, William Penn.   Immediately
following this is a conveyance[14] dated 24 April 5
William and Mary 1693, recorded 22 July 1693, whereby Robert Webb of the County of Talbot in the Pro-
vince of Maryland, merchant, conveyed land in Phila-
delphia to William Salsbury of the Town and County of
Philadelphia, carpenter, land patented to Webb by
William Penn.

On 7 May 7 William and Mary 1695, Robert Webb of
the Town and County of Philadelphia, gent., and
Elizabeth his wife who had been the widow of John
Barber, conveyed land to William Buckman of Bucks
County, husbandman, recorded 11 8th mo. 1697.[15] The
Board of Property on 3 Oct. 1691[16] granted a patent
for 40 acres of Liberty Land to Robert Webb in the
right of Elizabeth his wife, late Barber. Granted
High Street lot proportional to John Barber's 2500

acres, he (Webb) having married the said Barber's widow. The same body at the session of 17-18 3rd mo. 1703,[17] discussed the grant of John Barber of Shipley. Robert Webb was by now also dead, and on 4 May 1703 the widow had sold parts to David Lloyd and John Guest, and they now requested patents. At the session of 3 5th mo. 1704[18] it was recorded that Elizabeth Webb, formerly wid'w of John Barber, conveyed the remainder to Thomas Fairman, 666 1/3 acres. Finally, as late as 20 3rd mo. 1739[19] bounds of the 40-acre patent were given, original date now stated to be 28 Sept. 1691.

At Philadelphia Monthly Meeting, 28 5th mo. 1704, Elizabeth Webb had leave to marry Samuel Richardson, undoubtedly the man of that name who, with wife and family, brought a certificate from Spanish Town Monthly Meeting, Jamaica, dated 10 3rd mo. 1687, the date of arrival not given.[20] His first wife Eleanor died 19 April 1703 and Samuel Richardson died 10 June 1719.[21] His will[22] was dated 6 4th mo. 1719 5 George, probated 19 June 1719, and was witnessed by Abraham Bickley [husband of daughter Elizabeth], John Ogden and John Cadwallader; inventory £289/9/4 taken by John Warder, Evan Owen. The will bequeaths various rents to dear wife Elizabeth; to daughter-in-law Elizabeth Richardson[23]; to son-in-law William Hudson of the City of Philadelphia, tanner [widower of daughter Mary]; son Joseph Richardson[24]; to daughter Ann Cartlidge, her 6 children by Edward Lane,[25] William, Samuel, James, Eleanor, Elizabeth, Anne, and her three children by Edmd Cartlidge, not named[26]; son Joseph's children: Aubrey, Edward, Richard, William, Eleanor, Barbara, Elizabeth[27]; great-granddaughter Hannah Cockfield, daughter of Joshua Cockfield; William Hudson's children: Samuel, William, John, Mary, Elizabeth, Susannah, Hannah, Rachel; grandsons Samuel Richardson and John Richardson; executors: William Hudson and his son Samuel.

NOTES

[1] TAG 38:152-154; see also the sketches of SONGHURST, WHITPAINE and OWEN.
[2] 2 PA 19:121.
[3] 1 PA 1:42.
[4] PMHB 11:176.
[5] 1 PA 1:40.
[6] 3 PA 3:328.
[7] PGM 23:71.

[8]Though called Barber in this will, two, perhaps all three, were already married.

[9]*The Quaker Ogdens* (Philadelphia 1898), p. 44.

[10]PMHB 49:99.

[11]*Colonial Records* 1:541.

[12]MQA 37, 33.

[13]2 PA 19:120-122 = PhD F, No. 6, pp. 15 f.

[14]2 PA 19:122-124.

[15]BD 2:143.

[16]2 PA 19:74.

[17]2 PA 19:375.

[18]2 PA 19:436.

[19]2 PA 19:765.

[20]MQA 12.

[21]See PGM 23:101. On this Samuel Richardson see Samuel W. Pennypacker, *Historical and Biographical Sketches* (Philadelphia 1883), 243-256; Governor Pennypacker did not know the name of the second wife; see also JCRFP 1:484 f.

[22]Described from a photograph of the original, correcting the abstract in PMHB 33:371-373.

[23]Wife of son Joseph, née Bevan.

[24]See JCRFP 1:136-146. This marriage is dated 30 4th mo. 1696. Joseph died in January 1752 (Jordan says Dec. 1751); m. Elizabeth Bevan, b. 1678, d. 27 Feb. 1740, daughter of John and Barbara (Aubrey) Bevan, and they had a daughter Sarah from whom descended Governor Samuel Whitaker Pennypacker of Pennsylvania (see GM 179). Jordan's list of the children is John, Samuel, Aubrey, Edward, Richard, William, Eleonor, Barbara, Elizabeth. Joseph Richardson of Providence, Co. Philadelphia, yeoman, made his will 6 Dec. 1745/6, probated 14 Jan. 1752 (I:468), names children: Samuel and his wife, Abrey, Edward, Ellinor Harmer, Barbara Davies, Elizabeth Pugh,; nephews and nieces: eldest son of Edward Richardson, Elizabeth, James, John Richardson, eldest son of John Richardson deceased, namely Samuel Richardson; executors: Abrey, Edward and Richard Richardson; witnesses: Thos Yorke, John White, David Thomas; codicils 6 Dec. 1745/6, 3 1st mo. 1749/50.

[25]His will calls him of Philadelphia County, yeoman, dated 4 Jan. 1709/10, probated 19 April 1710 (C:200), names wife Ann and friends James Shattick and Abraham Bickley, executors; children: James, William, Samuel, Elizabeth, Christian, Ellinor, Ann.

[26]Edmund Cartlidge of Darby, made his will 21 2nd mo. 1703, probated 12 June 1703 (B:304): daughter

Mary (minor); wife Mary; two sons John and Edmund (minors); Richard Smith and wife Mary, testator's eldest sister, and their sons Thomas and Richard; sister Helen Black; Matthew Smith, sister's son; brother-in-law Joseph Need.

[27]There were two William Hudsons in early Philadelphia. This one was not that William Hudson who married Ann Ways, 1st int. Philadelphia Monthly Meeting, 5 5th mo. 1686 (PGSP 2:96), 2nd int., and passed, 2 6th mo. 1686 (PGSP 2:98). He was a bricklayer. His will, #100 (PGSP 2:15), is dated 29 6th mo. 1694, probated 1 Sept. 1694, names son John, daughter Elizabeth Hudson, wife Ann Hudson; witnesses: John Hart, Mary Dunton, John Parsons.

On our William Hudson see JCRFP 1:114-116; Watson's *Annals of Philadelphia* 1:547; T. A. Glenn (PMHB 15:336-343; 16:108; 36:320). The grandfather and father of this man were both also named William Hudson and were both of the City of York. The father's will says he was dwelling near Walmgate Bar, York, tanner, and he made his will 23 June 1708, probated 20 May 1713. The will also states that his wife was Jane Waite, and alludes to the son William as then in Pennsylvania and with issue, and to another son Timothy who was made executor. Jane Waite was not, however, the mother of son William. She was thought to be named Head, according to Jordan, and she died 11 9th mo. 1681. In a codicil dated 23 Oct. 1711 allusion is made to Mary and Elizabeth, eldest daughters of son William Hudson and to his other children unnamed. The son of the mayor, as he later became, left a family record which says that his father, the mayor of Philadelphia in 1725-1726, was born in the City of York, 3 4th mo. 1664, and that his mother, Mary (wife of the mayor), not here identified as Mary Richardson, was born in the City of London, 19 4th mo. 1673, and that the parents were married on 28 12th mo. called Feb. 1688 (1688/9). She died 16 12th mo. 1708/9 in her 37th year and of the birth of her 14th child. The father died 16 10th mo. 1742 aged 78/6/13. An obituary of the father appeared in the *Pennsylvania Journal & Weekly Advertiser* of 11 Jan. 1742 which says that he died 16 Dec. 1742 (so PMHB 15:336) and the death is put on 12 Dec. 1742 by the same author (T. A. Glenn, PMHB 15:342) which must be an error. William Hudson m. (1) Mary Richardson, 1st int. 25 11th mo. 1688, 2nd int. and passed, 22 12th

1688, wedding on 28 12th mo. 1688 [1688/9] (PGSP
2:146 f.) and here the date of her death is given
as 17 12th mo. 1708/9. William married (2) 27 12th
mo. 1709/10, Hannah Ogden, widow of Robert Barber
of Chester, and sister of David Ogden, and she died
in the City of Philadelphia in 1759 aet. 99. Her
will dated 4 June 1743/4, probated 12 Sept. 1759
(PhW L:319, #203) names sister-in-law Martha Thomas
[David Ogden's widow remarried]; kinswoman Lydia
(wife of Thomas Vernon); cousin Lydia (daughter of
Isaac Vernon); nephew Isaac Williams; friends David
Ogden, Wm Moore, Mary Williams, Sarah Densey, Jane
Hatfield. A codicil dated 18 June 1743 names Lydia,
wife of Thomas Vernon. So far as known, none of the
heirs was a Hudson relative.

BARKER, SAMUEL   *improbable*

This name appears on no list but the claim was
made by Elizabeth Frye Barker, *The Barker Genealogy*
(New York 1927) where the following paragraph, also
printed in Oscar Frank Stetson, *The Art of Ancestor
Hunting* (New York 1936; 3rd printing 1956), p. 139,
appears:

> In 1682 William Penn came to America on the
> ship Welcome and with him came his friend Samuel
> Barker who belonged to the Society of Friends.
> On March 27th, 1685, a grant was made to William
> Penn of two hundred acres of land and purchased
> by Samuel Barker. It was located in what is now
> Newcastle County, Delaware.

The late date of this grant strongly argues against
this claim.

BLACKSHAW, RANDALL or RANDULPH   *disproved*

This name most surprisingly appears on List X
and there alone. That the man arrived on the *Submission* is abundantly proved by documentary evidence. He, his family and some of his servants, are
on the passenger list of that ship which accompanies its log, and the ages of these persons as shown
below are there given. In addition, Phineas Pemberton, who was also a passenger on the *Submission*,
inserted into Bucks Arrivals the following passage
concerning the Blackshaws:

> Randle Blackshaw of Hollingee in the County
> of Chester yeoman and Allis his wife arived in

Maryland the 2nd day of the 9th month 1682 in ye
ship the Submission of Liuerpoole the masters
name was James Settle and Randle arrived in this
Province att Apoquimene the 15th day the 11nd
month 1683 & pte of his Servants & Allis his wife
arrived at the sd place Apoquimene the 9th day of
the 3rd month & most of theire Children & Some of
the Servants 1683.

Children		servants
arrived with Randle	Phebe	William Bewsie[1]
arrived with Allis wife	Sarah	Ralph Nuttall &
	Mary	Ralph Cowgill
	Jacob	servants to Ran-
	Nehemiah	dle to serve
	martha	each of them 4

yeares & to be

[Ages from *Submission* log:]   provided for

Randulph Blackshaw	60	durein the term
Phebe	16	& to have land
Abraham	10	accustomed These
Mary	6	servants Came
Martha	1	in the Ship
Allis	43	friends adven-
Sarah	14	ture the mr
Jacob	8	Thomas Wall & ar-
Nehemiah	7	rived here the
Roger Bradbury	49	2nd of the 7th
Ellenor	46	1682 and to be
Jacob	18	from the time of
Martha	14	arrival Roger
Joseph	10	Bradbury & El-
Sarah	8	lenor Bradbury
Roger	2	& their Children

Sarah, Roger,
Jacob, Joseph,
Martha Bradbury
came in the Ship
Submission at
the time afore-

[*continuation of servants'*   said to serve 4
column to the right]   years a peice
except Sarah to
Joseph Martha Bradbury sold   serve 8 years to
in Maryland by Randle   have necessarys
Blackshaw.   dureing the term
& land accustomed
Roger Ellenor
Roger Jacob

Jordan states that Randall or Randulph Blackshaw was the son of a Captain Blackshaw and that Alice's maiden name was Burghes or Burges, but upon what evidence I do not know. It is obvious that Randall was born ca. 1622 as the *Submission* log reports him as aet. 60 in 1682. He must have married Alice, who was aet. 43 in 1682 and therefore born ca. 1639, by 1665. Jordan says that Alice died 18 11th mo. 1688/9. The first seven of the children were born in England and accompanied their parents to America on the *Submission* in 1682.

Issue: surname Blackshaw
i.   Phoebe, b. England ca. 1666, aet. 16 in 1682; d. 1701; m., as 1st wife, Falls Monthly Meeting, 13 1st mo. 1687/8, Joseph Kirkbride. See Kirkbride sketch below.
ii.   Sarah, b. England ca. 1668, aet. 14 in 1682; d. 15 7th mo. 1694; m. ca. 1689 Ralph Cowgill who came on the *Friends' Adventure* as servant to her father. See the Cowgill sketch below.
iii. Abraham, b. England ca. 1672, d. aet. 10 on 2 8th mo. 1682 while the *Submission* was at sea.
iv.   Jacob, b. England ca. 1674, not further found.
v.   Nehemiah, b. England ca. 1675, aet. 7 in 1682. Jordan dates his death 25 10th mo. 1731 but his will is dated 11 6th mo. 1743, probated 4 Jan. 1744 (BW file 504), naming dear and loving wife Mary; daughter Mary Linton; daughter Sarah Blackshaw; daughter Phebe; brother Josiah Blackshaw to be maintained; daughter Rebecca Wharton. Nehemiah m. (1) Falls, shortly after 1 7th mo. 1703, when he had leave to marry, Elizabeth Bye; (2) Falls 20 12th mo. 1716 Mary Linton.
      Issue: surname Blackshaw
      by first wife Elizabeth Bye
      1. Mary, b. 28 12th mo. 1705; m. Falls 16 12th mo. 1725 Joseph Linton; she mentioned in her father's will 1743.
      2. Sarah, b. 2 3rd mo. 1707, still unm. in father's will 1743.
      3. Martha b. 2 12th mo. 1707, not in will of father 1743.

    4. Nehemiah, b. 17 12th mo. 1712.
       by second wife Mary Linton
    5. Phebe, b. 25 10th mo. 1717; m. 19 8th
       mo. 1743 Joseph Wharton, son of John.
    6. Rebecca, v. 7 7th mo. 1719; m. 31 10th
       mo. 1740 Daniel Wharton.
vi.   Mary, b. England ca. 1676, aet.6 in 1682;
       had leave to m. 6 10th mo. 1710 Ephraim
       Fenton, b. ca. 1676.
vii.   Martha, b. England ca. 1681, bur. Falls
       26 2nd mo. 1731; m. Falls 3 9th mo. 1697
       George Biles who m. (2) 20 12th mo. 1726
       Mary Lynton.
viii. Josiah, mentioned in brother Nehemiah's
       will of 1743, then to be maintained.

NOTE

[1]PGM 23:46 reads this name as "Beasy." On the
Blackshaws see JCRFP 1:300-302.

BRADFORD, WILLIAM   *disproved*
BRADFORD, ELIZABETH TOWLE, his wife   *disproved*

The name of William Bradford appears on Lists A,
B, C, D, E (here with a long negative note), G (here
with a note of doubt at the end), H, I, J, K, L, M,
N, P, R, S, T, U (here rejected), W and X. On Lists
C, H, I and M, he is identified with the famous
printer of this name. Elizabeth Towle Bradford is
shown with her husband only on List U but there to
be rejected. If the William Bradford under discussion was the printer, then she was his wife; if we
are dealing with another William Bradford, then of
his wife nothing is known.

There were, in fact, two men named William Bradford in early Pennsylvania, one the celebrated printer, the other of Sussex County in the present state
of Delaware. We shall discuss the printer first.

In *Americana* 15:190 is an article on Henry Glover
in which we read: "William Bradford left England
Sept. 1, 1682, in the Ship Welcome, and arrived here
Oct. 27 of the same year." John F. Watson's *Annals
of Philadelphia* (Philadelphia, 1st ed., 1830; p. 521;
later ed., 1:543-547) has a sketch on the Bradfords
which dates their arrival in 1682 but does not mention the *Welcome*. An obituary of the printer, published in the *New York Gazette* of 25 May 1752, and

copied in the *Pennsylvania Gazette* of 28 May 1752,
says: "He came to America seventy years ago and
landed at a place where now stands Philadelphia, before that city was laid out or a single house built
there." The tombstone inscription says much the
same thing and specifically that he came to America
in 1682, before the City of Philadelphia was laid
out. So also Isaiah Thomas, *History of Printing*
(1st ed. 1810), 7, 286; Thomas I. Wharton, "Notes
on the Provincial Literature of Pennsylvania" (*MHSP*
1 [1826] 105; 2nd ed. [1864] 113), where, however,
the landing is dated in 1682 or 1683, and nothing
is said of the *Welcome*; William Hepburn Dixon, *Life
of William Penn* (1851), 208, who claims that Bradford did come on the *Welcome* with Penn.

Edward Armstrong, compiler of Lists A and B,
asked Benjamin Ferris of Wilmington what he knew of
Bradford's crossing on the *Welcome* and Ferris replied on 31 Dec. 1851 (letter in the Manuscripts
Collection, Historical Society of Pennsylvania)
that "I have no authority, . . . except as the assertion of some modern history--I suppose Dixon's."

In 1863 John William Wallace of Philadelphia, an
assiduous deliverer of commemorative addresses whose
bust now stands in the Library of the Historical
Society of Pennsylvania, commemorated the 200th an-
niversary of Bradford's birth, which had taken place
on 20 May 1663, and this address was shortly afterwards printed in the *Typographic Advertiser* (Albany
1863). A copy of this address is owned by the Historical Society of Pennsylvania but could not be
found when asked for in 1967. However, Joseph Jackson's *Encyclopaedia of Philadelphia* (Harrisburg
1933), 4:1181-1184, after citing this address, says
that Wallace concluded that Bradford came and looked
over the country, went back to England and then came
again in 1685. A similar view is expressed by T. F.
Henderson (*DNB* 6:164), but Victor H. Paltsits (*DAB*
2:563 f.) denies the *Welcome* claim and suggests that
there was another man of the same name, as, indeed,
there was.

The negative evidence is to be found in the records of Philadelphia Monthly Meeting under date of
4 11th mo. 1685 [really 1685/6], where William and
Elizabeth Bradford are received on a certificate
from Devonshire House Monthly Meeting in London,
dated 12 6th mo. 1685, and they brought also a letter from George Fox which shows that they were then

unknown in Philadelphia. This certificate is cited by Frank Willing Leach in *The North American* for Sunday, 8 Sept. 1907, p. xiv. It is quite clear that the printer William Bradford and his wife Elizabeth, daughter of Andrew Towle, to whom Bradford had been apprenticed, were not on the *Welcome* or they would have needed no introduction from Fox in 1685.

As for the other William Bradford, he was of Sussex County, now Delaware. Could *he* have been on the *Welcome?* C. H. B. Turner, *Some Records of Sussex County, Delaware* (Philadelphia 1909), shows the following entries for the Delaware Bradford:

p. 87 appointed one of the surveyors of highways and bridges, 9-11 Jan. 1682 (1682/3)
p. 96 action of the case, Bradford a defendant, 10 April 1683
p. 103 ordered to get bridge repaired, 12 4th mo. 1683
p. 106 petitions court as bridge surveyor, 11 7th mo. 1683
p. 116 John Barker chosen in room of William Bradford, 11 9th mo. 1684

Probably this William Bradford is the man recorded as owed 28 pounds for pork, 12 7th mo. 1683 (Minutes of the Provincial Council 1:82).

We conclude that this William Bradford of Delaware was probably there before the *Welcome* as only ten weeks later he is well enough known to be appointed to local office. Whether he died in 1684 or moved elsewhere is unknown, but there is no probate for him in Sussex County, and there is really no affirmative evidence to show that among the passengers on the *Welcome* there was any man named Bradford at all.

Probably it was the printer who brought as servant Edw'd Mayos (2 *PA* 19:586).

BRADSHAW, LEMUEL   *disproved*

This name appears only on List X, there spelled wrongly as Lemuel Bardlaw. Lemuel Bradshaw, however, came as servant to Robert Turner on the *Lion* of Liverpool, arriving 14 8th mo. 1683, to serve 4 years and get 27 (shillings?), 50 acres, on 14 8th mo. 1687. Lemuel Bradshaw of Salem County, husbandman, died intestate on 13 11th mo. 1689/90, administration being granted 14 April 1690 to Bartholomew Wyatt of Elsenburgh. Inventory dated 10 March

1689/90, £26/19/6, including a Bible and primer, and
debts due by Sam'l Carpenter, Thomas Budd, Thomas
Jones, James Scoles, John Beetle and Christopher
White, in all £19/7/7. Debts due the creditors,
£7/12/9, show them to be John and Andrew Thompson,
John Scoles, Benj. Acton and Wm Cooper. The inventory
was signed by Andrew Thompson, Joseph White and John
Thompson (*NJW* 1:56).

BREARLY, JOHN   *disproved*

This name appears on List X only, there mistakenly spelled Breasly. The truth is that John came as
servant to William Yardley on the *Friends' Adventure*,
arriving 28 7th mo. 1682, to serve four years, loose
on 29 7th mo. 1686. He appears a number of times in
Bucks Court records but by 22 June 1693 he begins to
appear in a series of New Jersey deeds[1] as resident
of Hunterdon County, either of Maidenhead or of Hopewell, a Quaker and a yeoman. He was chosen one of
two overseers of highways at Burlington Court, 19
Jan. 1694/5, and as constable of Maidenhead Township
on 21 Feb. 1697/8 and 15 March 1698/9.[2]

John Brealy or Braily, of Maidenhead, Hunterdon
County, yeoman, made his will 7 May 1722, probated
23 Oct. 1722,[3] in which he names wife Sarah and the
children: John, Benjamin, David, Joseph, Mary (wife
of John Oulden) and Ruth; mentions home farm near
Five Miles Run, a farm bought of Joseph Reeder and
a third farm on the Delaware River called Pardsee
Crage; names wife and son-in-law John Ouldden as
executors. Inventory dated 16 8th mo. 1722, made
by William Hixson, Benjamin Clarke, Joseph Worth,
and came to the large sum of £343/15/1 for the personal estate including £1/8 for books. The names
of the children harmonize with those in the wife's
will but he does not include the stepchildren.

Sarah's will calls her of Maidenhead in West Jersey, widow, being very sick, and is dated 16 Sept.
1731, probated 27 Oct. 1731,[4] and she leaves her apparel to Sarah Watson, Ruth Gumly and Ann Biles; re-
mits her "thirds" in a certain plantation to David
Brearley, and names her children as John Biles, E-
licksander Biles, John Brearly, David Brearly, Joseph Brearly, Benjamin Brearly, Sarah Watson and
Ruth Gumley; executor: John Brearly; inventory 23
Oct. 1731, £149/7/1. Ann Biles is left clothing but
is omitted from the list of children. As will be
seen, there were two Biles daughters and this Ann

may be one of them.

John Brearly married, first, Mary -----, and had a first child born 18 Sept. 1694,[5] but the date of her death and her maiden name are both unknown. He married, second, between 2 Nov. 1696, date of administration of her first husband, and 9 March 10 William III 1697 [1697/8], date of a deed in which she is called Brearly, Sarah Wood, born probably at Attercliffe, Parish of Sheffield, Yorkshire, youngest of three daughters--there were two sons--of John Wood of said Attercliffe who arrived on the *Shield* 10th mo. 1678. John Wood made his will when of Crookhorn [Crewkerne, now Morrisville, Pa.] on 20 March 1692, probated 12 Nov. 1692,[6] in which he mentions his daughter Sarah as wife of Charles Biles. By deed dated, as stated, 9 March 10 William III 1697,[7] [her brother] Joseph Wood of Bucks Co., yeoman, conveyed to Sarah and to her second son Alexander Biles, and this deed identifies her former husband and says she has two daughters not named. On the Biles family see the Biles Excursus at the end of this sketch; also articles by Lewis D. Cook.[8]

> Issue: surname Brearly
> > *by first wife Mary*
> i. Mary, b. 18 Sept. 1694 (Chesterfield record), d. 3 Aug. 1766 (*ibid.*); m. John Olden, b. 5 April 1687, d. 18 Feb. 1757 (*ibid.*); made his will 13 Jan. 1757, probated 3 May 1757[9] naming his wife Mary and the following:
> > > Issue: surname Olden (rec. Chesterfield)
> > > 1. William, b. 1719.   5. Joseph.
> > > 2. John.   6. David.
> > > 3. James.   7. Mary.
> > > 4. Thomas.   8. Benjamin, b. 1737.
> > *by second wife Sarah Wood*
> ii. John, in wills of both parents, probably d. intestate, admin. 4 March 1777 to a James Brierly.[10]
> iii. Benjamin, mentioned as 2nd son in father's will, 4th of the Brearlys in mother's; m. by N.J. lic. dated 24 March 1732 Elizabeth Cook, probably daughter of Henry Cook and wife Wineford; his will dated 15 Nov. 1723, probated 20 Jan. 1723/4,[11] shows him of Maidenhead with, among others, an unmarried daughter Elizabeth. Another daughter of said Cook must have m. George Rozell or Rossell of Maidenhead (d. 1773[12]) called

brother-in-law in wills of both Benjamin
and Elizabeth: Benjamin's dated 18 June
1756, probated 17 March 1757,[13] calls him
of Maidenhead, names wife Elizabeth, children: Benjamin (minor), Rachel, Sarah, Rebeckah, Elizabeth; brother John Brearly,
brother-in-law George Rossell; Elizabeth's
will is dated 7 Sept. 1759, probated 12
Sept. 1759,[14] also names Rossell and all
the children except Rebeckah.

iii. David, named 3rd in father's will, 2nd of
Brearlys in mother's; probably David Brearly the elder of Maidenhead, admin. to Joseph Brearly, fellow-bondsman David Brearly, 6 Dec. 1785[15]inventory £389/1/9 by Benjamin Mershon and Jonathan Phillip; probably the David prisoner in Hunterdon jail on
charge of treason when on 4 Dec. 1747 a
jail delivery took place; wife said to be
Mary Clarke.
      Issue: surname Brearly, perhaps others
   1. David, of Trenton, Esq., sometime surro-
      gate of Hunterdon and N.J. Chief Justice;
      will dated 13 Aug. 1790, probated 18
      Sept. 1790[16], names wife Elizabeth, bro-
      ther-in-law Joseph Higbee, children:
      William, David, Joseph, George, Eliza-
      beth, Esther; mentions swords and shows
      he had been a judge. The son George m.
      7 1st mo. 1791 Ann Gillingham, b. 29 1st
      mo. 1773, d. 1843.[17]

iv. Joseph, 4th son in father's will, 3rd in his
     mother's, of Maidenhead; inventory of per-
     sonal estate, £198/4/1, 2 Dec. 1740, by
     Samuel Hunt and John Ely[18]; widow Phebe
     renounced in favor of Benjamin Brearly
     brother of deceased whose bond is dated
     23 Jan. 1740, calls him of Maidenhead,yeo-
     man.

v.   Ruth, m. between 7 May 1722 and 16 Sept.
     1731, ----- Gumly. Nothing further found.

BILES EXCURSUS

Though not *Welcome* claimants themselves, the Biles
family merits discussion because of intermarriages
with claimants.

Dorothy Strong[19] of co. Dorset, England, married
----- Biles and was his widow living in the Parish

of All Saints, Dorchester, Dorset, when in 1693 she made a very informative will, signed by mark, and naming brother Thomas Strong executor.

Issue: surname Biles (with variants)

i.   William, in 1693 in Pennsylvania; a fell-monger, he arrived in the Delaware on the *Elizabeth and Sarah* of Weymouth, 4 4th mo. 1679, with wife Johannah [bur. 21 10th 1709], and the five eldest children. He was bur. 19 3rd mo. 1710, will 5 11th mo. 1705.[20]

Issue:surname Biles

1. Elizabeth, b. 3 4th mo. 1670; had leave to m., 1 6th mo. 1688, Stephen Beaks and had John, Mary and Grace Beaks; m. (2) Matthew Hewes.

2. William, Esq., b. 12 11th mo. 1671, had leave to m., Falls (1) 7 9th mo. 1688 Jane Atkinson; (2) 1 11th mo. 1695 Sarah Langhorn, daughter of Thomas and Grace. His will dated 3 10th mo. 1737, probated 27 Sept. 1739, names his wife Sarah and seven children and eight grandchildren. For the details see the article cited in Note 19.

3. George, b. 4 7th mo. 1673, bur. 27 10th mo. 1708/9; on 3 9th mo. 1697 had leave to m. Martha Blackshaw (d. 1720) who m. (2) Joseph Waite. George and Martha had Jeremiah, Phebe [of Philadelphia, m. by N.J. lic. dtd 11 Oct. 1733 John Plaskett of same], Sarah Biles.

4. John, b. 31 1st mo. 1678; on 2 2nd mo. 1707 gr. cert. to Chesterfield to m. Mary Lambert, daughter of Thomas and Mary.

5. Johannah, b. 1 1st mo. 1679; on 4 7th mo. had leave to m. Samuel Beakes and had Johannah and Rebeckah Beakes.

6. Rebeckah, b. 29 10th mo. 1680 in Pennsylvania though listed in Bucks Arrivals; on 18 6th mo. 1702 had leave to m. Joseph Janney, son of Thomas and Margery, and had Martha and Ann Janney.

7. Mary, b. 11th mo. 1682 in Pennsylvania though also listed in Bucks Arrivals; m. ----- Robbins and had son William.

8. Ann, b. 13 4th mo. 1685, not listed in

Bucks Arrivals; m. 12th mo. 1706/7 Thomas Yardley and reported m. contrary to
discipline, 3 10th mo. 1707.

ii. Charles, in 1693 in Pennsylvania or elsewhere (mother's will); came with brother
William on the *Elizabeth and Sarah* on 4
4th mo. 1679; m., as first husband, Sarah
Wood, born undoubtedly in England, youngest daughter of John Wood, sometime of
Attercliffe, Parish of Sheffield, Yorkshire, later of Crookhorn [Crewkerne, now
Morrisville, Pa.], Bucks County, whose
will dated 20 March 1692, probated 12 Nov.
1692,[6] names her as Sarah, wife of Charles
Biles. Administration was granted by Burlington Court, 2 Nov. 1696, to widow Sarah
Biles,[21] and Sarah m. (2) by 9 March
1697/8 (West Jersey Deed Book B:658),
John Brearly, on whom see above, p. 54.
Issue: surname Biles

1. John, of Maidenhead, yeoman, m. (1) ----
-----; (2) by N. J. lic. dated 13 Oct.
1738, Elizabeth Carpenter; made his
will 29 May 1740, probated 22 July 17
1740,[22] naming wife Elizabeth, children
Sarah, John, Charles, brother Alexander.

2. Alexander, appears a number of times in
New Jersey Wills and Mr. Cook assigns
to him an intestacy in Maidenhead
Township in Feb. 1782, bond of Benja-
min Biles as admin. 4 March 1782, John
Rozell as fellow-bondsman.[23]

3. Sarah, m. by 1731 ----- Watson.

4. Ann, unm. in 1731. Her mother certainly
had two daughters in 1698 and perhaps
Ann was one.

iii. Jonathan, in 1693 in New England or elsewhere (mother's will); doubtless the man
of this name (b. England ca. 1647) who m.
(1) probably in England, Sarah -----, d.
Beverly, Mass., 20 July 1674; (2) at Beverly, 15 Nov. 1674, Elizabeth Patch, a
daughter of John and Elizabeth (Brackenbury) Patch [see J. Savage, *Gen. Dict. of
New England* 3:368]. Elizabeth d. 20 June
1715; was named as granddaughter of Richard Brackenbury of Salem in his will 14

probably 4th mo. 1684 [Pope, *Pioneers of Mass.* 65].

Issue *by second wife* recorded Beverly:
1. Richard, bapt. 21 April 1678; m. int. 22 Jan. 1695/6 Mary Davis.
2. Rebeckah, bapt. 21 April 1678; m. 22 Dec. 1700 James Patch.
3. Alexander, bapt. 18 May 1679.
4. Mary, b. 27 March 1681, m. 1 July 1707 Nathaniel Roberts of Gloucester.
5. Jonathan, b. 1 May 1683, d. 28 April 1706 aet. ca. 23.
6. Elizabeth, bapt. 29 Nov. 1685, m. 19 Jan. 1709/10 Isaac Hull.
7. Sarah, b. 31 Aug. 1688; m. 31 Dec. 1712 Samuel Harris.
8. Nicholas, b. 8 Nov. 1695, d. 22 June 1725 aet. ca. 31/6; m. 3 Jan. 1716/17 Elizabeth Preston.
9. William, b. 4 May 1696; m. 15 Dec. 1715 Priscilla Morgan.

iv. John, in 1693 in London; had daughter Elizabeth.

v. Rebecca, wife of Robert Scutt in 1693, had William, Rebecca and Elizabeth Scutt.

vi. Thomas, by 1693 had d. leaving widow Mary and children: Thomas, Mary, Rebecka, all minors. The widow Mary appears in both her mother-in-law's will and in that of her brother-in-law William in Pennsylvania, 1705.

NOTES

[1] 1 NJA 21:466, 483, 577 f., 531. There is a very poor account in Eli F. Cooley, *Genealogy of the Early Settlers of Trenton and Ewing* (Trenton 1883) 13-16.

[2] TAG 40:212 citing *Burlington Court Book 1680-1709*, pp. 170, 180, 183.

[3] NJW 1:59 f.   [4] NJW 2:59 f.   [5] TAG 40:212.

[6] BW A-1:61.   [7] West Jersey Deeds B:658.

[8] TAG 40:210-213; GMNJ 40:47 f.

[9] PMHB 45:393.   [10] NJW 5:62.   [11] NJW 1:106.

[12] NJW 5:436.   [13] NJW 3:39 f.   [14] NJW 3:38.

[15] NJW 6:58.   [16] NJW 7:29.

[17] Harrold Edgar Gillingham, *The Gillingham Family, Descendants of Yeamans Gillingham* (Philadelphia 1901), p. 73. This shows ten children of George and Ann and also descendants.

[18]NJW 2:59.

[19]On her and her descendants see Miles White's "William Biles" (PMHB 26:58-70, 192-206, 348-359); also Lewis D. Cook's articles cited in Note 8.

[20]A fuller account will be found in Miles White's article.

[21]J. E. Stillwell, *Historical and Genealogical Miscellany* 2:27; also NJW 1:79 under Byles.

[22]NJW 2:45.

[23]NJW 6:44. The fact that the first name Alexander appears in the Charles Biles family in New Jersey and also in the Jonathan Biles family of Beverly, Massachusetts, goes a long way in confirming our identification of the Jonathan of Beverly with the Jonathan in Dorothy (Strong) Biles' 1693 will as cited above.

BUCKMAN, WILLIAM[1]	*proved*
BUCKMAN, SARAH, his first wife	*proved*
BUCKMAN, SARAH, his daughter	*proved*
BUCKMAN, MARY, his daughter	*proved*
*BUCKMAN, THOMAS, his son	*possible*
+BUCKMAN, JOAN BAGHAM, his mother	*proved*
+*BUCKMAN, EDWARD, his brother	*proved*
+*BUCKMAN, THOMAS, his brother	*proved*
BUCKMAN, RUTH, his sister	*proved*

William Buckman appears on all lists but on List I is called William Bruckman. His wife Sarah is wrongly called Mary on Lists A, B, C, D, E, F, G, H, I, M, Q, U, X, Y and Z, and is included in the phrase "and family" on Lists J, K, L, N, P, S, T and W. She appears correctly on Lists O and V. The daughters Sarah and Mary are on Lists A, B, C, D, E, F, G, H, I, M, O, Q, U, V, X, Y and Z and included in "and family" on Lists J, K, L, N, P, S, T and W. The son Thomas is on no lists. The widowed mother Joan is on Lists O, Q and V, and the sister Ruth on Lists F, O, Q, U and V. William Buckman appears correctly, as stated, on List S, but in the List of Members of the Welcome Society which accompanies that list, the ancestor of Mrs. Theodore Aylward (Joan Buckman), of The Orchards, Langhorne, Pa., who became a member on 25 Oct. 1954, is given as John, an error corrected immediately. The account of this family accompanying List U is badly mixed up.

The surname is spelled Buckman in all primary documents except three, two of which are contemporary copies made in the early 18th century, and one an original, and these three all have Buckmate for a reason not apparent or explainable. All three of these examples occur in connection with William's son-in-law Henry Couper, and will eventually be discussed.

The nature of the proof for the Buckman family's presence on the *Welcome* is such that the family must be divided into two groups. The proof for William, his first wife Sarah, and their daughters Sarah and Mary is to be found in Bucks Arrivals,[2] where these four are stated to have come on the *Welcome* from Billingshurst, Sussex, as the Doylestown version has it correctly, or Billinghurst, as the Philadelphia version spells it. No other member of the family is registered in this source, though Dr. Arthur Edwin Bye claims that the sister Ruth is so registered.

The proof for William's widowed mother Joan, for his brothers Edward and Thomas, and for his sister Ruth, is of a different character. Of these four only Ruth can be found recorded in America, so it is assumed that the mother and the two brothers died during the crossing. The proof for all four is to be found in Dr. E. D. Buckman's 47-volume manuscript genealogy of the Buckman family, now in the Genealogical Society of Pennsylvania. In the first volume is transcribed the text of an account book originally belonging to the widow and continued by her son William, which was last seen by Dr. Buckman in the possession of a descendant, Benjamin Wiggins (1808-1881) before his death. The note book was also seen by William F. Corbett, who died in 1882, in the possession of Thomas Warner of Wrightstown, Pa., but whether Warner had it before or after Wiggins is not clear.[3] In the Buckman Genealogy Benjamin Wiggins was originally #1274 but later he was #1692, without the discrepancy being changed by the compiler. A search for the note book was long ago made by the late Albert Cook Myers and by myself more recently without discovering it. It is certainly in neither the Historical Society of Pennsylvania or the Bucks County Historical Society in Doylestown. Benjamin Wiggins was born 29 10th mo.

1808, died 12 9th mo. 1881, son of Benjamin and Margaret (Buckman) Wiggins; married 16 11th mo. 1836 Mary Ann Chapman of Wrightstown, Pa., and they had four daughters: #5460 Margaret, born 6 5th mo. 1838; #5461 Elizabeth, born 6 12th mo. 1839; #5462 Rachel, born 6 8th mo. 1842; and #5463 Sarah, born 6 11th mo. 1848. It is obvious that all these daughters are now dead and if any left issue, their children must now be extremely old, so that it would be difficult to trace them, since they would doubtless have other surnames than Buckman or Wiggins.

The note book contained "An Account of the widow Buckman's goods put up for Pennsylvania the 20th of the 5th mo. 1682," and similar lists of the goods of Edward Buckman, Thomas Buckman, William Buckman (24 5th mo. 1682), and of Ruth Buckman's box, contents of all itemized and weights duly noted. William Buckman had used the book for further vital records but he did not include the maiden name of his first wife or identify satisfactorily the second wife. The date of his own death was added later, but whether further vital records appeared is unknown, for at least Dr. Buckman did not transcribe them unless on the pertinent pages of his Genealogy.

The brothers Edward and Thomas Buckman were First Purchasers[4] of 300 acres together, but there is no record that William bought any land as a First Purchaser. There is also no record that Edward and Thomas arrived in Pennsylvania, but their brother William took up their rights. See a warrant of William Penn in the hand of Secretary Lehnmann, 22 Nov. 1683, to William Buckman "on the right of his 2 brothers deceased, city lot in proportion to their purchases."[5] The city lot is probably that in the Blackwell Rent Roll of 1689, 47 feet, 1/- for 5 years, on Chestnut Street, in the name of William Buckman.[6] The Buckman family, which certainly had eight members on the *Welcome*, perhaps even nine, is the largest single family with one surname who crossed on the vessel, and the only proved family in which three generations started the voyage. Though two of the eight died without issue, the family has been prolific in many branches and there are probably more descendants of the Buckmans now living than of any other family among the true passengers.[7]

THE BUCKMAN FAMILY

The original home of the Bucks County Buckman family was the parish of Billingshurst, Sussex, the registers of which were examined for me in 1961 by the Vicar, the Rev. R. Evans Hopkins. A number of entries were found which could not be placed in the family, although they are undoubtedly of members of the same family. These were as follows:

Dec. 1584	Thomas Buckman m. (indecipherable)
28 May 1638	William Buckman m. Elizabeth (indecipherable)
16 Oct. 1639	Richard Greenfield m. Elizabeth Buckman
2 Feb. 1641/2	Susan Buckman, daughter of (indecipherable)

The Thomas who married in 1584 was probably the great-grandfather of the immigrant William Buckman. The William who married in 1638 was probably an uncle of the immigrant. Whether the Elizabeth who married William Buckman in 1638 was the same person who married Richard Greenfield in 1639 is unknown, but the Susan who was baptized in 1642 may well have been the Susan Buckman recorded in Quaker records as buried at Ninnyhurst in 2nd mo. 1668.

No success has been had in locating any English probate records of this family.

1. Edward Buckman, the first of this line of whom we can be sure, was married in the Parish of Billingshurst, Sussex, 3 Oct. 1648, to a woman of whom the first name was certainly Joan and whose last name was read by the Vicar as possibly Bagham.[8] Besides the entries cited above, there were also births of two sons of Edward and Joan, and of one granddaughter, but after that the name Buckman does not appear in the Billingshurst registers until the last half of the nineteenth century. Either the Buckmans all became Quakers or moved away or died out in Billingshurst.

Some, if not all, of the Buckmans of Billingshurst did become Friends, including Edward and Joan who had recorded in the records of the Quarterly Meeting of Sussex and Surrey, as of Shipley Meeting, the births of three daughters named Mary, Ruth and Sarah, but as yet we have no birth record for William Buckman in either Anglican or Quaker records.

He was, however, associated with his brothers Edward and Thomas and his sister Ruth so closely that it is certain that he also was a son of Edward and Joan. It is quite possible that he was baptized by Anglican rite in a neighboring parish.

According to Quaker records Edward Buckman died on 13 5th mo. 1670 and was buried at Chiltington on the 15th of the same month. His widow did not remarry but in 1682 she embarked with her son William and his family, sons Edward and Thomas and her daughter Ruth, on the *Welcome* to come to Pennsylvania, but as neither the widow nor Edward and Thomas have ever been found alive in any American record, it is presumed that all three died of the smallpox on the way.

In the account book already cited was this: "William Buckman the elder came into Pennsylvania in the year of our Lord 1682 the 25th of the 6th Month." This has been thought by some to negate the *Welcome* claim, since the ship did not arrive until late October, but the date here recorded is probably either that on which the Buckmans left Billingshurst for some coastal port, or, more probably that on which they were about to embark.

The account book, already mentioned, contained the following:

An account of the widow Buckman's goods put up for Pennsylvania the 29th of the 5th mo. 1682:

In the least chest 2 pais of Sheets, and two pairs of pillow coats; weaving linen, weighed 78 lbs: marked B.

In the bigest chest 3 pairs of Sheets, 3 Small clothes, one bolster tick; other linen clothes, weighed 138 lbs.

In an old meal trough, 4 suits of clothese and other old things, weighed 175.

In a powdering tub, woollen yard weighed 33.

In an old sack, 2 Blanketts, a tongs, a yard of Curtain, 3 hand wipers, hops, weighed 69.

In a new cooler, Some bacon weighed 90.
The bounate [bonnet?] hat capes and --- weighed 32 lbs. One bed and blankets and pillows and a pair of sheets, weighed 85 lbs.

Two bolsters, a pair of Sheets, 2 blankets, 2 coverlets weighed 70 lbs.

Below this the total weight was computed (with digits running the other way of the page): 78, 138, 175, 33, 69, 90, 32, 85, 70 = 770 + 29, 54 = 843 [really 853], and then, "Widow Buckmans goods weighed 843 lbs" and

An account of Edward Buckmans goods put up for Pennsylvania ye 20th of 5th mo 1682 and Thomas Buckmans.

In the bigest chest, 3 suits of clothes, 14 shifts, 5 pairs of shoes, 3 pairs of stockings, marked EB [i.e. the chest, not the stockings].

In the Old Iron chest, 3 spitters, 2 mattocks, 2 Sledges, 2 hoes, and chisels, and augers and axes, and a hand saw, fire pan, tongs, and cleaver; weighed by gross 300. One iron bar weighed 27 lbs.

Thomas Buckmans goods, iii boiling tubs, Brass Kettle, 24 pewter dishes; Some porringers and other things, weighed 132 lbs, marked B. Two hand Saws and one cross Curf [cut, of course] Saw.

The addition, running as before the other way of the page, was: Ed. B. 223, 38, 26, 27, 140 = 554 [sic]; Thos. B. 160, 132, 60 = 352, and "Edward Buckmans goods weighed 374 [sic] and Thomas Buckmans 353." The discrepancy in the totals of Edward Buckman's weights may be due to carelessness in copying. Then follows:

An account of William Buckman's goods, put up for Pennsylvania ye 24th of [remainder of date illegible, which is surprising, for it could only have been "5th mo. 1682"].

In the bigest chest, 9 sheets, 12 napkins, 3 Table Cloths, Some Shifts and old Linen weighed 132 lbs marked WB.

In the least chest 3 suits of clothes and Old things weighed 72.

In ye old cou[n]ting box, 5 blankets, one rug, 2 candlesticks, one flagon and other odd things weighed 170 lbs.

2 Iron Pots weighed 35 lbs.

2 Spits, 4 crane rods, and a powderer weighed 20 lbs in a box, some linen goods weighed 37 lbs. In a firkin, Old things weighed 21, Old Sacks weighed 23 lbs, Some old firkins, weighed 36 lbs.

2 Beds, 4 Bolsters, 3 pillows, 2 sheets, 2 Blankets, weighed 289 lbs, Frying pans weighed 11 lbs, 2 Crane Irons, weighed 85 lbs.

In the longest box of William Buckmans goods some tools and axes, and pot hooks weighed 253 lbs.

Of Edward Buckmans goods, one gun and a chain, six Iron Wedges, weighed in all 60 lbs.

Of the widow Buckmans goods one posnet and leaden weights in all 348, one iron pot, one Kettle, a Brass sickle, one Basket, one cross curf [cut] saw, one pair of belts, one bag of nails, one box marked WB, one Sack, 2 lbs shot, 5 lbs powder.

Ruth Buckmans box--Some linen Clothes, weighed 54 lbs.

The total, as before running the other way of the page, was Will B.: 132, 72, 170, 35, 37, 21, 23, 36, 289, 21, 85, 253 = 1064 [sic] + 7 = 1071 [sic], and "William Buckmans goods weighed 1071 lbs."

The historical value of this series of memoranda is immense, for it does much to illuminate us on the kind of possessions persons migrating from England to Pennsylvania in the 17th century brought with them. These goods were not intended for sale, since they were not entered in the London Port Book, but there are some items in the inventory which do cause wonder.

Since Edward and Joan (Bagham) Buckman had children named Edward, Thomas and Ruth, as well as the daughters Mary and Sarah not named here, it becomes certain that William Buckman was also their son, especially since the evidence of the warrant shows that he was a brother of Edward and Thomas.

Issue: surname Buckman
2 i.   William, b. Sussex, probably ca. 1650, d. Bucks Co., Pa., 9 8th mo. 1716.
   ii.   Edward, bapt. Billingshurst, Sussex, 7 Nov. 1651; d. at sea, unm., early fall of 1682; with brother Thomas a First Purchaser of 300 acres which right went afterwards to their brother William.
   iii. Thomas, bapt. Billingshurst, Sussex, 5 Nov. 1654; d. at sea, unm., early fall of 1682; Mr. Colket, having found reference to a Thomas Buckman at a Friends Meeting held at the house of John Shaw in Shipley, 8 9th mo. 1682, after the *Welcome* had arrived in America, concluded that this man had intended to come but changed his mind.

The evidence of the devolution of Thomas's
share in the 300-acre right to his brother
William forces us to regard the Thomas in
England on 8 9th mo. 1682 as another man
whose wife Elizabeth died 30 10th mo. 1682,
bur. Fishlake.

iv.   Mary, b. 7 7th mo. 1656 (Shipley record),
      no further trace. She would have been 26
      in 1682 and perhaps already married.

3 v. Ruth, b. 4 Feb. 1659/60 (Shipley record),
      d. New Jersey, probably by 27 Nov. 1716.

vi.   Sarah, b. Sussex, 16 9th mo. 1669, d. there,
      4 8th mo. 1670.

2. William Buckman, the immigrant, was born,
probably at or near Billingshurst, Sussex, about the
year 1650, son, probably the eldest, of Edward and
Joan (Bagham) Buckman. Though no record of his
birth or baptism has been found, he is associated
with the other children of his parents in the baggage memoranda already quoted, and he inherited the
land rights of his brothers Edward and Thomas when
they died without issue. There can be no doubt of
his position in this family. He came to America on
the *Welcome* with his first wife Sarah, whose maiden
name has not been discovered, their daughters Sarah
and Mary, his two brothers Edward and Thomas, his
sister Ruth, and their widowed mother, Joan Buckman.
There is a possibility that his eldest child Thomas
started the voyage with the others but died of the
smallpox en route.

General W. W. H. Davis, author of the *History of
Bucks County, Pennsylvania,* appears to have seen
the baggage memoranda cited above but believed that
the first name of the widow was Ruth, rather than
Joan. He believed that the Buckmans of the baggage
memoranda, who did not in his view include our William but another of the same name, spent their
first winter in a cave south of Fallsington. In
the Strawn family, who descend, of course, from the
Buckmans, there was a strong tradition that their
ancestors, supposed usually to have been Strawns,
lived out the first winter in a cave on the bank of
the Delaware. It is certain that many early Pennsylvanians did live for a time in such places, so
this may represent a genuine tradition.

The Middletown Monthly Meeting minutes show 2 8th
mo. 1690 the names of contributors to the meeting
house fund and among them we find Willm Buckman with

0-05-01. He was appointed one of several to lay
out a road from Newtown to the ferry on the second
Wednesday in December 1693, reappointed 10 June
1696, on which day the work was reported done.[9]
Similarly, on 5 Oct. 1697, he was appointed to lay
out a road from Wrightstown to Neshamineh Meeting
House, and he was a juror in 1684,[10] on the grand
jury in 1688, 1689, 1691 and 1698, a witness on
14 April 1698.[11]

Bucks Deeds 2:142, dated 7 Sept. 1697, recorded
14 April 1697, show that William Buckman of Newtown,
yeoman, sold to John Shaw of the same, yeoman, for
£24, land which had been granted to William Buckman
by the Proprietor, 13 Sept. 1686. Bucks Deeds 2:
143, dated 7 May 7 William and Mary 1695, recorded
11 Oct. 1697, show that William Buckman of Bucks,
husbandman, bought for £30 from Robert Webb of the
Town and County of Philadelphia, gent., and Elizabeth his wife, who had been the widow of John Barber [a *Welcome* passenger, as were Elizabeth and her
father John Songhurst]. Bucks Deeds 3:242, dated
12 March 1704/5, recorded 3 Dec. 1705, show that
John Rowland and wife Priscilla of Bristol [Town-
ship and they were both *Welcome* passengers also],
he a yeoman, she formerly Priscilla Shepperd [and
as such a First Purchaser], sold to William Buckman
land which Priscilla had bought from William Penn,
19 Aug. 1681, before her marriage to John Rowland.
Bucks Deeds 4:34, dated 7 Dec. 11 Anne 1708, acknowledged same date, show that Henry Cooper [a
son-in-law of William Buckman] of Newtown, blacksmith, signed bv mark a deed to William Buckman,
consideration £90. We should also add the patent
to William Buckman mentioned above in the preceding
sketch whereby he was granted a city lot in the
right of his two deceased brothers. These are all
the deeds of William Buckman found in either Bucks
or Philadelphia counties.

In Thomas Holme's "Mapp of ye Improved Part of
Pensilvania," undated but in the mid-1680s, the name
Buckman appears on a rectangular plot, with the
southeast corner cut off, which lies in the second
tier of properties from the Bucks-Philadelphia
line two or three miles west of Neshamineh Creek,
and approximately where the U of Bucks appears on
the map. On a "Map of Newtown 1703,"[12] William
Buckman is shown as owner of a country lot of 668
acres, a Town lot of 59 acres, total 727 acres,

on the west side of Newtown, precisely where, on
Holme's map, appears the name Elizabeth Barber, i.e.
this was the property purchased in 1695 from the
Webbs, originally granted to John Barber who did
not survive to enjoy it.

The first wife Sarah died 10 5th mo. 1690, probably as the result of childbed, and William Buckman waited sixteen years before he married again.
His first intentions to marry Elizabeth Wilson
were made at Middletown, 1 6th mo. 1706, second
intentions 5 7th mo. 1706, but of her ancestry we
know nothing. W. H. J. asked in PMHB 8:441 who
this Elizabeth Wilson was but no reply was ever
printed. Dr. Buckman's Genealogy 1:25 says that she
was probably a daughter of Stephen and Sarah (Baker)
Wilson but that there is no proof. Quite so, for
this is a guess and wrong. Stephen Wilson and Sarah
Baker were married at Falls Monthly Meeting in 6th
mo. 1692, recorded also at Middletown Monthly Meeting: they had a son Stephen born 29 2nd mo. 1695/6
and a daughter Mary born 1 1st mo. 1696/7, and
their children are shown in Mrs. Brey's book, *A
Quaker Saga*, page 415. The Wilsons continued to be
recorded at Middletown until on 5 3rd mo. 1698 we
learn that Stephen Wilson had removed out of the
province. Fortunately, we know where he went, merely to Hopewell Township, then Burlington, now Hunterdon County, New Jersey, where, as yeoman, he
made his will on 26 March 1707, probated 19 May
1708,[13] naming wife Sarah, minor children Stephen,
Sarah, Mary, Rebecca, John, Samuel; executors: wife
and brother-in-law Samuel Baker; John Routledge to
assist in educating the children; witnesses: William Bryant, John Routledge, John Reading. No
Buckman connection appears, and a child of this
couple would not have been more than fifteen years
of age when William Buckman's first child by his
second wife was born. At the wedding of Stephen
and Sarah (Baker) Wilson, no Elizabeth Wilson appears, and, of course, at that date Elizabeth
Wilson was not to become Elizabeth Buckman for
fourteen years. If Stephen Wilson was the father
of Elizabeth Buckman by an earlier marriage, there
is no evidence of it.

Elizabeth (Wilson) Buckman married, second,
Thomas Story of Falls Meeting, who was not the
well-known Quaker of the same name. They declared
their first intentions at Middletown on 5 10th mo.

1717 and were advised "to try affections a little
further." "A little further" they again declared
their intentions on 6 12th mo. 1717 and second
intentions [the first time obviously did not count]
on 6 1st mo. 1717/18, and Thomas Story had a certificate from Falls Monthly Meeting to marry Elizabeth Buckman at Middletown dated 5 12th mo. 1717/18.
    Of this marriage they had only one son, John
Story, born 26 11th mo. 1718/19. It has been said
that he died unmarried on 30 1st. mo. 1732/3, but
this may be a garbled report of his father's death.
John Story was living much later when on 18 4th mo.
1788 he was named as brother in the will of David
Buckman (#11 below), and he then had sons David and
Samuel Story who are also mentioned in David Buckman's will. When of Newtown "far advanced in years"
he made his own will, 23 3rd mo. 1801, probated 19
Jan. 1805.[14] He mentions sons John [hardly the man
who married at St. Paul's Protestant Episcopal
Church, Philadelphia, 24 March 1760, Elizabeth Green],
Thomas [married at Middletown, 19 10th mo. 1786,
Rachel Jenks], and David Story [married at Middletown, 19 4th mo. 1792, Rachel Richardson]; son Samuel; daughter Mary Smith (wife of Edward); children
of daughter Mary Smith: Amos Briggs, Phineas Briggs,
Thomas Briggs, James Briggs, David Briggs, Elizabeth
Ashton formerly Briggs, Ann Briggs, Mary Briggs, Rachel Briggs; executors: sons Thomas and David; witnesses: Hamton Wilson, Anne Wilson, Anne Wilson,
Phineas Jenks. It would appear that Mary Story had
married, first, ----- Briggs, father of all her
children, second Edward Smith.
    Elizabeth (Wilson)(Buckman) Story died 13 March
1732/3.
    The account book already mentioned contains the
notation, naturally in a different hand from William's, that he died in Makefield, 9 8th mo. 1716.
According to Middletown Monthly Meeting records,
he was buried on 11 8th mo. 1716. His will dated
4 7th mo. 1716, probated 26 Oct. 1716,[15] had as
witnesses Stephen Twining, John Frost and Joseph
Scott. It reads as follows:

    William Buckman of newtown in the County of
    Bucks: to eldest son William Buckman plantation
    in Newtown purchased from Samuel Hough and also
    piece of meadow and woodland by Neshamineh Creek
    to the extent of 50 acres, and if William lack
    heirs of his body, then to son David Buckman or

to son Thomas Buckman; to wife Elizabeth Buckman
remainder of lands until son Thomas is aged 21
and one-third part afterwards during life or
widowhood. To sons Thomas Buckman and David
Buckman the last mentioned lands from the time
Thomas is 21, he to have the town lot in his
share, subject to the life interest of his mother
as stated above; if either Thomas or David die
in their minority, then the survivor shall have
the whole, paying £10 current money of the province to each of the two daughters Elizabeth
Buckman and Rebeckah when they are 21. To son-
in-law edward Beck five shillings to be paid 12
months after testator's decease; Beck is indebted
to testator about eleven pounds old Currency
which debt and also thirty shillings more current
money of the province is to go to each of the
three children of said Edward Beck, Sarah, Fran-
ciss and Edward, to be paid when they are respectively aged 21. To daughter Mary Strawhen fifty
shillings current money to be paid 12 months after testator's decease and to her five children
Ruth, Sarah, William, Henry and John fifty shillings when they respectively arrive at the age
of 21. To daughter Ruth Blaker fifteen pounds
current money to be paid 12 months after testator's decease. To two youngest daughters Elizabeth and Rebeckah Buckman fifteen pounds current
money each to be paid at age of 21 years. To
three sons William, Thomas and David, all the
carpenter toolls equally divided. To son William Buckman one Cowe called prissy and her calf.
To wife Elizabeth Buckman all rest and residue
of personal estate as long as she remains a widow
but if she marry, then this to the two daughters
Elizabeth and Rebeckah one-half to be equally
divided between them. [Apparently he intends
that each shall get half and not that they shall
share a half, for no provision is made for the
other half.] Wife Elizabeth Buckman and son William Buckman, joint executors.

Though he signed by mark, the mark is "Will" and he
was able to write, as other documents show.

  Issue: surname Buckman
   by first wife Sarah
4 i.   Thomas, b. in England, probably at Billings-
    hurst, Sussex, 4 7th mo. 1676; death date

                    unknown.
5 ii.   Sarah, b. in England, probably at Billings-
           hurst, Sussex, 10 9th mo. 1677; d., prob-
           ably v.p., in Bucks County, before 4 7th
           mo. 1716.
6 iii.   Mary, b. in England, probably at Billings-
           hurst, Sussex, 23 9th mo. 1680, bapt.
           at Billingshurst, 13 Jan. 1680/1; d. in
           Bucks County, 1739-40.
7 iv.   Ruth, b. in Bucks County, 22 4th mo. 1688;
           d. ca. 1750.
8 v.   William, b. in Bucks County, 28 4th mo.
           1690; d. shortly before 13 Jan. 1755.
      by second wife Elizabeth Wilson
9 vi.   Thomas, b. Bucks County, 8 7th mo. 1707,
           d. shortly before 12 Sept. 1734.
10 vii.   Elizabeth, b. Bucks County, 14 4th mo. 1709,
           d. 29 11th mo. 1793.
11 viii.   David, b. Bucks County, 22 9th mo. 1711,
           d. 10 11th mo. 1791.
    ix.   Rebecca, b. Bucks County, 24 11th mo.
           1712/13, d. 11 2nd or 3rd mo. 1717. The
           printed list of marriages of Middletown
           Monthly Meeting shows a Rebecca Buckman
           married to Joseph Wildman, 15 Nov. 1709.
           This marriage cannot be fitted into the
           Buckman family and the entry of the same
           marriage under Joseph Wildman's name
           gives Rebecca's maiden name as Bunting
           and this is probably correct.

     3. Ruth Buckman, daughter of Edward and Joan (Bag-
ham) Buckman, was born in England, probably at Billingshurst, Sussex, on 4 Feb. 1659/60, and came to
America in 1682 with the rest of the family. Though
it is claimed by Dr. Arthur Edwin Bye[16] that her
arrival was registered by Phineas Pemberton in Bucks
Arrivals, along with her brother William and his
family, this is not so. She was recorded in Pennsylvania as witness to the wedding of Thomas Rutter
and Rebecca Staples which took place at Pennsbury
on 11 10th mo. 1685, recorded at Middletown Monthly
Meeting. The Land Office at Harrisburg[17] has a request dated 17 8th mo. 1695 for head rights for
Jacob Turner and Ruth Buckman.
     Ruth married 4 3rd mo. 1687 at the house of Josh-
ua Wright in Nottingham Township, Burlington County, New Jersey, recorded at Chesterfield Meeting,

Richard Harrison, who was a witness at Middletown
Monthly Meeting on 27 9th mo. 1716 of the wedding
of Ruth's nephew William Buckman to Esther Penquite, but as Ruth was not present, she was probably
dead by then.

Dr. E. D. Buckman states that Richard Harrison
was from Burlington, Yorkshire, and was a passenger
on the fly boat *Martha*, arriving in the fall of
1677. We have not seen the document which proves
this statement, but in the list of passengers of the
Martha which will appear in connection with an account of early shipping to the New Jersey bank of
the Delaware in Welcome Society Publications, vol.
1, the name of Richard Harrison is included and the
sources cited are Samuel H. Smith, *History of Novo-
Caesaria or New Jersey* (Burlington 1765; reprinted
1890) and E. M. Woodward and J. F. Hageman, *History
of Burlington and Mercer Counties, New Jersey* (1883).
No connection has been seen with James Harrison of
Pennsbury Manor or with any other Harrison family
in New Jersey or New England, where the first name
Richard seems to be unusually frequent.

Richard Harrison married, second, 5 3rd mo. 1720,
Alice (Wright) Steward, widow of Joseph Steward who
had married her, 2nd intentions at Chesterfield, 7
12th mo. 1694/5.[18] He had arrived in America aged
14 years, on the *Submission* as a member of James
Harrison's household. Alice was probably a member
of the Quaker Wright family of Nottingham, but how
is unknown. She is mentioned in the will of her
first husband Steward dated 3 July 1715, probated
20 Oct. 1715,[19] which also names their children:
John, Joseph, Josiah, Elizabeth and Ellen. One of
the witnesses, who also made the inventory, was
Richard Herrison, her second husband, whose own
will was dated 20 Dec. 1739, probated 5 Oct. 1742.[20]
This will names wife Alse and children William, Peter, George, Richard, Ruth Starkey, Sarah Rogers and
granddaughter Rebeckah Harrison. In the file are
receipts from the widow, from Sarah Rogers, Richard
Harrison, Ruth Starkey and William Harrison, but
none from sons Peter or George. The will of Alice
Harrison, of Hanover Township, Burlington County,
dated 24 April 1759, probated 11 Feb. 1761,[21] names
son John and his sons William and John; son Josiah's
two sons Joseph and Josiah; granddaughter Martha
Chapman; son Joseph Steward, Elizabeth Reckless,
Alice Fowler, Alice Feagins, Elizabeth Parent and

Susannah Steward, all of these children or grandchildren of Alice by her first husband except possibly Elizabeth Reckless and Alice Feagins who have
defied identification. Joseph Burch of Chesterfield in his will dated 27 Nov. 1703, probated 4
May 1704[22] names among other heirs the children of
Joseph Steward, not named, but what relationship
there was, if any, is unknown.

All of Richard Harrison's children appear to be
by Ruth Buckman.

    Issue: surname Harrison

i.   William, eldest son in father's will; m.,
       2nd int. Chesterfield, 2 11th mo. 1728
       Sarah Bullock who is called Sarah Harri-
       son in will of her father John Bullock
       of Burlington Co., yeoman, dated 4 May
       1741, no date of probation,[23] naming
       wife Sarah and other children besides
       Sarah Harrison. This William may have
       been the William Harrison of Monmouth
       Co., intestate, admin. 8 Nov. 1768 to
       Thomas Harrison of Upper Freehold, said
       co.[24]

ii.   Peter, b. 8 10th mo. 1691; m. 2nd int.,
       Chesterfield, 2 11th mo. 1723/4, Sarah
       Starkey. He made his will as of New Han-
       over, weaver,[25] naming children Isaac,
       Joseph, Thomas, Sarah Fox, Mary, Ruth
       and Deborah; father Richard Harrison;
       executors: wife Sarah, son Thomas; wit-
       nesses: Joseph Rogers, William Rogers,
       Thomas Earl.

         Issue: surname Harrison, order uncer-
           tain

       1. Isaac.
       2. Joseph.
       3. Thomas.
       4. Sarah, m. before 1748 ----- Fox.
       5. Mary.
       6. Ruth, probably m. by N.J. lic. dated
          17 Jan. 1759 Benjamin Wright of Bur-
          lington.
       7. Deborah.

iii.   George, no probate and no marriage record
       were found but in 1733 he had an unnamed
       wife and four children of whom one was a
       minor named Rebeckah. This information
       comes from the will of a Joseph Steward

dated 11 June 1733, probated 21 July
1733,[26] which leaves the residue to the
wife and four children of George Harrison. This Joseph was not, however, the
stepbrother of the same name who was living in 1759 but probably the son of a
Simon Steward (probably a brother of
Alice Wright's first husband), whose
will dated 17 Dec. 1708, probated 12
Feb. 1708/9,[27] mentions unnamed wife and
minor children Samuel, Joseph, Esther;
inventory by Joseph Steward. The wife
was named Mary as is shown by the will
of her next husband, Richard Chappill
of Freehold, dated 17 Nov. 2 George I,
probated 28 April 1715,[28] which names
wife's children Hester, Samuel and Joseph Stuard; Alice Steward a witness.
Mary (-----)(Steward) Chappill m. again
----- Woodel, and had by him Girshom
and John Woodel, called brothers under
age in the will of their half-brother
Joseph Steward the testator. No more has
been found about them.

iv.   Richard, m. (1) by N.J. lic. dated 21 June
1736, Rachel Everingham of Monmouth Co.;
(2) Mary -----, mentioned in his will
dated 19 May 1777, probated 19 May 1777,
which[29] calls him of New Hanover; mentions minor grandson Israel Harrison;
granddaughter Rachel Harrison; wife Mary;
daughter-in-law Edith Harrison; friend
John Rogers and daughter Edith Harrison
[the same as the daughter-in-law?].
    Probable issue: surname Harrison
1. Richard, d.v.p., m. by N.J. lic. dated
   14 Aug. 1765 Edith Wright, perhaps
   widow of Joseph Wright of Salem Co.,
   whose will dated 19 April 1758, probated 14 Feb. 1761,[30] mentions wife
   Edith but no daughter Edith. This
   pair may have been parents of the two
   grandchildren mentioned in the will
   cited above.

v.   Ruth, m., 2nd int. Chesterfield 4 9th mo.
1714 James Starkey of New Hanover whose
will dated 22 Feb. 1748/9, probated 18
April 1749,[31] names wife Ruth, children:

Nathan, Sarah, Ruth, Edith, Mary, Alice,
Phebe; Richard Harrison a witness.
Issue: surname Starkey
1. Nathan, probably m. by N.J. lic. dated
   1 Nov. 1736 Edith Wilson.
2. Sarah, probably m. by N.J. lic. dated
   25 March 1746 William Mount of Monmouth Co.
3. Ruth, probably m. by N.J. lic. dated 29
   Sept. 1748 Charles Collins.
4. Edith.
5. Mary.
6. Alice.
7. Phebe.
vi.   Sarah, m., 2nd int. Chesterfield 4 3rd mo.
       1721 Joseph Rogers of New Hanover whose
       will dated 23 Aug. 1764, probated 16 Dec.
       1771,[32] names daughters Mary Rogers, Sa-
       rah, Ruth, Amy; sons Michael, William,
       John; Thomas Harrison a witness. Joseph
       Rogers was probably a son of John Rogers
       of Nottingham, whose will was dated 13
       April 1698, probated 30 March 1700,[33]
       and directs that son Joseph be appren-
       ticed to a weaver.

4. Thomas Buckman, eldest child of William Buckman (Edward) by his first wife Sarah -----, was born
in England, probably at Billingshurst, Sussex, on 4
7th mo. 1676, one of the three children whose birth
dates appear in the account book. That is all that
is certain about this Thomas. He was not included
in the family when his father registered them in
Bucks Arrivals which may mean no more than that at
the date of registration [1684 or a little later]
Thomas was no longer living in his father's home and
would be expected to be registered where he was then
living. On the other hand, in 1684 this Thomas was
eight, rather young to be apprenticed, and as he was
then the only son, it seems improbable that the father would be willing to lose the services of his son
by apprenticing him elsewhere. But on 8 7th mo.
1707 the firstborn son by the second wife was also
given the name Thomas, so that there seems some like-
lihood that the elder Thomas had by then died. We
have seen, however, instances when the same first
name is given to brothers, both living, and particularly when they were only half-brothers. If death
had occurred, it may have taken place in England

at any time between 1676 and 1682, or it may have
occurred on board the ship as the result of smallpox
or even in Pennsylvania, but before his father made
the entry in Bucks Arrivals. Dr. Bye is sure this
Thomas died at sea, but I see no real evidence.

The argument that the same name would not have been
given to two sons is weaker than one would think,
for this phenomenon can be paralleled. There was,
however, a Thomas Buckman of Gloucester County, New
Jersey, whose will was dated 28 June 1708, probated
13 May 1713,[34] that is, executed when our Thomas
would have been only 32 and the younger half-brother
only one. This man of Gloucester had a wife Elizabeth named executrix, and five daughters named Sarah
(wife of George Homack or Hamack, and they had a son
John), Mary, Elizabeth, Judy and Ruth, all five with
names common in our Buckman family. If this man who
died in 1713 was the Thomas born in 1676, he was rather young to be a grandfather. Moreover, we have a
deed of Thomas Buckman of Gloucester County, blacksmith, 1 March 1696/7, for 29 acres sold to Martin
Jarvis,[35] bought back on 1 7th mo. 1701, as well as
a deed to Thomas Buckman of Gloucester County, blacksmith, 12 Dec. 1699.[36] In 1697 our Thomas would
have been just 21 when he sold land to another.
Moreover, if Thomas of Gloucester was the Thomas born
1676, then William Buckman's will completely over-
looks the five granddaughters in Gloucester County.
The Beck and the Cooper grandchildren were not forgotten, so we conclude that the Thomas born in 1676
was not the man in Gloucester County, though the
latter was probably a member of the Billingshurst
Buckman family.

5. Sarah Buckman, second child and eldest daughter of William Buckman (Edward) by his first wife
Sarah -----, was born in England, probably at Billingshurst, Sussex, and on 10 9th mo. 1677, as the
account book cited above tells us. She is registered as a *Welcome* passenger, having arrived when
she was about five years of age. She was not mentioned as living in her father's will in 1716, but
her husband and her three children are mentioned, so
that it is probable that Sarah had died *vita patris*
some years before. At an unknown date she had married Edward Beck who is named as son-in-law in William Buckman's will and in such a position that we

must conclude that it was Sarah who had married Edward Beck. When Edward Beck died at Solebury in
1736 he left a wife named Sarah but she was probably
not Sarah Buckman. The will of Edward Beck Sr. is
signed by mark and named children as Edward, Jeffry,
Mary, Jane, Rachel, Susanna and Ellen; inventory
made at Solebury, 15 11th mo. 1736/7[37]; bond of
Sarah Beck, widow, 8 11th mo. 1736/7, with William
Saterthwaite, yeoman, of Solebury. Sarah was made
administratrix and signed her account by mark on 8
Feb. 1736/7. The estate came to £50/11/10. Of the
children named in the will of Edward Beck, only the
eldest had been named in the will of their grandfather Buckman, so the other children must have been
by the second wife.

Issue: surname Beck
i.   Sarah, named as eldest in Grandfather Buck-
        man's will; m. William Griffon of Upper
        Makefield, farmer, whose will dated 2
        9th mo. 1743, probated 14 Dec. 1744,
        names sons Peter, Aaron, daughter Eliza-
        beth; wife Sarah; brother-in-law Edward
        Beck.
ii.   Francis or Frances, sex unknown, mentioned
        as living in Grandfather Buckman's will
        in 1716; not mentioned in father's will
        in 1736; no further trace.
iii.   Edward, mentioned in grandfather's will
        in 1716, in father's will in 1736, and
        in brother-in-law's will in 1743; no
        further research done on him.

   6. Mary Buckman, third child and second daughter
of William Buckman (Edward) by his first wife Sarah
-----, was born in England, probably in Billingshurst, Sussex, and on 23 9th mo. 1680, and she was
baptized by Anglican rite in Billingshurst on 13
Jan. 1680/1, which fact may suggest that her mother
was not a Friend. With the rest of the family she
came to America on the *Welcome* in 1682. Tradition
among her Strawn descendants says that she sat on
the lap of William Penn while at sea, and since she
was then a child of two, his interest in her would
make this plausible. There has been handed down in
the Strawn family through ten generations of Strawns,
all of whom were named Jacob, a sea shell which she
brought with her as a toy.
   She married, first, on 30 Nov. 1703[38] under the

auspices of Middletown Monthly Meeting but at the
house of William Twining in Newtown, Henry Cooper
or Couper, as the name was often spelled in contemporary documents. He had been baptized by Anglican
rites in Low Ellington, Yorkshire, on 13 Jan. 1674/5,
son of William Cooper by a wife who may or may not
have been the wife Thomasine, mother of the six
younger children of William Cooper. William Cooper
the father had himself been baptized at Low Ellington on 16 Aug. 1649, son of another William Cooper
of whom we know no more. Besides Henry, William
Cooper the younger had a daughter Elizabeth baptized at Low Ellington, 13 April 1673. It is to be
presumed that the Coopers became Friends only after
the baptism of Henry. In any case, when William
Cooper the younger decided to emigrate, he obtained
from Robert Banks, then parish clerk of Low Ellington, a certificate for the three Anglican baptisms
and also a Friends certificate of removal from the
Massham or Masham Monthly Meeting in Yorkshire dated
26 1st mo. 1699. Both the Anglican and the Friends
certificates were duly deposited at Middletown Monthly Meeting where he also entered the births of his
other children, namely: Jonathan (b. 11 11th mo.
1676/7); Hannah (b. 28 11th mo. 1678/9); Anne (b.
18 2nd mo. 1681); Abraham (b. 24 6th mo. 1684);
Sarah (b. 24 6th mo. 1684, evidently a twin); Joseph (b. 5 8th mo. 1686/7).

The following deeds of Henry Cooper have been
found: Henry Nelson to Henry Cooper, blacksmith,
1 May 3 Anne, acknowledged 15 June 1704, recorded
(BD 3:169) 18 Nov. 1704; Edmund Cowgill to Henry
Cooper of Newtown, blacksmith, 9 Sept. 6 Anne 1707,
acknowledged same day, recorded (BD 3:359) 25 Oct.
1707; Mary Cowper of Newtown and William Buckmate
[sic] of Newtown, yeoman, 1 May 1711 (BD 4:155-157).
This last deed was part of the settlement of Henry
Cooper's estate. The strange signature of William
Buckman as William Buckmate is puzzling.

Henry Cooper's will calls him of Newtown, blacksmith, and is dated 6 12th mo. called Febby 1709,
signed by mark, and probated not in Bucks County
but in Philadelphia County (C:209f.). He leaves to
well-beloved wife Mary Couper £20 current money of
Pennsylvania; also the mare and saddle on wch she
useth to ride, and one Bedd & furniture Suitable;
the rest to be sold for the education of the children who are to have what remains at age 21. The

executors are wife Mary and father-in-law William
Buckmate [sic: both docket copy and original have
this spelling]; witnesses: Robert Heaton Junr.,
John Penquite (by mark), John Cutler. Cutler and
Heaton probated the will on 17 May 1710 and admin-
istration was granted to William Buckmate and Mary
Couper, sole executrix.

Following the death of Henry Cooper in 1710, Mary
remained a widow for about six years, and then married, second, Lancelot Straughan or Strawhen, most
of whose descendants have spelled the name Strawn.
Lancelot was not a Friend and thus far all efforts
to discover his origin have failed. The marriage
took place in 1716. As was seen, Mary was called
Mary Strawhen in the will of her father. There is
also a document in the Middletown Monthly Meeting
records, specifically in the Women's Meetings of
5 5th mo. and 2 6th mo. 1716, when Mary was dealt
with and the following condemnation was drawn up
against her:

> ffrom our Men and Women's Monthly Meeting in
>   Middletown in Bucks County the 6th of the 7th
>   month 1716,
>   Whereas shee that was lately known by the name
> of Mary Couper (Widow of Henry Couper deceased
> being then owned as one of our Society) hath been
> for some time since concerned in Intent of Mar-
> riage with Lancelot Strawhen one who was never
> owned amongst us, And although shee was season-
> ably advised by friends and Relations both pub-
> lickly and in private, And often exhorted both
> by the Overseers of the Meeting and other friends
> not to be concerned with him in that respect,
> And much labour and paines being taken with her
> to bring to a sense of friends dissatisfaction
> with the matter, yet still Shee resisted all
> their advice and Councell, And now at last hath
> marryed the said Lancelot Strawhen contrary to
> the order and Method of our Society; Wee do
> therefore give forth this as a Testimony against
> her for her Misdemeaner, And do disown her (by
> the name of Mary Strawhen) to be any more of our
> Society untill she come to a true sight of her
> disorder, and a sincere Repentance for the same,
> which we heartily wish for the good of her Im-
> mortal Soul.
> Signed by order and in behalf by John Cutler
> of our said Meetings   Margery Cutler

Here a young widow with five children to support
has succeeded in finding a second husband but the
good Friends of the meeting cast her out in the
very month of her father's death, and nothing is
said against Lancelot Strawhen save that he was not
a Friend. No record has been found to show that in
the sequel she ever complied with the demands of the
meeting and returned, though some of her descendants
have been Friends.

There was a Richard Strawhen who witnessed the
marriage of Joseph Lupton to Mercy Twining at Middletown Monthly Meeting on 10 7th mo. 1713, and is
thereafter not found. An attempt to find the original of this certificate in order to verify the
first name has failed. Lancelot Strawhen similarly
signed as witness the marriage certificate of Mary's
brother William Buckman to Esther Penquite, as 21st
name in the lefthand column, 27 9th mo. 1716, two
months after the condemnation.

We hear nothing more of Lancelot until he is dead
and there are no deeds of record and no will, for he
died intestate, administration granted to the widow
in Bucks County on 10 June 1720.[39] Thomas Baynes
signed her bond with her. The inventory was taken
8 4th mo. 1720 by John Wildman and Thomas Thwailes
and came to £34/16/6, one item of unusual interest
being a desk, so Lancelot Strawhen was undoubtedly
literate.

After the death of Lancelot in 1720 Mary and such
of her brood as had not flown the nest probably removed about 1728 to Kent County, Delaware, where
her son-in-law Dennis Pursell owned land, but by
1738 she was in New Jersey for she made her will in
Bethlehem Township, Hunterdon County, 7 Jan. 1738
(1738/9). She names daughters Ruth and Sarah, sons
William Cooper, Henery Cooper, John Cooper and Jacob Starwhen [sic] who is named executor. This will
was written by an exceptionally poor speller, and
it was probated in Bucks County on 10 Sept. 1740 by
the oath of Daniel Ashcraft and on 2 Oct. 1740 by
the affirmation of Richard Mitchell. The third
witness, Robert Hazlet, did not appear. She had
survived the making of her will by about a year and
a half.

    Issue:
      by first husband Henry Cooper
12 i.   Ruth, b. probably ca. 1704.

```
13 ii.    Sarah, b. probably ca. 1705-6.
14 iii.   William, b. probably ca. 1707, d. ca.
             1793.
15 iv.    Henry, b. 25 Jan. 1707/8.
16 v.     John, b. 19 April 1709, d. 1783.
          by second husband Lancelot Strawhen
17 vi.    Jacob, b. 1717-1720, d. 20 Dec. 1800.
```

7. Ruth Buckman, fourth child and third daughter, and first child born in Pennsylvania, of Wiliam Buckman (Edward) by his first wife Sarah -----, was born in Bucks County, 22 4th mo. 1688, and died ca. 1750. She is mentioned in her father's will in 1716. She married at Middletown Monthly Meeting, 24 9th mo. 1708, Peter Blaker, born at sea on the Ship *Concord* in 6th mo. 1683, recorded at Abington, who was still living in 1750, son of Johannes Bleicker by his wife Rebecca, of Northampton Township, Bucks County.[40] The Bleickers were also probably the parents of Catherine who married, as first wife, 29 May 1702, Edmund Cowgill (son of Ellen Cowgill), and he married, second, in October 1707, Ann Osborne. The Bleickers were also parents of a son Paul who is called uncle in the will of Peter's son John. The only Blaker deeds found are those which are shown for Peter, son of John, below.

```
Issue: surname Blaker
i.     John, d. 15 5th mo. 1778; m. (1) 16 8th
          mo. 1735 Catherine Williams, (2) ca.
          1754 Mary Briggs, who was mentioned in
          his will probated 4 Jan. 1777.[41] This
          will also mentions sons Peter Blaker
          and Paul Blaker; uncle Paul Blakers,
          probably then deceased; cousin Peter
          Blakers; son John Blaker; son Acchilles
          Blaker; beloved wife Mary Blaker; five
          daughters: Ruth Hibbs, Sarah Hibbs,
          Pheaby Wiggens, Catherine Weismer; Mary
          Hamton; executors sons Peter and Paul
          Blaker; witnesses: John Story, Henry
          Cooper, Paul Blaker. The second wife
          is identified by Dr. Buckman as the
          daughter of John and Mary (Watson)
          Briggs, but Mr. Colket, who puts the
          second marriage after 6 1st mo. 1757,
          says that she was a widow Briggs. If
          so, Bucks file 760 shows the estate of
          William Briggs Jr., admin. granted 7
```

Dec. 1750, bond signed by the widow Mary Briggs, Edmund Briggs of Middletown, yeoman, James Briggs, yeoman, and William Croasdale of Newtown, and Thomas Nelson of Middletown.

Issue: surname Blaker

1. Peter, who may or may not be the Peter Blaker with wife Sarah whose admin. is in BA 2112 (1788). The latter was father to Rachel, wife of John Erwin of Newtown who jointly sold to William Cooper of Horsham, 4 April 1811 (rec. BD 40:7, 22 May 1811). He was also father to Ruth, wife of Andrew McKee of Bucks, saddler, who jointly sold to John Johnson of Newtown, weaver, 24 July 1806, (rec. BD 36: 337, 24 July 1806). Peter Blaker and wife Sarah of Upper Makefield gave a mortgage to Letitia Baker of Lower Makefield, 13 May 1776, rec. (BD 18: 342) 13 June 1776.
2. Paul.
3. John.
4. Achilles.
5. Ruth, m. ----- Hibbs.
6. Sarah, m. Wrightstown, 21 4th mo. 1762 James Hibbs.
7. Phebe, m. Wrightstown, 12 12th mo. 1764 Isaac Wiggens.
8. Catherine, m. ----- Weismer.
9. Mary, m. Wrightstown, 20 12th mo. 1775 Joseph Hamton.

8. William Buckman, fifth child of William Buckman (Edward) by his first wife Sarah -----, was born in Bucks County, 28 4th mo. 1690, about a fortnight before his mother's death. He died shortly before 13 Jan. 1755, the date of probation of his will executed 15 Sept. 1751.[42] He married at Middletown Monthly Meeting, 27 9th mo. 1716, Esther Penquite, born 21 2nd mo. 1694, died 20 11th mo. 1758, daughter of John and Agnes (Sharp) Penquite, of Wrightstown. Seventy persons signed their marriage certificate, including John Penquite, Agnes Penquite, Elizabeth Buckman, John Penquite Jr., Nicholas Penquite, Mary Strawhen, Jane Penquite and Lancelot Strawhen as the 21st signer in the lefthand column.

His will calls him of Newtown, yeoman, and names
wife Hester and son Jacob as executors. Jacob is to
provide for his mother; son William, who has wife
Jane and minor son William; sons John, Joseph,
Thomas, Isaac and daughter Sarah Taylor; witnesses:
Charles Stewart, Thomas Buckman Jr., Wm Ashburn.
William and Esther Buckman conveyed to their eldest
son William Buckman Jr., 15 May 1752, acknowledged
12 June 25 George II 1752, recorded 1 Sept. 1752.[43]

Issue: surname Buckman
18 i.   Sarah, b. 15 3rd mo. 1718, d. by 13 10th
          mo. 1785.
19 ii.   William, b. 19 1st mo. 1719, d. 6 9th mo.
          1782.
20 iii.   John, b. 15 5th mo. 1721.
21 iv.   Joseph, b. 16 5th mo. 1723.
22 v.   Thomas, b. 28 5th mo. 1725.
23 vi.   Isaac, b. 29 3rd mo. 1729.
24 vii.   Jacob, birth record not found.

9.   Thomas Buckman, eldest child of William
Buckman (Edward) by his second wife Elizabeth Wilson, was born in Bucks County, 8 7th mo. 1707 and
was therefore still a minor when his father made
his will in 1716. He died by 12 Sept. 1734, date of
probation of his will which was executed in 5th
mo. 1734,[44] naming wife Agnes and Abraham Chapman
as executors; minor son Thomas; daughters Rebeckah
and Agnes; witnesses: Esther Buckman, Mary O Gibson,
David Buckman. He married in 3rd mo. 1726 Agnes
Penquite, born 22 8th mo. 1705, daughter of John
and Agnes (Sharp) Penquite.   The will alludes to
Agnes's pregnancy.

Issue: surname Buckman
i.   Rebecca, b. 11 1st mo. 1727, not mentioned
        in uncle David's will in 1788.
25 ii. Thomas, b. 12 4th mo. 1729.
iii.   Agnes, b. 6 2nd mo. 1732; m. Wrightstown,
        27 9th mo. 1750 Jacob Hewlings of Eves-
        ham, Burlington Co., N.J. His will is
        dated 31 March 1758, probated 30 May
        1758,[45] and names wife Agnes, children
        Jacob, Theodosia, Sarah, Agnes, all
        minors; brother Wm Hewlings, brother-in-
        law Micajah Wills; Elizabeth Buckman a
        witness. This Jacob was son of another
        Jacob who d. just before the son.

iv.   Elizabeth, b. 1734, unborn in her father's
      will, so perhaps posthumous; said to
      have m. John Inskeep of Evesham by N.J.
      lic. dated 26 June 1758, the printed
      record of the bond calling her Buchanan.
      Dr. Buckman made Elizabeth m. a John
      Inskeep, son of Abram and Sarah, but
      as this man was b. 29 Jan. 1757, this
      is an impossible identification.

10.   Elizabeth Buckman, daughter of William
Buckman (Edward) by his second wife Elizabeth Wilson, was born in Bucks County, 14 4th mo. 1709,
died there 29 11th mo. 1793. She married at Wrightstown, 22 4th mo. 1726, Zebulon Heston, born 4 11th
mo. 1702, died 12 3rd mo. 1776, son of Zebulon Heston of Middletown. His will dated 26 6th mo. 1773
mentions all of his children except Rebecca. There
is a periodical called *The Heston Historian,* founded
by John P. Heston, 9377 Chatham, Allen Park, Mich.,
in which much information about the Hestons has been
published.

Issue: surname Heston
i.   Elizabeth, b. 30 4th mo. 1727, m. 2 9th
      mo. 1747, Titus Fell.
ii.   Jemima, b. 27 8th mo. 1728, m. (1) 2 10th
      mo. 1751 Jonathan Kinsey; (2) 22 11th
      mo. 1758 Benjamin Doan.
iii. Rebecca, b. 3 5th mo. 1730, probably d.y.
iv.   Rachel, b. 30 11th mo. 1731/2; m. 29 1st
      mo. 1750 Samuel Merrick.
v.   Zebulon, b. 18 11th mo. 1733/4; m. Buck-
      ingham 27 10th mo. 1756 Sarah Burgess.
vi.   Mary, b. 23 4th mo. 1737; m. Wrightstown
      30 4th mo. 1760 John Hirst or Hurst,
      perhaps Hayhurst; if so, not easily
      identified in that family.
vii. William, b. 7 5th mo. 1739; m. Wrights-
      town, 14 12th mo. 1763 Mercy Cutler.
viii. John, b. 15 5th mo. 1742, m. (1) recorded
      Abington, 24 5th mo. 1770 Hannah Jar-
      rett; (2) Mary Dickerson.
ix.   Isaiah, b. 20 8th mo. 1744; m. Middletown
      10 6th mo. 1767 Ann Leonard of Hunterdon
      Co. Isaiah is called Joshua in the will
      of his uncle David Buckman.
x.   David, b. 30 9th mo. 1748; m. (1) 24 4th

1771 Rachel Briggs, d. 12 4th mo. 1786;
(2) Rachel Hough; (3) Wrightstown 21
5th mo. 1800 Phebe Smith, widow.

11. David Buckman, youngest son of William Buckman (Edward) by his second wife Elizabeth Wilson,
was born in Bucks County, 22 9th mo. 1711, and died
there, without issue, between 18 4th mo. 1788 and
25 March 1791,[46] dates of execution and probation
of his will. Dr. Buckman gives a death date, 10
11th mo. 1791, which is impossible as it is later
than the date of probation, but death may have occurred on 10 11th mo. 1790. He married at Byberry,
28 8th mo. 1744, Mary Knight, born 13 11th mo.
1719/20, daughter of Daniel and Elizabeth (Walker)
Knight, and sister of Jonathan (born 5 7th mo. 1722)
and Joseph (born 4 2nd mo. 1725). David Buckman's
will is very informative. He mentions brother John
Story; nephew David Heston (son of sister Elizabeth
Heston); late father William Buckman deceased; cousin Isaac Buckman (son of Isaac Buckman deceased);
trustees named for a school: Isaac Wiggins of the
Township of Northampton, David Buckman and James
Briggs of Newtown, and Joseph Hamton and Isaac
Chapman of Wrightstown; Thomas Powell my apprentice;
nephew Zebulon Heston; nephew William Heston; nephew
John Heston; nephew Zebulon (son of nephew Zebulon
Heston); nephew Mahlon Heston (son of nephew Zebulon
Heston); Joshua Heston (son of Isaiah Heston decd);
brother John Story; nephew Thomas Story; nephew
David Story; nephew Samuel Story; William Buckman
(son of cousin William Buckman deceased); James
Buckman (son of cousin William Buckman deceased);
Ann Osmund (wife of John); Jesse Buckman (son of
cousin Thomas Buckman deceased); David Buckman (son
of cousin John Buckman); Joseph Buckman (son of Joseph Buckman); Abraham Buckman (son of Isaac Buck-
man); Sarah Buckman (widow of cousin Isaac Buckman
deceased); Mary Briggs (wife of James Briggs); two
nieces Agnes and Elizabeth (daughters of brother
Thomas Buckman deceased); Phebe Wiggins (wife of
Isaac); Mary Hamton (wife of Joseph); Phebe Scott
(wife of Timothy). Residue goes to nephews Zebulon
William, John, Joshua Heston, Thomas and David Story,
and friends Joseph Hamton and Isaac Wiggins; executors: brother John Story, friends Isaac Wiggens,
yeoman, and Joseph Chapman; witnesses: Daniel Hunt,
Edward Chapman, Amos Briggs. On 2 Sept. 1755 David

Buckman conveyed the Barber-Webb property, which his
father had bought many years before, to his nephew
Thomas Buckman, recorded 20 July 1791 after the
death of David. It may be that David had retained
control of the property after the paper sale of
1755.

12. Ruth Cooper, eldest child of Mary Buckman
(William, Edward) by her first husband Henry Cooper,
was doubtless born ca. 1704, though no record of her
birth has been found. She was named first in the
wills of her maternal grandfather in 1716 and of her
mother in 1739. By New Jersey license dated 18
Sept. 1728[47] Ruth Cooper, spinster, married Dennis
Pursell, yeoman, both of Bucks County. He had been
baptized as Dinnes at the Raritan Dutch Church, 28
April 1708, youngest child of Thomas and Christiana
(Van Woggelom) Pursell.[48] Dennis was the brother of
John Pursell, the father of Christiana Pursell who
later married Ruth Cooper's half-brother, Jacob
Strawhen. Thus, Ruth became aunt by marriage of her
half-brother. On 28 Jan. 1732/3 Dennis Pursell is
said to have exchanged land which he owned in Kent
County, Delaware, with his brother Daniel for land
which the latter owned in Wrightstown Township,
Bucks County.[49] The subsequent history of Dennis
and Ruth (Cooper) Pursell is shrouded in mystery.
I have elsewhere suggested that they may have had
children named John, Daniel and Lydia, but nothing
is really certain.[50] Dr. E. D. Buckman misunderstood the Strawhen paragraph in William Buckman's
will and supposed that the five Cooper children of
Mary Strawhen were really Strawhens. As a result,
his long search for a Ruth Strawhen was doomed to
failure. The same error was made by the late Warren
S. Ely in a genealogical report to a client which
has been shown us.

13. Sarah Cooper, second child of Mary Buckman
(William, Edward) by her first husband Henry Cooper,
was born ca. 1705 or 1706, but no birth record has
been found. She appears second among the children
of her parents in the wills of her maternal grandfather in 1716 and of her mother in 1739. She was
still living on 22 Dec. 1769 but had apparently
died by 17 July 1772 when she was not mentioned in
her husband's will. She married, first, ca. 1727,
Joseph Strickland, a tailor born in Dublin, Ireland,
15 Aug. 1705, died between 1 May and 13 Aug. 1737,

dates of execution and probation of his will.[51] He
was the fourth child of Miles and Frances (Wharton)
Strickland who were married in Dublin, 7 Sept. 1698.
Miles Strickland was born at Craighouse, Lancashire,
3 12th mo. 1674/5, died in Philadelphia, 18 6th mo.
1751, son of John and Janet Strickland. Joseph's
children are mentioned in Miles Strickland's will
dated 8 3rd mo. 1751/2, probated 22 8th mo. 1752,[52]
and all five of them were living on 4 April 1759
when the property of Miles Strickland was sold by
the other heirs to one of them, Joseph Hilborn.
Joseph Strickland's will names the children Miles,
Mary, Ruth, Sarah and Rachael, among whom £50 is to
be divided when they come of age; wife Sarah; executor: John Hilborn; witnesses: Samuel Blaker (by
mark), William Cooper (by mark), Abraham Chapman.
Sarah (Cooper) Strickland married, second, by New
Jersey license dated 17 Nov. 1738, Jonathan Abbott,
of Northampton Township, Bucks County, cordwainer,
whose will dated 17 July 1772, probated 24 Aug.
1772, mentions no wife but does name son William;
grandsons Jonathan (son of son Jonathan deceased),
William, Henry and Dennie [Dennis] (sons of son
William); brother Edward Abbett, living in the government of Virginia, if alive; executors: Richard
Leedom, Jacob Twining; witnesses: John Addis, Phineas Paxson. Five pounds are left to the overseers
of Wrightstown Friends Meeting, ten pounds to the
overseers of the Southampton Baptist Church. The
only deed of Jonathan Abbott found is dated 15 April
1767 when he, of Northampton, and wife Sarah [she
by mark] convey for £202/10 to John Cooper of the
same place, yeoman.[53] Like her sister, Sarah was
mistaken by Dr. Buckman and Mr. Ely for a Strawhen.

    Issue:
        by first husband Joseph Strickland
    i.   Miles, b. 12 March 1730, d. 27 Aug. 1823;
          m. 24 Dec. 1760 Phebe Van Sant, b. 1736,
          d. before 1823. He was named for his
          paternal grandfather, and the name Miles
          passed in the fourth generation into
          the Strawn family, probably as a tribute
          to this one, since the Strawns had no
          Strickland ancestry. In 1790 Miles re-
          sided in the Manor of Moreland, Montgom-
          ery Co. (2/0/6). When of Lower Make-
          field Township, Bucks Co., he made his
          will 24 Jan. 1813, probated 29 April

1823,[54] naming children: Sarah Bennitt (wife of John), Mary Addis (wife of John), Ann Wynkoop (wife of Gerrit), son Joseph Strickland, son Amos Strickland, executor. The following is drawn largely from Bible records at the Bucks County Historical Society.

Issue: surname Strickland

1. Sarah, b. 2 June 1761, d. 21 March 1845 aged 83/9/19; m. 27 Nov. 1782 John Bennett, d. 26 July 1836 aged 78/5/19. Eleven children in theBible records.
2. Mary, b. 31 March 1763, m. John Addis.
3. Ann, b. 19 Nov. 1765, m. Gerrit Wynkoop.
4. Joseph, b. 2 July 1767, in 1790 in Moreland Manor (1/1/16).
5. Amos, b. 5 Feb. 1773, in 1790 in Moreland Manor (2/0/4), d. 26 Jan. 1812.

ii. Mary, mentioned in father's will; m. 9 2nd mo. 1746 John Martindale, b. 22 June 1719, son of John Martindale by his wife Mary Bridgman, daughter of Walter and Blanche (Constable) Bridgman. On the Martindales see Marjorie Seward Cleveland and Charles Henry Roe, *John Martindell (or Martindale) Cordwainer, of Philadelphia, and Some of His Descendants* (1953).

Issue: surname Martindale

1. Joseph, b. 20 6th mo. 1747, m. (1) Hannah Buckman (Isaac, William, William, Edward); (2) Falls, 22 May 1788 Sarah Merrick.
2. John, b. 15 12th mo. 1749, m. Ann Lambert.
3. William, b. 2 6th mo. 1751, m. Esther Buckman (Jacob, William, William, Edward).
4. Rachel, b. 1 10th mo. 1752, m. Charles Reader, probably the one b. 15 June 1743, son of Charles Reader (Joseph, Isaac, John) and Eleonor Merrick.
5. Sarah, b. 13 10th mo. 1754, m. Matthias Harvey, no issue.
6. Miles, b. 2 6th mo. 1757, m. Susanna Harvey.

   7. Strickland, b. 19 6th mo. 1759, m.
        Sarah Sands.
   8. Amos, b. 10 8th mo. 1761, d. 1 Aug.
        1841, m. Martha Merrick, b. 22 Nov.
        1768, d. 17 Oct. 1813, daughter of
        Thomas Merrick.
   9. Jonathan, b. 10 7th mo. 1763, m. Rachel
        Morgan.
  10. Thomas, b. 1765, m. (1) Mary Boothe,
        5 ch.; (2) at age 82, Sarah Ann Con-
        rad aged 22, by whom he had two or
        three daughters.
  11. Isaac, b. 2 12th mo. 1767, m. Rachel
        Bonham.
  12. Mary, b. 16 1st mo. 1769 m. Isaiah
        Morgan.
  iii. Ruth, mentioned in father's will; marriage
        bond dated April 1756 to m. John Leed-
        ham (as bond spells the name) or Latham
        alias Leatham (as deed for Miles Strick-
        land's property in 1759 has it).
  iv.   Sarah, mentioned in father's will; m. 1
        Dec. 1755 William Carver, d. 27 Sept.
        1803, son of William Carver (William)
        by his wife Elizabeth Walmsley.
  v.   Rachel, mentioned in father's will; m. by
        1759 Thomas Wilson of Middletown, yeo-
        man.
        by second husband Jonathan Abbott
  vi.   William, living 1772.
           Issue: surname Abbott
        1. William, living 1772.
        2. Henry, living 1772. Did he m. at Glor-
           ia Dei Church, Philadelphia, 9 June
           1777, Elizabeth Marshall?
        3. Dennis, living 1772; name shows rela-
           tionship to his uncle by marriage,
           Dennis Pursell.
  vii. Jonathan, d. by 1772.
           Issue: surname Abbott
        1. Jonathan, living 1772.

   14. William Cooper, son of Mary Buckman (William,
Edward) by her first husband Henry Cooper, was named
third in the will of his maternal grandfather in
1716 and in that of his mother in 1739. No birth
record has been found but he was clearly the eldest
son. No evidence has been located to show that he

ever married and there are indications that he did
not.[55] He witnessed the will of his brother-in-law
Joseph Strickland in 1737, and in old age William
Cooper Sen[r] of Northampton, yeoman, conveyed to
William Cooper of the same, husbandman, his nephew,
13 May 1783, a property bought from Samuel Blaker.[56]
The will calls him William Cooper the elder of
Northampton Township, Bucks County, 3 Nov. 1788,
probated 3 Oct. 1793.   No wife or child is mentioned
but he names brothers Henry Cooper and Jacob Strawen
as executors; also cousins John Cooper and Miles
Strickland; Sarah wife of George Cammell [Campbell];
Mary wife of John Atkinson.   The 1790 Census of
Bucks County, which is not subdivided into townships,
has two William Coopers, one not living next to the
other Coopers (2/4/5), the other between John and
Henry Cooper (3/3/5).   It is probable that the William Cooper now being discussed was neither of
these two householders but one of the three males
above 16 in the house of the second William Cooper
found recorded. As was the case with his sisters
Ruth and Sarah, Mr. Ely and Dr. Buckman supposed
that this William was William Strawhen.

15. Henry Cooper, son of Mary Buckman (William,
Edward) by her first husband Henry Cooper, was born
25 Jan. 1707/8 (Middletown record), and is mentioned
as fourth child in the wills of his maternal grandfather in 1716 and of his mother in 1739. He married
by New Jersey license dated 8 July 1732 Mary Sherman, but whether he had issue and when he died we
do not know. He was living on 3 Nov. 1788 when he
was named an executor of his brother William. In
the past I have supposed that he was the testator
of a will dated 10 June 1785, probated 26 Nov. 1805,
but now think this will belongs to his nephew.

16. John Cooper, youngest child of Mary Buckman
(William, Edward) was born 19 April 1709 (Middletown record), and was mentioned as the youngest
child of his parents in the wills of his maternal
grandfather in 1716 and of his mother in 1739.   He
died in 1783, leaving a will dated in Northampton
Township, 4 April 1783, probated 3 May 1783, in
which he names as executors sons John and Henry;
also elsewhere in the will sons John, William and
Henry; daughters Margaret Tomlinson, Sarah Campbell and Mary Atkinson.   In 1790 the three sons
lived in adjacent houses in Bucks County, but there

was another John Cooper (2/6/6), not adjacent to
them, and, of course, not their father who was then
dead. On 10 Oct. 1767 George Cambell of Newtown,
cooper, who signed his name, and wife Sarah, who
signed by mark, sold land to John Cooper of Northampton, yeoman.[57] It seems probable that the grantor was his son-in-law but it is certain the
grantee was this John Cooper. Though it is clear
that this John Cooper had married, we have found no
record of his marriage or his wife's name.

Issue: surname Cooper

i.   John, mentioned in his father's will,
       1783; in 1790 living in Bucks County
       adjacent to his brothers (2/4/6). A
       John Cooper is credited with having
       married Esther Buckman (Joseph, William,
       William, Edward) and may or may not be
       this one.

ii.   William, mentioned in father's will,
       1783; living 1790 in Bucks County ad-
       jacent to his brothers (3/3/5). One of
       the three males above sixteen may have
       been his uncle William Cooper who in
       1788 had conveyed to him.

iii.   Henry, mentioned in his father's will,
       1783; in 1790 living in Bucks County
       adjacent to his brothers (1/1/1). On
       12 Oct. 1786 when of Upper Makefield,
       schoolmaster, he conveyed to Joseph
       Hart of Warminster, in a deed which
       states that his father was John Cooper
       late of Northampton.[58] On 9 Aug. 1803
       when of Northampton, yeoman, with wife
       Martha (both able to write), he con-
       veyed to Francis Irvin and John Irvin,
       both of Newtown and masons, the proper-
       ty which his father had bought from
       George Campbell in 1767. He made his
       will in Northampton Township, 10 June
       1785, probated 26 Nov. 1805, in which
       he names wife Martha, son Phineas and
       daughter Martha. The son would be the
       male under 16 in 1790 but the daughter,
       living in 1785, was not shown in 1790.

iv.   Margaret, mentioned, without her husband's
       name, in the will of her father, but
       as Margaret Tomlinson; not mentioned
       in her uncle William's will in 1788

and she may then have been dead. No
Margaret Tomlinson appears in Bucks
County in the 1790 Census.

v.　Sarah, m. perhaps by 1767 and certainly
by 1783, George Campbell; living 1788
when mentioned in her uncle William's
will. The 1790 Census has several
George Campbells in Pennsylvania but
none in Bucks County.

vi.　Mary, m. by 1783 John Atkinson; living
1788 when mentioned in her uncle William's will. Her husband is not iden-
tifiable in the 1790 Census of Bucks
County or in the Atkinson genealogies.

7. Jacob Strawhen, as he generally spelled his
name, or Strawn, as most descendants spell it, was
the only child of Mary Buckman (William, Edward)
by her second husband Lancelot Strawhen. He was
born, probably in Middletown Township, and in the
year 1717, since in 1739 he was old enough to be
named his mother's executrix. As his father died in
1720 and his parents were married in 1716, he can
not have been born before 1717 or after 1721.

Aside from his mother's will, the earliest record of Jacob is found in a Middletown marriage certificate dated 22 3rd mo. 1740, when Robert Lucas
married Sarah Croasdale of Newtown, daughter of William Croasdale. The name of Jacob Strawhen is next
to the last among the men, but neither his mother,
who was dead by September of that year, or his wife
signed. He probably remained with his mother until
her death and accompanied her, if not to Kent County, Delaware, at least to Bethlehem Township, Hunterdon County, New Jersey, where she made her will.
He married about 1741, probably in Bethlehem Township, Christiana Pursell, baptized at the Dutch
Church at Readington, that county, daughter of John
Pursell (Thomas) by his wife Henah or Hannah whose
maiden name has not been determined. Thus, Jacob
Strawhen became the nephew by marriage of his half
sister, Ruth (Cooper) Pursell, since John Pursell,
her father, was an older brother of Ruth's husband
Dennis. [60]

Christiana had been named for her paternal
grandmother, Christiana Van Woggelom, who in Dutch
records was regularly ·called Stintje Jans, that is,
in English, "little Christina, daughter of John." [61]

By coincidence this Stintje Jans was daughter of another, and Christiana Pursell, being daughter of a
John, could also be called Stintje Jans by the Dutch
and, at any rate, was called Stintje. To the English
ears at Richland Meeting, this sounded like "Staun-
chy," and she was so recorded as such for many years.
As a result, some descendants have supposed that she
was so called from staunchness of build or charac-
ter--she did survive the birth of twelve children.
In any case, Jacob and Stintje began having children
while living in New Jersey, since the births of the
first three children are not found recorded at Richland Meeting, Quakertown, Pa.

    If this supposition is correct, the move to Hay-
cock Township, which lies east of Richland Manor and
Township, and now the Borough of Quakertown, took
place between the spring of 1748 and the fall of
1749. It would appear that the family must have
lived first on rented property. There is an unrecorded deed dated 6 May 1752[62] whereby Joseph Tomlinson of Makefield, Bucks County, Pennsylvania,
yeoman, sold to Jacob Strawhen of the Haycock Township, aforesaid county, for a consideration of five
shillings [doubtless a fictitious sum used to conceal the real price], a certain Messuage, plantation and Tract of Land in Haycock Township, containing 255 acres and 98 perches, deed witnessed
by Samuel Twining and Tho: Chapman.

    In the year 1784 Jacob Strawhen erected a fine
stone house near the village called Strawntown
about three miles east of Quakertown. The house
remained in possession of Jacob to his death in 1800
and then became the home of his youngest son Enoch
until it was sold after his death in 1849. The
house has been owned in late years by Mrs. Natalie
Platoff Nichols and her sister, Mrs. Ahlum, who
operate the property as a farm, having inherited it
from their father, Col. Platoff, U.S.A. As this is
being written, there are reports that the property
may be condemned in order to build a highway and
how long this beautiful building will be allowed to
remain standing is therefore doubtful. The entire
structure is now well preserved and the wing added
to it on the east was constructed of stone salvaged
from an original wing attached to the house on the
northwest. The large barn nearby is a new one, re-
placing one built in 1809 which was not long ago
destroyed by fire. In the neighborhood of Strawn-

town are a number of similar stone houses, some of
which were occupied by sons of Jacob Strawhen, the
one immediately to the west having been the residence of Enoch's next older brother, Abel Strawn,
until his death in 1848. These houses can be approached by driving south from the village of
Pleasant Valley on what used to be called the Bethlehem Pike to a point where a road leads off to the
left. In the northeast angle of this intersection
is the stone house formerly occupied by Ed and Laura
Roudenbush. Shortly farther on, a road runs west
from a point just beyond the Roudenbush house, and
on this lane, as it really is, Jacob Strawhen's house
is the first on the right, his son Abel's the next
on the left.

At the formation of the Bucks County Committee
of Safety on 15 Dec. 1774[63] Jacob Strawhen was the
member for Haycock Township, but when it became evident that the colonies would resort to arms, he and
Thomas Foulke, the member for Richland, resigned on
21 July 1775, unable, as Friends, to serve further.
This brief service, however, has been accepted as
qualifying female descendants for membership in the
Daughters of the American Revolution.

In 1779 Jacob Strawhen Sr. was recorded as the
owner of 350 acres in Haycock Township, with four
horses and six head of cattle[64]; in 1781, 360 acres
and three horses and seven head of cattle[65]; in 1782
350 acres, two horses and seven head of cattle[66];
in 1783, taxed £4/14/6[67]; in 1784, 360 acres, five
horses, five head of cattle, five dwellings, five
outhouses, inhabited by 25 whites[68] and in 1785
he had 360 acres, three horses, nine head of cattle[69]. At this period, of course, several of the
children must already have married and had children
of their own. It is obvious from the acreage stated
that Jacob Strawhen had added to his original 255+
acres, and in 1767 he bought 167 acres adjoining,
but no deeds of sale or purchase are on record at
Doylestown.

Jacob and Christiana were faithful members of
Richland Meeting, as were at least some of their
children, but the Strawn family was not uniformly
Quaker in background. The parents are undoubtedly
buried in the graveyard at Richland Meeting, no
stones now visible for them. The earliest Strawn
stone now visible is for Jacob's grandson John,
who died in 1868. The earlier graves were opened

in rows as deaths occurred, and husbands and wives might be separated from each other by considerable distance.

In addition to farming, Jacob Strawhen is said to have engaged in pottery making, a trade followed by several descendants. His grandson, John Straughan (son of Daniel), recorded in 1848 that his grandfather was a man of veracity and candor, five feet, ten inches, tall, stout of brain and limbs. He also says that Jacob died at age 86, which is too high, and that Christiana died at age 97, which is all of fifteen years too many.

Jacob Strawhen died on 20 Dec. 1800, not 1801 as often deduced from the probate record that administration was granted, 13 Jan. 1801,[70] to his son Daniel Strawhen and to Israel Foulke [1760-1824][71] the securities being John Cooper and Henry Cooper, undoubtedly his nephews. The inventory of 13 Feb. 1801 came to £942/18/8. Christiana Strawhen also died intestate, administration granted 28 April 1807 to Israel Foulke,[72] with inventory made by Israel Lancaster and George Sheive, £300/8 and 3/4 pence.

Issue: surname Strawn

i.   Thomas, b. 1742, d. Madison Co., Kentucky, late in 1814; m. (1) at Richland, 8 June 1769, Mary Heacock, b. 11 July 1752, d. in childbed, 27 March 1770, daughter of William Heacock (Jonathan) by his wife Ann Roberts (Thomas); (2) Sophia, perhaps a Chisholm. One ch. by Mary; seven by Sophia.

ii.   John, b. 1744, d. Greene Co., Pa., shortly before 29 Aug. 1808; m. at Richland, April 1770, Kezia Dennis, b. 22 Feb. 1753, survived her husband, daughter of John Dennis (Joseph) by his wife Kezia Ball (John). Usually said to have had 19 children but there probably were all of twenty and by one wife.

iii.   Jacob, b. 23 March 1747/8, d. Greene Co., Pa., 28 Aug. 1809; m. Susanna Van Buskirk, b. 2 Sept. 1754, d. 2 Sept. 1829, daughter of George Van Buskirk (John, Andries, Lourens Andriesen) by his first wife Sarah -----, and sister of Joseph Van Buskirk who m. Jacob's sister Mary. Thirteen ch.

iv. William, b. 17 Jan. 1749/50, d. 12 June
1809; m. (1) Ann Van Horn, d. by 1780,
daughter of Garret Van Horn (Peter,
Barent, Christiaen) by his wife Mary
Neal; (2) Mary Raudenbush, d. 1821. One
ch. by Ann, seven by Mary.

v. Daniel, b. 27 May 1752, d. 10 Nov. 1819;
m. (1) ca. 1774, Ann Lloyd, probably
daughter of John and Eleanor (Foulke)
Lloyd; (2) ca. 1780, Margaret Pursell,
probably daughter of John and Ann
(Coomb) Pursell; (3) Sarah Shaw, d. in
Plumstead, Jan. 1829, daughter of Jonathan and Sarah (-----) Shaw and widow
of Edward Moore of Plumstead. Four ch.
by Ann, 14 by Margaret.

vi. Mary, b. 21 Feb. 1754, d. 1782 in what is
now Chestnut Hill Township, Monroe Co.,
Pa.; m. Joseph Van Buskirk, b. ca. 1751,
d. 21 May 1821, as first wife. Three ch.
by Mary, five more by his second wife
Mary Levers.

vii. Hannah, b. 8 April 1756, d. Madison Co.,
Kentucky, 9 Nov. 1823; m. John White,
b., possibly in Maryland, 1 March 17--,
d. Madison Co., 23 April 1825. He had
14 ch. of whom the first four may have
been by an earlier wife.

viii. Isaiah, b. 28 Oct. 1757, d. 2 Aug. 1843 in
either Florida Township, Putnam Co.,
Ill., or Deer Park Township, LaSalle Co.,
Ill.; m. in Turkey Foot Township, Somerset Co., Pa., 12 Aug. 1781, Rachel
Reed, b. 1 July 1763, d. in Illinois,
2 April 1843, daughter of Capt. John
and Thankful (Honawell) Reed. Six ch.
Isaiah served in the Revolution and was
disowned by Richland Meeting.

ix. Job, b. 12 Oct. 1760, d., probably 5 Sept.
1825, in Indiana; m. (1) 4 Nov. 1791
Mary Cooper, b. 12 April 1775, d. Perry-
opolis, Pa., 12 Feb. 1812, daughter of
John Cooper (1742-1797) by wife Martha
----- (1750-1831); (2) Hannah Bowers,
b. 29 July 1779, widow of ----- McColley.
By Mary ten ch., by Hannah three.

x. Jerusha, b. 14 Dec. 1762, d. Perry Co.,
Ohio, 1834; m. ca. 1785 Jeremiah Reed,

son of Capt. John and Thankful (Honawell) Reed. and brother of Isaiah's
wife. Eleven ch.

xi.   Abel, b. 12 March 1765, d. 17 Nov. 1848;
       m. ca. 1786 Elizabeth Raudenbush, b. 26
       Dec. 1764, d. 6 Dec. 1841, parentage
       unknown but perhaps sister of the wives
       of William and Enoch Strawn. Ten ch.
xii.   Enoch, b. 1 Sept. 1768, d. 7 Nov. 1849;
       m. (1) ca. 1791 Rebecca Raudenbush. b.
       7 Feb. 1770, d. 14 Nov. 1821; (2) 14
       Nov. 1822, Margaret Carty, a widow, she
       still living 1851. Ten ch. by Rebecca.

18. Sarah Buckman, daughter of William Buckman
(William, Edward) by his wife Esther Penquite, was
born 15 3rd mo. 1718 and died by 13 10th mo. 1785.
She had leave to marry, first, at Wrightstown, 7
8th mo. 1741, Benjamin Taylor; and married, second,
28 11th mo. 1752, Thomas Lancaster, son of Thomas
and Phebe (Wardell) Lancaster, born near Wrightstown, 16 12th mo. 1727, died on the mainland near
Biles Island in the Delaware (Falls Township), 27
1st mo. 1808, having married, second, 13 10th mo.
1785, at Abington Monthly Meeting, Martha Lloyd,
daughter of John and Eleonor (Foulke) Lloyd, born
20 2nd mo. 1756, died 16 8th mo. 1843. See Clarence
Vernon Roberts, *Early Friends Families of Upper
Bucks* (Philadelphia 1925), pp. 331 f.; Harry Fred
Lancaster, *The Lancaster Family* (Columbia City, Ind.,
1902), p. 23. Thomas Lancaster had four children
by his second wife.

       Issue: surname Lancaster
       i. Thomas, b. 11 3rd mo. 1754, d. 7 6th mo.
          1811; m. at Makefield Meeting, 21 11th mo.
          1782, Ann Knowles, b. 1 10th mo.1760, d.
          9 3rd mo. 1850; lived in Whitemarsh Town-
          ship, Montgomery County, Pa.

19. William Buckman, son of William Buckman (William, Edward) by his wife Esther Penquite, was born
19 1st mo. 1719 and died 6 9th mo. 1782. He married
at Wrightstown, 3 11th mo. 1744, Jane Briggs, born
14 12th mo. 1720 in Upper Makefield, died 21 2nd mo.
1777, daughter of William and Margaret (-----)
Briggs.[73]*Pennsylvania Marriages Prior to 1810* gives
the year correctly on 2:276 under William's name
but incorrectly as 1774 on p. 275 under Jane's.

This William Buckman was commissioned as sheriff, 3 Oct. 1767.[74] He died intestate, and administration bond was filed 20 Sept. 1782 by William Buckman of Northampton, Abner Buckman, James Buckman, Jacob Buckman, yeoman, and Thomas Buckman, farmer of Newtown,[75] probably three sons, two brothers.

Issue: surname Buckman
i.   William, b. 24 7th mo. 1745, d. 10 1st mo. 1810; m. Horsham 13 5th mo. 1770 Hannah Dilworth.
ii. Sarah, b. 2 9th mo. 1747, d. 9 9th mo. 1752.
iii. Elizabeth, b. 2 1st mo. 1750; m. Wrightstown 21 2nd mo. 1769 Joshua Vanzant.
iv. Abner, b. 19 10th mo. 1752; m. (1) Mary (Yardley) Lambert, a widow; (2) 2 12th 1778, Elizabeth Bailey.
v.   Sarah, b. 7 6th mo. 1755; m. Wrightstown 21 12th mo. 1774 William Chapman.
vi. James, b. 6 10th mo. 1758, d. 12 12th mo. 1840; m. 1780 Sarah Burroughs.
vii. Jane, b. 17 2nd mo. 1761, d. 18 10th mo. 1826; m. Joseph Tomlinson.
viii. Eleanor, b. 14 12th mo. 1765, d. 28 2nd mo. 1769.
ix. Phineas, b. 14 2nd mo. 1767; m. (1) Falls 22 4th mo. 1790 Susannah Leedom; (2) Catherine Sheriff.

20. John Buckman, son of William Buckman (William, Edward) by his wife Esther Penquite, was born 15 5th mo. 1721, died 27 2nd mo. 1790. He was a husbandman and, according to Dr. E. D. Buckman, also a miller. He married ca. 1747 Eleanor Briggs, born in Lower Makefield Township, 19 11th mo. 1722, the daughter of William and Margaret (-----) Briggs. Her father's will dated 15 Aug. 8th mo. 1758, probated 9 Sept. 1758[76], calls her Ellen Buckman. By deed dated 25 May 1750 his father conveyed to John[77] who made his own will 2 3rd mo. 1789, probated 6 March 1790[78], and mentions wife Elenor, sons John, David, Jonathan, Samuel, Abdon, daughters Ruth Buckman, Margaret Lee; witnesses: Phinehas Buckman [his nephew], Deborah White and John Story.

Issue: surname Buckman
i.   John, b. 24 7th mo. 1748, d. 3 11th mo. 1837; m. Wrightstown 21 4th mo. 1773 Susannah Chapman.

ii.   David, b. 14 4th mo. 1750, d. 1 9th mo.
      1810; m. 14 11th mo. 1779 Esther White.
iii. Margaret, b. 10 4th mo. 1753, m. Falls
      3 5th mo. 1774 Daniel Lee; removed to
      Catawissa, Pa.
iv.   Jonathan, b. 29 4th mo. 1755, d. 4 10th
      mo. 1826; m. Falls 16 5th mo. 1778
      Sarah Kirkbride.
v.   Rachel, b. 21 1st mo. 1757, perhaps the
      Rachel who m. at Falls 16 10th mo.
      1800 Jacob Knowles.
vi.   Samuel, b. 2 6th mo. 1763, d. 3 2nd mo.
      1847; m. 7 2nd mo. 1785 Rachel White.
vii. Ruth, b. 3 2nd mo. 1766, d. 17 4th mo.
      1846; m. Falls 12 4th mo. 1792 Joseph
      Winder.
viii. Abdon, b. 28 7th mo. 1768, d. 14 8th mo.
      1856; m. Sarah Harvey.

21. Joseph Buckman, son of William Buckman (William, Edward) by his wife Esther Penquite, was born 16 5th mo. 1723, and died in 1794. He married 13 9th mo. 1746 Martha Carr, daughter of John and Mary (-----) Carr. Dr. E. D. Buckman remarks that living descendants did not know where this man lived. As Joseph's will says he was of Newtown, it is probable that the good doctor had encountered someone who could not say on what farm Joseph lived. Joseph and Martha conveyed to Joseph Tomlinson on 28 April 1768.[79] They also conveyed on 10 1st January 4 George III 1764[80] to John Hamton of Wrightstown, yeoman, and to the same grantee again on 3 8th mo. 1768.[81] Joseph Buckman's will was dated 9 12th mo. 1794, probated 12 March 1798,[82] and mentions daughter Ester Cooper; granddaughter Martha Briggs; grandson Joseph Pownal; son-in-law John Carver; daughter Mary Carver, Agnes Blaker, Latitia Briggs, Sarah Blaker, Elizabeth Pownal, Assenath Warner; son Joseph Buckman, residuary legatee and executor; witnesses: William Buckman [by mark], Abner Buckman, Elizabeth Buckman [by mark].

Issue: surname Buckman
i.   Esther, b. 22 8th mo. 1747, d. 28 12th
      mo. 1812; m. John Cooper who may be
      the one shown on p. 92, #i.
ii.   Mary, b. 1 10th mo. 1748, d. 8 2nd mo.
      1812; m. Wrightstown 22 5th mo. 1771
      John Carver.

    iii.   Agnes, b. 15 2nd mo. 1750, m. 1771 Paul
           Blaker.
    iv.   Letitia, b. 5 3rd mo. 1751, d. 17 9th mo.
           1833; m. 1769 John Briggs.
    v.   Joseph, b. 30 8th mo. 1752, d. 17 9th mo.
           1828; m. 16 5th mo. 1792 Elizabeth Lin-
           ton.
    vi.   Sarah, b. 22 11th mo. 1753, m. Achilles
           Blaker.
    vii. Mahlon, b. 24 4th mo. 1755, and the Mahlon
           who m. Falls 16 5th mo. 1805 Hannah Tay-
           lor was probably a younger man.
    viii. Elizabeth, b. 12 9th mo. 1756, m. 12 6th
           mo. 1782 Levi Pownall.
    ix.   Martha, b. 25 2nd mo. 1758, d. 18 4th mo.
           1760 aet. 2/1/23.
    x.   Asenath, b. 2 4th mo. 1761, d. 31 12th mo.
           1837; m. 26 12th mo. 1787 David Warner.

    22. Thomas Buckman, son of William Buckman (William, Edward) by his wife Esther Penquite, was born 28 5th mo. 1725 and died intestate in 1785. He married at Falls Meeting, 24 9th mo. 1747 Priscilla Bunting, born 22 5th mo. 1722, daughter of Samuel Bunting (son of Job and Rachel [Baker] Bunting) by his wife Priscilla Burgess (daughter of Samuel and Ellen Burgess). Administration was granted 17 Nov. 1785 on Thomas Buckman's estate,[83] Precilla Buckman renouncing in favor of her son Benjamin Buckman, blacksmith.

    Issue: surname Buckman
    i.   Phebe, b. 2 4th mo. 1748, d. 5 2nd mo.
           1832; m. Joseph Kelley.
    ii.   Hannah, b. 12 7th mo. 1750; m. (1) 1771
           Abraham Hibbs; (2) Benjamin Leedom.
    iii.   Samuel, b. 25 7th mo. 1752, d. 18 6th mo.
           1754.
    iv.   Thomas, b. 15 7th mo. 1754, d. 22 10th
           mo. 1837; m. Mary Harding.
    v.   Benjamin, b. 26 7th mo. 1756, d. 28 12th
           mo. 1808; m. 27 7th mo. 1781 Ann Janney.
    vi.   Timothy, b. 15 1st mo. 1759, d. 2 9th mo.
           1759.
    vii. Amos, b. 10 1st mo. 1762, d. 8 8th mo.
           1762.
    viii. Daughter, b. 5 6th mo. 1763.
    ix.   Jesse, b. 21 11th mo. 1764, m. 13 12th
           mo. 1787 Hannah Taylor.

23. Isaac Buckman, son of William Buckman (William, Edward) by his wife Esther Penquite, was born 29 3rd mo. 1729 and died intestate in 1785. He married first, on 18 Nov. 1751 at Christ Church, Philadelphia, Mary Hilborn; second, at Wrightstown, 28 10th mo. 1762, Sarah Cutler, daughter of Thomas Cutler. The widow Sarah Buckman renounced administration by mark (witnessed by William Buckman) in favor of son-in-law [stepson] Isaac Buckman and son Abraham Buckman. The bond is signed by Isaac Buckman of Buckingham, Abraham Buckman of Upper Makefield, Joshua VanSant of Upper Makefield and Wm Buckman of Newtown, yeoman, 1 Feb. 1785.[84]

Issue: surname Buckman
by Mary Hilborn
i.   Isaac, d. 14 12th mo. 1807; m. Buckingham 13 10th mo. 1779 Joyce Fell, b. 7 1st mo. 1753, d. 18 9th mo. 1823, daughter of Titus and Elizabeth (-----) Fell.
ii. Hannah, m. 1774 Joseph Martindale, b. 20 6th mo. 1747, her second cousin once removed (see p. 89).
iii. Ann.
by Sarah Cutler
iv. Abraham, b. 24 3rd mo. 1777, d. 23 3rd mo. 1847; m. Eleanor Comfort, d. 27 8th mo. 1823.

24. Jacob Buckman, though, for want of a birth record, placed last among the children of William Buckman (William, Edward) by his wife Esther Penquite, may perhaps have been born earlier as he was executor of his father's estate. Dr. Buckman's date for his marriage to Mary Taylor, died 14 3rd mo. 1777, daughter of Peter and Jane (Scott) Taylor, is 24 3rd mo. 1757, but the marriage was reported at Falls Meeting on 2 2nd mo. 1757. Jacob and wife Mary conveyed land inherited from William Buckman to William Buckman Esq. of Newtown, 5 Sept. 1768.[85] Jacob made his will 14 8th mo. 1794, probated 20 Sept. 1796, calling himself of Newtown, yeoman, and naming daughter Ester Martindell; friends John Buckman, Joseph Buckman Jr. and Thomas Story, as trustees for daughter Sarah Smith who has children; son-in-law Wm Martindell and cousin William Buckman executors; witnesses: Samson Cary, Moses Kelley. Jacob married, second, in 1779, Rebecca Smith, daughter of William and Rebecca (Wilson) Smith, but had no children by her.

    Issue; surname Buckman
i.   Mary, b. 15 4th mo. 1758, d. 26 8th mo.
       1771.
ii.   Esther, b. 7 11th mo. 1759, d. 19 11th
       mo. 1809; m. 5th mo. 1779 William
       Martindale, her second cousin once re-
       moved, for whom see p. 89.
iii.   Sarah, b. 7 10th mo. 1761, d. 8 10th mo.
       1831, m. 12 4th mo. 1780 William Smith.

    25. Thomas Buckman, son of Thomas Buckman (William, Edward) by his wife Agnes Penquite, was born 12 4th mo. 1729 and died 1 4th mo. 1804. He married at Christ Church, Philadelphia, 11 Dec. 1753, Elizabeth Carver, daughter of William and Elizabeth (Walmsley) Carver of Byberry. There was no issue by her. They conveyed 5 Dec. 1772 to Patrick Hunter,[87] this deed wrongly making him son of David Buckman; again on 30 July 1776 to Thomas Sharkey, tanner,[88] this deed correctly identifying him as Thomas's son. He was probably the Thomas Buckman of Solebury, yeoman, who gave a power of attorney to collect debts to John Rose, yeoman.[89] When of Newtown, farmer, "now upwards of seventy," on 5 July 1799, he made his will[90] with a codicil added 19 June 1802, probated 9 April 1804. He mentions his wife Elizabeth and names as executors Abraham Chapman, attorney at law, Benjamin Chapman, miller, and Archibald McCorkle, shoemaker. The codicil adds son Thomas, and he states that he had but three children, all born out of wedlock by Mary Wisener with whom he had lived many years.

    Issue: surname Buckman
i.   Thomas, m. Martha Richards.
ii.   Stacy, d. unm.
iii.   Mary, m. ----- Flanagan.

NOTES

[1]See TAG ?8:154-157; 41:40. While no very satisfactory accou.: of the Buckmans has appeared in print, there is in the Genealogical Society of Pennsylvania a 47-vol. manuscript genealogy made by the late Dr. E. D. Buckman (b. 1823) which has been used with due caution. There is a brief sketch in Clarence Vernon Roberts, *Early Friends Families of Upper Bucks* (Philadelphia 1925), pp. 532 f.; another in W. W. H. Davis's *History of Bucks County, Pennsyl-*

vania (Doylestown, 1st ed., 1876), pp. 64, 85, 249; still another in William J. Buck's *History of Bucks County* (Doylestown 1858), p. 96; a highly imaginative sketch in Dr. Arthur Edwin Bye's "The Widow Buckman" (*The Historian* 3 [1965] 61-68) and in his *A Friendly Heritage* (New York 1959), 224-228. In both references he cites an address of George Pownal Orr (Welcome Society, 24 Oct. 1957), printed in *The Germantown Crier* (May 1958) which we have not seen.

[2]PMHB 9:225; BHBC 673. Dr. Bye is quite wrong in claiming that William's sister Ruth is also listed in Bucks Arrivals.

[3]Mr. Corbett also began a Buckman Genealogy, in a volume now in the Genealogical Society of Pennsylvania.

[4]1 PA 1:45, Group 49.

[5]Old Rights DD 66, Land Office, Harrisburg; 3 PA 3:74 #74.

[6]PGM 23:79.

[7]Mrs. Ruth John, 220 Stuart Avenue, Downingtown, Pa., claims in *The Heston Historian* #17, p. 7, that there is no evidence that any Buckmans died of smallpox. This is quite right but the circumstantial evidence is strong. Mrs. John appears to know nothing of Ruth Buckman's later history.

[8]Dr. Bye (*Historian* 66; *Heritage* 219) conjectures that the Widow Buckman was a sister of John and Thomas Rowland, also from Billingshurst and on the *Welcome*. This disregards the fact that they were a generation younger and Joan's true maiden name was Bagham, as I published before *The Historian* article appeared. Having made the conjecture in one column, in the next he would have us believe the Buckman sons of Joan were the nephews of the Rowlands!

[9]*Records of the Courts of Quarter Sessions and Common Pleas for Bucks County, Pennsylvania 1684-1700* (Meadville, Pa. 1943), pp. 281, 299, 301.

[10]*Ibid.* 76f.   [11]*Ibid.* 93, 193, 255, 349.

[12]The original is said to be owned by C. Arthur Smith of Wycombe, Pa.; a photograph was supplied me through the kindness of the late A. L. Morgan of Windsor, Conn.

[13]NJW 1:515.   [14]BW file 3305.
[15]BW 1:27-30.   [16]*The Historian* 3:38.
[17]Old Rights D 67   [18]PMHB 9:350.
[19]NJW 1:441.   [20]NJW 2:223.
[21]NJW 4:180.   [22]NJW 1:74.
[23]NJW 2:752.   [24]NJW 4:181.

[25]NJW 2:223. [26]NJW 2:457. [27]NJW 1:441.
[28]NJW 1:89. [29]NJW 5:232. [30]NJW 4:490.
[31]NJW 2:452 [32]NJW 1:431. [33]NJW 1:393.
[34]NJW 1:70; see also NJW 1:397 where the same estate is repeated under the spelling Ruckman. I have examined the original documents in the State Library at Trenton and find that Buckman is correct though Ruckman appears in one endorsement.
[35]1 NJA 21:678. [36]1 NJA 21:671. [37]BW file 671.
[38]This date is shown in Middletown Minutes.
[39]BW file 192.
[40]Collections of Genealogical Society of Pennsylvania: Geneal. Notes BL-BR 13.
[41]BW file 1607. [42]BW 2:274, file 864.
[43]BD 8:352. [44]BW 1:217, file 367.[45]NJW 3:156.
[46]BW 5:258, file 2359. [47]GMNJ 14:81.
[48]See TAG 36:139-148, 204-213, on the Pursells; on the Van Woggeloms, 32:204-210.
[49]This deed is cited by Clarence Vernon Roberts, but I have never located it at Doylestown. Perhaps it is an unrecorded deed.
[50]See TAG 36:147 f. [51]BW 1:234-6.
[52]PhW I:418. See TAG 38:2249-234 on Stricklands.
[53]BD 19:258, ackn. 22 Dec. 1769, rec. 25 Jan. 1781. William Cooper signed by mark as witness.
[54]BW 10:169.
[55]A William Cooper, with wife Mary, of Philadelphia County, conveyed to John Morris, 18 April 3 George II 1730, receipted same date, recorded 7 May 1771, property originally bought from the Van Buskirks. I feel reasonably certain this was a different man.
[56]The Blaker deed is BD 3:116; the Cooper-Cooper deed, BD 21:131, signed by mark, recorded 20 May 1783.
[57]BD 21:109, 111. [58]BD 23:77, rec. 7 Nov. 1786.
[59]BD 33:148. [60]See p. 87.
[61]See Note 48.
[62]A photostat of this deed was sent me by Miss Bernice Strawn who got it from the late Mrs. F. B. Strawn, then living in Hollywood, California. The deed descended through Jacob, Enoch, Miles, George Washington to Frank Brookbank Strawn, whose widow she was.
[63]PMHB 14:259, 262. [64]3 PA 13:75.
[65]*Ibid.* 179. [66]*Ibid.* 301. [67]*Ibid.* 402.
[68]*Ibid.* [69]*Ibid.* 556.

[70]BA 3:10, file 2992.
[71]Foulke #32 in Clarence V. Roberts, *Early
Friends Families of Upper Bucks* (Philadelphia 1925),
p. 135.
[72]BA 13:107, file 3517.
[73]See the Buckman Genealogy 1:39.
[74]BD 12:29, rec. 23 Nov. 1767.
[75]BW file 1725.
[76]BW 2:338. See also Buckman Genealogy 1:39.
[77]BD 11:542.   [78]BW 5:164, file 267.
[79]BD 15:247, rec. 10 March 1774.
[80]BD 12:195, rec. 5 Aug. 1768.
[81]BD 12:197, rec. 5 Aug. 1768.
[82]BW file 2816.   [83]BW file 1960.
[84]BW file 1937. [85]BD 13:125, rec. 30 Oct. 1769.
[86]BW file 2673. [87]BD 14:393, rec. 16 May 1773.
[88]BD 18:421.   [89]BD 13:310.   [90]BW 6:559.

BURCHEL, JOHN[1]   *possible*

John Burchel or Burchall has not hitherto been
suggested as a possible *Welcome* passenger. He was
a First Purchaser of 500 acres in Group 50,[2] but
no evidence has been found to show that he ever
reached Pennsylvania, though he may have survived
long enough to claim his land.

Warrants and Surveys 2:152 show John Burchal
with lot 41 in back of the Front of Schuylkill, beginning along the east side of Schuylkill Second
Street. Cuthbert Hayhurst had lot 40 and John
Snashfold lot 49. Snashold was, of course, already
dead when the *Welcome* arrived, so Burchel may also
have died. Blackwell's Rent Roll of 1689[3] also
shows John Birchall, next to John Songhurst, as the
owner of an old purchase 51-foot lot, 2/- for five
years, on Mulberry Street, but this Roll had names
of many deceased persons on it, and we can be sure
that Burchel was dead by 1686 and therefore dead
in 1689 when the Roll was made.

Warrants and Surveys 3:222 show a survey 17 6th
mo. 1684 by virtue of a warrant dated 10 6th mo.
1683, for a city lot (#72) in the right of John
Burchall, bounded by John Songhurst and Benjamin
Chambers and by Delaware Front Street. This was
warranted by William Penn to John Songhurst by Warrant 2130 of the date given, whereby city lots for
a number of persons were included in one piece:
Songhurst himself; his daughter Elizabeth Barber;
William Wade, a deceased *Welcome* passenger; John

Burchall; Humphrey Killingbeck, who was definitely
not deceased and not even in Pennsylvania; and Jno
Snashfold, another deceased *Welcome* passenger. A-
part from Songhurst and his daughter, both *Welcome*
passengers, these persons include two definitely
deceased *Welcome* passengers, another who was still
living and never came to America at all, and John
Burchall, status not clearly known. Thus far, nothing really indicates any connection between John
Burchel and the *Welcome*, but, on 30 9th mo. 1686,
Penn wrote from England to J.H. a letter in which
he said that R. Snashfold, a brother of John, was
complaining about Songhurst's failure to render an
accounting of Snashfol's estate, and then come the
words: "& so doe Jo Burchall's kindred & others."
By this time Burchel, or however the name should
be spelled, was surely dead.

Finally, on 22 Xber 1720 John Songhurst [Jr.]
came to the Board of Property[4] with his father's
original deed from Penn, 250 acres, 23-24 May 1682,
also with a deed 24-25 July 1685, Thomas Burchall,
brother and heir of Jno Burchall, 500 acres, 15-16
May 1682, which Songhurst had bought. He now asked
a patent but the Board was hesitant and there is no
indication of the final disposition of the case.

From English Friends records we learn that Jane
Burchall of the Parish of Shipley, Sussex, married
23 11th mo. 1677 at John Snashfold's house in the
parish of Thackham or Hackham, John Quinby, among
the witnesses being John Songhurst, Sarah Fuller
[a First Purchaser], Thomas Buckman Sr., Thomas
Buckman Jr. and John Burchall.

It would seem at least possible that John Burchel was on board the *Welcome* and died during the
crossing.

NOTES

[1]The principal research on this sketch was done
by Walter Lee Sheppard.
[2]1 PA 1:45.   [3]PGM 23:76   [4]2 PA 19:707.

CALES, ALICE   *disproved*

This name appears on List X only. The truth is
that this woman--the spelling of the name in the
Philadelphia Arrivals seems to be "Aiolce"--came on
the *Lion* of Liverpool, arriving 14 8th mo. 1683, as
servant to Robert Turner, to serve four years and
get £3 and fifty acres, loose on 14 8th mo. 1687.

Nothing further has been found concerning this person but she was not a *Welcome* passenger.

CARVER, JOHN   *rather improbable*
CARVER, MARY LANE,   *rather improbable*

John Carver appears on Lists A, B, C, D, E, F, G, H, I, J, L, M, O (here doubtful), R (here controversial), U (here probable), W, X, Y and Z. His wife Mary Carver appears on Lists A, B, C, D, E, F, G (here identified as Mary Lane), H, I, M, O (here doubtful), R (here controversial), U (here probable), Y and Z, and, without her first name, called merely John's wife, on Lists J, L and W.   No affirmative evidence of any kind has been found.

Though Comly[1] says that the Carvers "came over with William Penn in 1682," he does not mention the *Welcome* in this connection. That the Carvers were, however, on the *Welcome* is claimed by Elias Carver, *Genealogy of William Carver from Hertfordshire, England, in 1682* (Doylestown 1903), on the unpaged page before page 1: John Carver and wife Mary Lane came from Hartford [sic], England, with William Penn on the *Welcome*, and Joseph Carver, William Carver (the main name in the volume) and Jacob Carver, came "about the same time," and in their cases nothing is said of the *Welcome*. Elias Carver was followed by Mrs. Miranda S. Roberts, *Genealogy of the Descendants of John Kirk*, edited by Gilbert Cope (Doylestown 1912-13), p. 72. No *Welcome* claim is made, however, by Joseph C. Martindale, M.D., *The Gilbert Family, The Carver Family, and The Duffield Family* (Frankford 1911), p. 9, and so also in his *History of the Townships of Byberry and Moreland* (2nd ed., no date, rev. by Albert W. Dudley),[2] pp. 263-269, where the four Carvers, John, William, Joseph and Jacob, are made to be brothers who arrived in 1682. Mrs. H. W. Naylor[3] also treats the Hertfordshire Carvers without mentioning the *Welcome*.

John Carver was a First Purchaser of 500 acres in Group 7[4] and is mentioned in Besse's *Sufferings* 1:196. In Blackwell's Rent Roll of 1689, John Carver appears as an Old Purchaser, 49-foot lot, 2/- for 5 years, a city lot on Walnut Street between Second and Third Streets from the Delaware.[5]

The will of John Carver of Byberry, Philadelphia County, maltster, was executed 26 2nd mo.

1713, probated 8 Nov. 1713, and names wife Mary and son John as executors; mentions also sons James, John, Richard, daughter Mary Knight; witnesses: John Dunkan, Joseph Gilbert, George Dunkan. Comly says of the daughter Mary that she married Isaac Knight of Abington, and "is stated to have been 'one of the first children born of English parents in Pennsylvania.' Her birth is dated 28 8th mo. 1682, which is four days after Penn's landing at Chester." Penn, however, was not at Chester until 29 Oct. 1682. The same claim for priority of birth in Pennsylvania is made for Mary (Carver) Knight in the sketch devoted to her in *Collection of Memorials Concerning Divers deceased Ministers and Others of the People Called Quakers* (1787), p. 264. Now if the date of her birth is right, then she could not have been born in Pennsylvania unless her parents had arrived on some other ship than the *Welcome*, for Penn did not arrive, as stated, at Chester until 29 Oct. 1682, the day after her birth, and if on the *Welcome*, then she was born on shipboard. It therefore seems probable that the Carvers came on another vessel and arrived before the *Welcome*.

Issue:
i.   James.
ii.   John, served as executor to his father in
       1713; had a certificate to m. Isabella
       Weldon of Philadelphia from Abington,
       dated 26 9th mo. 1716, received 26 8th
       mo. 1716.[6]
iii.   Richard.
iv.   Mary, m. Isaac Knight of Abington.

NOTES

[1]MHSP 2:181.
[2]Both the works cited were printed, of course, long after Dr. Martindale's death.
[3]*Old Northwest Quarterly* 11:46.
[4]1 PA 1:40.
[5]PGM 23:77.
[6]MQA 67.

*CHAMBERS, BENJAMIN   *highly probable*

This name appears on all lists but the line has been extinct since 1715. The evidence is the fact that Chambers was named executor of William Wade,

whose will was executed aboard the *Welcome*. This
is not quite so clear a proof as if some document
testified to his presence there, but it is very
probable that Wade would not have chosen as executor
a person not present. He may well have made Chambers' acquaintance during the voyage, for Wade was
a Sussex man and Chambers came from Kent.

Benjamin Chambers was a First Purchaser of 1000
acres in Group 30[1] and according to his certificate
was from Rochester, Kent,[2] or of Bearsted, also in
Kent, a turner, when he bought from Penn, 24-25
11th mo. 1681.[3] He subscribed £50 to the Society of
Free Traders,[4] of which he was afterwards the president, as shown by a document dated 20 7th mo.1686.[5]

If he brought with him a wife, there is no evidence of it, but he married at Philadelphia Monthly
Meeting, 3 3rd mo. 1686, now called yeoman, Hannah
Smith, of Philadelphia, almost certainly the Hannah
Smith, daughter of Robert, who was received on a
certificate from Worcester City, dated 4 6th mo.
1685, and arrived on the *Unicorn* of Bristol, Thomas
Cooper, commander, 16 10th mo. 1685.[6] Hannah was
buried in Philadelphia, 27 1st mo. 1693, and Benjamin Chambers seems never to have married again.
They had only two children:

    i.   Hannah, d. Philadelphia, 2 3rd mo. 1689.
   ii. Sarah, bur. Philadelphia, 13 12th mo.
         1690/1, the record here, as printed, cal-
         ling the mother Sarah, probably in error.

On 5 4th mo. 1683 Benjamin Chambers was one of
six appointed by Philadelphia Monthly Meeting "to
meet together at some convenient time and draw up
a Brief yet full account of the good order of
Truth as it was practised in the men and women
meetings of friends in England." In 1683 Chambers
was sheriff of Philadelphia County,[7] and on 22 3rd
mo. 1684 he was receiver of the Public Aid, i.e.
treasurer, of the county. He was in debt, 19 6th
mo. 1685[8]; was on petitions dated 7 6th mo. 1686
and 28 6th mo. 1689[9]; was water baly, 30 5th mo.
1690.[10] His first home was in a cave and when,
in 1686/7, Penn by proclamation ordered abandonment
of such caves, he made an exception in the case of
Chambers' cave which "was more costly than ordina-
ry," and Chambers was still occupying the cave on
29 5th mo. 1687.[11] He was remiss about caring
for Penn's timber and was replaced by Evan Oliver

on 7 9th mo. 1691.[12] He owned a ferry over the
Schuylkill, rented to a tenant, and this had to com-
pete with another ferry owned by two Swedes who had
been in the area before Penn's time, Andrew Rudman
and Andrew Sandel.[13] In 1693 Chambers' taxable
property was valued at £100.

Benjamin Chambers died in Philadelphia, 27 9th
mo. 1715, and administration was granted on his
estate to Elizabeth Jackson, shopkeeper.[14] The file
now contains only her bond of £500 with William
Robinson, saddler; Richard Robeson, tallow chandler
[signed by mark], with no indication of any relationship. This Elizabeth Jackson was not Elizabeth
(Palmer)(Ricketts) Jackson, stepdaughter of the *Welcome* passenger, Thomas Fitzwater, for she was by
this time long dead,[15] but the daughter of Benjamin
Chambers' brother John, and an account of her father
and herself will be given in the next sketch and
must, of necessity, include more information about
Benjamin Chambers.

NOTES

[1]1 PA 1:43. [2]MQA 5, 18 5th mo. 1682.
[3]2 PA 19:438.
[4]PMHB 11:177. The Constitution of the Society,
which was what we should now call a company, was
reprinted, PMHB 5:37-50. For a brief sketch of
Chambers, see PGM 23:101. On Chambers' property
in Philadelphia, see. 3 PA 3:346, 367f., 376f., 388,
392; surveys 3 PA 3:385, 387.
[5]Col. Recs. 1:190; 2:154, 163. [6]PMHB 8:338.
[7]Col. Recs 1:74, 86. [8]*Ibid.* 1:152.
[9]*Ibid.* 1:189, 298. [10]*Ibid.* 1:342.
[11]2 PA 19:17. [12] PA 19:77.
[13]2 PA 19:515f., 553, 560, 562; Col. Recs. 2:137,
147, 149f., 258, 477, 525.
[14]PhA B:124, No. 39.
[15]See the Fitzwater sketch.

CHAMBERS, JOHN   *possible but*
CHAMBERS, ELIZABETH   *rather improbable*

This man was the brother of Benjamin Chambers,
and, with his daughter, may have been on the *Welcome*
with Benjamin, though this has not previously been
suggested. The fact is, however, that we can neither prove nor disprove the claim.

The evidence may be adduced from the Minutes of
the Board of Property, session of 8 10th mo. 1701,[1]

which may be summarized as follows: There was a problem over ownership of 1100 acres in Plymouth Township belonging to Jonathan Hayes and also claimed by Penn himself. The land consisted of two contiguous tracts, of which the first was 500 acres sold by Penn, 19-20 11th mo. 1681/2, to John Chambers,[2] who afterwards came to America[3] and had a warrant, 28 4th mo. 1686 for 490 acres, which, John Chambers dying, his sole daughter Elizabeth by deed dated 30 8th mo. 1686 sold her right to Benjamin Chambers. Benjamin Chambers and the said Elizabeth now Clemson, by deed dated 29 4th mo. 1699, conveyed the tract to Jonathan Hayes. The other tract was 610 acres of a 1000-acre tract which Benjamin Chambers had bought from Penn, 24-25 11th mo. 1681/2.[3]

Here we have Benjamin Chambers in close association with Elizabeth Chambers, wife, in 1699, of one Clemson, and daughter of a John Chambers who had come to America and died there, both events between 20 11th mo. 1681/2 and 30 8th mo. 1686. As will have been seen in the preceding sketch, Benjamin Chambers was a highly probable *Welcome* passenger, and it is entirely possible that he brought with him his brother John and the latter's daughter Elizabeth. There is no proof, however, and the fact that the warrant for the property was not dated soon after the arrival of the *Welcome* but more than three years later, throws something of a cloud on the possibility. In any case, all that can be said of John Chambers' career in America is that he came, claimed land, and died.

To turn now our attention to the daughter, at Philadelphia Monthly Meeting on 25 8th mo. 1689,[4] James Taylor and Elizabeth Chambers declared, for the first time, their intention to marry, presented by Melissant Hodgkins, Hannah Carpenter and Hannah Chambers, the last of whom must be the wife of Benjamin Chambers. James Taylor was instructed to get his father's assent and a certificate from his meeting--he was clearly not of Philadelphia. We find no further record of this James Taylor alive, but he may have been a son of John Taylor of Gloucester County, New Jersey, whose probate[5] contains an accounting of John's estate dated 15 March 1713/14, showing payment made to Will Biddle (due him from James, dec'd son of John). There is also an inventory made in Waterford Township, 26 May 1704,

so John was dead by then, and if a debt of son James
could be charged against his father's estate, then
he must have died first. Confirming this is the
fact that John's will dated 13 Dec., year not given,
mentions no James or Elizabeth Taylor.[6] It seems
probable that Elizabeth Chambers never married James
Taylor at all, for there is no record of second intentions.

She did, however, marry, in succession, Matthew
Clemson and Stephen Jackson. No record of the marriage to Clemson has been found, but administration
on the estate of Matthew Clemison of the Town and
County of Philadelphia, merchant, was granted, 3
Dec. 1698, to his widow Elizabeth,[7] and coupling
this administration with the evidence from the
Board of Property, we can be sure that this is the
right Clemson. She now married, again, at Philadelphia Monthly Meeting House, 15 8th mo. 1702,
Stephen Jackson of Philadelphia, formerly of Chester,[8] and it was probably she who departed this
life in Philadelphia on 6 5th mo. 1746. No record
of Clemson children has been found but by Jackson
she had the following, order of births unknown:

    i.   Benjamin, d. 31 1st mo. 1730.
    ii.   Elizabeth, d. 22 5th mo. 1712.
    iii. John, d. 3 8th mo. 1710.
    iv.   Mary, bur. 23 6th mo. 1738, record calling
          her daughter of Stephen.

Stephen Jackson died 1 July 1740, leaving a nuncupative will deposed to on 20 July 1741 by his sister Precilla Williams, the executrix, and by Elizabeth Jackson who is not specifically called the
wife but probably was. No wife was mentioned in
the deposition.

In addition to the ·evidence cited above, John
Chambers is shown to be a brother of Benjamin by a
letter of Penn dated 1 6th mo. 1700. He must have
been dead by 30 8th mo. 1686, so the warrant dated
4 2nd mo. 1688 for 490 acres must have been surveyed for one of his heirs.[9] The Blackwell Rent
Roll of 1689 shows[10] John Chambers as owner of an
old purchase lot of 51 feet on Mulberry Street, 2/-
for five years.

We now turn to Howard Williams Lloyd's well-
known book with the misleading title of *Lloyd
Manuscripts* (Lancaster 1912), wherein on pages 133-
139 we find more on the Chambers family. Eliza,

daughter of John Chambers who was brother to Benjamin Chambers, of Philadelphia and Bearsted, Kent,
was the first wife of James Hunt, born ca. 1640,
probably at or near Bearsted, Kent, died at Kingsessing, Pennsylvania, 31 1st mo. 1717, leaving a will
with which we have only minor concern, dated 29 1st
mo. 1716/17, probated 3 April 1717. It will be remembered from Note 2 that James Hunt's name is all
that separates the name of Benjamin Chambers from
that of his brother John in the roll of First Purchasers. Though Mr. Lloyd did not know it, we can
give the marriage record:[11] James Hunt of Berstead,
linenweaver, bachelor age 33, and Eliza Chambers,
spinster, age 22, whose father consents, at St. Mar-
g[t], Canterbury, 9 October 1676.[12] The authority
given by Mr. Lloyd was Gilbert Cope, letter of 15
9th mo. 1893, but Cope's source was not stated.
Eliza (Chambers) Hunt must have died early, probably about 1682 in England, for Hunt married, second,
10 9th mo. 1686, at ye house of John Blunston, Elizabeth Bonsall [daughter of George Wood, on whom see
Lloyd's page 343], and she died at Darby, 28 6th
mo. 1703, after which Hunt married, third, in 1707,
Sarah Wildman of Falls Township, Bucks County, 2nd
intentions, 3 10th mo. 1707.
     As has been stated, James Hunt was also a First
Purchaser of 1000 acres, twice as much as his father-in-law could buy.[13]
     Thus we have John Chambers as the father of two
daughters living simultaneously, Eliza (Chambers)
Hunt, who died in or about 1682, and Elizabeth
(Chambers)(Clemson) Jackson, who was old enough to
contemplate marriage in 1689 and had executed a deed
in 1686. In 1701 she stated that she was her father's sole daughter, and this was quite true at that
time, for her older sister, or perhaps half-sister,
had by then been dead nearly two decades. In 1701,
however, the older sister had living issue by James
Hunt, as follows:

     i.   Elizabeth, b. in England, d. 1701; m. 27
           3rd mo. 1696 at Darby, William Bartram,
           on whom see Gilbert Cope and H. G. Ash-
           mead, *Genealogical and Personal Memoir
           of Chester and Delaware Counties* pp.
           124-128. This William Bartram m. (2)
           8th mo. 1707 Elizabeth Smith, b. 17 1st
           mo. 1689/90, daughter of William and

Elizabeth Smith, and she m. (2) John
Smith of Burlington County. Bartram's
will dated 18 Oct. 1710, probated 17
Jan. 1712/13, calls him of Darby, Chester County, yeoman, about to remove
with wife and youngest child to Carolina; sons John and James; uncle Benjamin Chambers; father-in-law William
Smith and Joseph Harvey of Ridley, executors; witnesses: John Maris, Jonathan
Hood, William Smith.[14] His brother
Isaac's will dated 7 March 1707/8, probated 3 April 1708[15] mentions, among
others, his brother William and the
latter's sons John and James. See also
Francis D. West, "The Mystery of the
Death of William Bartram, Father of John
Bartram the Botanist."[16] Bartram's issue by his first wife were:
1. John, the celebrated botanist, b. 23
    3rd mo. 1699, d. 22 9th mo. 1777.
2. James, b. 6 8th mo. 1701, living 1765.

ii.   Mary, b. England, d. 4 3rd mo. 1769, West
       Bradford Township, Chester Co., Pa., m.
       Darby, 17 1st mo. 1702/3 Abraham Mar-
       shall.

We have no concern here with James Hunt's younger
offspring, a daughter and a son, since they had no
Chambers inheritance.
    While it is strictly true that in 1701 Elizabeth
(Chambers) Clemson was the sole living daughter of
her father, she was not the sole heir, for the two
Bartram boys and their then unmarried aunt Mary Hunt
shared in the right to an inheritance. This fact
was later recognized by two deeds,[12] the first of
which is Philadelphia Deeds, Book G-7, p. 248, dated
31 Dec. 1720:

    John Bartram of Chester Co., yeoman [the bot-
    anist], son and heir of Eliza Bartram of said
    county, decd, to Stephen Jackson of Philadelph-
    ia, merchant: Whereas Benjamin Chambers late of
    Schuylkill in Philadelphia County in his life-
    time was seized of messuage and 600 acres in
    Blockley Township and Kingsessing township, al-
    so sundry lands in Pennsylvania and counties of
    Newcastle, Kent and Sussex on Delaware; said
    lands descended to Elizabeth Jackson, wife of

said Stephen Jackson, one of the daughters of
John Chambers, brother of Benjamin Chambers,
dec'd, and to aforesaid John Bartram, in right
of his mother Elisa Bartram, granddaughter of
said John Chambers, that is to say John Bartram,
son and Heir of Elisa Bartram who was a daughter
of Elisa Chambers who was a daughter of said
John Chambers, brother of said Benjamine Chambers, . . . Now for £60 releases rights.

**The second deed is Chester Deeds F-9, p. 179, 11
Jan.** 1716/17:

Stephen Jackson of Philadelphia, merchant,
and Elizabeth his wife, she daughter of John
Chambers, late of Philadelphia, decd, who was
a brother of Benjamin Chambers, late of Philadelphia, gent., also decd, to Abraham Marshall
of Bensalem, Chester Co. [sic], and Mary,
daughter of Elizer who was wife of James Hunt,
late of Darby, yeoman, decd, said Elizer being
the other daughter of said John Chambers . . .

NOTES

[1]2 PA 19:208.

[2]As First Purchaser of 500 acres in Group 30
(1 PA 1:43), between James Hunt, who was, as will
be seen, his son-in-law, and his brother Benjamin
Chambers.

[3]1 PA 1:43; 3 PA 3:390, 29 4th mo. 1686.

[4]PGSP 2:158.

[5]NJW 1:455.

[6]On this Taylor family see Walter Lee Sheppard
(NEHGR 111:275 f.).

[7]PhA A:272, abstracted in PGM 19:270.

[8]HEAQG 380.

[9]W&S 3:581, rec. 21 2nd mo. 1688.

[10]PGM 12:76. This John Chambers cannot have been
the servant in the will of Joseph Shaw of Brandywine
Creek, New Castle Co., Delaware, 14 March 1689/90,
probated 19 April 1690, will filed in Philadelphia.

[11]Cowper's *Canterbury Marriage Licenses*, ser. 3,
p. 244.

[12]I owe my knowledge of these facts to Mrs. Hannah Benner Roach.

[13]See Note 2.

[14]PhW C:335, abstr. in *Chester Co. Coll.*   340 f.

[15]PhW C:82.   [16]PGM 20:253-255.

8

CLAYPOOLE, JAMES   *disproved*

This is in some ways the most ridiculous claim
yet found. The name has appeared on no list but the
claim is made inferentially in W. W. H. Davis, *History of Bucks County, Pennsylvania* (Doylestown, 1st
ed., 1876), p. 67, where a paragraph claims Joseph
Kirkbride as a *Welcome* passenger, after which Davis
goes on to say that Jane [sic] Claypoole, descendant
[sic] of Oliver Cromwell through his daughter, may
never have come to Bucks County. This may mean that
Davis thought James Claypoole was also on the *Welcome*. The error of "Jane" for "James" was corrected
in the second edition of this work. We should point
out that James Claypoole was not a descendant of
Oliver Cromwell but that his brother John married
Oliver Cromwell's daughter Elizabeth.

As a matter of fact no Claypoole came on the
Welcome. Abundant proof exists that James did not.
Mrs. Rebecca Irwin Graff, *Genealogy of the Claypoole
Family of Philadelphia 1588-1893* (Philadelphia 1893),
p. 32, cites a letter to John Goodson written by
Claypoole in England on 21 7th mo. 1682, when the
Welcome was nearing America; on p. 35 a letter
from Claypoole to William Penn, written at London,
1 2nd mo. 1683; and on p. 42 she states that Claypoole arrived on the *Concord*, 8 8th mo. 1683, with
his wife and seven of his children, the eldest son
John having already sailed on the *Amity*, 23 April
1682. Claypoole himself registered this arrival
in Philadelphia Arrivals as "on Capt. Jefferies
Ship."[1]

THE CLAYPOOLE FAMILY[2]

1. John Claypoole, the son of Adam, grandson of
James, and great grandson of James, married at the
Church of St. Thomas the Apostle, 8 June 1622, Mary
Angell and she died 10 April 1660/1, having given
birth to the following issue:

i.	Mary, m. 26 Dec. 1655 William Shield Esq.
ii.	John, m. Elizabeth Cromwell, daughter of Oliver Cromwell.
iii.	Elizabeth, d. 1681 in Ireland; m. Dr. Alexander Staple.
iv.	Robert, d. unm.
v.	Wingfield, captain of Horse.
vi.	Granely, cornet.
vii.	Dorothy.

      viii. Frances.
2 ix.   James, b. 8th mo. 1634, d. 6 6th mo. 1687.
     x.   Edward, d. Barbadoes 11 Sept. 1699.
     xi.   Martha, d.y.
     xii. Martha, d. unm.
     xiii. Norton, d. 1688; m. 1677 ---- ----.
     xiv. Benjamin, bapt. 15 Feb. 1642/3.

    2. James Claypoole, ninth child of John and
Mary (Angell) Claypoole, was born 8th mo. 1634,
died in Philadelphia, 6 6th mo. 1687. He married at
Bremen, Germany, Helena Mercer. He became a prosperous merchant in London and migrated to Pennsylvania on the *Concord*, 8 8th mo. 1683. For a full
account see Mrs. Graff's Claypoole Genealogy.

    Issue: surname Claypoole
    i.   John, b. Nicholas Lane, London, 15 9th
           mo. 1658; d. 8 7th mo. 1700; came to
           America on the *Amity*, 23 2nd mo. 1682;
           m. Mary -----.
    ii.   Mary, b. Minsing Lane, London, 14 8th mo.
           1660, d. 1726; m. 11 Oct. 1688 at the
           house of Wm Hare, Philadelphia (rec. by
           Register General), Francis Cooke of New
           Castle County, now Delaware.
    iii.   Helen or Helena, b. Scots Yard, London,
           6 9th mo. 1662, d. 1691; m. 2 Feb.
           1687/8 (rec. by Register General),
           William Bethell, bricklayer of Amboy,
           East Jersey.
    iv.   James, 12 6th mo. 1664, d. in or before
           1706.
    v.   Priscilla, b. 25 2nd mo. 1666, d. in or
           before 1706; m. Dr. John Crappe.
    vi.   Nathaniel, b. 23 7th mo. 1668 at Horsly
           Down.
    vii.   Josiah, b. Scots Yard, London, 9 9th mo.
           1669, d. 2 3rd mo. 1670 at Kingston up-
           on Thames.
    viii. Samuel, b. 19 1st mo. 1670/1, d. 11 1st
           mo. 1680/1.
    ix.   Nathaniel, b. 4 8th mo. 1672, d. by 1726.
    x.   George, b. 14 11th mo. 1674, d. Phila-
           delphia, 23 10th mo. 1730; had leave to
           m. (1) at Philadelphia Monthly Meeting,
           Mary Righton who d. 28 2nd mo. 1702; (2)
           had leave to m., same meeting, 29 3rd
           mo. 1704, Martha Hoskins, daughter of

Richard, her death not recorded; had
leave to m. (3) same meeting, 2 9th mo.
1715, Deborah Hardiman, daughter of
Abraham and Diana (-----) Hardiman and
she d. as Widow Claypoole, 26 5th mo.
1785 aged 93.

Issue: surname Claypoole
by Mary Righton
1. William, d. 25 2nd mo. 1706.
by Martha Hoskins
2. Martha, bur. 1 6th mo. 1714.
by Mary Righton or Martha Hoskins
3. Elizabeth, d. 22 12th mo. 1730.
4. Isaac, d. 22 12th mo. 1730.
by Deborah Hardiman
5. Deborah, b. 1 8th mo. 1716, d. 12 12th mo. 1730.
6. Mary, b. 21 12th mo. 1717, d. 18 12th mo. 1730.
7. Hanah, b. 3 10th mo. 1719, d. 2 5th mo. 1721.
8. Samuel, b. 6 2nd mo. 1721, d. 1 9th mo. 1728.
9. Hannah, b. 24 2nd mo. 1722, d. 12 12th mo. 1730.
10. Abraham, b. 20 1st mo. 1722/3, d. 10 12th mo. 1750. Mrs. Graff says he was the only one to survive his father which is not quite so, but he was the only one to survive his father an appreciable length of time.
11. John, b. 5 7th mo. 1724, d. 18 3rd mo. 1725.

xi. Stillborn son b. about end of 1673.
xii. Joseph, b. 29 1st mo. 1676, d. 20 6th mo. 1676 at Lambeth.
xiii. Joseph, b. 14 5th mo. 1677.
xiv. Elizabeth, b. 25 5th mo. 1678, d. 31 5th mo. 1678, bur. Moorfields.[3]

NOTES

[1]PMHB 8:331. See Milton Rubincam, 'The Identity of Helena "Merces" Mercer, wife of James Claypoole, (1634-1687), of Philadelphia! (TAG 18:201-206). also PGM 17:39; 18:141d.; 24:74; PMHB 14:86-88; TAG 39:12 f. See also Marion Balderston, ed., *James Claypoole's Letter Book, London and Philadelphia, 1681-1684* (San Marino, Huntington Library, 1967).

[2]This material is based largely on Mrs. Graff's Genealogy, except for the list of George Claypoole's marriages and children.
[3]Claypoole brought with him on the *Concord* a total of seven of his fourteen children. No. 1 had crossed alone in the preceding year; Nos. 7, 8, 11, 12 and 14 were dead. This makes six of the missing accounted for, but there must be another who had died earlier.

CLAYTON, JOSHUA[1]   *disproved*

This name was added in 1910 to the original list of qualifying ancestors of the Welcome Society of Pennsylvania and appears on Lists J and K by rubber stamp, and also on Lists N, S, T and V, in this last as a *Submission* passenger, however.

The proof that Joshua Clayton did not cross on the *Welcome* was long obscured by the fact that in the printing of the primary documents which would have revealed the truth, the name Joshua was twice read as Joseph, though it was in one instance correctly printed. In the end, the incorrect reading had far more influence than the correct. These documents are as follows:

BUCKS ARRIVALS

James Clayton of	with these
middle witch in	Children
in the County of Chester	James
black Smith & Jane	Sarah Clayton
his wife Came in y[e]	John
Said Ship Submission	Mary
at the time aforesaid	Josuah
[i.e. the 1682 voyage]	Lydia

The name Josuah was correctly read in the transcript of this document which appears in J. H. Battle's *History of Bucks County, Pennsylvania* (Philadelphia 1887), p. 675, but in the transcript which appears in *Pennsylvania Magazine of History and Biography* 9:231, the name Josuah was read as Joseph and the erroneous reading was allowed to stand for many years without challenge.

THE LOG OF THE SUBMISSION[2]

James Clayton   50   Jane Clayton   48

James Clayton	16	Sarah Clayton	14
John Clayton	11	Mary Clayton	8
Josuah Clayton	5	Lydia Cleaton	5

It will be seen that the *Submission's* log is in harmony, in regard to the name Josuah, with the actual letters of Bucks Arrivals, but here again the printed version[2] wrongly reads Josuah as Joseph. Thus, it is clear that Joshua Clayton arrived on the *Submission* in 1682, then aged five and hardly the head of a household. It may well be that he and Lydia, both recorded as aged five, were twins.

The original documents were, in 1910 as now, in the custody of the Historical Society of Pennsylvania, but when the question of eligibility of Joshua Clayton as a qualifying ancestor for the Welcome Society came up, the committee probably assumed that the records which printed the name as Joseph were correct and did not examine the originals. Since Joshua spent his adult life in Delaware, it was unlikely that anyone would find him in a Bucks County record.

An affidavit was, however, submitted in support of an application for membership. This was sworn to at Edgewater Park, Burlington County, New Jersey, 23 June 1910, by Mrs. Belinda Jane Thomas, then residing with her daughter, Mrs. George DeB. Keim. She deposed that she was then aged 86 [i.e. b. 1824], and daughter of Henry Mitchell and Mary Tuly Mitchell, his wife, and that she had heard her aunt, Belinda Tuly Strothers, say that "their ancestors came to America in the ship Welcome in company with William Penn, the Founder of the State of Pennsylvania." The affidavit does not identify "their ancestors" more particularly or mention Joshua Clayton. Further, she deposed that Mary Tuly Mitchell, her mother, was aged 75 when she died in 1860, so was born in 1785. There is here no proof that Joshua Clayton came on the *Welcome* or even that the applicant was descended from him. Assuming, as I do, that the deponant was entirely honest and even entirely accurate and careful in what she said, it may well be that she was descended from some genuine *Welcome* passenger not named Joshua Clayton.

Henry F. Hepburn of Philadelphia printed in 1904 an elaborate account of a Clayton family in Yorkshire, "The Delaware Branch of the Clayton Family" (*Papers of the Historical Society of Delaware* 41:21-27). How accurate the English part of

this article is, I do not know, nor do I know whether
the Yorkshire family was ancestral to the Claytons
of Virginia or the Claytons of Chichester Township,
present Delaware County, Pennsylvania, as Hepburn
claims. As a matter of fact, he asserts more than once
that the founder of the Chichester Claytons, William, was a cousin of the man whom he calls "Joshua
(1) Clayton," that is, the James Clayton who was
aged 50 in 1682, wrongly called by his son's name.
The name James is found in the Yorkshire family described by Hepburn as borne by a son of a John and
grandson of a William, etc., born 1620, but this
man is claimed to have become a doctor of divinity,
hardly likely to be identical with the blacksmith
from Middlewich, Cheshire, in 1682. We may therefore confidently reject all that Hepburn has to say
on the origin of Joshua Clayton.

The discovery of the family home in Middlewich,
Cheshire, led to George Ormerod's monumental *History
of the County Palatine and City of Chester* (London,
3 vols., folio, 1882), a huge work where (1:747)
the Manor of Thelwall in the Hundred of Bucklow is
said to have been held, from the time of Edward III
to that of Elizabeth I, by a family named Clayton.
Our James Clayton is, of course, not mentioned, but
this is a more likely clue for research than are
the Yorkshire Claytons of Hepburn's article.

The following pedigree of the Delaware Claytons
is in part based on information kindly supplied by
a Clayton descendant, George Valentine Massey II,
F.A.S.G., of Dover, Delaware.

THE CLAYTONS OF DELAWARE

1. James Clayton, of whose parentage nothing is
known, was born about 1632, probably in or near
Middlewich, Cheshire, where he practiced his trade
of blacksmith and married Jane -----, aged 48 in
1682, of whose maiden name we know nothing. With
his wife and the children listed below he came to
America in 1682 on the ship *Submission*, one of
Penn's 1682 fleet.

   Issue: surname Clayton
   i.   James, b. England ca. 1666, aged 16 in
         1682. Further research on this man
         in Delaware records might prove fruit-
         ful.
   ii.   Sarah, b. England ca. 1668, aged 14 in

        1682. Not traced further.
  iii. John, b. England ca. 1671, aged 11 in
        1682. Further research in Delaware rec-
        ords might prove profitable. With his
        brother Joshua he bought land in Dela-
        ware in 1698.
  iv.   Mary, b. England ca. 1674, aged 8 in 1682.
        No further trace.
2 v.   Joshua, b. England ca. 1677, aged 5 in
        1682, possibly twin of Lydia; d. ca.
        1761.
  vi.   Lydia, b. England ca. 1677, aged 5 in
        1682; possibly twin of Joshua; no
        further trace.

     2. Joshua Clayton, fifth child of James and Jane
(-----) Clayton, sometime of Middlewich, Cheshire,
was born about 1677, possibly a twin, and was five
years old when he and his family came to America
in 1682 on the *Submission*.
     At the age of 21 years, Joshua and his older
brother John bought 200 acres of "Shoemaker's Hall"
in Kent County, Delaware, on the south side of Walker's Branch on Dover River, 15 June 1698. This had
formerly been taken up by Isaac Webb and was sold
by Thomas Bidewell, attorney for Wm Lawrence and
Michael Walton of Philadelphia, and Joshua later
sold and acquired land in Little Creek Hundred at a
place later known, and still known by old inhabitants, as Cowgill's Corner--named for his descendants.
     Joshua Clayton married, first, before 12 4th mo.
1699, Sarah (Needham) Bedwell. The date of the marriage must have been subsequent to 14 June 1698 when
the will of her former husband, Henry Bedwell, was
probated.[3] Proof that the marriage was before 12
4th mo. 1699 is a deed from Joshua and his wife Sarah, executrix of the will of Henry Bedwell, selling
a tract called "Longreach."[4] Joshua married, second,
at Little Creek, 21 5th mo. 1747, Sarah Cummins,
widow, née Miers, of Sussex County,[5] who had been
married several times before this.
     All of Joshua Clayton's children were by his
first wife. The evidence for her maiden name is
circumstantial, but her possible brother or nephew,
Ralph Needham, signed Joshua's second marriage certificate next to her son and Joshua Clayton's sons-
in-law, directly under the groom and bride. Ralph's
name is signed directly under the bride's parents
on the marriage certificate of Jane Cowgill, the

granddaughter of Joshua Clayton, to Daniel Smith,
21 5th mo. 1747.[6]

The will of Joshua Clayton of Little Creek Hundred, dated 2 Sept. 1760, probated 26 Jan. 1761,[7]
names his wife Sarah and his deceased daughter Sarah Cowgill; grandchildren, who can be identified
by other records: John Cowgill, Henry Cowgill, Clayton Cowgill, Sarah Register (wife of John) and Elizabeth Neal (wife of Francis), who were the children
of John and Lydia (Clayton) Cowgill.[8] Also Thomas
and Ezekiel Cowgill, Sarah Hand [married Samuel
Hand, 22 12th mo. 1756], Eleanor [called Ellen in
her mother's will], Rachel [married Jonathan Grew-
ell], and Jean [called Jane in her mother's will],
who married Daniel Smith, as stated above, these
four being children of Thomas and Sarah (Clayton)
Cowgill. Other grandchildren in the will were Eunice Osburn and Lydia Durburrow, the former child
of the testator's daughter Elizabeth who had married Mark Manlove Jr., 3 Sept. 1730, and Joshua also mentioned her husband, Jonathan Osburn.[9]

The tradition that Joshua Clayton was a minister among Friends is recorded on a plaque on a
Cromwellian type chair that belonged to him. The
brass plaque says that the chair's owner had been
"the venerable Joshua Clayton, an eminent and distinguished minister of the Society of Friends . ."
The chair came into the Corbit family through
Joshua's great-granddaughter Mary Cowgill, wife of
William Corbit (1746-1818) who built the now inter-
nationally known Corbit-Sharp House at Odessa, Delaware, owned by Winterthur Museum.[10]

Sarah (Miers)(Cummins) Clayton's birth record
is in an old Cowgill Bible, and the birth of Sarah
Needham is in an old Needham Bible that came down
in the Cowgill family but has disappeared, printed
in 1728 and purchased by the Cowgill family in 1829.
It contained the births of the children of Ezekiel
Needham, son of Edmund, born the last of 5th mo.
1644, who married Sarah King, 27 Oct. 1669. The
children of Ezekiel and Sarah were:

        Sarah Needham, b. 27 May 1674
        Ezekiel Needham, b. Dec. 1676, d. Dec. 1676
        Ezekiel Needham, b. 15 Nov. 1677
        Daniel Needham, 15 March 1679/80
        Ralph Needham, b. 26 Aug. 1682

Ralph, whose wife was Phebe, died intestate in Kent

County, before 7 March 1752 when letters were issued
to his widow.[11] The Needham family can be traced
to England where Edmund's mother, Mary Needham, left
£200 to her son Edmund "now residing in New England."[12] She lived at Hampstead, Middlesex, and her
will was dated 12 April 1660, probated 26 March 1661.
It sounds like a prosperous family, for she wills
considerable property and the sister of Edmund, her
daughter Katherine Needham of Chipping Barnett, Herefordshire, in her will[13] dated 1 Feb. 1691 directs
that she be buried in the vault of the parish church
of St. Martin's, Ludgate, as near her parents as
possible.

The Cowgill family Bible, then owned by Mrs. Susan C. Bowes, of Ridley Park, Pa., is quoted in Turner, and gives the birth of Sarah Miers, daughter of
John and Mary, as 30 Sept. 1695, died 19 10th mo.
1766.

Ann Wharton Smith's *Genealogy of the Fisher Family 1682 to 1896* (Philadelphia 1896), p. 22, says
that Joshua Fisher (son of Thomas and grandson of
John), born 1707, died 1 Feb. 1783, married 27 July
1733, Sarah Rowland, born 6 Dec. 1716, died 4 Jan.
1772, daughter of Thomas Rowland and his wife Sarah
Miers. This Sarah (Rowland) Fisher was Joshua Clayton's stepdaughter, of course, and Joshua Fisher,
with his brother-in-law Samuel Rowland, made the
first survey and chart of Delaware Bay, used for
many years until the government survey was made.

A footnote on the same page of the Fisher Genealogy says that Sarah Miers (later Mrs. Joshua Clayton) was daughter of John Miers and Mary Haworth,
his wife, the latter of whom came from England with
Dr. Thomas Wynne in 1682. She, Sarah (Miers)(Rowland)(Cummins) Clayton was five times married, and
always an honored member of the Society of Friends.
"She is remembered as a woman of uncommon excellence
in mental and personal advantages, an efficient manager of her own estates, and extensively esteemed
for her usefulness and virtues."

Issue: surname Clayton
i.   Lydia, m. 16 12th mo. 1720 John Cowgill,
      b. 8 5th mo. 1698, son of John and Brid-
      get (Croasdale) Cowgill [Middletown
      recs.] He m. (2) Hannah -----, and d.
      intestate, admin. to widow Hannah, 29
      July 1752,[14] and Hannah m. (2) Robert
      Hall.

Issue: surname Cowgill
1. John, m. Mary Worrell.
2. Clayton.
3. Sarah, m. John Register.
4. Elizabeth, m. Francis Neal.
5. Henry, m. Elizabeth Osborne.
6. Lydia, m. ----- Durborow.[15]

ii.   Sarah, m., 2nd int.. Duck Creek Meeting,[16]
11th mo. 1727, Thomas Cowgill, also son
of John and Bridget (Croasdale) Cowgill,
b. Bucks Co., Pa., 21 4th mo. 1696[17];
removed to New Castle Co., Del., ca.
1713 when his father bought land in Duck
Creek Hundred; d. Kent Co., Del., before 7 Dec. 1749 when his widow and administratrix Sarah Cowgill (Cowgle)
passed an account. Additional proof of
the marriage is given in a deed of Joshua Clayton[18] to his "loving daughter,
Sarah Cowgill, widow of Thomas Cowgill,"
for part of "Willingbrook," 11 3rd mo.
1750.[19] This land abuts the present
Cowgills Corners. After Sarah's death,
son Ezekiel was named administrator d.
b.n. of his father's estate.[20] Sarah
d. 16 Aug. 1750,[21] naming her children:
Ezekiel, Thomas, Sarah, Ellen, Rachel
Cowgill, and Jane Smith; executors: son
Ezekiel and son-in-law Daniel Smith.

    Issue: surname Cowgill, order uncer-
    tain
1. Ezekiel, executor of his mother and
admin. of his father; not mentioned
in grandfather Clayton's will 1760.
2. Thomas, in his grandfather's will he
is to get the share left to his
cousin John Cowgill if the latter
d.s.p.
3. Sarah, named conditional heir after
her brother Thomas; m. 22 12th mo.
1756 Samuel Hand.
4. Elenor or Ellen, named in grandfather's
will as conditional heir after sister Sarah.
5. Rachel, named as conditional heir after sister Elenor; m. Jonathan
Grewell.
6. Jane, m., Little Creek Meeting, 21 5th

mo. 1747[22] Daniel Smith, b. 11 11th
mo. 1722 in Kent Co., Md.,[23] d. 27
2nd mo. 1769.[24] Their daughter Sarah
b. 11 5th mo. 1752, m. Joseph Nock,
b. 15 6th mo. 1750, son of Daniel
and Barthia (Hales) Nock, and Sarah
Nock d. 17 10th mo. 1790,[25] Joseph
Nock, intestate 1793.[26] His estate,
divided by Orphans Court, lists his
minor daughter Jane who petitioned
that Samuel Smith, her uncle, be
her guardian (May 1795); Joseph
Knock's heirs recorded in Orphans
Court E-1:151. [He had changed the
spelling because he had a double
first cousin named Joseph Nock.] Jane
m. 17 11th mo. 1796, John Woodall
(d. testate, 19 2nd mo. 1847), and
their son John Jr., b. 27 2nd mo.
1810, d. 18 10th mo. 1886, m. 16 6th
mo. 1836 Anna Matilda Calley (1818-
1911). They were parents of Mary
Woodall, wife of George Valentine
Massey I.

iii. Elizabeth, m. 3 Sept. 1730 Mark Manlove
Jr. They had a daughter Eunice who in
1750 m. Jonathan Osborne and as such is
mentioned in Joshua Clayton's will.[27]
John Clayton (b. 1671), Joshua's brother,
named his land "Middlewick," and this
land, or part of it, his son John sold
to his uncle Joshua Clayton, 8 May 17
1732.[28] James Clayton Jr. (b. 1666),
brother of John and Joshua, named his
land "Clayton Hall."[29] He was called a
blacksmith when he bought this land
8 9th mo. 1687 at age 21. Joshua Clayton's will, already cited above, leaves
to granddaughter Eunice Ozburn "all my
now Dwelling Plantation being part of a
Tract called Willen Brook, Bounded on
the South with the land given to af[sd]
Daughter Sarah Cowgill, On the West and
North with the land of the af[sd] Ralph
Needham and on the East with the land
left here=in before to my grandson John
Cowgill Together with Improvements
w[torn]=soever . . ." In failure of

lawful heirs, to grandson Thomas Cowgill
and in failure, etc., then to his sisters Sarah Hand, Elenor Cowgill and Rachel Grewell in equal shares. . ." Eunice Manlove is named in the will of
her grandfather Mark Manlove dated 16
March 1747, probated 8 Jan. 1749, as the
daughter of his son Mark.[30]   She d. intestate, with heirs, in Little Creek
Hundred, ca. 1793, when Henry Cowgill
(1741-1810) administered her estate.[31]
Her husband Jonathan Ozburn had d. testate in 1773 (will dated 24 Aug. 1773,
probated 11 Nov. 1773),   naming wife
Eunice, son Jonathan and daughters Eunice and Tabitha Ozburn; Elizabeth Cowgill and Mary Alstone and her husband
Izrael Alstone.

NOTES

[1]TAG 39:10-12.

[2]PGSP 1:10, transcribed by L. Taylor Dickson.

[3]Kent Wills Ae-141, Hall of Records, Dover, Del.

[4]*Ibid.* C:237.

[5]Duck Creek MM, p. 186 of records, copy at the
Genealogical Society of Pennsylvania.

[6]*Ibid.* at back of p. 186.

[7]Kent Wills A9, 121f. He also freed his Negroes
Phillis, Dick, Hannah and Charles, at 21, and before this he had said: "My will further is that my
Negro man, Patrick, shall continue free during his
good behavior."

[8]See MS Cowgill Family by the Rev. J. B. Turner,
Hall of Records, Dover, Del.

[9]See John A. Sweeney, *Grandeur on the Appoquin-
imink: The House of William Corbit at Odessa, Delaware* (University of Delaware Press 1959), 111, 119
note, 125.

[10]Kent Wills K:55.

[11]Henry F. Waters, *Genealogical Gleanings in England* (Boston 1901) 1:543.

[12]*Ibid.* 2:1239-40.

[13]See Leon de Valinger, ed. *Calendar of Kent
County, Delaware, Probate Records 1680-1800* (Dover,
Del., 1944), p. 150.

[14]She can hardly be the Lydia Cowgill of Talbot
Co., Md., who m. William Webb, 1 8th mo. 1753, at
Third River Meeting, witnessed by a Henry Cowgill.

[15]Minutes 3:78.
[16]Neshamina Meeting rec. p. 163.
[17]Kent Deeds O-1:46.
[18]Called Willen Brook.
[19]Kent Admin. A-11:119.
[20]Kent Wills A-11:116.
[21]Duck Creek Minutes p. 94.
[22]Cecil Co. Meeting recs. 1:11.
[23]Duck Creek minutes 26.
[24]*Ibid.* 12, 28, 83.
[25]Kent Wills N-1:52.
[26]See also papers of the late Miss Alice Cowgill
cited by Turner.
[27]Kent Deeds K:131.
[28]*Ibid.* B-2:62.
[29]*Calendar* 137.
[30]*Ibid.* 467.
[31]Kent Wills A-38:166f.

CLIFT, BENJAMIN   *disproved*

This name appears on List X only. The truth is
that Benjamin Clift crossed the Atlantic on the ship
Lion of Liverpool, arriving 14 8th mo. 1683, in the
capacity of servant to Joseph Fisher, to serve four
years and get the customary fifty acres.

If Benjamin Clift was at the crossing only a boy,
then there is no reason not to identify him with
the Benjamin Cliffe of Darby who died in 1750, leaving his estate to Benjamin Lobb, his sister's son.
Mrs. Balderston, who provides this intelligence,[1]
speaks of an Isabel Clift who came as a servant to
Joseph Fisher in 1682. The "evidence" for such a
servant of Joseph Fisher is confined to the record
of a grant of fifty acres made to Isabel Clift by
the Board of Property on 7 3rd mo. 1705. It happens,
however, that Joseph Fisher left in Philadelphia
Arrivals a list of his servants then brought into
the province, and there is no Isabel Clift and no
Isabel with other surname among them. Mrs. Balderston accepts Isabel Clift as a servant in 1682 with
no doubt of her existence and supposes that she was
wife to Benjamin Clift.

Now the grant in 1705 may have been made to Isabel Clift on the basis of her own service, if genuine, or on the basis of the service of a deceased
husband. It is not impossible that the clerk of the
Board of Property could have misunderstood the proceedings and have thought the grant was on the basis

of Isabel's own service when it really was on the
basis of her husband's. If so, this is the first
instance where I have found the Minutes of the Board
of Property mistaken and provably so.

There is a possibility, however, that the grant
really was made on the basis of Isabel's own service
and not on her husband's. The last servant of the
Fisher group was "Eliz. Johnson." No success has
been had in tracing such a person further, though
this is perhaps not too significant, since several
of the servants who wrongly got placed on List X
have not been found thereafter in American records.
It has, however, been suggested to me that the
first name should be read as "Eliezer," though it
does not seem to me possible to do so on the basis
of the palaeography of the passage. But in the
17th century the name "Elizabeth" was sometimes used
interchangeably with "Isabel," and I therefore suggest with some caution that a woman named Elizabeth
alias Isabel Johnson came on the *Lion* as servant to
Joseph Fisher and that she afterwards, before 1705,
married Benjamin Clift, and in 1705 applied for and
received the grant of fifty acres in her own right,
being called Elizabeth Johnson when entered on the
Fisher list and Isabel Clift when applying for the
grant. If this supposition be correct, then it
would be possible for the woolcomber Christopher
Lobb who, in Mrs. Balderston's view, probably married Isabel born Clift, and became the father of
Benjamin Lobb, nephew and heir of Benjamin Clift,
to have married another sister of Benjamin Clift.

While it is not clear that this is what happened, it seems the best explanation of the evidence
presented. In any case, no success has been had
in locating an Eliezer Johnson.

NOTES

[1]PGM 24:93, note 88. See CW C;98.
[2]2 PA 19:450.

COLVERT, MARGARET   *disproved*

This name appears only on List X and there with
the first name given wrongly as Mary. The truth is
that in Philadelphia Arrivals, immediately below
the entry for Joseph Fisher and his household, Margaret Colvert "late of Dublin came in ditto ship,"
that is, in the *Lion* of Liverpool, arriving 14 8th

mo. 1683. As she is not shown in the servants column,
she had obviously paid for her passage. With good
reason Mrs. Balderston has identified[1] her as probably daughter of Thomas Calvert of Chester County,
husbandman, who made a nuncupative will, 15 1st mo.
1685, probated 17 12th mo. 1685,[2] in which he names
no wife but does mention two daughters Elizabeth
and Margaret.

NOTES

[1]PGM 24:93, note 88.
[2]PhW A-30, #23, 1685; PGSP 1:55; MIQ 316.

COMLY, HENRY   *highly improbable*
COMLY, JOAN TYLER, his wife   *highly improbable*
COMLY, HENRY, his son   *highly improbable*

This family is on no list but that they were
on the *Welcome* is claimed in Albert W. Dudley's revised edition of Dr. Joseph C. Martindale's *A History of the Townships of Byberry and Moreland* (Philadelphia, no date), pp. 270-301, especially 270 for
the claim. On the other hand, George Norwood Comly
in his excellent work, *The Comly Family in America*
(Philadelphia 1939), states the claim only to deny
it. The *Welcome* claim is likewise denied by Mrs.
Balderston,[1] who apparently did not find any record
of Comly's loading on any ship but did find record
of a loading by Edward Comly, perhaps a relative,
on the *Samuel and Mary* of Bristol, which arrived in
America by November 1683. Mr. Comly found evidence
that the family was in America by 25 9th mo. 1683
when the daughter Mary, who remained in England,
was married. It therefore seems probable that the
family crossed the Atlantic on the *Samuel and Mary*
but this lacks proof.

Henry Comly was a First Purchaser of 500 acres,
in Group 11[2] and another record calls him of the
City of Bristol.[3] There was a warrant dated 26 9th
mo. 1683, soon after the arrival of the *Samuel and
Mary*, for 200 acres and another the next day for a
city lot laid out 29 9th mo. 1683 on the east side
of Schuylkill Second between Chestnut and Walnut
Streets.[4] In the Blackwell Rent Roll of 1689[5]
Henry Combly appears as owner of a city lot of
sixty feet, fifth name on Schuylkill Second north
of Walnut Street, and this is marked as an Old Purchase.

Mr. Comly believed that Henry Comly was son of

another Henry. He married, first, in England, a
wife named Judith ----- who was buried at Bristol
on 22 7th mo. 1670; second, at Bristol Meeting, 25
10th mo. 1673, Joan Tyler, who accompanied her husband and son to America and was buried at Middletown, 20 10th mo. 1689, having married, second, 26
2nd mo. 1685, Joseph English, another *Welcome*
claimant.[6] Henry Comly died in Bucks County and
was buried at Middletown, 14 3rd mo. 1684. He left
a will[7] dated 26 2nd mo. 1684 which mentions wife
Joane, daughter Mary and son Henry.

Issue: surname Comly
by first wife Judith
i.   Mary, b. Bedminster, England, 23 6th mo.
        1656, bur. Bristol, 22 12th 1686; m.
        25 9th mo. 1683 John Crew of Bedminster,
        bur. Bristol 29 1st mo. 1710.
        Issue: surname Crew
        1. John, b. 11 10th mo. 1686, bur. Bris-
           tol 27 5th mo. 1720.
ii. John, b. Bedminster 14 8th mo. 1661.
iii. Sarah, b. Bedminster, 24 4th mo. 1665,
        bur. 20 11th mo. 1678.
iv. George, bur. 3 6th mo. 1662.
by second wife Joan Tyler
v.   Henry, b. Bedminster 1674, d. 16 1st mo.
        1726/7, Moreland; m. Middletown Meeting
        17 8th mo. 1695 Agnes Heaton, b. 12 9th
        mo. 1677, d. 30 10th mo. 1743, Moreland,
        daughter of Robert and Alice (-----)
        Heaton, also *Welcome* claimants, all
        three of them.
        Issue: surname Comly
        1. Alice, b. 14 1st mo. 1696/7, d. 26 9th
           mo. 1759; m. 28 7th mo. 1719 Thomas
           Gill; 6 ch.
        2. Mary, b. 12 12th mo. 1699/1700, d. 4
           3rd mo. 1782; m. (1) 28 7th mo. 1719
           Thomas Harding, 6 ch.; (2) 17 10th
           mo. 1731 George Randall, 5 ch.
        3. Henry, b. 26 2nd mo. 1702, d. 21 9th
           mo. 1772; m. 26 7th mo. 1728 Phebe
           Gilbert, 8 ch.
        4. Robert, b. 12 June 1704, d. 13 3rd mo.
           1770; m. 30 8th mo. 1727 Jane Cad-
           wallader, 6 ch.
        5. John, b. 20 3rd mo. 1706, d. 15 1st
           mo. 1761; m. 20 4th mo. 1728 Hannah

Mason, 11 ch.
6. Joseph, b. 21 Aug. 1708, d. 21 6th mo.
   1774; m. 1731 Elizabeth Mason, 9 ch.
7. Walter, b. 12 Nov. 1710, d. 30 3rd mo.
   1759; m. 1st mo. 1731 Susanna Mason,
   2 ch.
8. Agnes, b. 20 Feb. 1712/13, d. 22 9th
   mo. 1779; m. 27 1st mo. 1738 Nicholas Randall, 8 ch.
9. James, b. 14 June 1715; m. 27 7th mo.
   1737 Mary Paul, 7 ch.
10. Isaac, b. 4 June 1717, d. 8th mo. 1747;
    m. 2nd mo. 1738 Abigail Walmsley, 4
    ch.
11. Grace, b. 24 1st mo. 1721/2, d. 12 1st
    mo. 1800; m. Benjamin Cadwallader.

NOTES

[1]PGM 24:107, note 148.
[2]1 PA 1:41.
[3]3 PA 3:330.
[4]3 PA 2:679; W&S 3:503. An indentured servant
named George Sheave may have come with this family
(see Col. Recs. 1:92).
[5]PGM 23:91.
[6]Middletown, 1st int., 3 10th mo. 1684, passed
1 11th mo. 1684. Dr. Martindale's accounts of the
Comlys seem to think Joseph's first name was Henry.
[7]BW A-1:8, abstracted PGSP 1:203; photograph in
the Comly Genealogy.

CONDUIT, WILLIAM   *disproved*

This name appears on List X only. The truth is
that he came on the *Lion* of Liverpool, arriving 14
8th mo. 1683, as servant to Joseph Fisher, to serve
four years and get £3 and fifty acres, loose on
14 8th mo. 1687. No success has been had in finding further trace of this man. The name Condit is
frequent among Presbyterian families in northeast
New Jersey.

COWGILL, ELLEN[1], widow   *disproved*
COWGILL, RALPH, her son   *disproved*
COWGILL, JANE, her daughter   *disproved*
COWGILL, JENNETT, her daughter   *disproved*
COWGILL, JOHN, her son   *disproved*
COWGILL, EDMUND, her son   *disproved*
COWGILL, MARY, her daughter?   *disproved*

COMLY

The widow Ellen Cowgill was accepted as a *Wel-come* passenger on Lists A, B, C, D, E, F, G, H, I, J, K, L, M, N, P, Q, R, S, T, W, X, Y and Z, but List O denies the.claim and List V puts her on the *Lamb*. The unspecified family appears on Lists A, B, C, D, E, G, H, I, M, P, U (most probably on the *Lamb*), Y and Z, and Lists F and X say there were five children, though List Q shows only two. List V says the family *was* on the *Lamb* and names the children as John, Edmund, Jane, Mary, Jennett. Mr. Myers (List Q) collected no data on the Cowgills, a rare occurrence in his Welcome Papers, which may suggest that he was inclined to be negative to the claim, though he did include the mother and two children on the list.

The son Ralph, who is known to have come on the *Friends' Adventure* as servant to Randall Blackshaw, appears only on List X--whether he is to be presumed covered by the Settle certificate, which will be mentioned in a moment, is doubtful, since it does not specify the names of the children.

The daughter Mary (shown above and on List V) has not been found in any primary document and she is probably fictitious. W. W. H. Davis, *History of Bucks County, Pennsylvania* (Doylestown, 1st ed., 1876), p. 66, speaks of a Mary Cowgill who married John Gilbert, but this is the only indication found to suggest that such a woman even existed.

The son John, doubtless included in the certificate, even if Ralph were not, came on the *Lamb* as servant to Cuthbert Hayhurst, so that we have documentary proof to show that two of the children, at the least, did not come on the *Welcome*.[2]

This brings us to the question of whether the Widow Cowgill and some of her children were really on the *Welcome*, a topic fully discussed above in the Introduction, Section E, to which reference is now made. The conclusion there reached is that all of the Cowgills except Ralph came on the *Lamb*.

John W. Jordan, *Colonial and Revolutionary Families of Pennsylvania* (New York 1911), 1:297-300, prints within his account of the Pembertons one on the Cowgills. Some bad accounts of the Delaware Cowgills are refuted and it is expressly stated that no trace of the Cowgills had been found in any Yorkshire Friends records, nor any trace of the widow's deceased husband, not even his first name. Jordan thought, however, that Thomas Stackhouse, whose

will mentions sisters Ellen and Jennett, was probably referring to Ellen Cowgill who had a daughter
Jennett. It is also claimed that Ellen Cowgill had
died by 1701 but on what evidence is unknown to me.

THE COWGILL CHILDREN

1. Ralph Cowgill, born, says Jordan, ca. 1668,
apparently the eldest, came on the *Friends' Adventure* as servant to Randall Blackshaw who so recorded
in Bucks Arrivals. Jordan also says that he died
between 13 and 20 6th mo. 1756, on what evidence I
do not know, but Ralph was still living on 19 2nd
mo. 1733 when present at the marriage of his daughter Jane. It would appear that at the time of the
crossing Ralph was in his teens, for he married,
first, in 1689, Sarah Blackshaw, daughter of Randall
Blackshaw, his former master, and Sarah died 15 7th
mo. 1694, after which Ralph married, second, at
Burlington, New Jersey, 2 7th mo. 1697, Susanna
Pancoast, daughter of John Pancoast, deceased, of
Burlington, formerly of Ashton, Northamptonshire,
England.

Issue: surname Cowgill
    by first wife Sarah Blackshaw
i.   Abraham, b. 15 May 1690, according to a
        1716 Bible cited in JCRFP 302; m., 2nd
        int., Chesterfield, 1 April 1725, Doro-
        thy Turner.
ii.   John, d. inf. 30 Dec. 1692, rec. Middle-
        town Monthly Meeting.
iii.   Nehemiah, b. 13 March 1692/3, m. (1) at
        Burlington, 21 Nov. 1717 Joyce Smith,
        daughter of Thomas Smith; (2) 1 8th
        month 1738 Esther (-----) Davis, widow,
        whose estate is in NJW 3:74, admin. to
        William Harrison, William Harrison Jr.,
        fellow-bondsman. The marriage to her
        is in GMNJ 18:23. Admin. on Nehemiah's
        estate had been granted to Esther on
        14 June 1750 (NJW 2:117), and he is
        called innholder of Gloucester County.
        See Charles S. Boyer, *Old Inns and Inn-
        holders,* of which I know only through
        the kindness of Dr. E. G. Van Name.
        Probable issue: surname Cowgill
        1. Nehemiah, m. St. Paul's P. E. Church,
            Philadelphia, by lic., 18 May 1773,
            Mary Middleton.

iv.   Sarah, b. 3 Sept. 1694, d. 1 Aug. 1724;
       m. 1715 Thomas Clifford.
      by second wife Susanna Pancoast
v.   Rebecca, b. 10 Oct. 1698, d. 15 March
       1758; m. 2nd int., Chesterfield,3 1st mo.
       1725/6, wedding 17 1st mo. 1725/6, Rich-
       ard Gibbs, son of Isaac Gibbs.
vi.   Mary, b. 7 Jan. 1700/1, d. 3 Nov. 1767;
       m. 2nd int., Chesterfield, 7 2nd mo.,
       wedding 14 2nd mo. 1720 Archibald Sil-
       ver.
vii. Isaac, b. 4 June 1703, d. 6 Dec. 1766; m.
       at St. Mary's, Colestown, 14 Oct. 1730,
       Rachel Briggs. This marriage is con-
       firmed by her father's will: John Briggs
       of Northampton, 10 March 1752 (NJW 3:41):
       daughter Rachel Cowgill, son-in-law
       Isaac Cowgill, grandson George Cowgill.
       Isaac's will (NJW 4:94), of Chester-
       field, 9 Jan. 1765, probated 31 Dec.
       1766: wife Rachel, sons George, Isaac,
       John, daughter Rachel Hall, granddaugh-
       ter Lydia Cowgill (daughter of John and
       Jemima), her sister Rachel, both minors.
viii. Rachel, b. 5 Sept. 1705, d. 8 Sept. 1750;
       m. 16 Sept. 1728 Samuel Woodward.
ix.   Jane, b. 20 Feb. 1707/8, d. 28 Oct. 1791;
       m. 19 2nd mo. 1733 Benjamin Linton of
       Bucks County. Their wedding certificate
       was signed by Joseph and Mary Linton
       who may have been his parents. This Ben-
       jamin was probably the man of that name
       whose son Benjamin of Lower Makefield m.
       Hannah Satterthwait at Chesterfield, 21
       11th mo. 1764.
x.   Jacob, b. 29 May 1710, d. 18 May 1735.
xi.   Susanna, b. 16 Jan. 1718/19, d. 19 Jan.
       1744; m. 24 Sept. 1737, John King of
       Monmouth County (GMNJ 17:48).

2. Jane Cowgill was buried 26 9th mo. 1699. She
had married, 25 8th mo. 1685, 1st intentions, Middletown, 3 7th mo. 1685, passed 1 8th mo. 1685,
Stephen Sands, of Bucks County, who also came on the
Lamb. His will, dated 25 11th mo. 1730, probated
15 Feb. 1732/3,[3] names wife Elizabeth [a second
wife, of course, and she had been Elizabeth Norcross, married at Middletown 9 8th mo. 1701], sons
Richard and John as executors; also sons Edmund and

William and daughter Elinor Hough; witnesses: Tho:
Stackhouse, Wm Atkinson, Margaret Eastburn. Whether
all of his children were by Jane Cowgill is not certain but Edmund and Elinor have Cowgill names and
Richard had a daughter Jane. Five children are not
too many to be born between 1685 and 1699. We have
therefore accepted all five as Jane Cowgill's, with
the caveat that some may really have been Elizabeth
Norcross's.

In 1892 T. S. [Sands?] printed[4] the text of an
undated letter from two of Stephen Sands's grandsons,
which we shall shortly present. He does not say
where the letter was but that with it was another
letter with almost the same text and this one was
dated 15 June 1790. Both letters appear to be copies
of missives sent to England in an effort to locate
relatives of Stephen Sands and, of course, to obtain
some pecuniary value, if possible. The undated letter was addressed "To Joseph Sands, a Farmer, Living
in Lancashire or Lincolnshire if he can find himself
to be a relative To the family of Stephen Sands from
Lancashire to Pennsylvania In the year Sixteen Hundred & Eighty Two or to any of the name of Sands,
that can, In England, these with Care and Speed p^r
favour of . . . "   The letter runs as follows:

> Pennsylvania Bucks County Middletown Township
> Cawly Town 23 miles from the City of Philadel-
> phia We Benjamin & Abraham Sands the Grand Sons
> of Stephen Sands who came into this province
> from Lancashire in England In the year of our
> Lord one Thousand Six Hundred and Eighty two
> with others from the same place viz Henry Wamsly
> the name of Wood &c some of Wamsleys Children
> are yet living. These will inform that our
> Grandfather departed this Life before our Memory
> & our parents when we were Children also Died
> but we remember the Spring 1758 a few days be-
> fore our father's Death there came a Letter from
> England that Informed that if there was any of
> the race of Stephen Sands our Grandfather Living
> that would come or send that they would meet
> with something Greatly to their Advantage but
> what went with the letter after we cannot tell
> but it was supposed a careless nurse threw it away
> which leaves us at a loss who sent it or who
> to Direct these to but hoping these may meet
> with some relative of the family that will do us
> the favour to Speculate & Enquire about it, &

let us know by a few lines, We have to remember
once that we have heard our Father often say
when he was alive & when the letter came, that
our Grandfather had left a wealthy parentage behind & that he came away to this province to Enjoy Liberty of Concience among people called
Quakers being one, Henry Wamsleys Children also
remember the like as their Father came with him
& knew our Great Grand parents Now as Humble
petitioners we beg the favour if these should
find any way to any of the family that they
would Convey the first opportunity some account
to us about it by some way to Philadelphia where
it will soon be conveyd to us, if it be sent by
the Care of any of the people called Quakers,
to any of that Denomination in Philadelphia, we
are Informed by Inquiry of One of the Name near
the place, Called Joseph Sands a farmer, And
honoured friend, we have made free to direct
these to thee, or any of the name of Sands that
Can find they are of the above said family,
flattering ourselves that if there was any thing
when this letter we mention came, that it may
perhaps remain for us, And if we can be Informed
by any friend that would do us the favour, we
shall take it as a favour not soon to be forgotten, & if any thing should turn out in our favour, we shall be very free to retaliate the
kindness of the Enquirer we are able to send a
Character very Clear of blemish but as yet we
think it of little use unless something should
turn out in our favour then it may be satisfactory to any that may correspond with by Letter or any way Else we have sent two letters to
an acquaintance one Abraham Praul in Rotherhite
hoping he would do some Enquiry for us but we
are informed that he is Dead we Conclude ourselves your humble Petitioners.
                    Benjamin & Abraham Sands

**Note that Benjamin and Abraham Sands neglected to
tell us their father's first name.**

Issue: surname Sands, order uncertain
i.   Richard, executor of his father in the
        will of 1730; made his own will when of
        Bensalem Township, 7 Jan. 1758, codicil
        dated 27 Feb. 1758, probated 5 June
        1758[5], naming wife Mary; daughter Jane

(wife of Thomas Bains); grandchildren:
Mary Jones, Richard Sands, Jesse, Phebe
and Elizabeth Bains; children of daughter Elizabeth Roberts; Stephen Bains
(son of daughter Jane), and, again,
granddaughter Mary Jones. This will
fits chronologically the father of
Benjamin and Abraham, above, but they
are not mentioned in the will.

ii.   John, named an executor in his father's
will in 1730. On the basis of data now
at hand, it is possible that he also d.
in 1758, leaving the following children,
some of them then minors.
Issue: surname Sands, order uncertain
1. Edmund, of Bensalem, farmer, made will
2 5th mo. 1773, probated May 1773[6]:
wife Mary, cousin John Mitchell, executors; brothers Thomas, William, Abraham, Benjamin Sands; sisters Jennet Clauson and Mary [Sands?].
2. Thomas, mentioned in Edmund's will.
3. William, mentioned in Edmund's will.
4. Abraham, mentioned in Edmund's will;
co-author of the 1790 letters.
5. Benjamin, mentioned in Edmund's will;
co-author of the 1790 letters.
6. Jennet, m. ----- Clauson by 1773.
7. Mary, mentioned in Edmund's will.

iii.   Edmund, mentioned in father's will in
1730; may have been father of the children tentatively assigned to his brother
John, above.

iv.   William, mentioned in father's will 1730;
may have been father of the children
tentatively assigned to his brother John.

v.   Elinor, m. Middletown, 1 4th mo. 1714
John Hough Jr.

3. Jennett Cowgill, not identical with Jane,
though Jordan seemed to have thought so, married at
Burlington Monthly Meeting, 2nd intentions, 25 12th
mo. 1687/8, Bernard Lane, whose will dated 25 June
1715, probated 6 Oct. 1715,[7] mentions the three
daughters.

Issue: surname Lane
i.   Elin, by 1715 had m. ----- Cutler, not
identified in the Cutler Memorial but

that book is very weak on Bucks County
Cutlers.
ii. Mary, by 1715 had m. John Naylor, on whom
see Mrs. H. W. Naylor.[8] She asserts
that the Cowgills were on the *Welcome*.
A Jane Cutler had m. a John Naylor at
Middletown, 11 5th mo. 1685, but is
not easily identified. No study of the
Naylors has been made for this book.
iii. Sarah, in 1715 unm.; on 8 Dec. 1715 chose
uncle Ralph Cowgill as guardian, so she
was b. 1695-1701, as she must have been
aged 14 to choose a guardian.

4. **John Cowgill** came as servant to Cuthbert Hayhurst on the *Lamb*.[9] He married, first, 19 8th mo.
1693 at Neshamineh, Bridget Croasdale, born 7 8th
mo. 1671, died 26 2nd mo. 1701, daughter of Thomas
and Agnes (Hathornthwaite) Croasdale[10]; second, in
11th mo. 1703/4, Rachel (Baker) Bunting, widow of
Job Bunting and daughter of Henry Baker, she born
in West Darby, Lancashire, 23 2nd mo. 1669. John's
Bucks County patent was issued 14 June 1712 but he
had already removed to New Castle County. On 18 Dec.
1707, when of Trevore in Bensalem Township, he and
wife Rachel, widow and executrix of Job Bunting,
gave a deed.

Issue: surname Cowgill
by first wife Bridget Croasdale
i. Elizabeth, b. 24 6th mo. 1694, m. 1715
William Brown.
ii. Thomas, b. 21 3rd mo. 1696, d. Kent Co.,
Del., before 7 Dec. 1749, when his
widow passed an account on his estate;
m., 2nd int., Duck Creek Meeting, 11th
mo. 1727, Sarah Clayton, daughter of
Joshua and Sarah (Needham) Clayton, on
whom see the Clayton sketch, above.
Issue; surname Cowgill
1. Ezekiel, perhaps d. by 1760.
2. Thomas, living 1760.
3. Sarah, m. 22 12th mo. 1756 Samuel Hand.
4. Elenor or Ellen, living 1760.
5. Rachel, living 1760; m. before 1760
Jonathan Grewell.
6. Jane, m., Little Creek Meeting, Del.,
21 5th mo. 1747, Daniel Smith.
iii. John, b. 8 6th mo. 1698, m. 16 12th mo.

1720, Lydia Clayton, daughter of Joshua and Sarah (Needham) Clayton, on whom see the Clayton sketch, above; (2) Hannah -----, to whom admin. was granted on his estate, 29 July 1752, after which Hannah m. (2) Robert Hall.

Issue: surname Cowgill

1. John, m. Mary Worrell.
2. Clayton.
3. Sarah, m. John Register.
4. Elizabeth, m. Francis Neal.
5. Henry, m. Elizabeth Osborne. He was probably the Henry who was the only Cowgill witness to the marriage of his sister Lydia (see below).
6. Lydia, probably the Lydia who m. at Third Haven Monthly Meeting, Talbot Co., Md., 1 8th mo. 1753, William Webb; by 1760 had m. (2) ----- Durborough and as such had been mentioned in Grandfather Clayton's will.

iv. Ellen, b. 14 10th mo. 1700, d. 15 Jan. 1772; m. (1) 1719 Thomas Browne; (2) Lewis Clothier.

by second wife Rachel Baker

v. Henry, b. ca. 1704; m. (1) 4 4th mo. 1724, Burlington Monthly Meeting when of New Castle, Mary Boulton, daughter of Edward and Sarah Boulton of Burlington; (2) 1 June 1741 Alice Pain.

Issue: surname Cowgill, perhaps others

1. Sarah, mentioned in grandmother Boulton's will dated 25 Feb. 1740/1;[11] perhaps m. at Buckingham, 11 4th mo. 1753, Thomas Smith.
2. Rachel, also mentioned in Grandmother Boulton's will.

vi. Rachel, b. 3 3rd mo. 1706, d. 19 10th mo. 1729; m. Thomas Sharp.

vii. Mary, b. 23 11th mo. 1707/8, m. 1724 Alexander Adams Jr.

viii. Ebenezer, b. 19 10th mo. 1709, d. 1743; m. 1742 ----- -----.

ix. Eleazer, b. 21 1st mo. 1711, m. 29 6th mo. 1739 Martha Pain.

5. **Edmund Cowgill** married, first, at Middletown, 29 3rd mo. 1702, Catherine Blaker, died 2 2nd mo. 1703, probably daughter of Johannes Bleicker of

Northampton Township, Bucks County, by his wife Rebecca; second, at Burlington Monthly Meeting, 6 8th
mo. 1707, Ann Osborne. He is said to have removed
to Burlington after the second marriage and was already dead when his daughter Jennet married in 1743.
No probate has been found. He got a patent for 300
acres in 1702.[12]

    Issue: surname Cowgill, order uncertain
      by first wife Catherine Blaker
  i. Edmund, b. 10 1st mo.1702/3, d. 22 1st mo.
     1702/3.
    by second wife Ann Osborne
 ii.   Jennet, d. by 2 1st mo. 1760; m. Burling-
     ton Monthly Meeting, 8 10th mo. 1743,
     Joseph Atkinson, son of William Atkin-
     son of Bucks County. Joseph m. (2) 13
     April 1762 Sarah Silver. On the At-
     kinsons see Oliver Hough (PMHB 30:482).
     Joseph's will is dated 11th mo. 1780,
     probated 4 May 1781.[13]
      Issue: surname Atkinson
    1. William, mentioned in aunt's will in
      1770.
    2. Mary, m. by 1787 ----- Watson.
    3. Elizabeth, unm. in 1787.
    4. Ann, m. by 1787 ----- Shaw.
    5. Jennet, unm. in 1770.
iii.   Edward, m. Margaret ----- who is a lega-
     tee as simply the wife of Edward Cow-
     gill in the will of Thomas Leeds dated
     20 April 1741.[14] All of the children
     are mentioned in the will of their
     aunt in 1770.
     Issue: surname Cowgill
    1. Joseph, m. St. Mary's, Colestown, 9
      11th mo. 1748, Ann Arnold.
    2. Sarah.
    3. Margaret.
    4. Septima, m. 13 5th mo. 1773 at Bur-
      lington Monthly Meeting, Samuel Bun-
      ting Jr., son of Samuel and Hannah
      (-----) Bunting of Bucks County.
    5. Elizabeth.
    6. Mary.
 iv.   Elizabeth, of Burlington, shopkeeper; her
     will dated 30 Nov. 1770, probated 28
     Jan. 1772,[15] names nephew Joseph Cow-
     gill; nieces Sarah, Margaret and Sep-

tima Cowgill, Mary Watson, Elizabeth, Anna and Jennet Atkinson, seven in number specified; nephew William Atkinson; Elizabeth and Mary Cowgill are mentioned and they may be nieces but are not counted among the seven.

v.   ?Edmund, d. intestate, of Wrightstown, Bucks County, when widow Rebeckah, 1 Aug. 1768, signed renunciation to administer[16] in favor of Benjamin Hamton, one of the greatest creditors. Rebeckah Cowgill[17] appears as mother of a person recorded as Jeremiah Cooper on 12 Nov. 1770 when said person renounced administration of administration on the estate of mother Rebeckah Coughan [sic] in favor of John Mier, but the indorsement calls this person Jemimah Cooper and the bond dated 13 Nov. 1770 says John Mire. NOTES

[1]As two of the grandsons married daughters of Joshua Clayton, see the Clayton sketch.
[2]2 PA 19:586. [3]BW 1:197. [4]PMHB 16:462f.
[5]BW 2:334. [6]BW 3:327. [7]NJW 1:281.
[8]*Old Northwest Quarterly* 11:41.
[9]2 PA 19:586. [10]See the Croasdale sketch.
[11]NJW 2:54. [12]2 PA 19:318. [13]BW 4:112.
[14]NJW 2:296. [15]NJW 5:114. [16]BW file 1252
[17]BW file 1301.

CROASDALE, THOMAS		*disproved*
CROASDALE, AGNES HATHORNTHWAITE wife		*disproved*
CROASDALE, WILLIAM son		*disproved*
CROASDALE, JOHN son		*disproved*
CROASDALE, ELIZABETH daughter		*disproved*
CROASDALE, MARY daughter		*disproved*
CROASDALE, BRIDGET daughter		*disproved*
CROASDALE, ALICE daughter		*disproved*
CROASDALE, EZRA not his son		*disproved*

The spelling here given appears to be standard but for some reason "Chroasdale" appears on Lists A, C, E, I and M, all of which include Thomas, his wife Agnes and six unnamed children. Thomas Croasdale appears on Lists B, D, F, G, H, J, K, L, N, O (here denied), P, Q (here cancelled), R, S, T, U (here said to have come on the *Lamb*), W, X, Y and Z. The

wife Agnes Croasdale is on Lists B, D, F, G, H, Q
(here cancelled), U (on the *Lamb*), V (also on the
Lamb), X, Y and Z, and she and the children are called
"and family" on Lists J, K, L, N, P, S, T, W and X.
The children are called six in number but are never
named except on List V. On List Q the last two
children are not cancelled like the rest, but this
is certainly due to the fact that they are at the
top of the next page and were overlooked. On List
V the children are, like their parents, credited to
the *Lamb*, and are given the names William, John,
Elizabeth, Mary, Ezra, Bridget and Alice. The in-
clusion of Ezra on this list is an error for which
I myself am to blame, having put the name on a list
made before I had made a thorough study of this
family. I understand that the name was removed from
later printings of List V.

The spelling Croasdill is frequent in the primary records though not found on any of the hypothetical lists. Specifically, it is the spelling
in the Middletown Meeting copy of the original certificate issued by Settle Monthly Meeting in Yorkshire on 7 4th mo. 1682, in which the Croasdills
appear between the Walmsleys and the Stackhouses.
A full discussion of this certificate and its bearing on the *Welcome* claims of the persons mentioned
in it will be found in the Introduction Section E.
The conclusion there reached is that the Croasdales
came on the *Lamb*, though he loaded no goods on it.

Of the seven families named in the Settle certificate, the Croasdales are the only ones who can
not be shown to be related in some way to the others, but there may have been an unknown relationship. As will be seen later, Thomas Stackhouse
had given Thomas Croasdale money to buy land for
him. The Roberts version of the certificate omits
the Croasdales, probably from design, as Mr. Roberts
was not concerned with them; the children are left
out in the Buckman-Potts version, though Thomas and
Agnes are there.

Mrs. Balderston strangely says[2] that of the
Croasdale children only William, John and Alice can
be found later in Bucks County and suggests that
that the others died during the crossing. As a matter of fact, all six children are recorded in Bucks
County, and five of them lived to marry.

Thomas Croasdale was a First Purchaser of 1000
acres in Group 44,[3] and there was a survey in his

name dated 8 4th mo. 1702.[4] In Warrants and Surveys
2:152, lot No. 64-20 High Street, corner of 20th
Street, is granted to Wm Lloyd, Thomas Croasdale,
George Pownall, William Banner; Lot No. 41, Schuylkill Front, 1683, granted to Charles Jones, George
King, John Jones, Thomas Croasdale; *ibid.* 2:34, 4
5th mo. 1692, survey to widow Ann Croasdale,[5] purchaser of 500 acres, warrant dated 25 11th mo.
1683, 2nd Street from Delaware, west back lots,
north by Robert Lodges, return dated 10 7th mo.
1693.

THE CROASDALE FAMILY

The late Thomas Allen Glenn stated[6] that the
immigrant Thomas Croasdale was that Thomas baptized
at Waddington, 20 May 1644, son of Edward Croasdale,
and that he later married in May 1664 Agnes Hathornthwaite, daughter of William Hathornthwaite of Lancashire. He also provided more data on the ancestry without reaching any definite conclusion, and
though the marriage seems to be right, the identification of the father is almost certainly wrong.

Though proof is lacking it seems highly probable that the immigrant was a son of that William
Croasdale of Newah, who died 29 11th mo. 1666 and
was buried 31 11th mo. 1666, with a wife Elizabeth
who died 18 4th mo. 1672, buried 20 4th mo. 1672,
both in the graveyard of Settle Meeting which was
at a place called Newton. In that graveyard was
buried also a Thomas Croasdale of Lower Newhah
who died according to Settle Meeting records on 28
11th mo. 1676, date of burial not stated. It at
least may be suggested that he was a younger brother of the aforesaid William.[7]

It seems possible, indeed, rather probable, that
William and Elizabeth Croasdale aforesaid had at
least the following children:

Issue: surname Croasdale
1 i.   Thomas, the immigrant to Bucks County.
   ii.   Ezekiel, of Shipley (Brighouse Meeting),
          d. 11 3rd mo. 1708 aged 63.
2 iii.   William, of Bradford.
   iv.   ?Mary, of Bradford, m. Hugh Jackson of
          Bradford, 16 11th mo. 1675.

1. Thomas Croasdale, probably the son of William
and Elizabeth (-----) Croasdale of Newah, Yorkshire,

rather than of Edward Croasdale, was born probably somewhat earlier than 1644, since he married in May 1664 Agnes Hathornthwaite, daughter of William Hathornthwaite of Lancashire. They came to America with six children in 1682 on the *Lamb*. They settled at Middletown, Bucks County, Pennsylvania, but Thomas was buried there on 2 2nd mo. 1682 and Agnes on 20 8th mo. 1684, and not, as stated by Mrs. Blanche (Moore) Haines[8] in 1684 and 1685, respectively. There is no mention of Thomas in the probate of Agnes Crossdale, late of Neshamineh, on whose estate administration was granted to her sons William and John Crossdale on 1 9th mo. 1686.[9]

Several Bucks deeds have been found whereby the two sons dispose of property of their father Thomas Croasdale, e.g. 2:62 f., 100 acres to Jonathan Scaife of Bucks County, yeoman, 10 6th mo. 1695; 2:63, to Robert Heaton Jr., receipt dated 12 10th 1694; 2:148, William Croasdell to John Croasdell, which deed says that of 670 acres on Neshamineh laid out by the Commissioners of Property on 28 June 1692 to Thomas Crosdell dec. his heirs William and John have sold 270 acres, leaving 400 acres remaining, of which William now sells 197 acres to John, acknowledged 5 8th mo. 1697, recorded 12 8th mo. 1697; 2:234 f., to John Cowgill for £140 part of the same tract, acknowledged 9 1st mo. 1698, recorded 28 1st mo. 1699; 3:103, William Crosdell of Buckingham, yeoman, son and heir of Thomas Crosdell late of New Hey [Newah?] in Co. York, England, yeoman, and John Crossdell of Bucks, yeoman, the other son, recite that Penn granted by lease and release dated 21 and 22 April 1682, 1000 acres to Thomas Crosdell, 250 acres whereof were purchased with money of Thomas Stackhouse and included to save charge. [The minimum "First Purchase" was 250 acres but there may have been fees saved by this method.] These 250 acres were later sold but not conveyed by Stackhouse to Nicholas Walne who sold his interest to Robert Heaton of Bucks yeoman. The Crosdells now at the request of Thomas Stackhouse and Nicholas Walne convey to Robert Heaton, and the deed is signed by both Crossdells, Thomas Stackhouse and Nicholas Walne, witnessed by Samuel Hough and John Stackhouse, acknowledged 10 4th mo. 1702, recorded 18 11th mo. 1702.

In Mrs. Jane W. T. Brey's *A Quaker Saga* (Philadelphia 1967), p. 166, is a photograph of an inden-

ture dated 21 2nd mo. 1682 signed by both William
Penn and Thomas Croasdale. The book does not say
where the indenture is but it is in Mrs. Brey's own
possession.

The six children were all, of course, born in
England but their births were later recorded in the
minutes of Middletown Monthly Meeting. The dates in
some cases differ from those in the records of Settle Meeting as transcribed by the late Gilbert Cope.
In what follows the Cope dates are given first and
then the Middletown in parentheses.

Issue: surname Croasdale

3   i.   William, b. Yorkshire, 12 7th mo. 1664
           (7 12th mo. 1664), d. Bucks Co. between
           30 1st mo. 1715 and 10 Jan. 1715/6.
4   ii.   John, b. Yorkshire 11 5th mo. 1666 (about
           14 5th mo. 1666), d. Bucks Co., shortly
           before 26 12th mo. 1706/7.
     iii. Elizabeth, b. Yorkshire 5 11th mo. 1667
           (15 11th mo. 166[7]), bur. Bucks Co.,
           4 6th mo. 1683.
5   iv.   Mary, b. Yorkshire, 30 8th mo. 1669 (31
           9th mo. 16[69]); bur. Bucks Co., 16
           10th 1716.
     v.   Bridget, b. Yorkshire, 30 6th mo. 1671
           (8 9th mo. [1671]); m. Middletown, 19
           8th mo. 1693, John Cowgill. For their
           issue, see above, pp. 140 f.
6   vi.   Alice, b. Yorkshire, 3 8th mo. 1673 (a-
           bout 26 7th mo. 1673).

2. William Croasdale, probably son of William
and Elizabeth Croasdale of Newah, and therefore,
if so, brother of the immigrant, lived at Bradford,
sometimes called Bradford Moorside, and attended
the Brighouse Monthly Meeting. Late in life he
lived at Shipley where he died 4 9th mo. 1691 and
was buried at Bradford 7 9th mo. 1691. His wife
was named Grace and she died 24 7th mo. 1679.[10]

Issue: surname usually spelled Croysdil

7   i.   Ezra, b. 21 6th mo. 1655; d. Bucks Co.,
           probably in 1740.
     ii.   Martha, b. 11 9th mo. 1657, m. Knares-
           borough Monthly Meeting, 26 2nd mo.
           1693, John Hird.
     iii. Jeremiah, b. 24 10th mo. 1659, d. 23 or
           30 5th mo. 1667, bur. at Horton.
     iv.   Sarah, b. 5 12th mo. 1661.

     v.   William, b. 6 4th mo. 1664.
     vi.   John, b. 22 10th mo. 1666.
     vii.   Hannah, b. 16 11th mo. 1668.

    3. William Croasdale, eldest son of Thomas and Agnes (Hathornthwaite) Croasdale, was born in York- shire, 12 7th mo. 1664, according to the Settle rec- ord or 7 12th mo. 1664, according to the Middletown record. With his parents and their other children he came to America in 1682 on the *Lamb*, and died in Bucks County between 30 1st mo. 1715 and 10 Jan. 1715/16, dates of execution and probation of his will:[11] William Croasdale of Bristol mentions no wife; grandson William Hill, minor; daughter Agnes Hill, life interest; sister Mary Smith's eight children; brother John Croasdale dec. two daughters; sister Alice Potts' ten children; sister Bridget Cowgill's four children; friends George Clough and John Hall to care for £4 left to Bristol Friends; brother John Croasdale's son and two daughters; brother-in-law John Cutler's daughters; brother Wil- liam Smith; brother David Potts; son Richard Hill's two 'prentices; sister Marah Wildman and her daugh- ter Ruth Croasdale; witnesses: Joseph Bond, James Moon, Wm Atkinson, probated by Bond and Atkinson, 10 Jan. 1715. William Croasdale married, first, at Middletown, 10 2nd mo. 1690, Elizabeth Hayhurst, born 3 9th mo. 1669, died before her husband, eld- est child of Cuthbert Hayhurst by his wife Mary Rudd. According to Mrs. Brey,[12] he married, second, Sarah Milner, but she cites no evidence and we have found none. A William Croasdale married at Middle- town, 16 7th mo. 1713, Grace Harding, but I am in- clined to think this was Ezra's son.

     Issue; surname Croasdale, probably by first
       wife in both cases
     i.   Thomas, b. 1691, bur. 16 11th mo. 1691.
     ii.   Agnes, m., by 1715, Richard Hill.
          Issue: surname Hill, all discovered
          1. William, minor in 1715.

    4. John Croasdale, second son of Thomas and Agnes (Hathornthwaite) Croasdale, was born in Yorkshire on 11 5th mo. 1666, according to the Settle record, or about 14 5th mo. 1666, according to the Middletown, and came to America in 1682 on the *Lamb*. He died in Bucks County shortly before 26 12th mo. 1706/7, though Mrs. Brey says he was buried 16 10th mo. 1706. He married at Middletown

28 2nd mo. 1697 Marah Chapman, daughter of John and Jane (-----) Chapman, to whom administration was granted on his estate 26 12th mo. 1706/7.[13] She married, second, John Wildman, son of Martin and Ann (Ward) Wildman,[14] and his will was dated 28 9th mo. 1738, probated 9 Sept. 1739,[15] naming wife Marah, son-in-law John Woolston, executor; brother Joseph Wildman; sister Alice Nelson; brother Joseph's six children: Rebecca, Mary, Rachel, Joseph, John and Isaac; nephew James Woster; brother Matthew Wildman; wife's son Thomas Croasdale. Marah is sometimes called Morah. Mrs. Haines[16] wrongly calls her a daughter of Thomas Croasdale, but in 1715 she was Marah Wildman with daughter Ruth Croasdale, and in 1738, still Marah Wildman, she had a son Thomas Croasdale.

> Issue: surname Croasdale, order unknown
> i.   Thomas, the Thomas of Middletown in a deed[17] whereby Isaac Penington Esq., Sheriff of Bucks, states that he levied on the goods and chattles of Thomas Croasdale, late of Newtown, yeoman, called Thomas Croasdale of Middletown, for a debt of £9/5/2 due Thomas Howard and James Hamilton, administrators of John Beaks, dec., plus 65/11 damages. The sheriff had seized 250 acres of Thomas Croasdale in Middletown and now sells them to John Watson, 20 Sept. 7 George II 1733, for £256, receipted 12 Feb. 1733/4, acknowledged 14 March 1733, recorded 23 April 1747. Mrs. Brey makes much of this sale, as she is concerned with the Watsons. She says Thomas was disowned for marrying out on 12 3rd mo. 1731/2, had one daughter, but names neither wife nor daughter. The wife was Susannah Hamilton and the marriage was at Christ Church, Philadelphia, 24 Aug. 1731. Susannah was buried from Christ Church, 6 Jan. 17 1742/3. Thomas died 13 4th mo. 1747.
>   Issue: surname Croasdale
>   1. Mary, bur. from Christ Church, 13 Aug. 1751.
> ii. Ruth, mentioned 1715 in uncle William's will; d. unm.
> iii. Agnes, mentioned but not named, 1715, in

uncle William's will; m. Middletown,
16 2nd mo. 1723, Joseph Warner, b. 15
2nd mo. 1701, d. 1746, son of John and
Anne (Campden) Warner, on whom see Jordan.[18]
    Issue: surname Warner
1. John, b. 16 12th mo. 1723/4.
2. Mary, b. 28 11th mo. 1725/6.
3. Joseph, b. 10 11th mo. 1727/8.
4. Croasdale, b. 5 12th mo. 1729/30.
5. Ruth, b. 8 8th mo. 1732.
6. Abraham, b. 14 7th mo. 1735.
7. Sarah, b. 7 11th mo. 1737/8.
8. Nancy, b. 28 9th mo. 1741, d. 28 Nov. 1829.
9. Thomas, b. 6 10th mo. 1746, d. 19 Feb. 1821.

    5. **Mary Croasdale**, daughter of Thomas and Agnes
(Hathornthwaite) Croasdale, was born in Yorkshire,
30 8th mo. 1669, according to the Settle record, or
31 9th mo. 16[69], according to the Middletown which
originally had the qualification of "about" before
this date, later cancelled. She came with the family to America in 1682 on the *Lamb* and was buried
in Bucks County on 16 10th mo. 1716. She declared
intentions to marry William Smith at Middletown
Monthly Meeting on 7 6th mo. 1690, was passed 4 7th
mo. 1690, and the marriage took place at the house
of John Chapman in Wrightstown. The certificate
has signatures of 24 persons, none named Smith except the bridegroom and bride, as follows:

William Croasdell	Thomas Stackhouse	Richard Lundy
John Croasdell	Israel Harris	Elizabeth
John Chapman	William Buckman	Croasdell
Jonathan Scaife	Jacob Janney	Alis Croas-
Nicholas Waln	Joseph Sharpe	dell
John Palmer	Seaman Gillingham	Jane Chapman
Robert Heaton	Nicholas Randall	Mary Walley
William Paxton	William Hayhurst	Jane Lyon
James Heaton	Samuel Coats	

This William Smith appears to have been the man of
that name who came as servant of Phineas Pemberton
on the *Friends' Adventure* though Pemberton himself
came on the *Submission*.[19] William Smith married,
second, a woman named Mercy -----. His will is
dated 10 Dec. 1740, probated 20 April 1743, inventory 29 March 1743, and shows seven children by

each wife, not counting the first wife's daughter
Elizabeth who married in 1718 Thomas Watson and was
dead by 1730. William Smith of Wrightstown in the
County of Bucks purchased of John Rowland 100 acres
"about 20 years ago" and "hath ever since claimed
that quantity, joining on his other land in the
same T'p and now craves Resurvey. Granted for £5,"
in a warrant dated 10 3rd mo. 1718 at the session
of the Board of Property on 18 1st mo. 1717/18.[20]
On the Smiths see Josiah B. Smith, *Genealogy of the
William Smith of Wrightstown, Bucks County, Pennsylvania* (Newtown 1883); Blanche (Moore) Haines,
Ancestry of Sharpless and Rachel (Roberts) Moore
(1937), pp. 177 f.

Issue: surname Smith (Mary Croasdale's children
    only)
i.   Margaret, b. 20 8th mo. 1691; m. -----
        Pearson.
ii.   Mary, b. 9 2nd mo. 1696, m. John Atkinson.
iii.   William, eldest son; m. Middletown, 8 2nd
        mo. 1723, Rebecca Wilson?
iv.   Sarah, b. 26 11th mo. 1700.
v.   Thomas, 2nd son.
vi.   Hannah, m. William Lee (see TAG 24:76).
vii.   Lydia, m. ----- Heaton.
viii. Elizabeth, d. by 1730, m. 1718 Thomas Wat-
        son. She was probably not the youngest
        child of her mother.

6. Alice Croasdale, youngest child of Thomas
and Agnes (Hathornthwaite) Croasdale, was born in
Yorkshire, 3 8th mo. 1673, according to the Settle
record or about 26 7th mo. 1673, as the Middletown
record has it. With the rest of the family she
came to America in 1682 on the *Lamb*. Her marriage
to David Potts was recorded at Philadelphia Monthly
Meeting as having occurred on 26 11th mo. 1693/4
but the Middletown date for the same marriage is
22 1st mo. 1693/4. If the actual marriage took
place shortly before the first date, then the discrepancy may be explained by supposing that the
marriage occurred after the Middletown Monthly Meeting of 11th mo. but before the Philadelphia Monthly
Meeting of the same month, so that the clerk of the
latter meeting was able to get his entry in a month
ahead of the clerk at Middletown. The will of the
eldest brother, William Croasdale, says Alice had
ten children in 1715. The following list of them

has been taken from Thomas Maxwell Potts, *Historical Collections relating to the Potts Family,* etc.
(Canonsburg, Pa., 1901), corrected in part by Milton Rubincam. Mr. Potts says (pp. 232, 278) that
Alice died on Monday, 16 Nov. 1730.

Issue: surname Potts
i.   Thomas, b. 27 3rd mo. 1695; m. 1715 Rachel
       James.
ii.   John, b. 8 8th mo. 1696, d. 1766; m. 1726
       Elizabeth McVaugh.
iii.   Daniel, b. 19 2nd mo. 1698, d. by 1729;
       m. 1721 Sarah Shoemaker.
iv.   Elizabeth, b. 30 10th mo. 1699; m. 1722
       Peter Cleaver Jr.
v.   Jonathan, b. 23 9th mo. 1701; m. 1729
       Sarah Wood.
vi.   Mary, b. 3 2nd mo. 1703/4; m. 1727 Jere-
       miah McVaugh.
vii.   Stephen, b. 20 11th mo. 1704/5, d. 1758;
       m. Anne -----.
viii. Rebecka, b. 16 11th mo. 1705/6.
ix.   Ezekiel, b. 30 1st mo. 1708, d. 1781; m.
       (1) 1734 Magdalen Miller, (2) Barbara
       Vogdes.[21]
x.   Nathan, b. -----, d. 1754; m. 1736 Esther
       Rhoads.

    7. **Ezra Croasdale,** eldest son of William Croas-
dale of Bradford alias Bradford Moorside, Yorkshire,
was born on 21 6th mo. 1655, as was recorded at Brighouse Monthly Meeting, from which meeting he brought
a certificate which was dated on 20 1st mo. 1683,
which was signed by many Friends including nine
named Croasdill.   Mrs. Brey says he came on the
Shield of Stockton but we have found no evidence
of this and as that vessel is not recorded as having
made a crossing in 1683, we think it probable that
Ezra was an unrecorded passenger on some ship that
did cross in 1683.[22]   He married at Middletown
Monthly Meeting, 6 2nd mo. 1687, Ann Peacock, of
Killdeale in Yorkshire, who did come on the *Shield*
of Stockton, Daniel Foos, master, which arrived in
Maryland the beginning of the 8th month 1684[23] and
in "this River" [the Delaware] the latter part of
the same month.   Ezra's will, dated 17 2nd mo. 1727,
not probated until 2 Aug. 1740,[24] mentions but does
not name his wife who was not living at the date of

probation. He mentions an elder son William who is
to get 200 acres [sic] and has a minor son John who
gets 100 acres adjoining the said 300 acres [sic];
another son Jeremiah who has a son Ezra who gets a
piece of land in Salbury; witnesses: Jonathan Car-
lisle (who proved the will in 1740), Elizabeth Car-
lisle and Elizabeth Randall.

   Issue: surname Croasdale
   i.   William, mentioned as father of a son in
         1727; probably the William who m. at
         Middletown, 16 7th mo. 1713, Grace Har-
         ding. We have found no probate.
            Possible issue: surname Croasdale
         1. John, a minor in 1727, b. after 1713.
         2. Sarah, m. at Middletown, 22 3rd mo.
            1740, Robert Lucas, of Falls. Her
            father was a William, probably this
            one.
         3. ?Rebecca, m. Middletown, 22 10th mo.
            1748, Henry Hough.
         4. ?Rachel, m. Middletown, 19 1st mo.
            1757, Joseph Watson.
         5. ?Jeremiah, m. Buckingham, 13 5th mo.
            1772, Ann Quimby.
   ii.   Jeremiah, mentioned 1727 as a father; m.
         22 7th mo. 1720 at Middletown, Grace
         Heaton. Jeremiah's will[25] is dated 23
         11th mo. 1748, witnessed by John Evans
         and by one whose name is broken off the
         paper, probated by Evans and by Abraham
         Chapman Jr. and John Woolson, 8 March
         1748, i.e. 1748/9. He mentions beloved
         wife Grace; daughters Grace, Mercy and
         Ann [she should have been named Peace
         or at least Irene!]; four youngest: Eber,
         Abijah, Marcy [probably error for Marci],
         Achsah, all minors and unmarried; sons
         Ezra and Robert, the latter a minor;
         executors: son Ezra and friends James
         Thackery and Cuthbert Hayhurst.
            Issue: surname Croasdale
         1. Ezra, undoubtedly the eldest son; b.
            before 1727 when heir of grandfather,
            executor of father 1748.
         2. Grace, of age 1748; m. Middletown, 22
            10th mo. 1748, Jonathan Knight. This
            cannot be a second marriage of her
            mother as her father was not yet dead.

3. Mercy, mentioned in father's will in
   1748, apparently then of age.
4. Ann, apparently of age in 1748.
5. Robert, minor in 1748.
6. Eber, minor in 1748.
7. Abijah, minor in 1748.
8. Marcy, as the will calls her, really,
   in all probability, Macre, m. at
   Wrightstown, 20 3rd mo. 1765, Thomas
   Wilson.
9. Achsah, minor in 1748.

NOTES

[1]This sketch has benefitted from a careful scrutiny of an earlier draft by Milton Rubincam.

[2]*Huntington Library Quarterly* 26:40.

[3]1 PA 1:45.   [4]3 PA 3:390.

[5]The names Ann, Anna, Annis and Hannah were in the 17th century frequently interchanged with Agnes.

[6]PMHB 36:322.

[7]The following items are probably concerned with the same family but are not easily placeable:

William Croasdale and wife Dorothy of York had Chris b. 14 9th mo. 1664; Ann, b. abt 12th mo. 1667 (York Meeting).

John and Mary Croasdale of Bradford had the following recorded at Brighouse Meeting and he may have been the brother of Ezra, #7):
John, b. 12 5th mo. 1693, d. 11 4th mo. 1694.
Jeremiah, b. 5 6th mo. 1696, d. 7 10th mo.
   1698.
Mary, b. 26 3rd mo. 1695, d. 14 6th mo. 1695.
Hannah, birth not rec., d. 29 3rd mo. 1705.

Daniel Croasdale of Shipley, Yorkshire, son of William, late of Shipley, m. Alice Parker, d. of John, late of Slateburn, at Brighouse Meeting, 2 8th mo. 1700. (This man would also be thought a brother of Ezra #7 but`for the fact that he is not listed among the children of his putative father.)

[8]*Ancestry of Sharpless and Rachel (Roberts) Moore* (1937), pp. 180 f.

[9]PGSP 1:212.

[10]This paragraph has been supplied by Milton Rubincam.

[11]BW file 165.

[12]Jane W. T. Brey, *A Quaker Saga* (Philadelphia 1967), pp. 363-366.
[13]PhA B:53. [14]So Mrs. Brey, 560 f.
[15]BW 1:273. [16]See Note 8. [17]BD 7:323-326.
[18]JCRFP 1:236. [19]PMHB 9:230; JCRFP 1:571.
[20]2 PA 19:637.
[21]See Philadelphia Orphans Court Recs. 7:190 f.
file a b Roll 307, which shows by petition dated
8 May 1765 of Jacob Vogdes that Barbara, widow of
Reinard Vogdes, married, second Ezekiel Potts. Mary
Thomas Seaman, *Thomas Richardson of South Shields,
Durham County, England, and His Descendants in the
United States of America* (New York 1929), claims
that the second wife of Thomas Fitzwater the younger was Mary, daughter of David and Alice (Croasdale) Potts, but Clarence Vernon Roberts has her
father as John Potts, and as will be seen from the
above, David's daughter Mary has a different history.
[22]On the 1683 ships see PGM 24:69-114.
[23]Philadelphia Arrivals.
[24]BW file 444.
[25]BW file 614.

CURTIS, RICHARD   *disproved*

This name appears on List X only. The truth is
that he came on the ship *Lion* of Liverpool, arriving
14 8th mo. 1683, as servant to Robert Turner, to
serve four years, loose on 14 8th mo. 1687, and to
get £3 and fifty acres.
The name was read by Mrs. Balderston as Curlis,[1]
doubtless because she could see no crossing of the
t. I have examined all of the handwriting on this
page of Philadelphia Arrivals and conclude that the
reading of Curtis may be supported palaeographical-
ly. It therefore becomes necessary to inquire whether we can find confirmation of this reference in
other documents. No success as yet has been had in
locating elsewhere anybody named Richard Curlis and
I therefore conclude that Curtis is right.
The will of Richard Curtis of Mispillion Creek
Hundred, present Kent County, Delaware, was dated
20 May 1695, probated 14 Dec. 1695.[2] He names as
heirs: Jehu Curtis; Winlock, son of Jehu Curtis;
sister-in-law Elizabeth Jones; Nathaniel Hun, Samuel Low; son Samuel Curtis, daughter Elizabeth Curtis; James Howell, John Arriskin; father-in-law John
Curtis; executors: John Curtis and James Haven.

This abstract of the will bristles with questions not easily answered but it appears that, having served out his time with Robert Turner, Richard Curtis married a daughter of John Curtis who was probably related to him; that, having given birth to two children, Samuel and Elizabeth, the wife died, and now at an early age Richard himself is facing death which came to him sometime in the next few months.

From other wills in the Kent County Calendar we learn a little more. When Samuel Low died in 1707, leaving a will dated[3] 19 Aug. 1707, probated 23 Sept. 1707, he remembered, among others, Elizabeth Curtis, daughter of Richard, but not her brother. The will of John Curtis, gent., presumably the "father-in-law" of Richard Curtis's will, was dated 22 April 1698, probated 3 May 1698,[4] does not mention either of the two supposed grandchildren, Samuel and Elizabeth, but does mention unnamed wife, son Caleb, daughters Elizabeth and Ruth, grandson Jehu Curtis, and Samuel Low. Jehu Curtis's wife Mary is shown as daughter of William Brinckle in the latter's will dated 1 April 1722, probated 8 May 1722[5]; of Elizabeth Hammitt, wife of John Hammitt, in her will dated 31 Oct. 1725, probated 8 Dec. 1725.[6]

NOTES

[1]PGM 24:92, note 88.   [2]KC 18.
[3]KC 28.   [4]KC 21.
[5]KC 43.   [6]KC 47.

CUTLER, EDMUND   *disproved*
CUTLER, ISABEL, his wife   *disproved*
CUTLER, ELIZABETH, his daughter   *disproved*
CUTLER, THOMAS, his son   *disproved*
CUTLER, WILLIAM, his son   *disproved*

This family has appeared on no list but in the Albert Cook Myers Papers accompanying List Q there is a page for this family which provides birth dates for the children, as follows: Elizabeth, born 14 3rd mo. 1680; Thomas, born 23 9th mo. 1681; and William, born 19 10th mo. 1682. Mr. Myers may at one time have thought this family were on the *Welcome* but he never added their names to List Q.

There is a brief and unsatisfactory account of this family in Nahum S. Cutler's *A Cutler Memorial and Genealogical History* (Greenfield, Mass., 1889), pp. 559 f., which calls Edmund Cutler a planter, identifies his wife as Isabell, and says he bought land in Bucks County, 5 4th mo. 1686, but gives nothing on the date of arrival or the ship they came on.

The Cutlers were definitely not *Welcome* passengers but recorded themselves as passengers on the *Rebecca* of Liverpool, the Mr James Skiner, arriving "in the river 31 8th mo. 1685."[1] Edmund Cutler was of Slateburn in Bowland, Yorkshire, webster, and brought with him Cornelius Netherwood to serve one year; Richard Mather to serve two years; and Ellen Wigreen to serve four years.

This reference in Bucks Arrivals would seem to be the ultimate source of Mr. Myers' information, and if so, one wonders why he ignored the definite information concerning the ship and year of arrival. Perhaps he learned of this from another person and neglected to check the statement, or the sheet may have been prepared for some other purpose and have gotten mistakenly placed among the Welcome Papers.

Edmund Cutler had a brother John who also came on same ship and afterwards married Margery Hayhurst.[2]

The son William Cutler left a will dated 23 5th mo. 1714, probated 14 July 1714,[3] in which he names his brother Thomas, his mother Isabel Cutler (£4 annuity), sister Ellen Cutler (executrix), sister Jane Cutler, but not his older sister Elizabeth, and he also names the three children of John Cutler. A Jane Cutler married at Middletown on 11 5th mo. 1685 John Naler or Naylor. As this date is before the arrival of the Cutlers on the *Rebecca*, we are at a loss to identify this Jane.

NOTES
[1]Bucks Arrivals in PMHB 9:232, 8:335 f., also BHBC 680.
[2]See the Hayhurst sketch.
[3]BW 1:8.

DAVID, HUGH   *highly improbable*

This name had appeared on no list but was included by Mr. Colket among the claimants for whom he had no evidence either way. He cited Bonamy Dobree, *William Penn Quaker and Pioneer* (Boston-New York 1932), p. 139, where there is the claim that aboard the *Welcome* William Penn addressed Hugh David about a goat seen eating a broomstick.

It was on this occasion that Penn is supposed to
have made the oft-quoted remark, "I am a Welshman
myself." The story seems quite apocryphal but can
be traced back as far as Hazard's 1887 edition of
John F. Watson's *Annals of Philadelphia* (1:119) and
doubtless to the earlier editions as well, where it
is stated that this conversation took place during
Penn's second voyage to Pennsylvania.

Thomas Allen Glenn[1] tells us that Hugh David of
Haverford made his will 27 April 1709, probated 9
June 1709 by his wife Martha, naming children David,
Ruth, Mary, Jonathan, Caleb and Samuel. There is
a delicious story of how Hugh David was handled by
Thomas Penn, but this can hardly be the same man.

Peare's life of Penn (p. 11) does not mention
Hugh David but quotes the "I am a Welshman myself"
remark as occurring on the *Welcome*.[2]

NOTES
[1]GWF 1:164.
[2]Brigadier O. F. G. Hogg, "Further Light on the
Ancestry of William Penn," cites also *Notes and
Queries,* 1st ser., 3:454.

DAVIS, JACOB	*disproved*
DAVIS, ANN ASHMEAD, his wife	*disproved*

On this couple see what is said under Ashmead.

DIMSDALE, DR. ROBERT	*disproved*
DIMSDALE, LUCY ROBINSON, his wife	*disproved*
DIMSDALE, JOHN, his son	*disproved*
DIMSDALE, WILLIAM, his son	*disproved*
DIMSDALE, MARY, his daughter	*disproved*

The Dimsdales appear on no list but Mr. Colket
called attention to the claim as quoted by Mr. Rubincam without apparently noticing that, though
Mr. Rubincam did not state the fact in so many
words, he included disproof of the claim. The wife
has been listed above on the supposition that she
would have accompanied the family, but her presence
in America has not been recorded. There is proof
that Mary Dimsdale did come to America but it is
not quite certain that she was Robert's daughter.

For Dr. Dimsdale and the two sons, the claim
was made by Robert Dimsdale's great-granddaughter,
Susannah Dimsdale, in a manuscript note quoted by
Mr. Rubincam:[1]

He was a flourishing Doctor of Medicine,
practicing at Hoddesden, Herts,[2] and was a Quaker. He was a great friend of William Penn's.
He went out to America in 1680 [sic][3] taking
his two Sons, John and William, with him. While
out there, large tracts of land were granted to
him. Nearly 1/3rd of the Present City of Philadelphia was part of it[4] and much land in New
Jersey. The latter land was later sold to M[r]
Burr, a Cousin. The Pennsilveninan [sic] Property was lost from Neglect. He returned to
England, and went to live at Theydon Gernon,
Essex; where his father had been a Doctor.

Robert Dimsdale and his sons did not come on
the *Welcome*. The negative evidence is to be found
first in a survey of 500 acres in New Jersey made
for Robert Dunsdale [sic] on 13 Oct. 1682,[5] a date
when the *Welcome* was at sea. If Dimsdale was present in America on that date, he had arrived before
the *Welcome* but this survey might have been entered
by a representative. This is probably what happened, for on 20 Jan. 1682/3 Hugh Lambe, now or late
of the Parish of St. Martins in the ffields, Co. of
Middlesex, hosyer, conveyed to Robert Dimsdale of
Edmonton, co. Middlesex, physician, one-half of
one-seventh of one-ninetieth share in West New Jersey, the one-seventh having been bought of John Bull
on 27 March [i.e. 1681/2], to whom, with Francis
Collins and Richard Mew, Edward Byllinge had conveyed one full ninetieth share at some previous
date.[6] In the next month, on 27 Feb. 1682/3, Nicholas Lucas conveyed to Robert Dimsdale of Edmonton,
Co. of Middlesex, physician, one-third of a share
in New Jersey which Lucas had bought, when of Hertford, Herts, maulster, on 3 April 1677, from John
Kinsey, late of Great Hadam, Co. of Hertford, gent.[7]
These two deeds show that in the months of January
and February 1682/3, Robert Dimsdale was in England
and had not come to America on the *Welcome* in the
preceding autumn. While it would have been barely
possible that a *Welcome* passenger might have landed
and then immediately started back on another vessel,
we can hardly imagine why anyone should do this.
As will be shown later, a Mary Dimsdale whom we
take to have been Dimsdale's daughter was one of
seven women among witnesses of a wedding at Burlington, New Jersey, on 20 1st mo. called March 1683/4.[8]
The presumption is that this daughter came with her

father, though it is a bit strange that her mother
was not one of these seven witnessing women. We
therefore are inclined to believe that the Dimsdale
family must have crossed the Atlantic sometime in
the year beginning with March 1682/3.

Dimsdale was certainly in New Jersey on 21 Aug.
1688 on which date, intending to sail back to England, he gave a power of attorney to John Tatham of
Tatham House, Penna, Samuel Jenings and Symon
Charles, both of Burlington County, as general a-
gents.[9] While his name is also recorded numerous
times in New Jersey before and after that date,
this is the only evidence found to show his move-
ments. Susannah Dimsdale was right in saying that
he did come to America but the year 1680 is, of
course, quite wrong.

Sometime before 4 April 1677 Robert Dimsdale
had bought land in New Jersey of William Biddle,
trustee for Thomas Ollive,[10] his home being then in
Bishop Starford, co. Hertford [now Bishop's Stort-
ford], but in 1682/3 he was, as we have seen, living
at Edmonton, co. Middlesex. He was a First Purchaser of 5,000 acres in Pennsylvania in Group 7,[11]
and he subscribed £100 to the Society of Free Traders.[12] He had a survey for 1600 acres in 10th mo.
1684,[13] and still another for 500 acres in 4th mo.
1689,[14] by which time he was, of course, back in
England. The earliest record of him as an abutter
is dated 4 June 1689 and these references continue
to 1700,[15] during all of which period he was in England. Besides the power of attorney cited above,
there were others on 24 Jan. 1692/3, when he was of
Bishop Stafford,[16] and on 2 Feb. 1699/1700.[17]
There are at least four references to him as one of
two trustees of Francis Collins,[18] the earliest
being dated 21 Dec. 1686, and the others all during
the period when Dimsdale was in England.

In an article devoted to Francis Collins, who
was Robert Dimsdale's second father-in-law, Mr. F.
J. Dallett[18] asserts that Robert Dimsdale probably
came to America soon after the Collins family and
in his view they were probably on the *Shield* in
1680. H. Stanley Craig,[19] whose passenger lists
are filled with all manner of error, would put the
Collins family on the *Amity* in 1682. Mrs. Balderston, however, has found that Francis Collins loaded
goods on 26 July 1681 on the ship *Thomas and Anne*,
Thomas Singleton, master, which probably arrived

in New Jersey in October 1681 and then continued to
Virginia.[20] As we have seen, all of these dates
are too early for Robert Dimsdale who was still in
England in the early months of 1682/3, but he came
to America a second time after his first wife had
died, as she did, as we shall see, on 16 or 17 4th
mo. [June] 1705.   Before his own death, however,
he returned once more to England, so that, like
Penn, he made two trips to America but lived out
his life in England.

THE DIMSDALE FAMILY

> Arms: Argent on a Fesse, dancetté Azure, be-
>   tween three Mullets sable, two Bezants.
> Crest: an Eagle's Head, Argent.

1. Robert Dimsdale, barber-surgeon of Hoddesden, Herts, appears to have gotten into trouble
with the authorities for practicing as a grocer:[21]

> 5th April 1630. Presentment that Robert
> Dimsdale, late of Hodsdon, in the parish of
> Broxbourne, barber, had practiced the art
> and mystery of a grocer, without having
> served apprenticeship of seven years.

His wife's name was Sarah and both of them were
living in 1635 and doubtless much later.

Issue: surname Dimsdale
2 i.   Robert, b. shortly before 1630, d. 25
           10th mo. 1713, the immigrant.
   ii.   John, bapt. Broxbourne, Herts, 17 May
           1635; mayor of Hertford 1675, 1682,
           1688, 1697-1700; bur. All Saints,
           Hertford, 18 July 1725; his wife Martha
           bur. there 1 Dec. 1702. See William
           Berry, *County Genealogies. Pedigrees of
           Hertfordshire Families* (London 1844),
           211 f., a photograph of which has been
           kindly supplied me by Mr. Rubincam.
           Issue: surname Dimsdale
     1. Robert, M.D., of Hertford; m. Eliza-
        beth Clarke of Hertford, bur. at All
        Saints, Hertford, 29 April 1748,
        having m. (2) at Hertingfordbury in
        1726, Henry Cooley of St. George the
        Martyr, co. Middlesex.
        Issue: surname Dimsdale

      a. John, b. 17 Oct., bapt. 27 Oct.
        1703, All Saints, bur. there,
        9 Aug. 1710.
      b. Bringfield, d.y.
      c. Elizabeth, b. 31 Jan., bapt. 15
        Feb. 1704/5, d. unm., bur. 18
        Nov. 1737.
      d. Martha, bapt. 27 July, bur. All
        Saints, 11 Sept. 1710.
   2. Sir John, M.D., mayor of Hertford 1706,
      1711; knighted 20 Jan. 1725; d.s.p.
      27 Sept. 1726 aged 61; m. (1) 2 Aug.
      1709 Martha Lucas of Hitchin, Herts;
      (2) Susanna -----, living 1727.
   3. Joseph, b. 26 June, bapt. 10 July, bur.
      All Saints, 26 Aug. 1666.
   4. Margaret, bapt. All Saints, 29 March
      1668; m. Thomas Clarke M.D. of Hert-
      ford, d. before 8 March 1724.
  iii. Daughter.

    2. Robert Dimsdale, born at Theydon Guernon, co. Essex, not Hoddesdon, Herts, and probably somewhat before 1630, died at Bishop's Stortford, Herts, 25 10th mo. 1713, not, as in Mr. Rubincam's article, 1733, and was buried in the Bishop's Stortford Friends cemetery. He married, first, at Little Berkhamstead, 15 Nov. 1650, Lucy Robinson (her name unknown to Berry), who died at Bishop's Stortford, 16 or 17 4th mo. 1705, in the period between her husband's two trips to America. He married, second, in America, probably not long after his first wife's death, Sarah Collins, born 16 10th mo. 1665, died at Haddonfield, New Jersey, between 23 May and 9 Nov. 1739, dates of execution and probation of her will,[21] eldest child of Francis Collins by his first wife Sarah Mayham, on whom see Mr. Dallett's article cited above. The date of the second marriage is wrongly stated by William Nelson[22] as by 1686 and results from the confusion of the second marriage of Francis Collins in that year with that of Robert Dimsdale. It is not probable that it was as late as 1713, which is given by both Berry and Rubincam, for this is the year in which Dimsdale died, as we have seen.
    Robert Dimsdale was, of course, a Friend, and suffered persecution as such. He was the pioneer

settler of Lumberton, New Jersey, having settled
south of Mount Holly on both sides of what became
known as Dimsdale's Run. At London in 1684 he
published a book, *Robert Dimsdale's Advice: How to
Use his Medecines,* etc. It is not known that any
of his descendants settled permanently in America.

    Issue: surname Dimsdale, all by first wife
3   i.   John, d. 9 July 1730.
4   ii.   William, d. 19 May 1713.
   iii. Mary, probably the Mary who witnessed, as
        third of seven women, the wedding of
        Peter Jenings to Ann Nott at Burlington,
        N.J., 20 1st mo. 1683/4.[8] The others in
        order were JoAnna Pryor, Sarah Basnett,
        Sarah Collins Sr. & Jr., Mary Cripps,
        Margaret Collins. Why her mother did
        not also witness this wedding, which
        was before a justice and not according
        to Quaker ceremony, is not clear. It
        may be that this Mary was an unknown
        second wife of Dr. Dimsdale and that
        it was she who died in 1705.

    3.   John Dimsdale, the elder son of Dr. Robert
Dimsdale by his wife Lucy Robinson, is styled by
Burke,[23] without giving the date of knighthood, Sir
John Dimsdale Knt. It may well be that he has been
confused with his first cousin of the same name who
was knighted in 1725 shortly before his death. In
any case, this John is supposed to have come to
America with his father, though it must be admitted
that we have no documents to prove it except the
testimony of Miss Susannah Dimsdale. John was living at Epping in 1726, and died 9 July 1730. Not
much else is known of him save that he married, 25
June 1700, Susanna Bowyer, born 14 Nov. 1682, died
1754, eldest daughter of Thomas Bowyer of Albury
Hall, co. Hertford, and sister of Elizabeth Bowyer
who married his brother William.

    Issue: surname Dimsdale
   i.   Mary, b. 23 June 1701, d. 27 June 1702.
   ii.   John, b. 6 April 1703, d. 26 Nov. 1719.
   iii. Robert, of Theydon Gernon and Epping,
        surgeon, b. 3 Nov. 1705, d. by 11 Feb.
        1765; m. dau. of John Burr of Ware, co.
        Herts.
   iv.   Susannah, b. 13 Dec. 1707, d.s.p. 20 Feb.
        1731/2.

    v.   William, b. 25 June, bur. 28 July 1710.
5 vi.   Thomas, b. 29 May 1712, d. 30 Dec. 1800.
   vii.   Joseph, of Hertford, b. 13 Aug. 1716, d.
         26 April 1779, bur. Friends Ground, at
         Bishop's Stortford; m. (1) at Chipping
         Norton, co. Oxford, 16 Sept. 1741, Mary
         Clarke, dau. of Henry Clarke of that
         place, and she d.s.p. there; (2) at
         Cheshunt, co. Herts, 4 Jan. 1744, Eliza-
         beth Ball, dau. of Daniel Ball of Tot-
         tenham, co. Middlesex, and had issue not
         shown by Berry.
  viii. Calvert, b. 6 March, d. 16 May 1718, bur.
         Friends Ground.

    4. William Dimsdale, of Theydon Gernon and also
of Bishop's Stortford, surgeon, younger son of Dr.
Robert Dimsdale, presumably accompanied his father
to America though he is not recorded here. He married, 12 June 1706, Elizabeth Bowyer, born 17 Oct.
1685, died 29 May 1707, second daughter of Thomas
Bowyer of Albury Hall, co. Herts, and sister of his
brother John's wife. William died, according to
Berry, 19 May 1733 and not 1713, as had been supposed.

    Only issue: surname Dimsdale
    i.   Joseph, of Bishop's Stortford, surgeon,
         b. 16 May 1707, d. 1744, leaving a will
         dated 27 Jan. 1744 (cited by Berry, not
         examined), bur. Friends Ground, Bishop's
         Stortford; m. Elizabeth Appleby, daugh-
         ter of Anthony Appleby of Bishop's
         Stortford, and she d. 2 Jan. 1780.
         Issue: surname Dimsdale
    1. Robert, left issue but not shown by
       Berry.
    2. John, of Hitchin, m. Priscilla Pitts,
       and had son Joseph who m. Sarah
       Cockfield (daughter of Joseph). This
       latter Joseph Dimsdale was of Upton
       and had a son, Joseph Cockfield Dims-
       dale, b. 2 April 1813, d. 2 March
       1879, having had with others listed
       in Burke, 104th ed. (1967), p. 763,
       a son Joseph Cockfield Dimsdale, 1st
       Bart., b. 19 Jan. 1849, d. 10 Aug.
       1912, created baronet 23 July 1902;
       m. 11 Feb. 1873, Beatrice Eliza Bow-

er, d. 15 March 1948, daughter of
Robert Hunt Holdsworth. The present
and 3rd Bart. is Sir John Holdsworth
Dimsdale, b. 31 Dec. 1901. Further
details will be found in Burke.
3. William.
4. Mary.
5. Susan.
6. Elizabeth, b. 29 April 1732, d.s.p.
16 Oct. 1812; m. Nov. 1779, as 3rd
wife her 2nd cousin once removed
the first Baron Dimsdale (No. 5).

5. Thomas Dimsdale, 1st Baron Dimsdale of the
Russian Empire, was of the Priory of Hertford, M.D.,
fourth son of John Dimsdale by his wife Susanna
Bowyer; was born at Theydon Gernon, 29 May 1712,
died at Hertford, 30 Dec. 1800, buried in the Quaker Burying Ground at Bishop's Stortford. Like his
grandfather and uncle, he was a physician, in which
profession he had a singularly eminent career. At
the time of the Scottish rebellion in 1745, he vol-
unteered his services as a military surgeon. Having
become proficient inoculating for smallpox, he was
in 1762 invited by Catherine the Great, Empress of
Russia, to come to Russia to inoculate herself and
her son. The inoculation proving successful, the
Empress rewarded Dr. Dimsdale by appointing him
Councillor of State and Physician to Her Imperial
Majesty. By letters patent dated 13 Feb. 1769 she
created him a Baron of the Russian Empire, and the
same honors were conferred on his second son Nathaniel who, however, died in 1811. Dr. Dimsdale married, first, in July 1739, Mary Brassey, only child
of Nathaniel Brassey Esq. of Roxford House near
Hertford by his first wife, and she died without
issue, 4 Feb. 1744/5, buried in Friends Ground;
second, 17 June 1746, Anne Iles, daughter of John
Iles Esq., and she died 9 March 1779; third, in
Nov. 1779, his second cousin once removed, Elizabeth Dimsdale, born 29 April 1732, died 16 Oct.
1812, daughter of Joseph Dimsdale by Elizabeth
Appleby (as shown at the top of this page).[24]

Issue: surname Dimsdale, by second wife
i.   John, 2nd Baron Dimsdale, b. Priory of
Hertford, 11 March 1746/7, d. unm. May
1820; assumed the title of Baron of the
Russian Empire by Royal Sign Manual in

1813.
ii. Nathaniel, b. at the Priory of Hertford,
     11 April 1748, d. unm. 3 July 1811,
     bur. St. Andrew's Church; M.P. for Hert-
     ford; accompanied his father to Russia
     and there received a title at the same
     time as his father; had he survived his
     elder brother, he would have been the
     3rd Baron Dimsdale.
iii. Thomas, 3rd son, d. inf.
iv. Susanna, d.y. Was it she who made the
     Welcome claim?
v.   Joseph, b. 1751, M.D., of Bloomsbury Squ.
     London, d. 16 June 1784, bur. Quaker
     Burying Ground, Bishop's Stortford; m.
     1776 Mary, dau. of Nehemiah Champion
     and widow of Joseph Beck.
vi. Richard, b. 7 March 1753, d.s.p., bur. 31
     Aug. 1812, St. Andrew's Church, Hert-
     ford; assumed the name of Iles before
     that of Dimsdale.
vii. Thomas, 6th son, d. inf.
viii. Robert, 3rd Baron Dimsdale, b. 26 Dec.
     1756, m. at Bath, 10 July 1794, Finetta
     Pye, eldest daughter of Charles Pye of
     Wadley House, Berks.
         Issue: surname Dimsdale
     1. Thomas Robert, 4th Baron Dimsdale.
     5. Charles John, 5th Baron Dimsdale. In
        1956 the then present and 8th Baron
        Dimsdale was Thomas Edward, b. 11
        Oct. 1911, son of Edward Charles
        Dimsdale by his wife Katherine Joan
        Dimsdale, and Edward Charles was the
        son of the 7th Baron and died during
        the lifetime of his father, so that
        the 8th Baron was grandson of the
        7th.

NOTES

[1]"Dr. Robert Dimsdale: Pioneer Physician and
Colonial Legislator" (*Proc. N.J. Hist. Soc.* 47
[1939] 98-107). The document was furnished Mr.
Rubincam by Mrs. Katherine J. Dimsdale of Meesden
Manor, Buntingford, Herts., mother of the 8th Baron
Dimsdale.

[2]It was at Hoddesden that Gulielma Maria Springett, first wife of William Penn died, and the death

occurred at a time when Dr. Dimsdale may have been
living there.

[3]William Nelson (1 NJA 21:467) and Burke, *Peerage*, 104th ed. (1967), p. 763, both give the year
as 1683, which is not far from the truth, but, like
DNB 5:997, which says 1684, all three are wrong in
saying that Dimsdale accompanied William Penn.

[4]Probably a gross exaggeration. We have not attempted to trace the Dimsdale holdings in Pennsylvania.

[5]1 NJA 21:353.   [6]*Ibid.* 424.
[7]*Ibid.* 423 f.   [8]Stillwell, *Hist.M.*2:35.
[9]1 NJA 21:467.   [10]*Ibid.* 400.
[11]1 PA 1:40.   [12]PMHB 11:77.
[13]1 NJA 21:372.   [14]*Ibid.* 366.

[15]*Ibid.* 385 (4 June 1689), 370 (1693), 458 (1695),
484 (1696), 502 (1697), 527 (1700).

[16]*Ibid.* 467.   [17]*Ibid.* 522.

[18]*Proc. N. J. Hist. Soc.* 67 (1949), 62-74. See
PGM 25: 192-194 for Garwood Bible Records which begin with Francis Collins' son John (1690-1761).

[19]Salem County, New Jersey, Records p. 292.

[20]On this ship see Welcome Society Publications,
Vol. 1.

[21]Quoted by Mr. Rubincam.

[22]NJW 2:143 f.

[23]1 NJA 21:467. Nelson wrongly puts the death
date in 1718.

[24]Extended accounts of Baron Dimsdale appear in
DNB 5:997 f. and in Burke's *Peerage*, 101st ed.
(1956), p. 2403. In the 104th edition (1967) allusion was made to the "Foreign Titles Section"
omitted here but in 1956 edition, p. 2403.

DOYLE, EDMUND   *disproved*

This name appears on List X only. The truth is
that Ed[mund] Doyle came on the *Lion* of Liverpool,
arriving 14 8th mo. 1683, as servant to Joseph
Fisher, to serve four years, loose on 14 8th mo.
1687.

General Da is[1] says he came to Pennsylvania from
Newport, Rhode Island, where he had married a daughter of the Rev. Thomas Dungan. He did marry such a
wife but obviously not in Rhode Island but somewhere
in Bucks County after the Dungans arrived there from
Rhode Island. There is a fair account of this man
in Alfred Rudolph Justice, *Ancestry of Jeremy Clarke
of Rhode Island and Dungan Genealogy* (Philadelphia

no date), p. 121, on which we heavily lean:
  Edmund Doyle married ca. 1687 in Bucks County,
Rebecca Dungan, born ca. 1670, died 1722, daughter
of the Rev. Thomas Dungan, Baptist clergyman, by
his wife Elizabeth -----, who married, after Edmund
died in 1702/3, second, on 29 Sept. 1706, David
Griffith. Edmund and Rebecca were baptized by Baptist rite at Cold Spring, Bucks County, in 1696
(Penny Pack Church). His will dated 16 Sept. 1702,
probated in Philadelphia County, 12 March 1702/3,
names sons Edmund and Clement. Edmund was at one
time deputy sheriff of Bucks County.[2] It was for
later generations of this family that Doylestown,
county seat of Bucks County, was named.

  Issue (following Justice):
  i.   Elizabeth, b. 1688, d. 17 4th mo. 1784 in
       her 97th year; m. Buckingham but recorded
       at Falls, 10 3rd mo. 1711, Joseph Fell,
       widower of Bridget Willson whom he m. 2
       3rd mo. 1700, place unknown, he b. 19 8th
       mo. 1668, Longlands, parish of Uldale,
       Cumberland, England, d. 9 4th mo. 1748
       in Buckingham, son of John and Margaret
       (-----) Fell. Elizabeth's will was dated
       30 10th mo. 1777, probated 24 May 1784,
       mentions daughters Sarah Church, Rachel
       Kirk; grandson Zenas Fell; granddaughters
       Rachel Fell, Cynthia Fell; and son Thomas.
       Joseph Fell's account of his life says he
       had seven children by his second wife.
  ii. Edward, b. ca. 1690, d. Philadelphia 1770;
       m. ca. 1731, Martha Hellings, daughter of
       Nicholas and Ruth (-----) Hellings; (2)
       Mary -----, mentioned in his will dated
       9 Sept. 1768, probated Philadelphia 14
       March 1770.
         Issue: surname Doyle
       1. Elizabeth, m. ----- Rees.
       2. William, b. 1712, d. 26 Oct. 1800 aet.
          88, lived at Doylestown.
       3. Jeremiah.
       4. Edward, m. by license dated 11 Dec. 1751
          Hannah Eaton.
       5. Rebecca, m. ----- Freeman and had Eliza-
          beth and Isaac Freeman, mentioned in
          her father's will in 1768.
  iii. Clement, bur. 11 Feb. 1772; m. Margaret
       -----.

NOTES

[1]DHBC 2nd ed., 3:454.
[2]PGM 24:93, citing Bucks Court Records 391.

| DUCHÉ, ANTHONY | *highly improbable* |
| DUCHÉ, -----, his wife | *highly improbable* |

These names appear on no list but the *Welcome*
claim was alleged for them by John F. Watson,[1] and
in the A. C. Myers Welcome Papers at the Chester
County Historical Society, there is a cryptic reference which leads to the *Penn-Logan Correspondence* 1:273, where Mrs. Deborah Logan, wife of
George Logan whose grandfather James Logan was the
close friend of Penn, prints a note in which she
attributes to Charles Thompson Esq., an eighteenth-
century Philadelphian, the following tale: According
to this, Anthony Duché, a respectable Protestant
refugee from France, came with his wife on the same
ship with William Penn, name of ship not stated.
Penn had borrowed a small sum of money (under £30)
from Duché and after the landing Penn offered to re-
pay it with a city lot but Duché replied, "You are
very good, Mr. Penn, and the offer might be advantageous enough, but the money would suit me better."
Then Penn is supposed to have expressed an unfavor-
able opinion of Duché's preference and the latter
said later that he had regretted his folly. Note
that though this comes from an annotation to a letter of Penn to Logan dated 10 1st mo. 1703/4, there
is no mention of the Duchés in the letter. What
incited the remark was something Penn said about the
value of central Philadelphia real estate. The editor of the *Correspondence* (Edward Armstrong) adds
his note that the same tale was told with reference
to one Ladd and that Penn had punned on his name
when he refused the city lot in payment. We have
not found the Ladd version elsewhere.

The Rev. Edward Duffield Neill printed an article
on "Rev. Jacob Duché, the first Chaplain of Congress,"[2] in which without referring to the previous
reference he says as follows:

> The following anecdote has often[3] been prin-
> ted. William Penn on the voyage borrowed from
> Duché about thirty pounds. After landing, Penn
> offered a valuable square of land in the centre
> of the City, in lieu of the money. "You are very
> good, Mr. Penn, and the offer might prove ad-

vantageous, but the money would suit me better."
[The name of Duché does not appear on any of the
lists of persons who came over on the Welcome.
--Ed.]⁴

Mr. Neill's version differs from the Logan-Armstrong
one, in that, according to the latter, it was quite
possible for the loan to have been made to Penn before the voyage began, whereas Mr. Neill puts the
loan on the ship, hardly a place where Penn would
be likely to have needed funds. Surely, he was not
playing poker en route! Neither version specifies
the ship, whether the *Welcome* in 1682 or the *Canterbury* in 1699, but the editor of the Neill version
brings in the *Welcome* and its passenger lists but
he does not definitely declare for the first voyage.
Only Watson has done that.

The first record of Anthony Duché in Pennsylvania is to be found in the marriage register of the
First Presbyterian Church in Philadelphia, where
on 19 4th mo. 1705 Anthony Duchel married Anne Doz,
elsewhere⁵ said to be daughter of Andrew Doz. The
marriage record does not say that Anthony was a
widower but he probably was, as in his will he names
his son Anthony first, though the baptism of son
Andrew comes so soon after the marriage that we
can be sure he was the firstborn of Anne Doz.

Since no record of Anthony Duché has been found
before the arrival of the *Canterbury*, we think it
probable that if he did cross with Penn on any ship,
it was on Penn's second voyage and not the first.
As for the loan, that appears to be apocryphal. It
would hardly seem possible for a refugee to lend
money to a friend; indeed, refugees generally need
to borrow themselves.

Anthony Duché was a potter when he made his will
on 2 May 1761, probated 1 June 1762, in which he
names no wife, appoints executrix daughter Anne who
is specified as the sole daughter then living, and
names three sons Anthony, Andrew and Jacob in that
order; also granddaughter Ann Meares, grandsons
James J. and Andrew.

In the following reconstruction of the family,
we have been unable to place certain Duchés who undoubtedly belong to the family:

    Joseph Duché who m. at Gloria Dei, 4 July 1761
        or 1762 Margaret Blake
    Peter Duché who m. there 13 May 1779 Hannah

Shanks

Ann Duché m. Christ Church 16 Sept. 1784 Thomas
   Moore

Maria Duché m. St. Michael's and Zion, 19 Dec.
   1783 John Pollard

James [sic] Duché of Southwark, widow, will dated
   24 Dec. 1827, probated 1 March 1829, names
   Jane Duché Hozey, daughter of late Isaac and
   Jane Hozey decd; Margaret Hozey, daughter of
   same. Letters of administration were granted
   24 May 1825 to Margaret Jones.[6]

Issue of Anthony Duché:

   by presumed first wife

i.   Anthony, first son named in will, living
      5 Dec. 1774 when he joined in a multi-
      partite deed of partition; no probate
      found. He m. (1) Catherine Swanson,
      daughter of Christopher and Christian
      Swanson of Wiccacoe, mother of all the
      children; and probably m. (2) at Gloria
      Dei, 3 Jan. 1758, Sarah Evans; and proba-
      bly (3) at Christ Church, 24 April 1770,
      Sarah Falconer. If he did not marry the
      two Sarahs, then we are unable to identi-
      fy their husband or husbands.
         Issue: surname Duché
         all by first wife Catherine
   1. Anthony, d. before 1774, m. Gloria Dei,
      11 Nov. 1758 Lydia Millane who m. (2)
      at Gloria Dei, 19 July,1774, Richard
      Paul. He must be the cutler of South-
      wark whose will is dated 15 May 1772,
      probated 7 July 1772, naming wife Lydia,
      and the children listed below; execs.
      friends John Johnson of Germantown, sad-
      ler, and Andrew Doz of Philadelphia,
      merchant.
         Issue:
      a. Andrew, named in father's will 1772.
      b. Anthony, named in father's will 1772,
         and living Dec. 1788 (Orphans Court
         record).
      c. Sarah, named in father's will 1772.
      d. Mary, named in father's will 1772,
         probably m. Gloria Dei, 10 Jan.
         1782, John Dennys.
   2. Jacob, d. before 1774, no other record.

3. John, of Southwark, boatbuilder, will
   dated 12 March 1802, probated 11 Jan.
   1810, names wife Jane sole heir. She
   possibly was the unidentified widow
   "James" mentioned on p. 171. No issue.
4. Swanson, of Southwark, shipwright, will
   dated 19 Sept. 1780, probated 28 Oct.
   1780, names wife Ann, executors brother
   John and wife; also nephews Andrew and
   Anthony, son of brother Anthony.
5. William, house carpenter, of Southwark,
   will dated 18 May 1779, probated 1
   July 1779, unnamed wife sole heir and
   executrix; m. Gloria Dei, 11 Jan. 1779
   May Price.
6. Rebecca, m. (1) Gloria Dei, 28 Dec. 1752,
   Thomas Janvier; (2) Christ Church, 7
   July 1768, George Griffith, taylor, of
   Southwark

by second wife Anne Doz

ii. Andrew, bapt. First Presbyterian Church,
     Philadelphia, 14 Aug. 1706; m. (1) Hannah
     ----- who was bur. from Christ Church,
     7 Oct. 1731; (2) Christ Church, 12 Dec.
     1731, Mary Mason. His will dated 18 Aug.
     1778, probated 19 Sept. 1778, calls him
     of the City of Philadelphia, gent., ad-
     vanced in years, names nephew John Duché
     and nephew Swanson Duché, sons of brother
     Anthony; niece Ann Estler, her husband
     Henry Estler and her daughter Elizabeth
     Johns when 21; Elizabeth Duché daughter
     of nephew Jacob with remainder to her
     brother Thomas; niece Ann Estler and Ann,
     wife of Swanson Duché to divide wearing
     apparel; executors: Andrew Doz, Edward
     Duffield, Benjamin Wynkoop.
iii. Jacob, b. 26 April 1708, as his will tells
     us; baptism not found; d. 28 Sept. 1788,
     parish of Lambeth in Surrey; left a will[7]
     dated 1 Aug. 1786, probated (PCC 477
     Calvert) 8 Oct. 1788, in Philadelphia,
     7 March 1789. He calls himself late of
     the city of Philadelphia, now of the
     Parish of Lambeth, Surrey, and gives his
     birthdate as stated; names beloved son
     Rev. Jacob Duché, chaplain and Secretary

to the Asylum for female orphans; daughter-in-law Elizabeth Duché; granddaughter Esther Duché; granddaughter Elizabeth Sophia [Duché]; grandson Thomas Spence Duché; executors son Jacob and grandson Thomas Spence Duché. This testator had been colonel of a Philadelphia regiment and a vestryman of Christ Church. He married (1) at Christ Church 13 Jan. 1734 Mary Spence, the mother of his children; (2) at Christ Church, 5 June 1747, Esther Duffield, b. 19 April 1701, d. 22 June 1779, daughter of Benjamin and Elizabeth (Watts) Duffield and widow of ----- Bradley, the marriage to whom has not been found.

Issue: surname Duché

1. Sarah, bapt. Christ Church, 14 Nov. 1734, aged 1 mo.; bur. from there, 25 Sept. 1735.

2. Spence, bapt. Christ Church, 21 July 1736, bur. from there, 17 Sept. 1736.

3. Jacob, bapt. Christ Church, 12 Feb. 1738 aged 1 mo.; d. Philadelphia, 3 Jan. 1798, a clergyman. He m. at Christ Church, 19 June 1760, Elizabeth Hopkinson, daughter of Thomas Hopkinson and sister of Francis Hopkinson, the Signer of the Declaration of Independence, and she d. in 1797. He was a member of the first graduating class of the University of Pennsylvania in 1757; studied theology at the University of Cambridge; was licensed by the Bishop of London as an assistant minister and served at Christ Church 1759-1775. At the outbreak of the Revolution he at first exhibited enthusiasm for the patriot cause, made the opening prayer at the First Continental Congress, 7 Sept. 1774, was chosen the chaplain to Congress on 9 July 1776. But on 8 Oct. 1777 he wrote a letter to General Washington in which he expressed Tory sentiments and attempted to induce the general to resign. When this letter was laid before Congress, Duché was exiled and his property confiscated. He

went to England, followed by his wife
and children and remained there until
1790 when he returned to Philadelphia.
He was granted the D.D. degree and was
the author of two books. He made his
will 29 March 1797, probated 13 Jan.
1798, mentioning his two daughters.[8]
    Issue: surname Duché
a. Thomas Spence, was a pupil in painting
   of Benjamin West, and portraits of
   his parents by him are said to be in
   the Historical Society of Pennsylvania. He died at the age of 26 years,
   six months, buried at Lambeth.
b. Esther, m. Christ Church, 7 Aug. 1798,
   William Hill.
c. Elizabeth Sophia, m. Christ Church, 23
   May 1799, John Henry.
4. Mary, bur. from Christ Church, 5 July
   1743.
iv. James, no baptism found; m. Christ Church,
    8 May 1737, Hannah Preston. He was bur.
    from Christ Church, 1 Jan. 1750/1. Admin.
    granted 27 Feb. 1750/1 to widow Hannah,
    and two minor children are mentioned.
    The widow was probably the Ann who m. at
    Christ Church, 28 April 1763, John Moyes,
    to whom admin. was granted 21 June 1768
    on James's estate. Perhaps Hannah had by
    that date died.
        Probable issue:
    1. James J., mentioned in grandfather's will
       in 1761 as minor.
    2. Andrew, mentioned in grandfather's will
       in 1761 as minor.
v. Elizabeth, bapt. First Presbyterian Church,
    Philadelphia, 6 April 1712; m. Christ
    Church 15 Aug. 1741 John Meares.
        Issue: all known, surname Meares
    1. Ann, mentioned in grandfather's will 1761
       and m. (1) Christ Church, 13 June 1767,
       Joseph Johns, (2) Christ Church, 17
       Sept. 1774, Harry Esler. She had by
       her first husband:
       a. Elizabeth, minor in 1778 in the will
          of Andrew Duché; m. Christ Church,
          26 Dec. 1794 John H. Cheyney.
vi. Ann, only living daughter on 2 May 1761.

vii. Susanna, m. Christ Church, 5 Feb. 1744, William Winkle, but was dead by 2 May 1761
when sister Ann was the only living daughter.[9]

NOTES

[1]*Annals of Philadelphia* 1:413.
[2]PMHB 2:58-73.
[3]I have found it only in the places cited.
[4]The bracketed material appears thus in PMHB.
[5]*Our Ancestors* (a periodical that was short-lived),
vol. 1, no. 2, pp. 56-59.
[6]For this and other Duché probate see PMHB 12:485.
[7]PMHB 29:92.
[8]See the articles on this man in DAB and in the
*Twentieth Century Biographical Dictionary of Notable
Americans,* s.v. Jacob Duché.
[9]Marion Balderston (PGM 24:79) reports a Daniel
Duchais who loaded on the *America* of London, 31 May
1683, and suggests he was possibly related to a
Jacques Duché said to have fled from LaRochelle to
London in 1682 with wife Mary and eight children
(*Proc. Huguenot Soc. of Penn'a* 28:125).

DUFFIELD, BENJAMIN   *disproved*

This name appears on no list but we understand
that the claim is made in a "Duffield Genealogy"
which we have thus far never found in any library,
including the Genealogical Society of Pennsylvania.
There is, however, a small work bearing the name of
Joseph C. Martindale, M.D., *The Gilbert Family, The
Carver Family, The Duffield Family* (printed at Frankford, 1911, long after Dr. Martindale's death), in
which mention is made of Benjamin Duffield but with
no reference to the *Welcome* and a statement which
precludes the claim, namely that Duffield was at
Burlington, New Jersey, in 1679. It has been stated
to me that the sentence, "Benjamin Duffield came to
Pennsylvania October 27, 1682 and was 21 years of
age," has been found in some Duffield account but it
definitely is not in the Duffield Bible Record in
the Genealogical Society of Pennsylvania, nor in an
account of the Duffields by the late Alfred Rudolph
Justice in the same collection (Justice Coll. 7:81).
While we have not found primary evidence that Duffield was in Burlington in 1679, that seems to be
the consensus and, if correct, then the claim is
false.

From a Bible record in the Collections of the
Genealogical Society of Pennsylvania and an account
of the Duffields by A. R. Justice, the following
information has been compiled.
Benjamin Duffield, son of Robert and Bridget
(-----) Duffield, was born 29 Sept. 1661 and died
1 May 1741 aged almost 81 years, buried in the old
Christ Church Graveyard at 5th and Arch Streets,
Philadelphia. His wife Elizabeth, who was daughter
of Arthur and Susanna (-----) Watts, was born 1 10th
mo. (Dec.) 1658. In some way Benjamin Duffield became the brother-in-law of Allen Foster of Philadelphia, now Montgomery County. The children were:

i.   Suzanna, b. 22 Jan. 1682/3.
ii.   Mary, b. 25 Oct. 1684, m. Benjamin Black-
        ledge [marriage said to be proved by
        PhD H-9:163].
iii.   Robert, b. 20 Oct. 1685.
iv.   Benjamin, b. 21 June 1687.
v.   Elizabeth, b. 22 June 1688.
vi.   John, b. 13 Oct. 1689 [d. 1756, m. Martha
        Maddock].
vii.   Thomas, b. 20 Feb. 1690/91 [d. 1758, m. (1)
        Phebe Chamberlin; (2) at Christ Church,
        15 Feb. 1734, Mary Lee].
viii.   Joseph, b. 22 Sept. 1692, d. Feb. 1747, of
        whom more below.
ix.   Peter, b. 8 May 1694 [d. 1752, m. Elizabeth
        -----].
x.   Stephen, b. 28 May 1696.
xi.   Abraham, b. 28 Jan. 1698.
xii.   Esther, b. 19 April 1701, d. 22 June 1779,
        [m. (1) ----- Bradley at unknown time and
        place; (2) as 2nd wife, at Christ Church,
        Col. Jacob Duché, on whom see p. 173.
xiii.   Isaac, b. 8 April 1705.

Joseph Duffield, the eighth child of Benjamin
and Elizabeth (Watts) Duffield, was born 22 Sept.
1692, died 6 Feb. 1747, married, first, Sarah
-----, born 21 May 1694, died 4 Sept. 1736; second,
Hannah ----- who died 22 July 1748. Her name is
said to have been Leach and she was a widow, but
the record does not make clear whether she was born
Leach or married a Leach. The children were all
by the first wife:

i.   Benjamin, b. 13 April 1716, d. 31 Aug. 1756.
ii.   Elizabeth, b. 31 Dec. 1717, m. Christ

             Church, 25 June 1733, Dr. Samuel Swift.
    iii. Mary, b. 23 Feb. 1719, d.23 Aug. 1756.
    iv.   Sarah, b. 26 Feb. 1719, d. 6 Nov. 1802,
             11:30 AM, aged 81/8, m. Ebenezer Kinners-
             ley.
    v.   Hannah, b. 19 May 1724.
    vi.   Joseph, b. 28 Dec. 1726, d. 24 Aug. 1736.
    vii. James, b. 28 Oct. 1728, d. 31 Aug. 1736.
    viii. Edward, b. 30 April 1730, d. 12 July 1803,
             bur. in front of All Saints Church, in
             Holmesburg, Pa., together with his wife,
             his daughter who was wife of Stacy Hep-
             burn, and his son Edward; m. Christ
             Church, 10 June 1751, Catherine Parry.
    ix.   Tiz or Uz (male), b. 4 May 1733, d. 26 Aug.
             1736.

DUTTON, JOHN   *improbable*
DUTTON, MARY DARLINGTON? his wife   *improbable*

     John Dutton's name appears with unnamed wife on
Lists E, M, R (here among controversial names) and
X.   A qualified claim is made by George Smith, M.D.,
History of Delaware County, Pennsylvania (Philadelphia 1862), p. 457: the Duttons arrived "with the
proprietary, when he made his first visit, or shortly afterwards." This claim was not, however, adopted by that astute genealogist, Gilbert Cope, *Genealogy of the Dutton Family* (West Chester 1871), one
of his earliest works.
     Cope thought that it was not improbable that
Thomas Brassie, Robert Taylor and John Dutton all
crossed the Atlantic together, and he cites a deed
of Thomas Rowland of the Co. Palatine of Chester,
yeoman, who sold on 22 May 1682 to John Dutton of
Overton, Cheshire, yeoman, and wife Mary, part of
a tract which he had bought from Penn as a First
Purchaser. John Dutton's 500 acres were laid out
on 8 Oct. 1682, and if this was not done for him
by an agent, Dutton had arrived on an earlier vessel, for on that day the *Welcome* was at sea.
     Cope prints at the head of his book a lengthy ac-
count of English Duttons but does not claim to have
placed John among them. The date of John Dutton's
death is unknown but his widow married, second,
either in 1694 or 1695, John Neild, for the Chester
Women's Monthly Meeting of 1 5th mo. 1695 made an
attempt to get Mary to acknowledge her fault in

marrying Neild who was not a Friend. Mr. Cope was
of the opinion that Mary was a sister of Job Darlington of Darnhall, Cheshire, who wrote letters to
his children in Pennsylvania which mention Mary Dutton in such a way as to suggest this. Mary had died
by 2 May 1717 for a letter of Job Darlington of that
date shows that Job was not aware of what John Neild's
wife was named. Her name was Elizabeth on 18 May
1724 and she married, second, William Jefferis.

Issue: surname Dutton
i.   Elizabeth, b. England, d. Pennsylvania, 23
     10th mo. 1682.
ii. John, supposedly b. 1675 in England, left a
     will dated 21 1st mo. 1735/6 and probably
     d. that very day, as the will was never
     signed; m. 1st int. Concord, 11 7th mo.
     1704, 2nd int. 13 9th mo. 1704, reported
     11 10th mo. 1704, Elizabeth Kingsman, b.
     6 9th mo. 1685, living 1745, daughter of
     John and Hannah (Simcock) Kingsman.
     Issue: surname Dutton
     1. John, m. 4 8th mo. 1733, Chichester,
        Prudence Reynolds, b. 16 1st mo. 1713,
        daughter of Francis and Elizabeth (Ac-
        ton) Reynolds.
     2. Hannah, d. 31 12th mo. 1782, m. 29 8th
        mo. 1730 Chichester, Nathaniel Scar-
        lett, son of Humphrey and Ann (-----)
        Scarlett.
     3. Mary, m. "by a priest" shortly before
        4th mo. 1733, Joseph Cobourn.
     4. Kingsman, d. ca. 1765, carpenter, m. out
        shortly before 7 1st mo. 1736/7, Anne,
        living 1774, probably daughter of
        Francis and Barbara Routh .
     5. Jacob, disowned 4 11th mo. 1741 for m.
        out, Hannah -----, to whom admin. was
        granted 16 Aug. 1749 after which she
        m. (2) Charles Henszley.
     6. Joseph, millwright, m. out, 21 10th mo.
        1742, Elizabeth Smith, daughter of
        Thomas Smith of Birmingham. He d. 14
        6th mo. 1773 and she before that.
     7. Robert, b. by 1719, m. out, acknowledged
        1 6th mo. 1743 ----- Crosby.
     8. James, m. out by 8 10th mo. 1753, Hannah
        -----, who d. 1 Oct. 1798 aged 65; he
        d. Northern Liberties, Philadelphia, 1

Aug. 1769, aet. 45.
9. Isaac, m. out, Mary Coates, daughter of
John Coates, brickmaker, and widow of
----- Wright. Isaac's will dated at
Kensington, 9 Oct. 1760, was probated
2 March 1761; Mary's will was dated
29 Sept. 1786, probated 26 May 1791.
10. Amy, m. ----- Tally by 7 6th mo. 1749
and was disowned.
iii. Edward, left will dated 24 10th mo. 1731,
probated 14 March 1731/2; m., 1st int.,
9 4th mo. 1701, 2nd int., 11 6th mo. 1711,
no report, Gwin Williams, and she m. by
Justice of the Peace shortly before 7 3rd
mo. 1744, ----- Bennett, and d. ca. 1753.
Issue: surname Dutton
1. Mary, m. 27 9th mo. 1728, Daniel Davis,
son of John and Mary (-----) Davis of
Thornbury.
2. John, d. intestate 1748/9, m. out by 7
12th mo. 1736/7, at Christ Church, 4
Nov. 1735, Elizabeth Dunlap.
3. William, complained of for not paying his
debts, 3 9th mo. 1735, and seems to
have resigned from meeting.
iv. Thomas, b. England, 1 3rd mo. 1679, d. of
smallpox, 10th mo. 1731; m. 1st int., 10
1st mo. 1700/1, 11 2nd mo. 1700/1, a curious approval by John Neild, 2nd int., 14
2nd mo. 1701, Leusy Barnott [= Lucy Bar-
nard], b. 2nd mo. 1681, d. 10th mo. 1728
of measles in 48th year, daughter of Richard and Frances (-----) Barnard of Aston.
Issue: surname Dutton
1. Thomas, b. 3rd mo. 1702, d. 10th mo. 1728
of measles, unm.
2. Rebeckah, b. 19 8th mo. 1709, d. 10th mo.
1731 of smallpox, unm.
3. Richard, b. 8 10th mo. 1711, d. 18 2nd
mo. 1795, m. 7 8th mo. 1733 Mary Martin, b. 30 6th mo. 1711, d. 26 1st mo.
1782, daughter of Thomas and Mary (---)
Martin.
4. David, b. 28 12th mo. 1713/14, d. 25 3rd
mo. 1798, m. Jane, perhaps McClaskey.
5. Lydia, b. 14 2nd mo. 1716, d. 11 4th mo.
1748, m. 30 6th mo. 1739, William
Hewes, son of William and Mary (-----)

Hewes.

6. Jonathan, b. 11 6th mo. 1721, d. 18 10th mo 1745, unm. and s.p.

7. John, b. 6 7th mo. 1721, twin, d. 6 2nd mo. 1759, probably unm.

8. Mary, b. 6 7th mo. 1721, twin, m. out by 3 4th mo. 1745 ----- Grubb.

9. Sarah, b. 22 8th mo. 1725, d. 20 2nd mo. 1795; m. John Power (d. 1 2nd mo. 1791) and was disowned 3 6th mo. 1747.

v.   Robert, m. 1st int., 8 7th mo. 1707, 2nd int. 13 8th mo. 1707, reported 13 9th mo. 1707, Ann Brown, daughter of William and Ann (Mercer) Brown. She m. (2) 23 9th mo. 1736, John Underhill of Cecil Co., Md., and she was also then of Cecil County.

Issue: surname Dutton

1. Mary, b. 15 8th mo. 1708.

2. Ann, b. 10 10th mo. 1711.

3. Robert, b. 26 8th mo. 1713.

4. Elizabeth, b. 25 1st mo. 1722, m. 20 2nd mo. 1742, East Nottingham, Joseph England of Kent Co., Md, son of Lewis England.

EMLEN, GEORGE   *disproved*

This name appears on no list but Jordan[1] says clearly that Emlen "came in 1682 with William Penn." Though not on List Q, the name had a page in the A. C. Myers Welcome Papers reserved for it, and included with this was a copy of Frank Willing Leach's *North American* article on Emlen which states that Emlen's sons said "he came over the sea with William Penn," but that Emlen is not found of record in Pennsylvania before his marriage in 1684 or 1685.

The sons Joshua and Samuel reported that their father was born at Shepton Mallett, Somersetshire. At his first marriage he was recorded as a husbandman but was afterwards a vintner. His first grant was not until 3 12th mo. 1687/8, and on the Blackwell Rent Roll of 1689,[2] Emlen is shown as a renter of a lot on Chestnut Street, north side, between Second and Third Streets from the Delaware, for one year, rent 7/6.

He married, first, 1st intentions at Philadelphia Monthly Meeting, 3 6th mo. 1685, 2nd intentions, 12 7th mo. 1685, and the wedding was on

12 9th mo. 1685, recorded by the Register General,
the bride Eleanor Allen, daughter of Nathaniel Allen
of Bucks County, and she died 22 1st mo. 1690 without surviving issue; second, 5 4th mo. 1694, Hannah
Garrett, born at Harby, Leics., 23 4th mo. 1674,
daughter of William and Ann (Kirk) Garrett, and she
married, second, 20 10th mo. 1716, William Tidmarsh,
and died 24 6th mo. 1738. George Emlen himself died
on 7th day [Saturday], 24 10th mo. 1710.

Issue: by second wife, surname Emlen
i.   George, b. 7 5th mo. 1695, d. 24 10th mo.
       1754; m. 24 2nd mo. 1717, Mary Heath, b.
       11 4th mo. 1692, d. 2 6th mo. 1777, daugh-
       ter of Robert and Susanna (-----) Heath
       from Staffordshire ca. 1701. He was a
       brewer.
       Issue: surname Emlen
       1. George, b. 21 6th mo. 1718, d. 3 1st mo.
          1776; m. Anne Reckless.
       2. Hannah, b. 1 4th mo. 1722, d. 30 1st mo.
          1777; m. 24 1st mo. 1740 Philadelphia
          Monthly Meeting, William Logan, son of
          James and Sarah (Read) Logan.
       3. Joseph, b. 1 5th mo. 1728, d. 17 11th
          mo. 1750, unm.
ii.   Samuel, b. 15 2nd mo. 1697, d. 28 10th mo.
       1783; m. 2 10th mo. 1731 Rachel Hudson,
       b. 11 9th mo. 1707, d. 12 9th mo. 1771,
       daughter of William and Mary (Richardson)
       Hudson.
       Issue: surname Emlen
       1. Hudson, merchant, d. 26 3rd mo. 1768,
          unm.
       2. Sarah, d.s.p. 16 12th 1813 in 80th year;
          m. 12 1st mo. 1773 Thomas Moore, son
          of Richard and Margaret (Preston) Moore.
iii.   Caleb, b. 9 4th mo. 1699, d. 13 10th mo.
       1748, unm.
iv.   Joshua, b. 14 2nd mo. 1701, d. 22 5th mo.
       1776, tanner; m. (1) 25 9th mo. 1726
       Mary Holton, widow of Samuel Hudson, and
       daughter of Arthur and Elizabeth (Guest)
       Holton, and she d. 23 12th mo. 1726; (2)
       29 9th mo. 1728, Deborah Powell, daughter
       of Samuel and Abigail (Wilcox) Powell.
       Issue: surname Emlen
          by second wife
       1. Samuel, b. 15 1st mo. 1730, d. 30 12th

mo. 1799; m. (1) 6 7th mo. 1761 Elizabeth Moode, daughter of William Moode;
(2) 1 2nd mo. 1770 Sarah Mott who d.
26 10th mo. 1796, daughter of Asher
Mott.

    Issue: surname Emlen
      by first wife

a. William, b. 17 5th mo. 1765, d. minor.
b. Samuel, b. 4 9th mo. 1766, d.s.p. 29
    12th mo. 1837.
      by second wife
c. Deborah, d. 17 4th mo. 1789 aet. 17.
d. Elizabeth, d. 19 6th mo. 1820, aet.
    47, m. 20 9th mo. 1800, Philip Syng
    Physick, M.D.

v.   Hannah, b. 3 12th mo. 1703/4, d. 6 8th mo.
      1711.
vi.   Ann, b. 19 3rd mo. 1705, m. 26 3rd mo. 1732,
      William Miller of Chester Co., son of
      John and Mary (-----) Miller.
vii. Mary, b. 1 11th mo. 1707/8, d.s.p. 18 3rd
      mo. 1791; m. 1728, John Armitt, b. 8 10th
      1702, d. 20 5th mo. 1762, son of Robert
      and Sophia (Johnson) Armitt.
viii.Sarah, b. 19 1st mo. 1709/10, d. 2 8th mo.
      1752; m. 25 3rd mo. 1738 James Cresson,
      son of Solomon and Anna (Watson) Cresson.

NOTES

[1]JCRFP 1:190-199. See also an unpaged section
on Emlen in Alexander DuBin, *Old Philadelphia Families* (Philadelphia 1939).
   [2]PGM 23:78.

ENGLISH, JOSEPH   *disproved*

    This name appears on no list but the claim is
made in Dr. E. D. Buckman's 47-volume manuscript
Buckman Genealogy (1:30) now in the Genealogical
Society of Pennsylvania that Joseph English, the
brother of Mary, wife of Giles Knight, came on the
Welcome. This is probably merely an inference to
be drawn from the belief that the Knights had come
on that ship. If Dr. Buckman attempted to convince
William J. Buck, he did not succeed, for List F,
compiled by Buck with the assistance of Dr. Buckman,
does not have the name. It is probable that the
Joseph English involved was the father and not the
brother of Mary Knight, so he should be styled the

elder.

In any case, a Joseph English, whatever relation he bore to Mary Knight, loaded on the *Society* of Bristol, 2 May 1682, 2½ cwt of wrought iron, 2 pcs English fustians, 10 lbs tammy.[1] This is the same ship on which the Knights can be shown to have come and there is the greatest probability that Joseph English crossed on it also.

At Middletown Monthly Meeting, 3 10th mo. 1684, Joseph English and Joan Comely, widow of Henry, declared 1st intentions and were passed, 1 11th mo. 1684. Joseph C. Martindale, M.D., *History of the Townships of Byberry and Moreland* (revised ed., undated), says that Joseph English came with Penn in 1682 and gives the date of his death as 10 8th mo. 1686 and says Joan died 20 10th mo. 1689.

C. A. Hoppin, *The Washington Ancestry and Records of the McClain, Johnson and Forty Other Colonial American Families* (Greenfield, Ohio, 1932), 2:335-390, has an account of the English family which declares that Joseph English and Joan Comly were married 26 2nd mo. 1685 at John Otter's house, and that Joseph was buried at John Hart's in Byberry. Hoppin also states that this Joseph had a brother Tobias who had a son Joseph who died in England in 1708. He also says that Joseph English Sr. was still in England in 1683 but Hoppin had no way of knowing about the goods loaded on the *Society* in 1682 and this may well be an error.

There was a Joseph English, more probably another than this one, who is mentioned in the will of Samuel Clifte of Bucks County, dated 23 9th mo. 1682, less than a month after the *Welcome* had arrived.[2] This Joseph is left "30 acres of land, beginning up the Creek where he has begun to build his house . . ." Hoppin[3] prints a long account of Samuel Clift, Quaker, from Horsley, England, who as Samuel Clift of Shortwood, Parish of Horsley, married 4 2nd mo. 1667 Joane Betterby of Hampton Rhoads. Their daughter married Joseph English the younger, probably son of Joseph English the elder. Joseph the younger, not a Friend, came to America in 1677 or 1678 and settled at Burlington, making a will 4 7th mo. 1725 which we have not seen. It is not abstracted in *New Jersey Wills*, vols. 1-2, and where Hoppin saw it is unknown to me. Hannah Clift, wife of Joseph English the younger, cannot have been the daughter of Joane Batterby, but might have been by

an earlier wife of Samuel Clift, not discovered by
Hoppin.

NOTES

[1]PGM 23:43.   [2]PGSP 1:47.   [3]*Op. cit.* 2:393-410.

FISHER, JOHN   *highly improbable*
FISHER, MARGARET, his wife   *highly improbable*
FISHER, JOHN, his son   *highly improbable*
FISHER, THOMAS, his son   *highly improbable*

John Fisher's name appears on Lists A, B, C, D,
E, F, G, H, I, M, N, O (here doubtful), R, S, T, U
(here denied), X, Y and Z. His wife Margaret is on
Lists A, B, C, D, E, F, G, H, I, M, U (here denied),
X, Y and Z. The son John is on Lists A, B, C, D, E,
F, G, H, M, U (here denied), X, Y and Z, and the
family is listed on Lists J, K, L, N, P, S, T and W.
List V puts the family probably on the *Lamb* and names
the children as John, Thomas, James, Rachel, Sarah,
Alice and Annis.
        Ann Wharton Smith, *Genealogy of the Fisher Fami-
ly 1682 to 1896* (Philadelphia 1896), pp. 9-14,
twice categorically states that John Fisher, his
wife Margaret (probably born a Hindle), and at least
the two eldest children, came on the *Welcome*. His
descendant, Joshua Fisher (1707-1783), wrote about
1762: "My grand father, John Fisher, removed from
Clithero in Lancashire, Old England, in the year
1682, with all his children to Philadelphia." On 22
2nd mo. 1839 William Logan Fisher, grandson of the
said Joshua, published his grandfather's account in
a 24-page Fisher Genealogy, not having a title-page,[1]
and amplified the statement somewhat: "John Fisher,
my great great grandfather, accompanied William Penn
in his first voyage to America, October 1682." In
1929 Sophia Cadwallader edited [she calls herself
"arranger"] the *Recollections of Joshua Francis
Fisher* in which on page 4 we read: "My ancestors
of the name of Fisher emigrated from Yorkshire in
the year 1681" [sic].   List B alleges as proof of
the Fishers' presence on the *Welcome* "papers in the
possession of Mr. Thomas Gilpin of Philadelphia."
Mrs. Isaac H. Shelly, when secretary of the Welcome
Society, informed me that the "proof" submitted in
support of an application was "partly taken from a
Family Bible and partly from a family tree by Thomas
Gilpin."

An article[2] in the *Morning News* of Wilmington, Delaware, 31 Aug. 1967, p. 20, concerning the house of John Fisher's son Thomas, at Cool Spring, Sussex County, Delaware, says that Thomas Fisher was private secretary to William Penn but we have seen no evidence of that. The article says the house is 239 years old and also that John Fisher and wife Margaret arrived at New Castle on the *Welcome* on 24 Oct. 1682.

Our John Fisher was a glazier and may well have been the John Fisher in a dispute at Philadelphia Monthly Meeting, 1 4th mo. 1685,[3] but was hardly the John Fisher received at the same meeting on certificate from Pardsaye Crag Monthly Meeting dated 26 3rd 1700, who was probably the father of a Sarah Fisher married at Philadelphia Meeting House, 12 2nd mo. 1716, to Joseph Taylor; of a John Fisher who married there, 30 3rd mo. 1708, Mary Hodge, daughter of Henry; and of Hannah Fisher, daughter of John and Sarah Fisher, buried 16 5th mo. 1714.

The will of our John Fisher is dated 6 Feb. 1685/6 and was probated 30 April 1685,[4] and names wife Margaret, eldest son Thomas, other sons John and James; daughters Rachell, Sarah, Allis (youngest), Annie Adkins (wife of Samuel); also mentions Thomas Scott; executors: wife Margaret, eldest son Thomas; witnesses: William Emmott, Richard Coore [Turner reads as Richard RC Coon], Anna Dougdull.

At a Provincial Council Meeting, 25 Sept. 1688, Margaret ffisher of ye Co. of Sussex had indicted one John Barker for Theft of 3 head of cattle from her and her son Thomas.[5]

The Blackwell Rent Roll of 1689 shows a John ffisher in reight of Mary Smith, owner of an old purchase lot of 51 feet, 2/- for five years, on Walnut Street.[6] This is probably our man but what the connection with Mary Smith was we do not know.

Warrants and Surveys show the following:

2:46 f.   By warrant dated 21 1st mo. 1683, surveyed 28 1st mo. 1683 to John Fisher, purchaser of 250 acres, lot bounded on north by Walnut Street, west by Robert Holgate, east by 3rd Street, No. 115.

2:29   Surveyed to Edmund Cartlidge by virtue of warrant 2 5th mo. 1683, surveyed 14 5th 1683, lot in city, bounded north by Walnut Street, etc. east by Robert Holgate, recorded 3 3rd mo. 1688, No. 63, Cart-

lidge declared on 10 7th mo. 1683 that
he had sold to John Fisher.

6:31   Warrant 25 11th mo. 1683, surveyed 24 3rd
mo. 1684 to John Fisher, 300 acres in
Philadelphia County, not identified,
250 acres on old purchase, 50 acres on
new purchase, bounded by Henry Jones
and by Company land, recorded 25 3rd mo.
1688.

Another John Fisher obtained land in 1733-4 (*ibid.*
2:174, 9:49, 51; 5:106).

Still another John Fisher, of Hirsington, is
shown as a servant sailing to Pennsylvania on the
Maryland Merchant, 15 Oct. 1684.[7]

The probability is that the Fishers came on the
Lamb on which ship came Charles Lee, also of Clith-
eroe.

The son Thomas[8] is said to have been born in 1669,
and he married at Lewes, Delaware, in 1692, Margery
Maude, daughter of Joshua Maude by Elizabeth (Chorley) (Rowden) Maude who was afterwards the second
wife of Dr. Thomas Wynne,[9] the *Welcome* passenger.
As Elizabeth Wynne was almost certainly also on the
ship, her descendants in the Fisher family would
thus have a *Welcome* line even if the Fishers were
themselves not on the vessel. This would explain
how there may have been a persistent tradition in
the Fisher family that their ancestors came on the
famous ship, as it would be an easy error to transfer the claim from the Wynne ancestors to the Fishers.

The will of Thomas Fisher is dated 17 Nov. 1713
with date of probate not recorded.[10] It names son
Jabez Maude Fisher [who married Sarah -----]; son
Joshua Fisher [born 1707, died 1 Feb. 1783; married
Sarah Rowland]; daughter Margaret Fisher [married
Joseph Booth Jr.]; two daughters Margery [who married James Miers, son of John and Mary (Haworth)
Miers, and had Esther, wife of Charles Draper; Mary,
wife, in succession, of John Clarke and Andrew Collins; Sarah, wife of Nehemiah Draper; and Elizabeth
wife of Jonathan Manlove] and Hester Fisher; uncle
John Hindle, son of Bryan Hindle of Clitheroh;
daughter Elizabeth Fisher [who married Daniel Eyre
of Virginia and died without issue]. The executrix
was the wife Margery who by 8 2nd mo. 1717[11] had
become Margery Green; witnesses: Cornelius Wiltbanck, Richard Williams, John Lupercues or Lukecues,

depending on which abstract of the will is followed. The Sussex Calendar abstract reads the name of the son as James but the one in *Publications of the Genealogical Society of Pennsylvania* calls him Jabez Maude Fisher, and he inherits the island called Bright's Island which had been conveyed to his parents in February 1683 by his grandmother Elizabeth Wynne.

Jabez Maude Fisher made his will 13 Sept. 1742[12] and names wife Sarah, sons Joshua, Edward, Finwick Fisher; daughters Margaret, Elizabeth, Sarah Fisher; executors: wife Sarah and brother Joshua Fisher; codicil dated 30 Sept. 1742, probated 8 Dec. 1742. The identity of the wife Sarah has not been investigated but the Fenwick family of New Jersey should be examined for her origin, though it is probable that she was not born a Fenwick but was related to the Fenwicks.

The other son of Thomas and Margery (Maude) Fisher, Joshua, was born in 1707, died in February 1783. He married 27 July 1733 Sarah Rowland, born 6 Dec. 1716, died 4 Jan. 1772, daughter of Thomas and Sarah (Miers) Rowland. He was first a hatter, then a surveyor, and importer.[13] He had a son Thomas, born 6 May 1741, died 6 Sept. 1810, married 17 3rd mo. 1772, Sarah Logan, born 6 11th mo. 1751, died 25 1st mo. 1796, this couple being parents of Hannah Logan Smith, born 6 11th mo. 1777, died 25 6th mo. 1846, married 10 6th mo. 1810, James Smith.[14]

Of John Fisher of the second generation Ann Wharton Smith says that he married Elizabeth Light[15] and had a son John whose first wife was named Catherine, his second Grace Lloyd; a son James who "settled west of Harrisburg"; a son William who likewise "settled west of Harrisburg"; and a daughter Ann who married Enoch Cummings.

NOTES

[1]According to KPC 17 it was Hannah Logan Smith (on whom see p.187) who caused this genealogy to be printed.

[2]I owe my knowledge of this article to the kindness of George Valentine Massey II.

[3]PGSP 1:284, 286.

[4]See Historical Society of Pennsylvania AM 2013, 63-65; abstracted also PGSP 12:24 f., and in C. H. B. Turner, *Some Records of Sussex County, Delaware* (Philadelphia 1909), p. 136; more recently in SC 10.

[5]Turner, *op. cit.* 35.

[6]PGM 23:75.

[7]*Bristol and America, A Record of the First Set-tlers in the Colonies of North America 1654-1685* (London no date).

[8]See Ann Wharton Smith, *op. cit.*, 14-20.

[9]On Margery Maude see the sketch devoted to her sister below, also the sketch of Elizabeth Wynne, their mother.

[10]PGSP 12:24 f.; SC 23.   [11]2 PA 19:678.

[12]SC 48.

[13]See Francis J. Dallett cited in the Elizabeth Wynne sketch.

[14]KPC 17.   [15]Ann Wharton Smith, p. 20.

FISHER, JOSEPH	*disproved*
FISHER, ELIZABETH, his wife	*disproved*
FISHER, MARTHA, his daughter	*disproved*
FISHER, MARY, his daughter	*disproved*
FISHER, MOSES, his son	*disproved*

These names appear only on List X. The truth is that Joseph Fisher registered himself, his wife, his daughters Martha and Mary, and his sons Moses and Joseph, as having crossed on the *Lion* of Liverpoole, arriving 14 8th mo. 1683. Note that List X has overlooked the son Joseph who not only was registered in Philadelphia Arrivals but is afterwards recorded in Pennsylvania, as son Moses is not. With the family were also eleven servants, as follows:

Edward Lancaster	4 years	loose	14	8mo	1687
Wm Robertson	4 years	loose	14	8mo	1687
Ed. Doyle	4 years	loose	14	8mo	1687
Ben: Clift	4 years	loose	14	8mo	1687
Tho: Tearewood	4 years	loose	14	8mo	1687
Robt Kilcarth	8 years	loose	14	8mo	1691
Peter Long	2 years	loose	14	8mo	1685
Phill: Packer	4 years	loose	14	8mo	1687
Wm Conduit	4 years	loose	14	8mo	1687
Mary Toole	4 years	loose	14	8mo	1687
Eliz: Johnson	4 years	loose	14	8mo	1687

Each of these eleven servants will be discussed in the alphabetical position.

Joseph Fisher had recorded in Philadelphia Arrivals the fact that he was late of Stillorgin near Dublin in Ireland but was "borne in in [sic] Elton Cheshire in old England." It is also significant

that the entry of Joseph Fisher yeoman is just below the entry of Robert Turner of Dublin in Ireland
merch[t], who came on the same ship with his daughter
Martha and seventeen servants. It seems probable
that Joseph Fisher was the brother of Martha, second
wife of Robert Turner, who had died in Ireland shortly before the voyage. Note that he had a daughter
Martha and that Martha Turner is said to have come
from Cheshire.

Though only a yeoman, this Joseph Fisher, who can
have had no connection with John Fisher of Lancashire in the preceding sketch, was an affluent one,
as the number of his servants shows. He also made a
First Purchase of 5,000 acres in Group 45, the only
other person in the group being Robert Turner, also
with 5,000 acres.[1] On Blackwell's Rent Roll of 1689
Joseph Fisher is shown as owner of an Old Purchase
lot of 102 feet, 5 shillings for five years.[2] He
settled in Dublin Township, Philadelphia County, now
Montgomery County. On 13-14 2nd mo. 1702 his tract
of 4420 acres was now found to be 5062 acres, and
he was charged £2/14 for the overplus.[3] On 4 3rd
mo. 1702 Joseph Fisher and others complained about a
road in Dublin Township and about 500 acres in the
Township.[4] As executor of the estate of Thomas
Tearwood, his erstwhile servant, he is recorded on
28-29 Xbr 1702 as having sold land.[5]

He made his will in Dublin Township, 12 Dec. 1711,
probated 21 Jan. 1714,[6] naming his son Joseph sole
devisee and executor; if dead, then to his eldest
son, if any, and if none, then to his daughter Isabell. Mary Archer and Martha Ball are called "sister's daughters." Witnesses were Daniel Derio,
John Swift, Edward Farmar. The son Joseph made a
nuncupative will in Dublin Township, 23 Oct. 1717,
probated 2 Dec. 1717.[7] He names wife Mary and brother Edward Farmar; children: Isabell, Mary, Martha;
witnesses: John Swift, Edward Farmar.

The other children of Joseph Fisher Sr. have not
been found of record.

Lewis D. Cook's excellent article on the Farmar
family[8] says that Joseph Fisher the younger married
in 1709-10 Mary (Swift) Morgan, widow of Evan Morgan
of Dublin, and as the will names wife Mary, she was
undoubtedly the wife married seven years previously.
Mr. Cook identifies the Edward Farmar of this will
as the youngest son of Major Jasper Farmar and by

his second wife Mary, the widow Batsford. This Edward died testate on 3 Nov. 1745 aet. 73, buried in the original St. Thomas's Episcopal Church, Whitemarsh. The will mentions no wife but from 18 May 1714[9] to 30 Nov. 1731[10] Edward's wife was named Rachel, and presumably before and after that period, as we are relying here on deeds in which Rachel is joined with Edward, but the marriage has not been found of record.

Farmar and Fisher could have been brothers-in-law if Farmar had married Fisher's sister. In this case, Fisher had sisters Mary and Martha who were living in 1683 but are not found of record later, and specifically are not mentioned in their father's will in 1714. Farmar could have married one of them by 1694--his first child was born in 1695--and then have lost her. Second, Fisher could have married one of Farmar's sisters, and again we have two, a half sister named Katherine and a full sister named Sarah, both recorded in 1685 but not found thereafter. There is, of course, the third possibility: Farmer and Fisher could have married sisters. In this case, we have evidence to show that from 1710 Joseph Fisher had a wife named Mary Swift. Whether Mr. Cook investigated the Swift family to see whether there was a Rachel available to marry Edward Farmar, I do not know.

NOTES

[1]1 PA 1:45.   [2]PGM 23:72   [3]2 PA 19:300.
[4]2 PA 19:303.   [5]2 PA 19:344f. [6]PhW D:24.
[7]PhW D:89.   [8]PGM 21:89-124.[9]PhD E7-9, 222.
[10]PhD F-5, 383. Mr. Cook located another Edward Farmar whom he was unable to place in the family, namely, one who d. intestate, bur. from Christ Church, Philadelphia, 17 Oct. 1755, who had married there, 2 June 1734, Hannah Morgan, died testate in 1765, daughter of William and Mary (-----) Morgan. This man seems too late to have been Joseph Foster's brother-in-law.

FITZWATER, THOMAS		*proved*
+FITZWATER, MARY CHENEY, first wife		*proved*
FITZWATER, THOMAS, son		*proved*
FITZWATER, GEORGE, son		*proved*
+*FITZWATER, JOSIAH, son		*proved*
+*FITZWATER, MARY, daughter		*proved*

Six Fitzwaters started the voyage to America but
only the father, Thomas, and the two sons, Thomas
and George, lived to reach Pennsylvania, the mother
and the daughter and one son having succumbed to the
smallpox at sea. The family appears, of course, on
all lists, Thomas being called Fitzwalter on List E,
and it is probable that this was the original spelling meaning "son of Walter." The wife Mary appears
on Lists A, B, C, D, E, F, G, H, I, M, O, Q, U, V,
X, Y and Z but not on Lists J, K, L, N, R, T and U,
although perhaps included on List S. The "children"
are included on Lists J, K (here spelled "childern"),
L, N, P, S and T, and as "family" on U and W. They
are specifically named Thomas, George, Josiah and
Mary, on Lists A, B, C, D, E, F, G, H, I, M, O, Q,
V, X, Y and Z.

The proof is in the following entry in Bucks Arrivals where the information is set down in three
columns too wide for the margins of this book:[1]

first column

Thomas ffitzwater of | Hanworth in the County
of | Midlesex [near Hampton | Court[2]] Husband-
man | Arived in this River | in the welcom of
London | the master Rob[t] Green | away the 28
day of the | 8th month 1682 |

Mary his wife and Josiah & Mary | his children
dyed coming over Sea.

second column: children's names

Thomas & | George his | Children

third column: servants' names

John Ottey to serue | 6 yeares from his | ar-
rival to be found | with necessarys dure | ing
the terme & | Land att outcome.

THE FITZWATERS[3]

The quotation just given shows the residence of
the Fitzwaters in England as Hanworth, Middlesex,
which is placed near Hampton Court in the Doylestown version of Bucks Arrivals, but Mrs. Balderston
says[4] that when he loaded on the *Welcome*, 27 July
1682, 4 cwt of iron, 4 cwt of nails, duty 2s, he was
of Kingston-on-Thames. He apparently applied for a
Friends certificate of removal and one such was
filed with Middletown Monthly Meeting in Bucks County, dated 11 7th mo. 1682, a day when the *Welcome*

was at sea, so this must have followed the family
to America. The certificate says he was of Lammark,
Middlesex, husbandman, and includes four children.
Mr. Colket says that Fitzwater was an active member
of Longford Monthly Meeting. Neither Lammark nor
Longford appears on eighteenth-century maps but Hanworth, Hampton Court and Kingston-on-Thames are all
in the same neighborhood.

Thomas Fitzwater married, first, at Devonshire
House Monthly Meeting, London, 8 6th mo. 1672, Mary
Cheney of Hodgson near London, and she died at sea,
mother of all the four children; second, presented
to Philadelphia Monthly Meeting by Ellin Claypoole
the elder, 1st intentions, 1 2nd mo. 1684,[5] when he
was not of Philadelphia Monthly Meeting [he was then
living in Bucks County], also discussed 6 3rd mo.
1684,[6] 2nd intentions, 3 4th mo. 1684,[7] Elizabeth
Palmer, widow of George Palmer of Nonesuch, Parish
of Ewell, Surrey, whose will was signed on the ship
Isabella Anne Katherine,[8] 4 Sept. 1682 (date of probate not recorded). This will leaves 1000 acres to
wife Elizabeth Palmer, and 800 acres each to daughter
Elizabeth Palmer and sons George, John, Thomas and
William Palmer; to the wife all moveable goods; executors: wife Elizabeth Palmer and son George; witnesses: Thomas Hutson, William Clarke, Enoch Coose
(?). George Palmer was a First Purchaser of 1000
acres in Group 52,[9] and so far as is known to me,
had only this land--in any case, a man who died at
sea would have had no opportunity to acquire land
afterwards--and this error in the will in disposing
of 5000 acres when he owned but 1000 is doubtless
one of the causes for the difficulties between the
widow and both of her sons-in-law, as we shall see.
The second wife, Elizabeth (-----)(Palmer) Fitzwater, by whom there were no Fitzwater children, died
30 7th mo. 1720, administration being granted 12
Nov. 1720 to William Palmer of the County of Philadelphia, millwright.[10]

Elizabeth Palmer, the step-daughter called the
daughter-in-law in Thomas Fitzwater's will shortly
to be described, had leave to marry 29 2nd mo. 1687,
Isaac Ricketts, snuffmaker, and did marry him on 31
2nd mo. 1687 at the Philadelphia Meeting House.[11]
He was buried 26 4th mo. 1692,[12] leaving a son John
born 13 11th mo. 1689, buried 3 10th mo. 1712, a
locksmith. As stated above, Elizabeth Palmer is
mentioned in the will of her stepfather but is then

called Elizabeth Jackson,   As Elizabeth Ricketts of
Philadelphia she married at the house of John Parson
in Philadelphia, 2 8th mo. 1695, Ralph Jackson, and
she died 26 5th mo. 1704, he on 27 10th mo. 1725.
Being long dead, she was not the Elizabeth Jackson
who was administratrix of Benjamin Chambers in the
year 1715.[13] Ralph Jackson had brought a certificate from the Monthly Meeting at West River, Maryland, dated 1 5th mo. 1692, recorded 29 5th mo.
1692.[14]

Thomas Fitzwater and the two husbands of his step-
daughter, Isaac Ricketts and Ralph Jackson, had a
great deal of trouble with Thomas's second wife
Elizabeth, as the following entries in vol. 1 of
the minutes of Philadelphia Monthly Meeting will
show:

29 1st mo. 1695 at Robert Ewer's (p. 176):
Several friends being dissatisfied that Thomas
Fitzwater and his wife live apart, therefore
Thomas Fitzwater is desired to get an house in
order to Entertain her, and that she may have
no Excuse to stay from him.

30 8th mo. 1696 (p. 197): This meeting
taking into their consideration the Ill president [sic] of Thomas Fitzwater and his wife in
living apart from each other, desires Thomas
Duckett & George Gray to speak to them that
they may live together, & that Thomas may provide an house or room to entertain her in, and
return their answers to the next monthly meeting.

29 11th mo. 1696/7 (p. 197): Thomas Fitzwater appeared at this meeting & signifyed to
friends that he would Endeavour to get a room
or two furnished in 2 or 3 months time, to receive his wife, if she will then come to dwell
with him, and to take off the reproach whereby
Truth and friends suffer.

27 11th mo. 1698 (p. 200): Thomas Fitzwater
laid before this meeting that he with John
Goodson & William Southeby went to his wife In
order that the said Thomas and his wife might
be Reconciled and live together, but could not
prevail with her; whereupon this meeting desires
Griffith Owen, Thomas Duckett, Nicholas Walln,
and James Fox to Endeavour to bring them to a

reconciliation, and that they do for the future
live together in Love, and likewise to desire
some women friends to be assisting in this Concern.

> *24 12th mo. 1698/9 (p. 230):* The friends that
> were appointed the last meeting to Endeavour a
> reconciliation between Thomas Fitzwater and his
> wife makes [sic] report that they are in hopes
> they will live in Love together for the future.

This seems to be the last entry on the matter and
in the following October Thomas Fitzwater died.
Elizabeth also had, as stated, a controversy with
her successive sons-in-law:

> *30 4th mo. 1689 (p. 108):* Isaac Ricketts laid
> before this meeting some difference between him
> and his mother Elizabeth Fitzwater. The meeting
> considering thereof, Requested William Southerby,
> Francis Rawles, Benjn Chambers & Richard Whit-
> field to endeavour to put an end to the said
> difference, and if not Ended, then to request her
> to come to the next monthly meeting.

> *25 5th mo. 1689 (p. 110):* There being a dif-
> ference between Isaac Ricketts and his mother-in-
> law, Elizabeth Fitzwater, laid before the meeting,
> they having considered the matter, she being wil-
> ling to let him have his part in the liberty land,
> upon which the meeting desires the said Isaac
> to forbear for the present, and leave the matter
> till a further opportunity.

> *30 6th mo. 1689 (p. 111):* The difference be-
> tween Isaac Ricketts and his mother was again
> heard at this meeting, she not being here. The
> meeting desires Robert Turner, John Goodson,
> William Southerby, Alexander Beardsley, Richard
> Whitefield & Samuel Carpenter to speak with her
> in order to the ending of the said difference
> between them, which if they cannot perform, then
> to advise her to come to the next Quarterly meet-
> ing.

As stated above, Isaac Ricketts died in 1692, so it
should not surprise us to learn that the next entry
concerns his successor as husband to Elizabeth Palmer, Ralph Jackson:

> *29 11th mo. 1696/7 (p. 200):* Ralph Jackson
> brought in a Complaint to this meeting against

his wife's mother for refusing to let her [his
wife] have her right, according to her father's
will, and friends desire John Goodson, Thomas
Duckett & David Lloyd to speak to Elizabeth
Fitzwater and Endeavour to get her to Comply with
her former husband's will, and bring her answer
to the next monthly meeting.

   26 12th mo. 1696/7 (p. 202): The friends appointed to speak to Elizabeth Fitzwater have accordingly done it and return her answer that she
thinks herself not well used by Ralph Jackson's
bringing it to the meeting before he had given
her Gospell order, which this meeting advises
the said Ralph to perform before he proceeds any
further therein.

   In Joseph Besse's famous *Sufferings* 1:366 is a
long passage concerning persecution of Quakers in
1660, by Richard Brown, Lord Mayor of London, which
states that the names of said Quakers are included
in the index with reference to this page.   Thomas
Fitzwater's name so appears.   He represented Philadelphia in the General Assembly of February 1683
and again in 1688, and in 1690 he represented New
Castle.   In 1688 he was coroner of Philadelphia
County.[15]   On 3 7th mo. 1687 he was appointed to
represent Philadelphia at the Quarterly Meeting.
On 29 8th mo. 1686 he sent a man to work on the
meeting house roof, credit to be given for this
man's time to the meeting house.   On 29 11th mo.
1691 at Philadelphia Monthly Meeting he made an attack on the theology of George Keith and he was ad-
monished to forbear, but on 26 3rd mo. 1692 various
Friends supported his testimony against Keith, and
among them Benjamin Chambers.
   The Blackwell Rent Roll of 1689[16] shows Tho:
Fitzwater as owner of a 49-foot lot on Sassafras
Street, term 5 years, no statement as to whether
this was an old or new purchase, and amount of payment omitted.   On 7 5th mo. 1694 a deed for 100
acres with highway allowance, on the south branch
of Cropwell River, in New Jersey, was granted to
Thomas Fitzwater.[17]
   Thomas Fitzwater died 6 Oct. 1699, not, as Mary
Thomas Seaman has it, 6 August--she has obviously
misread the Old Style Quaker date.   He left an undated will[18] probated 2 Nov. 1699, in which he mentions only sons Thomas and George and daughter-in-

law [stepdaughter] Elizabeth Jackson, omitting all
reference to his second wife who was living; witnesses: Anthony Morris, George Gray, William Southbee.

Issue: surname Fitzwater, all by first wife
1 i.   Thomas, b. England, 3 3rd mo. 1673, d. 1748.
2 ii. George, b. England, 28 8th mo. 1674, d. in
       Philadelphia, 19 3rd mo. 1750.
iii. Josiah, b. England, 28 11th mo. 1676, d. at
     sea, 1682.
iv. Mary, b. England, 6 11th mo. 1678, d. at
     sea, 1682.

1. Thomas Fitzwater, eldest child of Thomas Fitzwater the elder by his first wife Mary Cheney, was
born in England, 3 3rd mo. 1673, came to Pennsylvania with the family on the *Welcome* in 1682, and
died in 1748, probably in Upper Dublin Township,
then Philadelphia, now Montgomery County. He married twice, both wives being named Mary. The first
wife was not discovered by Clarence Vernon Roberts,
able as he was. She was undoubtedly Mary Foster,
third daughter of Allen Foster of Lower Dublin Township, Philadelphia County, who was a First Purchaser
of 1100 acres in Group 52,[19] by his wife Lydia.
The will of Allen Foster dated 30 July 1725,
probated 13 Sept. 1725,[20] names as third daughter
Mary Fitchwater, and also mentions son-in-law Thomas
Fitchwater. No other Thomas Fitzwater is available
at the right time to be this son-in-law. This wife
was the mother of all the children. Thomas married,
second, 2nd intentions at Abington Monthly Meeting,
25 10th mo. 1732, Mary (Potts) Tyson, widow of
Matthew or Matthias Tyson (son of Reynier), whom
she had married, first, 29 1st mo. 1708, 2nd intentions at Abington. According to Mr. Roberts, her
father was John Potts who came to America as an or-
phan, and this, I think, is correct, but Mary Thomas
Seaman says that Mary was daughter of David and
Alice (Croasdale) Potts, and that Alice had come to
America with her father on the *Welcome*.[21] I have
disposed of this *Welcome* claim in the Croasdale
sketch. David and Mary (Croasdale) Potts did have
a daughter Mary but she has contrary history.[22]
Mary (Potts)(Tyson) Fitzwater is called Mary Fitz-
walter in the will of John Tyson of Philadelphia
County, yeoman, dated 28 Feb. 1741/2, probated 10
April 1743,[23] which also names brothers Reynier,
Isaac and Matthew; sisters Margaretta Howell, Mary

Lewis and Elizabeth Tyson.[24]

The will of Thomas Fitzwater of the City of Philadelphia, yeoman, dated 16 Nov. 1742/3, probated 8 April 1748,[25] mentions wife Mary, children John, Thomas, George, Hannah, Sarah, Deborah Lucans, son-in-law John Davis; executor: John Fitzwater; witnesses: George Fitzwater [testator's brother] and William Coleman and Hannah Coleman [son-in-law and daughter of said George].

This Thomas Fitzwater was an executor of the will of William Rennells of Horsham, co. Philadelphia, dated 9 April 1730/1, probated 30 April 1730,[26] and was called friend in that of Sarah Ironmonger of Philadelphia County, widow, 29 Jan. 1730/1, probated 26 April 1731.[27] He and his son Thomas Jr. also witnessed the will of Will Robeson of Philadelphia County, 24 2nd mo. 1746.[28] On this last occasion, the elder Thomas made his mark, probably an indication of age or illness.[29]

Issue: surname Fitzwater, all by first wife
3   i.   Thomas, gets only 5/- in father's will.
   ii.   Sarah, gets only 5/- in father's will; m. at First Presbyterian Church, Philadelphia, 23 Dec. 1718, William Robinson or Robeson, whose will is cited above on this page.
  iii.   Martha, not mentioned in father's will but her husband in called son-in-law and gets 5/-; m. at First Presbyterian Church, Philadelphia, 29 Dec. 1729, John Davis. As he had overlooked this marriage, Mr. Roberts could not explain Davis's presence in the will.
  iv.   Deborah, gets 5/- in father's will; m. at Abington, 26 6th mo. 1734, John Luckens; called Deborah Lucans in father's will.
4   v.   John, b. 29 1st mo. 1715, d. 28 March 1794.
5 vi.   George, bequeathed £120 in Pennsylvania currency in father's will.
  vii.   Hannah, mentioned in the will; m. First Presbyterian Church, Philadelphia, 16 June 1740, Robert McCurdy.

2. George Fitzwater, second son of Thomas Fitzwater the elder by his first wife Mary Cheney, was born in England on 28 8th mo. 1674, came with the family on the *Welcome* in 1682, and died in Philadelphia, 19 3rd mo. 1750.[30] Though he was a prom-

inent merchant in Philadelphia and the grandfather
of a Signer of the Declaration of Independence,
family accounts have neglected him because, though
he had sons, none survived him and his descendants
all stem from daughters.[31]

He married under the care of Philadelphia Monthly Meeting, 10 10th mo. 1707 (1st intentions, 28
9th mo. 1707), Mary Hardiman who died 19 8th mo.
1731, daughter of Abraham Hardiman (died 19 9th mo.
1699) by his first wife Dyana (buried 27 8th mo.
1697). Abraham Hardiman's will dated 28 6th mo.
1699, probated 10 Sept. 1702,[32] mentions wife Rebecca, mother of only one child, and the children
are Mary, Hannah, Deborah and Rebecca, all minors.[33]
Abraham Hardiman was doubtless related to Hannah
Hardiman of near Haverford West, co. Pembroke, who
came to Pennsylvania in 1683 as a spinster and married Samuel Carpenter of Philadelphia, merchant, who
in 1693 had the highest assessment (£1300) on the
tax roll.[34]

Mary Fitzwater was mentioned as friend in the
will of Abraham Carpenter of Philadelphia, merchant,
dated 26 March 1708.[35] She appears to have been
the mother of all the Fitzwater children, and, so
far as has been discovered, the only wife of George
Fitzwater, though Mary Thomas Seaman claims that he
married, for second wife, a daughter of George Claypoole. This is certainly wrong. George Claypoole's
third wife was Deborah Hardiman, a sister of Mary
Hardiman, George Fitzwater's wife. The men were
brothers-in-law. Furthermore, as we have shown in
the Claypoole sketch (pp. 118 f.), all of the issue
of George Claypoole by his three wives died young,
and his widow Deborah lived a long time after him,
never remarrying.

As a merchant, George Fitzwater appears in a
considerable number of Philadelphia wills as executor, trustee, or friend, from 1711 to 1740, after
which his name disappears from this kind of record,
suggesting retirement.[36]

George Fitzwater of the City of Philadelphia,
Gent., signed his own will 11 Oct. 1748, probated
15 June 1750.[37] The instrument is curious in that
he names first his sons-in-law and then his daughters, five of each, but the daughters are not named
in the order of their respective husbands. The
sons-in-law are Joseph House, Isaac Griffits, William Coleman, Francis Richardson and Joseph Morris;

the daughters: Hannah, Mary, Martha, Sarah and Elizabeth; then the grandchildren: George Clymer; Phebe
and George Morris; Mary and Elizabeth Griffiths;
Peregrine and Mary Hogg; Mary, Grace and Hannah Richardson; executors: William and Hannah Coleman, Francis and Mary Richardson; witnesses: Thomas Hopkinson, Tench Francis Jr., Thomas Biles.

The order of birth is quite uncertain so for this
reason we list the dead children first.

    Issue: surname Fitzwater
    i.   Abraham, d. 12 1st mo. 1723/4, named for
        maternal grandfather.
    ii. George, d. 1 7th mo. 1718, named for father.
    iii. Thomas, d. 22 10th mo. 1725, named for uncle.
6 iv. Deborah, bur. 6 May 1740.
7 v.   Rebecca, d. 22 7th mo. 1744.
8 vi. Hannah, d. after 1769.
9 vii. Mary, d. 30 9th mo. 1771.
10 viii.Martha.
11 ix. Sarah, d. 19 7th mo. 1764.

3. Thomas Fitzwater, son, probably eldest, of
Thomas Fitzwater (Thomas) by his first wife Mary Foster, received from his father only a token bequest
of 5/-. It is probable that he already had had his
portion. He died in Whitpaine Township, then Philadelphia, now Montgomery County, yeoman, leaving a
will signed by mark and dated 24 Sept. 1761, probated 14 Oct. 1761,[38] in which he names wife Rosannah and son Thomas as executors; children: John,
Thomas, William, Mary, Martha, Catherine, Deborah,
Joseph, Jeremiah; witnesses: William Dehaven, Frederick Kern, Jno Robinson. In her petition of 1762
the widow says that her four children were all then
under seven years of age. She married, second, ca.
1763, John McCommons or McCummins. Rosannah was,
of course, a second wife to Thomas Fitzwater, and
we derive the name of the first wife, Martha, from
the birth record of her daughter Mary, but neither
of Thomas's marriages are recorded and we do not
know the surnames of his wives. It is possible
that Rosannah married, third, ----- Karn.[39]

    Issue: surname Fitzwater
     by first wife Martha
    i.   John, left will dated 1791, probated 1794,
        which shows that he had a daughter Sarah,
        wife of Abraham Lukens; executor was
        Matthew Fitzwater.

ii. Thomas, d. 1797, of Whitpaine Township; m.
     Sarah ----- who d. 1822. There is nothing
     on this man in the Tyson-Fitzwater Genea-
     logy.
          Issue: surname Fitzwater
     1. George, b. 11 April 1759; ca. 1799 to
        Jerusalem, Ontario Co., N.Y., thence
        to Milo, Yates Co., N.Y.; d. 1842 aet.
        82; wife d. 1823 aet. 75. In 1944
        Maude C. Reno deposited in the Iowa
        Historical Library in Des Moines a
        typed Fitzwater Family which traces
        further from this couple.
     2. John.
     3. William.
     4. Thomas.
     5. David.
     6. Rachel.
     7. Mary.
iii. William, living 1773.
iv. Mary, m. 1 May 1753 Matthias or Matthew Ty-
     son, son of Matthew and Mary (Potts) Ty-
     son.
          Issue: surname Tyson
     1. Martha, b. 7 4th mo. 1756.
     2. Mary, b. 11 8th mo. 1757.
     3. Grace, d. unm., March/April 1809.
     4. Thomas, living 1809.
     5. Priscilla, m. ----- Butler.
     6. Elizabeth.
v.   Martha, m. Abijah Wright, both living 1766.
     by second wife Rosannah
vi. Catherine, b. ca. 1755.
vii. Deborah, b. ca. 1757, m. ----- Moyer and
     was living 1784.
viii.Joseph, b. ca. 1759, living 1794.
ix. Jeremiah, b. ca. 1761.

4. John Fitzwater, son of Thomas Fitzwater (Thomas) by first wife Mary Foster, was born 29 1st mo.
1715 and died 28 March 1794. He married 31 3rd mo.
1742 his stepsister Elizabeth Tyson, daughter of
Matthias and Mary (Potts) Tyson. He was executor
of his father's will in 1748, witnessed that of
John Johnson dated 19 Oct. 1760.

     Issue: surname Fitzwater
i.   Thomas.
ii. Matthew.

```
        iii.  John.
        iv.   John.
        v.    Mary.
        vi.   Sarah.
```

5. George Fitzwater, son of Thomas Fitzwater
(Thomas) by his first wife Mary Foster, was bequeathed in his father's will the large sum of £120
whereas the others had to be content with five shillings. The explanation is probably that the others
had already had their portion, he had not. He married at the First Presbyterian Church, Philadelphia,
6 10th mo. 1739, Mary Walker. He left a will signed
in Upper Dublin Township, then Philadelphia, now
Montgomery County, dated 14 8th mo. 1760, probated
3 Dec. 1760,[40] in which he names his children as
Joseph (executor), Martha, Thomas, Abel, Mary, Ruth
and Elizabeth; witnesses: Peter and Nathan Clever
and John Fitzwater, doubtless his older brother.

```
        Issue: surname Fitzwater
        i.    Joseph.
        ii.   Martha.
        iii.  Thomas.
        iv.   Abel, m. Neshaminy Presbyterian Church, 24
                Dec. 1801, Esther Foster.
        v.    Mary.
        vi.   Ruth.
        vii.  Elizabeth, m., probably, Joshua Tyson.
                Issue: surname Tyson
                1. Maria, b. 11 11th mo. 1796, d. 1797.
                2. Charlotte, b. 1798, d. unm.
                3. Matilda, b. 1800, d. unm. ca. 1850, re-
                    sided with brother-in-law Samuel H.
                    Traquair in Philadelphia.
                4. Edwin, b. 13 11th mo. 1802, d. 19 4th
                    mo. 18    m. Eleonor Hallowell, b. 17
                    11th mo. 1805, d. 7 2nd mo. 1866.
                    Issue: surname Tyson
                    a. Joshua.
                    b. Isaac Alfred.
                    c. Charlotte.
                    d. James Paul.
                    e. Edwin.
                    f. Franklin.
                    g. Mary Elizabeth.
```

6. Deborah Fitzwater, daughter of George Fitzwater (Thomas) by his wife Mary Hardiman, was buried

in Friends Graveyard, Philadelphia, 6 3rd mo. 1740.
She was dismissed by Philadelphia Monthly Meeting
on 27 4th mo. 1735 for marrying out of unity. We
should have expected to find this marriage recorded
in Christ Church registers but it is not there. The
husband was Capt. Christopher Clymer, baptized at
Christ Church, 4 Aug. 1711 aet. 3 days, buried from
Christ Church, 27 July 1746, second son of Richard
and Elizabeth (-----) Clymer. Richard Clymer was a
blockmaker and merchant and was, with his wife Elizabeth, in Philadelphia by 30 July 1710 when their
son John was baptized at Christ Church aet. 6 days,
and they had also Sarah, baptized there, 30 Sept.
1713 aet· 1 month, buried there 19 May 1714, and
Richard, buried 4 Jan. 1715/16, as well as William
and Daniel, mentioned in the will of their uncle,
Capt. William Clymer, buried from Christ Church, 26
April 1751, leaving a will dated 22 March 1749/50,
probated 29 April 1751,[41] in which he names wife
Margaret (died 29 May 1781), no issue, but does name
nephews William, son of late brother Richard; George,
son of late nephew Christopher, and Daniel, son of
Richard; executors: Margaret Clymer and George Willing. The nephew William was probably the William
Clymer Jr. whose son Richard was buried from Christ
Church, 31 July 1744. The father-in-law óf Deborah
Fitzwater, Richard Clymer, made his will 8 July
1734, probated 19 Aug. 1734, in which his wife Elizabeth, who had been buried from Christ Church, 4 July 1733, is naturally not mentioned. The grandfather of Capt. Christopher Clymer was another Christopher Clymer of Bristol, England, whose wife Catherine was still living when her son made his will
on 8 July 1734. Richard's son William married Anne
Judith Roberdeau. In a sketch of the Clymers[42]
Deborah Fitzwater's name in one place is spelled
"Deborah Fitzabeth," an error which may in part be
responsible for Mary Thomas Seaman's incorrect remark that it was Elizabeth Fitzwater who married
Christopher Clymer, though the death of the daughter shown below may have something to do with this
error.

    Issue: surname Clymer
    i.   Elizabeth, bur. Friends Graveyard, Phila-
          delphia, 16 Feb. 1739/40.
13 ii.   George, b. 11 March 1739 [probably 1739/40],
          d. 23 Jan. 1813.

7. Rebecca Fitzwater, daughter of George Fitzwater (Thomas) by his wife Mary Hardiman, died 22
7th mo. 1744. She is not mentioned, therefore, in
her father's will which does, however, name as heirs,
grandchildren Peregrine and Mary Hogg, her children.
Rebecca Hogg late Fitzwater was dismissed by Philadelphia Monthly Meeting for marrying out, 27 4th
mo. 1735. Her husband was probably Thomas Hogg who
was finally of London, mercer. On 27 Aug. 1750[43]
Peregrine and Mary Hogg petitioned the Orphans
Court, as their father was about to take them out
of the country. The claim has been made[44] that
Peregrine was Rebecca's husband and her mother Mary
Fitzwater. As a matter of fact, her mother *was* a
Mary Fitzwater [Mary (Hardiman) Fitzwater] but it
appears that Peregrine and Mary were really Rebecca's children.

Issue: surname Hogg
i.   Peregrine, living 1750, not found later.
ii. Mary, if taken out of the country, she re-
     turned, for she m. as 1st wife, James
     Wharton (John, Thomas, Richard), bur. in
     Philadelphia, 4 May 1785 aet. 53.[45]
iii. Rebecca, d. 4 7th mo. 1747, probably a
     daughter of Thomas and Rebecca.
iv. Thomas, son of Thomas, d. 16 7th mo. 1741.

8. Hannah Fitzwater, daughter of George Fitzwater
(Thomas) by his wife Mary Hardiman, was the first
named of the daughters in her father's will. No
birth or death record has been found but she survived her husband. She married at Philadelphia
Meeting House, 26 11th mo. 1737, William Coleman,
who died 13 1st mo. 1769 aet. 64, son of William
and Rebecca (-----) Coleman. His will[46] calls him
of Philadelphia, merchant, and is dated 26 March
1768, codicil dated 13 Dec. 1768, probated 19 Jan.
1769, and names wife Hannah, mother Rebecca, kinsman George Clymer. Coleman's obituary is in *Pennsylvania Gazette*, 19 Jan. 1769. There is no record
of issue but the Colemans had raised Hannah's nephew
George Clymer, if they had not legally adopted him.

9. Mary Fitzwater, daughter of George Fitzwater
(Thomas) by his wife Mary Hardiman, died 30 9th mo.
1771, and was the second of the daughters named in
her father's will. She married, 30 10th mo. 1742,
Francis Richardson, fourth of the sons-in-law named

in her father's will, born 18 12th mo. 1705/6, buried 2 10th mo. 1782 aet. 76, son of Francis Richardson (Francis, Thomas) by his wife Elizabeth Growdon. On this family see Mary Thomas Seaman, *Thomas
Richardson of South Shields, Durham County, England,
and his Descendants in the United States of America*
(New York 1929), pp. 40-42, #14. The birth dates
below come from Hinshaw's abstracts of Philadelphia
Monthly Meeting records; the other information from
Seaman.

    Issue: surname Richardson
    i.   Mary, b. 13 4th mo. 1743, not in Seaman.
    ii.   Grace, b. 6 2nd mo. 1745, m. Dr. Jonathan
          Potts and had Mary, Edward, Francis.
    iii. Frances, b. 15 3rd mo. 1746, m. Clement
          Biddle and d.s.p. Hinshaw spells the
          name Francis.
    iv.   George, b. 27 2nd mo. 1747, not in Seaman
          or in grandfather Fitzwater's will.
    v.   Hannah, b. 4 2nd mo. 1748; m. Samuel Fair-
          lamb, and had John, Francis, Maria, Sam-
          uel.
    vi.   Elizabeth, b. 29 3rd mo. 1749, not in Sea-
          man.
    vii. Thomas, b. 16 5th mo. 1750, d. 20 6th mo.
          1752, not in Seaman.
    viii. John, d. 6 1st mo. 1752.
    ix.   Deborah, b. 29 8th mo. 1753; m. Joseph
          Mifflin and had Lloyd, Thomas, Mary, Deb-
          orah, Hannah, Rebecca, Joseph.

    10. Martha Fitzwater, daughter of George Fitz-
water (Thomas) by his wife Mary Hardiman, is named
third among the daughters in her father's will. She
married, as first wife, 18 12th mo. 1741/2, Joseph
Morris, the fifth named of the sons-in-law in her
father's will, born 10 1st mo. 1714/15, buried 1
7th mo. 1785 aet. 71, son of Anthony Morris (Anthony, Anthony) by his wife Phoebe Guest. His will
calls him of the City of Philadelphia, merchant,
dated 28 Aug. 1784, probated 19 July 1785,[47] names
second wife Hannah, and the children: Phebe, James
(who had Joseph and Hannah), and Martha Mifflin
(who had Elizabeth and Thomas). Joseph Morris had
married, second, at Philadelphia Meeting House, 7
11th mo. 1765, Hannah Mickle, daughter of Samuel
Mickle of Philadelphia, and by her had Joseph, died
15 8th mo. 1768 aet. 10 months; Elizabeth, buried

30 1st mo. 1772 aet. 3. On this family see Robert
C. Moon, M.D., *The Morris Family of Philadelphia*
(Philadelphia 1898), 1:274, #24, which, however,
has an incomplete list of the children.

Issue: surname Morris
i. Joseph, d. 3 6th mo. 1747, not in grandfather's will.
ii. James, d. 10 6th mo. 1747, not in grandfather's will.
iii. Phebe, b. by 1748, mentioned in grandfather's
  will in 1748.
iv. George Anthony, d. in North Carolina, of
  bilous fever, 5 Oct. 1773; called George
  in grandfather's will in 1748.
v. Martha, b. probably ca. 1751, d. 13 9th mo.
  1757.
vi. James, b. 1753, according to the genealogy,
  d. 10 7th mo. 1795; m. at Gwynedd, 1 10th
  mo. 1772, Elizabeth Dawes.
    Issue: surname Morris
  1. Joseph, b. 1775, bur. at Plymouth Meet-
    ing, 1 7th mo. 1796.
  2. Hannah, b. 12 9th mo. 1773, d. 27 7th
    mo. 1842, m. 10 6th mo. 1802, Dr.
    Thomas C. James.
vii. Martha, said by the genealogy b. 1751 but
  it knows only one daughter Martha, d. 9
  1st mo. 1792; m. 15 Oct. 1772 George
  Mifflin (John, John, John), who d. 14
  July 1785. See KPC 368-370.
    Issue: surname Mifflin
  1. Joseph, b. 1773, d. 19 8th mo. 1775.
  2. Elizabeth, b. 28 11th mo. 1775, d. 7 9th
    mo. 1816; m. as 2nd wife, 28 Nov. 1798,
    Caspar Wister, M.D., who d. 14 Jan.
    1818.
      Issue: surname Wister
    a. Richard M., M.D.
    b. Mifflin, M.D., d.s.p. 1872.
    c. Elizabeth, d. unm. 1832.
  3. Thomas, b. 1777, d. 1 April 1820; m. 20
    June 1799, Sarah Large, daughter of
    Ebenezer; 4 sons, 3 daughters.

11. Sarah Fitzwater, daughter of George Fitzwater (Thomas) by his wife Mary Hardiman, is named
fourth among the daughters in her father's will,
and died 19 7th mo. 1764. She married, 25 5th mo.

1745, Isaac Griffits, born 17 April 1719, died in
July 1755, son of Thomas and Mary (Norris) Griffits.
Isaac Griffits, sometime sheriff[48] of Philadelphia
County, is mentioned in the will of his brother
Joseph, silversmith, dated 17 Aug. 1784, codicil
dated 11 Oct. 1784, probated 11 Oct. 1784.[49] Sarah
(Fitzwater) Griffits' will[50] is dated 13 July 1764,
probated 3 April 1773, and mentions brother Joseph
Morris as executor; sisters-in-law Mary and Hannah
Griffitts; cousins George Anthony and James Morris;
nieces Phebe and Martha Morris; friend Hannah Rolfe;
witnesses: Ann Howell and Mary Hood.

Issue: surname Griffits
i. Mary, d. 8 1st mo. 1750.
ii. Elizabeth, d. 25 9th mo. 1751. She and Mary
    were both in their grandfather's will in
    1748.
iii. George, d. 9 10th mo. 1751, not in grand-
     father's will in 1748.

12. Elizabeth Fitzwater, daughter of George Fitzwater (Thomas) by his wife Mary Hardiman, is named
fifth among the daughters in her father's will but
died soon afterwards on 7 1st mo. 1749/50. She married, by Pennsylvania license, in Oct. 1746, Joseph
House, who was dismissed for disunity, 25 8th mo.
1745. Elizabeth House late Fitzwater was dismissed
for marrying out of unity on 26 4th mo. 1747, and
it is probable that the entry of 29 3rd mo. 1747,
which condemns Rebecca House late Fitzwalter, is an
error for her, as we can find no Fitzwater Rebecca
who married a House. Joseph House is called mariner
in his will dated 27 Nov. 1758, probated at Anti-
gua, 12 July 1759. When George Fitzwater made his
will in 1748, the Houses had no children living.

Issue: surname House
i. George, d. 27 12th mo. 1747, not mentioned
    in his grandfather's will, as already
    dead.
ii. Elizabeth, d. 7 1st mo. 1749. As she is not
    mentioned in her grandfather's will of
    11 Oct. 1748, she was probably b. shortly
    before her death.
iii. George, probably b. between 11 Oct. 1748
     when not mentioned in his grandfather's
     will and 7 5th mo. 1754, on which day he
     died, father's name not stated.

iv. Esther or Hester, bur. 11 9th mo. 1776 aet.
30, so b. ca. 1746. If so, she was ignored by her grandfather's will and perhaps her age at death was less than thirty. On 6 Sept. 1776 Esther Pemberton of
Philadelphia made an informative, though
puzzling, will, probated 15 Oct. 1776,[51]
which names father[-in-law] Israel Pemberton and Thomas Fisher as executors; mentions grandfather George Fitzwater [long
dead]; "mother" Mary [probably stepmother-
in-law, who, as widow Mary Jordon of Philadelphia m. 10 10th mo. 1747, Israel Pemberton, son of Israel, and as Mary wife
of Israel Pemberton was bur. 20 10th mo.
1778 aet. 73]; brother-in-law Joseph Pemberton; daughter Mary; sister[-in-law]
Sarah Rhoads [as Sarah Pemberton, daughter of Israel, she had m. 27 6th mo. 1765,
Samuel Rhoads Jr.]; cousin Hannah Rhoads;
cousin William Morgan (son of Aunt Mary)
[who must be the Mary House who m. at
Christ Church, Philadelphia, 23 Dec. 1749,
Morris Morgan, and was the Mary Morgan
late House dismissed for marrying out of
unity, 23 12th mo. 1749/50]; and then
she names nephews and nieces: Elizabeth,
George, Samuel and Isaac, children of her
uncle Samuel House [they were really her
first cousins. Samuel and Mary House were
dismissed for marrying contrary to discipline, 15 8th mo. 1751, and Elizabeth was
b. 18 Sept. 1751, and she, George, Samuel
and Joseph, not Isaac, were all bapt. at
Christ Church, 2 Nov. 1760. The birthdays
of George, Samuel and Joseph, were, respectively, 12 Dec., 25 April and 10 May,
but the clerk did not know the years[52]];
Sarah, Ann, Israel, Charles, Joseph, the
children of Joseph and Ann Pemberton.
Testatrix was Esther House Jr. who m. 8
3rd mo. 1770 Charles Pemberton, son of
Israel, and she was then called daughter
of Joseph House of Philadelphia. On 30
3rd mo. 1770 she was reported to have m.
Charles Pemberton. Esther Pemberton and
daughter Mary were on 30 12th mo. 1774
given a certificate to South District

Monthly Meeting but this was merely a paper
transfer when Philadelphia Monthly Meeting
was being divided. Finally, her burial
record, cited above, also identifies her
husband.

13. George Clymer, only son and only surviving
child of Deborah Fitzwater (George, Thomas) by her
husband, Capt. Christopher Clymer, was born on 11
March 1739/40 but lost his parents at an early age.
As a boy he was taken by his aunt, Hannah (Fitzwater) Coleman, wife of William Coleman, to be raised.
He married at Christ Church, Philadelphia, 18 March
1765, Elizabeth Meredith, who died at Northumberland, Pa., in February 1815, daughter of Reese
Meredith, and she was dismissed for marrying out of
unity on 28 6th mo. 1765. Clymer became a prominent
merchant and statesman, signed both the Declaration
of Independence and the United States Constitution.
He died at Morrisville, Bucks County, Pa.,[53] 23 Jan.
1813. On his career, see John Sanderson, *Biography
of the Signers of the Declaration of Independence*
(Philadelphia 1823), 4:171-246; DAB 4:234 f.; James
R. McFarlane, *George Clymer, Signer of the Declaration of Independence, Framer of the Constitution of
the United States and of the State of Pennsylvania,
and His Descendants* (Sewickley, Pa., 1927); also
Valeria E. Clymer and Emily Ellsworth Clymer, *A
Record and Genealogy of the Clymer Family (Descendants of Christopher Clymer of Bristol, Rngland)*
(1949).[54]

Issue: surname Clymer
i.   William Coleman.
ii. Henry, b. 31 July 1766, d. near Morrisville,
     Pa., 17 April 1830; m. Christ Church, 9
     July 1794, Mary Willing, b. 15 Sept. 1770,
     d. 25 Oct. 1852, daughter of Thomas and
     Anne (McCall) Willing. Four daughters, four
     sons. See KPC 99-101. Henry Clymer was a
     graduate of the College of New Jersey, now
     Princeton University, Class of 1786. He
     read law with James Wilson and was admitted
     to the Philadelphia bar. From 1800 to 1813
     he lived at Morrisville, then moved to North-
     umberland, Pa., and later to Wilkes-Barré,
     Pa., but in 1819 moved to Trenton, N.J. and
     in 1822 again to Morrisville.

iii. Meredith, graduate of the College of New
     Jersey, Class of 1787; joined the First
     Troop, Philadelphia Cavalry, 12 Sept.
     1794; participated in the "Western Exped-
     ition" which put down the Whisky Rebellion,
     and lost his life, 18 Nov. 1794, at Par-
     kinson's Ferry, now probably part of Pitts-
     burgh where he is bur. in Trinity Churchyard.
iv. Elizabeth, d.y.
v. Margaret, m. Christ Church, 21 May 1794,
     George McCall, b. 2 May 1767, d. 17 April
     1799 in Philadelphia, and she d. a few
     days later. He was son of Archibald and
     Judith (Kemble) McCall. George and Mar-
     garet left infant sons named George Cly-
     mer McCall and William Coleman McCall.
vi. Julian, d.y.
vii. George, d. 28 July 1848; m. 13 June 1816,
     Maria Gratiot O'Brien, d. Sept. 1853,
     both bur. in Friends Graveyard in Trenton.
     One son, Meredith Clymer.
viii.Ann, d.s.p. Trenton, N.J. 9 Aug. 1810, bur.
     Friends Graveyard; m. Philadelphia, 17
     Nov. 1807, Charles Lewis of England.

NOTES

[1]Badly copied, PMHB 9:228; correctly copied,
BHBC 679.

[2]Bracketed words are in the Doylestown version.

[3]Accounts of the Fitzwaters appear in Clarence
Vernon Roberts, *Roberts-Walton Ancestry* (1940), pp.
60-68; Alexander DuBin, *Old Philadelphia Families*
(Philadelphia 1939); Samuel Traquair Tyson, *A Contribution to the History and Genealogy of the Tyson
and Fitzwater Families* (1922), pp. 35-59; Mary Thomas Seaman, *Thomas Richardson of South Shields, Durham County, England and his descendants in the United States of America* (New York 1929), pp. 103-105.
In 1944 Maude C. Reno deposited in the Iowa Historical Library in Des Moines a typescript Fitzwater
Family which follows a line through George Fitzwater
(Thomas, Thomas, Thomas, Thomas).

[4]PGM 23:58.   [5]PGSP 1:364. [6]PGSP 2:266.
[7]PGSP 2:267.   [8]PGSP 1:265; PhW N:343.

[9]1 PA 1:46. For an account of George Palmer, see
Roberts-Walton Ancestry, 205-209. Another is to be
found in the voluminous Palmer Genealogy compiled
by the late Horace W. Palmer. See TAG 45:143-152.

[10]PhA C:7, #34.

[11]The Register General puts it on 31 May. On the man see PGM 23:102. He was a weaver who in 1690 bought from Griffith Jones a portion of the latter's bank lot near Walnut Street (PhD E-2, p. 5, 18 6th mo. 1690).

[12]PhA A:163 #104 (1692), admin. to widow.
[13]See p. 111.   [14]MQA 16.
[15]*Colonial Recs.* 1:228.   [16]PGM 23:85.
[17]1 NJA 21:281.   [18]PGSP 3:33.
[19]1 PA 1:43.   [20]PhW D:429.
[21]See the Croasdale sketch.
[22]She married Jeremiah McVaugh.
[23]PhW F:293.

[24]The Tyson family is discussed in both the *Roberts-Walton Ancestry* and in the Tyson-Fitzwater Genealogy cited above in Note 3.

[25]PhW G:340.   [26]PhW E:129.
[27]PhW E:153.   [28]PhW H:117.
[29]Tyson-Fitzwater Genealogy, pp. 40 f.
[30]HEAQG 362.
[31]Tyson-Fitzwater Genealogy, pp. 41 f.
[32]PGSP 3:250   [33]PGM 23:119.
[34]GWF 171; PGM 23:96.   [35]PhW C:97.
[36]PhW D:6, 73, 118, 131, 330, 393, 446; E:309; F:44, 172.
[37]PhW I:275   [38]PMHB 16:449.
[39]*Historical Sketches* (of Montgomery Co. Hist. Soc.) 6 (1920) 139.
[40]PhW L:547.   [41]PhW I:393.
[42]PMHB 9:353-355.
[43]Philadelphia Orphans Court 3:130.
[44]PMHB 1:325-327.   [45]For children *ibid.*
[46]PhW E:294   [47]PhW O:315-317.
[48]MIQ 262f., KPC 184. [49]PhW T:167.
[50]PhW P:381 #267.   [51]PhW Q:407.
[52]PhW Q:358.
[53]Not Berks County, as Sanderson has it.
[54]In the New England Historic Genealogical Society Library at Boston is a study made by Mrs. Winifred Lovering Holman Dodge of another Clymer line, during which research it was necessary to investigate this one so as to eliminate it from the possibilities.

FURNACE/FURNISS, HENRY	*disproved*
FURNACE/FURNISS, JOSEPH	*disproved*
FURNACE/FURNISS, RACHEL	*disproved*

These three names appear on List X only. The truth is that these three and two other persons of the same surname, came on the *Lion* of Liverpool, arriving 14 8th mo. 1683, as servants to Robert Turner. Henry Furnace was second name on the list of servants, to serve four years, receive £3/8 and 50 acres. John Furnace was eighth on the list, to serve four years, get £3 and 50 acres. Dan: Furnace was to serve nine years, get no money but 50 acres, the ninth name on the list. Rachel Furnace was the sixteenth on the list, to serve six years and get only the 50 acres, no money, and, finally, Jos: Furnace is seventeenth and last on the list, to serve four years and get £3 and 50 acres.[1]

At the session of the Board of Property on 26 9ber 1701,[2] John Furnese of Philadelphia, barber, produced a certificate of Samuel Carpenter and Joseph Fisher dated 13 8ber 1701, that Robert Turner late of Philadelphia, deceased, transported as servants from the port of Dublin to Pennsylvania in the *Lyon* of Liverpool, John Crumpton, master, landed 8 8th mo. 1683: Henry, John, Mary, Sarah, Rachel, Joseph and Daniel, all named Furnis. The said John has purchased their head rights and wants 350 acres. Note that the five servants listed by Turner himself soon after arrival have grown to seven by the addition of Mary and Sarah. No women of these first names appear on Turner's list, though Mary Toole appears on Joseph Fisher's list of servants who arrived on the same vessel. It is possible that Mary and Sarah came unmarried and had since married men of the Furniss family.

Philadelphia Monthly Meeting records the burial of Daniel, son of Henry Furniss on 31 3rd mo. 1696. John (the barber?) died 21 2nd mo. 1730. Mary, wife of Joseph, was buried 14 6th mo. 1735. Among non-Quaker burials is that of Ann, wife of Henry, 19 7th mo. 1699, and of Henry himself, buried 10 11th mo. 1701.

The will of Henry Furnis of Philadelphia, saddler, was dated 30 Dec. 1701, probated 20 Jan. 1701/2.[3] He names no wife, of course, but mentions son Samuel and his four eldest children; son John; daughter Sarah and her two eldest children; daughter

Mary and her two eldest children; daughter Rachel; daughter Brigett; cousin Jane Burland in England; son-in-law William Robinson; James Paulter of Philadelphia, wheelwright.

This will forces us to conclude that when Henry Furniss came on the *Lion* in 1683, not all his children were with him. Some may have come later or even earlier, though we have not found record of them. Bridget may well have been born in America but Rachel came on the *Lion*, as did John. Samuel could hardly have been born after 1683 and have by 1701 four children. Indeed, his position in the will suggests he was the eldest. Whether Joseph was also a son, rather than a brother, is not clear. The wife Ann was curiously overlooked by Turner, if she came with her husband.

NOTES

[1]Mrs. Balderston (PGM 24:92) thought Daniel was perhaps Samuel, and she misread Rachel as Catherine. The name is abbreviated "Rach:" and the first letter does resemble K, and the kind of C used may be mistaken for T, but this one is recorded at least twice elsewhere as Rachel.

[2]2 PA 19:200.   [3]PhW B:179.

GIBBONS, ANNA   *possible*

This name appears on no list but I am informed by Mr. Harold A. West of Philadelphia that in the Sellers family there is a strong tradition that Henry Gibbons' daughter Anna, who married at Darby Meeting, 1st intentions 13 5th mo. 1684, Samuel Sellers of Belper, Derbyshire, and Upper Darby, now in Delaware County, came on the *Welcome*. Thomas A. Glenn[1] shows Henry Gibbons of Paverage, co. Derby, coming to Darby in 1684, and shows that this is the right man by remarking that his daughter married Samuel Sellers. Jordan, however, in a Sellers sketch[2], identifies Anna's parents as Henry and Eleanor who came in 1682, but says nothing of the *Welcome*. Elsewhere,[3] the same work alludes to the certificate brought from Parwich, Derbyshire in 1682. In attempting to find this certificate I have been unsuccessful, but I have located a transcript of it made by Gilbert Cope who says that it was issued at Matlock Monyash and Ashford on 27 5th mo. 1682. This date is about the time when certi-

ficates for *Welcome* passengers would have been issued, but as this was an upper Midlands county, it
seems probable that a ship from another port would
have been chosen.

NOTES

[1]GWF 168 f.   [2]JCRFP 3:1412.   [3]JCRFP 1:497.

GILBERT, JOHN   *highly improbable*

    This name appears on List X only but the claim
is also made by W. W. H. Davis, *History of Bucks
County, Pennsylvania* (Doylestown, 1st ed., 1876),
p. 66 where it is stated that John Gilbert married
Mary Cowgill, a person otherwise unknown, and settled in Bensalem. In the small work bearing the
name of Joseph C. Martindale, M.D., *The Gilbert
Family, The Carver Family, The Duffield Family*
(Frankford, 1911, printed long after Dr. Martindale's
death), p. 1, we read: "John Gilbert who came on
the ship 'Welcome' from England in 1682," died at
Philadelphia, 13 8th mo. 1711, married in England
Florence -----. The same author's *History of the
Townships of Moreland and Byberry* (rev.ed., no date,
also printed after Dr. Martindale's death), contains
on pp. 308-317 an account of John Gilbert which puts
John on the *Welcome* but says nothing of "Mary Cowgill." Note 17 to p. 308 says: 'From Gilbert Cope
I learn that John Gilbert, in all probability, did
not come on the ship "Welcome."' No evidence has
been found to settle the matter one way or another,
but we understand that descendants of John Gilbert
are of the opinion that John Gilbert came as early
as 1679. John Gilbert Sr. of Bucks County, yeoman,
bought a hundred acres at Great Egg Harbor, New
Jersey, on 29 Nov. 1695.[1] His will[2] dated 8 8th mo.
1711, probated 19 Nov. 1711, calls him John Gilbert
of Philadelphia, merchant; names son Joseph executor; daughters Sarah Elfreth, Mary Ballard, Abigail
Gilbert; grandson Joseph, eldest son of son Joseph;
grandson John, son of deceased eldest son John;
other unnamed children of son John; unnamed grandchildren, children of Henry and Sarah Elfreth;
grandsons William and Samuel Ballard; granddaughter
Elizabeth, daughter of deceased son Joshua; Daniel
England, Susannah Harwood and Richard Sutton; witnesses: Thomas Batson, Joshua Hastinges, John Parsons, John Cadwallader. The son Joshua, born 10

6th mo. 1684, married 19 8th mo. 1707 Elizabeth Old-
ham and died 19 7th mo. 1711, about two months before his father. The eldest son John died at Philadelphia 7 1st mo. 1701/2; Joseph, who married Sarah
Livesey, died in 1765 aet. 90; Sarah, who married
Henry Elfreth in 1702, died in 1728. We have not
seen documentary proof of the wife's name but Florence seems a bit early.

NOTES

¹1 NJA 21:665.   ²PhW C:280.

GILLETT, THOMAS   *proved*

This name appears on all lists and on Lists K,
N, P, S and T, the name is given as above but with
a variant spelling "Gillott" in parenthesis. The
proof of this man's presence aboard the *Welcome* is
his signature as witness on the will of John Barber,
executed aboard the vessel and here we see that the
proper spelling is really "Gillett" and not "Gillott", and the e is not even of the type which may
be easily mistaken for an o.

It is probable that this is the Thomas Gillett
whose name appears numerous times in the *Records of
the Court of New Castle on Delaware* (Meadville, Pa.,
1935), as follows:

69	Thoṁ Gillett on a jury 17 Oct. 1683
77	again on a jury 4 Dec. 1683
83	300 acres 19 Feb. 1683/4
102	same, 18 March 1684
114	on jury 15 10th mo. 1688
122	300 acres, Christiana Creek
155	15 March 1686/7 he and Elizabeth Ogle ac-knowledge deed of enfeoffment to James Claypoole Sr.
167	he acknowledges mortgage, 17 Jan. 1687, on plantation called Devises to Nicholas Al-len and Mathyas Matess
171	300 acres, North Christiana Creek, 1687

He appears to have had no probate in New Castle
County but there was a Thomas Gillett deceased before 14 Feb. 1719/20, when his widow Ann was called
a granddaughter in the will of Ellinor Fowke of
Dark Creek Hundred, probated 5 March 1719/20. This
will names among others a daughter Ann and a grandson Owen Fowke, besides the granddaughter Ann, widow

of Thomas Gillett.

This Ellinor was probably widow of Owen Foulke of Bettws-y-Coed, Caernarvonshire, tanner, who is recorded as having loaded on the *Lion* of Liverpool at Chester, 2 May 1682: 1 bundle qty 60 yards of flannel, 2 sack qty 8 Winchester bushels of oatmeal, duty 2s 4½d.[1]   He purchased on 23 1st mo. 1681/2,[2] for £3/2/6 a 2/30 share of the 5000 acres sold to John ap Thomas and Thomas Wynne by William Penn. On 12 4th mo. 1683 Foulke obtained a warrant for taking out 200 acres, survey returned five days later.[3] On 13 July 1686 he had another warrant for 400 acres, to be laid out in New Castle County.[4] On 27 4th mo. 1692 Owen folke sold 150 acres in Darby Township to Samuel Levis.[5]   He was buried 5 6th mo. 1695, recorded among non-Quaker burials at Philadelphia Meeting.

From what has been said, it seems probable that the Thomas Gillett who came on the *Welcome* was too old a man to be a likely grandson-in-law of Ellinor Fowke.   There was also another Thomas Gillett, much too young to be the *Welcome* passenger, since he was yet to be brought up when he was mentioned in the will of his father, Joshua Gillett, of Penn's Neck, Salem County, New Jersey, yeoman, dated 15 Dec. 1691, probated 10 Nov. 1692.[6] He might well have married Ellinor Fowke's granddaughter Ann.

NOTES

[1]PGM 23:252 and note 4.   [2]PhD C-1:291.
[3]3 PA 3:125.   [4]2 PA 7:196.
[5]*Records of the Courts of Chester Co., Pa. 1681-1697*, p. 268.

[6]NJW 1:186.

GREEN, BARTHOLOMEW   *proved*

This name appears on all lists except I   alone. The proof is in Philadelphia Arrivals where Bartholomew Green is shown as servant to Richard Townsend who was himself a servant of the Society of Free Traders.   It would appear probable that Green was a mechanic of some kind. He could not have died on the *Welcome* or he would not have been listed as an arrival.   No further trace of him has been found and he may have returned to England.

GREENWAY, ROBERT   *proved*

This man was the commander of the *Welcome*, so recorded in numerous references to the vessel, and he took it back to England in 1683. We have seen the name spelled several times as "Greenaway" and once as "Greenman."

The *Welcome* was, of course, not Greenway's first command, for Norton Claypoole, younger brother of James Claypoole, got a ticket from Barbadoes to New York, 23 Feb. 1678, on the ship *Bachelor's Delight*, Robert Greenway, Com[m]ander.[1] It was suggested by Mr. Colket that Greenway was the author of an anonymous tract, *Christian Unity exhorted to bring a few words in tender love to all Professing of Christianity in Old England the land of my nativity*, 13 July 1678, and another in 1684, *Farewell, or a Salutation to Faithful Friends in Old England*.[2]

Robert Greenway was a First Purchaser of 1500 acres in Group 34,[3] 20 1st mo. 1682. Blackwell's Rent Roll of 1689[4] shows Greenway's lot as an old purchase, 30½ feet, 1/6 for 5 years, on Chestnut Street next to Griffith Jones. By that time he was, of course, long dead, for he died 14 2nd mo. 1685, leaving a will dated 9 2nd mo. 1685,[5] the executor of which, Morgan Druett, is to secure the estate for the use of Thomas Maly in England, apothecary, liver and dweller near London; witnesses: Wm Brown, Horner Brown. This will not being in order, letters of administration c.t.a. were issued 8 1st mo. 1686/7 to Morgan Druett of New Castle, husbandman. It is obvious that Greenway left neither wife nor child.

The late Henry Paul Busch was inclined to regard Greenway as merely a speculator and not entitled to be called "a *Welcome* passenger." In the strictest sense he was not a passenger, being master of the ship, but the Friends who travelled on the vessel owed their safe arrival in America to Greenway, and his name deserves to be remembered.

NOTES

[1]John Camden Hotten, *Original Lists*, p. 357.
[2]See John Whiting, *Catalogue of Friends Books* (London 1708), p. 60.
[3]1 PA 1:44.   [4]PGM 23:72.
[5]PGSP 1:85.

HALL, ROBERT		*highly improbable*
HALL, ELIZABETH, his wife		*highly improbable*
*HALL, ELIZABETH, his daughter		*highly improbable*
*HALL, GEORGE, his son		*highly improbable*

This name has appeared on no list. A qualified claim appears in an account of the family in *Pennsylvania Magazine of History and Biography* 11:314: 'Tradition credits him with having been a passenger on the "Welcome," or on one of the vessels of Penn's fleet,' etc.

Robert Hall was of St. Margaret's Parish, City of Westminster, and his wife was daughter of George and Elizabeth (-----) White. Both of these children died in childhood.

According to the records of Middletown Monthly Meeting in Bucks County, the son George was born in England on 18 2nd mo. 1682 but it is claimed that his birth has been found in an English parish register where the date of baptism is given as 11 Sept. 1682. A number of discrepancies have been found between dates given by American settlers and the English parish registers of baptism or Quaker birth registers. In such instances it is wiser to accept the English record set down near the time of the event, whereas the American record must have been entered some time later and is therefore subject to error through forgetfulness. If George Hall was, indeed, baptized on 11 Sept. 1682, then the family was not on the *Welcome* which was on that day in mid-Atlantic. See *The American Genealogist* 39: 13.

HALLOWELL, JOHN   *disproved*

This name has appeared on no list but is admitted by Meredith B. Colket Jr. as one on which he will not commit himself either way. The claim is, of course, false, as the Hallowells brought a certificate dated 19 12th mo. 1682, some four months after the *Welcome* arrived.

See William Penrose Hallowell (7-45): *Record of a Branch of the Hallowell Family* (Philadelphia 1893), p. 13, who says that John and Mary Sharpe [sic] Hallowell came to Darby, Pa., from Hucknow Parish of Sutton, Nottinghamshire, on a certificate bearing the date given above. Mary was the daughter of Thomas Sharpe. No *Welcome* claim is made.

Mary Paul Hallowell Hough: *The Hallowell-Paul*

Family History (Philadelphia 1924), likewise makes
no reference to the *Welcome* and agrees with Mr.
Hallowell on the date of the certificate. She says,
however (p. xii), that John Hallowell married (1)
Sarah Clay; (2) 27 10th mo. 1675 at Mansfield Quarterly Meeting, Mary Holland of Millnepey, Derbyshire.
We have made no further research on the Hallowells
but the discrepancy in the wife's maiden name might
be resolved if this were a second marriage for her
also.

HAMBIDGE, ROWLAND   *disproved*

This name appears on List X only, as Hambridge.
The truth is that Hambidge came on the *Lion* of Liverpool, arriving on 14 8th mo. 1683, as servant of Robert Turner, to serve four years, loose on 14 8th mo.
1687, to get 50 acres. No further trace of him has
been found.

HARRISON, NATHANIEL   *proved*

This name appears on all lists except List I, on
Lists A, C, F and M, at the end. The proof is to
be found in Philadelphia Arrivals where Harrison
is a servant to Richard Townsend who was, himself,
a servant to the Society of Free Traders. It is
probable that Harrison was some sort of mechanic.
He cannot have died on the *Welcome* or he would not
have been registered as an arrival. He may have
returned to England as no trace of him further has
been found. List X thinks the first name was Nathan.

HAWKINS, JEFFREY		*proved*
HAWKINS, DOROTHY, his wife		*proved*
HAWKINS, ROGER, his son		*proved*
HAWKINS, JAMES, his son		*proved*
HAWKINS, DANIEL, his son		*proved*
HAWKINS, JEFFREY, his son		*proved*
HAWKINS, ?SUSANNA, his daughter		*proved*
HAWKINS, ?ELIZABETH, his daughter		*proved*

The following certificate was published by W. J.
Buck[1] who does not say where he saw it:

> These are to certifie all Friends in Truth and
> others whom these concern, that Jeffry Hawkins of
> Norton-Bavant in the County of Wilts being desir-
> ous to Transport himself Beyond the Seas with his
> wife and six children, hath behaved himself hon-
> estly and that he is under no engagement of Debts

nor any other Misdemeanour as far as we know. In Testimony whereof we have hereunto set our hands this 12th day of the 6th month, 1682.

Will. Chandler	John Benet
James Hodges	Tho. Holt
William Forest	Overseers
Richard Hedge	Timothy Thorne
John French	William Vew

I being in the Country and having made inquiry into the Truth of the Contents of the above written Certificate, I do not find anything Contrary thereunto.

Lawrence Steel

The wording of the certificate and Steel's endorsement suggest that perhaps Jeffrey Hawkins was not well known to the signers. Perhaps he had only recently come to Norton-Bavant, or perhaps he was of Norton-Bavant and the signers were of some larger place. On the other hand the one who drew up the certificate may have been unusually careful not to commit himself by saying what he supposed, rather than what he knew to be true. The document also bore the following unusual endorsement:

Tho. Holmes let the within named Jeffry Hawkins have his head-rights set out to him with what speed can be.
13th 8 month '82   Wm Penn.

It was pointed out by Francis J. Dallett that on the 13th of the 8th month 1682, the *Welcome* was at sea, so that it may be presumed that Jeffrey Hawkins was on board the ship.[2] Though Albert Cook Myers knew of the certificate, he did not put the Hawkins family on List Q.

The name of the first wife is derived from the Makefield Monthly Meeting record of her death in 1685, day and month not stated. Jeffrey Hawkins had leave to marry from Falls Monthly Meeting, 2 9th mo. 1687, by certificate to Neshaminy Monthly Meeting [i.e. Middletown], Elizabeth [sic] Pierson, and the marriage took place at Middletown, 21 9th mo. 1687, when he is called husbandman and she Ellin [sic] Pierson, spinster. In this period the word 'spinster' meant 'single woman' and included widows as well as women never married, but the word 'widow' is not used in any record found of Ellen Pierson.

Ellin Pearson of Kirklydam in the County of York,

aged about 54 years, came on the *Shield*, Mr Daniel
Foos, to Maryland, arriving at the beginning of 8th
mo. 1684.[3] Penn's Receiver General in 1692 paid
13/6 to Ellen Hawkins for work done by her husband
at Pensberry formerly.[4] Ellen Hawkins died 30 12th
mo. 1708/9, recorded at Falls Monthly Meeting.

The land records for Jeffrey Hawkins are as follows: On 25 9th mo. 1683, 288 acres in Bucks County,
"at Purchase," were surveyed and laid out to Jeffrey Hawkins, "by Vertue of two Warrant [sic] from
the Governor the 1st dated the 13th of the 8th month
1682 [i.e. the endorsement on the certificate], the
other the 11th of the 9th mo. 1683," land adjoining
John Luff, survey returned 15 of 6th mo. 1685.[5]
Luff, also a First Purchaser, was from Market Laving-
ton, Wiltshire.[6]

Jeffrey Hawkins, planter, conveyed to his brother
Roger Hawkins, planter, for £8/15/0, 100 acres, part
of a grant confirmed by William Penn to Jeffrey Hawkins and heirs, date of deed 4 7th mo. 1685, signed
by mark.[7] Jeffrey Hawkins conveyed to John Collins
and wife Susannah Collins, 1 7th mo. 1686, for
£9/12/6, 110 acres, part of the same property as
the preceding deed.[8] Jeffrey Hawkins, laborer, conveyed to son Daniel Hawkins, 1 10th mo. 1687, for
£5, all land on the west side of a run of water on
Jeffrey Hawkins' land, 100 acres ± (no recital but
bounds indicate part of same property), all in Falls
Township. The mark of Roger Hawkins appears as a
witness but Jeffrey Hawkins was able to sign his
own name.[9]

On 29 Dec. 11 Anne 1712 Roger Hawkins, late of
Bristol, Bucks County, laborer, for 5/-, grants to
Jonathan Nutt of Falls Township, a release and quitclaim for 210 acres in possession of Jonathan Nutt,
granted to Jeffrey Hawkins, "my father," by William
Penn, 7th mo. 1685, 110 acres of which were sold to
John and Susannah Collins, 1 7th mo. 1686, sold by
said Susannah, widow of John, to John Liddell, 11
10th mo. 1690; the other 100 acres Jeffrey conveyed
to son Daniel, 1 10th mo. 1687, confirmed and conveyed by Thomas Croasdale being sole executor to
his brother-in-law, said Daniel, to Henry Liddell,
10 7th mo. 1689. Then these two pieces were taken
in execution at the suit of Isaac Meritt by Wm
Croasdale, then High Sheriff of Bucks County, and
sold to Jonathan Nutt.[10]

Jeffrey Hawkins had on 6 2nd mo. 1686 witnessed

the wedding of Joseph Chorley. Administration on
the estate of Jeffrey Hawkins of [blank] was granted 16 Jan. 1711/12 to Rodger Hawkins of Bucks
County,[11] and on 14 Aug. 1712 administration was
granted to Roger Hawkins and two others.[12] Jeffrey
Hawkins was an abutter, 12 June 1723, of Samuel
Dark, Robert Lucas, Richard Hough, Henry Marjoram
and Jonathan Nutt.[13] This may pertain to the son
Jeffrey but as deeds sometimes name as abutters
persons long dead, we cannot be sure.

Issue: surname Hawkins
i. Roger, reported to have m. out, 4 4th mo.
1684, Falls Monthly Meeting, wife's name
not stated or found; was admin. of father,
1712; may have m. (2) 11, 14 or 15 June
1712, at St. Mary's, Burlington, Elizabeth
Holman.[14] He gave release and quitclaim
to Jonathan Nutt, 29 Dec. 11 Anne 1712;
1712 was also admin. of Jonathan Graves.
ii. James, first recorded as having leave to m.
Mary Ellot from Falls Monthly Meeting, 4
5th mo. 1705, which puts him in the family under discussion. Then he moved to Abington Monthly Meeting which gave a certificate to him with wife Mary to return
to Falls, 30 11th mo. 1709; next Mary,
wife, not widow, of James, was granted a
certificate at Falls, 7 1st mo. 1711; after that in 1734 James was among the land-
holders of Moreland Manor, with 50 acres
of land.[15]
iii. Daniel, witnessed 23 3rd mo. 1688 will of
Joshua Boare.[16] On 1 10th mo. 1687 his
father conveyed to him 100 acres.[17] Upon
Daniel's death, date unknown, his brother-
in-law Thomas Croasdale was sole executor, as stated in the deed quoted above,
but no record of this administration has
been found. Moreover, who this Thomas
Croasdale was is puzzling. The immigrant Thomas Croasdale [see p. 146] died
in 1682, had no son Thomas and the grandsons were hardly old enough by 1712 to
have married and served as executor of a
brother-in-law's estate.
iv. Jeffrey, of Philadelphia, laborer, on 1 Mar.
1706 when he gave release to Elizabeth,

           relict of William Darby, to sell property
           formerly belonging, in succession, to his
           father and his uncle Roger.
     v.   ?Elizabeth, m. William Darby (heir to Roger
           Hawkins the elder on whom see the next
           sketch) who was dead by 1706. The ? in
           front of this name is intended to express
           doubt as to whether this Elizabeth was a
           child of Jeffrey Hawkins. He undoubtedly
           had six children with him on the *Welcome*.
     vi.   ?Susanna, m. John Collins who was dead by
           11 10th mo. 1690 when as his widow she
           sold property purchased from Jeffrey Haw-
           kins the elder on 1 7th mo. 1686. As in
           the case with Elizabeth, the doubt is as
           to whether we have correctly identified
           Susanna as a child of Jeffrey Hawkins.

                         NOTES

   [1]PMHB 8:430. The principal research for this
sketch was done by Walter Lee Sheppard Jr.
   [2]TAG 41:220.   [3]PMHB 9:227; BHBC 678.
   [4]PMHB 35:205.   [5]W&S 3:165.
   [6]3 PA 3:336.
   [7]BD 1:14, ackn. 10 1st mo. 1685/6, rec. 1 3rd mo.
1687.
   [8]BD 1:48, ack. 8 7th mo. 1686, rec. 12 7th mo.
1686.
   [9]BD 1:135, ackn. 14 10th mo. 1687, rec. 1 11th
mo. 1687.
   [10]BD 4:254.   [11]PGM 20:50.
   [12]PGM 20:51.   [13]PGSP 6:276.
   [14]PGSP 2:245.   [15]PGSP 1:176.
   [16]PGSP 1:220.   [17]BD 1:135.

  *HAWKINS, ROGER the elder   *possible*
  *HAWKINS, SARAH, his wife   *possible*

    This man is identified as a brother of Jeffrey
Hawkins the elder by a record of Falls Monthly Meeting dated 6 9th mo. 1689, shortly after the death
of Roger. On 4 7th mo. 1685, Jeffrey Hawkins, planter, conveyed to Roger Hawkins, planter, for £8/15,
100 acres, part of a grant confirmed to Jeffrey Hawkins by William Penn.[1] This deed does not call the
grantee a brother but on 1 March 1706, Jeffrey Hawkins of Philadelphia, laborer, gave a release to
Elizabeth, widow of William Darby, in which he re-
cites that his father Jeffrey had sold to his bro-

ther Roger [uncle of the younger Jeffrey] the property mentioned in the deed of 1685.[2] In a deed of
Jeffrey Hawkins to his son Daniel dated 1 10th mo.
1687, the mark of Roger Hawkins appears as witness.[3]
Roger Hawkins was also a witness on 17 4th mo. 1683
to the marriage of Samuel Dark and Ann Knight and
again in 1684 to the marriage of Richard Lundy.

Now Jeffrey Hawkins was from Norton-Bavant, Wiltshire, and brought a certificate, which, from William
Penn's endorsement made on it during the voyage of
the *Welcome*, proves that Jeffrey, his first wife and
their six children, were passengers on that vessel.
Roger is not included in this certificate but he may
have brought one of his own which has not come to
light. There is no proof that he was on the *Welcome*
but he and his wife remain possibilities. No Hawkins
can be found in Friends records of Gloucestershire
or Wiltshire.

The Makefield Monthly Meeting records the death
of Sarah, wife of Roger Hawkins, 20 5th mo. 1687. On
4 4th mo. 1684, Roger Hawkins had been disowned by
Falls Monthly Meeting for marrying out of unity, but
it seems most probable that the man disowned was his
nephew and not the elder Roger, since Friends seem
to have been interested enough to record Sarah's
death and also to report on 2 8th mo. 1689 that Roger
Hawkins was then dead and buried. In the release by
his nephew Jeffrey, cited above, reference is made
to a will of this Roger, "dated" but the date is left
blank, in which the 100 acres bought from his brother
were willed to William Darby. No Hawkins will has
been found in the counties of Bucks, Chester or Philadelphia, or in New Jersey. Perhaps Roger Hawkins
made a nuncupative will and the witnesses neglected
to record it by deposition, hence the need for the
release by his nephew in 1706 to clear the title. In
any case, no surviving issue of Roger and Sarah Hawkins has been found.

                            NOTES

[1]BD 1:14. The principal research for this sketch
was done by Walter Lee Sheppard Jr.
   [2]BD 3:313.   [3]BD 1:135.

HAWORTH, MARY   *improbable*

The claim is made by Ann Wharton Smith, *Genealogy
of the Fisher Family 1682 to 1896* (Philadelphia 1896),
p. 22, where it is alleged that Mary Haworth came to

America with Dr. Thomas Wynne in 1682, though the
Welcome is not mentioned. Evidence to support this
claim may exist but has not been discovered.

In Charles R. Hildeburn's manuscript pedigrees
on file in the Genealogical Society of Pennsylvania
there is one of the Haworth family (p. 130). He
begins with James and Isabel Haworth who are said
not to have come to America but are credited with
the following children:

   i.   Mary, m. John Miers, a hatter, who came to
        America and settled at what is now Lewes,
        Delaware. They are credited with the
        following issue: surname Miers
        1. Sarah m. (1) Thomas Rowland; (2) in 1724
           Jonathan Osborne; (3) in 1733 James
           Blundell; (4) in 1740 Enoch Cummings;
           (5) in 1747, Joshua Clayton, the *Wel-*
           come claimant.
        2. John.
        3. Mary.
        4. James.
  ii.   Sarah m. Isaac Collins.
 iii.   Susanna, d. during the passage.
  iv.   George, who may have been the George Hay-
        worth of Buckingham, Bucks Co., Pa., whose
        will was dated 27 11th mo. 1724, probated
        6 May 1725 (BW 1:88), naming wife Sarah,
        mentioning but not naming children; exe-
        cutors: wife and brother-in-law John Fish-
        er.
   v.   Daughter, d.y.
  vi.   James m. his cousin Elizabeth Haworth.

What evidence Mr. Hildeburn had is unknown to me.
It is possible that the John Fisher in George Hayworth's will may have been John, son of John, already
discussed above as a *Welcome* claimant. This John
Fisher the elder had several daughters, one of whom
may have married George Hayworth.

If so, the claim that Mary Haworth was on the
Welcome may have been derived from misplacing a family tradition of descent from a genuine *Welcome*
passenger. Dr. Thomas Wynne is a proved passenger,
his second wife Elizabeth, a highly probable one.
It would be easy for one who had heard talk in the
family of the Wynnes on the *Welcome* to have transferred the tradition to one to whom it did not apply.

HAYHURST, CUTHBERT   *disproved*
HAYHURST, MARY RUDD, his wife   *disproved*
HAYHURST, ELIZABETH, his daughter   *disproved*
HAYHURST, WILLIAM, his son   *disproved*
HAYHURST, MARGERY, his daughter   *disproved*
HAYHURST, JOHN, his son   *disproved*
HAYHURST, CUTHBERT, his son   *disproved*
HAYHURST, ALICE, his daughter   *disproved*
HAYHURST, MARY, his reputed daughter   *disproved*
HAYHURST, WILLIAM, his brother   *disproved*
HAYHURST, ARTHUR   *mythical*[1]

Cuthbert Hayhurst is on Lists A, B, C, D, E, F, G, H, J, K, L, M, N, O (here denied), P, Q, R, S, T, W, X, Y and Z. List I calls him "Arthur Hayhurst" and List U puts him on the *Lamb*. The wife is called Mary on List Q, is unnamed on Lists A, B, C, D, E, F, G, H, I, J, K, L, M, N, P, S, T, W, X, Y and Z, and List U, of course, puts her on the *Lamb*. Elizabeth, William, Margery, John, Cuthbert, Alice, are called "children" on List F, are included in "family" on Lists A, B, C, D, E, G, H, I, M, X, Y and Z. List Q allows only four unnamed children, and Lists U and V put them all on the *Lamb*. The reputed daughter Mary is quite doubtful. No primary record of her has been found, and without her, we have found six children, and it is generally agreed that there were six children in this family. W. W. H. Davis, *History of Bucks County, Pennsylvania* (Doylestown, 1st ed., 1876), p. 66, says that a Mary Hayhurst otherwise unidentified married William Carver. The Carver Genealogy makes William Carver marry, first, 11th mo. 1689 at Middletown, Joan Kinsey, mother of six Carver children; second, at Falls in 1723, Grace (Paxson) Carter, mother of one. His son William, born 22 3rd mo. 1694, died Jan. 1759; married 28 10th mo. 1719, Elizabeth Walmsley, daughter of Henry and Mary (Searle) Walmsley, and she died in 1772. There is thus little probability that there was such a Mary Hayhurst. The brother William Hayhurst, who was a childless widower, appears only on Lists F and H, and on List V he is put on the *Lamb*.

The name "Hayhurst" was probably pronounced almost as a monosyllable so that "Hairst," "Hearst" and "Hurst" appear frequently in the records. Cuthbert is always put first of all people named in the Settle certificate of 7 4th mo. 1682[2] and when his brother William appears at all, he is always last.

The names of the six children are never given in any
version of the Settle Certificate. For a full discussion of this certificate, see the Introduction,
Section E.

The family was long believed to have come on the
Welcome and Mr. Albert Cook Myers never cancelled
their names on List Q, but allowed four unnamed
children. Cuthbert Hayhurst, however, loaded on the
Lamb of Liverpool on 26 June 1682, 2 casks, 1 pack,
1 box, 1 bag qty 6 cwt wrought iron; 7 cwt nails;
35 doz. woolen stockings for men; 5 doz. felts [hats]
English making; 35 pots qty 3½ barrels butter; 462
cheeses qty 3 tons; 2 cwt cheese; 40 grindle stones
qty 2 chalders; 5 millstones; 3 doz. sieves value
£5. This evidence now seems conclusive to put him
on the *Lamb* with his family and the rest of the
Settle party.

The first record of Cuthbert Hayhurst in America
was discovered independently by both Albert Cook
Myers and Walter Lee Sheppard Jr., though Mr. Myers
did not comment on its significance. This was an
Old Rights warrant in Bucks County for 250 acres,
issued 12 8th mo. in a year not stated. Since Cuthbert Hayhurst died in Pennsylvania, 2 1st mo. 1682/3,
the only year possible is 1682, and this date was
two weeks before the *Welcome* arrived. Mrs. Balderston's date for the arrival of the *Lamb* has been
22 Oct. 1682, but perhaps it arrived a week earlier.

Cuthbert Hurst was a First Purchaser of 500 acres
in Group 44,[2] and the widow received another warrant
for 250 acres, 12 5th mo. 1683, and return for 200
acres on the first warrant, 9 1st mo. 1683.

The following account of the Hayhurst family draws,
for the English part, on a manuscript in the Genealogical Society of Pennsylvania, presented by Miers
Busch and Henry Paul Busch and bearing the title
Palmer, Cutler, Hayhurst . . . Families,[3] as well
as upon information found in the A. R. Justice
Collection (11:77). The English data have not been
verified by me.

THE HAYHURST FAMILY

Cuthbert Hayhurst of Newton-in-Bolland, Yorkshire,
died at Newton in 1623; married Isabell Rangill, the
daughter of George Rangill of Slaidburn. He made his
will 26 Nov. 1622, probated 27 Aug. 1623, naming
daughter Jennett and her husband Richard Hide; youngest son Christopher; daughter Elizabeth and her hus-

band John Bond; executrix: wife Isabel. Mr. Justice
remarks that Cuthbert's heirs were Isabell Hairst,
Jennett Stackhouse, Margaret Bawden, wife of John.
How this last was involved, does not appear.

    Issue: surname Hayhurst or Hairst
1 i.   William, eldest son.
  ii.   Jennet, m. Richard Hide. Did she m. (2) ----
        Stackhouse?
 iii. Christopher, youngest son.
  iv. Elizabeth, m. John Bond.
   v.   ?Margaret, m. John Bawden.

    1. William Hayhurst or Hairst, eldest son of Cuth-
bert Hayhurst or Hairst by his wife Isabell Rangill,
married Jennet ----- and made his will 30 July 1647,
probated 17 April 1650, naming sons Cuthbert, William (minor), Richard, daughters Isabel, Jenet, Elizabeth.

    Issue: surname Hayhurst or Hairst
2 i.   Cuthbert, eldest son.
  ii.   William, minor 1647, b. ca. 1635, m. 1665
        Grace Bond aet. 24.
 iii. Richard.
  iv. Isabel, m. 6 Jan. 1655/6 Stephen Wilkinson.
   v.   Jenet.
  vi. Elizabeth.

    2. Cuthbert Hayhurst, eldest son of William Hay-
hurst (Cuthbert) by his wife Jennet -----, died 19
1st mo. 1676, buried at Newton, "aged"; married
Alice ----- who died 17 11th mo. 1667, buried at
Newton. They were the parents of the immigrant
brothers.

    Issue: surname Hayhurst or Hairst
  i.   Alice, m. at John Driver's house in Bolland,
       2 7th mo. 1665, Thomas Wiglesworth, no
       issue. They came to America on the *Lamb,*
       were covered by the Settle certificate of
       7 4th mo. 1682, and he d. testate between
       13 9th mo. 1682 and 11 1st mo. 1683 when
       the inventory of his estate was taken. See
       the sketch devoted to him.
  ii.   William, m. at James Harson's [or Harrison's]
       house in Waddington, 15 7th mo. 1666, Do-
       rothy Rudd, daughter of Edward Rudd, and
       sister of Mary Rudd who m. his brother
       Cuthbert, and of Jane Rudd, wife of Rich-

ard Waln and mother of Nicholas Waln, on
whom see the sketch devoted to him. This
Dorothy d. in England and she does not appear in the Settle certificate, though Myers thought she had come to Pennsylvania,
survived her husband, and had meetings at
her house (things true of her sister Mary).
William was bur. at Middletown, 15 10th
mo. 1682, and William Penn's letter to Margaret Fox, dated 29 8th mo. 1684, says:
"Poor Cut Hurst & Brother deceast soon after arrivall, fixing on a low marshy place
(tho a dry banck was not a Stone's cast
from ym) for ye rivers sake: they had ye
Ague & feaver but [there has been] no
Sickening in any other settlements." [I
owe this quotation to Mrs. Marion Balderston.] In the A. C. Myers Welcome Papers
is a letter from Warren S. Ely describing
a 1652 Bible once belonging to this William Hayhurst. The details suggest that
Mr. Ely had the Bible in his hands but the
letter does not say where it was at the
time, and it cannot be found in the Historical Society of Pennsylvania or the Bucks
County Historical Society.

3 iii. Cuthbert, d. in Pennsylvania 1683.
  iv. ?Margery, b. 1643, m. 1668 John Parker, b.
      1644, both of Slaidburn (Pavor's Marriage
      Licenses). This is the most reasonable
      place to enter this woman--Mr. Justice
      made her a daughter of her brother Cuth-
      bert.

    3. Cuthbert Hayhurst, son of Cuthbert Hayhurst
(William, Cuthbert) by his wife Jennet ----, came
to America, as stated above, on the *Lamb,* but after
he had been in Jamaica first.[4] He died in Pennsylvania, buried at Middletown, 2 1st mo. 1682/3. He
married in England, at John Driver's house, 28 8th
mo. 1666, Mary Rudd, daughter of Edward Rudd, and
she was buried in Pennsylvania, 24 7th mo. 1686.
She was the sister of Dorothy Rudd who had married
her husband's brother William, and of Jane, the wife
of Richard Waln and mother of Nicholas Waln to whom
a sketch has been devoted. For the details of Cuthbert's illness and death, see above, this page. Inventory was taken on his estate, 11 1st mo. 1682/3,

by Nicholas Waln, James Dilworth, Thomas Stackhouse
and John Eastbourne, and includes three manservants
[one was John Cowgill] and one maidservant. Inventory was taken on Mary's estate 1 9th mo. 1686, and
administration was granted 1 9th mo. 2 James II 1686
to William Hearst and Alles Wigglesworth, both of
Neshamineh, the decedents being parents of said
William, with Thomas Stackhouse and Nicholas Waln
also signing the bond.[5]

    Issue: surname Hayhurst
    i.   Elizabeth, b. 3 9th mo. 1669, m. Neshaminy
           Meeting, 10 2nd mo. 1690, William Croas-
           dale, eldest son of Thomas and Agnes (Ha-
           thornthwaite) Croasdale, on whom see the
           Croasdale sketch.
4 ii.   William, bur. 2 6th mo. 1713.
5 iii. Margery, b. Yorkshire, 29 1st mo. 1671.
    iv.   John, b. Yorkshire, 7 4th mo. 1673, bur. at
           Middletown, 8 6th mo. 1727. He was over-
           seer of Middletown Meeting. An inventory
           of his estate was exhibited 30 Xber 1727,
           bond of Cuthbert Hayhurst and Cuthbert
           Hayhurst Jr., 14 Oct. 1727.[6] No evidence
           of wife or child has been found and Bucks
           Deeds 9:484 say that he d. intestate and
           without issue.
6 v.   Cuthbert, b. Yorkshire, 30 2nd mo. 1678,bur.
           22 6th mo. 1733.

7 vi.   Alice, b. Yorkshire, 20 1st mo. 1679.

    4. William Hayhurst, second child and eldest son
of Cuthbert Hayhurst (Cuthbert, William, Cuthbert)
by his wife Mary Rudd, was doubtless born in Yorkshire but his birth record is curiously omitted from
the list of the children recorded at Middletown Monthly Meeting. Perhaps it was he who had these births
entered after his parents' death and forgot to include himself. He administered his parents' estates
in 1686; in 1687 signed the memorial on selling liquor to the Indians as Willm Hayhurst[7]. He married
17 10th mo. 1702 Rachel Radcliffe, daughter of James
and Mary (Holden) Radcliffe, a marriage which also is
proved by Bucks Deeds 3:411, which sells land late
of James Radcliffe of Wrightstown to Jonathan Cooper,
15 12th mo. 1704, recorded 21 March 1707/8. This
deed shows that Rachel's mother Mary had by then married ----- Baker, and Mary signed the deed by mark.

William sold some of his father's property to
Philip Howell,[8] and the following deeds are of record in Doylestown:

Bucks Deeds

1:218 William Hayhurst of Bucks, eldest son of
Cuthbert Hayhurst, to Henry Huddleston
husbandman, £10, 23 12th mo. 5 James II
1688, rec. 27 1st mo. 1689.

2:250 same parties, 11 7th mo. 1699, rec. 16 7th
mo. 1699.

3:188 William Hayhurst of Middletown, to John
Cutler, land laid out to Cuthbert Hayhurst,
9 10th mo. 1704, rec. 7 Jan. 1703/4.

3:238 William Hayhurst of Bucks, yeoman, son of
Cuthbert Hayhurst, to Joseph Growdon et al.
1 Dec. 1704, rec. 2 Dec. 1705.

3:308 William Hayhurst of Middletown, yeoman,
son of Cuthbert Hayhurst, to brother John
Hayhurst, 27 11th mo. 1706, rec. 27 Jan.
1706 i.e. same day.

3:310 William Hayhurst to Cuthbert Hayhurst [his
brother], 27 11th mo. 1706, rec. 27 Jan.
1706.

3:312 Jno Hayhurst batchelor and Cuthbert Hayhurst to William Hayhurst "our eldest
brother" land laid out to Cuthbert Hayhurst and confirmed to their mother, date
of deed 26 11th mo. 1706/7.

The will of Rachel Hayhurst of Middletown dated
6 9th mo. 1714, probated 18 July 1715[9] shows that
she had administered her husband's estate [no record found], names as executors brothers-in-law John
Cutler and John Hayhurst. Several children are
mentioned but not named; witnesses: Cornelius Mac-
Carthy, Susanna Carver, Margery Cutler.

Issue: surname Hayhurst

i.   Mary, b. 1703, d. 22 1st mo. 1729/30; m.
24 2nd mo. 1722 at Middletown, Matthew
Wildman, b. 11 12th mo. 1678/9, bur. 8
2nd mo. 1741, son of Martin and Ann (Ward)
Wildman. That Mary Wildman was William
Hayhurst's daughter is proved by Bucks
Deeds 11:179. Though she did not live
long, her six children included twins.
See Jane W. T. Brey, *A Quaker Saga* (Phil-
adelphia 1967), pp. 560-564.

                    Issue: surname Wildman
          1. Martin.   4. Elizabeth.
          2. James.   5. Rachel.
          3. Ann.   6. Mary.
    8 ii. Cuthbert, probably b. 15 7th mo. 1706 (so
           Justice).
      iii. Elizabeth, m. Middletown, 20 11th mo. 1731
           [1731/2], John Linton.
      iv. Rachel, m. 23 2nd mo. 1735, Bezaleel Wig-
           gins, son of Benjamin Wiggins.

    5. Margery Hayhurst, daughter of Cuthbert Hayhurst
(Cuthbert, William, Cuthbert) by his wife Mary Rudd,
was born in Yorkshire, 29 1st mo. 1671 and was still
living when executrix of her husband's will. She married at Middletown, 17 4th mo. 1702/3, John Cutler,
who had come on the *Rebecca* of Liverpool, the M^r
James Skiner, arriving in this river 31 3rd mo. 1685,
with his brother Edmund Cutler of Slateburn.[10] See
the sketch devoted to Edmund Cutler. John Cutler of
Middletown made his will 7 11th mo. 1718, probated[11]
6 June 1720, naming wife Margery sole executrix;
minor son Benjamin; daughters Elizabeth and Mary Cutler, brother-in-law John Hayhurst. The will of Margery Cutler of Middletown, widow, 22 12th mo. 1722,
probated 20 Aug. 1723[12], names son Benjamin and
daughters Elizabeth and Mary; executors: brothers
John and Cuthbert Hayhurst. John Cutler had brought
with him servants: William Wardle to serve 4½ years,
loose on 30 2nd mo. 1688; James Molinex, son of James,
late of Liverpool, about three years of age, to serve
to the age of 22 years. William Croasdale's will
in 1715[13] mentions John Cutler's daughters. The
Cutler Memorial (p. 550) wrongly makes this John a
son of his brother Edmund. In 1685 Edmund had no
John, and as Margery Hayhurst was aged 24 in 1685,
her husband is unlikely to have been born later than
that year.

       Issue: surname Cutler, order unknown
       i.   Benjamin.
       ii. Elizab th.
       iii. Mary.

    6. Cuthbert Hayhurst, son of Cuthbert Hayhurst
(Cuthbert, William, Cuthbert) by his wife Mary Rudd,
was born in Yorkshire, 30 2nd mo. 1678. It was probably he who was buried at Middletown, 22 6th mo.
1733. He married 1 4th mo. 1723 Mary Harker, who
was still living in 1772, and she married, second,

8 11th mo. 1734/5 Robert Stockdale. Mr. Justice was
inclined to think Mary Harker a second wife, for her
husband was 51 when he married in 1723, but the children all seem to be minors. Cuthbert's will is dated
20 6th mo. 1733, probated 6 Nov. 1734,[14] and he names
wife Mary, eldest son William, a minor, sons John,
James, eldest daughter Elizabeth, daughter Ruth;
trustees Cuthbert Hayhurst [who must be his nephew,
only son of William] and Benjamin Cutler [another
nephew, son of Margery]. No executor being named,
letters of administration c.t.a. were issued to the
widow Mary. The trustees petitioned Orphans Court
at the session of 10 March 1734/5, asking that Robert
Stockdale and wife Mary be directed to render an account and it was so ordered.[15] On 4 Aug. 1735 the
Court appointed the two trustees as guardians of the
children, and on 9 Xber 1734 Mary Hayhurst--she had
not yet married Stockdale--was ordered to produce an
inventory. It must have been this Cuthbert Hayhurst
who was of Southampton, yeoman, when he conveyed to
[his nephew] John Hayhurst of the same, yeoman, on
10 June 1712.[16] He also quitclaimed to his nephew
Cuthbert Hayhurst.[17]

    Issue: surname Hayhurst
    i.   William, b. 1 1st mo. 1723/4 (so Justice),
          minor in 1733, d. between 7 Sept. 1795 and
          15 Oct. 1795, dates of execution and pro-
          bation of his will[18] naming wife Rebeckah,
          executors: son John and cousin Joseph Hay-
          hurst of Middletown; son John ¼; to daugh-
          ter Rebeckah Spencer [who m. 27 5th mo.
          1779 Abel Spencer, b. 8 8th mo. 1753, son
          of William and Elizabeth (Lewis) Spencer
          of Abington and Middletown] ¼; to son
          Cuthbert [b. 26 11th mo. 1745/6] ¼; and ¼
          to grandchildren Joseph, William, Rebeckah
          and James, all named Carter; witnesses:
          Joseph Thornton, Joseph Croasdale. He m.
          Christ Church, Philadelphia, 14 Nov. 1745,
          Rebecca Searle, identified by Mr. Justice
          as daughter of Arthur and ----- (Naylor)
          Searle. William and his brother John or
          perhaps his son John were executors of the
          estate of son-in-law William Carter.[19]
          Issue: surname Hayhurst
       1. John, named first in his father's will
          and perhaps child of an earlier wife
          than Rebecca.

    2. Rebeckah, m. 27 5th mo. 1779, Abel Spencer, b. 8 8th mo. 1753, son of William and Elizabeth (Lewis) Spencer of Abington and Middletown.

    3. Cuthbert, b. 26 11th mo. 1745/6, undoubtedly firstborn of the wife Rebeckah but named third in the will; probably the grantee of a deed of 10 Oct. 1793, rec. 12 Oct. 1793[20], grantors John Leedom and wife Mary, widow of William Carter of Northampton, miller, and William and John Hayhurst, executors to said Carter.

    4. Mary, b. 25 10th mo. 1747; m. (1) William Carter of Northampton, miller; (2) John Leedom.

        Issue: surname Carter
     a. Joseph.
     b. William.
     c. Rebeckah.
     d. James.

ii.   Elizabeth, b. 14 2nd mo. 1726/7, m., according to Mr. Justice, Bezaleel Wiggins.

iii. John, b. 1728, in father's will 1733; m. at Wrightstown, 9 6th mo. 1762, Mary Wiggins, b. 26 10th mo. 1742, d. 11 7th mo. 1818, daughter of Bezaleel and Rachel (Hayhurst).

iv. Ruth, b. 5 7th mo. 1730, m. Joseph Warner.

v.   James, b. 3 9th mo. 1732; d. 1783; m. 7 4th mo. 1757, at Horsham, Ann Spencer, b. 16 11th mo. 1737, daughter of William and Elizabeth (Lewis) Spencer. James Hayhurst of Middletown, cordwainer, and wife Ann conveyed to John Mitchell, 10 June 1760, rec. 9 Jan. 1769[21], and on 1 June 1774 he conveyed to Samuel Mitchell of Middletown, yeoman, rec. 11 March 1782.[22] This last identifies James as son of Cuthbert, late of Northampton, dec., who had bought the land 4 Nov. 1729 from Cuthbert Hayhurst Jr., Elizabeth Hayhurst and Rachel Hayhurst, late of Middletown [obviously the children of William (Cuthbert, Cuthbert, William, Cuthbert)]. Ann Hayhurst of the Co. of Harford, Maryland, who was sick in the township of Northampton, Bucks Co., Pa., when on 6 May 1789 she signed by mark her will, probated 25 May 1789,[23] names children James Hayhirst, David Hayhirst, Hannah Hayhirst, grandchild Ann Hanaway,

daughter Sarah Newberry, granddaughter Ann
Newberry; witnesses: Hugh Edames, Thomas
Spencer, James Spencer. See Addenda, p. 609.
- iv. Elizabeth, b. 14 2nd mo. 1726/7, m., according to Mr. Justice, Bezaleel Wiggins.
- v.   Ruth, b. 5 7th mo. 1730, m. Joseph Warner.

7. Alice Hayhurst, youngest child of Cuthbert
Hayhurst (Cuthbert, William, Cuthbert) by his wife
Mary Rudd, was born in Yorkshire, 29 lst mo. 1679;
m. 16 12th mo. 1708, Henry Nelson. The will of
Henry Nelson of Middletown was dated 11 April 1744,
probated 4 May 1745,[24] and names daughter Alice Carter and her children, Henry, John and James Carter,
minors; son Thomas Nelson, minor; wife Alice; daughter Ann Wilson and her children, Henry and Elizabeth
Wilson, minors; daughter Letitiah Joly and her children Nelson and Alice Joly; daughter Jemimah Heaton's
children Robert and Thomas Heaton, minors; nephew
Edward Worstill, minor; negro man, name illegible,
to be set free; executors: wife Alice, well-beloved
son Thomas, trusty friend Euclydus Longshore; witnesses: John Watson, John Woolson, Edward Worstil.
The inventory taken 13 3rd mo. May 1745 came to
£924/7/3½.

Issue: surname Nelson, order unknown
- i.   Alice, m. ----- Carter and had
     Issue:surname Carter
     1. Henry, minor in 1744.
     2. John, minor in 1744.
     3. James, minor in 1744.
- ii. Thomas, minor in 1744.
- iii. Ann, m. ----- Wilson and had
     Issue: surname Wilson
     1. Henry, minor in 1744.
     2. Elizabeth, minor in 1744.
- iv. Letitia, m. ----- Joly and had
     Issue: surname Joly
     1. Nelson, minor in 1744.
     2. Alice, minor in 1744.
- v.   Jemima, not living 1744, m. ----- Heaton and
     had
     Issue: surname Heaton
     1. Robert, minor in 1744.
     2. Thomas, minor in 1744.

8. Cuthbert Hayhurst, known generally as Cuthbert
Jr., to distinguish him from his uncle, only son of

William Hayhurst (Cuthbert, Cuthbert, William, Cuthbert) by his wife Rachel Radcliffe, was born, according to Mr. Justice, 15 7th mo. 1706 but did not
die, as the same authority says, on 26 12th mo. 1795
for he must be the Cuthbert whose widow Deliverance
--her maiden name was Bills--and two oldest sons
John Hayhurst Jr. and Cuthbert Hayhurst renounced
administration on 4 1st mo. 1754 in favor of Bezaleel Wiggins [brother-in-law of deceased] and Robert
Croasdale.[25] The recital in Bucks Deeds 9:484 makes
clear that this man was the only son and heir of
William Hayhurst and that he died intestate, having
had seven children, of whom, by 1758, two had died,
one being the eldest, the other presumably though
it is not specifically stated, the second son, and
that, as a result, another Cuthbert Hayhurst, the
grantor of this deed, became the eldest surviving
son of his father. Who the others were is told us
by Bucks Orphans Court file 220 where the five surviving children are listed as Cuthbert Hayhurst the
petitioner, William, Margery, Thomas and Joseph (a
minor).

Issue: surname Hayhurst
i.   John, whose estate included cooper's tools.
      The file 846 contains only the bond of
      Cuthbert Hayhurst yeoman of Middletown and
      of Abraham Harding of Southampton, 6 Jan.
      1754. Doubtless the administrator was his
      brother.
ii.   Another son, d. 1754-1758.
iii. Cuthbert, ultimately the eldest surviving
      son of his father, perhaps d. 1795.
iv.   William, in whose estate (file 2190) there
      is nothing but the bond of Cuthbert Hay-
      hurst and William Hayhurst, dated 30 Dec.
      1789.
v.   Joseph, in whose estate (file 2191) there
      is the bond of Cuthbert Hayhurst and
      William Hayhurst, dated 30 Dec. 1789.
      Note that the signatories to the bond
      and the date are the same as for brother
      William above.
vi.   Thomas.
vii. Margery.

NOTES

[1]See PGM 23:52, note 92.   [2]1 PA 1:45 .
[3]Coll. Gen. Soc. Pa. 1.   [4]So Mrs. Balderston.

[5]BD 1:81. This would have been expected in the
Register of Wills' office but it is in a deed book.
    [6]BW file 260.   [7]Middletown Min. 170.
    [8]2 PA 19:229, session of 29 10th mo. 1701.
    [9]BW file 163.   [10]PMHB 9:232 f.
    [11]BW 1:50   [12]BW 1:75.
    [13]See p. 148 above; the will was dated 30 1st mo.
1715.
    [14]BW 1:219, file 368   [15]Bucks Orph. C. file 50.
    [16]BD 4:192.   [17]BD 9:484.
    [18]BW 5:452, file 2599.   [19]See BD 27:173.
    [20]*Ibid.*   [21]BD 11:179.
    [22]BD 21:377.   [23]BW file 2200.
    [24]BW file 514.   [25]BW file 844.

HEATH, ANDREW   *disproved*

This name appears on List X only. The truth is
that Andrew Heath came on the *Friends' Adventure*,
arriving 28 7th mo. 1682, as servant to William
Yardley, to serve four years, loose on 29 7th mo.
1686. It is probable that he was a relative, perhaps a nephew, of William Yardley's wife Jane Heath
but we have not seen documentary evidence to prove
this. Andrew Heath was about twenty on 9 10th mo.
1 James II 1685.[1]

He married, first, by 2 12th mo. 1701/2, Elizabeth Barret, sister of Thomas Barret and widow of
two earlier husbands. She had come with her first
husband, William Venable of Chatkill, parish of Ec-
cleshall, Staffordshire, who died in Bucks County,
17 10th mo. 1683; their daughter Joyce, who by 1699
had married John Richardson, once servant to John
Clowes,[2] and their daughter Frances, but no servants,
also on the *Friends' Adventure*, arriving, as stated,
on 28 7th mo. 1682, but after Venable's death had
married Lawrence Bannor of whom we know no more.[3]
Heath married, second, Hannah -----, widow of -----
Clark by whom she had in 1716 three children, Daniel,
Samuel and Hannah Clark, and this second wife Hannah
survived him. He made his will[4] on 3 Jan. 1716/7 when
of Hopewell Township, Hunterdon County, yeoman, and
it was probated 29 Dec. 1720, so that he probably
died in the latter year. He mentions wife Hannah,
daughter Martha under 18; and the following children:
John, Elizabeth, Andrew, Sarah (under 21), Richard;
also grandchildren Elizabeth, Abigail, Andrew Peittet,
John Heath; son-in-law Nathaniel Pettet; wife's child-

ren: Daniel, Samuel and Hannah Clark; executors:
Thomas Lambert and Robert Heaton; witnesses: John
Plumly, Nathaniel Pettet.

   Issue: surname Heath
   i.   John, mentioned in father's will 1717.
   ii.   Elizabeth, mentioned in father's will 1717.
         She, or possibly a sister dead in 1717, m.
         Nathaniel Pettit, son of Nathaniel Pettit
         Sr. who mentions the son in a will dated
         15 March 1714/15[5]; the son Nathaniel was
         mentioned in Andrew Heath's will of which
         he was also a witness, and may have been
         the man of this name who died intestate in
         Hunterdon County, administration granted
         to Aaron Pettit as late as 3 Dec. 1779.[6]
           Issue: surname Pettit
         1. Elizabeth.
         2. Abigail.
         3. Andrew, all mentioned in their grandfather
            Andrew Heath's will in 1717.
   iii. Andrew, made his will of Amwell Township,
         Hunterdon Co., N.J., 23 Aug. 1745, probated
         5 Oct. 1745,[7] naming sons Andrew, John,
         Richard, David, Timothy; daughters Eliza-
         beth Ketchum, Mary, Catherine, Sarah; exe-
         cutors: wife and son Andrew; witnesses:
         Ephraim Quimby, Daniel Ketchum, John Lew-
         is M.D.
           Issue: surname Heath
         1. Andrew, probably the man of this name who
            d. intestate, admin. 24 June 1777 to
            Magdalene Heath, John Heath, fellow-
            bondsman; inventory 20 June 1777 came
            to £226/1/3.[8]
         2. John, probably the fellow bondsman of
            brother Andrew's estate in 1777.
         3. Richard, d. intestate of Hunterdon Co.,
            admin. to David Heath [his brother?],
            fellow bondsman Walter Cane; witness
            Benjamin Yard Jr.; inventory 8 Nov.
            1769, account 1 July 1771, date of ad-
            min. 1 Nov. 1769.[9]
         4. David, admin. of brother Richard 1769.
         5. Timothy, mentioned in father's will 1745.
         6. Elizabeth, m. ----- [perhaps Daniel] Ket-
            chum by 1745.
         7. Mary, mentioned in father's will 1745.
         8. Catherine, also mentioned in the will.

        9. Catherine, mentioned in the will.
       10. Sarah, mentioned in the will.
  iv. Sarah, under 21 in 1717.
  v.   Richard, mentioned in father's will 1717 as
      youngest son; administration, when of Beth-
      lehem, Hunterdon Co., 10 April 1747, to
      Mary Heath of Bethlehem, Daniel Ketchum,
      fellow bondsman, witnesses: Wm Peirson,
      Joshua Howell; Mary Heath shown to be a
      Friend; her account 16 May 1757 calls her
      Mary Park, formerly Mary Heath.[10]
  vi. Martha, under 18 in 1717.

NOTES

[1]PGM 23:46 f., note 75.   [2]PGM 24:82, note 49.
[3]PGM 23:49, note 80; 2 PA 19:243, 264, 326 f.,
523; *Records of Bucks County Courts* 238, 258, 261,
291.
  [4]NJW 1:219 f.   [5]NJW 1:363.
  [6]NJW 5:392.   [7]NJW 2:228.
  [8]NJW 5:237.   [9]NJW 3:185.
 [10]NJW 2:228.

HEATON, ROBERT[1]	*disproved*
HEATON, ALICE, his wife	*disproved*
HEATON, GRACE, his daughter	*disproved*
HEATON, ROBERT, his son	*disproved*
HEATON, JAMES, his son	*disproved*
HEATON, AGNES, his daughter	*disproved*
HEATON, EPHRAIM, his son	*disproved*

    According to a manuscript folder marked "HEATON"
in the Genealogical Society of Pennsylvania library,
"Robert Heaton is believed to have arrived on the
Welcome with William Penn." The claim also is made
in the second edition of W. W. H. Davis, *History of
Bucks County, Pennsylvania* (New York 1905), 3:545.
    The disproof comes from the fact that Robert "Ea-
ton" shipped 1 pack qty 350 ells English linen, on
the *Lamb* of Liverpool, John Tench, master, and so
undoubtedly travelled himself with his wife and five
children, arriving in the Delaware River on or about
22 Oct. 1682.[2] The certificate given to Robert and
Alice Heaton--the children are not mentioned but undoubtedly accompanied their parents--was issued by
the Settle Monthly Meeting in Yorkshire on 7 4th mo.
1682. On the same date the same meeting issued another certificate covering a large party of Friends,
most of whom, if not all, were related to each other,

and these Friends also crossed the Atlantic on the
Lamb. Upon arriving both certificates were recorded
in the minutes of the Middletown Monthly Meeting in
Bucks County, the Heaton certificate after the other
one but on the same page.[3] In this connection, Section E of the Introduction should be read.

Robert Heaton was born ca. 1635-1645, almost certainly in Yorkshire and very probably at Settle in
the parish of Giggleswick, co. York, in which parish
the registers show Heatons from 1560. It seems likely that our Robert was a nephew of another Robert
Heaton, "of Setle in the parish of Gigleswick,"
singleman, whose will was dated 25 Feb. 1635, proved
in July 1636,[4] though the younger Robert is not mentioned in this will. Perhaps he had not yet been
born or was very small in 1636.

By 1667 our Robert was a member of the Settle
Monthly Meeting, in which year the birth of his eldest child was recorded, as were those of all the
children born later. In 1670 and 1671 Robert Heaton
of Settle Meeting was fined £14-12-0 and £8-15-0 in
corn, hay, household goods, etc.[5]

Having come to America, Robert Heaton was present
at a Meeting held in the home of Nicholas Waln in
Bucks County, on Neshaminy Creek, 1 of 11th mo.
(Jan.) 1682/3.[6] A meeting was held at Robert Heaton's house in Bucks County in 1683.[6] According to
Davis,[7] Robert Heaton built the first mill in Bucks
County, on Chubb Run, "in the lower corner of Langhorne Manor," about 1683. He was a representative
elected for Bucks County to the Assembly of Pennsylvania, 10 3rd mo. 1698; 14 Oct. 1700; 1 6th mo.
1701.[8] He and Nicholas Waln were administrators of
the estate of Alexander Giles of Bucks County, 10
10th mo. 1684, and he made an inventory of the estate of Mary Hayhurst of Bucks County, 1 9th mo.
1686.

The will of Robert Heaton of Middletown Township,
Bucks County, yeoman, was signed by mark and dated
16 2nd mo. 1716, probated 16 July 1717.[9] He married,
no doubt in Yorkshire, England, about 1666, Alice
-----, who was named in the certificate of 1682 and
in his will of 1716. She was buried in the Friends
Burial Ground, Middletown, Bucks County, Pa., 7 2nd
mo. 1727.

    Issue: surname Heaton (all probably b. Settle)
    i.   Grace, b. 14 1st mo. 1667, d. in Bucks Co.,
             8 8th mo. 1708; m. in Bucks County, 27 2nd

          1688, Thomas Stackhouse the younger who
          m. two later wives, Ann, widow of Edward
          Mayos, and Dorothy, widow of Zebulon Hes-
          ton.

ii.   Robert, b. 3 6th mo. 1671, d. 1743; will
          dated Hampton Township, 17 March 1743,
          probated 23 July 1743,[10] naming wife Su-
          sanna; son Robert; daughters Sarah Walker,
          Grace Crossdale, Elizabeth Noble, Alice
          Plumly, Anna Heath; codicil 25 March 1743.
          He was elected to the Pennsylvania Assem-
          bly in 1709 and 1710.[11] He married (1) in
          Bucks Co., 8 3rd mo. 1700 [intentions at
          Philadelphia Monthly Meeting, 26 2nd mo.
          1700], Grace Pearson, b. at Keighley, co.
          York, 31 3rd mo. 1680, daughter of Thomas
          and Grace (Veepon) Pearson, and she d. in
          Middletown Township, 30 9th mo. 1719 [see
          Jane W. T. Brey, *A Quaker Saga* (Philadel-
          phia 1967), p. 125.] He m. (2) 3 9th mo.
          1720, Susanna (Griffith) Carter, widow of
          James Carter and daughter of John and E-
          lizabeth Griffith of Woodbridge, N.J.
          Eight children by the first marriage: Sar-
          ah, Grace, Elizabeth, Alice, Robert, Mary,
          Thomas, Isaac; three children by the sec-
          ond marriage: Robert (again), Alice (again)
          and Anne. Susanna Heaton of Northampton
          Township, "ancient," made her will 15 Jan.
          1766, probated 24 Jan. 1771,[12] naming son
          Joseph Carter executor; son William Car-
          ter dec.; late husband Robert Heaton dec.,
          bond dated 2 March 1731/2; son-in-law
          John Plumly also an executor; grandsons
          Richard and William Carter, sons of Joseph;
          Katherine Hayhurst, daughter of Sarah Hay-
          hurst; granddaughter Mary Plumly; Ann Car-
          ter, daughter of Rachel and Joseph; grand-
          children Isabel, Susanna and John Heaton
          at age 21; daughter Ann Hibbs and grand-
          daughter Susanna Hibbs.

iii. James, b. 25 12th mo. 1674; m. (out of meet-
          ing) in 1696, Ann Griffith, daughter of
          John and Elizabeth Griffith of Woodbridge,
          N.J.

iv.   Agnes, b. 22 9th mo. 1677; d. at Moreland,
          Pa., 30 10th mo. 1743; m. at Middletown
          Meeting House, Bucks County, 17 8th mo.

1695, Henry Comly the younger of Byberry,
Pa., d. at Moreland, Pa., 16 1st mo.
1726/7, on whom see the Comly sketch and
also George Norwood Comly, *The Comly Family in America* (Philadelphia 1939).
v. Ephraim, b. 17 6th mo. 1679, d. -----; living in Upper Dublin Township, Philadelphia
Co., 1743; m. at the house of Richard Worrell in Bucks Co., 13 11th mo. 1703, Sarah Parker, daughter of Humphrey Parker,
of Dublin Township, Philadelphia County.

NOTES

[1]This sketch is largely based on information
kindly furnished by John Insley Coddington, F.A.S.G.,
a Heaton descendant. See the Heaton sketch in
George Norwood Comly, *The Comly Family in America*
(Philadelphia 1939), 884-890.
[2]PGM 23:53, note 95.
[3]Middletown Monthly Meeting minutes, p. 1 of
certificates.
[4]Original will, York Probate Registry, bundle
for July 1636.
[5]Joseph Besse, *Sufferings* 2:130 f.
[6]Middletown Monthly Meeting minutes.
[7]DHBC
[8]2 PA 9:753; 8 PA 1:201, 243, 277; also 2 PA 9:
754; 8 PA 1:206 f., 212, 265.
[9]BW 1:33.
[10]2 PA 9:754; 8 PA 1:921, 924 f., 1003 f., 1010 f.
[11]BW 2:26.   [12]BW 3:227.

†HERIOTT, THOMAS   *proved*

This name appears, of course, on all lists but
the line has been extinct since the death of Thomas
Heriott on board the *Welcome*. He was of Hurst-pier-
pont, Sussex, yeoman, son of John Heriott who had
died 20 2nd mo. 1672, buried at Twiniham. John was
also father of Mary, second wife of Dennis Rochford,
both *Welcome* passengers, and of Ann, wife of Richard
Scrase. Thomas Heriott was a First Purchaser of two
purchases of 2500 acres each in Group 20.[1] Mrs.
Balderston informs me that he was a friend of William
Penn and that he died 19 Sept. 1682, but this is
merely the date of his nuncupative will which is the
proof of his presence on the *Welcome*.

The Last Will & Testament Nuncupative of Thomas
Heriott | late of Hurstpre=Poynt in y^e County of
Sussex in Old England Yeoman, | Lately deceased,
as it was spoken & delivered by him, the nineteenth
day of | y^e seventh Moneth commonly called Septem-
ber Anno One Thousand Six | Hundred & Eighty two,
on Board y^e Ship Welcome Robert Greenaway | Comman-
der then Bound by permission of God for Pennsil-
vania. | The aforesaid Thomas Heriott being sick &
weak in body, | but of sound memory & understanding,
as, by several sensible words of good | Counsel &
Advice then given, it was evident; Amongst which,
for y^e disposal | and settlement of his worldly
Estate, he did to us declare his last Will | & Tes-
tament as followeth, | viz That he did desire That
his Brother | in law Dennis Rochford should have
his goods & Man=Servant then on Board | ye said Ship,
& also what he had in money or moneys worth else=
where, | excepting threescore pounds which he had
in London wch he did desire, y^t | his Sister Anne
Scrace [not Strate, as printed] should have: And
this he declared, delivered, & | confirmed, as his
Last Will & Testament the day and Year above=said |
in y^e presence of US whose names are hereunto Sub-
scribed as Witnesse our | Hands.
George Thompson Grocer
Thowynne, Chyrurgeon
David Ogden waver
Joshua Morris Tine plate worker

This will was proved by before Christopher Tayler
Regist^r gen^ll [three illegible words cancelled] by
Dennis Rochford the second day of | the ffifth
Month | leave graunted him to administer | he
bringing in a true Inventory of the deceased's
Estate | within Three monthes next after the date
hereof.

The omitted year was 1683, the scrivener a good one,
and the will may have been put on paper after the arrival in Philadelphia. Perhaps Heriott died in Pennsylvania. The printed version[2] has the sister as Anne
Strate. The unnamed manservant may have been Thomas
Jones, afterwards registered by Rochford as his servant.
The inventory was as follows:

An Inventory of the goods of Thomas Heriott

The Last Will & Testament Nuncupative of Thomas Heriott
late of Hurstpre=Poynt in y{e} County of Sussex in Old England Yeoman,
lately deceased, as it was spoken & delivered by him, the nineteenth day of
y{e} seventh Moneth commonly called September Anno One Thousand Six
Hundred & Eighty two, on Board y{e} Ship Welcome Robert Greenaway
Commander then Bound by permission of God for Pennsilvania.

The aforesaid Thomas Heriott being sick & weak in body,
but of sound memory & understanding, as, by several sensible words of good
Counsel & Advice then given, it was evident. Amongst which for y{e} disposal
and settlement of his worldly Estate, he did to us declare his last Will
& Testament as followeth, viz. That he did desire That his Brother
in law Dennis Rochford should have his goods & Man servant then on Board
y{e} said Ship, & also what he had in money or money's worth else=where,
excepting threescore pounds which he had in London, w{ch} he did desire, y{e}
his Sister Anne Grace should have. And this he declared, delivered, &
confirmed as his Last Will & Testament the day and Year above=said
in y{e} presence of US whose names are hereunto Subscribed as Witnesse our
Hands

George Thompson (Greene)
Thowynne Chyrurgeon
David Ogden [word]
Joshua morrell Tinnplate=worker

This Will was proved in oepore Christopher Taylor Regist{r}
gent{le} _____ by Denny Rochford the second day of
the fifth Month, yleave granted him to administer —
he bringing in a true Inventory of the decease's Estate
within three months next after the date hereof

as truly taken as we could to y^e Best of our skill
and knowledg this 14th of y^e 7th mo 1683

6 Beads [beds] worth aboute	016: 00: 00
3 couerlitt 2 Rugs: 6 Blankitt aboute	003: 15: 00
~~2 pair of Curtanes~~ & some wearing clothes	015: 00: 00
A Chest of Linin, worth aboute	016: 00: 00
some Cushions, 2 paire of curtains at	002: 05: 00
30^{lb} of ould puter & som iron things	003: 10: 06
Som new puter & new iron ware	020: 02: 00
Som Chests: & new nails	006: 00: 06
some new bodys & som colering Shiff [?]	004: 15: 07
som seeds of meale & beans & some new spades	002: 00: 04½
in bread & som new saws	001: 02: 03
some new hatts and Linin Cloath	022: 05: 08
in grocery ware and som Brasiers goods	007: 09: 00
Som haberdashery ware and Cutlers ware	025: 00: 00
Som new shoose	013: 10: 00
Rece^d in Depts Due to him	058: 00: 00
Som netts to fish with	002: 18: 06
one Iron pott: 1 gridiron & 2 warming pans	000: 17: 00
a sadle and A watch	003: 08: 00
in money when he Dyed in his pocketts	003: 00: 00
in Land purchased of Wm Penn	100: 00: 00
som new Blankitts and Couerlide	002: 01: 00
one Dept more Recd on his account	013: 00: 00
	340: 10: 04½
more in goods and mony	030: 00: 00
	370: 10: 04½
Som made up glass which came to	002: 00: 00
some new fishing nets Cost	002: 18: 06
	375 -08 -10½

Wee whose names are hereunder written
doe hereby certify that Dennis Rochford
~~& his wife~~ does attest this to be
true Inventory of the Estate of the
said Thomas Herriott, before me Christop^h
Taylor Regist gen^{ll} of the Province of
Pennsilvania &c   Philip England
                       Geo Langhorn

**This inventory raises the interesting question of
whether many of the items shown were not intended
for sale and should therefore have been listed in a
port book and duty paid. Thomas Heriott's name does**

not appear as loading on the *Welcome* in the London
port book. Perhaps he joined the ship at some other
port in the Channel like Brighthelmston (now Brighton) where his brother-in-law Dennis Rochford had resided.

Besse's *Sufferings* 1:721, under date of 21 Nov.
1676, shows Thomas Heriott of Hurstpierpont, after
long imprisonment for tithes at the suit of Manred
Shaw, priest of that parish, had £25 worth of cattle
taken away. A record of Lewes Monthly Meeting describes Heriott as one who "walked orderly and hon-
estly Amongst us since his conuincement and have
borne his testimony for ye truth Against the Nation-
all Priest on ye Account of Tythes."

At Lewes Monthly Meeting 21 4th mo. 1682 Thomas
Heriott, Denis Rochford of Brighthelmston and John
Cheesemen (alias Chisman) of New Shoreham, applied
for certificates, being minded, if the Lord permit,
to go to Pensillvana. On 9 5th mo. 1682 Heryot's
certificate was enrolled but John Chisman's deferred
because of his wife's sickness, and later records
show him still in England on 20 12th mo. 1683, and
therefore the Cheesemans were not on the *Welcome*.
Herriott's certificate dated 19 5th mo. 1682, and
granted by Lewes and recorded in the Minute Book,
is in PGSP 12:273.f. Thomas Herriot subscribed £50
to the Society of Free Traders,[3] this item marked
"P.F." which probably means that Philip Ford had received the money according to the constitution of
the Society.

At Lewes Monthly Meeting, 21 9th mo. 1683, Richard Scrase produceth a letter from Mary Rochford,
his wife's sister, in wch Letter shee saith that her
Brother Thomas Heryot made a will in which he gave
his sister Ann Scrase some money due on a bond from
James Mathew, his unkel, which bond was produced to
this meeting by John Snaishfold [not the *Welcome*
passenger who was then dead] and the said John
Snaishfold promised to deliver the said bond as the
meeting should advise. And because the said Richard
Scrase desireth to right to Philadelphia in Pennsil-
vana for a coppy of ye said will, wee now desire
Ambrose Galloway and his son Ambrose Galloway and
Thomas Mosely to right, etc.

THE HERIOTT FAMILY

John Heriott died 20 2nd mo. 1672 and was buried
at Twiniham. His unknown wife may have been a sis-

ter of James Mathew who owed Thomas Heriott a bond
of £60 when Thomas died in 1682, and Mathew is designated "unkel" of Thomas in the passage quoted
above. As it is possible that John Heriott's sister had married Mathew, or that both Mathew and
Heriott had married sisters, this is not certain.
By his unknown wife John Heriott had, at least:

Issue: surname Heriott, perhaps others
i.   Thomas, d. unm. at sea shortly after 19 7th
        mo. 1682 or perhaps in Pennsylvania but
        in any case before 2 5th mo. 1683.
ii.   Anne, declared 1st intentions, 21 4th mo.
        1676, and m. at Coufeld, 15 7th mo. 1676,
        under the care of Lewes Monthly Meeting,
        Sussex, England, Richard Scrase who was
        still living 21 9th mo. 1683 but was dead
        by 20 1st mo. 1694/5, when his widow Ann
        was granted, late of Blechington, Sussex,
        a certificate by Lewes Monthly Meeting to
        go to Philadelphia with such of her five
        children as were willing to go. This rec-
        ord states that she was sister of Mary,
        widow of Diones Rochford.[4] The Scrases
        are a well-known Sussex family, on whom
        see John Comber, *Sussex Genealogies: Lewes
        Centre* (Cambridge 1933), pp. 237-247, on
        Scrase of Blatchington; M. A. Lower, "Gen-
        ealogical Memoir of the Family of Scrase"
        (*Sussex Archaeological Coll.* 8:1); J. H.
        Round, *Peerage and Pedigree* (London 1910)
        2:99, who denies that the Scrases were
        Danish and begins with a Richard Scrasce
        who died 1499. Richard Scrase, husband
        of Anne Heriott, probably d. ca. 1691 when
        admin. was granted to widow Ann, with Wal-
        ter Scrase of Bletchington one of the
        sureties. The only Richard Scrase with a
        close relative named Walter was a Richard
        of Pangdean in Piecombe and Hurstpierpont
        who had a brother Walter. They were Qua-
        kers and sons of Henry Scrase (Richard,
        Edward, Richard, Richard, Richard, which
        last d. 1480/1) of West Blatchington by
        his wife Joan Andrewes. Comber puts the
        birth of this Richard in 1635/6 and says
        that he d. ca. 1733, perhaps with a wife
        named Elizabeth, daughter of Thomas Tur-
        ner of Oldland. They had a daughter Mary

who m. by lic. dated Lewes, 12 May 1705,
when of Westmeston, at Clayton, Richard
Whitpaine of Hurstpierpont, gent., by
whom she had a son Richard who had the
manor of Pakyns from his maternal grandfather's will. Whether these Whitpaines
were kin to Richard Whitpaine of London,
who is discussed in the Whitpaine sketch,
is not certain but it is at least possible. Henry and Joan (Andrewes) Scrase
had also a son Henry punished as a Quaker
in 1660 and 1670; a son John, bapt. 2 Oct.
1638, d. ca. 1716, m. Philippe -----; a
son Walter, bapt. 4 April 1640, West
Blatchington, punished as a Quaker, d.
1718; and a daughter Susan, bapt. 28 Sept.
1628 at Hove, bur. there, 2 Feb. 1628/9.
It is strongly suspected that the Richard
who d. in 1733 was not the son of Henry
and Joan (Andrewes) Scrase, but that their
son was the one who m. Anne Heriott. Whether Anne (Heriott) Scrase used her certificate to come to America is unknown.[5]
    Issue: surname Scrase
1. Richard, d. in Pennsylvania, testate,
   1715, on whom see the Rochford sketch
   for further details.
2. Anne, m. by 1720 John Older or Houlder.
3. Elizabeth, m. by 1720 Jonas Revett.
4. Susanna, m. by 1720 James Larford/Lur-
   ford/Lasford or some other spelling.
5. Another, living 1695, not living 1715.
iii. Mary, d. by 28 10th mo. 1694 at Philadelphia; m., as 2nd wife, ca. 21 2nd mo. 1680,
   Dennis Rochford, b. Enniscorthy, co. Wexford, Ireland, ca. 1647, son of William
   Rochford; d. Philadelphia, 7 2nd mo. 1693.
   They came to America on the *Welcome* in
   1682. For a fuller account see the Rochford sketch.
    Issue: surname Rochford
1. Mary, d. at sea, aged 6 mos., 1682.
2. Mary, b. in Pennsylvania at Egely Point,
   22 8th mo. 1683, d. 9 3rd mo. 1702/3.
3. Heriott, d. by 1715.
4. Solomon, b. ?1689, d. 7 6th mo. 1765.
5. Dennis, d. 10 11th mo. 1739.
6. Another, counted in the five who survived

the parents, d. by 1715.

NOTES

[1]1 PA 1:42; 3 PA 3:388, 391, survey 30 7th mo. 1684.

[2]PGSP 1:46, Wills A-4.   [3]PMHB 11:175-180.

[4]The name Dennis is derived from that of Dionys-ius the Areopagite, a convert of St. Paul (Acts 17: 34). The name Dionysius is in turn derived from the name of the god Dionysus, which ultimately goes back to Zeus himself, so it is not surprising that Dennis is here called Diones.

[5]I owe thanks to Timothy Field Beard of the New York Public Library for photostats of Comber and Lower's works on the Scrases.

HEY, JOHN   *mythical*

This name appears on Lists A, B, C, E, G, H, I, J, K, L, M, N, P, Q, R, S, T, W, X, Y and Z. List F has it as John Otley and Lists O, U and V, as John Ottey, which is correct. The man was servant to Thomas Fitzwater and his further history is presented under his correct name. List D, however, prints the name as John Key, which see. There was no such person as John Hey or John Key in connection with the *Welcome*. The Doylestown copy of Bucks Arrivals shows the name as "O ttey," the space between the O and the rest being a little greater than it should be but perhaps not enough for a full space of separation. Through the letter O a line is drawn. I suspect this is a much later "correction", perhaps even in pencil, but as the page is laminated, it is impossible to determine the full truth.

HOLLINGSWORTH, VALENTINE   *disproved*
HOLLINGSWORTH, HENRY, his son   *disproved*

The name Valentine Hollingsworth appears on no list, that of his son Henry only on List X. In re-gard to Henry, the truth is that he crossed the At-lantic on the *Lion* of Liverpool, arriving on 14 8th mo. 1683, as servant to Robert Turner, the 14th of his 17 servants in the list, to serve two years, receive fifty acres, loose on 14 8th mo. 1685.

As for Valentine Hollingsworth, William B. Hol-lingsworth, *Hollingsworth Genealogical Memoranda in the United States from 1682 to 1884* (Baltimore, Md. 1884) says (p. 6) that he "came to America with

William Penn in 1682 with his family." An anonymous work called *Historical, Genealogical, and Biographical Account of the Jolliffe Family of Virginia, 1652 to 1893; also Sketches of the Neill's* [sic], *Janney's, Hollingsworth's, and other Cognate Families* (Philadelphia 1893), says on p. 145:

> Valentine Hollingsworth, a member of the Society of Friends, was born in Cheshire, England, about 1630 to 1640. He married Catherine, daughter of Henry Cornish, High-Sheriff of London, who was executed (unjustly) during the reign of James II, October 23, 1685. Valentine H. came with his family to America in the year 1682: he came before William Penn in the bark "Welcome."[2]

In a newspaper clipping of unknown source is found[3] an article by Emily Anderson Lantz, "Hollingsworth Lineage" and dated 26 Feb. 1905, which has much the same account as William B. Hollingsworth's. In George Norbury MacKenzie, *Colonial Families of the United States of America* 7:292-300, is a sketch of Hollingsworth which says he arrived "a few months after William Penn's arrival in the good ship *Welcome*." Finally, Joseph Adger Stewart, *Descendants of Valentine Hollingsworth, Senior* (Louisville, Kentucky, 1925), p. 1, we read:

> In 1682, Valentine Hollingsworth, Sr., and his family, accompanied by his son-in-law, Thomas Connaway, and by John Musgrave, an indent[ur]ed servant, sailed from Belfast for the Delaware River, arriving a few months after William Penn's arrival in the good ship "Welcome."

As a matter of fact we find nobody actually saying that Valentine actually came on the *Welcome*, but most of them somehow managing to mention the ship as if to allow some prestige to rub off on to Hollingsworth. It is generally believed that he did come, and such of his family as came with him, though not, as we have seen, his son Henry, on the ship *Antelope* which arrived on 10 10th mo. 1682 and brought at least one passenger from Ireland, namely, Ann Milcom of Armagh, Ireland, widow.

In 1735 during the dispute over the boundary with Maryland, testimony was given and recorded in the "Breviate"[4] by Samuel Hollingsworth, son of Valentine, then aged 67, who said he had come to the Province of Pennsylvania in 1682. Likewise, John

Musgrave, aged 73, gives the same year for his arrival and states that he was an indentured servant of
Valentine Hollingsworth; that he lived for four
years at New Castle; that he first saw William Penn
in the year 1682 at Robert Wade's house in the town
now called Chester in Pennsylvania. Now Penn was
entertained at his arrival by Robert Wade, and if
Musgrave, and his master Hollingsworth, had been on
the *Welcome*, they ought to have seen Penn at the
start of the voyage at the very latest. We conclude
that Hollingsworth and Musgrave arrived on a ship
which preceded both the *Welcome* and the *Antelope*.[5]

THE HOLLINGSWORTH FAMILY

1.   Henry Hollingsworth the elder, who by his
wife Katheran, was father to the immigrant Valentine
Hollingsworth, was of Ballyvickcrannell, Parish of
Seagoe, Co. Armagh, Ireland. In the Quaker records
in which the family is enrolled, the name of the
townland was regularly spelled Bellevickcrannell
and this was misread by Albert Cook Myers as Bellen-
iskcrannell, an error copied by Joseph Adger Stewart. The father was probably born in England and is
recorded in a Muster Roll of the Ulster Plantation[6]
ca. 1631 as fifth in a list of 24 tenants of Richard Cope, Esqr, and Mr. [Michael] Obbins, undertakers of 2,000 acres. Henry is assessed with a sword
and a Caliver (a primitive calibrated pistol).
     Whether Henry and Katheran had other children and
when, where and how they died, is not known, but
they had at least, the following

     Issue: surname Hollingsworth
2   i.   Valentine, b. at Ballyvickcrannell, 6th mo.
         1632.[7]

     2. Valentine Hollingsworth, son of Henry and Ka-
theran (-----) Hollingsworth of Ballyvickcrannell,
Parish of Segoe, Co. Armagh, Ireland, was born there
in 6th mo. 1632. When he was about 32 he purchased
Ballyvickcrannell which had the following history:
The plantation called Ballyworran was first granted
to William Powell of Staffordshire, 13 June 1610.[8]
The Rev. Richard Rolleston or Roulsten purchased
this grant but was financially unable to keep it,
and sold it to Richard Cope of Loughgall, Co. Armagh, who was the son of Sir Anthony Cope, knight,
High Sheriff of Oxfordshire, who himself was one of
the principal undertakers of Armagh. Richard Cope's

son Anthony was regranted this property 20 Sept.
1639, and it passed to the next in line, another
Anthony Cope, who sold that part containing Ballyvickcrannell to Michael Harrison of Magherleane, Co.
Antrim, 23 June 1662. Harrison deeded the 120 acres
of Ballyvickcrannell by indenture made 22 Aug. 1664,
for ten pounds sterling ("Harrison & his Heirs to
dig for and carry away any Mineral or Quarry"), to
Valentine Hollingsworth, yeoman. The townland of
Ballyvickcrannell thus became the farm of Hollingsworth by title. After he removed with his family
to the Delaware River, it was sold, and it may be
that when his son Henry returned to Ireland in 1688
he came as much to sell his father's property as to
marry his sweetheart Lydia Atkinson. There was in
1688 a suit between Valentine Hollingworth and Henry Jenney.[9] Other later deeds[10] prove that the Jenney or Janney family were in possession of Ballyvickcrannell.

Ballyvickcrannell is a rural area a few miles
east of the town of Portadown, which was founded by
the Obins or Obbyns family in the early part of the
seventeenth century. Early in the life of Valentine
there was an outbreak of violence in this part of
Ireland, and the English residents were badly treated by the native Irish. Many were murdered, many
went back to England and never returned. The period
was turbulent for many years.

Some time in the 1660s Valentine Hollingsworth
became a devoted member of Lurgan Monthly Meeting.
He had his family records entered into the books of
that meeting. William Stockdale's *A Great Cry of
Oppression* contains eight references to Hollingsworth's sufferings, deprivation of goods or stock
as payment for tithes to the English church in the
period 1672-1681.

Perhaps to escape persecution, he requested a
certificate of removal to Pennsylvania, and this was
granted at the meeting of 25 5th mo. 1682.

Valentine Hollingsworth married, first, on 7 June
1655, Ann Ree, daughter of Nicholas and Ann (-----)
Ree of Tanderagee, Co. Armagh, and by her had four
children; second, 12 4th mo. 1672, in Friends Meeting House, Co. Armagh, Ann Calvert, born Nov. 1650,
at Kilwarling, Co. Down, daughter of Thomas and Jane
(-----) Calvert of Drumgor, Parish of Seagoe, Co.
Armagh. Ann's grandfather, John Calvert, came from
Great Moorsholm alias Moresome near Guisborough, in

North Riding, Yorkshire, to Legacory, Co. Armagh,
before 1617.
As stated above, the ship on which the Hollings-
worths crossed the ocean was one which arrived before either the *Welcome* or the *Antelope*.
Valentine Hollingsworth died about 1711 and was
buried at Newark, Delaware.

Issue: surname Hollingsworth
  by first wife Ann Ree
i.   Mary, b. Ballyvickcrannell, 25 1st mo. 1656;
      d. 1746 in America; m. (1) Thomas Conoway
      or Conway; (2) Randal Malin.
ii.   Henry, b. 7 2nd m.1658, Ballyvickcrannell,
      d. Cecil Co., Md., 1721; m. in Ireland,
      22 6th mo. 1688, Lydia Atkinson, Parish of
      Segoe, Co. Armagh.[11]
iii. Thomas, b. ca. 1 3rd mo. 1661; d. New Castle
      Co. 2 2nd mo. 1727; m. (1) Margaret -----;
      (2) Grace Cook. He did not die by being
      killed by a buffalo or bison, in Virginia
      in 1733, as popularly understood.
iv.   Catherine, b. ? 5th mo. 1663, d. 29 6th mo.
      1746 in America; m. George Robinson.
  by second wife Ann Calvert
v.   Samuel, b. Ballyvickcrannell, 27 1st mo.
      1673, d. 1748, Chester Co., Pa.; m. Han-
      nah Harland.
vi.   Enoch, b. Ballyvickcrannell, 7 6th mo. 1675,
      d. 1687 in Delaware.
vii. Valentine, b. 12 11th mo. 1677/8, d. 1757
      in Chester Co., Pa.; m. in New Castle Co.
      Pa., not Ireland, as some accounts say,
      Elizabeth Heald.
viii. Ann, b. 28 Dec. 1680, d. in America; m. James
      Thompson.[12]
ix.   John, b. 19 2nd mo. 1684, d. New Castle Co.,
      Delaware, Aug. 1722; m. Catherine Tyler,
      daughter of William and Elizabeth (-----)
      Tyler of Salem County, N.J. This couple
      converted to the Welsh Tract Baptists ca.
      1713, Catherine being baptized in that
      year at Cohansey. After John's death she
      m. ----- Edwards and removed, ca. 1735,
      to the northwest branch of Cape Fear Riv-
      er in Bladen Co., North Carolina, where
      her oldest son, Rev. Stephen Hollingsworth,
      preached the hard-shell doctrines and bap-
      tized many famous men in his time.

x. Joseph, b. 10 1st mo. 1686, d. ca. 1732 in
Orange Co., Virginia; lived in Cecil Co.,
Maryland, until he moved to Virginia; m.
Elizabeth -----, and after his death she
m. (2) ----- Rentfro. No record of issue.
xi. Enoch, b. ca. 1688, d. 26 9th. mo. 1690.

NOTES

[1]Although this sketch owes much to Mr. Henry Hollingsworth of Inglewood, California, the sketch of Valentine Hollingsworth in his *Hollingsworth Register*
5:87-100 appeared too late for use in this book.

[2]The account of the connection with the Cornishes
is, of course, entirely without validity and contains
insuperable chronological difficulties. On this see
MIQ 311-316.

[3]Filed in Genealogical Notes, vol. 10, p. 21 at
the Genealogical Society of Pennsylvania.

[4]2 PA 16:525, 530; see also *McFarlon-Stern Genealogy* 58 f.

[5]PGM 23:62: Valentine Hollingsworth "might have
come on the *Antelope*." Mary Jamar, *Hollingsworth
Family*, p. 5, says that Myers states plainly that
Hollingsworth came on the *Antelope*, but this is not
true.

[6]British Museum Addit. MSS 4770, folio 29, Co.
Armagh.

[7]Lurgan Monthly Meeting, Book of Births & Deaths,
p. 203, Public Record Office, Belfast. This also
contains records of the births of those children who
were born in Ireland.

[8]Hill, *Plantation in Ulster*, pp. 261 f.

[9]The Calendar of Fines & Recoveries, Public Record Office, **Four Courts**, Dublin, Entry Books 1688.

[10]Vol. 62, p. 112, #42130, Jenney to Archbishop
of Meath and others.

[11]PGSP 2:60 f.

[12]This child and all before her were born at
Ballyvickcrannell and are recorded in the Lurgan
Monthly Meeting records as stated in Note 7. All
following her were born in Delaware and are recorded
in the Newark or Kennett books.

HOSKINS, JOHN   *disproved*
HOSKINS, MARY, his wife   *disproved*
HOSKINS, JOHN, his son   *disproved*

    This man was a First Purchaser of 250 acres in
Group 41.[1] The claim that he was a *Welcome* passenger was first brought to my attention by my friend,
Mr. George Ely Russell, of Bowie, Maryland, who only passed on to me a statement that the three Hoskins "are said to have sailed from England 30 August
1682 on the 'Welcome' with Wm Penn, arriving at Upland (Chester), Pa., 27 Oct. 1682." More information on Hoskins was included but no proof of the
claim. Later the writer of this statement was i-
dentified as Dr. Fred H. Hoskins, 3040 Madeira
Drive, Baton Rouge, La. 70810. He, being asked for
the proof, replied on 18 Aug. 1966 that the "claim
has arisen from several sources which I have pieced
together in my search of *HOSKINS* records over the
past few years" and made specific reference to an
unidentified history of Chester, Pa., to a "Hoskins
Family Tree," Mrs. Opal Lausin, 1009 George Street,
Sharon, Pa., a "Fairfield, Iowa, Hoskins Genealogy,"
Mrs. C. C. Day, Box 61, Bloomfield, Iowa; and Mrs.
H. H. Hoskins, 1544 Main Street, South Windsor,
Conn. Having previously corresponded with Mrs. Hos-
kins, I knew she was primarily concerned with the
Connecticut family. Mrs. Lausin did not reply to
my query. Mrs. Day stated that her "ancestor John
Hoskins came over on the steamship [sic] *Mary and
John* to Dorchester, Mass., in 1635." Dr. Hoskins
also remarked that the name is sometimes spelled
Hodgkins.
    Meanwhile, I found an account of this Hoskins
family in Mary Thomas Seaman's *Thomas Richardson
of South Shields, Durham County, England, and his
Descendants in the United States of America* (New
York 1929), pp. 121-128. She says that John Hoskins came from Cheshire to Chester, Pa., in 1682,
but makes no mention of the *Welcome* claim. In 1688,
however, he built a house on what is now Edgemont
Avenue, Chester, and left a will dated 2 Jan.
1694/5, probated 15 Aug. 1698.
    At this juncture, Mr. Walter Lee Sheppard sup-
lied me with notes from Mrs. Hannah Benner Roach.
She cites the First Purchase mentioned above, and
also another by a John Hodgkinson in Group 39, 500
acres.[2] Though the name is spelled differently,
the group number different and the acreage different,
she feels that the two references are to the same
man, as the associates are the same and mostly from
Cheshire. John Hodskin had a warrant for a house

lot 9 2nd mo. 1683 (city), survey not made until 30 6th mo. 1684.[3] Also rights to John Hoskinson for 250 acres.[4]

In Marion Balderston's article on Penn's 1683 ships[5] we find that John Hodkinson shipped goods on the *Friendship* of Liverpool, 21 9th mo. 1683, loaded 3 August: 3 cayles, qty 3 cwt cheese, 3 pots, qty ½ bbl butter; duty 1s 6d.

This demolishes the *Welcome* claim and even the year 1682 for the arrival. John Hoskins or Hodgkinson or Hotkinson or Hodkinson did not come with Penn on the *Welcome* or even in 1682.

NOTES

[1] 1 PA 1:44. [2] See 3 PA 3.
[3] Exemplification Book 1:127.
[4] 3 PA 3:130; also W&S 3:238.
[5] PGM 24:102, also Note 124 on same page.

HOULSTON, JOHN   *possible but improbable*

This name appears on no list but was mentioned by Meredith B. Colket Jr. among the cases of which he could find no evidence to decide. A qualified claim is made by Howard Williams Lloyd in his well-known book, *Lloyd Manuscripts* (Lancaster, Pa., 1912), pp. 121 f., on Houlston: "John Houlston removed to Pennsylvania very early; according to tradition in the Welcome, with William Penn, in 1682." Houlston had a warrant of survey for 250 acres in Middleton Township, Chester County, 9 Dec. 1684, and he was certainly in Pennsylvania in the summer of 1683. As the survey is dated rather late for a *Welcome* passenger, the preponderance of evidence seems to be on the negative side. As it happens, his daughter Martha afterwards married a proved *Welcome* passenger, and therefore that branch of the Houlstons which descended from Martha Ogden might well have had a genuine *Welcome* tradition which might easily have been transferred in error to the Houlstons.

John Houlston was born in or near Shrewsbury, England. He was present at a Friends Meeting at Shrewsbury on 5 10th mo. 1660, was imprisoned in 1664, shown to be a Friend in 1670, and again in prison in 1672. He and his wife were still living on 17 4th mo. 1698 when his son John made his will. John the elder died, according to Lloyd, on 12 3rd mo. 1699. His wife, whose name was Elizabeth, died

8 3rd mo. 1702. Her maiden name is stated by Lloyd
to have been Serrill. Whether he had proof of this
fact is not known but he probably derived the conclusion from the statement in his son John's will
that he had "cousin James Serrill & cousin Mary Serrill" who had two children. This is, of course, in-
sufficient proof in view of the fact that "cousin"
in this period more often means niece or nephew than
child of uncle or aunt. Moreover, the relationship
may have been through the younger John's wife Ann
Gibbs whose family has not been investigated in this
connection. Even if the connection was through the
senior Houlstons, it is possible that Houlston and
Serrill had married sisters.

    Issue: surname Houlston (order unknown)
    i.   Elizabeth, on 6 2nd mo. 1685 at Chester
           Monthly Meeting to m. James Swaffer. Her
           birth record has not been found.
    ii.   John, birth record not found; m. Philadel-
           phia Monthly Meeting, 7 8th mo. 1684, Ann
           Gibbs. He d. at Edgmont,leaving will dated
           17 4th mo. 1698, probated 14 March 1701/2
           (PhW B:254) in which he is called John
           Houldstone of Edgemont, Chester Co., and
           states that his father and mother are still
           living; he has four sisters unnamed; names
           wife Ann and son John as executors; cousin
           James Serrill and cousin Mary Serrill and
           their two children; children of Peter Tay-
           lor and William Gregory [who had m. his
           sisters]; witnesses: John Goulding, John
           Musgrave, Edward Jones, Peter Taylor (he
           by mark). The will was protested in 6th
           mo. 1701 by Joseph Baker, John Worrilaw,
           John Bowater, David Ogden, Edward Jones,
           Frances Bowater, Elizabeth Houldstone,
           Francis Worrill, Sarah Taylor, Rebecca
           Gregory, that is, by one brother-in-law
           (Ogden), by testator's mother (Elizabeth
           Houldstone) and two sisters (Sarah Taylor
           and Rebecca Gregory), as well as by others
           whose interest does not appear. Orphans
           Court in Feb. 1701/2 shows that the will
           was examined and he found to be not of
           right mind when he made it. At the same
           court the son John chose James Swaffer and
           William Gregory as guardians which shows
           that the son was between the ages of 14

and 21 on that day and harmonizes with a date of birth given by Lloyd as 19 9th mo. 1686. Lloyd, however, has a theory that there were two sons named John, one of whom, he says, was aged 25 in 12th mo. 1701/2. What evidence he had for such an age is unknown and I have seen no evidence there were two sons John, and believe that Lloyd assumed that because son John was named joint executor in 1698, he must then have been of age.

Issue: surname Houlston

1. John, b. 19 9th mo. 1686 (Chester record), d. Edgmont, 1732, leaving will dated 1 6th mo. 1732, probated 16 Aug. 1732: names wife Sarah maiden name Phipps, sister of Samuel Phipps ; sons Benjamin and John; daughters Sarah, Ann, Elizabeth, Rebecca, Hannah; son-in-law John Ireland [which was his wife?], cousin Peter Taylor.

iii. Sarah, b. 7 8th mo. 1660 at Heath House farm near Stenton [Stanton]; declared 2nd int. Chester Monthly Meeting, 1685, to m. Peter Taylor.

iv. Rebecca, b. 2 2nd mo. 1663 at Abbey Foregate Shrewsbury; m. 1685, 2nd int. Chester, William Gregory.

v. Martha, b. 1 2nd mo. 1667, Preston Boats, which record, as also those of the births of Sarah and Rebecca, was seen by Gilbert Cope (Gen. Soc. of Pa. Cope Coll., 42:61) in the Friends Records of Herefordshire, Worcestershire, Wales. She m., 2nd int. Chester Monthly Meeting, 1 1st mo. 1685/6, David Ogden, the *Welcome* passenger; (2) 1st int., 28 6th mo. 1710, 2nd int., 26 7th mo. 1710, James Thomas of Whiteland, yeoman who d. intestate in 1727. For her children see the Ogden sketch.

vi. ?Henry, perhaps. A Henry Houlston is called brother-in-law, with children Mary, Stephen and Sarah, in the will of John Stephens of Radnor, bachelor, dated 1 2nd mo. 1721, probated in Chester Co. 1 May 1722 (rec., however, in PhW D:311). Testator also had a sister Phoebe James who had a son John; a niece Mary, daughter of Thomas More of

Marple; a brother-in-law Stephen Evans and
a brother Stephen Evans, perhaps the same;
brothers Evan Stephens and David Stephens.

HOWELL, THOMAS	*disproved*
HOWELL, DANIEL, his son	*disproved*
HOWELL, MORDECAI, his son	*disproved*
HOWELL, MIRIAM, his daughter	*disproved*
HOWELL, PRISCILLA, his daughter	*disproved*
HOWELL, KATHARINE, his daughter	*disproved*

These names appear on no list but the *Welcome*
claim was made by that indefatigable manufacturer of
false claimants, the late Josiah Granville Leach, in
his *Genealogical and Biographical Memorials of the
Reading, Howell, Yerkes, Watts, Latham and Elkins
Families* (Philadelphia 1898), p. 139:

On 31 August, 1682, he [Thomas Howell], with
his sons and daughters, embarked at Deal, England,
in the "Welcome," for the voyage made historic
by the presence of William Penn, proprietor of
Pennsylvania, then on the way to place himself
at the head of his government established in his
province.

No positive evidence has been found and there is
strong negative evidence.
Mordecai Howell, one of the sons of Thomas, deposed before the Boundary Commission in 1740, when
he was aged 78, as follows:[1]

That about 1682 he came up the Bay of the Delaware in company with the ship in which the Plain-
tiffs Father [William Penn] was. That he landed,
some time before Mr. Penn at New Castle Town,
and was there when he landed at said Town.

The ship on which Mordecai Howell crossed has now
been identified as the *Bristol Factor* on its second
trip,[2] and it is clear that the Howell family are
not *Welcome* passengers.
Thomas Howell of Gloucester County, New Jersey,
left an undated will which was probated 9 March
1686/7.[3] His wife was not living with him and he
did not know whether she was alive or dead. He names
the two sons Daniel and Mordecai and mentions three
daughters. Mr. Leach says the wife was named Katharine.

Issue: surname Howell
i.   Daniel, b. ca. 1660, d. Bucks Co., Pa., in
     September 1739; m. Hannah Lakin.
ii. Mordecai, b. ca. 1662; m. (1) Elizabeth ----;
     (2) widow Frances Garret; (3) Elizabeth
     Morgan.
iii. Miriam, m. Henry Johnson.
iv. Priscilla, m. Robert Stiles.
v.   Katharine, m. James Robinson.

NOTES

[1]2 PA 16:719.
[2]See p.7, #17.
[3]NJW 1:242.

INGALS/INGOLS, THOMAS   *highly improbable*

This name appears on no list unless it be, as we
think possible, a confused form of the name of Richard Ingelo, a genuine *Welcome* passenger. The claim
is made by W. W. H. Davis, *History of Bucks County,
Pennsylvania* (Doylestown, 1st ed., 1876), p. 66, who
says also that Ingols settled in Warrington Township.
We have not found other evidence for his existence.

*INGELO, RICHARD   *proved*

This name appears on all lists except List I,
where it is unaccountably missing, and Lists D and
F where the surname is spelled Ingels. The proof
of his presence on the *Welcome* is the fact that he
signed as witness the wills of Isaac Ingram and William Wade, both executed aboard the vessel. It is
possible that it was his hand that penned the will
of Ingram. Whenever his occupation is given, he is
always called gentleman, and he is the only passenger who can be clearly shown not to have been a
Friend, though there may have been others. He was
colonial secretary 1684-5[1] and the Historical Society of Pennsylvania preserves a letter dated 19 7th
mo. 1685, complaining that his salary has not been
paid.

Mr. Pemberton and Mr. Janney, I thinke I need
not write much to ye for you have been mightly
kind for Mr. Biles promised me he would send yt
when he was here in Town Last. The sonner I
have it the [illegible] good it will doe me for
I want it. I remaine yr friend and Servt

Richard Ingelo
19th 7th mo. 1685

This document was indorsed to W. Markham, same date.
Soon after that, Ingelo probably left for England,
as a letter from Penn dated at Warminghurst, 28 11th
mo. 1686 says: "I hear by R. Ingelo thou takest great
care and pains about my husbandry."[2]
Ingelo had property in New Castle, Philadelphia
and Bucks Counties, was on the New Castle tax list
1685-6, and on 22 11 th mo. 1685/6 had 1200 acres
in equal halves in Philadelphia and Bucks.[3]
When Charles II died, Ingelo functioned as a sort
of herald in America:

> Pennsylvania
> By the President and Councell--
> These are to give General Notice, That our
> Present Soveraign King James the Second, will be
> Published in the Front Street upon Delaware Ri-
> ver, Over against the Governours Gate to Morrow
> Morning at the Ninth hour upon the Wringing of
> the Bell.

Philadelphia the   Signed by Order
11th 3d month 1685.   Richard Ingelo
                                       Cl Councill

Richard Ingelo was son of a clergyman of the English Church, Nathaniel Ingelo (1621-1683).[4] The father took an M.A. at Edinburgh, was Fellow of Queens
College, Cambridge, Greek lecturer in 1644; junior
bursar; was a person to whom Andrew Marvell dedicated a poem; took his D.D. at Oxford in 1658. He died
in August 1683, while Richard was in America, aged
62, and was buried in Eton College Chapel. By his
wife Mary he had four or five sons and one daughter.
Two of the sons, Nathaniel and John, were scholars
of Eton and Fellows of Kings College, Cambridge.
The old gentleman was greatly devoted to music and
when this predilection for what seemed to Puritans
an unchristian occupation aroused criticism, he said,
"Take away music, take away my life!"
The will of Richard Ingelo is dated 9 May 1695 5
William. He is of the Towne of Busleton in Somersetshire and leaves to his nephew Nathaniel Ingelo
four pounds to buy him mo[u]rning and names his sister Elizabeth Ingelo sole executrix and residuary
legatee; witnesses: Tho: Langton, Robt Langton,

George Hudson. The will was probated 24 Aug. 1697 by
the oath of Elizabeth Ingelo, sister and sole executrix of testator, before the Prerogative Court of
Canterbury. She afterwards married John Gibb of Bristol, clerk.

The brother Nathaniel Ingelo of Eaton [sic] College
was at age 26 licensed to marry Ann Evans, 21 May
1678.[5] They were the parents of the nephew Nathaniel,
who, as Nathaniel Ingelo of the Parish of St. Mary
le Bow, London, clerk, with wife Margaret, conveyed
for £120 two 600-acre tracts in Pennsylvania, 24
Sept. 1719.[6] He had inherited the land from Richard
Ingelo.

The Blackwell Rent Roll of 1689 shows Rich: Inge-
low as owner of a 51-foot lot on Walnut Street, 2
shillings for five years.[7]

                        NOTES
[1]*Colonial Records* 1:81.
[2]Norman Penney, *My Ancestors*, p. 276.
[3]For a survey see 3 PA 3:390.
[4]DNB 10:432 f.
[5]Joseph Foster, *London Marriage Licenses*.
[6]PhD G-8, p. 256.   [7]PGM 23:75.

+*INGRAM, ISAAC*   *proved*

This name appears, of course, on all lists but
Lists J and L which spell the name Ingham and List W
which appears to have been copied in general from L,
but spells it Inghram. The proof is his will executed
on board the *Welcome*.

vpon the twenty sixt day of ye seauenth month |
one thousand six eighty & two· I Isaak | Ingram late
of Garton [sic] late of Surrey yeoman, | Being
weake of body yet of perfect mind and | memory doe
make this my last will and testament | on board the
wellcome Robt Greenaway M^r· | bound for Pensilvania
(viz) as foll. | Item I giue & bequeath vnto my
Sister miriam | short late deseased her three child-
ren Adam | short miriam short & Anne short all that
| thirty pownds lying in Ambrose Riggs hands | live-
ing at Garton [sic: for Gatton] in ye county of
Surrey to | be equally deuided betweene them viz
ten | pownds a peece further it is my will & mind |
that my Sisters children aforesd haue all the |
goods on board the wellcome equally devided | be-
tweene them. [Line and a half cancelled, illegible.]
| It I giue & bequeath to Jane Batchler fiue | pownds.

It I giue & bequeath to Thomas fitzwaters | fiue
pownds. | I giue & bequeath to david ogden forty
shillings. | It I giue & bequeath to John Song-
hurst ten pownds. | I giue & bequeath to Thomas
wynne | fiue pownds. | Item I giue & bequeath all
ye remainder of my | money euery where to the
poore of our freinds called quakers [line and a
half cancelled, illegible]. | Item I doe consti-
tute & apoint John Songhurst | And Thomas wynne
to be my Sole Executors | of this my last will &
testament in wittnes | whereof I haue herevnto
put my hand and seale | the day & yeere a boue
writen. |
Signed sealed & deliued in ye
presence of Vs
Richard Ingelo   Themarke of I I Imgram
Zechariah Whitpaine   Isak
Geo: Thompson   [seal]

The handwriting of this will is not very legible
(see page 263) but a comparison of it with specimens
of Richard Ingelo's handwriting seems to suggest
that he was the scrivener.[1]

As will be apparent, Isaac Ingram was the uncle
of the three Shorts, one of whom, Miriam the younger,
in the end chose George Thompson, the *Welcome* passenger, as the first of her three husbands. For this
reason, the sketches on the Shorts and on Thompson
should be read in this connection.

                              NOTE
[1]For an abstract of the will see PGSP 1:48 f.; also TAG 38:159-162; 41:218.

JOHNSON, ELIZABETH   *disproved*

This name appears on List X only. The truth is that
this person came on the *Lion* of Liverpool, arriving
14 8th mo. 1683, as servant to Joseph Fisher, to
serve four years and get fifty acres, loose on 14
8th mo. 1687. Nothing further has been found on
Elizabeth. It has been suggested to me that the first
name should be read rather as Eliezer but the handwriting does not support this view, and I have found
no record of an Eliezer. Moreover, the name is last
on the list, the two females being at the end.

upon the twenty first day of [the] second month
one thousand six eighty & [eighty] two I Isaak
Ingram late of Carton [vale] of [Surrey] yoeman
Being weake of body yet of perfect mind and
memory doe make this my last will and testa[ment]
on board the wellcome Robt Greenaway m[aste]r
bound for Penfilbania. (viz) as foll[oweth]

Item I give & bequeath unto my sister mirian
ghost late of [ ] her three children [viz]
ghost mirian ghost & Anne ghost all that
thirty pounds lying in Ambrose Rigge hands
living at Gatton in [the] county of Surry to
be equally devided betweene them [ ] ten
pounds a peece further it is my will & mind
that my sisters children aforesd haue all the
goods on board the wellcome Equally devided
betweene them [ ]

It I give and bequeath to Jane Batchler fiue
pounds

It I giue & bequeath to Thomas fitzwaters
fiue pounds

It I giue & bequeath to dauid ogdon forty shilling

It I giue & bequeath to John Longhurst ten pound

Item I giue & bequeath to Thomas wynne
fiue pound

Item I giue and bequeath all [the] remainder of my
money euery where to the poore of our
freinds called quakers [ ]

Item I doe [ ] & appoint John Longhurst [ ]
[ ] to be my [sole executor]
of this my last will & testament in wittnes
whereof I haue hereunto put my hand and seale
the day & yeare aboue writen.
Signed sealed & deliuered
presence of vs
[ ]
[Zecharia Williamo]   Thompson [ ]   [Ingram]
Jno: Thompson

JONES, THOMAS   *proved*

This name appears on all lists except List I. The
proof is to be found in Philadelphia Arrivals where
Jones is shown as servant to Dennis Rochford. As
such he may originally have been servant to Thomas
Heriott whose service was bequeathed to Dennis Rochford.

Dennis Rochford's servant, Thomas Jones, is identified by Charles H. Browning, *The Welsh Settlement
of Pennsylvania*, pp. 214 and 499, as the Thomas
Jones, gent., of Glascombe, Radnorshire, Wales, who
in 1682 purchased 100 acres from Penn. It is extremely improbable that a servant could have been in a
position to purchase a hundred acres in the same
year as he crossed the Atlantic, or that a servant
would have been called "gent." Thomas Allen Glenn,
The Welsh Founders of Pennsylvania, 1:187, lists
seven Thomas Joneses in early Pennsylvania but our
man is probably not among them.

He may or may not have been the Thomas Jones of
Penn's Neck, Salem County, New Jersey, husbandman,
whose inventory dated 16 Aug. 1694 shows personal
estate of £28/9/3, taken by John Hughes and John
Scoggin, administration being granted to the widow
Hannah Jones.[1] Another Thomas Jones, probably one
younger, was of Kent County, Delaware, shoemaker,
on 30 Dec. 1728 when mentioned as husband of Margaret Johns alias Pope, step-daughter in the will
of Samuel Dark of Greenwich, Cohansey Precinct,
Salem County, New Jersey.[2]

NOTES

[1]NJW 1:268.   [2]NJW 1:127.

KEY, JOHN   *mythical*

This name appears only on List D where it is a
misprint, in all probability, for John Hey, which
name is in turn a misreading of John Ottey, the correct name of the servant of Thomas Fitzwater. The
error having been created by the carelessness of J.
Futhey Smith and Gilbert Cope in their *History of
Chester County, Pennsylvania* (Philadelphia 1881),
pp. 21 f., they were followed by Mrs. Julian C. Lane,
Key and Allied Families (Macon, Georgia 1931), p.
75, who makes of the error a "John Key, who with
his wife, came to America on the ship Welcome, landing Oct. 27, 1682, on a high bluff, the west bank

of the Delaware River." To this couple she gives a
son, also named John Key, the first born child of
European parents in Philadelphia. She locates the
birthplace as a cave at "Penny Pot near Sassafras
Street," and says that this first-born died at Ken-
net Square, Chester County, 5 July 1767 aet. 79. The
not impeccable mathematics is, of course, Mrs. Lane's
and "Penny Pot" is not a place but the name of an
inn or tavern in the vicinity of the bank. In de-
signating John Key as "mythical" I do so with reference to the *Welcome* only. There was such a first
born named John Key and he was granted land by the
Board of Property on 22 8th mo. 1705, "being the
first born in Philadelphia, now of age."[1] I have
not attempted to determine the names of his parents
or to trace him further.

NOTE
[1] 2 PA 19:466. John F. Watson, *Annals of Philadelphia* 1:511, mentions the first born but not the
Welcome in this connection.

KILCARTH, ROBERT   *disproved*

This name appears on List X only. The truth is
that he came on the *Lion* of Liverpool, arriving 14
8th mo. 1683, as servant to Joseph Fisher, to serve
eight years and get fifty acres, loose on 14 8th mo.
1691. Mrs. Balderston (PGM 24:93, note 88) concludes from the length of service that he was aged
thirteen. Nothing more has been discovered about
him.

KILLINGBECK, HUMPHREY[1]   *disproved*

This name has appeared on no list and no one has
claimed in writing that Humphrey Killingbeck was a
Welcome passenger. During this investigation, however evidence was uncovered which caused us for a
time to think that he had been a passenger who died
during the crossing. Further research made it clear
that this was illusory, but because it is necessary
elsewhere to quote this document, we think it wise
to discuss the evidence so that no one will misun-
derstand it.

In Warrants and Surveys 4:43 is a survey return
of Edward Penington, Surveyor General, certifying
survey to Thomas Wickersham in the right of Humphrey
Killinbeck, purchaser of 1,000 acres, a tract on
Brandywine Creek in Marlborough Township, Chester
County, for 480 acres, surveyed 10 2nd mo. 1701, re-

turned 18 5th mo. 1701, no abutters mentioned. In
the same source 1:864 No. 2140 is a warrant:

> William Penn, Proprietor and Governor, at re-
> quest of Jno Songhurst that I would grant him to
> take up within the Liberties of the City for the
> proposition of purchase the land of his own 500
> acres, 10 acres; for his daughter the widow Bar-
> ber 2500 acres, 50 acres; for William Wade 1000
> acres, 20 acres; for John Burchall, 500 acres,
> 10 acres; for Humphrey Killingbeck 1000 acres,
> 20 acres; for Jno Snashold 500 acres, 10 acres.
> These are to will and require thee forthwith to
> to survey or cause to be surveyed for him the
> Land of the said persons within the Liberties of
> the City in all 120 acres where not taken up ac-
> cording to the method of townships by me appoin-
> ted and make return thereof unto my Secretary's
> office.   Given at Phila the 10th 6th month 1683
> for Thoms Holme, Surveyor General.
>   Wm Penn.

As, except for Killingbeck, all of the above named
persons are either known *Welcome* passengers or most
probably such, and as Mrs. Barber's husband John,
Wade, Snashold, and probably Burchall, were persons
who died during the crossing, the first sight of
this warrant raised the thought that perhaps Killingbeck was also a passenger who died during the
crossing.

Humphrey Killingbeck's name appears among the
First Purchasers of Group 49,[2] with purchase of 1000
acres by Henry [sic] Killingbeck, and in this group
were also John Rowland, 1250 acres; Edward and Thomas Buckman, together, 300 acres; and others, those
named being proved *Welcome* passengers, the others
not.

From the records of the Surrey and Sussex Quarterly Meeting in Lewes and Chichester Monthly Meeting, we find the following Killingbeck entries:

Elizabeth Killingbeck of Twiniham, Sussex, m. 8 2nd
    mo. 1666, Richard Mercer, at Jno Graves house.
Ann Killingbeck of same, m. 4 7th mo. 1667, John
    Grover, at his house.
Elizabeth Killingbeck, bur. 18 7th mo. 1684, very
    aged, widow, lived at Balney.
Cassandra Killingbeck, bur. 13 4th mo. 1697, wife
    of Humphrey, bur. Horsham.

The A. C. Myers Papers at the Chester County Historical Society provide further entries:

Humphrey Killingbeck among witnesses to Quaker marriage 16 8th mo. 1660
12 5th mo. 1678 Cassandra Killingbeck and Mary Songhurst were noted among witnesses to William
Woods' marriage, bride not named, at Shipley.

Humphrey Killingbeck has also been seen among witnesses to English Quaker marriages 1679-1683, in
1681 with wife Cassandra.

The warrant first cited above is referred to in
proceedings before the Board of Property[3] as follows:

> Humphrey Killingbeck by deed 13 April 1682
> 1000 acres bought from William Penn, sold by said
> Humphrey 12 7ber 1700 to kinsman Thomas Wicker-
> sham 500 acres thereof and city lot to Thomas
> himself; the other 500 to his four children, 200
> to eldest son Humphrey, and to Thomas, John and
> Ann 100 acres when they come of age. Thomas took
> up his 500 acres [the warrant cited above for on-
> ly 480 acres] and liberty land deducted from the
> whole 21 1st mo. last near the Brandywine, re-
> quests the balance of 500 for his children.
> Granted. P. 392: surveyed 480 acres on south
> side of Brandywine per warrant dated 21 1st mo.
> 1700/1. Patent ordered.

This document rather strongly suggests that Killingbeck was transferring this property to the Wicker-
shams because Thomas Wickersham was son-in-law to
Killingbeck, but no attempt has been made to check
this surmise by research into the Wickersham history.

Philadelphia Deeds C-2, vol. 3, p. 185, shows a
conveyance signed 12 10th mo. Dec. 1699, recorded
18 6th mo. 1702, of which the grantors were Thomas
Baldwin and wife Mary, both of Chester County, Pa.,
she lately wife of one Richard Linwell of ye Co.
of Sussex, England, dec'd, and John Linwell and
Thos Linwell, sons of said Richard and Mary Linwell;
grantees: Humphrey Killingbeck of the parish of
Bolney, co. Sussex, Nicholas Cox of the parish of
fflething in co. Sussex. The land sold was "all
that messuage or tenement, barn, lands, premises,
etc., called the Northern or North Lands," containing estimated 14± acres lying between Doane
Hill in the parish of fflething, co. Sussex, and

now in the occupation of Nicholas Cox. The deed was
signed by TB mark of Thomas Baldwin, Mary Baldwin,
Ɨ mark of John Linwell, TL mark of Thomas Linwell;
witnesses: Jona. Heayes, Walter Marten, John Childe.
This deed was doubtless recorded in Philadelphia so
that a certified copy might be sent to England for
further use.

The last two documents, together with the items
cited from English records, make it abundantly clear
that the purchaser of the 1000 acres in 1682, Humphrey Killingbeck, was still living in England in
1702, having lost his wife Cassandra in 1697, and
that, so far as is known, he never came to America
at all.

NOTES

[1]The basic research for this sketch was done by
Walter Lee Sheppard, Jr.
[2]1 PA 1:45.   [3]2 PA 19:217.

KIRKBRIDE, JOSEPH   *disproved*

This name appears on List X only but W. W. H. Davis, *History of Bucks County, Pennsylvania* (Doylestown, 1st ed., 1876), p. 67, says of Joseph Kirkbride, aged 19, son of Mahlon [sic] Kirkbride and
his wife Magdalena, from Kirkbride, Cumberland, that
"one account says he came on Mary and John but family records say he came on Welcome." So also Battle
says he came with Penn in 1682.[1]

Though the primary document proving otherwise
has thus far eluded us, he is stated to have come
on the first trip of the *Bristol Factor* by John W.
Jordan,[2] Sherman A. Kirkbride,[3] and Jane W. T. Brey.[4]
The father's name is given by Mr. Kirkbride as not
Mahlon but Matthew, and this is probably correct as
it seems highly likely that the name Mahlon entered
the Kirkbride family with the marriage of Joseph to
Mahlon Stacy's daughter. Mr. Kirkbride also says
that Joseph was a third son, was already bound as
an apprentice when he was invited to sail on the
Bristol Factor in 1681, that he arranged his affairs
so as to accept the invitation and arrived with this
ship on 29 7th mo. 1681. He was thus in Pennsylvania over a year when the *Welcome* arrived. Mrs. Brey
alludes to his return to England,says that he came
back to Pennsylvania on the *Welcome* some time before
2 2nd mo. 1701. This is the only reference found to
a second voyage of the *Welcome* and is probably a

confusion of the false 1682 *Welcome* claim with the
truth about the second trip of Kirkbride. What is
certain is that Joseph Kirkbride was received at
Falls Monthly Meeting from Pardsey Cragg Monthly
Meeting in England on 7 6th mo. 1700.

Joseph Kirkbride married first, having leave to
marry from Falls Monthly Meeting on 7 1st mo. 1688/9,
at Middletown on 13 1st mo. 1688/9, Phebe Blackshay
or Blackshaw, who had come to America on the *Submission* in 1682, then aged 16, with her parents,
Randulph Blackshaw of Hallingee in the Co. of Chester and his wife Alice.[5] As we have seen in the account of her father,[6] Phebe accompanied her father
from Choptank, Maryland, to Pennsylvania, while the
rest of the family came later. Joseph Kirkbride
married second, second intentions at Chesterfield
Monthly Meeting in Burlington County, New Jersey,
3 Dec. 1702, Sarah Stacy, daughter of Mahlon Stacy
of Balifield, Nottingham Township, Burlington County, New Jersey, and his wife Rebecca. Mahlon Stacy's will dated 11 11th mo. 1703/4, probated 24
April 1704,[7] does not mention his daughter Sarah
Kirkbride, as she was already dead, but does mention her minor son Mahlon Kirkbride as grandson of
testator. Joseph Kirkbride married third, at Falls
Monthly Meeting, 17 11th mo. 1706/7, Mary Fletcher,
daughter of Robert Fletcher of Abington and widow
of Enoch Yardley who had died 23 11th mo. 1702/3,
leaving three daughters, all of whom were dead by
the time their mother married Joseph Kirkbride.

Phoebe Blackshaw Kirkbride must have died by 1702;
Sarah Stacy Kirkbride was buried 29 9th mo. 1703,
while Mary Fletcher Yardley Kirkbride survived her
second husband who died 1 1st mo. 1737 and was buried 4 1st mo. 1737/8, leaving a will of which the
date is now illegible but it was probated 18 April
1738.[8] Joseph Kirkbride of Bucks County, yeoman,
mentions his three sons Joseph, Mahlon and John;
his wife Mary Kirkbride; his son-in-law Thomas Mar-
iat and his wife testator's daughter Martha; daughters Sarah Kirkbride and Jane Kirkbride; granddaughter hanah Marffee; daughter Phebe's children; cusins
Thomas Kirkbride and Joseph Kirkbride. Inventory of
£2989:11:6, a large sum for those days, was taken
by Edward Livesey, John Hutchinson, Wm Atkinson.

Living in Falls Township and as member of Falls
Monthly Meeting, was Thomas Kirkbride, said to be
a nephew of Joseph, who married at Falls, the widow

Elizabeth Derby, 25 9th mo. 1707, and had recorded at
Falls: Matthew (b. 3 3rd mo. 1705/6), Thomas (b. 13
6th mo. 1712, m. 31 3rd mo. 1738, Grace Woollston,
daughter of Jonathan, and had five children 1739-47);
Elizabeth (b. 13 6th mo. 1712, evidently twin) and
Joseph (b. 18 8th mo. 1715).

Issue: surname Kirkbride
  by first wife Phoebe Blackshaw
i.   Joseph, m. (1) 26 8th mo. 1720, Hannah
      Sotcher (daughter of John Sotcher); (2)
      1 2nd mo. 1724 Sarah Fletcher, daughter
      of Robert Fletcher.
         Issue: surname Kirkbride *by Sarah*
      1. Phebe, b. 12 12th mo. 1724/5. Davis[9]
         says that Joseph Kirkbride, probably
         father of this girl, had two daughters
         by wife Sarah who m. Abel Janney and
         Reuben Pownall. This can hardly be
         true of the first Joseph Kirkbride, as
         his wife Sarah lived less than a year
         after their marriage. It therefore
         seems probable that this woman m. Abel
         Janney but we have not found proof.
      2. Daughter, name unknown, b. 23 9th mo.
         1726; perhaps m. Reuben Pownall, cer-
         tainly not the son of the immigrant.
      3. Joseph, b. 13 6th mo. 1731, d. Borden-
         town, N.J., 21 Oct. 1803.
ii.   Martha, on 7 8th mo. 1713 had leave to m.
      Thomas Marriott and is called his wife in
      her father's will.
iii. Phebe, on 1 3rd mo. 1706 had leave to m.
      John Hutchinson.¯ Her children are refer-
      red to, not by name, in her father's will.
iv.   Hannah, bur. 4 10th mo. 1703.
v.   Jane, probably d. young.
  by Sarah Stacy
vi.   Mahlon, b. 3 9th mo. 1703, d. 7 11th mo.
      1776; m. 12 9th mo. 1724 Mary Sotcher,
      daughter of John Sotcher, who d.22 9th mo.
         Issue: surname Kirkbride   [1778.
      1. Stacy, b. 2 9th mo. 1725, d. 6 3rd mo.
         1789 aet. 63, bur. Haverford; m. Fran-
         ces Smith.
      2. Mary, b. 22 12th mo. 1727, m. 31 10th mo.
         1736, Bernard Taylor.
      3. Hannah, b. 29 9th mo. 1726, d. 30 5th mo.
         1728.

4. Sarah, b. 13 10th mo. 1729, m. 31 3rd mo. 1756, William Yardley.
5. Rebecca, b. 14 8th mo. 1731, d. 15 1st mo. 1731/2.
6. Ruth, b. 10 11th mo. 1732, d. 14 6th mo. 1745.
7. Letitia, b. 23 4th mo. 1734, m. 27 12th mo. 1752, Timothy Taylor, son of Benjamin Taylor.
8. Mahlon, b. 9 3rd mo. 1736, d. 2nd mo. 1778; m. 30 11th mo. 1757, Ann Rickey, daughter of Alexander Rickey.
9. Robert, b. 23 11th mo. 1737, m. 27 3rd mo. 1758, Hannah Bidgood, daughter of William Bidgood.
10. Jonathan, twin, b. 10 6th mo. 1739, d. 5 11th mo. 1824; m. Chesterfield, 18 11th mo. 1767, Elizabeth Curtis. Their marriage certificate was signed by Frances, Mahlon Jr., Sarah, Mary and Joseph Kirkbride.
11. David, twin, b. 10 6th mo. 1739, d. 14 12th mo. 1764.
12. Joseph, b. 27 4th mo. 1745, d. 31 5th mo. 1745.

by Mary Fletcher Yardley[10]

vii. John, b. 13 11th mo. 1706/7, m. Springfield, 16 1st mo. 1730/1, Hannah Sykes, bur. 12 10th mo. 1732, daughter of John and Johanna (-----) Sykes.
Issue: surname Kirkbride, perhaps more
1. John, b. 2 9th mo. 1732.
viii.Robert, b. 5 12th mo. 1708, living 1731.
ix. Thomas, b. 31 11th mo. 1712, d. by 1716.
x. Mary, d. 18 2nd mo. 1714, living 1731.
xi. Sarah, b. 11 4th mo. 1714, m. 7 1st mo. 1737, Israel Pemberton.
xii. Thomas, b. 30 10th mo. 1716, living 1731, not living in father's will ca. 1737.
xiii.Jane, b. 28 12th mo. 1719, m. 13 11th mo. 1741, Samuel Smith, son of Richard Smith Jr. of Burlington.

NOTES

[1]BHBC 906.
[2]*Encyclopaedia of Pennsylvania Biography* 4:1226.
[3]*A Brief History of the Kirkbride Family, etc.* (1913).

[4]*A Quaker Saga, the Watsons of Strawberryhowe, the Wildmans and Other Allied Families*, etc. (Philadelphia 1967), pp. 102, 116, 151-153. The reference to the *Welcome* is on p. 116. See also BHBC 369; Lawrence Buckley Thomas, *The Thomas Book* (New York 1896), 382.

[5]PMHB 9:229 f.   [6]See pp. 48-51.
[7]NJW 1:437.   [8]BW file 409.
[9]DHBC 67.

[10]The Kirkbride Genealogy cited (p. 17) says that the third marriage was in 1740, a misprint for 1704, and says the wife was Mary Yardley Fletcher instead of Mary Fletcher Yardley.

KNIGHT, GILES	*disproved*
KNIGHT, MARY ENGLISH, his wife	*disproved*
KNIGHT, JOSEPH, his son	*disproved*

Giles Knight appears on all lists but on List O the verdict is negative; on List Q, Giles, Mary and Joseph, are crossed out; and all three persons are said on Lists U and V to have come on the *Society* of Bristol. Mary is merely called wife on Lists J, K, L, N, P, S, T and W; is named on Lists A, B, C, D, E, F, G [here the maiden name is given], H, I, M, X, Y and Z. Joseph appears on Lists A, B, C, D, E, F, G, H, I, M, X, Y and Z.

Comly[1] says the Knights came "in company with Penn but does not mention the *Welcome*.

> On the passage, Mary was extremely sick, so that her survival to the end of the voyage was very doubtful. On their arrival up the Delaware she was carried ashore in a blanket and laid on the bank; she then observed that she had been fully persuaded in her mind she should not die until she saw America, but now she had landed here, she could not tell how it would go with her.

She need not have worried for she lived until 24 7th mo. 1732 when she was 77, and Giles died 20 8th mo. 1726 aged 73.

Joseph C. Martindale, M.D., *The Knight Family* (no date), p. 1, has a statement similar to Comly's but the same author's *History of the Townships of Byberry and Moreland* (revised ed., no date), p. 318, makes the full claim of the *Welcome* (the Knights are discussed pp. 317-336). Lawrence Buckley Thomas, *The Thomas Book* (New York 1896), p. 383, also makes the *Welcome* claim, as do Battle[2] and C. A. Hoppin,

The Washington Ancestry (Greenfield, Ohio, 1932),
pp. 337-339, where Hoppin says Knight was son-in-law
to Joseph English Sr.; on p. 340 he says Giles is
in the list of passengers arriving on the ship *Welcome* which is true enough if one understands him to
mean one or another of the hypothetical lists.

Giles Knight of the parish of Rodbarrow, co.
Gloucester, broad-weaver, married at Nailsworth
Monthly Meeting, 24 2nd mo. 1679, Mary English of
Horsley. Son Joseph was born 10 3rd mo. 1680, son
Giles on 18 10th mo. 1681, but the latter probably
died soon as no one claims that he came to America.
Giles and wife had a certificate from Nailsworth
Monthly Meeting dated 11 2nd mo. 1682, rather early
for *Welcome* passengers.[3] The Abington Friends book
of Births Deaths [original at Friends Historical
Library, Swarthmore, Pa.] contains the following
Knight entries:

> Thomas, s. Giles & Mary, b. 9 4th mo. 1685
> Thomas, s. Thomas & Elizabeth, b. 22 3rd mo. 1687

In the A. C. Myers Welcome Papers at the Chester
County Historical Society is a pedigree of the family which begins with a Giles Knight born 9 May 1614,
who married first Elizabeth Williams, daughter of
Thomas, and she was mother to Thomas, Benjamin, Abel
and John; second, Elizabeth Payne, mother of Giles,
the immigrant to Pennsylvania. I suspect this pedigree and doubt if Mr. Myers compiled it himself.

The negative evidence begins with the will of
Thomas Fream of Avon in co. Gloster, dated 5 Sept.
1682, signed by mark, probated 10 8th mo. 1682, the
first will probated in Philadelphia County.[4] Ann
Knight is named executrix; Giles Knight is to receive £6 owed testator by James Crofts; Thomas
Knight, brother of Giles, is to receive the same sum
also owed by Crofts; residue to loving friend Ann
Knight; witnesses: John Somers, Thomas Madox [by
mark], Thomas Williams [by mark], William [surname
illegible; it has been read as Herron and as Mor-
row, but my guess is hains]. In this estate is a
bond of Samuel Darke of Bucks, husbandman, 9 6th mo.
1683, witnessed by Thomas ffitzwater and Will Darke.

Ann Knight, executrix and residuary legatee of
Thomas Fream, recorded her arrival on the *Society*
of Bristol, Thomas Jordan, master, in 6th mo. 1682,
in Bucks Arrivals.[5] The original document states
that she was Samuel Dark's wife, a fact omitted in

the printed abstract. The marriage certificate dated 17 4th mo. 1683 is now preserved in the Historical Society of Pennsylvania,[6] and shows only one person who could be obviously related to either party,
namely, William Dark. In Bucks Arrivals, immediately before Ann Knight, is Samuel Dark of London, cal-
lenderer, who came on the *Constant*, 8th mo. 1680,
with servants James Croft and Mary Croft. In the
same document William Dark aged ca. 58 years, of Ry-
sing Camden, Gloster, glover, is shown also to have
come on the *Constant*, mid 4th mo. 1680, and his wife
Alice aged ca. 63 came on the *Charles* in 6th mo.
1684, and with her, her son John, born 3 4th mo.
1667, i.e. aged 17 in 1684. What son John's surname was is not known, for Mr. F. J. Dallett has informed me that the records of the Gloucestershire
and Wiltshire Quarterly Meeting show that William
Darke and Alice Butcher were married 19 12th mo.
1670, that is, when the son John was already about
three years of age.

Thomas, son of Samuel and Ann Dark, was born 11
8th mo. 1683 and Ann, wife of Samuel Dark, was buried 13 8th mo. 1683, the transcript calling her originally Scaife but this is cancelled.[7] Having thus
lost his first wife in tragic circumstances, Samuel
Dark married, second, on 6 12th mo. 1685, Martha
Worrall who had arrived in Pennsylvania as servant
to the Pownalls in 1682, and is discussed in a separate sketch as a *Welcome* claimant. Whether this
Samuel Dark was the man of that name of Grinwitch
[Greenwich], Cohansey Precinct, Salem County, New
Jersey, fuller, who made his will 30 Dec. 1728,
probated 12 Aug. 1729, is not certain.[8] He was a
member of the Church of England; named his wife
Ruth executrix; had a daughter Ruth, then a minor,
had a daughter-in-law or step-daughter Margaret
Johns alias Pope, then wife of Thomas Jones of Kent
County, Delaware. The wife Ruth had probably been
first the wife of ----- Johns, secondly wife of
William Pope,[9] before she married Samuel Dark.

To make it certain that the Knight family was not
on the *Welcome* we may cite the fact that Giles Knight
loaded on the *Society* of Bristol, 2 May 1682, 3 cwt
of wrought iron, and that Thomas Freame made the
same load on that day, as well as 40 ells English
linen, ½ cwt of lead.[10]The Blackwell Rent Roll of
1689 shows Giles Knight in the reight of Robert
[sic] Freame, an old purchase of 49½ feet, 1/- for

5 years, on Fourth Street, west side, Sassafras to
Vine. Blackwell erred in calling the right that of
Robert Freame instead of Thomas. Evidently, Giles
Knight had inherited Ann Knight Dark's right, which
should prove that Ann Knight was sister to Giles and
Thomas Knight. She does not appear in the pedigree
in the Myers Papers, cited above, and this may not
be the only defect in that pedigree.

Dr. Martindale in his *Knight Family* says that
the Knights had twelve children of whom three died
in infancy, but he names only five, the same five
as listed by Dr. E. D. Buckman in his Buckman Genealogy (1:31), namely, Joseph, Thomas, Daniel, Jonathan and Ann. Of the last two nothing more is said
but Joseph, who is said to have died 26 4th mo.
1762,[11] had a certificate to marry Abigail Antill
dated 31 8th mo. 1715 from Abington Monthly Meeting
and she is said to have died 19 Nov. 1764 aet.
82,[12] having given birth to children named Giles and
Mary. She had arrived in America on a certificate
from Nailsworth Monthly Meeting dated 11 1st mo.
1713/4.[13] According to Martindale, Thomas was born
1685--as we have seen he was born 9 4th mo. 1685--
and died in 1774 aet. 89, having married Sarah Clifton in 1711. Daniel, according to the same source,
was born in 1697, married (1) in 1719 Elizabeth
Walker and (2) Esther, widow of Joseph Walton.

NOTES

[1]MHSP 2:179. See also Jane W. T. Brey, *A Quaker
Saga* (Philadelphia 1967), p. 460.
    [2]BHBC 1116.   [3]MQA 6.
    [4]Abstracted PGSP 1:45 but here described from a
photograph of the original will.
    [5]PMHB 9:228; BHBC 679.   [6]AM 10155, vol. 1, p.70.
    [7]BHBC 681 f.   [8]NJW 1:127.
    [9]NJW 1:370.   [10]PGM 23:43 f., note 56.
    [11]Thomas, *op. cit.* 383; also Martindale.
    [12]Martindale.   [13]MQA 61.

LANCASTER, EDWARD   *disproved*

This name appears on List X only. The truth is
that he arrived on the *Lion* of Liverpool, arriving
14 8th mo. 1683, as servant to Joseph Fisher, to
serve four years and receive £4/10 and fifty acres,
loose on 14 8th mo. 1687.

Edward Lancaster of Burlington County, New Jersey, miller, died intestate, administration being

granted 20 Feb. 1701/2 to William Hackney, Henry
Grubb, fellow-bondsman. The inventory of same date
was taken by George Gleave and Thomas Eve and came
to the small sum of £3/11.[1] It is obvious that Lancaster left neither wife nor child.

NOTE

[1]NJW 1:281.

LEECH, TOBIAS   *disproved*
LEECH, ESTHER/HESTER ASHMEAD, wife   *disproved*

These names appear on no list but the claim was
made by Josiah Granville Leach, *The Penrose Family
of Philadelphia* (Philadelphia 1903), p. 15, where
we read:

> There is a tradition in the [Penrose] family
> that . . . [Tobias Leech] . . . came in the ship
> "Welcome" with William Penn [, accompanied by
> Leech's wife Esther, her mother Mary Ashmead,
> and the latter's unspecified family], and this is
> possible, as in less than a month after Penn's
> arrival, Mr. Leech is known to have been in Phil-
> adelphia, and to have purchased two hundred and
> fifty acres of land [in Cheltenham township].[1]

The same account appears in Mr. Leach's *Chronicle
of the Yerkes Family, with Notes on the Leech and
Potter Families* (Philadelphia 1904), p. 206.

Tobias Leech and his party came, however, on the
Bristol Factor, on which he loaded on 1 July 1682,
one old mill for glover, value £3; on 14 August 1682
5 cwt nails; 3 cwt wrought iron; 3 cwt shot; 50 lbs
leather manufactured; 2 cwt¯haberdashery wares; 6
coverlets of wool and hair; 20 made garments; 28 lbs
brass manufactured; 20 bushels malt; 80 lbs gunpowder; 300 ells English-made linen; ½ chest window
glass; 40 lbs serges; 3 doz. men's woolen stockings;
20 pcs English fustians; 10 doz. plain sheepskin
gloves; ½ cwt cheese; ¼ chalder grindle stones.[2]
Such an inventory indicates that Leech was well off
as compared with the average passenger.

Toby Leech, as this Tobias was generally called,
was baptized at Cheltenham, Gloucestershire, 1 Jan.
1652, son of another Tobias Leech, and died in the
township of the same name in Philadelphia (now Montgomery) County, Pennsylvania, 13 Nov. 1726. He married in England, 26 10th mo. 1679, Esther Ashmead,
sometimes called Hester, who died in Cheltenham

Township, 11 6th mo. 1726, aged 66 years, daughter
of John and Mary (-----) Ashmead, the latter of whom
came to America with the Leech party. Toby Leech is
usually styled tanner, but he operated a corn and
fulling mill in connection with his farm.

Issue: surname Leech, order uncertain
i.   Esther, m. ca. 1703 Bartholomew Penrose, a
       shipwright who came to America about 1700
       and was buried in Christ Church graveyard
       17 Nov. 1711. Esther m. (2) Nathaniel
       Poole, also a shipbuilder, and she was
       buried in Christ Church graveyard, 1 Ap-
       ril 1713. This is the Penrose family who
       are the subject of Mr. Leach's genealogy
       cited above.
           Issue: surname Penrose
       1. Dorothy, b. ca. 1703, d. 11 Aug. 1764,
          m. Isaac Shoemaker.
       2. Sarah, b. ca. 1705, d. 28 April 1777, m.
          Richard Mather.
       3. Bartholomew, b. ca. 1708, d. 1 Feb. 1758,
          m. Mary Kirll.
       4. Thomas, b. prob. Jan.-Feb. 1709/10, d.
          17 Nov. 1757, m. Sarah Coats.
ii.   Tobias, d. March 1727, leaving widow and
       children.
iii.   John, merchant in Philadelphia, bur. Christ
       Church, 25 Dec. 1745, leaving widow and
       children.
iv.   Thomas, prominent Philadelphia merchant; was
       Clerk to the Assembly 1723-1727; member of
       the Assembly for twenty-five years, and
       Speaker 1758 and 1759; trustee of the Col-
       lege of Philadelphia 1749-1762; for 32
       years vestryman of Christ Church, for 5
       years a warden; was on the committee to
       purchase a bell, now Independence Bell; d.
       31 March 1762, leaving widow and children.
       He was probably the Thomas Leech of two
       Christ Church marriages: to Mary Rivers
       on 2 Sept. 1728 and to Mary Coatum on 27
       May 1758.
v. Isaac, J.P. in 1741, d. 10 Dec. 1744 leaving
       widow and issue.
vi.   Jacob, captain in provincial army, d. 28 Jan.
       1750; probably the Jacob of two Christ
       Church marriages, to Isabell Fisher 25

        July 1728 and to Eleanor Robison 4 April
        1733.
                        NOTES
        [1]The acreage is stated by Mrs. Balderston (PGM
23:54 f.) as 300 acres.
        [2]*Ibid.*

*LEHNMANN, PHILIP THEODOR   *highly probable*

   This private secretary to William Penn is on
Lists E, G [here probable], M, Q, R [here controver-
sial] and U. Mr. Colket was skeptical about Lehnmann's presence on the *Welcome* because the secretary
signed a document in London, 21 4th mo. 1682,[1] and
apparently his first signature in America was the
endorsement of the Frame of Government at Philadelphia, 2 April 1683.[2] Were it possible to make an extensive study of all documents signed by William
Penn after his arrival in Philadelphia and compare
the handwriting in them with the known handwriting
of Lehnmann, it might be possible to settle the matter, for Lehnmann might well have turned out many a
paper *for Penn's signature* before he had occasion
to sign his own name to a paper which has survived
to our time. While there is no direct evidence to
prove that he crossed on the *Welcome*, there is a
strong presumption that Penn would not have travelled without a secretary and Lehnmann was certainly in Pennsylvania on 22 9th mo. 1683 when he wrote
a patent for William Buckman.
   He was a First Purchaser of 1000 acres in Group
16.[3] Francis Daniel Pastorius's diary (ch. 16) has
the following:[4]

      On the sixteenth of August 1683, we came in
      sight of America, but reached the de la Ware
      River on the eighteenth of the same. On the
      twentieth of the same we . . . arrived toward
      evening safely at Philadelphia, where I was re-
      ceived by the Governor, William Penn, with af-
      fectionate friendliness, whose Secretary, Lehen-
      mann [sic], treated me with brotherly affection.

   Mr. Myers says that Lehnmann was son of Johann
Georg Lehnmann, farmer-general of Saxony, that his
wife Theophila lived at St. Philip's Parish, Bristol, and "He was Penn's private secretary on the
first visit of the Proprietor to Pennsylvania 1682-
1684, probably coming over on the *Welcome* in 1682."
He did not return to England with Penn in 1684, was

a Philadelphia merchant in 1685, and removed to
Broad Creek, not far from Lewes, Delaware.[5] Blackwell's Rent Roll of 1689 shows him as Phillip Le
mayn, an old purchase, 26 feet, 6d for 5 years, on
the northwest corner of High and Schuylkill Fourth
Street.[6]

Mr. F. J. Dallett informs me that Nailsworth
Monthly Meeting has the marriage of Phillip Theodor
Lehnmann of Bristol to Theophila Townend of Ciren-
cester, Gloucestershire, daughter of Roger Townend
of Tetbury, at Cirencester on 19 10th mo. 1678. Her
father or brother of the same name married as malt-
ster of Tetbury, Sarah -----, widow of John Boye of
Little Amwell, Ware, Herts, 6 1st mo. 1694, at Great
Amwell under the care of Nailsworth Monthly Meeting.
There was probably a relationship between Theophila
(Townend) Lehnmann and Richard Townsend, the *Welcome*
passenger.

Lehnmann was apparently not a perfect private
secretary. In a letter from William Penn to his
steward, James Harrison, at Pennsbury, dated Warminghurst, Sussex, 7 8th mo. 1684, four days after Penn
had arrived from America, we read:[7]

> Phil Lemain has, most carelessly, left behind
> the York papers that Thomas Lloyd brought, and
> should have come as the ground and very strength
> of my coming. He would not have done me a worse
> injury, nor balked a greater service, if he had
> taken the bribe of £1000 to do it. Wherefore,
> let him be quickened to send them by the first
> ship that comes out of Maryland or Virginia. . .
> Quicken T. Loyd and P. Lemain as aforesaid.

Lehnmann's will dated 26 10th mo. 1687, probated
31 Dec. 1687,[8] is signed by mark, showing, of course,
not illiteracy but illness. Neither wife nor child
is mentioned but Philip Th Lehnmann, being sick and
weak, leaves to Silas Crispin all right, title and
interest in 250 acres; to Ellinor Moss 250 acres;
to Capt. Thomas Holmes, all liberty land and plantation called Green Spring, co. Sussex; to Susannah
James, wife of John James, 300 acres; to William
Penn, Proprietary and Governor, plantation at Broad
Creek; to Charles Pickering, all land in Kent County
and my great horse called Brandy and my Camlet
Cloake, also a good feather bead & bolster & one
pillow 2 good Blankets & silver; to Samuel Bulkley
£5 of silver & clothing & a fowling piece & ½ a debt

due me from executors of John ffenwick late of West
New Jersey; to James Nevell of West New Jersey the
other half; to Cosen T B Kolkans 20 geanis; to John
Southworth £5; to John Hill mare & colt which John
Barker owes me; 2½ years of service of my maid Elizabeth Tucker to his wife Elizabeth; to William Dyre
my servant Ann Heckes for 2 years to his wife. . .
[The remainder runs off page that is broken]
Attested by William Salway, William Bethel, Elizabeth ffranc last day of Sept. 1687. "The mark was
on the margin. W Salway William Bethe[ll] Eliz
fframpton."

Philadelphia Wills A:72 contains the docket copy
which mentions also two other debtors, James Bradshaw and John Barber.

William I. Hull, *William Penn and the Dutch Quaker Migration to Pennsylvania* (Swarthmore Monographs
on Quaker History, No. 2, 1935), p. 411, makes a
curious error. In a list of Quaker immigrants from
Dutch and German lands he has "Lehnmann (Lehenmann)
Philip Theodor, one of Penn's private secretaries,"
which is right enough and then he adds that the man
was in Germantown before 1710. Apparently Hull had
found some German in Germantown with a similar name
and incorrectly identified him.[9] Our Philip Theodor
was, of course, in Germantown long before 1710 which
was twenty-three years after his death.

NOTES
[1]Samuel Hazard, *Annals of Pennsylvania* (1850),
p. 579.
[2]*Colonial Records* 1:47.
[3]1 PA 1:41; 3 PA 3:373, 380.
[4]Quoted from A. C. Myers, *Narratives of Early
Pennsylvania, West New Jersey, and Delaware 1630-1707*
(New York 1912), p. 390, note.
[5]See Marion Dexter Learned, *Life of Francis Daniel
Pastorius* (Philadelphia 1908), p. 127.
[6]PGM 23:90.
[7]William J. Buck, *William Penn in America* (1888),
p. 189; also partially quoted in Peare's life of
Penn, p. 285.
[8]Abstracted in PGSP 1:62 but described from a
photograph of the original.
[9]See TAG 39:14 f.

LEISTER, THOMAS   *disproved*

William Yardley brought with him on the *Friends'*

Adventure, arriving 28 7th mo. 1682, three servants, of whom the first and third were John Brearele and Martha Worrall, both discussed elsewhere in this book. The second servant had a name not read easily, but after repeated consideration, I have reached the conviction that the spelling as shown above is correct. The name in this form occurs, of course, on no list, but on List X, the faultiest list of all, there is a Robert Saylor who cannot otherwise be traced, and as the compiler of List X filched from Bucks Arrivals the entire household of William Yardley otherwise, I am convinced that the origin of "Robert Saylor" is a misreading of Thomas Leister's name. Mrs. Balderston (PGM 23:48) read the same name as "Robert Taylor" and it has even been suggested to me that the name should be "Laylor" or "Layler" but I am now unable to accept these readings. The first letter is L and this rules out "Taylor" entirely. No success has been had in locating this man later, though there were Lesters in Bucks County.

LLOYD, ROBERT   *disproved*

This name appears on List X only. The truth is that Robert Lloyd arrived on the *Lion* of Liverpool, 14 8th mo. 1683, as servant to Robert Turner, to serve four years, get £4 and fifty acres, loose on 14 8th mo. 1687. Extensive accounts are in Jordan[1], ·Glenn[2], and by R. L. Lloyd in *Chester County Collections* 1:379-381, 397-400, 420-25. Robert Lloyd was supposedly fourteen in 1683, died on a farm near Bryn Mawr, Pa., 29 3rd mo. 1714. An account of his ancestry is provided by Glenn, as follows:

I.   Coel ap Gweryf.
II.   Llewellyn Eurdorchog, Lord of Ial and Yat-
        rad Alun, who m. a daughter of Meredith
        ap David Lwch of Halchddyn in Deuddue.
III.   David, m. Dydgu, daughter of David ap Me-
        doc.
IV.   David Welw, m. Mallt, daughter of David ap
        Ritid.
V.   David Vair, m. Nest, daughter of Madoc ap
        Griffith.
VI.   Madoc Lloyd m. Taman, daughter of Edynfed
        ap Goronwy.
VII.   David ap Madoc of Hirnant in Mechain, Uwch

Coed, co. Montgomery, m. Maud, daughter
of Howel Gethin.

VIII.   Howell ap David, of Hirnant, m. Gwendhwy-
        far, daughter of Madoc ap Tudor.

IX.   Meredith ap Howell, m. Katharine, daughter
        of David ap Lewlln.

X.   David ap Meredith, m. Gwem, daughter of
        David ap Einion.

XI.   David Lloyd of Cowney, parish of Llanwd-
        dyn, Montgomeryshire, d. ca. 1693 [sic],
        m. Gwen.

XII.   John David Lloyd of Cowney, in Lay Subsidy
        1606, b. ca. 1568, d. July 1645, bur. 14
        July 1645; m. Jane, bur. 22 Jan. 1657.

XIII.   David Lloyd of Cowney, b. ca. 1601, bur.
        Llanwddyn Church, 9 March 1668; m. 12
        Feb. 1625, Mary, daughter of John Powell
        or John ap Howell Goch of Gadfa, Township
        of Rhinwagar, by his wife Sybil Gwyn.

XIV.   David Lloyd of Cowney, b. ca. 1645, living
        31 Aug. 1685, bur. in Quaker burying ground
        at Llanwddyn; m. Gwen, and had

        1. Robert Lloyd the immigrant.
        2. Thomas Lloyd, b. 1671, to Pennsylvania;
           m. 1697 Elizabeth, daughter of William
           ap Edward.
        3. Gainor, also came to Pennsylvania.

This pedigree has not been verified by me.
    Robert Lloyd married at Merion Monthly Meeting,
11 8th mo. 1698, Lowry Jones, born in Wales ca.
1681, eldest daughter of Rees ap John ap William,
i.e. Rees John William, by his wife Hannah Price,
and Lowry married, second, Hugh Evans.

    Issue: surname Lloyd
    i.   Hannah, b. 21 9th mo. 1699, d. Philadelphia,
          15 1st mo. 1762; m. (1) 3 9th mo. 1720,
          John Roberts, d. 1721; (2) William Pas-
          chall, 22 9th mo. 1722, d. 1732; (3) 6
          4th mo. 1734 Peter Osborne, d. 1765.
    ii.   Gwen, b. 20 8th mo. 1701, d. unm. 1783.
    iii. Sarah, b. 19 5th mo. 1703, d. 5 7th mo. 1739;
          m. 5 10th mo. 1729, Gerard Jones who d.
          21 3rd mo. 1765.
    iv.   Gainor, b. 5 2nd mo. 1705, d. 3 9th mo. 1728;
          m. 26 3rd mo. 1727, Mordecai James, d. 15
          8th mo. 1776.
    v.   David, b. 27 4th mo. 1707, m. Anne -----,

                    to North Carolina.
  vi.   Rees, b. 25 4th mo. 1709, d. 5 2nd mo. 1743,
        m. 12 12th mo. 1735, Philadelphia, Sarah
        Cox, d. 4 11th mo. 1775.
  vii. Robert, b. 25 8th mo. 1711, d. 27 8th mo.
        1786; m. 21 6th mo. 1735 at Gwynedd, Ca-
        therine Humphrey, d. 13 10th mo. 1782.
viii.Richard, b. 15 1st mo. 1731, d. 9 8th mo.
        1736; m. Hannah Sellers, d. 12 4th mo. 1810.

                              NOTES
[1]JCRFP 1:494-508.   [2]GM 81 f., 374-380.

   LONG, PETER   *disproved*
   LONG, WILLIAM   *disproved*

    Both these names appear on List X only. The truth
is that they both came on the *Lion* of Liverpool, arriving 14 8th mo. 1683, as servants to Robert Turner, Peter to serve two years, get £6 and fifty acres, loose on 14 8th mo. 1685; William, to serve
four years, get £3 and fifty acres, loose on 14 8th
1687. It seems highly probable that they were related to each other but what relationship it was is
unknown, though brothers would be the best guess.
    Peter Long was a carpenter and by 1688 was in
New Jersey when he bought 100 acres in "Second
Tenth" from Anne Salter, and was of Burlington in
1689 when he bought another 100 acres from Robert
Turner.[1] Early New Jersey deeds mention him in
various instances from 1691 to 1701, mostly in Salem
County.[2] He was son-in-law to Arthur Sturgis, felt-
maker, who had a warrant 2 9th mo. 1683[3] and died in
1702, leaving wife Dorothy, son Cornelius, daughter
Sarah (wife of Matthew Holgate), Esther Huntsman,
and son-in-law Peter Long.[4]
    On 9 Sept. 1698 Revel's Surveys included one for
Mr. William Long, 200 acres of land in Salem County,
East side of Cohansie River.[5] William Long married
Marie Jones, daughter of Henry Jones of Philadelphia whose will dated 19 6th mo. 1688, probated 16
8th mo. 1688[6], mentions them both.
    We have found nothing further on either Long.

                              NOTES
  [1]NJA 21:425, 439; PGM 24:93, note 88.
  [2]NJA 21:361, 365, 370, 425, 450, 460, 519, 672,
674, 682.
  [3]W&S 2:116.
  [4]PhW B:221, #83, 1702; PGM 23:102, 24:89.

[5]1 NJA 21:383.   [6]PhW A:83.

LUSHINGTON, WILLIAM   *proved*

This name appears on all lists except, unaccountably, List N. The proof is found in his signature
on the will of William Wade which was executed on
board the *Welcome*. The signature is beautiful and
firm, showing that if a member of the crew, he must
have been an officer. No other evidence of him has
been found, and Mrs. Balderston suggests that he may
have gone to a distant colony, been an officer of
the crew, or died at sea.

MADDOCK, THOMAS   *disproved*
MADDOCK, HENRY, allegedly his son   *disproved*

A writer in *The Colorado Genealogist* 26:89-96
quotes Pearl Baker (Mrs. F.F.), of Thomson, Georgia,
as saying that Thomas Maddock, when a very old man,
came from Cheshire, England, to Pennsylvania in 1682,
and that his son Henry came with him. He is said to
have married in Cheshire in 1646 and had two sons
by Elizabeth Simcock, Henry and a Nathan who died in
England in 1660. According to this story, Thomas
came to visit Penn's colony in America and witnessed
the first will in Chester County, Pa., 1681. It is
true that a Thomas Madox witnessed, by mark, the will
of Thomas Fream of Avon in co. Gloster, dated 5 7th
mo. 1682, probated 10 8th mo. 1682, the first will
probated in Philadelphia County. If this is the man
called Thomas Maddock, he was certainly not a *Welcome*
passenger because he was in Pennsylvania nearly two
months before the *Welcome* arrived. The Register
General issued a marriage license, date not recorded
but ca. 1685-6, for Thomas Maddox, husbandman, to
marry Jane Lee, spinster, both of Philadelphia County. A John Maddock married Margaret Kent at Philadelphia on 28 1st mo. 1690, but whether he was connected with Thomas I do not know. As for Henry
Maddock, who loaded on the *Endeavour* of Liverpool,
29 Sept. 1683 (PGM 24:82), he was in England about
a year after the *Welcome* crossed. Mrs. Balderston
says he was of Loom Hall, Cheshire, and probably
did not come on the *Endeavour*. He was brother of
James Kennerly.

MANN, [?THOMAS]   *highly improbable*

Whether this person existed at all is doubtful,

and, if he did, his first name is also highly doubtful. No evidence has been thus far been discovered
to settle either point, but I am informed by Mrs.
Mildred B. Midjaas, R.F.D. 6, Carbondale, Illinois,
that she has encountered among members of a Mann
family, in which she is interested, a tradition that
the immigrant ancestor of this family, which is supposed to be Scotch-Irish and not German in origin,
"arrived on the ship WELCOME, October 27, 1682, arriving at Delaware with William Penn."
     Mrs. Midjaas adds to this her belief that the
said ancestor did arrive very early, possibly married a Caldwell; possibly had a son John Mann who
married a Calhoun, and this John Mann followed the
Calhouns, first into Virginia, then into South Carolina when the Calhouns made that long trek to the
south.
     It may be said that in dealing with family tra-
ditions of this kind, the fact that a precise date
for the arrival of the *Welcome* is included does not
increase the credibility of the tradition, since a
date of this kind might easily be interpolated into
the story by a recent inheritor of the tradition.
Moreover, in the present instance the statement that
the Mann family under consideration was Scotch-Irish
and not German presents an added difficulty, since
1682 would be an extremely early date for the arrival of Scotch-Irish into Pennsylvania. The greatest
difficulty, however, is the vagueness of the data
supplied. ·
     The only man discovered with this surname was a
John Man or Mann of Cohansey, Salem County, New Jersey, in whose estate (NJW 1:303) there was a bond
of Daniel Dwight, late of Boston, merchant, dated
28 Oct. 1727; inventory 30 Dec. 1727, contains merchandise including silver goods and gold, stationery,
29 Testaments, 19 psalters, 11 psalm books, other
books. This does not appear to be a likely clue.

     MATTHEWS, JEANE   *proved*
     This name appears on all lists though on Lists
A, C, F and M, it is at the end. The proof is to
be found in Philadelphia Arrivals[1] where Jeane appears as a servant to Dennis Rochford. No further
trace of this woman has ever been found. Mrs. Balderston informs me that the Shipley Meeting in Sussex had several Matthews families. She may have married soon and be lost through change of name.

*MAUDE, JANE   } sisters   *disproved*
MAUDE, MARGERY   *disproved*

These two women were the daughters of Elizabeth
Chorley, the second wife of Dr. Thomas Wynne, by her
second husband, Joshua Maude. They were passengers
on the *Submission*, the log of which clearly states
that fact. That they were, instead, passengers on
the *Welcome*, is mistakenly claimed on List F, the
work of William J. Buck, assisted by W. F. Corbett
and Dr. E. D. Buckman. These gentlemen were doubtless well advised in claiming that the girls' mother was a *Welcome* passenger, but they overlooked the
evidence from the *Submission* log. A full account
of these women is included in the sketch on their
mother Elizabeth Wynne.

MENDENHALL, BENJAMIN   *disproved*
MENDENHALL, GEORGE   } brothers   *disproved*
MENDENHALL, JOHN   *disproved*

These names appear on no list and there is no
affirmative evidence for the claim made by Gilbert
Cope and Henry Graham Ashmead, *Genealogical and Personal Memoirs of Chester and Delaware Counties, Pennsylvania* (New York-Chicago 1904), 1:119: "Benjamin,
John and George Mendenhall, brothers, came to this
country from England in 1682 in compnay [sic] with
William Penn." George Smith, M.D., in his earlier
work, *History of Delaware County, Pennsylvania*
(Philadelphia 1862), p. 484, merely says that they
came in 1686 and this is much more probably true.

William Mendenhall and [his son] Edward Mendenhall,
hall, *History, Correspondence, and Pedigrees of the
Mendenhalls of England the United States* (Cincinna-
ti 1865), p. 9, print a letter sent to the said
William Mendenhall by Aaron Mendenhall of Fairfield
[Ohio] on 1 6th mo. 1828. In another letter Aaron
Mendenhall stated that his grandfather, Moses Mendenhall, was still living in Chester County, Pennsylvania, in 1829, aged 89, and that Moses was a
grandson to John Mendenhall the immigrant; that the
three brothers came "soon after or near the time
that William Penn located the site of" Philadelphia,
and that one of the three [most probably George] returned to England.

MILES, SAMUEL   *disproved*
MILES, MARGARET JAMES, his wife   *disproved*

In the course of research we came to think that
Samuel Miles might have been a *Welcome* passenger.
The clue that made us think so was a record of the
Board of Property, session of 27 6th mo. 1705,[1] at
which head land was granted to Samuel Miles on a
certificate signed by Benjamin Chambers that Miles
had come as a servant to the Free Society of Traders in 1682. As Chambers was himself very probably on the *Welcome*, this called for further research.

Earlier grants to Samuel Miles are of record: 31
1st mo. 1683, on warrant dated 24 1st mo. 1683, a
city lot bounded on the south by Poole Street [name
changed 1684 to Walnut], rear by back lots, vacant
both sides.[2] There is also a certificate of survey,
apparently for the same lot, between 5th and 6th
Streets from Delaware, south by Walnut, formerly
Poole Street (1684), apparently for a small lot No.
158-DB (1684).[3] By warrant dated 18 12th mo. 1701
there was a resurvey 28 3rd mo. 1703 to Samuel Miles
of 352 acres in Radnor in Welsh tract in Newtown,
bounds: William Davis, Richard Miles, Lewis Walker.[4]
With reference to the grant first cited above, William Marshall had 76 acres surveyed of which 50 are
in the right of Samuel Miles against his warrant of
3 7ber 1705 requiring Isaac Taylor, Surveyor, to lay
out to Samuel Miles, who came into this province a
servant of the Free Society of Traders in 1682 in
consideration of servitude, laid out to him 11 of
month in Township of Bensalem, now Bradford, Chester County. Balance was part of a piece warranted
to Richard Pierce & wife who came as servants to
William Stanley in 1682.[5]

But Minshall Painter[6] rightly says that Samuel
Miles and wife Margaret came from Radnorshire in
1683. The evidence is in Radnor Meeting records
where there is a certificate for this couple from
a monthly meeting in the parish of Llainhangel yr
helygen in co. Radnor, Wales, dated 27 5th mo.
1683, signed by Owen Humphrey, Edward Eyton, John
Jarman, Daniel Lewis and others. There is also a
certificate for James Miles from the same meeting,
on the same date, signed by the same men and by
Nathan Woodliffe.

Margaret James of the parish of Newchurch, co.
Radnor, Wales, spinster, married at Newchurch, 25
June 1682, Samuel Miles.[7] Samuel Miles of the parish of Llanfihangel Helyden, co. Radnor, was son
of James Miles of the same. Samuel and Margaret

James Miles had three daughters:

  i.   Tamar, b. 1687, m. 1708 Thomas Thomas, son
        of William Thomas.
 ii.   Phebe, b. 1690, m. 1715 Evan Evans of Hav-
        erford.
iii.   Ruth, b. 1693, m. 1715/16 Owen Evans.[8]

NOTES

[1]2 PA 19:462
[3]*Ibid.* 2:83.
[5]*Ibid.* 5:130.
[7]GWF 1:179.
[2]W&S 3:227.
[4]*Ibid.* 4:161
[6]PGSP 4:294.

[8]*Ibid.* 194 f. The research on warrants and surveys for this sketch was done by Walter Lee Sheppard Esq.

MOGERIDGE, HANNAH   *proved*

The proper spelling of this woman's name is as
shown above but the name appears as "Mogdridge" on
all lists owing to a misreading of the letter e
which is of the type which looks like a modern d.

The proof is to be found in Bucks Arrivals where
she is shown as a servant to John Rowland, to be
loose in 3rd mo. 1684, which would mean that she
had only to serve a year and nine months from the
arrival of the ship. Perhaps her period of servitude had begun in England; perhaps she had already
completed it by the time John Rowland registered her
as his servant. She married Thomas Rogers and had
a son Thomas by him, but the son's history after
1715 is unknown.

There is a curious statement about her in the
minutes of the Board of Property for 28 5th mo.
1720, repeated at the session of 9 4th mo. 1720.[1]
On these dates one James McVaugh presented to the
Board of Property a deed, the date of which is cru-
cial to the argument but is not stated, whereby
Thomas Rogers of Bensalem, Bucks County, conveyed
100 acres of servants' land, 50 acres on his own
account, 50 acres on his wife's formerly Hannah
Maugridge or Maugaridge, which fact should prove
the marriage. Also a certificate under the hand of
Benjamin Chambers [who in 1720 had been dead five
years] who asserted that Thomas Rogers served his
time to the Society of Traders but the said Hannah,
being dead long before the date of the above deed,
he [Thomas Rogers] cant pretend to have any land on

her account.

This is strange. If Hannah lived to 3rd mo. 1684,
then she was made free and entitled to her fifty acres of land. The marriage to Rogers must have been
later than 9 7th mo. 1686, on which date she signed
as Hannah Mugridg the wedding certificate of William
Berry to Naomy Wally, and the terminus ante quem was
12 1st mo. 1688, on which date Thomas and Hannah
Rogers, Jo Rowland and Piscilla Rowland, were among
witnesses to the wedding of Shadrach Walley and Mary
Sharpe at Middletown Monthly Meeting. Thomas Rogers
Jr., son of Thomas and Hannah, was born 11 4th mo.
1690, which shows that Hannah was still living in
1690, six years after the date when she should have
been free. In 1716 Thomas Rogers Jr. was an heir
of John Rowland.[2] All this would prove that Hannah
Rogers was the erstwhile servant of John Rowland,
Hannah Mogeridge.

Thomas Rogers's deeds in Bucks County do not indicate any wife: 2:139, 12 10th mo. 1694, 110 acres
bought from Charles Reed, sold to Edmund Lovett who
by the next deed sold the property on 7 7th mo.
1697; 2:45, 11 Sept. 7 William and Mary 1695, Thomas
Rogers, husbandman, sold for £31/10 225 acres in
Newtown Stead, land bought in 1695. Hannah therefore probably died between 11 4th mo. 1690 and 12
10th mo. 1694, which date must, on the basis of
Benjamin Chambers's note cited above, have been long
before the unknown date of the deed to James McVaugh.

Benjamin Chambers's statement is the only evidence
thus far found to show that Thomas Rogers was a servant of the Society of Free Traders. No one has suggested that Rogers was a *Welcome* passenger, and no
evidence has been found to show that he was.

He must, however, have been a different man from
the Thomas Rogers, merchant taylor, who subscribed
£100 to the Society of Free Traders.[3]

Following his appearance as one of the heirs of
John Rowland in 1716, nothing has been found concerning Thomas Rogers Jr. There is no probate or
land record for him in Bucks County thereafter, and
it is possible that the two Thomas Rogerses went
elsewhere, even back to England.

NOTES

[1]2 PA 19:671, 702.   [2]See below, p. 460.
[3]PMHB 11:175-180.

MORRIS, JOSHUA   *proved*

This name appears on all lists excepting, unaccountably, List I. Proof is to be found in the fact
that Joshua Morris, tynn-plate worker, witnessed the
will of Thomas Heriott executed aboard the *Welcome*.

Morris was buried in Philadelphia 6 2nd mo. 1696,
recorded in the list of non-Quaker burials kept by
William Hudson of Philadelphia Meeting,[1] which contains Keithians as well as persons who never were
Quakers at all. This may indicate that Morris had
become an adherent of George Keith; we really have
no evidence to show that he had been a Friend except
the presumption that an outsider would not have been
asked to witness a Friend's will, not a strong presumption, since George Thompson, who was almost certainly not a Friend, witnessed all wills executed
aboard the *Welcome*.

Administration was granted 18 Jan. 1696/7 on the
estate of Joshua Morris, tine-man, of the town and
county of Philadelphia, to Samuel Nichols, on behalf
of his brothers Henry, Richard, John Morris,[2] and
quietus est was given Nichols on 20 Aug. 1698/9.
File 110 for 1697 contains the bond of Samuel Nichols, sawyer, administrator of Joshua Morris, and
Joshua Carpenter, £50; inventory dated 27 Jan. 1699
[i.e. 1698/9], taken by Thomas Harris and John De-
plueys, recorded 19 Feb. 1698/9, £9/10/11 and sale
£2/13/6 "in Name and behalfe of [illegible name],
ye sd Morris's brother." The illegible words look
most like "Lareijj Riche" but I am far from satisfied with this reading, and it may be that the first
word should be "Henry," and the second "Rich.",
though even this is doubtful. On 18 9th mo. 1686[3]
Joshua Morris conveyed 200 acres to William Powell
for £6, the land being originally purchased from
Powell for £20. Morris was to live on the land until 2 Sept. 1688 when he must pay £6 or forfeit.
On 9 4th mo. 1687 he bought from Charles Bingham
for 40/- consideration some land in Philadelphia.[4]
On the Blackwell Rent Roll of 1689[5] Joshua Morris
is shown with a lot, rented, 47 feet, at the Center,
just east of Schuylkill Eighth, on the north side
of the Square.[6]

NOTES

[1]HEAQG 2:446.   [2]PhA A:223, 278.   [3]PhD E-1, 455.
[4]This deed is cited by Mr. Colket, not located.
[5]PGM 23:89.   [6]W&S 3:249, surveyed 1 8th mo. 1684.

NEWLIN, CHRISTOPHER   *disproved*
   This name appears on no list but Mr. Walter Lee
Sheppard informs me that Newlin is sometimes claimed
as a *Welcome* passenger, though for many years the
disproving evidence has been in print.[1] This consists of the text of a certificate dated 25 12th
mo. 1682, after the *Welcome* had arrived in America,
issued by the Friends of the Mt. Mellick Men's Meeting in Ireland, signed by Tobias Padwell, William
Edmundson, Christopher Rofer and others. The certificate asserts that there is nothing against him
but some dissatisfaction with his desire to move to
America, attributing this not to gain a livelihood,
which he already had in Ireland, but to escape persecution as a Friend! Sons Nathaniel and John are
clear of marriage.
   Newlin actually came on the *Levee* of Liverpool,
James Kilner, master, as we know because passengers
sued Kilner for diverting their property, and Newlin was a witness.[2] He was Justice of the Peace
for Chester, one of the first appointed, and died,
testate, in 1699.
   Neither of the two existing genealogies claims
Newlin as a *Welcome* passenger: Alexander du Bin,
Newlin Family and Collateral Lines (Philadelphia
copyright 1942), p. 1; Algie I Newlin and Harvey
Newlin, *The Newlin Family, Ancestors and Descendants
of John and Mary Pyle Newlin* (Greensboro N.C. 1965).

NOTES

[1]PMHB 6:174; MIQ 57f., 271-273.
[2]*Colonial Records* 1:80 f.

OGDEN, DAVID   *proved*
OGDEN, HANNAH, his sister   *possible*
OGDEN, SARAH, his sister   *possible*

   The name of David Ogden appears, properly, on
all lists; those of his sisters only on List F. He
signed as a weaver the will of Thomas Heriott which
executed aboard the *Welcome*, and he also received
a bequest of £2 in the will of Isaac Ingram, also
executed aboard the ship. It is possible that he
brought his two sisters with him, though they are
generally thought to have come a few years later.
As we have uncovered no evidence to prove their
coming on any particular ship, we have included
them as possible *Welcome* passengers.

David brought with him a certificate from London
Monthly Meeting dated 21 11th mo. 1681/2, the earliest date of any certificate brought by any proved
Welcome passenger.[1] He was born 1 2nd mo. 1655,
died 22 8th mo. 1705; married on 12 1st mo. 1686,
1st intentions 4 11th mo. 1685, 2nd intentions, 1
1st mo. 1686, Martha Houlston, born at Preston Boats,
Shropshire, 1 2nd mo. 1661, living 30 7th mo. 1717,
daughter of John Houlston whose wife's name has been
given variously. The mother is called Ann by Charles
Burr Ogden,[2] Margaret by Meredith B. Colket, and
Elizabeth Serrill by Howard M. Lloyd.[3] In the sketch
on John Houlston we have shown that the surname Serrill is probably only a possibility, and that John's
wife was named Elizabeth. Whichever of the three
names was correct for Martha's mother, Martha married, second, 1st intentions 28 6th mo. 1710, 2nd
intentions 26 7th mo. 1710, James Thomas of Whiteland, yeoman, on whose estate administration was
granted 27 Feb. 1727 to George Asbridge.

David Ogden was constable of Chester in 1694.[4]
His will was signed in Middletown Township, Chester
County, on 16 March 1705, probated 17 Nov. 1705,[5]
and it mentions wife Martha and the children
below. Chester Deeds D:62, 29 July 1717, acknowledged 5 6th mo. 1717 by testimony of the witnesses
Edward Lawrence of Middletown, yeoman, and Peter
Trego of Edgmont, carpenter, before Henry Pierce,
J.P., has grantors Jonathan Ogden of Middletown
Township, carpenter, and James Thomas of Whiteland,
yeoman, and his wife Martha who had been relict of
Jonathan's father David Ogden deceased. Another
deed of the same grantors and grantee, dated the
next day, acknowledged on that day (D:64), says
that William Penn granted to David Ogden by patent
dated 1 Aug. 1684, and he devised by will 16 July
1705 to Martha for a term and then to Jonathan. All
three grantors were able to sign their names.

Charles Burr Ogden[6] speaks of a mirror and a toy
glass hat (both illustrated), said to have been on
the *Welcome*, and he also quotes[7] an article from the
Philadelphia Press, 7 2nd mo. 1897, which includes
a story of arms granted to a weaver named John Ogden by Charles II, and says that John's son Jonathan or David was father to David Ogden of the *Welcome*. This story, which hardly seems impressive,
has not been verified.

Mr. Ogden also states that David had the two sisters listed above, of whom Hannah married, first,

Robert Barber of Chester County, and second, William
Hudson, sometime mayor of Philadelphia. Her first
intention to marry Barber was made at Chester Month-
ly Meeting, 13 8th mo. 1690, 2nd intentions, 3 9th
mo. 1690. By her second marriage to Hudson she be-
came connected with the widow of John Barber of the
Welcome, that is, Elizabeth (Songhurst)(Barber)(Webb)
Richardson, and the will of Hannah (Ogden)(Barber)
Hudson has already been discussed in the sketch on
John Barber.

Mr. Ogden was not quite sure that the other sister was named Sarah but says that she married Isaac
Williams and had a son Isaac who married and had
daughters Rachel and Hannah. The sister Sarah has
not been traced further.

The children of David and Martha (Houlston) Ogden were:

1 i.   Jonathan, b. 19 2nd mo. 1687, d. 6th mo.
        1727.
  ii.   Martha, b. 23 5th mo. 1689, unm. 1727.
2 iii. Sarah, b. 3 9th mo. 1691, death not found.
  iv.   Nehemiah, b. 15 10th mo. 1693, d. 14 11th
        mo. 1781, no further comment by Charles
        Burr Ogden.
3 v.   Samuel, b. 30 10th mo. 1695, d. 14 11th
        mo. 1748.
4 vi.   John, b. 4 5th mo. 1698, d. 6 12th mo. 1742.
  vii. Aaron, b. 31 3rd mo. 1700, no further com-
        ment by Charles Burr Ogden.
  viii. Hannah, b. 22 6th mo. 1702, m. out by 7
        6th mo. 1724, Joseph Hayes, formerly of
        Goshen Monthly Meeting, whose estate was
        admin. by widow Hannah, 29 July 1734.
5 ix.   Stephen, b. 12 11th mo. 1705, d. 16 9th mo.
        1760.

1. Jonathan Ogden, eldest child of David and Martha (Houlston) Ogden, was born 19 2nd mo. 1687, died
in 6th mo. 1727; married in 1720 Ann Robinson, daughter of George Robinson, whose will has not been discovered, by his wife Catherine -----. Jonathan's
will, dated in Chester Township and County, 17 6th
mo. 1727, probated 31 Aug. 1727, shows that his wife
was not living; mentions daughter Katherine, sons
David and Joseph, some of them, at least, minors;
loving father-in-law George Robinson, cousin Jacob
Howell. Witnesses include Martha Ogden, probably
his sister.

Issue: surname Ogden
i.   David, b. 1723, m. Wilmington Monthly Meet-
      ing, 16 12th mo. 1742/3, Zebiah Wollas-
      ton, daughter of William Wollaston of
      New Castle; 4 ch.
ii.   Joseph, b. 1725, d. Philadelphia, 18 1st
      mo. 1805; m. Philadelphia Monthly Meeting
      21 9th mo. 1751, Jemima Hewes, b. 1728,
      d. 30 6th mo. 1817, daughter of Moses and
      Sarah (Blythe) Hewes; 8 ch.
iii. Catherine, b. Chester Co., 1727, m. Old
      Swedes Church, Wilmington, Jan. 1747,
      Ebenezer Wollaston.

2. Sarah Ogden, third child and second daughter
of David and Martha (Houlston) Ogden, was born 3
9th mo. 1691, but her death date has not been discovered. She married, first, 21 9th mo. 1711, Evan
Howell (son of John Howell of Philadelphia), who
was of Edgmont when administration was granted his
widow, 28 June 1734; second, at Middletown Monthly
Meeting, 10 10th mo. 1741, William Surman, by whom
there was no issue.

Issue: surname Howell, all by first husband
i.   Israel, b. 1712, m. Middletown Monthly Meet-
      ing, 11 2nd mo. 1751, Elizabeth Swayne,
      daughter of William Swayne; (2) 12 11th
      mo. 1761, Springfield Monthly Meeting,
      Mary Hall, daughter of John Hall.
ii.   Esther, b. 30 1st mo. 1714; m. (1) Chester
      23 3rd mo. 1734, Daniel Few, b. 25 1st
      mo. 1706, of Kennett, son of Isaac and
      Hannah Few of Kennett Square.
iii. Abraham, b. 19 9th mo. 1716, removed to
      Sussex County, Delaware.
iv.   Jonathan, b. 5 6th mo. 1719, m. 28 4th mo.
      1750, Elizabeth Thomas.
v.   Isaac, b. 19 9th mo. 1721, perhaps m. Mary
      Baker, not Bartram.[8] The Isaac Howell
      who m. Mary Bartram, sometimes supposed
      to be this one, was son of Jacob and Sa-
      rah.
vi.   Mary, b. 3 1st mo. 1723/4.
vii. John, under 14 in 1741. He and the next
      are not in Charles Burr Ogden's book.
viii. Nathan, under 14 in 1741.

3. Samuel Ogden, fifth child and third son of Da-

vid and Martha (Houlston) Ogden, was born 30 10th
mo. 1695, died 14 11th mo. 1748, intestate. He married at Springfield, 26 3rd mo. 1720, Esther Lownes,
born 2 7th mo. 1703, died 11 11th mo. 1747, daughter of George and Mary (Bowers) Lownes.

Issue: surname Ogden
i. David, b. 15 4th mo. 1722, d. 16 4th mo.
    1798; m. Springfield, 20 9th mo. 1746,
    Alice Eachus, b. 11th mo. 1723, d. 12
    12th mo. 1791 aet. 68/0/23; 5 ch.
ii. Jane, b. 1 11th mo. 1724, d.s.p. 1748; m.
    Springfield, 21 6th mo. 1746, William Le-
    vis (1st int. 30 4th mo. 1746, 2nd int.
    28 5th mo. 1746).
iii. Mary, b. 8 8th mo. 1725; m. Philadelphia
    Monthly Meeting, 19 3rd mo. 1752, James
    Whitall; 2 ch.
iv. George, b. 26 9th mo. 1726, d. 20 9th mo.
    1762; m. Springfield, 25 2nd mo. 1751,
    Mary Low, b. 23 2nd mo. 1722, d. 20 5th
    mo. 1810, daughter of John and Janet
    (Hartley) Low; 5 ch.
v. Martha, b. 8 4th mo. 1729, m. ----- Thomp-
    son.
vi. Jonathan, b. 27 11th mo. 1731, m. 12th mo.
    1769 Martha Davis, b. 1748, d. 25 7th
    mo. 1813, daughter of Arthur and Esther
    P. Davis of Chester Co.; 6 ch.
vii. Hannah, b. 25 2nd mo. 1734, m. Swedes
    Church, Philadelphia, 15 July 1759 Wil-
    liam Lees; 1 ch.
viii. Sarah, b. 18 9th mo. 1737, d.s.p., 6 3rd
    mo. 1760.
ix. James, b. 10 10th mo. 1739, d.s.p. 10 8th
    mo. 1757.
x. Samuel, b. 8 5th mo. 1745, d. 21 4th mo.
    1821, m. Woodstown, N.J., rec. Salem
    Monthly Meeting, 1 3rd mo. 1770, Mary
    Ann Hoffman, b. 19 10th mo. 1752, d. 18
    1st mo. 1818, daughter of John and Mary
    (Fo) Hoffman; 10 ch.

4. John Ogd'n, sixth child and fourth son of David and Martha (Houlston) Ogden, was born 4 5th mo.
1698, died 6 12th mo. 1742. He married first, at
Philadelphia Monthly Meeting, 26 2nd mo. 1723, Hannah Davis, buried 22 5th mo. 1737; second, at the
same meeting, 23 8th mo. 1740 Hannah Owen, born 16

1st mo. 1720, died 1st mo. 1791, second daughter of Robert and Susanna (Hudson) Owen and granddaughter of Mayor William Hudson.[9] Hannah married second, 7 6th mo. 1754,[10] Joseph Wharton (Thomas, Richard), born 4 8th mo. 1707, buried 27 July 1776, who married, first, at Philadelphia Monthly Meeting, 5 1st mo. 1729/30, Hannah Carpenter, born Philadelphia, 23 9th mo. 1711, died 14 July 1751, daughter of John and Ann (Hoskins) Carpenter. There were seven Wharton children by Hannah Owen.[11]

Issue: surname Ogden
   by Hannah Davis
i.   Joseph, b. Philadelphia, d. 1749 in Barbadoes.
ii.   Rebecca, b. Philadelphia, d. by 1760.
iii.   John, d. 3 9th mo. 1725.
iv.   Sarah, d. 13 5th mo. 1727.
   by Hannah Owen
v.   William, b. by 31 1st mo. 1742, d. Camden, N.J., 13 5th mo. 1818; m. (1) 11 1st mo. 1769, Marie Pinniard, b. 1750, d. 14 7th mo. 1775; (2) St. Paul's, Philadelphia, 10 July 1777, Tacey David, d. 11 9th mo. 1809, daughter of Benjamin and Ann (----) David; 2 ch. by each wife.

5. Stephen Ogden, ninth and youngest child of David and Martha (Houlston) Ogden, was born 12 11th 1704/5, died 16 9th mo. 1760, intestate. He married Hannah Surman, born 5 2nd mo. 1722, died 10 10th mo. 1783, daughter of William Surman of the City of Worcester, England, by his wife Mary Barnes, who were married 16 10th mo. 1720.

Issue: surname Ogden
i.   Nehemiah, b. 12 12th mo. 1743/4, d.s.p. 29 8th mo. 1752.
ii.   John, b. 31 10th mo. 1746, d. 23 5th mo. 1825; m. Springfield, 15 4th mo. 1773, Sarah Crozer, b. 9 11th mo. 1747, d. 23 8th mo. 1822, daughter of James and Mary (Gleave) Crozer; 7 ch.
iii.   Stephen, b. 8 7th mo. 1748, d.s.p. 13 10th 1776.
iv.   Mary, b. 11 8th mo. 1750, d. 5 9th mo. 1809; m. Springfield, 29 6th mo. 1775, Edward Horne, b. 26 1st mo. 1752, son of William and Elizabeth Horne; 8 ch.
v.   Hannah, b. 21 6th mo. 1752, d. 17 4th mo.

1822; m. as 2nd wife, Springfield, 6 5th
1790, Philip Bonsall, son of Vincent
Bonsall and widower of Catherine Harrison; 2 ch.

vi. Aaron, b, 9 7th mo. 1754, m. Esther Preston; 8 ch.

vii. Martha, b. 20 10th mo. 1756, d.s.p.; m.
(1) Springfield, 5 4th mo. 1787, James
Arnold, son of David Arnold of Glouces-
ter, N.J.; (2) 27 11th mo. 1800, Thomas
Laycock, widower, son of William and
Hannah Laycock of Darby, Delaware County,
Pa.; (3) John Humphrey.

viii. Jonathan, said to have been a son but not
mentioned in Hannah's will.

ix. Abigail, b. 27 10th mo. 1760, d. 15 6th
mo. 1842; m. (1) Springfield, 23 11th
mo. 1786, Seth Pancoast; (2) Darby, 5
12 th mo. 1805, Israel Roberts, d. 29
7th mo. 1818, son of John and Susanna
Roberts; 4 ch. by Pancoast.

NOTES

[1]MQA 7.

[2]Charles Burr Ogden, *The Quaker Ogdens, David
Ogden of ye Goode Ship "Welcome" and his Descendants
1682-1897* (Philadelphia 1898); see also JCRFP 1:
681-688.

[3]*Lloyd Manuscripts* (Lancaster, Pa., 1912).

[4]Chester Court Records 311. [5]PMHB15:192.

[6]*Op. cit.*   [7]*Op. cit.* 23.

[8]*Op. cit.* 49, 56.   [9]GM 140.

[10]Wharton Genealogy says 1752. PMHB 1:326 f.

[11]PMHB 1:326 f.

OLIVER, EVAN	*disproved*
OLIVER, JEAN, his wife	*disproved*
OLIVER, DAVID, his son	*disproved*
OLIVER, ELIZABETH, his daughter	*disproved*
OLIVER, JOHN, his son	*disproved*
OLIVER, HANNAH, his daughter	*disproved*
OLIVER, MARY, his daughter	*disproved*
OLIVER, EVAN, his son	*disproved*
OLIVER, SEABORN, his daughter	*disproved*

Evan Oliver is on all lists but List O denies
his presence on the *Welcome* and Lists U and V put
him on the *Bristol Factor*. List X compounds its
peculiarity in this instance by calling him Evan

Mill Oliver and calls his wife Elizabeth. The wife Jean and the children named above are listed on Lists A, B, C, D, E, F, G, H, I, M, Q, Y and Z by name, and as "family" on Lists J, K, L, N, P, S, T and W, while Lists U and V put them, of course, on the *Bristol Factor*, that is, on the second trip of that vessel.

The alleged proof that the Olivers were on the *Welcome* is a statement in Edward Armstrong's Wilmington address printed in 1852 (p. 25) which asserts that Benjamin Ferris of Wilmington gave Armstrong a memorandum from a manuscript note-book of Evan Oliver, then called "Welcome passenger," as follows: "Wee arrived at Upland in Pensilvania in America, ye 28th day of ye 8th, month, '82." If this was not the very day when the *Welcome* arrived at Upland, it was very close. Albert Cook Myers appears to have seen the note-book and states in the Oliver section of his Welcome Papers that the note-book did not mention the *Welcome*. The seventh child was born during the voyage on 24 8th mo. 1682, "almost in sight of the capes of Delaware." In a letter in the Historical Society of Pennsylvania from Benjamin Ferris to Edward Armstrong, dated 29 12th mo. 1851, we read the following:

> I have had in my possession (and it is yet in my brother-in-law Merrit Canby's possession) an Old Manuscript Book, which had long served Evan Oliver of Radnorshire in Wales, as a Book of Records for pecuniary matters and the more momentous concerns of Marriages, Births, Deaths, and other weighty family affairs. Among other records is the following, which is copied in imitation of the original:

> Wee came out of Radnorshire about the beginning of ye 6 month 82 & arrived at Upland in pensilvania ye 28th of ye 8 month 82.

Another letter of Ferris to Armstrong, dated 3 1st mo. 1852, says:

> That Evan Oliver did come in the ship *Welcome* is certainly true, unless another ship arrived at Upland in Pennsylvania October 28th 1682, for this memorandum does not mention the name of the Ship which brought them to America.

Unfortunately for the Ferris-Armstrong theory, there

was just such another ship! Mordecai Howell, himself a *Welcome* claimant but not a *Welcome* passenger,
deposed before the Boundary Commission in 1740 when
he was aged 78, as follows:[1]

> That about 1682 he came up the Bay of the Dela-
> ware in company with the ship in which the Plain-
> tiffs Father [William Penn] was. That he landed,
> some time before Mr. Penn At New Castle Town,
> and was there when he landed at said Town.

The ship on which the Howell family arrived has now
been identified as the *Bristol Factor* on its second
trip.

The Oliver claim was accepted also by Henry Graham Ashmead,[2] by Horace E. Hayden,[3] and recently by
Dr. Arthur Edwin Bye,[4] but in view of Armstrong's
dependence upon Benjamin Ferris, it is surprising
that the latter's *History of the Original Settlements on the Delaware* (Wilmington 1846) says nothing
at all about the *Welcome* or any of its passengers.

The Olivers were from Radnorshire but they were
received in Pennsylvania on a certificate from Bristol dated 26 6th mo. 1682,[5] which is certainly a
very late date for the *Welcome* particularly in view
of the fact that the wife was pregnant during the
crossing. To go from Bristol to London in two or
three days, would, at that time, have been impossi-
·ble, and the same objection is valid even if we as-
sume that the family boarded the vessel at some
channel port nearer Bristol.

The suspicion with which this claim was long regarded was corroborated by the fact that Evan Oliver
loaded on the *Bristol Factor,* Roger Drew, master,
for Pennsylvania and Virginia, 14 Aug. 1782, 3/4
cwt wrought iron; 1½ bushels oatmeal; 1 firkin butter; 3 pails; 2 cwt nails; 14 cwt cheese; 1 3/4 cwt
iron; 2 cwt nails; 10 lbs brass manufactured; 1 doz
felt hats; ¼ cwt English soap; 18 lbs shoes; 15 lbs
pewter; 2 cwt nails more.[6] This is excellent evidence that the family intended to cross, and did so
cross, on the second trip of the *Bristol Factor*.

The Blackwell Rent Roll of 1689[8] shows Joane
Oliver as owner of an old purchase lot of 49 feet
on Chestnut Street, 2/- for five years. This is surprising, since Evan Oliver was still living, dying
on 31 11th mo. 1694/5, buried 2 12th mo. 1694/5.
His wife, who is said to have been probably a daughter of David Lloyd, was buried 5 1st mo. 1695/6,

having died two days earlier.
The first seven of the children were born before
the arrival in Pennsylvania.

        Issue: surname Oliver
        i.   David, b. 1 5th mo. 1670, d. 14 7th mo.
                1690, bur. Philadelphia 15 7th mo. 1690
                as Daniel.
        ii.   Elizabeth, b. 28 2nd mo. 1672; had leave to
                m. at Philadelphia Monthly Meeting, 25
                4th mo. 1697, George Gottschick or Godt-
                shant [probably Gottschalk].
        iii.   John, b. 24 12th mo. 1673, d. 15 8th mo.
                1685, bur. Philadelphia.
        iv.   Hannah, b. 21 11th mo. 1675, d. 12 8th mo.
                1688.
        v.   Mary, b. 9 10th mo. 1677, d. 26 1st mo.
                1721; m., according to Hayden, 2 June
                17--, as 2nd wife, Thomas Canby of Wil-
                mington.
        vi.   Evan, b. 27 1st mo. 1680, d. 8 8th mo.
                1688.
        vii.   Seaborn (female), b. at sea, 24 8th mo.
                1682, "almost in sight of the capes of
                Delaware," d. 28 9th mo. 1682.
        viii.   Benjamin, b. 7 6th mo. 1685, d. 19 8th mo.
                1688.
        ix.   Joseph, b. 14 5th mo. 1688.

                            NOTES
[1]2 PA 16:719.
[2]Henry Graham Ashmead, *History of Delaware County, Pennsylvania* (Philadelphia 1884), p. 20.
[3]Horace E. Hayden (PMHB 12:127; NYGBR 19:137f.).
[4]*The Historian* 3:68, also his *History of the Bye
Family and Some Allied Families* (Easton 1956), p.
424. Mrs. Jane W. T. Brey, *A Quaker Saga* (Philadelphia 1967), p. 415, does not make the same error.
[5]MQA 7.
[6]PGM 23:55, note 104, which says that the Oliver
certificate also included David James of Llandegley
and Glaseram, Radnorshire, Wales, weaver, and that
Oliver also came from Glaseram. David James's wife
Margaret and daughter Mary had to write back for
their certificate. See 2 PA 19:341; PGM 19:242.
On the "Explanation of the Map of Philadelphia" (3
PA 3:350), the names of Mary Oliver and Elizabeth
Gotschick appear.   [7]PGM 23:80.

OTTEY, JOHN   *proved*

Bucks Arrivals clearly show this man as servant
to Thomas Fitzwater with six years to serve.[1] List
F reads the name approximately as it should: John
Otley, but Lists A, B, C, D, E, G, H, I, J, K, L,
M, N, P, Q, R, S, T, W and X have it wrongly as
John Hey, and List D further compounds the error as
John Key. That the correct name was Ottey was discovered independently by both Meredith B. Colket Jr.
and me. John Ottey has sometimes been confused
with John Otter.[2] There are undoubtedly living descendants in the male line, for the name Ottey was
seen on a mail box on the road leading from the
Pennsylvania Turnpike northwest into Norristown.

A John Ottey, probably this one, died intestate,
administration granted 26 June 1717 to Ann Ottey of
Chester County, widow.[3] File 104 for 1717 has only
the bond of Ann Ottey [signed by mark], bondsmen
Thomas Ottey, David Thomas, all of Chester, £150,
inventory to be before 26 July, account before 26
June 1718, but no inventory or account was in the
file when it was examined.

Ann Ottey of Treduffrin, widow, signed by mark
her will on 5 Dec. 1737, probated 16 April 1753[4]:
the executor is Christopher Ottey, trustee is Richard Iddings and witnesses: John Jones, Mary Plain,
David Thomas; sons named are Thomas, Phillip, Richard, Christopher; Christopher's children: Ann, John,
Sarah, some, at least, minors. Now John Ottey of
the *Welcome* was not accompanied by a wife, so we are
at liberty to suppose that he could have married a
somewhat younger woman who could have survived to
1753. It may well be that John Ottey was only a boy
when he crossed the Atlantic, and he might well have
had a widow living seventy years later.

Issue: surname Ottey
i.   Thomas, bondsman in father's estate 1717;
        named in mother's will 1737; no further
        trace.
ii.   Philip, named in mother's will 1737; m. at
        St. Paul's Episcopal Church, Chester, Pa.,
        8 May 1730, Sarah Baker, daughter of Jo-
        seph and Martha Baker of Edgmont, as
        Gilbert Cope's Collections say, and he
        appears to have d. ca. 1750, for she m.
        (2) 5 Oct. 1750, James Maxwell. The
        birth dates also follow Cope.

Issue: surname Ottey
1. Ann, b. 22 June 1739, d.y.
2. John, b. 16 June 1741. In Chester County
   Deeds X:396 is a deed dated 19 April
   1783, John Ottey of Middletown, co.
   Chester, yeoman, and wife Ann, to Will
   Pennell of same, miller, for £20/15.
   The recital says that John was son of
   Philip Ottey dec., and the property
   was adjudged to him by the Orphans
   Court; acknowledged by Philip [sic]
   and Ann his wife, rec. 24 April 1784.
   The same couple gave another deed (D-2
   p. 345), 2 April 1789, to Samuel Black
   of same, wheelmaker, and they warrant
   his right to the property in the usual
   language of deeds against themselves
   and also against claims of the heirs
   of Thomas Pilkington dec. and against
   the said [sic] James Gibbons and Jacob Minshall, although nothing has
   been previously said about how any of
   these three men got any claim to the
   property; ackn. 2 April 1789, rec. 2
   April 1789. They also gave a third
   deed (E-2, p. 89), 9 3rd mo. 1789, to
   Anthony Masterson, ackn. 2 April 1789,
   rec. 19 Sept. 1789.
3. Martha, b. 10 March 1742/3.
4. Abigail, b. 30 May 1745.
5. Ruth, b. 30 March 1747.
6. Philip, b. 18 Aug. 1750.
iii. Richard, named in mother's will 1737, not
     found further.
iv. Christopher, named in mother's will 1737;
     m. at St. Paul's Episcopal Church, Ches-
     ter, Pa., 5 May 1729, Elizabeth Godfrey;
     the four children were mentioned in the
     will of their grandmother 5 Dec. 1737.
        Issue: surname Ottey, perhaps others
1. Ann, b. ca. 1730.
2. John.
3. Jane.
4. Sarah, b. by 5 Dec. 1737.
v.   John, of Kingsessing when he signed by mark
     his will dated 5 Jan. 1721, probated 17
     Dec. 1721/2[5] in which he mentions mother
     Ann Ottey, brothers Thomas, Philip, Rich-

ard, Christopher; executor brother Philip;
witnesses: Justa Justis, John Morton, Benjamin Cliffe.

There is also an unplaced James Ottey with wife
Ann, who gave a deed dated 24 Dec. 1748, when he was
of Goshen, mason, to Thomas Hoopes for £80, land
granted by the Proprietor 17 Oct. 1716. The spelling of this deed is Ottay and both husband and wife
could sign their names. Chester County will file
2339 has Ann Ottey's bond dated 22 Dec. 1786 in the
estate of James Otlay of Goshen, fellow bondsmen:
Joseph Pierce and Samuel Wall. Whether this man belonged to the same family is uncertain.

NOTES

[1]PMHB 8:228; BHBC 679.
[2]See TAG 38:157 f., 41:40. John Otter m. at Philadelphia Monthly Meeting, 29 8th mo. 1686, Mary
Blinstone, widow of Isaac Blinstone, as is shown in
the Middletown (Bucks) record of the same marriage,
passed 7 8th mo. 1686, 1st int. 2 7th mo. 1686.
Isaac Blinstone, late of the Parish of Eling, South-
[amp]ton County, maltster, made a will dated 15 May
1684, probated 25 7th mo. 1684 (PhW A:12), in which
he mentions wife Mary and daughter Mary, and several
other persons not his children. For a sketch of him
see PGM 23:99. He was probably the John Otter who
was granted a certificate at Horslydown or Southwark
Monthly Meeting, 5 2nd mo. 1682 (PGSP 3:227 f.), intending to Transport him Selfe & wife to Pencilvan-
ia. He probably came on the *Amity* (see PGM 23:35,
note 16).
[3]PhA B:147.   [4]CW 3:425.   [5]PhW D:205.

OWEN, Dr. GRIFFITH   *disproved*

This name appears on no list but the claim was
made by Caspar Morris, M.D., in "Contributions to
the Medical History of Pennsylvania," read before
the Medical Committee of the Historical Society of
Pennsylvania, 23 May 1826[1]: "With William Penn there
emigrated two Welsh gentlemen, Thomas Wynne and Griffith Owen, who appear to have been regularly educated to the [medical] profession . . ." The claim
is not quite so bold as it would have been, had the
Welcome been mentioned, but Wynne was on the *Welcome*
and "with William Penn" may not have been thought
elastic.

The disproof is in Philadelphia Arrivals: "Grif-

fith Owen, of Prescot [printed: Prescoe], Lancashire,
came on the Vine of Liverpool, 17 7th mo. 1684, with
his wife Sarah, son Robert, daughters Sarah and Ellinor, and seven servants."[2]

The following account is based in part on a sketch
by Gilbert Cope in his Collections at the Genealogical Society of Pennsylvania.[3]

Radnor Meeting Minutes (p. 27) show the certificate of Griffith Owen late of Prescott in Co. Lanc[s]
Doct[r] given by the Monthly Meeting at Hartshaw Sowth-
west in Lanc[sh], 27 3rd mo. 1684, family not specified. The first wife was Sarah, mother of all the
children, and she died at Philadelphia, 22 10th mo.
1702, after which on 13 9th mo. 1704 Griffith Owen
married, second, at Philadelphia Meeting House, Sarah Songhurst, daughter of John and Mary (-----)
Songhurst, *Welcome* passengers, all three, and the
widow of Zachariah Whitpaine, also a passenger, as
well as of Charles Sanders, her second husband. For
a fuller account of the second wife Sarah, see the
Songhurst and Whitpaine sketches.

Gilbert Cope thought that the first wife was possibly daughter of William Barnes of Hartshaw Monthly
Meeting by a mother who died in 1702, but he was far
from sure of it, and the fact that Dr. Owen's first
wife died in that year makes it wise to withhold
judgment on this point.

Though it is quite certain that Sarah Songhurst
bore no children to Dr. Owen, a writer in the *Utah
Genealogical Magazine* 24:147 f., presents a pedigree
tracing ancestry through her and her step-daughter,
Jane Owen, wife of Jonathan Coppock. At the Department of History and Archives, Des Moines, Iowa, is
a pedigree of Mrs. Nellie S. Owen Allen, born 16
Sept. 1891 at Slater, Iowa, which says that Dr. Owen
was born in 1647, died 19 6th mo. 1717, married "in
1693 in Lancashire" [sic] Sarah Barns who died 22
10th mo. 1702; married, second, Sarah Songhurst who
died 4 6th mo. 1733 without issue by Dr. Owen.   By
Sarah Barns he had a son, Dr. Griffith Owen, born
after 1694, died 4 1st mo. 1752, married Margaret
Thomas.   The death date and the marriage are, of
course, wrong, for when the younger Dr. Griffith
Owen died in 1733, not 1752, his probate shows his
sister acting as administratrix, which seems to argue against any surviving wife's existence.

The quotation from Philadelphia Arrivals quoted
above occurs at the bottom of a page at the top of

which is the registration of Robert Owen and wife
Joane, son Lewes, and the following servants: Edward
Edwards servant boy, to serve 8 years; Lowry Edwards
and Margaret Edwards, each to serve 4 years; Ann
Owen to serve 12 years, and Hannah Watts to serve
three years. All of these, coming from Merionethshire, crossed on the *Vine*, arriving 17 7th mo. 1684,
that is, the same ship on which Dr. Griffith Owen
of Prescot, Lancashire, also arrived.

Though it is not stated here that there was any
connection between these two Owen families, Griffith
Owen is accorded a sketch in the *Dictionary of National Biography* (14:1306), and he is there identified as son of Robert Owen who died 1684 by wife
Jane, born in Merionethshire. Glenn's *Merion* 385
f. accepts the Robert who died in 1684 as identical
with Robert of the *Vine* and he also says that the
said Robert had nine sons of whom he knows only of
a Robert who remained in Wales; our Dr. Griffith
Owen; Edward and Lewis who both settled in Newcastle
County; and, possibly, Rowland and Humphrey. He
further identifies Dr. Griffith Owen's mother as the
daughter of the celebrated genealogist and antiqua-
rian of Wales, Robert Vaughan of Hengrt. This man
also appears in the *Dictionary of National Biography*
but neither in his sketch nor in that of Dr. Owen is
the connection between them alluded to. It seems a
possibility that, as Glenn says, Griffith was a son
of Robert Owen of the *Vine*, but on the question of
Griffith's being a grandson of Robert Vaughan, I
should hope for more research in Wales.

In any case, Robert Owen of the *Vine* must not be
confused with another Robert Owen, son of Owen ap
Evan, who was born at Fron Gôch, a house in Merionethshire ca. 1657, and died in Merion Township,
Chester County, Pa., 8 10th mo. 1697, buried in the
graveyard at Merion Meeting, 10 10th mo. 1697, on
whom Glenn gives more details.

Dr. Griffith Owen had a distinguished career as
Friends' minister, was member of the Provincial
council, of the Board of Property, a Justice of the
Peace. It is claimed that he performed the first
surgical operation in Pennsylvania. As Dr. Thomas
Wynne preceded him to America by two years, this
claim is at best doubtful.

His will, dated 15 1st mo. 1716/17, probated 6
Jan. 1717/18, mentions two younger sons Edward and
Griffith; three sons John, Edward and Griffith; four

daughters: Sarah (wife of Jacob Minshall), Rebecca
(wife of Isaac Minshall), Jane (wife of Jonathan
Coppock dec.), and Ann (wife of John Whitpain);
daughter-in-law [i.e. stepdaughter] Mary, wife of
Samuel Marriott of Burlington.[5]

Issue:surname Owen, order uncertain, all by first
wife

i.   Robert, b. England, to America with his
      parents 1684; no further trace.
ii.   Sarah, b. England; to America with her
      parents 1684; m. Philadelphia Meeting
      House, 31 11th mo. 1706/7, Jacob Minshall,
      son of Thomas and Margaret (-----) Min-
      shall of Chester County. On this family
      see an anonymous *Thomas & Margaret Min-
      shall who came from England to Pennsyl-
      vania in 1682, and their early descen-
      dants; to which are added some account
      of Griffith Owen and descendants for a
      like Period* (1867). The will of William
      Sanders[6] who was a son of Sarah Songhurst
      by her second husband Charles Sanders,
      calls Sarah Owen the wife of Isaac Min-
      shall, an easy error as he was husband
      of her sister Rebecca Owen, below.
      Issue: surname Minshall
      1. Thomas, b. 3 1st mo. 1708, d. 12 9th mo.
         1783.
      2. Sarah, b. 21 5th mo. 1711; m. her first
         cousin, Griffith Minshall, son of Re-
         becca Owen by Isaac Minshall.
      3. Margaret, b. 28 10th mo. 1713.
      4. John, b. 21 8th mo. 1716, d. 8 1st mo.
         1784.
      5. Moses, b. 26 6th mo. 1718, d. 1761.
      6. Ann, b. 13 11th mo. 1727, d.y.
iii. Ellinor, b. England; to America with parents
      1684; no further trace.
iv.   Rebecca, b. Radnor, 19 2nd mo. 1687; m.(1)
      11 9th mo. 1707 Isaac Minshall,[7] d. 1731
      aged 46, son of Thomas and Margaret Min-
      shall, and brother of Rebecca's sister's
      husband; (2) 5 8th mo. 1748 Job Harvey.
      Issue: surname Minshall
      1. Aaron, b. 10 8th mo. 1708.
      2. Rebecca, b. 1 4th mo. 1710, m. Richard
         Blackham.
      3. Griffith, b. 1 4th mo. 1712, m. first

cousin Sarah Minshall, daughter of Sarah Owen by Jacob Minshall.

    4. Isaac, b. 29 8th mo. 1718, m. Lydia Ellis.

    5. Samuel, b. 26 8th mo. 1724, m. Jane ----.

    6. Edward, b. 28 4th mo. 1727, d. minor.

    7. Jacob, b. 10 5th mo. 1729, d. minor.

v.   Jane, b. 29 1st mo. 1689, Radnor; m. 3 1st mo. 1708/9,[8] Jonathan Coppock, son of Bartholomew Coppock of Chester County; (2) 9 7th mo. 1719 John Scholler; (3) 21 3rd mo. 1724 Robert Taylor.

vi. John, b. 25 1st mo. 1691, Radnor; m. 16 1st mo. 1714, Jane Harriott, daughter of Samuel Harriott, mariner, but in the Women's Minutes the name is twice spelled Harwood which probably had a very similar pronunciation at the time. Cope says the name was Marriott but this is probably one of his few errors. The will of Samuel Harriott, City of Philadelphia, mariner, dated 16 July 1733, probated 29 Sept. 1733[9]: among other daughters was Jane Owen; grandchildren: Samuel Owen, Sarah, Elizabeth, Griffith and John Owen; executrix Jane Owen. John's brother Edward's will of 2 Sept. 1729 names John's children as Sarah, Griffith, Elizabeth, John, Samuel.

Issue: surname Owen

    1. Sarah, living 1733.

    2. Griffith, d. 9 7th mo. 1741, cooper, testate, will dated 7 Sept. 1741, probated 18 Feb. 1741/2, naming two sisters Sarah and Elizabeth; mother Jane Owen, brother Samuel Owen.

    3. Elizabeth, living 1742.

    4. John, not named in brother Griffith's will 1742.

    5. Samuel, living 1742. From his must descend any living descendants of Dr. Griffith Owen, if such there be in the male line.

vii. Ann, b. 11 12th mo. 1692, Radnor; m. John Whitpaine (Zachariah), her stepbrother, and she was administratrix of her brother Dr. Griffith Owen, the younger. No issue. She was overlooked by Gilbert Cope.

   viii. Hannah, bur. Philadelphia, 22 11th mo.
         1694.

   ix.   Edward, b. 22 4th mo. 1696, Radnor; d. in
         1729; m. 15 8th mo. 1724, Susanna Kear-
         ney, daughter of Philip Kearney. He had
         been on a journey to England whence he
         was received at Philadelphia Monthly Meet-
         ing, 31 11th mo. 1717, from Hartshaw
         Monthly Meeting by certificate dated 20
         6th mo. 1717. Like his father and his
         younger brother, he was a physician. His
         will dated 2 Sept. 1729, probated 7 Oct.
         1729, names wife Susanna; mother Rebec-
         ca Kearney [i.e. mother-in-law]; brother
         Griffith Owen; mother Owen now living;
         brother John's children: Sarah, Griffith,
         Elizabeth, John, Samuel; sisters Sarah
         Minshall, Rebecca Minshall, Jane Taylor,
         Ann Whitpaine.

   x.   Catherine, d. Philadelphia, 19 5th mo. 1702.

   xi.   Griffith, physician, if not youngest child,
         at least youngest son; bur. Philadelphia,
         4 1st mo. 1732/3 [acc. to *DNB* 14:1306 on
         7 March 1731/2], administration to his
         sister Ann Whitpaine of Philadelphia,
         widow, sister and next of kin, and he is
         called late of Philadelphia surgeon.

NOTES

[1] MHSP 1 (1864 reprint), p. 352.

[2] PMHB 8:332 f. *Lancaster County Historical Society Historical Papers & Addresses* 2:23-25 has Owen
coming on the *Vine* in 1784 [sic].

[3] Griffith Owen is noted with Thomas Wynne by James
Thacher M.D., *American Medical Biography* (Boston
1828) 1:65.

[4] GWF 199; PMHB 13:168-183.

[5] See PGM 23:124; TAG 39:7-10.

[6] See below, p.

[7] MQA 39f.

[8] MQA 45.

[9] PhW E No. 337.

PACKER, PHILIP   *disproved*

    This name appears on List X only. The truth is
he crossed on the *Lion* of Liverpool, arriving 14 8th
mo. 1683, as servant of Joseph Fisher, to serve four
years, get fifty acres, loose on 14 8th mo. 1687.

He married 10 Nov. 1685, Hannah Sessions, marriage
recorded by the Register General,[1] and he was the
administrator in 1689 of the estate of his mother-
in-law Ann Sessions.[2] No further trace of him has
been found.

                              NOTES
[1] 2 PA 8:v.   [2] See PGM 19:255; 24:93, note 88.

PAIN, ELLINOR   *proved*

That Ellinor Pain was a *Welcome* passenger was
first discovered by Albert Cook Myers who put her
name on List Q and she has since then been put only
on List V.   The proof of her presence on board the
ship is found in the minutes of the Board of Property, session of 26 4th mo. 1704,[1] when at the request
of James Proteus and Ellinor Sykes (formerly Tain
[sic]), both servants to Wm Wade, for the Head land,
Order'd Two warrants.   So also at the session of 26
7ber 1704[2] Jam's Portes [sic] & Nathaniel Sykes &
Ellinor his wife, by deed 11 5th mo. Last [1704],
etc.   As Wade was a *Welcome* passenger, it is to be
presumed, failing evidence to the contrary, that his
servants came with him on that ship.

Ellinor Pain married at Philadelphia, 18 4th mo.
1686, Nathaniel Sykes of Philadelphia, carpenter.[3]
For a sketch of Sykes see *Pennsylvania Genealogical
Magazine* 23:107.   The Blackwell Rent Roll of 1689
shows John Love (in margin Nat: Sykes) as owner of
an old purchase lot of 20 feet on Chestnut Street,
1/- for 5 years,[4] and Nath: Sykes as renter of another 20-foot lot on the same street, 2/- for 1
year.   Nathaniel Sykes sold land to John Hart, 28
Jan. 7 Anne 1708,[5] and in this conveyance Ellinor
did not join with Nathaniel, so she was probably
then dead.

She was the daughter of James Paine of Brighton
by his wife Anne (the mother died 23 12th mo. 1669),
and sister of Edward Paine of Bishopston who appears in many of the same monthly meetings as Wade,
Songhurst, Barber, and who married at John Pearce's
house in Brighton, 6 9th mo. 1678, Mary Harrison,
daughter of William.

A monthly meeting at Bryhthelmston [Brighton],
16, 2nd mo. 1684, shows a division of goods of James
Pain or Paine between Richard Verall, John Cheeseman, Eleanor Paine, Henry Paine, effected 1st of
this month (1 2nd mo. 1684).   John Cheeseman is content to take his sister Elinor's part and pay 30s

for use of Elinor Paine to be returned to her in Penn'a, and Richard Verall will give the like to Henry Paine "when sent for or demanded." The material here divided was originally part of the estate of James Paine, in possession of Edward Paine, also of Brighton, when he died in 1682. There were queries from Elinor Pain in Pennsylvania, asking about her share of her father's estate, part from the sale of Edward's house. Elizabeth Cheeseman later apologized to meeting for accusing her sister Mary Verall of illegally taking items from the estate, and saying that she now knows the items were sent to Ellinor in Pennsylvania, apology dated 21 ye ---- mo. 1686.

At Lewes Monthly Meeting, 15 8th mo. 1684, there was an order to send a legacy of clothes and money from James Paine of Bishopstone dec'd to his daughter Elinor Paine in Pennsylvania, the legacy to be sent to Steven Adams in London for transport to America (consists of 2 pr sheets, 1 pr pillowcoats, 2 napkins, 1 silver tester, 29 shillings cash).

From the foregoing it will be seen that James Pain or Paine of Bishopstone had by his wife Anne the following

Issue: surname Paine
i.   Mary, m. Richard Verall.
ii.   Elizabeth, m. John Cheeseman, who originally intended to come to America with Thomas Heriott and others, but did not do so, owing to the illness of his wife.[6]
iii.   Ellinor, m. in Pennsylvania Nathaniel Sykes on 18 4th mo. 1686, and probably d.s.p.
iv.   James, d. in England 1682.
v.   Henry, living 1684, no further trace.

NOTES
[1]2 PA 19:434.   [2]2 PA 19:438.
[3]2 PA 8:vi.   [4]PGM 23:72.
[5]PhD E-5, no. 7, p. 154. See also 3 PA 3:385 for a survey to Sykes, 23 12th mo. 1688.
[6]See above, p. 246.

PARKER, RICHARD   *disproved*

In the Genealogical Society of Pennsylvania is a collection of papers made by one Henry Carvill Lewis for a history of the Bringhurst, Claypoole, DeVeaux, Evans, Foulke and Parker Families, on page 365 of which is a document copied 28 April 1840 from a paper given by "Aunt Rebecca Hallowell née Parker, widow of Judge Hallowell and sister of my grandmother Eleanor Foulke née Parker."

John Hallowell & Richard Parker came over with William Penn & Settled near Darby 1682.

It will have been seen under John Hallowell that he did not come until 1683. We may now say that Richard Parker came on a certificate issued by Rosley, co. Lincoln, Meeting at Willowby dated 6 5th mo. 1684. This certificate is included in a volume of abstracts of Darby Meeting records by Gilbert Cope, now in the Genealogical Society of Pennsylvania.

This Richard Parker may also be the man of that name who brought a certificate from Bristol, England, and was received at Philadelphia Monthly Meeting, 25 2nd mo. 1701 (MQA 27).

PARSONS, JOHN   *disproved*

This name is on no list and the claim has not appeared in print. In a letter dated 20 Jan. 1963, Mrs. Marion Balderston expressed to me her conviction that John Parsons was a *Welcome* passenger. She remarks that he was a friend and neighbor of Penn, got a warrant for 200 acres in January 1683 (Bd. of Property Minutes), and she thought some one, perhaps Davis, says something about him in Bucks County in the winter of 1682/3. Another John Parsons, who lived a little further away at Cowfold, Sussex, came with Penn in 1699.

Unfortunately, there is a certificate[1] for John Parsons and Tho: Kerell, 4 7th mo. 1681, from an unknown meeting, signed by, *inter alios*, John's parents, John and Florence Parsons.[2] *Mervine's Genealogical Register* (Lancaster 1913), pp. 141-149, is a sketch of this John Parsons, and the residence of the father is given as Middlezoy, Somerset. The marriage of John Parsons of co. Somerset, 23 6th mo. 1685, to Ann Powell of North Curry, co. Somerset, was performed at the Meeting House in the Parish of Greinton, but recorded in the minutes of Philadelphia Monthly Meeting. It seems certain that the certificate and the marriage record refer to the same man and that he had gone back to England to marry. Mervine's account also accepts this identification and further identifies him with the John

Parsons who was buried in Philadelphia, 19 6th mo.
1705, and left a widow Ann who died 25 6th mo. 1712,
and a son John who was buried 8 4th mo. 1714. This
John Parsons must be the testator of a will dated
10 7th mo. 1699, probated 22 Aug. 1705,[3] in which
mention is made of wife Ann, brother Thomas, brother-in-law William Tyler and his children William,
John, Mary and Jean, as well as William's kinsman,
Samuel Powell.   No son John is named in the will,
but if he were born after 1699, then his omission
might be an oversight.   It seems therefore possible
that we have to deal with two men named John Parsons, one who came in 1681, went back to England
and married Ann Powell in 1684; the other who came
with Penn in 1699, and happened to have a wife named
Ann also.

There is a letter of James Logan to William Penn,
dated 22 6th mo. 1705, cited by Mervine, which says
that on the 18th instant, Jno Parsons went to bed
and died. This would seem to show that the man who
died in 1705 was the close friend of William Penn
who came in 1699.

Mervine also states that John and Florence Parsons of Middlezoy, Somerset, were parents also of a
daughter Jane who married in Somerset, 15 2nd mo.
1677, William Tyler of Walton in Somerset; that they
came to Philadelphia and Salem County, New Jersey,
where he died in 1701.   This may be supported by a
reference to *New Jersey Wills* 1:474, where there is
the will of William Tyler of Allawayes Creek, Salem
County, yeoman, who made his will on 28 Feb. 1700/1,
recorded 20 June 1701.   He names children: Philipp,
John, William, Mary (wife of Abel Nicholson), Joan,
Katherine, Elizabeth and Rebecka.   Besides nearly
two thousand acres in New Jersey, there is land in
the Parish of Medlesse, co. Somerset, England, and
the inventory of 25 2nd mo. 1701 is signed by Roth-
orr Morris, Thos Parsons and John Parsons.

Mervine further says that John Parsons who died
in 1705 had a brother Thomas, born ca. 1665, died
1721 in New Jersey, who married, first Jane Culling
and second Mary Hinds. I do not find probate for
him but he must be the man who signed his brother-
in-law's inventory in 1701.

While the Board of Property minutes contain many
references to John Parsons, there is no reference
to a warrant of 1683,[3] and whoever may have written
of John Parsons as in Bucks County in the winter of

1682/3, it was not Davis. It therefore is clear that
there is really no evidence that any John Parsons was
a *Welcome* passenger.[4]

NOTES

[1]MQA 7.   [2]PMHB 15:191.
[3]2 PA vol. 19, *passim.*
[4]See PGM 23:106: John Parsons of Middlezoy was a
carpenter; a joint purchaser with Andrew Hoopper of
500 acres; attended Philadelphia Monthly Meeting on
1 1st mo. 1685/6; on 20 2nd mo. 1683 was granted a
warrant for the northwest corner of Second and Walnut (3 PA 2:765); was assessed £150 in 1693.

PASCHALL, THOMAS   *disproved*

This name has appeared on no list but the claim
was made by Caspar Morris, M.D., "Contributions to
the Medical History of Pennsylvania,', read before
the Medical Committee of the Historical Society of
Pennsylvania, 22 May 1826[1]:

> Connected, perhaps, as much with the present
> as with any other branch of investigation, permit
> me here to notice a fact which has not, hereto-
> fore, claimed attention. Among the gentlemen
> accompanying William Penn on his first visit to
> this country was one of French extraction, who,
> proud to have descended from the family of the
> recluse of Port Royal [i.e. Blaise Pascal (1623-
> 1662)], and to bear his honored name, had devoted
> his time and fortune to the study of the abstruse
> sciences, among others alchemy and astrology.
> Soon after his arrival, having provided himself
> with the requisite apparatus, he commenced the
> vain pursuit after that which has deluded so
> many, the Philosopher's Stone, and its necessary
> accompaniment, the Elixir Vitae. . . . His child-
> ren kept an apothecary's store, in which they
> vended many articles the produce of their father's
> laboratory. About fifty years ago [i.e. ca.1775]
> an old man [b. perhaps ca. 1700?], who recollected
> the gentleman referred to, narrated to one of
> his descendants the foregoing circumstances. . .

Though Dr. Morris did not clearly name Thomas Paschall, he must be the unfortunate target of this innuendo. It can safely be denied that there was any
close connection between the Paschalls of Bristol
and the philosopher of Port Royal. Indeed, if any

French connection existed at all, it must have been
very remote, for the Paschalls were from Bristol,
and though, as we shall see, there was some factual
basis for the story of the apothecary shop, the interpretation put upon it by Dr. Morris is arrant nonsense.

Howard W. Lloyd's sketch of the Paschalls[2] makes
no claim that they were on the *Welcome* but says they
came "either about the time of Penn's first visit or
just before." There is also a letter of Thomas Pas-
kel [the immigrant] to J. J. in Chippenham, England,
dated 10 Feb. 1683 n.s. [1682/3],[3] which does not
state the name of the ship on which he had arrived
but does say that a carpenter had been ill during
the voyage. Nothing is said of the epidemic of the
smallpox which had occurred on the *Welcome*, and it
would seem certain that if Paschall had witnessed
that epidemic with the deaths of thirty or thirty-
one passengers, he could not fail to mention that
fact. The letter also seems to imply that its
writer had been in Pennsylvania for some time, and
he speaks of the arrival of Penn and his party as
if he had even been on hand to greet them.[4]

The truth seems to be that the Paschalls came on
the *Society* of Bristol, for on that ship on 12 April
1682[5] Paschall loaded 3 cwt nails; 4 cwt wrought
iron; 3/4 cwt lead; 2½ cwt brass manufactured; 5 cwt
wrought pewter; ½ chalder grindle stones; 3 firkins
butter; 3 yards paving stones, 3s, and on 3 May of
the same year he loaded 28 lbs wrought pewter; 28
lbs brass manufactured; 2 cwt wrought iron; 1 firkin butter; 1½ bushels oatmeal; 1 small sadle; 3
parcels wares, £1/1/8. It therefore seems most
probable that this was their ship. However, Mr.
Meredith B. Colket reports that he saw a manuscript
in the Historical Society of Pennsylvania containing a list of early tradesmen in Philadelphia, with
five names checked as persons who arrived 11 10th
mo. 1681, on the first trip of the *Bristol Factor*,
Roger Drew master. An effort to examine this manuscript fails to discover it. It doubtless exists
somewhere in that magnificent collection but the
name of Paskall or other spelling has not been in-
dexed in the card catalogue of manuscripts. It seems
probable that the list of tradesmen is original and
that the checking of the five names and the note
about them is later. Without personal examination
of the document itself, I am unable otherwise to re-

solve the discrepancy.

There is a brief account of the Paschalls by Dr.
Jordan[6] in which it is stated that Thomas Paschall
and wife Joane, with children Thomas, William and
Mary, arrived in Philadelphia in February 1682, but
no evidence is cited and it seems to me impossible
that there can be any truth in that date. The *Society* is believed to have arrived in August 1682, and
whether "Feb. 1682" is to be taken New Style or Old
Style, it can't be right.

Thomas Paschall was a First Purchaser of 500 acres in Group 15[7] and he had a warrant as early as
18 7th mo. 1682, which date fits in nicely with the
belief he came on the *Society*. He was the son of
William Paskell, Pewterer,[8] and was born at Bristol,
3 8th mo. 1634, baptized by Anglican rite--this was
before there were Quakers---at St. Mary Redcliffe,
Bristol, on 29 Dec. 1634, and he died in Philadelphia on either 14 [so Jordan] or 15 [so Justice[9]]
7th mo. 1718 aet. 83/4. He left a will dated 12
7th mo. 1716, probated 18 Sept. 1718, in which he
mentions son Thomas and daughter Mary, and says,
without naming them, that he had 21 grandchildren
and great-grandchildren. His wife Joana had died
2 7th mo. 1707 aet. 72/9. It is claimed that Joane
was a Sloper. There is a letter in the Historical
Society of Pennsylvania dated 2 8th mo. 1718 from
Thomas Paschall the younger to his Cousin Sloper,
then in London, daughter of William Sloper, Paymas-
ter General to the Queens Foreign Forces, and this
states that the writer's mother was Joanna Sloper
and that she was nearly related to Squire Hook, son
of Humphrey. On these people the *Dictionary of
National Biography* is of no assistance.

Issue: surname Paschall
i.   Thomas, b. ca. 1655 in England, d. Phila-
       delphia, 14 2nd mo. 1743; m. Haverford
       Meeting, 15 9th mo. 1692 Margaret Jenkins,
       b. 23 3rd mo. 1674, d. 17 11th mo. 1728,
       daughter of William and Elizabeth (Grif-
       fith) Jenkins of Tenby, Pembrokeshire.
       Thomas undoubtedly came to America with
       his parents in 1682. A note in the Rogers
       Collection (53:399) in the Genealogical
       Society of Pennsylvania says that Thomas
       m. (2) at Abington, 1729, the widow Abi-
       gail Golden who d. 1 3rd mo. 1763. This
       has not been verified.

Issue: surname Paschall, all by first
wife:

1. Thomas, b. 22 7th mo. 1693, d. Goshen,
   ca. 1728; m. 6 10th mo. 1716 Margaret
   Jones.

2. Joanna, b. 19 12th mo. 1695, d. ca. 1731;
   m. John Marshall.

3. William, b. 8 1st mo. 1697, d. Goshen,
   ca. 1738; m. (1) 21 2nd mo. 1720,
   Grace Hoopes; (2) 22 9th mo. 1722,
   Hannah (Lloyd) Roberts, widow of John
   Roberts and daughter of Robert Lloyd
   and his wife Lowry Jones on whom see
   above, pp. 281-283.

4. Joseph, b. 23 1st mo. 1699, d. 1741; m.
   28 2nd mo. 1721 Elizabeth Coates. On
   this couple see Thomas Allen Glenn,
   *Some Colonial Mansions and Those who
   lived in them* (Philadelphia 1899) 1:
   119 f.

5. Elizabeth, b. 19 2nd mo. 1701, m. ca.
   1730 Jacob Jones.

6. Benjamin, b. 4 11th mo. 1703, d. 12 2nd
   mo. 1707.

7. John, b. 5 9th mo. 1706, d. 11 2nd mo.
   1779; m. 25 2nd mo. 1728, Frances
   Hodge, b. 15 4th mo. 1710, d. Philadelphia, 8 1st mo. 1781. Mr. Lloyd
   says he practiced medicine in that
   part of Chester County now Delaware
   County, manufactured "Golden Elixir"
   and "Paschal's Golden Drops." It may
   be that his success as a patent medicine tycoon aroused the ire and jeal-
   ousy of an orthodox practititioner like
   Caspar Morris M.D.

8. Benjamin, b. 16 2nd mo. 1709, m. Elizabeth Horne. It is hard to believe that
   his grandfather would have named him
   an executor at the age of seven.

9. Samuel, b. 2 5th mo. 1711, d. 11 12th
   mo. 1728.

10. Stephen, b. 3 8th mo. 1714, d. after
    1743, perhaps in 1800, m. 24 2nd mo.
    1738 Martha Humphreys.

11. Jonathan, b. 11 3rd mo. 1718, d. after
    1743, m. Mary Fisher.

ii. William, b. ca. 1667, d. Philadelphia 1696.

may have m. Susanna Budd, daughter of John
and Mary (-----) Budd, as Mrs. Rogers (32:
285) says, though Mr. Justice mentions the
marriage only to question it.
iii. Mary, b. England, d. Philadelphia 1732; m.
(1) William Say who d. 11th mo. 1714; (2)
Benjamin Paschall, probably a recent arrival and perhaps a relative but undoubtedly
the man of this name named the third of
three executors of Thomas Paschall in 1716.

NOTES

[1]MHSP 1 (1864 reprint), pp. 355 f.
[2]*Lloyd Manuscripts* (Lancaster 1912), 223-232.
[3]PMHB 6:323; A. C. Myers, *Narratives of Early
Pennsylvania* (1912), 243.
[4]JCRFP 1:500-505, especially 505.
[5]PGM 23:41, note on pp. 43 f.
[6]*Loc. cit.* in Note 4, above.
[7]1 PA 1:41.
[8]See A. R. Justice Collection 17:75 in the Genealogical Society of Pennsylvania.
[9]*Ibid.*

PEARSON, ----- or ROBERT or THOMAS   *mythical*

He is given no first name on Lists A, B, O [here
denied], and on Lists G, H and U, is called mythical. He is Thomas or Robert on List C; Robert on
Lists D, E, M, R [here called controversial] and X;
on Lists I, J, L, W and Y, he is Thomas; not on List
Z. Arthur Edwin Bye[1] accepts him and says he was son
of Lawrence and Elizabeth (Janney) Pearson.
List B cites Thomas Clarkson, *Memoirs of the Private and Public Life of William Penn* (Philadelphia,
1st ed., 1813, 1:259; 2nd ed., London, etc., 1849,
121). Clarkson did not get this from Proud's *History
of Pennsylvania* (Philadelphia 1797) which does not
mention Pearson. Clarkson says that Pearson, first
name not given, suggested to Penn that Upland be
called Chester, from which fact some lists deduce
he was from Cheshire. William Hepworth Dixon's *Life
of Penn* (1st ed. 1851, 195-198; 2nd ed., 1872, 203-
208) repeats the tale and it even appears in the latest biography of Penn, that of Catherine Owen Peare
(249), where it is accepted though called "according
to legend."
The following passage is taken from George Smith,
History of Delaware County, Pennsylvania (Philadelphia 1862), p. 139:

> He [William Penn] landed at Upland, but the
> place was to bear that familiar name no more for-
> ever. Without reflection, Penn determined that
> the name of the place should be changed. Turning
> round to his friend Pearson, one of his own soci-
> ety, who had accompanied him in the ship 'Wel-
> come,' he said, 'Providence has brought us here
> safe. Thou hast been the companion of my perils.
> What wilt thou that I should call this place?'
> Pearson said, "Chester,' in remembrance of the
> city from whence he came. William Penn replied
> that it should be called Chester, and that when
> he divided the land into counties one of them
> should be called by the same name. Thus for a
> mere whim the name of the oldest town, the name
> that would have a place in the affections of a
> large majority of the inhabitants of the new pro-
> vince, was effaced to gratify the caprice or va-
> nity of a friend. All great men occasionally do
> little things.

The tone of this passage suggests animosity towards
Penn's memory. The passage is also quoted with re-
jection by Henry Graham Ashmead, *History of Delaware
County, Pennsylvania* (Philadelphia 1884), pp. 20 f.,
since he shows that the name Upland continued to be
used for some time. He points out that Friends records ought to identify Pearson but do not, and he
calls him "this mythical person," saying that the
first was Thomas who came on the *Comfort*, 28 7th mo.
1683, sailing from Kingsroad, 25 5th mo. 1683, John
Read, master.

> The Pearson story for the first time appeared
> in our annals in Clarkson's "Life of Penn," a
> work which was not published until more than a
> century after the incidents therein first recor-
> ded are said to have occurred. Until the publi-
> cation . . . no writer makes any mention of the
> change of name having been suggested to Penn by
> his friend 'Pearson.'

An old time genealogist, Minshall Painter, says[2]
that Thomas and Margery Pearson came on the *Welcome*
and settled in Marple Township. See the query by
Horace E. Hayden (PMHB 3:358) and a very witty note
by Ashmead; Besse's *Sufferings* 1:105; Smith's *History of Delaware County, Pennsylvania*, p. 491; PGM
24:83 f., note 53.   Thomas Pearson was a mason from
Pownall with wife Margaret, brother John and sister

Mary Smith, arrival registered on the *Endeavour*.³
This man was probably the person referred to by Bye
as son of Lawrence and Elizabeth (Janney) Pearson,
but we have not attempted to verify this statement.
See also PGM 24:86, note 62. The Thomas Pierson on
the *Comfort* in 1683 must have been another man.

NOTES

¹Arthur Edwin Bye, *History of the Bye Family and
Some Allied Families* (Easton, Pa., 1956), p. 384.
²PGSP 4:296.   ³PMHB 8:330.

PENN, WILLIAM   *proved*

The great name of the Founder of Pennsylvania appears at the head of List I, and in alphabetical position on Lists G, J, L, N, O, P, Q, S, T, V, W, X
and Y, but was doubtless thought obvious to the compilers of the other lists.
Penn was not accompanied to America by his wife
or children, or by any known relative. When his friend
and associate, Philip Ford, says in an appendix to
his one-sheet *Vindication of William Penn* (London
1683), that a letter from Penn dated at Philadelphia,
1 Nov. 1682, immediately after Penn's arrival on the
Welcome, reports: "An House for William Penn is a
building, whose Family that went with him are all
come safe," the word 'family' must here be taken to
mean 'family of servants,' which, indeed, is the
first meaning listed in the Oxford Dictionary, citing
examples from 1641 and 1707. Penn's 1684 will, as
we shall see, makes clear that some servants had accompanied him to America, while others remained with
his wife at Warminghurst.
Of these servants we may suggest that one was Jane
Bachelor and another very probably the secretary,
Philip Theodor Lehnmann, both of whom are discussed
as *Welcome* claimants. There was, moreover, a family
of six persons called "servants of yᵉ Governor," Ellis
Jones aet. 45, Jane Jones aet. 40, Barbary Jones aet.
13, Mary Jones aet. 12½, Dorothy Jones aet. 10 and
Isaac Jones aet. 4 months.¹ They, however, had not
yet arrived in Philadelphia by 1 Nov. 1682; indeed,
they only reached Choptank, Maryland, on the next
day, with the burdensome land journey from the
Chesapeake to the Delaware yet to be performed,

320 PENN

so these cannot be reckoned in the 'family' alluded
to by Ford. There must have been other servants on
the *Welcome*, and we may really know the names of some
of them, though not that they were servants of Penn.

H. Stanley Craig, in a list of passengers on the
Fortune arriving from Wales in 1682, which is to be
found in conjunction with List X, has Thomas Lloyd
and William Penn as passengers. This is so far from
the truth that I am unable to explain how the error
could have started.

Independent investigation of the history of the
Penn family and of the life of Penn himself lies beyond the purpose of this study, but we shall present
a summary of what is known about the Penns, based
principally on the magnificent book of Howard M.
Jenkins,[2] augmented wherever possible by such information as has come to light since 1899, notably from
work by J. Henry Lea long in print, but more lately
by Brigadier O. F. G. Hogg,[3] a Penn descendant to
whom I am indebted not only for what he has printed
but also for valued correspondence, and still more
recently by Mrs. Hannah Benner Roach and Mr. Francis
James Dallett,[4] who also have enjoyed the collabora-
tion of Brigadier Hogg.

We should note here that Penn returned to England
on the *Endeavour*,[5] sailing 16 Aug. 1684, certainly
then intending to return to Pennsylvania rather soon
but he was prevented from doing so for fifteen years.
He again left England on the *Canterbury* which weighed
anchor at Cowes, 3 Sept. 1699, arriving on 1 December
following.[6] With him on his second trip were his second wife Hannah, his daughter Letitia, but the only
other child then surviving, the son William, did not
accompany them, and Hannah was fated to give birth
to her eldest, John "the American," in Philadelphia.
The second return to England was in the *Dolmahoy*,
leaving 3 Nov. 1701, arriving by 4 Jan. 1701/2, 26
days from the Cape to Soundings, 30 days to Ports-
mouth.[7] The name of this fourth ship used by Penn in
his crossings is interesting because at an earlier
period in his life, when he was attempting to help
Algernon Sidney campaign for Parliament, the can-
didate opposing Sidney was named Delmahoy.[8]

Whether Penn brought a Friends certificate with
him on the *Welcome* is unknown. He did bring one
on the *Canterbury*, from Horsham Monthly Meeting,
bearing the date of 12 5th mo. 1699, with a

supplementary certificate from the Men's Meeting,
Bristol, dated 31 5th mo. 1699.[9] No certificate
for him in 1701 has been found, but there was a request of Philadelphia Monthly Meeting for one for
his wife Hannah, his daughter and a nurse, to go to
Great Britain, 27 7th mo. 1701.[10] John the American
was not mentioned.

THE PENN FAMILY

1. JOHN PENNE, of Minety, co. Gloucester, England,
is the earliest ancestor of this family now known,
and was first discovered by Brigadier Hogg[11] who
effectively demolished all claims to connections
between the Founder's family and the Penns of Penn,
co. Bucks, and other Penn families, as well as a
Welsh origin. John is shown on two Subsidy Rolls,
one in 14-15 Henry VIII (1522),[12] when he is recorded as having paid a tax of 6s 8d on his chattels;
the other in 3 Edward VI (1550),[13] when he paid 6s
on moveable goods worth £6, after which his name
disappears from the rolls, and his supposed son William takes his place. This is the reason for be-
lieving that John was the father of the said William,
about whom more is known. The claim is made by Mr.
Dallett[14] that William may have had a brother Thomas
Penne, described as sub-prior of Bradenstoke Priory
at its dissolution in 1539, who signed the original
document of surrender as Thomas Pen, "superior."
Mr.Dallett believes that the sub-prior was identical with a man of the same name who was accused of
heresy in 1551, then vicar of Mickleton, Gloucestershire, suspended for simony but later restored.
There appears to have been a tradition among the
Penns of an ancestor who had been a secularized
monk and became a parish priest and married at the
dissolution. It has previously been believed that
this tradition was lifted from the history of the
Penns of Penn, co. Bucks, where it is authentic,
and Mr.Dallett admits that this is mere speculation.
It seems to me rather more probable that the tradition of the secularized monk was borrowed.

Only issue certainly known:
2 i.   William, d. Minety, 12 March 1591/2.

2. WILLIAM PENNE of Minety, co. Gloucester, yeoman, almost certainly the son of John Penne of the
same place, appears first in the Gloucestershire
Subsidy Rolls of 36-37 Henry VIII (1544-1546)[15]

assessed at 13 shillings. Then, in a deed dated 5
Feb. 1547/8[16] whereby Richard Andrewes of Hales, co.
Gloucester, grants one messuage, the fifth part of
a yard (*virgat*) [about 40 acres] and the moiety of
a croft, and one acre 3 roods of land in the tenure
of John Rydeler in Minety, co. Gloucester, late of
Lanthony Priory next Gloucester, to William Penn,
Y[e]oman of Minety. This would have been in addition to what he had inherited from his father. He
next appears on a Subsidy List in 2-3 Edward VI when
he paid 6s on personal belongings valued at £6[17].
2 Elizabeth I he had goods now worth £8[18] but in 25-
37 Elizabeth I no Penn is shown in Minety.[19] He had
died 12 March 1591/2, a date formerly cut into a
stone in the chancel of Minety Church (St. Leonard's)
but the stone was broken in John Aubrey's time, was
replaced by 1807 with a new slab which by 1890 had
also disappeared. It was claimed by one John George,
who was aged 73 when on 27 Jan. 1666/7 he wrote to
Admiral Sir William Penn the suggestion that the
latter should purchase his ancestral estate from one
Nicholas Pleydell, that this William Penn lived in
a "genteel ancient house" on a property then worth
£100 per annum, probably known as "Penn's Lodge,"
but Brigadier Hogg has demolished this tale on several grounds: (A) Penn's Lodge was not in Minety but
in Brinkworth; (B) it is not certain that it was already built in William's day; (C) no document really
connects this William with Penn's Lodge. It is also
shown that Dixon's *Life of Penn* is wrong when it
maintains that William Penn's property in Minety was
sold after his death to pay his debts, as his grandson continued to live there for some time.
  Willi'm Penne of Myntie in the County of Gloucester, yeoman, left a will[20] dated 1 May 1590, probated 21 April 1592 (PCC 31 Harrington):

> In the Name of God Amen The first day of May in
> the two and Thirtieth Year of the Reign of our
> Sovereign Lady Elizabeth by the Grace of God Queen
> of England France and Ireland Defender of the
> ffaith &c Et Anno Domini Millesimo quinqu[ag]e[si]-
> mo Nonagesimo I Willm Penne of Myntie in the Coun-
> ty of Glouc[ester] Yeoman being at this present
> time whole in Body and of good and perfect remem-
> brance (laud and praise be unto Almighty God) Do
> ordain and make this my last will and Testament
> in manner and form following viz. ffirst I commit
> and bequeath my Soul to my Lord and Saviour Jesus

Christ by whose Death and Merits and precious
Blood-shedding I hope to be saved And my body
to be buried within the Parish Church Chancels
or Church Yard of Minity where my ffriends shall
think meet. Item I give and bequeath unto the
poor people dwelling within the said Parish Twenty
Shillings to be distributed by my Overseers after
my Burial according to their Discretion. Item I
give and bequeath unto Giles Penn William Penn
Marie Penn Sara Penn and Susanna Penn being the
Children of my late son William Penn deceased
Twenty Pounds apiece to be paid unto them by my
executor as they shall come to and be of the age
of Twenty one Years apiece or at the day of their
Marriage (if any of them happen to be married before) So that such Marriage or Marriages be made
to the liking and with the Consents of my Overseers Provided always that if any of the said
Children shall fortune to departe this Life before the Age of Twenty one Years Then my Will is
that their portion or portions so dying shall be
equally divided among the Rest that shall be living. Item I give and bequeath unto Margaret Penn
Widow late Wife to William Penn my son deceased
the Sum of ten pounds to be paid unto her Yearly
during her natural Life by my Executor at the
ffeast of the Annunciation of the Virgin Mary and
St. Michael the Archangel by equal portions if
she shall and do so long keep herself sole and
chaste and unmarried The same Payment to begin
after my death at such time as my Heir shall come
to and be of the full age of Twenty one Years
provided always that if at any time the said Margaret shall happen either to marry or otherwise
to miscarry and not continue an honest Life Then
my Will is that the aforesaid ten pounds shall
surcease and be no longer paid unto her by my Executor. But that then upon either such Marriage
of her or other disordered Life being Known My
Will is that my Executor shall pay and deliver
unto her the Sum of Twenty Pounds in money and
also a good Bed with all manner of Furniture
thereunto belonging and so she quietly to depart
from my Executor. Item my will is that the said
Margaret Penn my Daughter-in-law and my Overseers
shall have the whole Charge Rule and Government
of my Heir and of all the Rest of the children
which were the Sons and Daughters of Willm Penn

my son deceased and of all such Lands and Tenements and Hereditaments and of all such Goods and
Chattels as I shall leave at my Death till such
time as my Heir shall accomplish and be of the
full Age of Twenty one Years and that the said
Margaret Penn shall continue with the said Children and help to breed them up during the time a-
foresaid And that she shall be maintained of the
whole and shall do and use all things in the
House for the use and benefit of my Executor in.
such manner or wise and sort as she did in my own
days used to do for me so that her doings and
Dealings therein be done with the Consent and Advise and good liking of my Overseers provided always that if the said Margaret Penn shall fortune
to marry or otherwise not live sole and chaste as
beforesaid before such time as my Heir shall be
of the Age of Twenty one Years Then my Will is
that my Executor with the Advice and Consent of
my Overser shall pay and deliver unto her the
said sum of Twenty Pounds and the said Bed with
all the ffurniture to the same as aforesaid and
that thereupon the said Margaret quietly to depart and have no more Rule and Authority of any
of my said Son's Children or of any Thing to them
belonging. But my Overseers only to do all Things
concerning the Children according to their own
Discretion and according to my true meaning herein expressed as my faithful Trust is in them
ffinalie the Rest of all my Goods and Chattels
Moveable and unmoveable not bequeathed my Debts
and Legacys being paid and my ffuneral discharged.
I give and bequeath to George Penn being the eldest Son of Willm Penn my late Son deceased whom
I do make my sole Executor of this my last Will
and Testament With condition that the said George
shall perform and do all Things herein contained
by and with the advices and consents of my Overseers Mr Robert George of Cirencester and Richard
Lawrence of Winthingeton in the County of Glouc:
and ffrancis Bradshaw of Wokely in the County of
Wiltshire Gent.[21] whom I desire to be my Overseers And I give to them hereby lawful authority
to see that all Things herein mentioned by my
said Executor with their helps and Consents performed. And I give to every of them for their
Pains so taken in and about the Premises ten
Shillings to be paid by my said Executor. In wit-

ness whereof to this my said last Will and Testament I the said William Penne have put my Hand
and Seal this day and Year above written. Item I
further give to Richard Bidle one Cow Item I give
to his Daughter Katherine Bidle one Heifer of two
years of Age Also I give to my [sic][22] Daughter
Ann Greene one Heifer and to Elizabeth Greene one
Heifer each of them to be Two Years old Item I
give to Willm Mallibroke one Yearling Heifer and
likewise I lastly give to Alice Thermor my old
white mare Those being witnesses--Francis Bradshaw Gent., Willim Taylor, and Richard Munden
with others.
Probated 1 April 1592 at Prerogative Court of
Canterbury by George Penn, executor.

The tone of the restrictions put upon the daughter-in-law in this will suggests that the testator
was a strict type, inconsiderate of the feelings of
others.

Issue:
3 i.   William, d. by 1587.

3. WILLIAM PENN, only son of William Penn (John)
of Minety, co. Gloucester, died *vita patris* by 1587.
By 1570 he had married MARGARET RASTALL, daughter of
Alderman John Rastall by his wife Ann George, the
said Ann being sister of Christopher George of Bawnton, counsellor-at-law, to whom this William Penn was
for many years law-clerk at Malmesbury and finally
chief clerk.   Christopher George had a brother John,
buried 6 Aug. 1571, who married Margaret, buried 12
Aug. 1578, daughter of Robert Strange.[23] John and
Margaret's third son, Robert George of Bawnton, baptized 5 Feb.   1564, died 1 Feb. 1633, married Margaret, daughter of Edward Oldsworth, and they had a
son John George who, as stated above, when aged 73,
wrote on 27 Jan. 1666/7 to Admiral Sir William Penn,
suggesting that he should purchase his "ancestral
lands" in Minety.   The George family was well recorded at Cirencester for nearly two hundred years. The
will[24] of John Restell, "one alderman of the City of
Gloucester, clothier," was dated 10 Aug. 1558, probated 10 Sept. 1558 (PCC 45 Noodles), and mentions
that decedent's two wives lie in the parish church
of the Trinity in Gloucester; names six daughters
Elizabeth, Anne, Alyce, Bridgett, Sara, Margaret;
sons Thomas and Edward; brothers Massinger and

and Christopher George; son John Rastall; executors:
Richard Pate, Thomas Massinger, John Rastel.

This William Penn was taxed in the Subsidy of 13
Elizabeth I for Malmesbury, 6s on goods, in 1570-71,
and again in 1580-81[25] and is in the roll for 1587.[26]
Though a law clerk, he died without probate, survived
by his father whose will names the widow and the
children of his deceased son. Despite the fact that
little is known of this William, in some ways he is
the most appealing of the earlier Penns.

As stated in the sketch for his grandfather John
Penn, no connection can be proved with a Thomas Penne
of Gloucester accused of heresy in the 16th century,
in a letter dated 25 May 1551 from Bishop Hooper to
Lord Trevor in Wiltshire, commending the bearer, Mr
Restell, Alderman of Gloucester, doubtless the father-in-law of this William Penn.

Issue: surname Penn
4 i.   George, b. ca. 1571. bur. 5 11th mo. 1632.
5 ii.   Giles, second son.
6 iii.   William, third son.
   iv.   Marie, perhaps m. at Quinton, 1614, Richard
          Compton.
   v.   Sarah.
   vi.   Susanna.

4. GEORGE PENN, eldest son of William Penn (William, John) of Malmesbury, by his wife Margaret Rastall, was born about 1571, died intestate at Brinkworth and was buried at Minety, 5 Jan. 1632. He was
heir and executor of his grandfather's will in 1592.
He became one of the Preservers, Keepers and Officers of the Forest of Braydon; appears in the Subsidy Rolls of Minety, 40 Elizabeth I (1597/8)[27],
again in 42 Elizabeth I (1599-1600)[28] and 1 James I
(1604-5)[29] but in 19 James I (1621-2), there is no
Penn in Minety.[30] He was a churchwarden in Minety
in 1608 but must soon have moved to Brinkworth, at
least by 1621. Mrs. Colquhoun Grant says he was
sent as envoy to Spain by Charles I as Prince of
Wales in 1623, but this seems to be a confusion
with his nephew George, son of brother Giles. He
married probably by 1600 a woman named ELIZABETH
-----, who was his administratrix on 15 Dec. 1632.[31]

Issue: surname Penn, order uncertain
   i.   William, ensign, d. Kinsale, Ireland, ca.
          April 1676, testate, will in Cork and
          Ross wills 1676 (not examined); men-

tioned in Admiral Sir William Penn's will,
1670; a letter of the ensign dated 1 Nov.
1670 to Sir Robert Southwell is printed
by Brailsford.[32] He calls himself clerk
of the Cheque at Kinsale, Ireland; has
held this post since the Restoration at
a salary of £40 p.a., in great part un-
paid, is fearful of losing this post but
was still there Feb. 1673.

ii.   Eleonor, bapt. Cirencester, 27 Oct. 1611,
then called daughter of George Penn,
gent. (the only Penn entry at Cirencester);
m. aged 24, 12 May 1635, Edward Keene of
Blackbourton, Oxfordshire, aged 27, who
had evidently d. by 1669 when she is
mentioned in Admiral Penn's will.[33] (An
Eleonor Penn, daughter of George [sic:
surely error for Giles] was bapt. at St.
Mary Redcliffe, Bristol, 26 May 1610, d.
24 Nov. 1612.)

iii.   ?Elizabeth, m. at St. Thomas, Bristol, 18
Sept. 1620, George Jones of Grittenham,
Wilts,[34] and his will dated 30 Feb. 1629,
probated 7 Oct. 1629, named George Penn
as overseer.

iv.   ?Christian, m. ----- Tucke of Charlton, co.
Wilts; on her estate admin. was granted
to George Penn 1630-1.[35]

v.   ?Margery, spinster of Brinkworth, m. there,
by lic. 17 Oct. 1622 John Sherer (Bishop's
Transcripts). He may have been the man
of this name who m. there, 24 June 1620,
Agnes Lewen.

vi.   ?Susanna, spinster of Brinkworth, m. there
by lic. 2 Aug. 1633, Richard Cusse of
Wootton Basset, co. Wilts, mercer.[36]

5. Captain GILES PENN, second son of William Penn
(William, John) of Malmesbury by his wife Margaret
Rastall, was born perhaps in 1573 and may have been
named for Giles, Lord Chandos, who became Lord of
Minety in that year. Giles was certainly dead by
1656 and may have been dead as early as 1641. He
married at St. Mary Redcliffe, Bristol, 5 Nov. 160C,
JOAN GILBERT of Somerset but originally from Yorkshire.[37] Egidius Penne, son of William Penne late
of Myntye in co. Gloucester deceased, apprenticed
himself to John Harte of the City of Bristol, draper,

and Juliana, his wife, for a term of eight years on
1 May 35 Elizabeth I 1593 A.D.[38] This record is in
Latin in the Bristol Apprentice Books and Egidius
is the Latin equivalent of Giles, but Giles was made
a member of the Drapers Guild on last day of April
1600, a bit earlier than we should expect.[39] With
his brother William he engaged in business in Bristol and in 1618 met with serious financial losses.
A State Paper dated 6 June 1618[40] says that the Mayor
of Bristol requested release and protection for five
years of Giles and William Penn of Bristol, merchants,
who had been reduced to poverty by great losses, so
that they could collect their debts and thereby pay
their creditors and obtain employment. A fuller account appears in the Acts of the Privy Council dated
24 June 1618:[41]

> A letter to the Mayor of Bristol, John Whitson,
> Alderman; John Doughtie; John Dowle and William
> Willett, gentlemen; or to any three of them. This
> enclosed petition, together with a letter from
> yourselves and other aldermen of that city, mer-
> chants; by both which it appeareth that the peti-
> tioners having heretofore been men of ability and
> means are by these divers casualties in their
> course of trade and otherwise become much indebted
> to their utter ruin, of whose miserable estates
> most of their creditors taking consideration have
> voluntarily subscribed to a letter of license for
> some respite and forbearance and divers merchants
> of that city are willing to employ the supplicants
> abroad whereby they are in hope to recover their
> estates, and be able to satisfy their creditors.
> Nevertheless, some few to whom they are indebted
> do refuse to join with the rest in that charitable
> course and by their rigour and severity seek to
> ruin the poor men, they having no means to employ
> their care and industry to discharge their debts,
> but are like to endure much misery and want un-
> less some good course be taken for their relief.
> Forasmuch as we conceive that the parties that
> now stand out may by persuasion be easily drawn
> to conformity with the rest especially since they
> can have no hope at all to recover their debts by
> any other means, we have been moved hereby to au-
> thorize and require you to call the petitioners
> together with the said refusing creditors before
> you and to use your effectual and best mediation
> to draw them to the like favourable conditions

as others have yielded unto. Wherein if you find
any persons obstinately bent to the poor men's
ruin and not yielding to such reasonable motions
as you shall think meet, we require you to certi-
fy their names unto us, and so etc.
   Lord Archbishop of Canterbury; Lord Treasurer;
   Lord Privy Seal; Lord Steward; Earl of Arundell;
   Lord Viscount Wallingford; Lord Viscount Fenton;
   Lord Bishop of Ely; Lord Zouch; Lord Carewe;
   Lord Hay and Mr. Secretary Naunton.

This document certainly speaks well of the ability of the Penns to inspire the confidence of others
in them; and it also shows on the part of these no-
blemen a Christian charity and good sense that is
sometimes thought to have been lacking in such cir-
cles in the seventeenth century.
   In any case soon afterwards Giles must have taken
on the life of a merchant adventurer and sailed for
the Barbary Coast, visiting all the ports from Tetuan to Sallee, at a time when this area was exceedingly dangerous to enter. The trade carried on in
the region by Giles Penn was not always successful.
On 24 Oct. 1630, Daniel Gorsuch of London, merchant,
petitioned the Council as follows:

   I shipped into Barbary in the *Harry* of London
   bound for Tetuan ten tons of iron. Giles Penn
   who carried letters from Charles I to the Governor of Tetuan agreed to sell the iron for me.
   However, it was sold by others and the money
   thereby made was brought back in the same ship to
   London. Richard Berrisford who had obtained a
   royal protection for Penn, pretending the money
   belonged to the latter, attached it to the factors. I pray that Richard Berrisford may be
   called before the Lords and ordered to withdraw
   his attachment.[42]

There followed an order in Council dated 25 May 1631
to the effect that if Giles Penn, merchant of Bristol, did not give satisfaction to Daniel Gorsuch
before the former's protection expired, the latter
might take such course for the recovery of the debt
as the law allowed.[43]
   In 1631 Giles Penn brought home to Charles I a
cast of Tetuan hawks,[44] and the king was so delighted
that he immediately demanded more hawks, whereupon
Penn told him that the royal wish could be more easily satisfied if he could be given letters of pro-

tection to the Moorish governor of Tetuan. Lord Conway drew up the letters and with these Giles returned to Tetuan with the king's order to purchase Barbary horses as well as additional hawks.

On his return to England, Giles came to London and made the acquaintance of Sir Robert Mansel, Edward Nicholas, Endymion Porter and other influential men at court, but in this year Penn was greatly in debt, for on 22 July 1631 Sir Robert Mansel wrote to Viscount Dorchester, Secretary of State, requesting him to procure a renewal of Captain Penn's protection for eight months, by which time he considered the latter's debts could be settled. Sir Robert added that he had a high opinion of Captain Penn.[45]

While in the Barbary Coast Penn became acquainted with the Moors, their customs and their language. At Sallee he was shocked to learn that hundreds of English captives were held as slaves, including some women. The native Moroccan court was powerless to act, as Sallee was in revolt. Penn made a full report to Charles I and suggested how the captives could be freed. The plans were laid before the Council and approved. A fleet was manned and victualled, and Admiral Rainsborough put in command. Penn was discussed as Rainsborough's deputy, and he came to London, lodged at the Black Boy in Ave Maria Lane, and saw Lords Cottington and Portland, who consulted him on every detail of the expedition, but after six months, Penn was politely dismissed with a modicum of money and thanks. The expedition was, however, successful.

To prevent a recurrence, London merchants prayed the king to appoint a consul in Sallee, offering to pay all the charges from their profits in trade, and when the Council asked a nomination, Penn was named, "a man well-experienced in the language and the customs of the said country." Ten days before, Penn had submitted to the Privy Council a full report on the States of Morocco, Tetuan and Fez,[46] and on 30 Dec. 1647 Penn was appointed a consul at Sallee,[47] to be His Majesty's consul at Sallee and to execute that office by himself and deputies in Morocco and Fez during the king's pleasure.

It is doubtful whether he ever revisited England, for his name disappears from the records at Bristol and in the State Papers. His son's monument says he was there "for several years." He doubtless died overseas and without leaving a will. In any case,

on 25 Feb. 1656 Nathaniel Luke, son of Sir Samuel
Luke, was appointed "Providore for the fleet in that
part of the Mediterranean."[48]   Giles Penn must by
then have been dead, and he probably passed away by
1641.

> Issue: surname Penn
> 7 i.   George, bapt. 1 Oct. 1602, d. 31 July 1664.
>   ii.   Giles, bapt. 4 Oct. 1603, St. Nicholas,
>   Bristol, son of Giles and Jane,[49] proba-
>   bly d. inf.
>   iii.   Henry, bapt. 26 Jan. 1604/5, Christ Church,
>   Bristol, son of Giles, merchaunt; d. be-
>   yond seas, unm., admin. to father, 7 June
>   1632.[50]
> 8 iv.   Rachel, bapt. 24 Feb. 1607.
>   v.   Eleonor, bapt. St. Mary Redcliffe, Bristol,
>   26 May 1610, then wrongly identified as
>   daughter of George; bur. 24 Nov. 1612,
>   then rightly identified as daughter of
>   Giles.[51]
>   vi.   Ann, bapt. St. Thomas, Bristol, 21 Jan. 1618,
>   bur. St. Mary Redcliffe, Bristol, 23 or
>   28 Feb. 1651.
> 9 vii.   William, the admiral, bapt. St. Thomas,
>   Bristol, 23 April 1621, d. 16 Sept. 1670.
> 10 viii. Daughter, name unknown, m. ----- Markham.

6.   WILLIAM PENN, third son of William Penn (William, John) of Malmesbury by his wife Margaret Rastall, was apprenticed 6 Aug. 1596 to John Aldworth
of Bristol, mercer, and his wife Martha, and was
made a burgess of Bristol on 5 June 1607.[52]   He
joined his brother in business, doubtless as drapers,
and suffered the same reverses of which we have reported the facts in the sketch on his brother.   By
1610 William had married a woman named MARGERY -----
who was living as his widow in the parish of St.
Mary Recliffe, Bristol, in 1628.

> Issue: surname Penn
>   i.   Catherine, bapt. St. Mary Redcliffe, 23
>   Dec. 1610.[53]
>   ii.   Martha, bur. 12 Aug. 1628, St. Mary Red-
>   cliffe, daughter of Margery Penn, widow.

7. GEORGE PENN, eldest son of Capt. Giles Penn
(William, William, John) by his wife Joan Gilbert,
was baptized at St. Mary Port, Bristol, 1 Oct.
1602[54] and died after a long illness, according to

Pepys (entry for 1 Aug. 1664), on 31 July 1664, on
which night Pepys was awakened by knocking on the
Admiral's door to report the death. On the 2nd the
diarist attended the funeral in an unnamed church,
attended also by the Admiral, fellow officers and
servants, and none else. The funeral was "nothing
handsome at all: and the body was laid under the
communion table in the chancel, about nine at night."
    George was a merchant of San Lucar, the port of
Seville; had married a Spanish Catholic at Antwerp,
and had her sisters in his house at San Lucar. In
1643 he was arrested by the officers of the Inquis-
ition, who excommunicated him "body and soul," imprisoned him for three years, two months and six
days; put him to torture until he confessed; then
forced him to divorce his wife in 1646, after which
she married another. It is said that he was about
to be sent on a diplomatic mission to Spain by
Charles II, with order to demand restitution from
the Spanish king, but he was prevented from going
by illness and death.
    No evidence has been found to show that he left
issue.

    8. RACHEL PENN, fourth child and eldest daugh-
ter of Capt. Giles Penn (William, William, John) by
his wife Joan Gilbert, was baptized at St. Mary Redcliffe, Bristol, 24 Feb. 1607,[55] and married by license dated 26 Oct. 1630, at the Church of St. Gregory by St. Paul, London, RAPHE or RALPHE or RANDALL
BRADSHAW, born ca. 1611, aged 53 on 16 March 1664,
buried at Eccles, 30 Oct. 1667, son of Lawrence
Bradshaw of Hope, parish of Eccles, Lancashire, by
his wife Sarah Hinchman of Andover, Southampton.
His will was probated 31 Jan. 1667/8 and called him
of Pendleton but is now missing. This family appears
in the 1664-5 Visitation of Lancashire (Chetham
Society, 84, pt. 1, p. 53).

    Issue: surname Bradshaw, order from Visitation
    i.   Robert, d.s.p., a merchant.
    ii.   William, d. inf.
    iii.   James, b. ca. 1646, d. 1691 (see 2 PA 19:
            66--he left a widow Mary); was surveyor
            for New Castle Co., Pa. In 1664-5 he was
            a merchant, then at sea, aged 18. He was
            a beneficiary of the Admiral's will, and
            is mentioned in that of Secretary Lehen-
            mann.

iv. John, b. ca. 1651, aged 13 in 1664-5; was a beneficiary of the Admiral's will.

v. Rebecca, d. ca. 1664-5, m. at St. Dunstan Stepney, Middlesex, 28 Sept. 1652, as 1st wife, William Crispin, merchant of London, bapt. Holy Trinity, Hull, Yorkshire, 3 Oct. 1627, d. beyond seas en route to Pennsylvania, bur. in chancel of a church in Carrickfergus, Ireland; letters of admin. granted 7 July 1682 in Ireland to John Suxbery and John Watts.[56] Crispin was to have been chief justice of Pennsylvania. On the Crispins see M. Jackson Crispin (PMHB 53:97-131, 193-202, 289-321). Mabel Richmond Brailsford, *The Making of William Penn* (London 1930), p. 13, wrongly makes Crispin husband of Anne Jasper, a hypothetical aunt of William Penn on his mother's side. She probably drew this from Dr. Jordan (JCRFP 1:357) who prints a sketch (pp. 346-394) which shows Capt. William Crispin marrying ca. 1650 Anne, daughter of John Jasper merchant of Rotterdam, and therefore an aunt of the Founder, and, second, Jane -----. What evidence lies behind this I do not know but it looks like a bad attempt to explain the relationship between Penn and Crispin. A. R. Justice, *Ancestry of Jeremy Clarke and Dungan Genealogy,* pp. 130 f., prints a chart showing that Giles Penn had an unknown daughter who had by an unknown husband a daughter Jane who married as 2nd wife, Capt. William Crispin, and had by him seven children named James, Joseph, Benjamin, Jane, Eleanor, Elizabeth and Amy. This also appears to be a bad guess at the relationship.
Issue: surname Crispin

1. Silas, d. 31 May 1711; m. (1) 1683 Esther Holme; (2) Mary (Stockton) Shinn.

2. Rebecca, m. (1) 24 Aug. 1688 at Ifield Meeting, Edward Blackfan, son of John Blackfan of Steyning, but he d. 1690 just before he was to sail to Pennsylvania. The widow and son William came to Pennsylvania ca. 1700 and she m. (2) Nehemiah Allen. The son William may

have been the man of this name who m. at
Philadelphia Monthly Meeting, 31 1st mo.
1721, Eleanor Wood, and they were probably
parents of Crispin Blackfan who m. at
Falls Monthly Meeting, 4 4th mo. 1756,
Martha Davis, and of Elizabeth who m. at
Falls, 30 9th mo. 1746, Hugh Ely Jr.
3. Ralph, surely a Bradshaw name.
4. Rachel.
vi.   Sarah, d.y., bur. Eccles, 28 July 1635.
vii. Mary, d.y.
viii. Anne.
ix.   Frances, m. after 1664, William Assheton,
attorney-at-law, coroner of Lancashire,
and deputy Herald of Arms. See KPC 281-
307 for an account of the Assheton family based in part on an affidavit sworn
2 July 1751 and said to be filed in Philadelphia Deeds, reference not stated.
Keith knew that Assheton's wife Frances
was a Penn relative but does not say how.
Issue: surname Assheton
1. Robert, b. 1669, invited to Pennsylvania
by William Penn about 1699, and for
many years clerk and prothonotary of
Philadelphia County; Provincial Councillor, July 1711; d. suddenly while
at the Council table, 29 May 1727 in
his 58th year, bur. under Christ
Church, 30 May 1727; m. (1) Margaret
----- who came with him and was the
mother of the children; (2) at Christ
Church, 12 Aug. 1725, Jane Elizabeth
Falconier, who m. (2) 8 April 1729,
the Rev. Archibald Cummings, (3) 17
April 1748, the Rev. Robert Jenney,
D.D., both rectors of Christ Church.
Robert Assheton's arms are #566 in the
Roll of Arms kept by the New England
Historic Genealogical Society (NEHGR
122:180).
Issue by first wife: surname Asshe-
ton or Ashton
a. William, of Gray's Inn, Esq., Judge of
the Admiralty in Pennsylvania, 1714;
Provincial Councillor, 18 May 1722;
d. 23 Sept. 1723, in 33rd year; m.
Christ Church, 11 Oct. 1716 Eliza-

beth Herring, perhaps daughter of
Judge John Herring of Barbadoes;
for 2 sons and 1 daughter, none
baptized at Christ Church, see KPC
cited.

b. Rachel, d.s.p.; m. Christ Church, 23
June 1720 Dr. Samuel Monckton, apothecary of Philadelphia who was
bur. from Christ Church, 29 Sept.
1720.

c. Ralph, b. Salford, Lancs., 30 Nov.
1695, d. in 51st year, bur. from
Christ Church, 20 Feb. 1745/6; m.
Christ Church, 24 Nov. 1716, Susanna Redman, bapt. there, 1 Jan. 1700
d. 24 Nov. 1767 in 66th year, daughter of Joseph Redman.

Issue: surname Assheton

α. Susannah, probably eldest, bur.
25 March 1753; m., according to
KPC, ca. 1741, James Humphries.
The date was, rather, by N. J.
lic. dated 14 Dec. 1740, the man's
name being omitted in the bond,
both in printed version and the
original at Trenton.

β. Elizabeth, bur. Christ Church, 10
Dec. 1718.

γ. Robert, bapt. 15 June 1726, bur.
8 Aug. 1727.

δ. Ralph, bapt. 16 April 1729 aet. 1
mo., bur. 2 July 1735.

ε. Robert, bapt. 17 Sept. 1731, aet.
5 weeks, bur. 7 Jan. 1736/7 (not
in KPC).

ζ. Ralph, bapt. 31 July 1736, aet. 6
weeks, d. 9 July 1773; m. 12 June
1766 Mary Price.

η. Thomas, bur. 27 July 1737 aet. 2
mos.

θ. Margaret, bapt. 31 Oct. 1740 aet.
11 weeks, d. unm., 20 Sept. 1761.

ι. Frances, bapt. 9 Apr. 1746 having
been b. 19 Dec. 1745; m. 12 March
1767 Stephen Watts.
and probably also

κ. Deborah, bur. 28 Feb. 1730/1.

λ. Mary, bur. 22 April 1731.

  μ. William, bapt. 8 Feb. 1733 aet.1
     mo., 3 days; bur. 16 April 1757.
  d. Margaret, d.s.p., m. (1) Christ Church
     9 Nov. 1727 Matthew Hooper; (2) at
     same church, 29 Aug. 1744, John Hy-
     att, sheriff of Philadelphia County;
     one son by first husband.
  e. Charles, bapt. 25 March, bur. 5 Aug.
     1710, Christ Church.
  f. Thomas, bur. 29 Sept. 1711, Christ
     Church.
2. Frances, bapt. Salford, Lancs., 15 March
   1675, m. (1) Robert Booth Esq.; (2)
   William Legh Esq., widow living at
   Manchester in 1751.
3. Mary, bapt. Salford, Lancs., 6 May 1680;
   m. Thomas Warburton gent. in Cheshire;
   a widow living in Salford in 1751.
4. Rachel, m. Andrew Ashton of Manchester,
   checkmaker, and d.s.p., bur. Trinity
   Chapel, Salford, 22 Jan. 1745.
5. John, d. by 27 10th mo. 1703 (2 PA 19:
   410); Penn granted, 30 May 1687, to
   cousins Robert, Frances, Rachel and John
   Assheton of the Co. of Lancaster.[57]

9. Admiral Sir WILLIAM PENN, youngest son and,
perhaps also, youngest child, of Capt. Giles Penn
(William, William, John) by his wife Joan Gilbert,
was born at Bristol in 1621, baptized at the Church
of St. Thomas the Apostle, 23 April 1621; died at
Wanstead, co. Essex, 16 Sept. 1670 aged 49/4, buried
"In Led" in St. Mary Redcliffe, Bristol, 3 Oct.
1670.[58] He was married at St. Martin, Ludgate, London, by Mr. Dyke, "Lecturer then," as witnessed later
by Mr. Roche, "churchwarden then," probably on 6 Jan.
1643/4,[59] to MARGARET JASPER, widow of Nicasius Van-
derschure or van der Schuren of Kilconry, Parish of
Killrush, co. Clare, Ireland, a Dutch merchant, whom
she had married before 1641. Her father, John Jasper of Rotterdam and Ballycase, co. Clare, Ireland,
was, according to Albert Cook Myers,[60] also a Dutch
merchant, though the fact that he was a Dutch merchant has been denied by some writers.[61] Her mother's
name was Marie, and Lady Penn died in February or
March 1681/2, buried 4 March 1681/2 at Walthamstow,
co. Essex.
  The Penns were, as is well known, intimately as-

sociated, both officially and socially, with the in-
comparable diarist, Mr. Samuel Pepys. Mr. Pepys
often saw the Penns on terms of what ought to have
been cordiality but he disliked them and did not
spare them in his cryptographic record. On 19 Aug.
1664 he went "to Sir W. Pen's, to see his lady the
first time, who is a well-looked, fat, short, old
Dutchwoman, but one that hath been heretofore pretty handsome, and is now very discreet, and I believe
hath more wit than her husband. . . very well pleased
I was with the old woman at first visit." It is
surprising that Mr.Pepys had not met Lady Pepys before this. At Lady Batten's on 12 April 1665 "Lady
Pen flung me down upon the bed, and herself and
others, one after another, upon me, and very merry
we were." On 29 June 1665 Lady Pen exhibited gold
fish to Pepys and Mrs.Pepys. On 21 May 1667 Mrs.
Turner is quoted: Lady Pen was "one of the sourest,
dirty women, that she ever saw; that they took two
chambers, one over another; for themselves and child,
in Tower Hill; that for many years together they eat
more meals at her house than at their own"; did call
brothers and sisters the husbands and wives . . ."
This passage is full of other vituperation against
the Penns, but we should remember that while we have
Pepys' frank opinions of the Penns, we are without
any secret diary of the Admiral in which he could
give his opinion of Pepys.
      The Admiral was "a merry fellow, and pretty good
natured, and sings very loose songs" (9 Oct. 1660);
got drunk (27 Dec. 1660, 19 April 1666); indulged
in foolish talk (1 May 1662); fawned on Pepys (29
June 1662); was a base rascal (3 June 1662); had
"base treacherous tricks" (5 July 1662); was "always
a conceited man, and one that would put the best side
outward but that it was his pretense of sanctity
that brought him into play" (27 March 1663); imitates
Pepys in everything (7 Jan. 1664); served "dishes
so deadly foul" (16 Jan. 1664); talked like a fool
and vexed his wife (28 May 1662); again had "old
dissembling tricks, he being as false a fellow as
ever was born" (8 March 1666); was "such a coward"
(29 March 1668) and a "very villain" (30 March
1669).
      If all this be true, then we are ready to have
the inscription on the Admiral's tomb in St. Mary
Redcliffe, Bristol, which reads as follows and was
doubtless composed largely by his son William:

To the just memory of S^r | Willm Penn, Kt. and | sometimes Generall; | Borne at Bristoll, An | 1621 | Son of Captain Giles Penn, severall | yeares Consul for ye English in ye Mediterranean; | of the Penns of Penns Lodge in ye County of Wilts, | and those Penns of Penn in ye C. of Bucks[62]; and | by his Mother from the Gilberts in ye County of | Somerset, Originally from Yorkshire: | Addicted from his Youth to Maritime Affaires; he was made | Captain at the yeares of 21; Rear-Admiral of Ireland at 23; | Vice-Admiral of Ireland at 25; Admiral to the Streights at 29; | Vice-Admiral of England at 31, and General in the first Dutch | Warres at 32. Whence retiring in A° 1655 he was chosen a | Parliament man for the Town of Weymouth, 1660; made Commissioner of the Admiralty and Navy; Governor of the Town and | Fort of King-sail; Vice-Admiral of Munster, and a Member of | that Provincial Counseil; and in Anno 1664 was chosen Great | Captain Commander under his Royall Highnesse in in y^t Signall | and most evidently successful fight against the Dutch fleet. | Thus he took leave of the Sea, his old Element; But | continued still his other employs till 1669; at what time, | through Bodely Infirmities (contracted by ye Care and   fatigue of Publique Affaires) | He withdrew | Prepared and made for his End; and with a gentle and Even | Gale, in much peace, arrived and anchored in his Last and | Best Port, at Wanstead in ye County of Essex 16 Sept. | 1670, being then but 49 and 4 months old. | To whose Name and merit his | surviving Lady hath erected this | remembrance. [63]

The will of Admiral Sir William Penn reads as follows:[64]

In the name of God Amen I Sir William Penn of London knight being of perfect minde and memorie doe make this my last Will and Testament this twentieth day of January in the yeare of our Lord God one thousand six hundred and sixtie and Nyne. And in the one and twentieth yeare of the reigne of our Sovereign Charles the Second by the Grace of God of England Scotland ffrance and Ireland King Defender of the ffaith etc in manner following And first I do hereby revoke admiss and make voyde all and every former and other Last

Will and Testament devise and devises bequest
and bequests by me heretofore at any tyme made
or published My soul I humbly recomend into the
merciful hands of my own beloved Lord and Saviour
Jesus Christ beseeching him that through his
meritts I may be made partaker of Life Eternal
My body I commit to the Grave to be buried in
the Parish church of Redcliffe within the Citty
of Bristoll as near unto the body of my deare
Mother deceased whose body lyes there interred
as the same conveniently may be And my will is
that there shall be erected In the said Church
as near unto the place where my body shall bee
buried as the same can be contrived A Hansome
and Decent Tombe to remain as a Monument as well
for my said Mother as for my Self[65] the charges
thereof To be defrayed by my Executor hereinafter named out of my personal estate I doe hereby
devise the same as followeth And first I doe will
and devise unto my deare Wife Dame Margaret Penn
to be paid unto her imediately after my decease
the summe of Three hundred pounds sterling together with all my jewells other than What I
shall hereinafter particularly devise And I doe
also give and bequeath unto my said Deare Wife
the use and occupation during her life of one
full moyety of all my Plate and household stuffes
all Coaches and Coach-horses or Coach-mares and
all such Cowes I shall happen to Have at the tyme
of my decease. Item I doe will and bequeath unto
my younger sonne Richard Penn the summe of four
thousand pounds sterling together with my Favritt
Dyamond Ring and all my Swords Gunns and Pis-
tolles The said four thousand pounds so bequeathed
unto my said sonne Richard to be paid and payeable
unto him so soone as He shall arrive at the Age
of one and twenty yeares and not sooner And my
Will is that in the meantyme And untill Richard
shall arrive at the said Age of one and twenty
yeares my Executor hereinafter named shall pay
unto my said sonne Richard out of my personal
estate the yearly summe of one hundred and Twenty
pounds which I hereby devise unto him for his support and maintenance untill He shall attain the
Age of one and Twenty yeares and no longer. Item
I doe will and devise unto my Deare Granddaughter
Margarett Lowther the summe of one hundred pounds
sterling unto my Two Nephews James Bradshaw and

William Markham to each of them tenn pounds sterling Unto my two Nephewes John Bradshaw and George
Markham to each of them five pounds sterling Unto
my Cosin William Penn son of George Penn late of
the fforest of Brayden in the County of Wilts gent
Deceased The summe of ten pounds sterling unto my
Cosin Elianore Keene The yearly summe of six
pounds sterling to be paid unto her yearly during
her life by my Executor out of my personall estate by quarterly payments at the four most usuall
quarterly feasts or quarterly days of payment in
the yeare. Item I will and bequeath unto my late
Servant William Bradshaw forty shillings to buy
him a Ring unto my servant John Wrenn five pounds
sterling unto the Poor of the Parish of Redcliffe
aforesaid in the Citty of Bristoll aforesaid
twenty pounds sterling I doe also Will and Devise
to my eldest Sonne William Penn my Gold Chain and
Medall with the rest and residue of all and singular my Plate household stuffe Goods Chattels
and personall estate not hereinbefore devised as
alsoe the said Goods Promised and devised to be
used By my said deare wife during her life from
and after the decease of my said Wife And I do
hereby Constitute Declare nominate and appointe
my said son William Sole Executor of this my
last Will and Testament and doe hereby appointe
at my ffunerall to give mourning unto my said
Deare Wife my said sonne Richard my Daughter Margaret Lowther And my sonne in lawe Anthony Lowther the husband of my said Daughter and unto
Doctor Whister and his wife and unto such of my
servants as my said Deare Wife shall for that
purpose nominate the said mourning to be paid
for out of my personall estate hereby devised
unto my said Executor And though I cannot appre-
hend that any difference may fall or happen Betweene my said Deare Wife and my said sonn William after my decease in regard to anything by
me devised or submitted by this my will in Relation to any other matter or thing Whatsoever
yet in Case any such difference should arise I
doe hereby request and desire and in my right
require conjoin and Direct my said Deare Wife
and my said sonne William by all the Obligations
of Duty affection and respect Which they have
and ought to have for me and my memory That all
Such Differences of what nature or kinde Soever

they shall bee by the joynt Consents and submission of my said Deare Wife and my said sonne William bee at all tymes and from tyme to tyme referred to the deliberation and finall judgment
and Determination of my worthy ffriende Sr William Coventry[65] of the parish of St. Martin in
the ffields in the County of Middlesex whom I
doe hereby instruct to take uppon himself the determination of all and every such difference and
differences as shall from tyme to tyme or at any
tyme after my decease shall be referred unto him
Awards and determinations by my said Deare Wife
and my said sonn William Penn for the totall pre-
vention of all suites in Lawe or equity which
upon any occasion or misunderstanding might otherwise happen betweene them. In Witnesse whereof
I have unto my last will and Testament sett my
hand and seal this day and yeare first above
written and doe publish and Declare this to be
my last will and Testament in the presence of
those whose names are subscribed as wittnesses
hereunto.

W. Penn

Signed sealed declared and Published after these
words viz the use and occupation during her life
of Betweene the seaventh and eight lines and these
words viz as also the said Goods and premises
devised to be used by my said deare wife during
her life from and after the decease of my said
wife betweene the seaventeenth and eighteenth
lines were intersigned in the presence of R.
Langhorn John Radford William Markham.[66]

Probatum fuit 1 Oct. 1670.

Issue: surname Penn
11 i.   William, the Founder, b. London, 14 Oct.
          1644, d. Ruscombe, 30 July 1718.
12 ii. Richard, b. ca. 1648-1650, d. April 1673.
13 iii. Margaret, b. ca. 1651, d. 15 Dec. 1718.

10. Daughter of unknown name and position among
the children of Capt. Giles Penn (William, William,
John) by his wife Joan Gilbert, this woman has thus
far defied all efforts to learn more of her. Her existence is, however, proved by the fact that Admiral
Sir William Penn left bequests to his nephews William
and George Markham. Moreover, the son William is

well known to have been a cousin of William Penn.
It is claimed that the said William Markham, cousin
of Penn, used a seal with the coat of arms of the
Markhams of Sedgebrook, Notts., from whom descended
the Markhams of Ollerton. It is possible, therefore, that the unknown husband was William Markham
of Ollerton, Nottinghamshire, but we have not been
able to prove it.

Issue: surname Markham, perhaps others
 i.   William, b. probably ca. 1635, d. testate
         at Philadelphia, 12 4th mo. 1704; m. (1)
         Ann (Nan) Wright, shortly before 5 Aug.
         1666[67]; (2) in Philadelphia, ca. Jan.
         1683/4, Joanna -----, widow of Capt. Eben
         Jobson by whom she had a daughter Eliza-
         beth Jobson who m. (1) Edward Robinson of
         Philadelphia, merchant, whose will was
         probated 4 Nov. 1699; (2) Jacob Regnier
         of Lincoln's Inn, barrister-at-law, and
         said Elizabeth (Jobson)(Robinson) Regnier
         d.s.p. before 3 Aug. 1715. As is well
         known, William Penn sent his cousin Wil-
         liam Markham to Pennsylvania in 1681 as
         lieutenant-governor. The fullest account
         of Markham is to be found in KPC pp.
         (1)-(6) [not 1-6]. See also PGM 25:75,
         note 17, where the KPC reference seems
         to have been overlooked. Markham ap-
         pears not to have been a Friend.
            Only issue: child of first wife
      1. Ann, d. after 1733, having m. between
         1690 and 1698, James Brown, alleged
         to have been a pirate in a letter of
         Edward Randolph dated 26 April 1698.
         James Logan had a low opinion of Ann.
            Issue: surname Brown
         a. William, d.s.p. by 19 Dec. 1726.
         b. James, d.s.p. by 19 Dec. 1726.
         c. Joanna, who, on 19 Dec. 1726, as Jo-
            anna Brown "of the city of New York
            only daughter of Ann Brown of the
            same City and granddaughter of Wil-
            liam Markham late of the City of
            Philadelphia, Esq., dec'd" sold
            property devised to her and her
            brothers. In 1767 the Penn family
            appears to have granted her a pen-
            sion and in 1774 Richard Hockley

> wrote that the "old gentlewoman is
> still living and hearty," and she
> appears to have m. one Barker.
> ii. George or possibly Charles George, heir in
> Admiral Penn's will, probably afterwards
> of Philadelphia, as Keith alludes to a
> Charles George Markham as witness to a
> Philadelphia deed, the reference for
> which he fails to give. At the First
> Presbyterian Church, Philadelphia, on 16
> 10th mo. 1734, a Hannah Markham married
> Anthony Sturgis. I feel reasonably sure
> that she belongs to this family and would
> cautiously suggest that she might have
> been a daughter, or even the widow, of
> George Markham.

11. WILLIAM PENN, sometime captain in the Royal
Army in Ireland, later Quaker and Founder of Pennsylvania, eldest child of Admiral Sir William Penn
(Giles, William, William, John) by his wife Margaret
Jasper, was born 14 Oct. 1644, probably in a house
on Great Tower Hill, in the Parish of St. Katherine
near the Tower, and was baptized in the Church of
Allhallows, Barking, 23 Oct. 1644, the parents then
being recorded as of the Tower Liberty.[68] After a
series of apoplectic strokes, the first occurring
probably in May 1712 in London, the second on 4 Oct.
1712 at Bristol during the writing of a letter to
James Logan, and the third shortly before 5 Feb.
1712/13 at Ruscombe near Twyford, Berkshire, in a
house which he had rented in 1710, Penn was incapa-
citated for serious work and died at Ruscombe, 30
July 1718 in his 74th year, buried at Jordans, 5
Aug. 1718, in the presence of thirty or forty "public Friends," i.e. ministers, and a vast number of
Friends and others.[69]
At this point in the narrative it may be of some
interest to give the items concerning him in Pepys'
Diary, as Pepys seems to have had a somewhat more
favorable opinion of him than of his father the Admiral. On 31 Nov. 1661 we learn that Mr William Penn
is lately come from Oxford, and on New Year's Day he
and his sister attend Pepys to the theater. On 25
Jan. 1662 Sir William is concerned about his son's
future and discusses with Pepys moving the young man
from Oxford to Cambridge, and the same topic appears
again on 1 February. On 16 March William Penn is at

home, not well. On 28 April 1662 we hear that Sir
William is troubled about letters he has in his possession which show that his son was influenced by
the nonconformist theologian, John Owen, D.D.[70] Then
there is nothing about young William until 26 Aug.
1664, when we hear that he has come back from France
and has called on Mrs. Pepys whose opinion is that he
is "a most modish person, grown a fine gentleman."
On 30 Sept. 1664 Pepys writes his own opinion, mentioning William's learning, "vanity of the French
garb," "affected manner of speech and gait," and
says "I fear all real profit he hath made of his
travel will signify little." On the 14th of the
same month, Pepys had been uneasy about the relations
of William with Mrs. Pepys! Then another long blank
and on 29 Dec. 1667 we hear that William Penn is
lately from Ireland, "Quaker again, or some very
melancholy thing." Nearly a year later, 12 Oct. 1668,
Penn has written a book (his *Truth Exalted*) which
Pepys calls a "ridiculous nonsensical book set out
by Will Pen for the Quakers; but so full of nothing
but nonsense, that I was ashamed to read in it."

As is well known, William Penn married twice, both
times to remarkable women but of very different character. When of Walthamstow, Essex, he declared first
intentions to marry GULIELMA MARIA [POSTUMA] SPRINGETT
on 7 12th mo. 1671 at Jordans Monthly Meeting. Daniel
Zachary and Thomas Ellwood were directed to make the
usual inquiries, and approval was given on 6 1st mo.
1672. The marriage was on 4 2nd mo. 1672 at Charlewood
or Chorley Wood, in King's Farmhouse, Parish of Rickmansworth, co. Hertford. Gulielma Maria Postuma
Springett, born in late 1643 or early 1644, posthumously, as the name shows, was daughter of Sir William
Springett, knight, by his wife Mary Proude, who by
this time was wife to her second husband, Isaac Penington.[71] Among the witnesses to this marriage were
James and Helena (Mercer) Claypoole, afterwards of
Philadelphia.[72]

Gulielma was frequently called "Guli" in the family, but whether we should pronounce this name as
"Julie" or with a hard G, we do not know. Her double
commemoration of the names of both her parents was
unusual in this period.[73] Though she had eight children, only three of them survived her when she died
in her husband's arms, at Hoddesdon, Herts., on 23
Feb. 1693/4, in her fiftieth year.[74]

Her ancestry was as follows. Her great-great-

grandfather in the male line was Thomas Springett who
married Margaret Roberts, daughter of Edmund Roberts
of Hawkhurst, Kent, and had, among other children,[75]
a son Herbert Springett, born ca. 1554, aged 40 in
1595 when a deponant in a lawsuit, died 7 May 1620
in his 66th year, leaving a will dated 30 Oct. 1617,
probated 20 May 1620. He was of Southover, afterwards of Lewes and Broyle Place, Ringmer, Sussex,
and married at St. Mary Westout, now known as St.
Anne's, Western Road, Westout, Lewes, Sussex, about
1580-83, Ann Stempe.

   This couple had, besides a son Thomas, afterwards
Sir Thomas,[76] and a daughter Elizabeth who married
Simon Stone, barrister-at-law of the Middle Temple,
a son Herbert Springett of Ringmer, Sussex, Esq.,
baptized at St. Michael's, Lewes, 14 Feb. 1590/1,
who married Katherine, daughter of Sir Edward Partridge of Bridge, Kent, knighted at Whitehall, 31
July 1641, son of Edward Partridge by his wife Susanna ?Stede. Herbert and Katherine had twin sons and
a daughter Katherine. The younger of the twins,
Herbert, born in Kent in 1621, afterwards of Oving-
dean, Sussex, was buried 11 June 1687 at St. Mary
Westout. His will was dated 31 July 1686, probated
at Lewes, 5 Jan. 1690/1. He married Elizabeth, the
daughter of Richard Tufnell of Clapham, Surrey, Citizen and Brewer of London, and M.P. for Southwark,
who married Elizabeth, daughter and heiress of William Humphries, and afterwards second wife of George
Thompson of Lee near Blackheath, Kent. Herbert and
Elizabeth had four sons: (1) Herbert, attorney-at-
law, Commissioner of Excise under James II, and who,
after many associations with William Penn, made a
will probated 30 Dec. 1724 (PCC 283 Bolton); (2)
Richard, Citizen and Apothecary of London, buried
6 Oct. 1718, St. Mary Westout; (3) Anthony, and (4)
William, all four being called of Plimpton or Plump-
ton, Sussex.

   The elder twin, Sir William Springett, knighted
in February 1641/2, died at Arundel, 3 Feb. 1643/4,
aged 23, of a fever contracted during the taking of
Arundel Castle, of which he was colonel commanding
for the Parliamentary forces. He had been present
at Edgehill and Newbury. When aged about 19 or 20,
he married about 1640 Mary Proude aged 18, daughter
and heiress of Sir John Proude, of whom more later,
and they had a son John Springett who died young,
leaving as only heir of Sir William, the daughter

Gulielma Maria Postuma. That the Springetts were
persons of gentle status will be clear. A sepulcral
inscription for Sir William is in the church at
Ringmer, Sussex,[77] which reads as follows:

> Here lyeth the body of | Sir William Springett,
> knt. | Eldest son and heir of Herbert Springett
> of Sussex, | who married Mary Proude, the only
> daughter and heir of | Sir John Proude, knt.,
> Colonel in the service of the United Provinces,
> | And of Ann Fagge, his wife, of the co-heirs of
> Edward Fagge | of Ewell near Feversham, in the
> County of Kent, Esq. | He had issue by Mary, his
> wife, one sonne, John Springett, and one | daugh-
> ter, Gulielma Maria Postuma Springett. | He, be-
> ing Colonel in the service of the Parliament at
> the taking of | Arundel Castle in Sussex, there
> contracted a sickness of | which he died Februa-
> ry the 3rd, Anno Domini | 1643, being 23 years
> of age. His wife, in testimony of her dear af-
> fection to him, hath erected | this monument to
> his memory.

Sir John Proude of Goodneston Manor, Kent, died
when his daughter Mary was aged three, while serving
under the Prince of Orange at the siege of Groll in
Gelderland. From the age of nine until her marriage
Mary Proude lived in the home of Sir Edward Partridge
in Kent, who had married Mary, daughter of Edward
Fagge, gent., of Faversham (died 1618) and sister
of Ann (Fagge) Proude. In that family lived also
Madame Springett (née Katherine Partridge) and her
three children William (afterwards Sir William),
Herbert and Catherine. After Sir William Springett's
death, his widow Mary married, second, at St. Margaret's, Westminster, 13 May 1654, Isaac Penington,
who died 8 Oct. 1679, buried at Jordans, and Mary
herself died 18 Sept. 1682 at Warminghurst, also
buried at Jordans, and on 21 7th mo. 1682, as James
Claypoole tells us.[78]

Her will was dated 10 3rd mo. called May 1680
"att my house att Woodside in Amersham parish and
County of Bucks." It was signed and sealed 5 July
1680 and probated 11 Oct. 1682 (PCC 121 Cottle):[79]
She refers to her husband Isaac Penington whose
administratrix she had been; to cousin Elizabeth
Dallison; to daughter Penn; to son William Pennington £500 sterling, £100 to bind himself to some
handsome trade that hath not much of labour, because

he is but weakly, and the other £400 at age of 21;
to son Edward Pennington the like sums upon like
conditions; to daughter Mary Pennington £30 a year
till she marry, and if she marry, £300 sterling[80];
to dear son William Penn £50 sterling; to friend
Thomas Elwood the like sum; to cousin Mary Smith,
wife to William Smith, £50; £20 towards a meeting
house if friends at Chalfont think it convenient to
build one; to Martha Sampson £2 a year for life; to
daughter Gulielma Maria Penn her choice of a suit
of damask except that marked I^{P}M; to her son Spring-
gett Penn my great plate with the Springetts and my
coat of arms and the silver two-eared cup made in
the fashion of his mother's golden one; to her
daughter Letitia Penn my silver chafin dish and
skimmer with a brasile handle and that large nun's
work box and a little basket of nun's work, and a
girdle of black plush and a black straw basket which
her father brought me out of Holand &c&c; to my son
William Pennington my dear husband's watch; other
bequests to son Edward Pennington, to daughter Mary,
to cousin Mary Smith the elder, to her daughter Mary; to son John Pennington my house and land at
Woodside and all my husband's horses at Kew, upon
conditions; reference is made to the will of testatrix's mother the Lady Prewed[81] "that is annext my
father's Sir John Prewed"; also "my mother's sister
the Lady Oxenden."[82] "I would have my son John Pennington lay mee in friends burying ground at Jordans
very neare my deare and precious husband Isaac Pennington." Son John is named executor and dear son
William Penn and loving friend Thomas Ellwood to be
overseers.[83]

After a courtship which seems to have made Friends
uneasy, possibly because of the difference in ages,
William Penn declared first intentions at Bristol
Men's Meeting, 11 9th mo. 1695, was passed 24 12th
mo. 1695/6 and was married 5 1st mo. 1695/6 to HAN-
NAH CALLOWHILL, born at Bristol, 11 12th mo. 1671/2,[84]
died 20 10th mo. 1726, only surviving child of Thomas Callowhill of Bristol, button-maker and later
linen-draper, by his wife Hannah Hollister, daughter
of Dennis Hollister of Bristol, grocer, by his wife,
first name unknown, a daughter of Edmund Popley, merchant. Thomas Callowhill was son of John Callowhill,
late of Bristol, gent.[85]

The will of Dennis Hollister of the City of Bristol, grocer, is dated 1 Sept. 1675, with a codicil

dated 6 July 1676, probated 21 July 1676 (PCC 91
Bence)[86]: It mentions only son Dennis Hollister;
daughter Hannah Callowhill, wife of Thomas Callowhill; granddaughter Sarah Callowhill, her eldest
daughter, with remainder to granddaughter Hannah
Callowhill; granddaughter Bridget Callowhill with
remainder to her sister Hannah Callowhill; grandson Dennis Callowhill, his eldest son, with remainder to Thomas Callowhill, 2nd son of said Hannah; daughter Lydia Jordan, wife of Thomas Jordan;
granddaughter Bridget Jordan, my daughter Lydia's
eldest daughter; and granddaughter Lydia Jordan;
daughter Mary Hollister's daughter Phebe Hollister;
Whitehart Inn, ¼ is my wife's inheritance; ¼ lately bought of Anne Yeomans dec., ¼ lately bought of
Edmond French, son and heir of Elizabeth French,
dec., ¼ lately bought of Henry Rowe and wife Judith,
Judith, Anne, Elizabeth and my wife daughters and
coheirs of Edmund Popley merchant dec.; Lydia, wife
of Edward Hackett; £10 each to George Fox and four
others; £5 each to five others; to each natural
brothers & sisters children that survive me except
Samuel Hollister, son of brother Thomas, and Nathaniel Tovie, only son of sister Margery Tovie dec.,
who are ill husbands[87] and like to misspend it, but
their share to Samuel Hollister's wife and Nathaniel
Tovie's children in England. Executors are Dennis
Hollister and sons-in-law Thomas Callowhill and Thomas Jordan. A codicil dated 6 July 1676 says that
granddaughter Lydia Jordan is dead, mentions grandchildren Hannah, Thomas and Elizabeth Callowhill;
Samuel Hollister, son of brother William; Dennis
Hollister, son of brother Abel; Samuel Hollister,
grandson of brother William and son of Jacob Hollister; Thomas Speed and others.
      The will of Thomas Callowhill of the City of Bris-
tol, linen-draper, dated 28 9th mo. 1711, probated
24 10th mo. 1712 (PCC 231 Barnes)[88], appoints as
trustees kinsman Brice Webb, linen-draper, and Charles
Harford of the said city, merchant, for his wife
Hanna als Anna; after her decease to granddaughter
Margaret Penn, daughter of Hannah Penn my daughter
by William Penn Esq. her husband. Property in Bristol, Somersetshire and other places in England and
Pennsylvania, is mentioned; an interest in Pennsylvania for £1000 due me by William Penn; provision
for Thomas and John Penn, sons of Hannah Penn. A gold
piece worth 23/6 to each of the following: my brother

Walter Duffield; my sister Elizabeth Javeling; my
nieces Elizabeth Javelin, Duffield Javelin, Sarah
Gurnay, Mary Gurney; wife Hanna als Anna, sole executrix; overseers: Brice Webb and Charles Harford.
On 19 Oct. 1738, administration was granted on this
estate to John Penn Esq., son of Hannah Penn, etc.
Who had been handling the estate before that is not
known.

William Penn the Founder of Pennsylvania executed
during his lifetime at least four, probably five,
and possibly still more wills. The first of these
four was doubtless prepared against the possibility
that Penn might not survive the voyage of the *Welcome*
in 1682 and was left in England where it must now be,
if extant. It would, of course, be quite idle to
look for it in the court records, since it was never
probated. It was mentioned and confirmed in the
second will, executed in Philadelphia on 6 6th mo.
1684, as Penn was preparing to leave Pennsylvania
after the first visit. This second will has, so far
as I can discover, not previously been printed. It
has had the signature torn off, either by an autograph hunter,[89] or even by Penn himself to render
the will invalid. In this period documents like
mortgages were sometimes rendered invalid by such an
act. Like the first will, the third, if there was
such, was made in England on the eve of departure,
this time for the second visit to Pennsylvania. No
proof has been found that such a will was really executed, but from what is known of the other wills,
it seems highly probable that Penn would not have
undertaken another ocean voyage without bringing up
to date his testamentary arrangements. Since the
second will, his first wife and his heir apparent,
son Springett, had died, and he now had a second wife
and would soon have a child by her. The fourth will
was again executed in America, at Newcastle on Delaware, 30 8ber 1701.[90] The fifth and final will,
probated 3 Nov. 1718 (PCC 221 Tennison), bore no date
when made in London while Penn was ill of a fever
but has a sort of codicil dated 27 3rd mo. called May
1712 at Ruscombe, as well as a postscript which had
to be proved by testimony, as will be seen.[91]

We now give the texts of the three wills still
extant.

SECOND WILL, PHILADELPHIA, 6 6th mo. 1684

For my dear wife[92] wth my last will & testam^t

[p. 2] My last will & Testem^t made this 6th day of ye 6th month 1684. Not knowing how the Lord may please to deal wth me least ye Sea be my grave & the deeps my Sepulchre, I had made this my last will & testem^t. 1 I confirm & ratefy all ye matter of my last will made in England. 2 I give this lott I live at in Philadelphia to my dr. wife for her life & then to Letitia Penn my dear daughter. 3 I give to my dear wife ye enjoym^t of Pennberry till my sonn Springett is of age, then to him & his for a Mannor. [p.3] 4 I bequeth to my sonn William Penn a lott runing through from Delaware to Skulkill on ye South side of ye Citty called commonly my sons lott, with 100^93 acres of ye overplus land of Passion. & ten thousand acres on Skullkill & four hundred Acres on delaware by Poquessen according to warrant, & I further guive him five thousand Acres in each County, & twenty thousand A^rs on ye Sasquehanah River with ye second best Island in it. 5 I do give to my daughter Letitia another town lott on Skullkill & two in the high street, as sett down in ye Citty platt, and all the land from ye Creek where the bridge is north of Pennberry towards the falls, to the land of James Harrison on ye main River called Sepasse, [p.4] and five thousand Acres on the Skullkill and So in each County & ten thousand on Sasquehanagh with an Island as also that Island in delaware Called oriction wch I call Letitias Isle, if y^t before Pennberry comes to y^t Seat [sic], else ye said oricton to belong to Pennberry. 6 I give to my Sonn william & my daughter Letitia one hundred pounds yearly for ever, yt is, to each of them one, out of my quit rents of the Province to be paid by my heir or his receiver, the paym^t to begin from my decease, & by thos I intrust or rather their dear mother to be kept or layed out in improveing their Plantations by labour & stock [p.5] 7 I give to my dear wife the Love of my youthe, & my Crown & blessing from ye lord, the enjoym^t of the rest of my rents till my Sonn Springett or my heir come to age, to enable her ye better to educate the children & live Comfortably together wth ten thousand Acres of land where she pleases & for w^t use she pleases. 8 I give fifty thousand Acres for poor famely, as one or two hundred apeice, as my executors please,

on ye Sasquehanagh River or neer yem paying y^e
shilling for each hundred wch I understand all
along. 9 I give ten thousand acres of land in
the County of Philadelphia towards the [p.6] support of a School, & as much for an hospitall in
yt Citty, & the like quantety on Sasquehanah,
for ye like uses in ye first Citty there to be
built. 10 I give all my servants I had before
I came & yt came wth me, two hundred acres, each
of them, my old servants yt stayd wth my wife,
the like proportion, & every one yt is with my
concerns in America an hundred Acres, as if they
had bought the same. The Lord bless my dear famely & keep them & the People of this Province &
terretory in his fear, yt in love & concord they
may live together while ye Sun & ye moon endureth.
Amen, Amen. [p.7]
wittnesses present
  Tho lloyd
  Tho Holme,
  James Harrison
  Wm; Clarke^{94}

FOURTH WILL, NEW CASTLE, 30 8br 1701^{95}

Newcastle on Delaware, 30 8br, 1701

     Because it is appointed for all men once to
dye, and yt their days are in the hand of ye Al-
mighty their Creator, I think fitt upon this present voyage to make my last will and testament,
which is as follows:
     Since my estate, both in England and Ireland,
are either entailed or incumbred, my wil is, that
wh^{ch} is saleable, be sould for payment of my just
Debts, and all my household stuff, plate, and
linen, not given or disposed of to my children
by their relations, and if there should be any
overplus, that it goe equally to my son William
and daughter Laetitia, as to my estate in Europe,
be it Land, houses, or moveables, except my gold
chain and meddall, wch I give to my son William;
and except such estate as I had with or since I
married this wife, ffor my estate in America, it
is also incumbered, but not with the tenth part
of the true value thereof--I mean of the Province
of Pennsylvania and counties annexed--when that
incumbrance is discharged, I give my son William
all my sayd Province and Territorys, to him and

his Heirs forever as Proprietary and Govern. But
out of or rather in the sayd soyle thereof, I give
to my daughter, Laetitia Penn, one hundred thousand acres, seaventy of wch out of or rather the
sayd Province, and ten thousand acres out of or
rather in each of the Lower Countys of the terri-
rorys.

I also give to my son John one hundred and
fifty thousand acres, of wch one hundred thousand
in the Province, and fifty thousand acres in the
Lower Countys; and I also bequeath to him my tenth
or Proprietary ship of Salem tenth or County in
West New Jersey, to my sayd son John and his heirs
forever, with all rents, Proffits, and Interests
therein.

I also will that the Childe my De: wife, Hannah Penn, now goes with, shall have one hundred
thousand acres if a boy, a seaventy thousand if
a Girle, in the Province aforesd; all which Land
so given shall lye between Susquehanagh River and
Delaware River, and to be taken up within twelve
months after my death. If my encumbrances can
be discharged in yt time, or so soon as they are;
but so as that the sayd Lands be not above = 80 =
miles above a due west line, to be drawn from
Philadelphia to Susquehanah River, and to be layd
out in ye way of townships, and to pay to my son
William one silver shilling for every township of
five thousand acres when taken up forever, in lieu
of all demands and services, hereby requiring my
sayd son William to erect all or any part of ye
aforesayd Lands into mannors, with due powers
over their own Tennants, according to my sayd
children's respective agreements with them, when
they or any for them require the same.

I also give to my De: Wife five thousand acres
of land as a token of my love, to be taken up as
before exprest, and upon ye same acknowledgment,
and within ye said limits, in my Province of Pennsilvania, to her and her heirs and assigns forever; and so I understand in my other afore-men-
tioned graunts to my children, viz., that I give
to them and their heirs and assignes forever. I
also leave my De: Sister and her children some
token of my love, such as my wife shall think fit
in memoriall of me. Also to her father and mother
the like.

I give to my Servts, John and Mary Sach . . .

three hundred acres between them; to James Logan
one thousand acres, and my blacks their freedom,
as under my hand already; and to ould Sam 100 acres, to be his children's after he and wife are
dead, forever, on common rent of one bushel of
wheat yearly, forever--for the performance of
which I desire my loveing friends, Edward Shippen,
Saml Carpenter, Edward Penington, and James Logan
in America, or any three of them, and Benjamin
Seal, Thomas Callowhill, Henry Goldney, Jos. Pike
in England, or any three of them, to see this my
last will observed, and that I have right done
me about my incumbrances, that my family suffer
not by impressive demands, but get me and myn
righted in law and Equity. And I do hereby
charge all my children, as their loveing dying
father's last command and desire, that they never
goe to law, but if any difference should arise,
wch I hope would not, that they be concluded by
ye Judgment of frds, to be chosen by the meeting
of sufferings of ye people called Quakers, in
England, for English and Irish concerns; and in
America, to ye ffrds of the quarterly meeting at
Philadelphia, in Pennsilvania, for a finall de-
cision.

I do further ordain by this will, that what
estate I here give to either or any of my child-
dren be never alienated from my family, for want
of heirs of their own body; but that debt being
payd, they may owe the rest to be inherited by
ye next of blood of my Body and discent, and for
want thereof, to my De: Sister and her Blood, in
such manner as she shall appoint.

And now, if ever I have done a wrong to any,
I desire their forgiveness; and for all ye good
offices I have ever done, I give God, yt Enabled
me, the honour and thanks; and for all my enemies, and their Evil reflections and reports and
endeavours to ruine me in name and estate, I do
say, ye Lord forgive them and amend them; for I
have ever, from a child, loved the best things
and people, and have had a heart, I bless the
name of Allmighty God, to do good, without gain,
yea sometimes for Evill and to consume my own, to
serve others, wch has been my greatest burden and
my infirmity; having a mind not only just but
kinde, even to a fault, for it has made me sometimes hardly so just by means of debts thereby

contracted, as my integrity would have made me.
    And now, for all my good friends, that have
loved and helped me, do so still, in my poor
children, wch you can, and God Allmighty be to
you and yours an ample reward. You have my hear-
ty and gratefull acknowledgments and commemoration, who never lived to myselfe from my very
youth, but to you and the whole world in love
and service. This I ordain to be (and accordingly
is) my last will and testament, revoaking all
other.
    Given under my hande and seal, the day and year
above written.
Sealed and Delivered   Wm. Penn
    in ye presence of
    Richd Halliwell
    Jos. Wood
    Rob Asheton[96]
    James Logan.
The interlineations were my writeing, they are
twelve in number, the pages 7 . . .[97]

There was, of course, happily no reason for the
foregoing wills to be offered for probate, as Penn
lived sixteen or more years after making the so-
called "fourth will."

FIFTH AND LAST WILL, LONDON AND RUSCOMBE 1712

    I William Penn Esq. so called Chief Proprie-
tary and Governor of the Province of Pensilvania
and the Territories thereunto belonging being of
sound mind and understanding for which I bless
God doe make and declare this my last Will and
Testament My eldest son being well provided for
by a Settlement of his mothers and my fathers
estate I give and dispose of my estate in manner
following   The Government of my Province of Pensilvania and Territories thereunto belonging and
all powers relating thereunto I give and devise
to the most Honorable the Earl of Oxford and Earle
Mortimer[98] and to Will Earle Poulet[99] so call'd
and their heires upon trust to dispose thereof
to the Queen or any other person to the best advantage and profit they can to be applied in such
manner as I shall herein after direct. I give
and devise to my dear wife Hannah Penn and her
ffather Thomas Callowhill and to my good ffriends
Margaret Lowther my dear sister and to Gilbert
Heathcote Physician Samuel Waldenfield John ffield

Henry Goldney all living in England and to my
ffriends Samuel Carpenter Richard Hill Isaac
Norris Samuel Preston and James Logan all living
in or near Pennsylvania and their heirs all my
Lands tenements and hereditaments whatever rents
and other profitts scituate lying and being in
Pensilvania and the Territories thereunto belonging or elsewhere in America upon Trust that they
shall sell and dispose of so much thereof as
shall convey unto each of the three children of
my son William Penn Gulielma Maria Springett and
William respectively and to their respective
heirs ten thousand acres of Land in some proper
and beneficial places to be let out by my Trustees aforesaid all the rest of my lands and hereditaments whatsoever scituate lying and being
in America I will that my said Trustees shall
convey to and amongst my children which I have
by my present Wife in such proportions and for
such estates as my said Wife shall think fit but
before such conveiance shall be made to my said
children I will that my said Trustees shall convey to my daughter Aubry whom I omitted to name
before ten thousand acres of my said lands in
such places as my Trustees shall think fitt all
my personall Estate in Pensilvania and elsewhere
and arreers of rent due there I giue to my said
dear Wife whom I make my sole executrix for the
equall benefit of her and her children. In Testimony whereof I have set my hand and seale to
this my Will which I declare to be my last Will
revoking all others formerly made by me.

Wm Penn   [L.S.]

Signed sealed and published by the Testator William Penn in the presence of us who set our names
as Witnesses thereof in the presence of the said
Testator after the interlineation of the words
above viz (whom I make my sole Executrix) Sarah
West Susanna Reading Thos Pyle Rob^{tt} Lomax Robt
West.
This Will I have made when ill of a ffeaver[100]
at London with a clear understanding of what I
did then but because of some unworthy expressions
belying Gods goodness to me as if I knew not what
I did[101] I do now that I am recovered through
Gods goodness hereby declare it is my last Will

and Testament at Ruscombe in Berkshire this 27 of
ye 3^m called May 1712.

                              Wm Penn   [L.S.]

Witnesses present Elizabeth Penn Thos Pyle Thomas Penn^{102} Elizabeth Anderson Mary Chandler Jo-
nah Dee Mary Dee.

Postscript in my own hand as a farther Testimony of my Love to my Dr Wife I of my own mind
give unto her out of the rents in America viz:
Pensilvania &c three hundred pounds a year for
her natural life and for her care and charge
over my children in their education of which she
knows my mind as also that I desire they may
settle at least in great part in America where I
leave them so good an Interest to be for their
Inheritance from generation to generation wch y^e
Lord preserve and prosper Amen.

      3 Nov^{ris} 1718°   Wm Penn   [L.S.]

Appeared personally Simon Clements of the Parish of St Margaret Westminster in the County of
Middl^x Esq^{r103} and John Page of George Yard in
Parish of St Edmund the King London Gent. and
being severally sworn upon the holy Evangelists
to depose the truth did depose and say as followeth Viz^t; That they knew and were well acquainted with William Penn late of Ruscombe in
the County of Berks Esqr deceased for many years
before his death and in that time have very often seen him write and subscribe his name to
Writeings and thereby became well acquainted
with his manner and character of handwriting and
having now viewed and diligently perused the
codicil wrote at the end of his Will or republi-
cation of his Will hereunto annexed beginning
thus Postscript in my own hand as a farther Testimony of my Love to my Dr Wife &c. and ending
thus, where I leave them so good an Interest to
be for their Inheritance from Generation to Generation wch ye Lord preserve and prosper Amen,
and thus subscribed Wm Penn, do verily believe
the same to be all wrote and subscribed by and
with the proper hand of the said William Penn
deceased.

            S. Clement   John Page
    Die p^{r}d.---dicti Simon Clements et Johannes
Page Jurat. de veritate p^{r}missorum coram me.

W. Phipps Sur.

Probatum fuit hujusmodi Testamentum apud London cum codicillo annexo coram venerabili viro
Gulielmo Phipps Legum Doctore Surrogato Venera-
bilis et egregii viri Johannis Bettesworth Legum
etiam Doctoris curia praerogativa Cantuar. Magis-
tri Custodis sive Comissarii legitime constituti
Quarto die mensis Novembris Anno Domini Millesi-
mo Septingenmo decimo octavo Per Affirmaconem
sive Declaraconem solennem Hannae Penn viduae
Relictae dicti defuncti et Executricis unicae
in dicto Testam^{to} nominatae cui commissa fuit
Administratio omnium et singulorum bonorum jurium
et creditorum dicti de functi Declaracone prae-
dicta in praesentia Dei Omnipotentis juxta actum
Parliamenti in hac parte editum provisum de bene
et fideliter administrando eadem per dictam Exe-
cutricem prius facta, etc.

Decimo sexto die mensis ffebruarii Anno Dni
1726 em^t como Johanni Penn Arm° filio et adstra-
tori cum Testo annexo bonor etc Hannae Penn Viduae deftae dum vixit Relictae extricis unicae
et Legatoriae Residuariae nominatae in Testo dicti Gulielmi Penn defti hen ad adstrandum bona
jura et credita dicti defti juxta tenorem et ef-
fectum Testi Ipsius defti per dictam Extricem
modo etiam demortuam inadstrata de bene etc.
Jurat.[104]

There remains to be given in this sketch an abstract of the will of Hannah Penn, dated 11 Sept.
1718, probated 16 Feb. 1726 by son John Penn (PCC
49 Farrant)[105] She calls herself late of the Parish
of St. Botolph, Aldersgate, widow, Relict of William
Penn, late of Ruscombe in Co. Berks, Esq., and refers
to her husband's will dated 27 May 1712. The lands
in America are to be divided into six parts of which
three go to the eldest son John Penn, he to pay his
sister Margaret £2000 at marriage or age 21; one
part to son Thomas; one part to son Richard; one
part to son Dennis, the survivors to share equally
the share of any dying. Witnesses: Susanna Perrin,
Mary Chandler, Hannah Hoskin, Thomas Grove, S. Clement.

Before listing the children, I should like to remark that as the result of considerable study of the
life and career of William Penn the Founder, I have
reached the firm conclusion that he was the greatest

single man who participated in the settlement of any
of the colonies of North America.

Issue:[106]

by Gulielma Maria Postuma Springett

i.   Gulielma Maria, b. Rickmansworth, Herts.,
      23 11th mo. 1672/3, d. there 17 1st mo.
      1672/3, bur. at Jordans.[107]

ii.   William, twin, b. Rickmansworth, Herts.,
      28 12th mo. 1673/4, d. there, 13 3rd mo.
      1674, bur. Jordans.[108]

iii. Mary or Margaret or Mary Margaret, twin,
      b. Rickmansworth, 28 12th mo. 1673/4, d.
      there, 24 12th mo. 1674/5, bur. Jordans.

iv.   Springett, b. Walthamstow, Essex, 25 11th
      1675/6, d. unm. at Lewes, Sussex, in his
      father's arms, 9-10 A.M., 10 2nd mo. 1696,
      bur. Jordans.[109] Until his death he was
      heir apparent of his father.

14 v. Letitia, b. Warminghurst, Sussex, 6 1st mo.
      1678/9, d.s.p. 6 2nd mo. 1746, bur. Jor-
      dans.

15 vi. William, b. Warminghurst, 14 1st mo. 1680/1,
      d. 23 June 1720.

vii. Daughter, perhaps named Hannah, b. Warming-
      hurst, Sussex, shortly before 13 1st mo.
      1683, d. aged ca. 3 weeks, while her fa-
      ther was in America, bur. at the Blue
      Idol, once an inn, then a meeting house,
      still in part standing, near Thakenham.
      The child was discovered by Dr. Cadbury.[110]
      The birth had occurred before 20-26 March
      when Bridget Ford, George Fox and James
      and Helena Claypoole had visited Guli at
      Warminghurst. Claypoole wrote 13 1st mo.
      1682/3 to Benjamin Furly in Holland: "Gu-
      li Penn is safe delivered of a daughter."
      Guli herself to Margaret Fox, Aug. 1683:
      the child died aged three weeks (both of
      the letters cited by Cadbury and Peare,
      p. 268). The only uncertainty is as to
      the name. The burial was not at Jordans,
      possibly because Guli was herself not
      well enough for the journey.

viii. Gulielma Maria, b. Warminghurst, 17 9th mo.
      1685, d. Hammersmith, Middlesex, 20 9th
      mo. 1689.

by Hannah Callowhill

ix. ?Child, name and sex unknown, and there is a possibility that there was a miscarriage and no child was born. Dr.Cadbury cites a letter of John Tomkins to Sir John Rodes of Barlborough, co. Derby, 26 Sept. 1696, who says: "I understand she [Hannah (Callowhill) Penn] is toward a litell one."

16 x. John, "the American," b. Philadelphia 28 or 29 11th mo. 1699/1700, d. unm. 25 Oct. 1746, bur. Jordans, 5 9th mo. 1746. The earlier birthdate appears in Hinshaw[111] and the discrepancy may be resolved if the birth occurred at night and there was doubt as to whether it was before or after midnight.

17 xi. Thomas, b. at house of Thomas Callowhill, Bristol, 9 1st mo. 1701/2, d. London 21 March 1775.

xii. Hannah Margarita, b. at house of Thomas Callowhill, Bristol, 30 5th mo. 1703[112], d. Bristol, 5 12th mo., bur. 10 12th mo. 1707/8[113].

18 xiii. Margaret, b. at house of Thomas Callowhill, Bristol, 7 9th mo. 1704, bur. Jordans, 12 Feb. 1750/51.

·19 xiv. Richard, b. 17 11th mo. 1705/6 at Thomas Callowhill's house in Bristol, d. 4 Feb. 1771.

xv. Dennis, b. Ealing near London, 26 12th mo. 1706/7[114], d. 6 11th mo. 1722/3, bur. Jordans, 8 11th mo. 1722/3 (Rebecca Butterfield's journal).

xvi. Hannah, b. 5 7th mo. 1708, Parish of Ludgate, London, d. Kensington, co. Middlesex, 24 11th mo. 1708/9, bur. at Tring, Herts.

12. RICHARD PENN, younger son of Admiral Sir William Penn (Gil , ;, William, William, John) by his wife Margaret Jasper, was born, according to Mrs Roach, ca. 164ᴜ, a date probably too early as he was called a minor in the will of his father dated 20 Jan. 1669/70. He died in April 1673, buried at Walthamstow, 9 April 1673. His will is dated 4 April 1673, probated 11 April 1673 (PCC 49 Pye)[115], and after the death of his mother, administration was

granted to William Penn, March 1681 (Admon. Act Book
1682, fol. 31). The will calls him younger son of
Sir William Penn, late of Wansteed in the County of
Essex, knight, deceased; to dear mother Dame Margaret Penn £40 yearly for life; to dear sister Margaret Lowther, wife of Anthony Lowther, Esq., £50
to buy a ring or any durable thing, to wear and keep
in remembrance; to said brother Anthony Lowther £30
(for the said purpose), also such two of my guns and
one pair of pistols as dear brother William Penn
shall appoint; to the poor of Walthamstow in Essex,
where I desire to be buried, £10; my will is that
my mother, my brother Anthony and sister Margaret
Lowther aforesaid, and her children; my said servant
George and the coachmen and footmen of my said mother
and brother and sister Lowther, and also their
coaches, shall have mo[u]rning in such manner as my
dear mother shall appoint; also unto loving sister
Gulielma Maria Penn £50 in testimony of my love and
affection unto her; dear mother sole executrix; witnesses: Richard Newman, George Haman, Michael Lee.
Pepys (14 Feb. 1665) notes that Dick Pen comes to be
MrsPepys' valentine, and was admitted to the bedchamber in which Pepys and wife were in the bed, and
Pepys tried to kiss him, "a notable, stout, witty
boy." Young Richard had been in Italy in the period
between his father's death and his own.[116]

13. MARGARET PENN, only daughter of Admiral Sir
William Penn (Giles, William, William, John) and his
wife Margaret Jasper, was born probably ca. 1651,
as she was aged 15 on 12 Feb. 1666/7, died 15 Dec.
1718 aged 73. Mrs.Roach makes her older than Richard
and puts the birth ca. 1645.[117] This approximate
date was probably reached from the age 73 at death,
but it seems more probable that the age given in the
marriage license is correct, since it would have been
of advantage in applying for the license to make the
bride older than fifteen, if she was. Death records
are notoriously likely to be faulty, especially as
to age of deceased. She was buried in Walthamstow
where the death date, as reported by Mr.Dallett, is
15 Dec. 1719.[118] It is certain, however, that she
died in 1718, since Hannah Penn reported that Margaret died of a lingering feaver about five months
after her brother.[119]
She was licensed to marry when aged 15 on 12 Feb.
1666/7, by the Archbishop of Canterbury, at either
St. Olave's, Hart Street, London, or Clapham, co.

Surrey, and she did marry at Clapham, where the Admiral then had a house, on 14 Feb. 1666/7, ANTHONY
LOWTHER of Mask or Marske in Yorkshire, then aged
24, born 1643, died 27 Jan. 1692 aged 52. Age at
marriage gives 1643 for his birth, age at death,
1640. He was the son of Robert Lowther of Maske,
and the monumental inscription at Walthamstow says
he was descended from the Lowthers of Lowther Hall,
co. Westmoreland, "baronets." There were, of course,
no baronets before the early reign of James I. In
the sketch of the 7th Earl of Lonsdale in *Burke's
Peerage, Baronetage and Knightage*, 104th edition
(1967), p. 1551, it is stated that Robert Lowther,
buried 9 Jan. 1655, was 7th son of Sir Christopher
Lowther, born 8 Sept. 1557, died 1617, by his second
wife Eleanor Musgrave, and Robert was alderman of
London. Robert married twice, first, Margaret, the
daughter of Thomas Cutler of Stainborough, co. York,
and second, Elizabeth, daughter of William Holcroft
of Co. Lancaster. While it is not clearly stated
which wife was mother to Anthony, onomastic considerations suggest the first.

Anthony Lowther was M.P. for Appleby in 1678-9.
Pepys called Mrs. Lowther, "Pegg, a very plain girl"
(28 July 1661); she painted pictures inferior to
those of Mrs. Pepys who enjoyed the same teacher (7
Aug. 1665, 3 Sept. 1665); at her wedding there were
no friends but 2 or 3 relations of his and hers;
they borrowed many things from Pepys' kitchen for
their dinner; the wedding was private owing "to its
being just before Lent, that they might see the
fashions as they are like to be this summer; which
is reason good enough. Mrs. Turner tells me that she
hears Sir W. Pen gives £4,500 or £4,000" (15 Feb.
1667). After two allusions to Mrs. Lowther's pride
in having her train held up (28 June, 14 July 1667),
we have this: "Mrs. Lowther is grown, either through
pride or want of manners, a fool, having not a word
to say; and, as further mark of a beggarly, proud
fool, hath a bracelet of diamonds and rubies about
her wrist, and a six-penny necklace about her neck,
and not one good rag of clothes upon her back (11
Sept. 1667), and the last shot: "ugly as she is"
(22 Feb. 1667). Rather a harsh judgment on a young
woman of fifteen.

    Issue: surname Lowther
20 i.   Margaret, b. 8 Feb. 1667/8, d. shortly be-
          fore 9 3rd mo. 1720.

ii.   William, d. ca. 1669 aged 6 mos., bur. at
        Walthamstow.
iii.   Elizabeth, b. ca. July 1670, probably d.
        by 1681. John Gay wrote William Penn a
        letter intercepted by the authorities and
        never delivered, dated 23 July 1670,[120]
        in which he reported that on the preced-
        ing first day, Lady Penn had told Gay
        that Penn's sister had been delivered of
        a girl a fortnight since.
iv.   Robert, b. ca. 1672, d. ca. 1693 in 22nd
        year, "A Gentleman of great hopes and
        learning," as the tombstone at Walthamstow
        states.
21 v.   William, b. ca. 1670-1674, d. April 1705,
        a baronet.
vi.   Ann Charlotte, b. ca. 1676, d. after 1681
        but in childhood; participated in a land-
        grant from William Penn in 1681.
vii.   Anthony, b. ca. 1678, d. age 1/8, bur. at
        Walthamstow.
viii.   John, b. ca. 1680, m. by 1720 Mary -----;
        then had a daughter, and was living in
        1731.[121]
ix.   Anthony, b. ca. 1682, d. ca. 1720 aged 20,
        bur. Walthamstow.

   14. LETITIA PENN, fifth child and third daughter
of William Penn (William, Giles, William, William,
John) by his first wife Gulielma Maria Postuma
Springett, was born at Warminghurst, Sussex, 6 1st
mo. 1678/9, died without issue 6 2nd mo. 1746, and
was buried at Jordans. She married at Horsham, Sussex, 20 6th mo. 1702, as second wife, WILLIAM AUBREY
or AWBREY of London,[122] who died ca. 21 3rd mo. 1731,
buried 23 3rd mo. 1731 at Jordans. Her will was
dated at Christ Church, Spitalfields, London, 20 July 1744, calls her widow, and mentions nephew William Penn; grandnieces Mary Margaretta Fell, Gulielma Maria Frances Fell; grandnephew Robert Fell; bequest to nephew William Penn for life, then to his
daughter Christiana Gulielma Penn of all property in
America. Letitia accompanied her father and stepmother to America in 1699 but was, like her stepmother, unwilling to stay there. Her husband was a
difficult problem for William Penn, demanding money
constantly, at times lending money to his father-in-
law and then pressing for its return. This William

was son of another William, of Llanelieu, Brecknock-
shire, Wales, by his wife and cousin Elizabeth Awbrey. In a letter dated 29 2nd mo. 1695, Rees Thomas,
who had married William Awbrey's sister, commented
on the recent death of "our brother William his wife,"
i.e. the first wife, name unknown to us.

15. WILLIAM PENN, often called Jr., eldest surviving son of William Penn (William, Giles, William,
William, John) by his first wife Gulielma Maria Postuma Springett, was born at Warminghurst, co. Sussex,
14 1st mo. 1680/1. He died of consumption in the
north of France or at Liege, present Belgium, on 23
June 1720, without probate. He did not accompany
his father to America in 1699 but was there, without his wife, in 1704. A Philadelphia Court record
dated 1 7th mo. 1704[123] is a presentment by the
grand jury for assault on James Wood, constable,
James Dough, watch, at the inn of Enoch Story, made
against William Penn jun., gent., John Finney, sheriff, Thomas Grey, scrivener, and Joseph Ralph, gent.
His father's letter to James Logan dated 16 11th
mo. 1704[124] calls this son "my greatest affliction
for my soul's and my posterity's sake."[125]

When William was not quite eighteen, he married,
12 11th mo. 1698/9, a girl of twenty-three, MARY
JONES, born 11 11th mo. 1676/7, died 10th mo. 1733,
buried 5 10th mo. 1733, daughter of Charles Jones
Jr. by his first wife Martha Wathers, the family
home of the Jones family being Bristol. The very
long will of John Jones of the City of Bristol,
linen-draper, dated 13 Aug. 1699, probated 4 Aug.
1702 (PCC 136 Herne)[126] shows that the said John
was the son of Charles Jones Sr. and his wife Ann,
and was thus uncle to the Mary Jones, here called
"cousin Mary, wife of William Penn," to whom he
leaves £100.

Issue: surname Penn

22 i. Gulielma Maria, b. 10 9th mo. 1699, d. 17
11th mo. 1739/40.

ii. Springett, b. 10 12th mo. 1700/1, at Warminghurst; d.s.p., unm., Dublin, 8 Feb.
1731 or 30 Dec. 1730 (Breviate).

23 iii. William, b. Warminghurst, 21 1st mo. 1702/3,
d. 6 12th mo. 1746/7.

16. JOHN PENN, "the American," ninth child of
William Penn (William, Giles, William, William, John)

and firstborn of the second wife Hannah Callowhill,
was born in Philadelphia, 28 or 29 Jan. 1699/1700,
the only Penn child of his generation born in America, hence the epithet by which he is known. He
died unmarried at Hitcham, co. Bucks, 25 Oct. 1746,
buried at Jordans, 5 9th mo. 1746. An obituary appeared in the *Oxford Flying Weekly Journal* for 1
Nov. 1746. On 17 Aug. 1715 he was apprenticed to
Brice Webb, linnen-draper, and Phebe his wife,[127]
this Brice Webb having been associated with his
grandfather Thomas Callowhill. He received as his
inheritance in his mother's will one-half of the
Proprietary grant. He came to Pennsylvania in September 1734, landing at Chester, together with his
his sister Margaret and her son Thomas Freame, but
returned to England in September 1735. On 24 Oct.
1746 he made his will, probated 13 Nov. 1746 (PCC
332 Edmunds).[127] He names as trustees William Vigor
of London, merchant, Joseph Freame citizen and banker of London,[128] and Lascelles Metcalf of Westminster, Esq. He leaves an annuity to sister Margaret
Freame; £100 to servant John Travers; 100 guineas
to each executor; old servants Thomas Penn[129] and
Hannah Roberts, Jane Aldridge, wife of Henry Aldridge of White Waltham, Berks; to nephew John Penn
provision for his education and testator's share of
manor of Perkasie; other nephews and nieces: Hannah
Penn, Richard Penn, Philadelphia Hannah Freame; brother Thomas Penn; late grandfather Thomas Callowhill;
brother Richard Penn to have properties in New Jersey; to brother Thomas Penn the half share of Pennsylvania for life and remainder to his sons in order of seniority,[130] then to brother Richard Penn
and his sons John and Richard; niece Hannah Penn,
only daughter of brother Richard Penn; sister Margaret Freame and niece Philadelphia Hannah Freame;
nephew of half blood, William Penn of Cork in Kingdom of Ireland, Esq.; his son Springett Penn; his
only daughter Christiana Gulielma Penn; grand nephew of the half blood, Robert Edward Fell, only
living son of Gulielma Maria Fell dec.; grand niece
Mary Margaretta Fell, eldest daughter of said Gulielma Maria Fell; grand niece Gulielma Maria Frances
Fell, only other daughter of Gulielma Maria Fell.
Brother Thomas was to serve as executor for America.
Of course, most of the persons named in the latter
part of the will inherited nothing, as Thomas Penn's
issue, as yet unborn, did not die out.

17. THOMAS PENN, tenth child of William Penn
(William, Giles, William, William, John) and the
second by the second wife Hannah Callowhill, was
born in Bristol at the house of his maternal grandfather, Thomas Callowhill, on 9 1st mo. 1701/2, and
died in London, 21 March 1775, buried at Stoke Poges,
having had a stroke of palsy in 1771. In 1716 Thomas was apprenticed to a London tradesman, Michael
Russell, mercer, in White Hart Court, Gracechurch
Street, and rapidly learned business methods, being
undoubtedly the ablest administrator of all the family of Penn, having gained at least some of these
qualities from his mother. [131]

At first he inherited a fourth of the Proprietary
grant but on the death of his brother John in 1746,
he acquired his half right, making in all three quarters, which he held from 1746 to his death in 1775,
his younger brother Richard having held the remaining fourth until he died in 1771. He spent some
nine years in America, arriving at Chester, 11 Aug.
1732, and departing in October 1741 from Boston for
England, still unmarried, accompanied by his sister
and nephew. Among the records of his American years
is one anecdote of considerable interest. The Rev.
Hugh David, not the man of this name who had come
to America in 1699 with William Penn, as he had died
in 1709, thought it proper to greet Thomas Penn with
complimentary words, but Thomas received him coldly,
and Hugh could afterwards report that Thomas had made
only three remarks: "How dost thou do?" "Farewell!"
and "The other door!"

In his fiftieth year Thomas Penn of St. Martin's
in the Fields, Esq., married, by special license, at
the fashionable church of St. George's, Hanover
Square, 22 Aug. 1751, Lady JULIANA FERMOR, of St.
James's, Westminster, born 1729, died at Ham, Surrey,
20 Nov. 1801, [132] fourth daughter of Thomas, 1st Earl
of Pomfret (created by George I, 1721) by his wife
Henrietta Louisa, daughter of John, Lord Jeffreys. [133]

Thomas Penn's will dated 18 Nov. 1771, probated
8 April 1775 (PCC 166 Alexander) [134] calls him of
Stokehouse in Co. Bucks, Esq. Executors are to be
Lady Juliana Penn and son-in-law William Baker of
Bayford Bury, Herts, Esq. Allusion is made to indenture tripartite dated 15 Aug. 1751, that is, an
ante-nuptial agreement. Trustees for holding Pennsylvania are named: James Hamilton, Esq., the Rev.
Richard Peters, Richard Hockley Esq., all of Penn-

sylvania.[135]   £20 annuity is to go to Mr. Duffield
Williams of Swansea, Glamorganshire [probably a relative of Thomas Callowhill in whose will persons
with the name Duffield appear].   Sons John and Granville Penn; daughters Sophia and Juliana. Agreements
had been made with his late brother [probably Richard
is meant as John died in 1746] on 8 May 1732, 31 Jan.
1750, 20 March 1750. Nephew Richard Penn, then the
lieutenant-governor of Pennsylvania, and Richard
Hockley are named executors for Pennsylvania. A codicil dated 11 July 1772 mentions that he has now made
advances to Juliana on the occasion of her marriage;
another on 18 July 1772 gives a £20 annuity to M[rs]
Harriot Gordon of Silver St., Golden Square; a third
on 23 June 1774 leaves £10 a year to Grace Armagh
and Mary Clarke.

A Reuters dispatch from London was printed in the
Des Moines Tribune of 14 June 1968 and reports that
the Vicar of Penn, Co. Bucks, has lately discovered
and opened the Penn vault in Penn Church. Correspondence has been had with the Vicar, the Rev. Oscar
Muspratt, but did not produce more details than were
printed in the newspaper. Such information as was
learned, however, has been included below.

Issue: surname Penn
i.   William, b. 21 June 1752, d. 14 Feb. 1753,
          age 7 mos. on the coffin, bur. at Penn,
          co. Bucks.
ii.   Juliana, b. 19 May 1753, d. 23 April 1772,
          bur. Stoke Poges; m. 23 May 1771 William
          Baker Esq, of Bayfordbury, Herts, an exe-
          cutor of his father-in-law.
          Issue: surname Baker
       1. Juliana, b. ca. 1772, d.s.p. 11 Sept.
          1849 at Gunters Grove, Stoke Courcy,
          Somersetshire; m. 18 Jan. 1803 John
          Fawsett Herbert Rawlins Esq.
iii.   Thomas, b. 17 July 1754, d. 5 Sept. 1757
          as Jenkins and Mrs.Roach have it or 6
          12th mo. 1759 as Lea gives it.[136] Age on
          coffin is 2 years.
iv.   William, twin, b. 22 July 1756, d. 24 April
          1760, bur. at Penn, co. Bucks. Age on the
          coffin is 5 years.
v.   Louisa Hannah, twin, b. 22 July 1756, d.
          10 June 1766, bur. at Penn, co. Bucks.
          Age on coffin is 9 years.
vi.   John, the Younger, b. London, 23 Feb. 1760,

bapt. 21 March 1760, St. Martin's in the
Fields; d. unm., Stoke Park, 21 June 1834;
M.A. (Cantab.) 1779; LL.D. (Cantab.),1811;
came to Philadelphia in 1783; auction of
his plate and furniture was held 21 May
1788 at Market and Sixth Streets, Philadelphia.[137] He was sheriff of co. Bucks
[England] 1798, M.P. in 1802, Governor
of the Island of Portland, 1805.[138]

24 vii.   Granville, b. New Street, Spring Gardens,
London, 9 Dec. 1761, d. Stoke, 28 Sept.
1844.

25 viii. Sophia Margaretta, b. 25 Dec. 1764, d. 29
April 1847, bur. Luton, Beds. Of all of
Thomas Penn's children, only she has de-
scendants living 1969.

   ix.   Probably stillborn child, name and date unknown, evidence from the Penn vault.

18. MARGARET PENN, thirteenth child of William
Penn (William, Giles, William, William, John) and
fourth by his second wife Hannah Callowhill, was
born at the house of her maternal grandfather, Thomas Callowhill, in James Parish, Bristol, 7 9th mo.
1704, and was buried at Jordans, 12 Feb. 1750/51.
She married between 5 July 1727[139] and 25 Oct. of
the same year[140]--Mrs. Roach says the date was 6 5th
mo. 1727--THOMAS FREAME, citizen and grocer of London, who died in March 1741, of fever, at Boccha
Chica, son of Robert Freame of London, grocer, by
his wife Ann[141] Vice. Thomas Freame came to America,
probably with Thomas Penn, in 1732, and his wife
and son joined him in 1734. Thomas turned soldier
during the War of Jenkin's Ear, was captain in Colonel Gooch's regiment, was stationed at Chester in
July 1740. "Thomas Freame, at present residing in
the City of Philadelphia in the Province of Pennsylvania, Captain of a company of Foot in the Honorable
William Gooch's Regiment of Foot, being ready to embark on a ship on an expedition against the enemies
of our sovereign Lord King George II."[142] In a
letter of Richd Hockley to Mr Jno Wragg, dated at
Philadelphia, 15 June 1741[143]: ". . . we have no
certain account as yet of the town of Carthagene
being in the Possession of our Troopes though we
daily Expect it, poor Captain Freame (Mrs Freames
Husband) after being at the Siege of all the Forti-
fications and in particular at Boccha Chico Castle,

and behaving himself gallantly so as to be excused
by Gen[1] Wentworth from any more Duty on this Attack
a few days after was seiz'd with a fever of which
he dyed in twenty four hours to the great Grief of
those nearly related to him as you may imagine,
since your Departure M[rs] Freame was delivered of a
fine Girl who is likely to live."

Freame's will was executed 22 Sept. 1740, probated 4 Sept. 1744 (PCC 214 Anstis), by Thomas Penn
Esq., and names wife Margaretta and her child; Hon.
Thomas Penn Esq. and one of the Proprietors and
Governor-in-Chief of said Province and Richard
Hockley of said city, merchant, executors. One
fifth to child wife now goeth with at 21; four
fifths to wife Margaretta and son Thomas; witnesses:
Willm Shaw, Wm Harper, Stephen Staples; at Philadelphia 10 July 1741, William Harper deposed as to
the sanity of testator.[144]

Issue: surname Freame

i.   Thomas, b. ca. 1730; to America with mother
       in 1734, returned to England 1741; bur.
       Jordans 2 6th mo. 1746.

ii.   Philadelphia Hannah, b. Philadelphia, 1740,
       not 1746 [see Jenkins' correction of his
       former error, p. x], d.s.p.s. at Stan-
       hope Street, Mayfair, London, 14 April
       1826 (so Jenkins) or 1825 (so Roach); m.
       8 May 1770, as 2nd wife, Thomas Dawson,
       b. 25 Feb. 1725, d.s.p. 1 March 1813,
       who in 1770 became Baron Dartrey and in
       1785 Viscount Cremorne, both Irish peer-
       ages, later of Castle Dawson, co. Monagh-
       an. When he died, the viscountcy expired
       but the barony of Cremorne was continued
       by a great nephew, Richard Dawson, whose
       son was created Earl of Dartrey in 1866,
       but they were not, of course, Penn de-
       scendants. Philadelphia Hannah was bur-
       ied in Stoke Poges Churchyard, and her
       funeral was attended by the Royal Prin-
       cesses; she had been a friend of Queen
       Charlotte. The will of the Rt. Hon.
       Philadelphia Hannah, Viscountess Cremorne,
       was probated in June 1826 (PCC 317 Swabey).
       On the Cremornes see Thomas Faulkner, *An
       Historical and Topographical Description
       of Chelsea and Its Environs* (Chelsea
       1829), 1:65-72.

Issue: surname Dawson
1. Thomas, d. 9 Oct. 1787.
2. Juliana Frances Anne, d. 8 June 1789.

19. RICHARD PENN, fourteenth child of William
Penn (William, Giles, William, William, John) and
fifth child of the second wife Hannah Callowhill,
was born at Bristol on 17 11th mo. 1705/6 and died
4 Feb. 1771, buried in Stoke Church.[145] He was the
only son of the Founder who reached manhood and yet
never came to Pennsylvania. When of the Parish of
St. Dionis Backchurch, he married by license of the
Vicar General, allegation bond dated 26 Oct. 1728,
HANNAH LARDNER of Woodford, Essex, above nineteen,
spinster, with the consent of her sister Frances
Lardner, the parents being both dead. Hannah herself signed the allegation and asked to be married
in St. Saviour's, Southwark, co. Surrey. She had
been born ca. 1709, and died at Laleham, Middlesex,
20 April 1785, daughter of Dr. John Lardner, physi-
cian of Gracechurch Street, London, and of Woodford,
Epping Forest, Sussex, by his wife who had been a
Winstanley. Hannah Lardner had a brother Lynford
Lardner,[146] who came to Pennsylvania in 1740, served
in the Proprietary Land Office, was Receiver-General,
Keeper of the Great Seal of Pennsylvania, and died
in 1774. A Robert Lardner who married at Christ
Church, Philadelphia, 1 Oct. 1748, Elizabeth Piles,
may have been another brother.
   The principal residence of Richard Penn was at
Stanwell, Middlesex, but he also owned Batavia House
in the Parish of Sunbury, co. Middlesex, and had a
house in Cavendish Square, London. He made a very
informative will on 21 March 1750, with codicils on
15 Jan. 1756, 13 March 1760, another in 1763, 13
July 1768, which was probated 4 March 1771,[147] and
named as executors William Vigor of Taplow, Bucks,
Esq., and Joseph Freame of London, banker [who had
been similarly named in 1746 by his brother John],
but they both had died and the wife Hannah was appointed in their place. For America the executors
were Lynford Lardner,[148] Richard Peters and Richard
Hackley [sic]. In the will Richard Penn names his
wife and his eldest son John, daughter Hannah Penn,
sons Richard and William, but the codicil dated 13
March 1760 says that William has lately died. Hannah Lardner's obituary appeared in *The Gentleman's
Magazine*, vol. 55, pt. 1, p. 326.

Issue: surname Penn
26 i.   John, the Elder, b. 14 July 1729, d. 9 Feb.
          1795.
   ii.   Hannah, b. ca. 1731, first mentioned in
          1732 or 1733; d.s.p. testate, Cavendish
          Square, London, bur. Stoke Poges, 2 Oct.
          1791; will probated 2i Oct. 1791, leaves
          all to brothers John and Richard and the
          latter's children; m. 19 July 1774, James
          Clayton, late of Sunbury, Middlesex, bur.
          Stoke Poges, 23 Jan. 1790.
27 iii.   Richard, b. 1735, d. 27 May 1811 in 76th
          year.
   iv.   William, b. shortly before 3 July 1747, d.
          4 Feb. 1760, bur. in Penn Church, co.
          Bucks. His father's codicil dated 13 July
          1768: his remains were to be removed to
          a vault in Stoke Church, but the coffin
          was in 1968 still in the Penn Church and
          the age of 12 was indicated.

20. MARGARET LOWTHER, eldest child of Margaret
Penn (William, Giles, William, William, John) by her
husband Anthony Lowther, was born 8 Feb. 1667/8, the
date supplied by Pepys and the name by the will of
her grandfather, Admiral Sir William Penn. Mrs Pepys
attended the christening (21 Feb. 1667/8): "It hath
made a flutter and noise, but was as mean as could
be, and but little company, just like all the rest
that family do." Margaret died before 9 3rd mo.
1720, on which date Hannah (Callowhill) Penn wrote
to Rebecca Blackfan in Pennsylvania a letter in
which she said that her "poor Niece Poole is also
dead since Deceas'd, of an uncommon Ayling & pain in
her Head, scarce understood by any, but as was sup-
pos'd proceeded from a Bruise on an overturn in a
Coach some months before: She has left one only
Daughter . . ."[149] She had married BENJAMIN POOLE,
Esq., who is said in J. Burke and J. B. Burke, *Extinct, Dormant Baronetcies* (London 1841), p. 411,
to have died in January 1656, an impossible date,
son of James Poole, Esq., of Poole, Cheshire, by his
wife Mary Mostyn.[150]

Issue: surname Poole
i.   Margaret, m. (1) John Keck, (2) John Nichol
       Esq. of Minchenden House, Southgate, Mid-
       dlesex.
           Issue by second husband Nichol:

1. Margaret, b. ca. 1736, d.s.p. at South-
gate, 14, bur. as Marchioness of Carnarvon, 29 Aug. 1768 at Whitchurch in
her 34th year. Administration on her
estate was granted 8 Sept. 1768 (PCC).
She had, "with £150,000," m. 22 March
1753, at St. George's, Hanover Square,
London, James Brydges, b. 16 Dec. 1731,
3rd Duke of Chandos and Marquess of
Carnarvon, Earl of Carnarvon and Visct
Milton, Baron Chandos of Sudeley, *de
jure* Lord Kinloss and a baronet, d.
at Tunbridge Wells, Kent, 29 Sept.
1789, bur. 10 Oct. 1789 at Whitchurch,
co. Middlesex. He had m. (2) 21 June
1777, Anne Eliza, daughter of Richard
Grace Gamon and widow of Roger Hope
Elletson, by whom he had an only daughter who succeeded him.[151] The dukedom
of Chandos has been extinct since 1889.

21. Sir WILLIAM LOWTHER, fifth child of Margaret
Penn (William, Giles, William, William, John) by her
husband Anthony Lowther, was born between 1670 and
1674, died in April 1705. On 15 June 1697 he was
created baronet of Mask or Marske. He was M.P. for
Lancaster 1702-1705, and married CATHERINE PRESTON,
daughter and heiress of Thomas Preston of Holker,
Lancashire.

Issue: surname Lowther
i.   Sir Thomas, 2nd Baronet, of Mask or Marske
        and Holker, Lancashire, M.P. for Lanca-
        shire 1722-1745, d. 23 March 1745; m. 2
        July 1723 Lady Elizabeth (d. 7 Nov. 1747),
        daughter of William, 2nd Duke of Devon-
        shire. This marriage is shown in the
        104th edition (1967) of *Burke's Peerage,
        Baronetage and Knightage* (p. 1551 under
        Lonsdale) but not under Devonshire (p.
        749) where it is said that the 2nd son of
        the 3rd Duke of Devonshire inherited Hol-
        ker from his cousin, Sir William Lowther,
        3rd and last baronet of Marske.
        Only issue: surname Lowther
        1.Sir William, 3rd and last baronet, b. 1727,
           d. unm. 3 Feb. 1753.
ii.   Catherine.
iii.   Margaret.

22. GULIELMA MARIA PENN, eldest child of William
Penn, Jr. (William, William, Giles, William, William,
John) by his wife Mary Jones, was born at Warminghurst on 10 9th mo. 1699, and so was older than all
the half-brothers and half-sisters of her father.
She died 17 11th mo. 1739/40, buried at St. Margaret's, Westminster, and married, first, at St. Mary
Magdalen, Old Fish Street, London, 14 Feb. 1720,
AWBREY THOMAS, born in Pennsylvania, 30 11th mo.
1694, died in England by 1724, second son of Rees
and Martha (Awbrey) Thomas who had married at Haverford, Pa., 18 4th mo. 1692, the said Martha being
sister to the William Awbrey who married Letitia
Penn.[152] The marriage record in Old Fish Street
strangely calls the bride "William Mary," as if the
clerk wished to display erudition. Gulielma Maria
(Penn) Thomas married, second, CHARLES FELL, who
died at Windsor, 1 Oct. 1748, son of Charles Fell
and grandson of Judge Thomas Fell of Swarthmore
Hall whose wife was Margaret Askew, later wife of
George Fox.[153] Administration was granted on the
estate of Charles Fell, late of St. Margaret, Westminster, widower, 17 Oct. 1748 (PCC), to his natural
and lawful son Robert Edward Fell.

Issue: *by first husband Thomas*
i.   William Penn, d. unm., intestate, ca. 1742.
        by second husband Fell
ii.   Mary Margaretta, bapt. 23 Aug. 1724, d. by
        1769; m. John Barron of Leeds, in 1774
        of Philadelphia, who may have d. intes-
        tate, Philadelphia, 3 Nov. 1794, bur. at
        St. Peter's Episcopal Church, recorded
        at Christ Church.
iii.   Gulielma Maria Frances, bapt. 10 Aug. 1725;
        m. by 26 May 1750 John Newcomb of Leir,
        co. Gloucester, who was dead by March
        1769 when she was living in Shrewsbury,
        co. Salop.
        Issue: surname Newcomb
        1. Gulielma Maria, probably living 1760 at
           Hackney.
        2. Susanna Margaretta, m. Richard Crompton,
           gent.
        3. Philadelphia, m. Thomas Brookholding of
           the City of Worcester; mentioned in
           her uncle Robert's will 1787. No
           proof has been found that she left no

surviving issue.
4. John Springett.
5. William Hawkins.
iv. Robert Edward, bapt. 29 Nov. 1726; d. testate, Bordentown, N.J., Nov. 1786; was
captain of marines, 1756; Lt. Col. R.A.,
of St. Martin in the Fields, 1770; last
appears in Army list for 1786, Lt. Col.,
79th Regt of Foot, original commission,
25 May 1772; will dated 24 March 1784,
calls him of Hamlet of Clitha, parish of
Lanarth, co. Monmouth, Esq., probated
22 Feb. 1787 (PCC 66 Major--see PGM 25:
125), and names nephew William Hawkins
Newcomb, £5000; niece Philadelphia Brookholding, wife of Thomas Brookholding;
sister Gulielma Maria Frances Newcomb;
niece Gulielma Maria Newcomb. Philadelphia Miscellaneous Book 1, p. 60, has
receipt by Robt Edwd Fell, 21 Nov. 1786,
recorded 28 Feb. 1787, £500 from Richard
Durdin Esq. for legacy from Ann Durdin
to Gulia Maria Frances Newcomb. The will
of John Penn (the Founder's son), 24 Oct.
1746, mentions Robert as the only son of
his mother then living. No record of
Robert's will has been found in New Jersey.

23. WILLIAM PENN, third child and younger son of
William Penn Jr. (William, William, Giles, William,
William, John) by his wife Mary Jones, was born at
Warminghurst, 21 1st mo. 1702/3, died at Shanagarry
or Shannagary, co. Cork, Ireland, of a dropsy, 6
12th mo. 1746/7. He had in 1730/1 inherited Shanagarry where he spent the remainder of his life.
When of Kingston Bowrey, co. Sussex, England, he
married at Wandsworth, Surrey, on 7 10th mo. 1732,
CHRISTIAN FORBES, born ca. 1715, died 1 9th mo. 1733
in childbed, daughter of Alexander Forbes, merchant,
by his wife Jane Barclay. Alexander Forbes, who
died 25 May 1740, was son of John Forbes of Aquhor-
thies near Aberdeen. Jane Barclay was the daughter
of Robert Barclay of Ury, author of the celebrated
Apology, born at Gordonstoun, Morayshire, 23 Dec.
1648, died at Ury, 3 Oct. 1690, son of David and
Catherine (Gordon) Barclay. He married in February
1670 Christian Mollison, daughter of Gilbert and

and Margaret Mollison, and Christian died 14 Dec.
1722, aged 75.[154] Col. David Barclay of Ury, father
of Robert, served under Gustavus Adolphus in the
Thirty Years War, and his wife Lady Catherine Gordon was the daughter of Sir Robert Gordon, 1st Baronet of Gordonstoune, born 14 May 1580, died March
1654, married 16 Feb. 1613 Louisa Gordon of Glenluce.
Sir Robert was the second son of the 12th Earl of
Sutherland and Sir Robert's second wife Jane was
daughter of the 4th Earl of Huntley and the divorced
wife of James Hepburn, Earl of Bothwell, husband of
Mary, Queen of Scots.[155]

William Penn of Withyan, Sussex, widower, married,
second, 7 Dec. 1736 at St. Paul's Cathedral, London,
by license, ceremony performed by W[m] Reyner, ANN
VAUX, born probably in London or co. Surrey, ca.
1710-1720, but not recorded in Friends records, the
daughter of Isaac Vaux, physician, who was born at
Reigate, co. Surrey, 10 8th mo. 1695, eighth and
youngest son of George and Lydia (Hitchcock) Vaux
of Reigate, and a prominent physician in St. Dionis
Backchurch, London, and brother of another physician,
George Vaux, who died in 1741.[156] This second wife
appears to have separated from her husband and went
to London, after which he charged her with desertion
and sued for divorce, which suit was pending on 12
Jan. 1742/3.   In his will dated 17 10th mo. 1743,
probated 15 March 1760, he says: "Whereas my present
wife, Ann Penn, otherwise Vaux, some years ago eloped
from me, and hath ever since continued without any
reasonable Cause to live separate from me . . .where-
by I am advised that she hath forfeited all Right
to Dower and Thirds out of my Real & Personal Estate," he leaves her one shilling.   That this marriage would end badly might have been predicted
from the opinion expressed in a letter of Margaret
(Penn) Freame to her brother John Penn, dated 18
April 1737,[157] in which she says: "Could I wonder
at his Conduct in anything I should that his Pride
would stoop so low."

For about twenty years Ann (Vaux) Penn remained
a widow, and then married, second, at Dublin, in
the latter part of February 1767, Alexander Durdin,
but died, of course without issue to this second
marriage, in Dublin, 13 April 1767, less than two
months after the wedding.

This Alexander Durdin was born in Co. Cork, in
1712, died in Dublin, 20 Sept. 1807, aged 95, buried

at Carrigtwohill, Ireland, son of John Durdin (Michael) by his wife Anne Cole, and Ann Vaux was his
third wife, the first two being Anne Heycock, mother
of two sons, and Mary Duncan, who died childless.
By his fourth wife whom he married when nearly or
quite 56, Barbara St. Leger, he had no fewer than
fourteen children of whom the names and something of
the subsequent history of eleven are known! [158]
    As will shortly be seen, this William Penn had
one child by each of his two marriages. Ann Vaux's
son Springett Penn died in 1766, leaving a will in
which he bequeathed his estate to his mother, and
she in the next year made a will in which she bequeathed the same property to her second husband,
Alexander Durdin, with the result that for the first
time Penn properties passed out of the Penn family,
causing a long lawsuit by the heirs of Christiana
Gulielma Penn against the Durdins. [159]

        Issue: surname Penn
            by Christiana Forbes
28 i.   Christiana Gulielma, b. 22 Oct. 1733, d.
                London, 24 March 1808 aged 69.
            by Ann Vaux
    ii.   Springett, b. Ballyphechane in the South
                Liberties of Cork, 1 1st mo. 1738, 8-9
                P.M.; d. of consumption, unm., Dublin,
                16 Nov. 1766 aged 28. When his father
                died, he was at a school in Lismore, co.
                Waterford. He was supposedly a ward of
                his great-uncle of the half blood, Thomas
                Penn, but is said to have regarded him-
                self as badly treated by Thomas. Benja-
                min Franklin, in a letter from London
                dated 9 May 1761, speaks of "Mr Springett
                Penn, a very sensible, discreet young man
                with excellent dispositions." [160]

    24. GRANVILLE PENN, seventh child of Thomas Penn
(William, William, Giles, William, William, John) by
his wife Lady Juliana Fermor, was born in the city
house of his father in Spring Gardens, 9 Dec. 1761,
and died at Stoke, 28 Sept. 1844, buried at Stoke
Park. [161] He enrolled at Magdalen College, Oxford,
11 Nov. 1780, but like many Penns, took no degree.
For many years he served as Assistant Chief Clerk of
the War Office, and left a considerable number of
volumes bearing his name, mostly on religious sub-
jects but also including the two-volume work on Ad-

miral Sir William Penn whom he seems to have pre-
ferred to the Founder. Before his marriage he became the father of an illegitimate son who was afterwards known as William Granville, born ca. 1785,
died January 1864 in Bath, aged 79, buried at Stoke
Park.[162] He was named as heir and kinsman in the
will of his half-brother, Granville John Penn, which
will, not signed, was held in the hand of Granville
John Penn when he died.[163]

Granville Penn married, 24 June 1791, ISABELLA
FORBES, born 1771, died 1847, eldest daughter of
General Gordon Forbes, sometime colonel of the 29th
Foot, by his wife Mary Sullivan of Cork. A warrant
of Queen Victoria dated 31 July 1838 permitted the
augmentation of the Penn arms.[164] The Historical
Society of Pennsylvania now displays at the top of
the stairs a fine oil portrait of Granville Penn.

Issue: surname Penn

i. Sophia, b. 1793, d.s.p. 1827; m., as 1st
    wife, Sir William Maynard Gomm, Field-
    Marshall, K.C.B., after which he m. (2)
    Elizabeth Kerr, daughter of Robert Kerr,
    and also d.s.p.

ii. Louisa Emily, b. 1795, d. unm., 27 May 1841,
    bur. Stoke Poges.

iii. Isabella Mary, b. 1795, d. unm., Brompton,
    28 Jan. 1856, bur. Stoke Poges.

iv. Henrietta Anne, b. 1797, d. unm., Brompton,
    13 June 1855, bur. Stoke Poges.

v. John William, d. inf., bur. 18 Dec. 1802,
    Stoke Poges.

vi. William, b. ca. 1800, d. unm., Brighton,
    7 Jan. 1848, bur. Stoke Poges; matricu-
    lated at Christ Church, Oxford, 5 June
    1818 aged 18, A.B. 1833, M.A. 1837. In
    1837 he was of Semoure Hall, Norfolk, a
    barrister of Lincoln's Inn, 1844.

vii. Juliana Margaret, d. inf., bur. Stoke Poges,
    21 March 1844.

viii. Granville John, b. Nov. 1802 (Mrs. Roach) or
    1803 (Jenkins); d. unm. at Stoke, 29
    March 1867, while holding his unsigned
    will in his hand. He visited Pennsylva-
    nia in 1852 and 1857. He had an M.A.
    from Christ Church, Oxford, and was a
    barrister. In 1848 he sold Stoke.[165]

ix. Thomas Gordon, clergyman, b. 7 May 1803,

d. unm., 10 Sept. 1869, at which time the
male line of the Penns became extinct.
For some time before his death he was regarded as incompetent to manage his affairs.

25. SOPHIA MARGARETTA or SOPHIA MARGARET JULIANA
PENN, eighth and possibly youngest child of Thomas
Penn (William, William, Giles, William, William,
John) by his wife Lady Juliana Fermor, was born 25
Dec. 1764, died 29 April 1847, buried in the Stuart
family vault at Luton, Bedfordshire. She married at
St. George's, Hanover Square, 3 May 1796, the Hon.
and Most Rev. WILLIAM STUART, D.D., born March 1755,
died 6 March 1822, of laudanum poisoning, inadver-
tently administered, fourth and youngest son of John,
3rd Earl of Bute, K.G., Prime Minister under George
III, by his wife Mary Wortley-Montague, daughter of
Lady Mary Wortley-Montague.[166] After 14 years as Vicar of Luton , he became Canon of Windsor, in 1800
Archbishop of Armagh and Primate of Ireland.

Issue: surname Stuart
29 i.   Mary Juliana, b. 3 April 1797, d. 11 July
         1866.
30 ii.   William, b. 31 Oct. 1798, d. 7 July 1874.
   iii. Louisa, b. ca. 1801, d. unm., 29 Sept. 1823.
         aged 22, bur. Luton.[167]
   iv.   Henry, b. 1804, d. unm., 26 Oct. 1854; M.P.
         for Bedfordshire.[168]

26. JOHN PENN the Elder, so-called because he
was older than his first cousin of the same name,
was eldest son of Richard Penn (William, William,
Giles, William, William, John) by his wife Hannah
Lardner, and was born 14 July 1729, died 9 Feb. 1795,
aged 66, buried from Christ Church, Philadelphia.[169]
While still a school boy, he contracted a marriage
about 1747 with GRACE COX, daughter of James Cox of
London, who may, according to Jenkins, have been the
silversmith of that name who made Thomas Penn's
wedding presents to Lady Juliana Fermor. Grace Penn,
wife of John Penn, Esq., died 17 March 1760, as reported in *The Gentleman's Magazine*.[170] The Penn family appears to have disapproved of this marriage and
forced the boy to repudiate his wife, and he was sent
to Geneva escorted by Robert Dunant and remained for
four years. He then came to America, 21 Nov. 1752,
arriving at Philadelphia on 1 Dec. 1752, and was made

a member of the Provincial Council on 6 Feb. 1753.
In 1755 he returned to England but came back to
Pennsylvania as lieutenant-governor in 1763, for a
period of three years, extended in 1766, 1769, 1772,
but in 1771 he again went back to England. At this
point his brother Richard produced a commission as
lieutenant-governor dated 16 Oct. 1771, and served
as such until August 1773, when John returned once
more, and became the last Proprietary Governor of
Pennsylvania. His first wife Grace having died in
1760, he married, second, 31 May 1766 in Christ
Church, Philadelphia, while lieutenant-governor,
ANN ALLEN, who died in Upper George Street, London,
4 July 1830, eldest daughter of Chief Justice William Allen of Philadelphia by his wife Margaret
Hamilton. There was no issue by either marriage.
John Penn's will was dated 2 Jan. 1795, probated 23
Jan. 1796, and mentions wife Anne, brother Richard
Penn's younger children; nephew William Penn, son of
Richard Penn; nephew Richard Penn, son of Richard;
and wife Anne's brother, Col. William Allen.[171]

27. RICHARD PENN, younger son of Richard Penn
(William, William, Giles, William, William, John) by
his wife Hannah Lardner, was born about 1736 and
died at Richmond, Surrey, 27 May 1811 in his 76th
year. He attended St. John's College, Cambridge,
but took no degree. He became a member of the Provincial Council on 12 Jan. 1764 but was in England
from 1769 to 1771. He served as governor of Pennsylvania during the absence in England of his older
brother John, with whom he was for a time not on
good terms. In 1775 he was sent to England as an envoy of the Continental Congress, a mission that did
not succeed, and he suffered severe financial straits
during the Revolution. He served as member of
Parliament, 1784-1790 for Appleby, Westmoreland;
1790-1796 for Haslemere, Surrey; 1796-1802 for the
Borough of Lancaster; and again 1806-1808 for Haslemere. In the years 1808-1809 he revisited Philadelphia. While governor, he married at Christ Church,
Philadelphia, 21 May 1772, MARY MASTERS, born 3 March
1756, died 16 Aug. 1829 at the house of her younger
son, Richard Penn Esq., in Great George Street, aged
73, daughter of William and Mary (Lawrence) Masters.
The lines from him are all extinct.[172]

Issue: surname Penn

i. William, b. England, 23 June 1776, d.s.p.
    Nelson Square, Southwark, 17 Sept. 1845,
    bur. St. Mary Redcliffe, Bristol; went
    to St. John's College, Cambridge[173] but
    took no degree; was m. by Dr. James Aber-
    crombie of Christ Church, Philadelphia,
    7 Aug. 1807, to Catherine Julia [or Ju-
    liana Catherine] Balabrega, b. 13 March
    1785, bapt. Christ Church, daughter of
    Jacob and Mary (-----) Balabrega of
    Philadelphia; went to England where he
    spent time in debtors' prison, was a
    writer for periodicals.

ii. Hannah, d. unm., Richmond, Surrey, 16 July
    1856. Her position among the children is
    uncertain but there were eight years be-
    tween William and Richard.

iii. Richard, b. ca. 1784, d. Richmond, Surrey,
    21 April 1863, aged 79; an official of
    the Colonial Department of the British
    government; made F.R.S., 18 Nov. 1824.
    At his death his fourth of the Proprie-
    tary rights, inherited from William in
    1845, went to Granville John Penn.

iv. Mary, b. 11 April 1785, d.s.p., 26 March
    1863; m. 1821, as 2nd wife, Samuel Payn-
    ter Esq. of Richmond, Surrey, J.P., High
    Sheriff for Surrey 1838, d. 24 July 1844.

v. Daughter, d. 17 June 1790, youngest daugh-
    ter.

28. CHRISTIANA GULIELMA PENN, only daughter of
William Penn (William, William, William, Giles, William, William, John) by his first wife Christian
Forbes, was born 22 Oct. 1733, died at Thornhaugh
Street, Parish of St. Giles-in-the-Fields, Middlesex, 24 March 1803 aged 69.[174] When of Sunninghill,
co. Berks and aged 26 and more, she was married on
14 Aug. 1761 by the Rev. William Nichols of St. Pan-
cras' Church, Middlesex, to PETER GASKELL of Bath,
born ca. 1730/1, died in Bath in January 1785. In
1778 he was a surgeon[175] and was the son of Peter
Gaskell of Bollington who was living on 20 Dec. 1783
when the son made his will (PCC 78 Ducarel) but died
shortly before the son. The son's death was reported in *The Bath Chronicle* of 27 Jan. 1785 which says
he died in Westgate Buildings "last week." Christiana Gulielma Penn Gaskell died intestate, administration being granted 25 Nov. 1803 to her son Thomas.[176]

Through her are descended all of the known descendants of William Penn by his first wife Gulielma Maria Postuma Springett.

Issue: surname Gaskell or Penn-Gaskell
  i.   Thomas, Esq., of Shanagarry, b. ca. 1762,
          d.s.p., Fitz-William Square, Dublin, 19
          Oct. 1823, aged 61; m. 1794 ----- Ward
          who d. after a few years leaving a son
          who d. inf. The wife was daughter of John
          Ward by his wife Jane Vesey, who m. (2)
          1 Nov. 1777 William Crosbie, Earl of Glan-
          dore, co. Cork, and Viscount Crosbie of
          Ardfert, co. Kerry, and she d. Sept. 1787.
31 ii.   Peter, b. 19 May 1764, d. 16 July 1831.
   iii.   Alexander Forbes, d.s.p. and unm. after
          1816 when he wrote letters from Gray's
          Inn.
32 iv.   William, of London, b. ca. 1769, d. England,
          17 Nov. 1842.
   v.   Jane, d.s.p. in England 19 May 1844 aged
          72; obituary in *The Gentleman's Magazine*,
          July 1844, p. 103. She resided in New Or-
          mond Street, Holborn above Bars; will is
          dated 27 April 1837, probated 1 June 1844
          (PCC #460 of 1844), abstracted PGM 25:100
          f.

   29. MARY JULIANA STUART, eldest child of SOPHIA
MARGARETTA PENN (Thomas, William, William, Giles,
William, William, John) by her husband, the Hon. and
Most Rev. William Stuart, was born 3 April 1797 and
died 11 July 1866. She married 28 Feb. 1815, THOMAS
KNOX, VISCOUNT NORTHLAND, afterwards 2nd Earl of Ran-
furly, of Dungannon Park, co. Tyrone, born 19 April
1786, died 21 March 1858, son of Thomas, 1st Earl of
Ranfurly by his wife, the Hon. Diana Jane Pery.[177]

Issue: surname Knox
  i.   Lady Sophia Diana, b. 18 Dec. 1815, d. 29
          Dec. 1815.
33 ii.   Thomas, 3rd Earl of Ranfurly, b. 13 Nov.
          1816, d. 20 May 1858.
34 iii.   Lady Mary Stuart, b. 21 July 1818, d. 14 May
          1903.
35 iv.   Lady Louisa Juliana, b. 9 Feb. 1820, d. 31
          March 1896.
   v.   Lady Elizabeth Henrietta, b. 5 April 1822,
          d. unm., 28 Jan. 1909.

vi.   Lady Juliana Caroline Frances, b. 18 Feb.
      1825, d. 11 Dec. 1906; m., as 2nd wife,
      15 Oct. 1862, General Sir Edward Forres-
      tier Walker, K.C.B., of the Manor House,
      Bushey, Herts, d. 27 July 1881, no issue.

36 vii. William Stuart, b. 11 March 1826, d. 15
         Feb. 1900.

viii. Lady Flora Sophia Anne Penn, b. 2 Aug. 1827,
      d. unm., 27 Feb. 1905.

ix.   Granville Henry Stuart John,[178] b. 1 Aug.
      1829, drowned in River Tamar, 18 Aug.
      1845.

37 x.   Lady Adelaide Henriette Hortense,[179] b. 23
         May 1833, d. 28 Aug. 1911.

30. WILLIAM STUART, second child and eldest son
of Sophia Margaretta Penn (Thomas, William, William,
Giles, William, William, John) by her husband, the
Hon. and Most Rev. William Stuart, was born 31 Oct.
1798, died 7 July 1874. He married, first, 8 Aug.
1821, HENRIETTA MARIA SOPHIA POLE, who died 26 July
1853, eldest daughter of Admiral Sir Charles Morris
[or Morrice] Pole, Bart., K.C.B., after which he
married, second, 31 Aug. 1854, GEORGINA ADELAIDE
FORRESTIER-WALKER, daughter of Sir Edward Forrestier-
Walker, and she married, second, 15 Dec. 1875, the
9th Earl of Seafield. William Stuart received the
degree of M.A. from St. John's College, Cambridge,
in 1820; was M.P. for Armagh 1820-1826, for Bedfordshire 1830-1834, J.P. and D.L. for Bedfordshire;
High Sheriff in 1846; his seats were at Aldenham
Abbey, Herts, and Tempsford Hall, Bedfordshire. In
1869, at the death of Thomas Penn, he became tenant
in tail general of the Penn property, and on 5 Aug.
1870 he barred the entail, and on 11 Nov. 1870 confirmed all conveyances previously made in Pennsylvania.

Issue: surname Stuart *all by first wife*
38 i.   Mary Pole, b. 3 Sept. 1822, d. 25 Jan. 1852.
39 ii.   Henrietta Pole, b. 10 Feb. 1824, d. 13 Feb.
         1881.
40 iii. William, b. 7 March 1825, d. 21 Dec. 1893.
41 iv.   Charles Pole, b. 7 May 1826, d. 26 Aug. 1896.
   v.   Clarence Esme, M.A. (Cantab.), b. 29 May
         1827, d.s.p. 8 Jan. 1913; m. 16 April
         1863 Catherine Cuninghame, d. 10 March
         1901, daughter of Col. John Cuninghame
         of Cadell Thornton, Ayrshire.

42 vi.   Louisa Pole, b. Aug. 1828, d. 5 Jan. 1858.

   31. PETER PENN GASKELL, later PENN-GASKELL, second son of Christiana Gulielma Penn (William, William, William, William, Giles, William, William, John) by her husband Peter Gaskell, was born 19 May 1764 and died in Pennsylvania, 16 July 1831 aged 67/2. Having come to America in 1785, he married on 5 Dec. 1793 at St. James's Episcopal Church, Perkiomen, ELIZABETH EDWARDS, born ca. 1773, died 19 July 1834 in her 62nd year, allegedly daughter of Nathan Edwards. The Penn-Gaskell Bible has the record of an Elizabeth Edwards dying on Tuesday, 26 Oct. 1819, perhaps the mother of Peter's wife of the same name. Both Peter and his wife were buried in the Baptist Church Cemetery in Lower Merion. By royal license of 31 May 1824 Peter Penn Gaskell assumed the name of Penn "in compliance with testamentary injunction of" his brother Thomas Penn Gaskell.[180]

Issue: surname Gaskell or Penn-Gaskell
i.   William Penn, b. Sunday, 29 June 1794, d. unm., 12 Oct. 1817 in 24th year, before the royal license cited above, so that it is incorrect to hyphenate his name.
ii.   Thomas, of Ballymaloe, co. Cork, and of Penn Hall, Montgomery Co., Pa., b. Wednesday, 6 Jan. 1795, d. at Penn Cottage, Lower Merion, 18 Oct. 1846, Sunday, 5 A.M., aged 52, bur. in vault at St. John's Roman Catholic Church, 13th Street, Philadelphia, 20 Oct. 1846; m. by Rt. Rev. Bishop White of Christ Church, 22 Dec. 1825, Mary McClenachan, daughter of George and Mary (Morris) McClenachan, and she d. Penn Cottage, 21 Dec. 1867, bur. 24 Dec. 1867 in the St. John's vault by her husband's side.[181] It was she who entertained Granville John Penn in 1852.[182]
iii.   Eliza, b. Wednesday, 28 Feb. 1798, d. unm. at Ashwood, Thursday, 23 Nov. 1865 in her 67th year, bur. Lower Merion Baptist Cemetery.
43 iv.   Peter, b. Thursday, 3 April 1800, d. 6 April 1866.
v.   Alexander Forbes, b. Monday, 20 Sept. 1802, d. unm. at Ashwood, Tuesday, 8 Sept. 1829 in his 27th year, bur. Lower Merion Baptist Cemetery.

44 vi. Christiana Gulielma, b. Monday, 27 May 1805,
        d. 20 March 1830 in her 24th year.
   vii. Jane, b. Tuesday, 13 Dec. 1808, d. unm.,
         Saturday, 7 July 1832 in 24th year, bur.
         Lower Merion Baptist Cemetery.
  viii. Isaac, M.D. (U. of Pa. 1834), b. Wednesday,
         9 Jan. 1811, d. unm., 24 Oct. 1842 in
         his 31st year, bur. Lower Merion Baptist
         Cemetery; called of Paris; his brother
         Thomas was of the opinion that Isaac was
         incapacitated but allowed his will dated
         23 Oct. 1842 to be probated 16 May 1843.

32. WILLIAM PENN GASKELL, fourth son of Christiana Gulielma Penn (William, William, William, William, Giles, William, William, John) by her husband Peter Gaskell, was born ca. 1769, died in England, 17 Nov. 1842. He resided at Cheltenham, a surgeon. His obituary appeared in *The Gentleman's Magazine* for January 1843, p. 106, his will in PGM 25:105. His wife's first name was Elizabeth but her surname is unknown. This family appears to have called themselves Penn Gaskell without the hyphen.

Issue: surname Penn Gaskell
45 i.   William, b. 20 Feb. 1808, d. 27 Dec. 1881.
   ii. Elizabeth, living 2 Aug. 1830, d.s.p.,
        not mentioned in father's will in 1835.

33. THOMAS, 3RD EARL OF RANFURLY, second child and eldest son of Mary Juliana Stuart (Sophia Margaretta, Thomas, William, William, Giles, William, William, John) by her husband Thomas, 2nd Earl of Ranfurly, was born 13 Nov. 1816, died 20 May 1858, less than two months after he had inherited the title from his father. He married 10 Oct. 1848, HARRIET RIMINGTON, who died 16 March 1891, daughter of James Rimington of Broomhead Hall, co. York.

Issue: surname Knox
   i.   Thomas Granville Henry Stuart, 4th Earl of
        Ranfurly, Captain in the Grenadier Guards,
        b. 28 July 1849, d.s.p., unm., on a hun-
        ting expedition in Abyssinia, 10 May 1875,
        aged 25.
   ii. Lady Agnes Henrietta Sarah, b. 19 March
        1851, d.s.p., 29 Dec. 1921; m. 1 Dec.
        1870, Nugent Murray Whitmore Daniell,
        Bengal Civil Service, d. 8 Aug. 1908.
46 iii. Uchter John Mark, 5th Earl of Ranfurly, b.

14 Aug. 1856, d. 1 Oct. 1933.

34. Lady MARY STUART KNOX, third child and second
daughter of Mary Juliana Stuart (Sophia Margaretta,
Thomas, William, William, Giles, William, William,
John) by her husband Thomas, 2nd Earl of Ranfurly,
was born 21 July 1818, died 14 May 1903. She married,
as second wife, 20 Sept. 1854, JOHN PAGE READE, D.L.,
of Crowe Hall, Stutton, Suffolk, born 1806, died 28
March 1880.

Issue: surname Reade
i.   Evelyne Helen Revell, d. unm., 24 March
        1909.
ii.   Hubert Granville Revell, b. 28 March 1857,
        d. unm., 13 Oct. 1938; educated at Eton.
iii.   Raymond Nathaniel Northland Revell, major
        general, C.B., C.M.G., b. London, 16 Feb.
        1861, d. 18 Oct. 1943, retired 1920; m.
        9 June 1894, Rose Frances Spencer, daugh-
        ter of Col. Almeric George Spencer and
        widow of Captain Greenway.
        Only issue: surname Reade
        1. Mary Spencer Revell, C.B.E., J.P., b. 7
           Aug. 1897, m. 1 Jan. 1918 Sir Fergus
           Graham of Netherby, Cumberland, 5th
           Bart., J.P., D.L., K.B.E., Captain,
           Irish Guards, severely wounded, World
           War I, b. 10 March 1893.[183]
           Issue: surname Graham
           a. Charles Spencer Richard, major, b.
              16 July 1919; m. 5 Feb. 1944, Susan
              Surtees, only daughter of Major
              Robert Lambton Surtees of Redworth
              Cottage, Littlestone-on-Sea, Kent.
              Issue: surname Graham
              α James Fergus Surtees, b. 29 July
                1946.
              β Malise Charles Richard, b. 19 Sept.
                1948.
              γ Susannah Anne Mary, b. 8 May 1951.
           b. Cynthia Mary, b. 13 Nov. 1923, d. 13
              Jan. 1927.

35. Lady LOUISA JULIANA KNOX, fourth child and
third daughter of Mary Juliana Stuart (Sophia Margaretta, Thomas, William, William, Giles, William,
William, John) by her husband Thomas, 2nd Earl of
Ranfurly, was born 9 Feb. 1820, died 31 March 1896.

She married, 14 Aug. 1839, HENRY ALEXANDER, of Forkhill, co. Armagh, born 16 Feb. 1803, died 1 Dec.
1877, barrister-ata-law, D.L., high sheriff of Armagh
1856.

Issue: surname Alexander
i.   Stillborn daughter, b. 21 July 1840.
ii.   Blanche Catherine Sophia Anne, b. 10 Dec.
      1841, d.s.p., 16 June 1878; m. 4 Sept.
      1877, the Rev. Frederick Anthony Hammond
      of Lauriston House, Dover, d. 1907, son
      of Col. Hammond.
iii. Alice Mary Juliana, b. 17 Aug. 1843, d. unm.
      13 Feb. 1921.
47 iv. Constance Henrietta Georgina, b. 23 April
      1845, d. 16 Oct. 1927.
48 v. Emily Louisa Jane, b. 19 Aug. 1850, d. 23
      Aug. 1900.
vi.   Granville Henry Jackson, of Forkhill, co.
      Armagh, b. 26 June 1852, d.s.p. 3 Sept.
      1930; was D.L., J.P. for co. Armagh, high
      sheriff 1883; lieutenant, 83rd Regt.,
      Captain 3rd Bn, Royal Irish Fusiliers;
      m. 25 Feb. 1880, Daisy Matthews, youngest
      daughter of M. Matthews of San Francisco,
      d. 20 Sept. 1939.
vii. Henry Nathaniel, b. 7 June 1854, d. 28 Jan.
      1923; in the Indian Civil Service: in-
      spector general of prisons, Bombay; m. 6
      Nov. 1883 Mary Stuart Erskine, d. 13 May
      1928, daughter of Claude Erskine of the
      Bengal Civil Service.
      Issue: surname Alexander
      1. Constance Mary, b. 2 June 1885, d. unm.
         5 Dec. 1956.
viii. Claude Henry, b. 31 May 1856, d. 19 March
      1915; m. 1 Oct. 1896, Irene Christine
      Templin, d. 25 Nov. 1958, daughter of
      Col. William Templin of Lennox Place,
      Brighton. He was a major in the Wiltshire
      Regiment.
      Issue: surname Alexander
      1. Dorothy Alice, b. 3 Oct. 1897.
      2, Rosemary Irene, b. 18 Dec. 1900, m., as
         2nd wife, 1 Oct. 1942, Count Gaston
         Dru, son of Colonel Dru, and he d.s.p.
         11 Aug. 1945.
      3. Nancy Stuart, b. 11 Sept. 1902, m. 16
         Sept. 1950 as 2nd wife, Rear Admiral

        Richard Ray Wallace, C.B.E., b. 14 Dec.
        1895, d. 24 Jan. 1963.
ix.   Ronald Henry, b. 15 Aug. 1858, d. unm., 2
        Aug. 1936; served in World War I.
x.   Frederick Henry Thomas, b. 30 Nov. 1860,
        d. 26 Sept. 1921, captain in the Leices-
        tershire Regt. and Army Pay Corps; m. 7
        June 1899 Blanche Bancroft, d. 25 Nov.
        1931, daughter of Lt. Gen. W. C. Bancroft
        Knellwood, Farnborough.
        Issue: surname Alexander
        1. Elizabeth Maude, b. 22 July 1902, d. Oct.
           1959; m. 12 April 1928, Kenneth Evers-
           Swindell.
           Issue: surname Evers-Swindell
           a. Penelope Ann, b. 8 Dec. 1930.
           b. Another daughter.
        2. Freda Alice, b. 1904, d. 25 March 1905.
xi.   Dudley Henry Blayney, b. 13 Jan. 1863, d.
        unm., 30 July 1931; major in the West
        Yorkshire Regt; private secretary to the
        5th Earl of Ranfurly as Governor of New
        Zealand 1897-1904 and as such accompanied
        the earl to Philadelphia in 1904.
49 xii. Edith Ellen, b. 1864, d. 27 May 1892.

    36. WILLIAM STUART KNOX, seventh child and second
son of Mary Juliana Stuart (Sophia Margaretta, Thomas,
William, William, Giles, William, William, John) by
her husband Thomas, 2nd Earl of Ranfurly, was born
11 March 1826 and died 15 Feb. 1900. He married 26
Aug. 1856, GEORGIANA [or GEORGINA] ROOPER, born
1832, died 4 Nov. 1926, youngest daughter of John
Bonfoy Rooper of Abbots' Ripton, Hunts. He was a
D.L., J.P. for co. Tyrone, major in the 51st Foot,
hon. colonel of the Mid Ulster Artillery, M.P. for
Dungannon 1851-1874.

    Issue: surname Knox
    i.   Violet Mary, b. 2 March 1864, d. unm., 23
          Dec. 1928.
    ii.   Florence May, b. 22 July 1865, d. 11 Feb.
          1943; m. 14 Nov. 1889 Col. Albert George
          Shaw of Hurst Grange, Twyford, co. Bucks,
          and of the Queen's Royal West Surrey Rgt.
    iii. Thomas Granville, b. 22 March 1868, d. 15
          Jan. 1947; captain 3rd Bn, Royal West
          Surrey Rgt; D.L., J.P. for co. Tyrone;
          m. 24 Feb. 1897 Hon. Harriet Georgina

Lucia Agar-Ellis, d. 4 July 1928, daughter of Leopold Agar-Ellis, 5th Viscount
Clifden.
Issue: surname Knox
1. Constance Georgina, b. 1898, m. 6 Oct.
1919 Dr.Henry Braund, M.R.C.S., d. 11
April 1954. They had a child b. July
1920.

37. Lady ADELAIDE HENRIETTE LOUISA HORTENSE KNOX,
tenth and youngest child and seventh daughter of
Mary Juliana Stuart (Sophia Margaretta, Thomas, William, William, Giles, William, William, John) by her
husband Thomas, 2nd Earl of Ranfurly, was born 23
May 1833 and died 28 Aug. 1911. She married 26 Sept.
1850, JOSEPH GOFF, M.A., of Hale Park, Hants, born
28 Oct. 1817, died 26 Dec. 1872.

Issue: surname Goff
i.   Joseph Granville Stuart, of Hale Park, b.
      7 June 1851, d. unm., 24 Sept. 1881, lieu-
      tenant in the 43rd Regiment.
ii.   Ada Mary, b. 1853, d. unm., 22 April 1932.
iii. Gerald Lionel Joseph, b. 8 March 1855,
      killed in action at Magersfontein, S.A.,
      11 Dec. 1899, no issue; m., as 1st hus-
      band, 23 May 1894, Ellen May Charlotte
      Dundas, d. 23 May 1927, 3rd daughter of
      Sir Robert Dundas of Arniston, 1st Bart.,
      who was of the same Knox family.[184] He
      was a lieutenant colonel in the 1st Bn,
      Argyll and Sutherland Highlanders.
iv.   Bertram Lyulph Joseph, captain Highland
      Light Infantry and Royal Garrison Rgt;
      b. 12 July 1857, d.s.p. 25 May 1911; m.
      2 July 1902, Helen Maria MacLeod, living
      1967, eldest daughter of Capt. Norman A.
      MacLeod of Orbost, Invernessshire.
v.   Cecil Willie Trevor Thomas, major, East
      Lancashire Rgt, D.S.O.; b. 26 March 1860,
      d. unm., 4 Aug. 1907.
vi.   Algernon Hamilton Stannus, of Standerwick
      Court, Somerset, major, Royal Field Ar-
      tillery, South Africa, 1900; World War
      I, C.M.G., b. 14 April 1863, d.s.p. 20
      June 1936; m. 24 Feb. 1906, Emily Dora
      Greenhill-Gardyne, d. 17 Sept. 1915, 5th
      daughter of Lt. Col. Charles Greenhill-
      Gardyne of Finavon. He purchased Stander-

wick in 1919, sold Hale Park, which he
had inherited, in 1920.
50 vii. Gwendoline Jane Eliza, b. 1869, d. 5 Sept.
         1951.

  38. MARY POLE STUART, eldest child of William
Stuart (Sophia Margaretta, Thomas, William, William,
Giles, William, William, John) by his first wife
Henrietta Maria Sophia Pole, was born 3 Sept. 1822
and died 25 Jan. 1852. She married, as first wife,
1 Aug. 1843, JONATHAN RASHLEIGH, of Menabilly, Cornwall; Fenitor Court Devon; and Lissadrone, co. Mayo,
born 7 Jan. 1820, died 12 April 1905, B.A., D.L. and
J.P. for Cornwall, High Sheriff 1877, and J.P. for
Middlesex and Westminster, son of William Rashleigh
by his wife Rachel Stackhouse.[185]

       Issue: surname Rashleigh
51 i.   Caroline Mary Stuart, d. 3 Jan. 1880.
   ii.   Jonathan, b. 26 May 1845, d. 8 Dec. 1872,
         educated at Harrow; m. 1 Nov. 1870, Mary
         Frances Labouchere, d. Feb. 1874, daugh-
         ter of John Labouchere of Broom Hall,
         Surrey.
         Issue: surname Rashleigh
         1. John Cosmo Stuart, of Throwleigh, Oke-
            hampton, Devon, formerly of Menabilly,
            Cornwall; b. 2 July 1872, d.s.p. 8
            Jan. 1961, educated at Eton and Trini-
            ty College, Cambridge, lord of many
            manors, J.P. Cornwall 1912, Devon
            1911, High Sheriff 1908, M.A., M.D.;
            m. (1) 1898 Gertrude Daniels, daughter
            of Henry Daniels; (2) 29 Aug. 1921,
            Elizabeth Evans, J.P. Devon 1937,
            daughter of William Evans of Cleveland,
            co. York.
   iii. Alice Henrietta, b. 16 April 1848, d. unm.,
         April 1934.
   iv.   Mary Anna, d. unm., 5 Aug. 1905.
52 v.   Evelyn William, b. 6 Jan. 1850, d. 29 April
         1921.

  39. HENRIETTA POLE STUART, second child of William Stuart (Sophia Margaretta, Thomas, William,
William, Giles, William, William, John) by his first
wife Henrietta Maria Sophia Pole, was born 10 Feb.
1824, died 13 Feb. 1881, married 4 Sept. 1845,
REGINALD THISTLEWAYTE COCKS, born 6 Oct. 1816, son
of Thomas Cocks. He matriculated at Christ Church,

Oxford, 15 May 1834.

Issue: surname Cocks
i.   Agnita Henrietta, b. 21 Oct. 1846, d. unm.
15 Sept. 1938.
ii.   Mary.
iii. Amabel Margaretta, b. 27 Nov. 1849, d., apparently s.p., 1891; m. 15 Dec. 1874,
William Newcome Nicholson, b. 22 May
1833, 4th son of John Armytage Nicholson
of Balrath-Burry, co. Meath.

40. WILLIAM STUART, third child and eldest son
of William Stuart (Sophia Margaretta, Thomas, William, William, Giles, William, William, John) by his
first wife Henrietta Maria Sophia Pole, was born in
London at the home of his grandmother, Sophia Margaretta (Penn) Stuart, 7 March 1825, died 21 Dec.
1893, and married 13 Sept. 1859, KATHERINE NICHOL-
SON, who died 16 Oct. 1881, eldest daughter of John
Armytage Nicholson of Balrath-Burry, co. Meath. He
was J.P. for Hertfordshire, J.P. and D.L. for Bedfordshire, High Sheriff in 1875, J.P. for Hunting-
donshire, and honorary colonel of the 3rd Battalion,
Bedfordshire Regiment. He was called to the bar at
Inner Temple, 1851. He sold Aldenham Abbey.

Issue: surname Stuart
i.   William Dugald, of Tempsford Hall, Bedfordshire, b. 18 Oct. 1860, d. 2 April 1922;
educated at Eton; 2nd Lt., King's Royal
Rifle Corps, Lt., 1 July 1881, Captain
13 Nov. 1889, served in Burma and India
until 1893 when put on the reserve list;
J.P. and hon. lt. col., 3rd Bn, Bedfordshire Rgt, having served as major; served
also in World War I as temp. major, 14th
Bn, K.R.R.C. Tempsford Hall was burned
in 1898, afterwards rebuilt. During the
fire an elm descended from the elm under
which Penn signed the treaty with the
Indians was badly scorched and pieces of
it were distributed among the family. He
m. 11 July 1895, Millicent Helen Olivia
Bulkeley Hughes, d. 2 Feb. 1933, eldest
daughter of Capt. G. W. Bulkeley Hughes.
Issue: surname Stuart
1. William Esme Montague, b. 22 Dec. 1895,
killed in action, 7 Oct. 1916.
ii.   Mary Charlotte Florence, b. Kempston, Beds,

   b. 2 May 1863m d. unm., 31 Jan. 1918, resided in London.

iii.   Henry Esme, b. Kempston, Beds, 15 July 1865,
       d. 21 Aug. 1905; m. 16 Dec. 1899 Emily
       Cornwall, d. 28 May 1922, daughter of
       James Cornwall.
       Issue: surname Stuart
       1. Margaret Esme Sylvia, twin, b. 17 Nov.
          1902, m. 1928 James Lyle.
       2. Winifred Hilda Muriel, b. 17 Nov. 1902,
          twin, m. Lawrence Desjardins.
       3. Dorothy Frances Irma, b. 28 June 1904,
          m. 11 June 1930, Clifford Frank But-
          cher. Issue.
iv.   Elizabeth Frances Sybil, b. Kempston, Beds,
       20 May 1868, d. unm., 15 Nov. 1931, lived
       at Farleigh Hungerford near Bath.

41. CHARLES POLE STUART, fourth child and second
son of William Stuart (Sophia Margaretta, Thomas,
William, William, Giles, William, William, John) by
his first wife Henrietta Maria Sophia Pole, was of
Sandymount House, Woburn Sands, Bedfordshire, barrister-at-law, born 7 May 1826, died 26 Aug. 1896.
He married 20 March 1860, ANNE SMYTH, born 18 June
1833, died 19 Oct. 1918, eldest daughter of Robert
Smyth, of Gaybrook, co. West Meath.

   Issue: surname Stuart
i.   Robert Alexander, b. 5 July 1862, drowned
       in the *Stella* disaster, 30 March 1899;
       m. 6 Jan. 1897, Nina Edith Margaret
       Stoker, b. 1 Nov. 1876, d. 30 Jan. 1963,
       daughter of the Rev. H. E. Stoker.
       Issue: surname Stuart
       1. Enid Frances Anne, b. 28 Nov. 1897.
53 ii. Reginald Pole, b. 22 July 1863, d. 20 April
       1934.
iii.   Charles Dudley, b. 26 Oct. 1864, d. unm.,
       13 March 1917.
iv.   Maud Frances, d. unm., 11 March 1889.
v.   Constance Mary, Sister of Mercy (Church of
       England), b. 11 July 1866, d. unm., 1
       March 1938.
vi.   James Francis, b. 16 Nov. 1867, d. 5 July
       1876.
vii.   Ralph Esme, major (R. Art.), b. 9 April
       1869, d.s.p., 27 Oct. 1927; m. (1) 30
       April 1907, Beatrice Kitchen, d. 28 Aug.

1913, daughter of John Kitchen of Scarborough, co. York; (2) 25 Feb. 1919, E-
lizabeth Thompson, d. July 1962, daughter of Samuel Thompson of Muckamore Abbey, co. Antrim.

viii. Florence Amabel, Sister of Mercy (Church
of England), b. 1 Nov. 1870, d. unm.,
4 May 1938.

ix. Grace Henrietta, b. 30 June 1872, d. unm.,
1 June 1955.

x. Frederick Clarence, b. 5 Aug. 1873, d. 12
Oct. 1879.

xi. Katherine Evelyn, b. 18 April 1877, d. 3
May 1887.

42. LOUISA POLE STUART, youngest child of William
Stuart (Sophia Margaretta, Thomas, William, William,
Giles, William, William, John) by his first wife
Henrietta Maria Sophia Pole, was born in August
1828, died 5 Jan. 1858, and married 3 Aug. 1852, as
first wife, the Rev. OLIVER MATTHEW RIDLEY, born 12
May 1824, died 10 Jan. 1907.

Issue: surname Ridley

i. Oliver Stuart, clergyman, b. 8 June 1853,
d. unm., 13 April 1935.

ii. Henry Nicholas, F.R.S., b. 16 Dec. 1855,
d.s.p., 24 Oct. 1956; m. 1941 Lily Eliza
Doran, daughter of Charles Doran.

iii. Charles William, clergyman, b. 28 Dec. 1856,
d.s.p., 23 May 1905; m. 1885 Jessie Dowdall, daughter of Thomas Dowdall.

iv. Mary Louisa, d.s.p., 23 March 1935, m. 14
Feb. 1912, Lt. Col. John Percy Graves,
Royal Guernsey Artillery, d. 13 Feb. 1916.

43. PETER PENN-GASKELL, fourth child and third
son of Peter Penn-Gaskell (Christian Gulielma, William, William, William, William, Giles, William,
William, John) by his wife Elizabeth Edwards, was
born 3 April 1800, died 6 April 1866. He was in business with Thomas Earle but in 1824 he failed,
it appears not seriously. His will says he was of
1613 Chestnut Street, Philadelphia, and of Shanagarry, co. Cork, Ireland. He was married by the rector
of Christ Church, 15 Feb. 1825, to LOUISA ADELAIDE
HEATH, born 2 Oct. 1805, died 7 Feb. 1878, daughter
of Charles P. and Esther (Keeler) Heath. She wrote
her will in Eastbourne Terrace, Hyde Park, London,

but was buried in Laurel Hill Cemetery, Philadelphia.

Issue: surname Penn-Gaskell

54 i.   Elizabeth, b. 19 Dec. 1825, d. 23 Oct. 1866.

ii.   Louisa, b. 12 May 1827, d. 28 March 1848,
        bur. Laurel Hill; m. 15 May 1845 at St.
        Stephen's Episcopal Church, Philadelphia,
        William Gerald Fitzgerald of Waterford
        and New York.
        Issue: surname Fitzgerald
        1. William Penn-Gaskell, b. 8 Feb. 1847, d.
           4 July 1847.

iii.   Mary Gulielma, b. 3 Aug. 1829, d. 21 June
        1830, bur. 25 Oct. 1847 in Laurel Hill.
        Where she was first bur. is unknown. An
        obituary is in *Philadelphia Inquirer,* 24
        Aug. 1847.

iv.   Gulielma, b. 29 May 1831, d. 25 Oct. 1850,
        bur. Laurel Hill.

v.   Hetty, b. 29 Jan. 1833, d. 23 Oct. 1847,
        bur. Laurel Hill.

vi.   Mary, b. 12 Sept. 1834, d. Delaware Co.,
        Pa., 22 Aug. 1877; m. 22 March 1865 Dr
        Isaac T. Coates of Chester, d. 23 June
        1883. Mary was bur. in Laurel Hill from
        her mother's residence, 4058 Chestnut St.
        Issue: surname Coates
        1. Peter Penn-Gaskell, b. 26 Feb. 1866, bur.
           26 Jan. 1869 aged 2/11/0, Laurel Hill.
        2. Harold Penn-Gaskell, b. ca. 1870; m.
           Florence Jarvis of Philadelphia. He
           was in Philadelphia in 1891, not found
           thereafter, perhaps moved to Virginia.
        3. Charles Morton, b. Oct. 1872, bur. 20
           May 1873 aged 7 mos, Laurel Hill.

vii.   William, b. 9 July 1836, captain in Civil
        War; d. unm., of consumption in the bosom
        of his family, 6 Dec. 1865 aged 29, obitu-
        ary dated New Orleans, 13 June 1866.

viii.   Jane, b. 4 July 1839, d.s.p., 1 Nov. 1863,
        bur. Laurel Hill; m. 15 Oct. 1862, Wash-
        ington Irving, said to have been nephew
        of the well-known author, and perhaps the
        paymaster, U.S.N., 1 June 1861, retired
        11 Feb. 1870.

ix.   Emily, b. 27 Jan. 1842, d. 17 Feb. 1869,
        bur. Laurel Hill; m. 13 Jan. 1864 John
        Paul Quinn, M.D., surgeon, U.S.N., d. 6
        June 1869, assistant surgeon 9 May 1861,

surgeon, 30 Oct. 1864.
Issue: surname Quinn
1. Hamilton, b. and d. Sept. 1865, aged 42
   hours, bur. Laurel Hill.
2. Granville Penn, b. 6 Jan. 1868, d. at
   Washington, D.C., bur. Laurel Hill,
   24 May 1892 aged 24. He had deeded his
   rights in the family home for $5000
   to Delia E. Quinn, relationship unknown.
55x.   Peter, b. 24 Oct. 1843, d. ca. 1905.

44. CHRISTIANA GULIELMA PENN-GASKELL, sixth child
and second daughter of Peter Penn-Gaskell (Christiana Gulielma, William, William, William, William, Giles, William, William, John) by his wife Elizabeth Edwards, was born ca. 1807, died 20 March 1830 in her 24th year, buried in the Baptist Cemetery in Lower Merion. She was married by the rector of Christ Church, 2 Jan. 1827, to WILLIAM SWABRIC or SWARTZ-BRICK HALL, born 1799, died 26 Sept. 1862 in his 63rd year, also buried in the Lower Merion Baptist Cemetery, possibly originally of Wavertree, Lancashire, son of a Liverpool merchant, Richard Hall, who is said to have sent the son to Philadelphia to manage a branch there.

Issue: surname Hall
i.   William Penn-Gaskell, b. 26 Nov. 1827, d.
       Camden, N.J., unm., Friday, 2 May 1862,
       in 35th year, bur. Lower Merion Baptist
       Cemetery.
56 ii. Peter, b. 16 March 1830, d. 1 Feb. 1905.

45. WILLIAM PENN GASKELL, eldest child of William Penn Gaskell (Christiana Gulielma, William, William, William, William, Giles, William, William, John) by his wife Elizabeth -----, was born at Burnham, co. Bucks, England, and died in England, 27 Dec. 1881. He was admitted pensioner, 4 July 1826, Corpus Christi College, Oxford. About 1840 he married by common law, with ceremony following, by license, 27 June 1842, St. John's Church, Paddington, by the Rev. J. Symons, rector of Radnage, Berks, MARY HOBBS, born at Sandhurst, ca. 1815, daughter of John Hobbs of Sandhurst, Gloucester, d. at Ealing, Middlesex, in a house called "Shanagarry" on Hamilton Road, 8 Aug. 1844. His will calls him of No. 1 Craven Terrace, Ealing, and was dated 16 Feb. 1877.

Issue: surname Penn Gaskell
i.   William, b. ca. 1840, d. 30 March 1886 at
        West Kensington, an accountant.
ii.   Thomas, b. 12 April 1841, Bayswater, Mid-
        dlesex, d. there 3 May 1928; m. 12 March
        1878, parish church of Mansfield, Notts,
        Ada Wallis, b. ca. 1854, daughter of Hen-
        ry Bell Wallis. Thomas was a civil engin-
        eer.
        Issue: surname Penn Gaskell
        1. Wallis William, killed in action, 26 May
           1915.
        2. Ada Phyllis, living 1945.
        3. Perhaps, Harold Edward who in 1945 had
           wife Winifred and daughter Gulielma,
           wife of Murdoch McLennan.
iii.   Jane, b. ca. 1843, Paddington, d. unm., 19
        Dec. 1923, Earls Court Square, Middlesex.
iv.   Alexander Barclay, b. 19 March 1845, Pad-
        dington, d. 30 Aug. 1930, West Kensington;
        m. St. John's, Notting Hill, 9 Oct. 1880,
        Miriam Da Costa, b. ca. 1847, d. 18 Feb.
        1927, daughter of Isaac Gomes Da Costa,
        dec'd. Alexander was a barrister-at-law.
        Issue: Penn Gaskell
        1. Leslie Da Costa, Lt. Norfolk Rgt, d. 4
           Feb. 1916 at Royal Flying Corps Hospital.
        2. William, b. 4 April 1883, Fulham, living
           1963 at Gardiners Ground, Beaulieu; m.
           26 June 1919, All Saints, Poole, Dorset,
           Iris Eleanor Burgoyne (Nedham) Deane,
           widow, daughter of Capt. Charles Sewell
           Nedham.
           Issue: surname Penn Gaskell
           a. Leslie de Nedham, Lt. Comm. R.N. in
              1963; m. Joyce Jessup and had Nigel
              William, b. 10 May 1963.
v.   Gulielma Maria, b. 6 Feb. 1847, Great Mar-
        low, Bucks, d. after 1882; m. 10 Nov.
        1877, Christ Church, Ealing, Edward Bowen,
        b. ca. 1851, probably d. 1922-24, son of
        John Bowen dec'd. Four of five children.
vi.   Elizabeth, b. ca. 1849, Great Marlow, Bucks,
        d. unm., 28 May 1947.
vii.   Mary, b. 1851, Great Marlow, Bucks, d. unm.,
        22 March 1885.
viii.   Frederick Octavius, b. 2 Nov. 1852, Great
        Marlow, d. 25 March 1890, Johannesburg,

S.A.
ix.   Alfred, d. unm., 17 March 1922, Brighton.
x.   George Edward, b. ca. 1857, d. 12 June 1946,
      Chalfont and Gerrards Cross Hospital,
      Bucks; m. Eleanor Charlotte (Lindsey?)
      who d. 8 May 1937. He was of Lincoln Col-
      lege, Oxford, a barrister but practiced
      as a solicitor. No issue surviving.

46. UCHTER JOHN MARK, 5th EARL OF RANFURLY,
second son and third child of Thomas, 3rd Earl of
Ranfurly (Mary Juliana, Sophia Margaretta, Thomas,
William, William, Giles, William, William, John) by
his wife Harriet Rimington, P.C., G.C.M.G., was born
14 Aug. 1856, died 1 Oct. 1933; married 10 Feb. 1880
the Hon. CONSTANCE ELIZABETH CAULFIELD, born 30 Nov.
1858, died 25 July 1932, only child of James Alfred,
7th Viscount Charlemont by his wife the Hon. Annette
Handcock.[187] He succeeded his older brother on 10
May 1875, was Lord in Waiting 1895-1897, Governor
of New Zealand 1897-1904; sworn of the Privy Council
of Ireland, 23 Aug. 1905; of the Privy Council of
Northern Ireland, 27 Nov. 1923, Officer of the Legion
of Honor; G.C.St.J. 1927; Director of the Ambulance
Department 1915-1919.

Issue: surname Knox
i.   Lady Annette Agnes, b. 21 Nov. 1880, d. 11
      July 1886.
ii.   Thomas Uchter Caulfield, Viscount Northland,
      b. 13 June 1882, killed in action at
      Cuinchy, 1 Feb. 1915; served as aide-de-
      camp to the Governor of New Zealand 1903-
      04; also served in the South African War;
      m., as first of four husbands, Hilda Su-
      san Ellen Cooper, youngest daughter of
      Sir Daniel Cooper, 2nd Baronet.[188]
      Issue: surname Knox
   1. Thomas Daniel, 6th and present Earl of
      Ranfurly, b. 29 May 1913, m. 14 Jan.
      1939, Hermione Poyntz Llewellyn,
      C.St.J., eldest daughter of Griffith
      Robert Poyntz Llewellyn of Llandapley
      Court, Baglan Hall, Monmouth Road,
      Abergavenny, co. Monmouth.[189] He was
      educated at Eton and Trinity College,
      Cambridge (M.A.); served in World War
      II and was a prisoner; Aide-de-camp
      to the Governor-General of Australia

1936-38; K.St.J.; Governor and Comman-
der-in-Chief, Bahamas, 1953-56; K.C.M.G.
1955.
Issue: surname Knox
Lady Caroline, b. 11 Dec. 1948.
2. Edward Paul Uchter, b. 23 May 1914, d.
   unm. 11 Dec. 1935.
iii. Lady Constance Harriet Stuart, b. 21 April
   1885, d. 29 April 1964; m. 7 Nov. 1905,
   Major Evelyn Milnes-Gaskell, D.L., J.P.,
   of the Queen's Own Dragoons, b. 19 Oct.
   1877, d. 14 Sept. 1931, eldest son of
   the Rt. Hon. Charles George Milnes-Gaskell of Thornes House, co. York, and Wen-
   lock Abbey, Salop.[190] She was D.C.V.O.,
   (1960), D.J.St.J.; Lady in Waiting to
   H.R.H. Princess Marina, Duchess of Kent,
   1953-1960; Woman of the Bedchamber to
   H.M. Queen Mary, 1937-1953.
   Issue: surname Milnes-Gaskell
   1. Mary Juliana, b. 2 July 1906, m. 12 July
      1934, Lewis Motley, younger son of
      Major Lewis Motley of Spen Hill, Far
      Headingly, near Leeds, co. York.
      Issue: surname Motley
      a. Christopher Steven, b. 7 Dec. 1935.
      b. Michael John, b. 21 Oct. 1937.
      c. Timothy Brooks, b. 22 Dec. 1941.
      d. Charles Osburn, b. 15 Dec. 1943.
   2. Charles Thomas, b. 5 Nov. 1908, killed
      in an aeroplane accident on active
      service as Lt. Col. with the Coldstream
      Guards, 5 Nov. 1943; m. 12 Nov. 1936,
      Lady Ethel Patricia Harl, b. 29 Oct.
      1912, elder daughter of Richard Gran-
      ville, 4th Earl of Listowell, and she
      m. (2) 4 Sept. 1945, Lt. Col. Robert
      Milnes-Coates, elder son of Sir Clive
      Milnes-Coates, 2nd Baronet, by his
      wife Lady Celia Hermione Crew-Milnes,
      and by him has a daughter and son who
      are not, however, Penn descendants.
      Issue: surname Milnes-Gaskell
      a. James, b. 13 Nov. 1937.
      b. Andrew, b. 20 Nov. 1939.
      c. Tom, b. 20 March 1942.
iv. Lady Eileen Maud Juliana, b. 3 May 1891,
   one of the trainbearers to H. M. Queen

Mary at the Coronation, 1911; m. (1) Major Charles Loraine Carlos Clarke, late of Royal Bucks Hussars, son of Charles Carlos Clarke, mar. dissolved 1934; (2) 3 Aug. 1935, Peter Stanley Chappell, only son of Thomas Stanley Chappell of Moreton House, Moreton Morrell, co. Warwick.
    Issue: surname Clarke
1. Charles Thomas Alexander, b. 1915.
2. Diana, b. 1917, d.s.p., 29 Dec. 1949; m. Fulke Walwyn of Saxon House, Lambourne, Berks.

47. CONSTANCE HENRIETTA GEORGINA ALEXANDER, fourth child and fourth daughter of Lady Louisa Juliana Knox (Sophia Margaretta, Thomas, William, William, Giles, William, William, John) by her husband Henry Alexander, was born 23 April 1845, died 16 Oct. 1927. She married 3 Oct. 1867, Col. GREGORY COLQUHOUN GRANT, of the Indian Army, born 1835, died 1902, son of Colquhoun Grant of Kirchirdy, Morayshire. Mrs. Colquhoun Grant was the author of one of the biographies of William Penn already cited.

Issue: surname Grant
i.   Stuart, O.B.E., b. 7 Feb. 1873, d. 26 Aug. 1946; served in South Africa 1900-02 and in World War I; m., as 1st husband, 24 Jan. 1906, Grace Potter, daughter of Frederick Potter of New York.
      Issue: surname Grant
1. Pamela, b. 23 Dec. 1906; m. (1) 9 April 1930, Col. Gordon Calthrop Thorne, D.S.O., d. 3 March 1942; (2) Kent Galbraith Colwell, 1 Aug. 1945; now of Morristown, N.J.
      Issue: surname Thorne
   a. Jennifer Clare, b. 22 Sept. 1931, m. 14 Sept. 1957 Lalcolm Scully Hayden.
      Issue: surname Hayden
   α Christopher Scully, b. 20 Oct. 1963.
   β Elizabeth Grace, b. 28 Jan. 1965.
   b. Frederick Gordon Potter, b. 18 July 1935; m. 8 Nov. 1957 Susan Whittlesey, daughter of Robert Taylor Whittlesey.
      Issue: surname Thorne
   α Gordon Potter, b. 11 Oct. 1958.
   β David Whittlesey, b. 12 Oct. 1960.

γ Stuart Kimball, b. 14 March 1962.
ii.   Alan, b. 1 July 1874, d. unm., 27 March
       1924, Chief of Police, Port Said.
iii.   Rose Vere, b. 19 July 1875, d.s.p. 3 April
       1941; m. 22 July 1909 Major Jack Davy,
       b. 1866, d. 24 Jan. 1927.

48. EMILY LOUISA JANE ALEXANDER, fifth child and
fifth daughter of Lady Louisa Juliana Knox (Sophia
Margaretta, Thomas, William, William, Giles, William,
William, John) by her husband Henry Alexander, was
born 19 Aug. 1850, died 23 Aug. 1900. She married,
25 March 1874, Col. ARTHUR MELVILL HOGG, of the 6th
Bombay Cavalry, born 20 Aug. 1845, died 21 Nov. 1901,
4th son of Charles Hogg of Eastwick Park, Surrey.

Issue: surname Hogg
i.   Conrad Charles Henry, colonel, Royal Engin-
       eers, b. 4 Aug. 1875, d. unm., 20 May
       1950; served in South Africa 1900-02,
       World War I, and the 3rd Afghan War, 1919;
       C.M.G.
ii.   Philip Granville Hardinge, lieutenant col-
       onel, D.S.O., b. 21 Dec. 1878, d. 17 Ap-
       ril 1951; m. 20 July 1905 Geraldine Pet-
       ley, b. 10 Oct. 1883, daughter of Capt.
       E. W. Petley, R.N.
         Issue: surname Hogg
       1. Cecily Irene Barbara, b. 14 June 1906;
          m. 5 Feb. 1931 Lt. Col. Robert B.
          Woods, R.A., b. 13 May 1900, son of
          Ernest Woods of Liphook, Hants.
            Issue: surname Woods
          a. Faith, b. 30 March 1934, m. 19 June
             1954 David Kenneth Tippett, b. 1927,
             son of Col. ----- Tippett.
               Issue: surname Tippett
             α Louisa Clare, b. 19 July 1956.
             β Piers Robert David, b. 14 Sept.
               1957.
       2. Granville Alexander, b. 28 Sept. 1907,
          d.s.p., 18 March 1961; m. (1) a Rus-
          sian lady, d. 1967, mar. dissolved;
          (2) 30 March 1957 Barbara Hargreaves.
       3. Peggy Patricia O'Neill, b. 10 Oct. 1911;
          m. as 1st wife, 7 Dec. 1932, mar. dis-
          solved, Douglas Creyke Maurice of
          Manton Grange, Marlborough, Wilts.
            Issue: surname Maurice

a. Tessa O'Neill, b. 1 Aug. 1934; m.
25 June 1955, David Kingsley Oliphant, son of Lt. Col. K. I. P.
Oliphant of Fittleton, Netheravon,
Wilts.
Issue: surname Oliphant
α Bruce Kingsley, b. 3 April 1957.
β Anthony David, b. 24 Oct. 1958.
γ James Robert, b. 20 May 1962.

iii.   Barbara Louisa Grant, b. 22 May 1881, d.
13 March 1963; m. 11 Jan. 1908, Col. Ar-
thur Anderson McNeight (I.M.S.), b. 9
July 1880, d. 14 Aug. 1966.
Issue: surname McNeight
1. Olive Maureen, b. 10 Nov. 1912, d. 8
Sept. 1961; m. 17 Oct. 1939 George
Kenneth Donald, d. 1 Oct. 1961, 2nd
son of Sir John Donald, K.C.I.E.,
C.S.I.
Issue: surname Donald
a. Jean Maureen, b. 22 Feb. 1944, m. at
Battle Church, 29 July 1967, John
Peter Fitzgerald, younger son of
Maurice Corbin Fitzgerald of the
Bungelow, Belsize Park Gardens,
London N. 63.
b. Heather Lynne, b. 19 March 1946.

iv.   Maud Edith Hammond, b. 17 March 1885, d. 4
May 1890.

v.   Oliver Frederick Gillilan, brigadier, retired, F.S.A., F.R.Hist.S., F.S.G.,
F.R.S.A., F.R.G.S., Leverhulme Research
Fellow; b. 22 Dec. 1887, m. 11 Feb. 1919,
Ella Harold Hallam, b. 20 June 1895, d.
3 Aug. 1968, elder daughter of Arthur
Harold Hallam of Shanghai. Brigadier Hogg
was educated at Bedford, R.M.A. Woolwich,
was commissioned in the Royal Artillery,
23 July 1907, retired as Brigadier in
1946. His vast knowledge of the history
of the Penn family has been generously
made available for this account.
Issue: surname Hogg
1. Niul Uchtred Alexander, late R.N., b. 5
Jan. 1922; m. (1) 5 Sept. 1946, Jane
Huddleston, b. 1 Oct. 1926, daughter
of Edward Huddleston, mar. dissolved
1951; (2) 5 Feb. 1966, Doris Faith

Lishman, b. 24 Aug. 1913, daughter of
Alfred Lishman and widow of Albert Les-
lie Harryman. No issue. Mr. Hogg was
educated at the Royal Naval College,
Dartmouth, and at Exeter College, Oxford (B.A., M.A.); a barrister-at-law,
Assistant Register, H. M. Land Register.

49.   EDITH ELLEN ALEXANDER, youngest daughter of
Lady Louisa Juliana Knox (Sophia Margaretta, Thomas,
William, William, Giles, William, William, John) by
her husband Henry Alexander, was born in 1864, died
27 May 1892. She married 15 Aug. 1891, as first
wife, Col. HENRY HERBERT SOUTHEY, of the 7th Bombay
Lancers, who died 30 Oct. 1926.

Issue: surname Southey
i.   Edith, b. 1892, d. 26 June 1955; m. 29 Ap-
       ril 1916, Lieutenant Commander Eustace
       Hallifax, of the Royal Naval Air Service,
       son of Admiral Hallifax.
       Issue: surname Hallifax
    1. Peter John de Courcy, b. 9 March 1917,
         m. 19 Dec. 1953, Blenheim, New Zealand,
         Helen Scott Johnstone, b. 15 Jan. 1924.
         Issue: surname Hallifax
       a. Charlotte Vanessa Jane, b. 4 Jan. 1955.
       b. Richard Granville de Courcy, b. 30
            Sept. 1957.
    2. Michael Eustace, b. 18 Sept. 1919, m. 11
         Dec. 1942, Elizabeth Howarth, daughter
         of Frederick Howarth.
         Issue: surname Hallifax
       a. Guy Stuart, b. 16 Oct. 1949.
       b. Clive Alexander, b. 13 Oct. 1951.
    3. Pamela Edith, b. 30 June 1922, m. 15 May
         1945, Michael Roland Leahy, b. 15 Sep-
         tember 1919, major in Royal Artillery,
         O.B.E., M.C., retired 1958.
         Issue: surname Leahy
       a. Christopher Michael, b. 8 March 1947.
       b. Anthony John, b. 24 March 1949.
       c. Jonathan Edmund, b. 22 Sept. 1950.
       d. Philippa Sarah, b. 14 June 1953.

50. GWENDOLINE JANE ELIZA GOFF, youngest child of
Lady Adelaide Henriette Louisa Hortense Knox (Mary
Juliana, Sophia Margaretta, Thomas, William, William,
Giles, William, William, John) by her husband Joseph
Goff, was born in 1869, died 5 Sept. 1951. She mar-

ried 12 June 1894, EDWARD SIDNEY WILBRAHAM, born 12
Aug. 1860, died 20 Dec. 1939, second son of Col.
Thomas Wilbraham. She succeeded her brother Algernon in the ownership of Standerwick Court in 1936
and disposed of it in 1946 to her younger son.

 Issue: surname Wilbraham
i.   Edward Jack, b. 18 Nov. 1895, m. St. Mar-
        tin's-in-the-Fields, Chestnut Hill, Pa.,
        24 Sept. 1927, Evelyn Martin, elder
        daughter of Carl Neidhard Martin of Llew-
        ellyn Farm, Bryn Mawr, Pa., by his wife
        Aline S. Taylor. He is a major in the
        Rifle Brigade, Military Cross.
        Issue: surname Wilbraham
     1. Elizabeth Joan, b. 12 Aug. 1928, m. 24
        Sept. 1949, Capt. Geoffrey Ernol Spar-
        row, M.C., Rifle Brigade, only son of
        Lt. Col. W. G. K. S. Sparrow of Birt-
        les Old Hall, Cheshire.
        Issue: surname Sparrow
        a. Geoffrey Randall John, b. 14 Aug.
           1951.
        b. Justin Maurice Andrew, b. 12 June 1953.
        c. Piers Christopher Martin, b. 15 March
           1958.
     2. Martin John, b. 4 June 1931, m. 1 Dec.
        1964 the Hon. Catherine Mary Sidney,
        2nd daughter of William Philip, 1st
        Viscount de L'Isle and 6th Baron de
        L'Isle and Dudley.[192]
        Issue: surname Wilbraham
        a. Alexander John, b. 22 Oct. 1965.
ii.   Thomas Roger, of Standerwick Court, b. 11
        March 1907, d. 14 Feb. 1966; m. 18 Dec.
        1945, Iris Janet Sarsfield Hill, youngest
        daughter of T. Sarsfield Hill of Calcutta.
        Issue: surname Wilbraham
        a. Ann, b. 30 Oct. 1946.

   51. CAROLINE MARY STUART RASHLEIGH, eldest child
of Mary Pole Stuart (William, Sophia Margaretta,
Thomas, William, William, Giles, William, William,
John) by her husband Jonathan Rashleigh, was born
ca. 1844 and died 3 Jan. 1880. She married 21 Nov.
1867, Major CHARLES POORE LONG, born 1834, died 2
Nov. 1871. He was of the 14th Foot, second son of
William Long of Hurt's Hall, Suffolk.

   Issue: surname Long

i.   Mary Eleanor, d.s.p., 1933, m. April 1892,
      John Martin Longe [sic], d. 5 Jan. 1933,
      2nd son of the Rev. John Longe, rector of
      Sternfield, Suffolk.
ii.   William Evelyn, of Hurt's Hall, Suffolk, b.
      10 Feb. 1871, d. 22 Jan. 1944, m. 22 Feb.
      1898, Muriel Hester Wentworth, youngest
      daughter of Thomas Frederick Charles Ver-
      nor Wentworth of Wentworth Castle, co.
      York.
            Issue: surname Long
      1. William George, of Hurt's Hall, b. 28
         March 1899, served in both World Wars.
      2. Aline Hester, b. 25 Jan. 1906, m. 27
         June 1928, Major Hugh Francis Travers
         Aldous, R.E., b. 30 Sept. 1900, 2nd
         son of Hugh Graham Aldous of Gedding
         Hall, Bury St. Edmunds, mar. dissolved
         1938.
               Issue: surname Aldous
         a. Evelyn Frances, b. 26 March 1930, d.
            24 June 1930.
         b. Judith Aline, b. 5 Nov. 1934.
         c. Hugh William, b. 2 Dec. 1935.
      3. Moyra Evelyn, b. 18 June 1908, d. 11 May
         1923.
      4. Louisa, b. 12 Nov. 1909, m. 22 Jan. 1938
         Capt. Alan Walmesley, M.C., Royal
         Welsh Fusiliers, no issue.

   52. EVELYN WILLIAM RASHLEIGH, fifth child of Mary
Pole Stuart (William, Sophia Margaretta, Thomas,
William, William, Giles, William, William, John) by
her husband Jonathan Rashleigh, was born 6 Jan. 1850,
died 29 April 1921, and married 29 April 1879, JANE
ELIZABETH SAVILL-ONLEY, died 13 Oct. 1947, daughter
of Onley Savill-Onley of Stisted Hall, Essex.

   Issue: surname Rashleigh
   i.   Jonathan Onley, b. 2 June 1880, d. 7 Dec.
         1880.
   ii.   William Stuart, of Stoketon, Saltash, Corn-
         wall, C.A. and J.P., Cornwall, A.M. Inst.
         C.E., b. 17 June 1882, m. 2 Sept. 1913,
         Dorothy Frances Howell, daughter of Fran-
         cis Butler Howell of Lostwithiel, Corn-
         wall.
               Issue: surname Rashleigh

1. Jonathan, b. 9 July 1914, d. Sept. 1914.
2. Gwendoline Oenone, b. 4 July 1915, m. Arthur Forbes Johnson, D.F.C., R.A.F., and has issue.
3. Daphne, b. 10 June 1916, m. 23 Aug. 1946 Major Arthur Henry Rede Buckley, O.B.E. Royal Marines.
4. Morwenna, b. 14 May 1917, m. 16 Dec. 1940 Lt. Peter Croome, R.N., and has issue.
5. William Francis, b. 4 Jan. 1920, drowned at Fowey, Cornwall, 25 June 1926.
6. Jennifer Mary, b. 21 March 1921, m. (1) 29 Sept 1939 Squadron Leader Michael Lawson-Smith, mar. dissolved 1947; (2) 26 Jan. 1948 Peter Carleton Rashleigh, son of Dr Hugh George Rashleigh.
    Issue: one by each husband
    a. Anthony Michael, b. 23 Dec. 1940.
    b. Hugh Carleton, b. 4 March 1950.
7. Philip Stuart, b. 15 Nov. 1924.
8. Honor, b. 18 Aug. 1927.

iii. Jane Henrietta, b. 1887, m. 8 Aug. 1914 Harry Rashleigh, b. 22 May 1880, d. 26 April 1950, J.P. for Corwall, served in both World Wars, 3rd son of Sir Colman Battie Rashleigh, 3rd Baronet.[193]
    Issue: surname Rashleigh
1. Elizabeth, b. 18 May 1915.
2. Mary Vivien, b. 9 Sept. 1917, m. 23 Jan. 1941 Commander Philip Joseph Kidd, R.N., 2nd son of Hugh Kidd of Weybourne Holt, Norfolk, and has issue.
3. Sir Harry Evelyn Battie, 5th Baronet, b. 17 May 1923, m. 8 June 1954 Honora Elizabeth Sneyd, only daughter of George Stuart Sneyd of the Watch House, Downderry, Cornwall.[193]
    Issue: surname Rashleigh
    a. Susanna Jane Battie, b. 19 April 1955.
    b. Frances Elizabeth Battie, b. 12 July 1956.
    c. Richard Henry Battie, b. 8 July 1958.
4. Peter, b. 21 Sept. 1924, m. 4 Dec. 1949 Lola Edwards of New South Wales.
    Issue: surname Rashleigh
    a. Margaret Anna, b. 16 May 1950.
    b. Edward Harry, b. 28 Nov. 1952, d.Jan.

1953.
c. Bettine Jane, b. 11 Oct. 1954.
d. Jim Owen, b. 2 April 1956.

53. REGINALD POLE STUART, second son of Charles
Pole Stuart (William, Sophia Margaretta, Thomas,
William, William, Giles, William, William, John) by
his wife Anne Smyth, was born 22 July 1863, died 20
April 1934; married 29 June 1895, HESTER MYBURGH,
died 30 March 1940, daughter of Gerhard Myburgh,
Consul General of the Netherlands in South Africa.
He was a lieutenant colonel in the South Stafford-
shire Regiment.

Issue: surname Stuart
i.   Kathleen Ann Pole, b. 20 Aug. 1899, the
        Stuart heir general; m. 7 July 1926,
        Frederick Robert Wynne, Group Captain,
        R.A.F., born 1895, son of Frederick Ed-
        ward Wynne.
        Issue: surname Wynne
        1. Lucy Elizabeth Anne, b. 17 March 1930,
           m. 14 Jan. 1961 Alan Turner.
        2. Frederick Owen Stuart, b. 17 June 1933,
           m. 6 Sept. 1955 Susan Sheils Bushell,
           daughter of Jack Reginald Bushell
           D.F.M.
           Issue: surname Wynne
           a. Owen Christopher, b. 30 Aug. 1959.
        3. Althea Kathleen, b. 6 Oct. 1936, m. 1
           Sept. 1961, Philip Dresman.
           Issue: surname Dresman
           a. Kathleen Beatrice, b. 11 Dec. 1962.
           b. Rebecca, b. 31 Jan. 1963.
           c. James Barnabas, b. 5 March 1966.
ii.   Rosalind Esme Pole, b. 28 Oct. 1900, Ph.D.,
        London University.

54. ELIZABETH PENN-GASKELL, eldest child of Peter
Penn-Gaskell (Peter, Christiana Gulielma, William,
William, William, William, Giles, William, William,
John) by his wife Louisa Adelaide Heath, was born 19
Dec. 1825, died at Pulaski, Tennessee, 23 Oct. 1866,
buried 3 Nov. 1866 in Laurel Hill Cemetery, Phila-
delphia. She married, 26 July 1855, SAMUEL RUFF
SKILLERN, M.D., born Huntsville, Alabama, 16 March
1834, died at Ardmore, Pa., 17 Feb. 1921 aged 87.
He married, second, Sarah Ross, daughter of William
H. Ross, former Governor of Delaware, and she died

ca. 1911, leaving three sons.
 Issue: surname Skillern
 i. [Peter] Penn-Gaskell, M.D. (U. of Pa.), of
    Philadelphia, b. Columbia, S.C., 28 April
    1856, d. 25 July 1931; m. St. James the
    Less, Philadelphia, 7 Oct. 1878, Anna
    Dorsey, b. 17 Oct. 1861, d. 8 Oct. 1900,
    daughter of Robert Ralston Dorsey, M.D.,
    of Philadelphia; (2) St. James the Less,
    after 1900, Theodosia Hartman, b. 19 Feb.
    1860, d.s.p., 23 June 1935.
    Issue: surname Skillern
   1. Violet Penn-Gaskell, b. 13 Nov. 1879,
    d. 20 May 1948.
   2. [Peter] Penn-Gaskell, M.D. (U. of Pa.)
    b. 26 March 1882, living 1961; m. at
    Kjoge, Denmark, 1 Oct. 1918 Lisa Mar-
    greta Valentiner, living 1961, daugh-
    ter of Julius Valentiner of Kjoge,
    Denmark.
    Issue: surname Skillern
    a. Penn-Gaskell, M.D., b. Philadelphia,
     26 July 1920; m. Cleveland, Ohio,
     4 April 1959, Nora Betty Morris of
     Crowthorne, England, b. 15 Dec.
     1930, daughter of Frederick George
     Morris.
    b. Anna Lisa, b. Philadelphia, 16 Sept.
     1922, m. 13 Sept. 1948 Carl Tasso
     Smith, b. Angola, Ind., 18 April
     1919--wedding at New Orleans.
     Issue: surname Smith, b. New Or-
     Leans
     α Lisa Suzanne, b. 13 Sept. 1949?
     β Richard Mark, b. 31 Oct. 1950.
     γ Christine, b. 10 Dec. 1951.
     δ Carl Tasso, b. 15 Feb. 1955.
     ε Nancy, b. 31 Dec. 1956.
    c. Scott Dorsey, M.D., b. 17 May 1924
     in South Bend, Ind., m. 9 March
     1957 Joyce McCullough of Gary, In-
     diana.
     Issue: surname Skillern
     α Dorsey (f.), b. South Bend, 1 June
     1958.
 ii. Irving H., b. 24 April 1858, d. 1 Oct. 1858
    aged 5 mos. 6 days.
 iii. Louise Fitzgerald, b. 17 May 1859, d. aged

3, bur. Laurel Hill, 11 March 1862.

55. PETER PENN-GASKELL, tenth child of Peter Penn-Gaskell (Peter, Christiana Gulielma, William, William, William, William, Giles, William, William, John) by his wife Louisa Adelaide Heath, was born 24 Oct. 1843, died ca. 1905. He was a major and cavalry officer in the Civil War. He was living in London 27 March 1877, where he had married, 6 July 1869, MARY KATHLEEN STUBBS, born 16 Nov. 18--, died 13 Nov. 1915, eldest daughter of Charles Edward Stubbs Esq. of Sussex Square, Hyde Park, London, formerly of Lima, Peru, by his wife Manuela R----- C-----, who was born in Bolivia, 2 June 18--. Peter Penn-Gaskell studied at the University of Heidelberg, was commissioned 2nd Lt., New Jersey Cavalry, 7 April 1862. He died in Folkestone, Kent. The dates without years come from the birthday book of Elizabeth Coddington who was a close friend of the daughter Winifred. The sketch of this Peter Penn-Gaskell and of his father owe much to Elizabeth Coddington's brother, John Insley Coddington, who was also acquainted with Miss Winifred Penn-Gaskell.

Issue: surname Penn-Gaskell
i.   William, of Shanagarry, co. Cork, a major, killed in action, Chemin des Dames, 12 Oct. 1916.
ii.   Winifred, b. 20 Sept. 1873, of Scobitor, Widecombe-in-the-Moor, Devon, d. unm. at Ashburton, Devon, 6 Nov. 1949 aged 76. She made her will 22 July 1937. At one time she was a close friend of the Coddingtons.
iii. Percy Charles, b. 1878, a major in the British Army in World War I, d. Folkestone, Kent, 26 Feb. 1937. He married after 1911 an actress not named or mentioned in his will.
      Issue: surname Penn-Gaskell
   a. Patricia Maud, under 30 in 1937, an actress, m. ----- Fox; in 1951 was of 38 Grenville Place, Brighton.

56. Col. PETER PENN-GASKELL HALL, younger son of Christiana Gulielma Penn-Gaskell (Peter, Christiana Gulielma, William, William, William, William, Giles, William, William, John) by her husband William Swabric Hall, was born on Tuesday, 16 March 1830, died

Wednesday 1 Feb. 1905 in his 75th year. In 1842-4
he was a member of the Class of 1846 at the University of Pennsylvania, the next two years being
spent in the Medical Department. It has been said
that he was a student at the College of New Jersey,
now Princeton University, but if so, he took no degree, as he does not appear in the *General Catalogue*
of 1906 which is limited to graduates. He was a Philadelphia lawyer, a Civil War officer and afterwards
in the Regular Army until 2 July 1891, a late date
for the retirement of a man born in 1830. He married
first, 24 Dec. 1861, ANNIE M. MIXSELL, born ca. 1841,
died Vicksburg, Mississippi, 14 Feb. 1868, aged 28,
daughter of Philip and Sarah (Deihle) Mixsell of
Easton, Pa., and second, at San Antonio, Texas, 13
Sept. 1871, AMELIA MIXSELL, born 13 Nov. 1847, died
in East Bradford Township, Chester County, Pa., 27
Oct. 1925 aged 78, buried 30 Oct. 1925 in the Lower
Merion Baptist Churchyard. She was presumably a
sister of the first wife.

Issue: surname Hall
   by first wife
i.   Christiana Gulielma Penn-Gaskell, b. Ash-
        wood, Sunday, 19 April 1863, d. unm., 25
        June 1938, bur. Lower Merion.
ii.   Eliza Penn-Gaskell, b. Baltimore, Md., 1
        Feb. 1865, d. ca. 1917; m. 1 July 1892,
        Henry J. Hancock, d. ca. 1906.
        Issue: surname Hancock
        1. Jean Barclay Penn-Gaskell, b. 2023 De-
        Lancey St., Philadelphia, 24 March
        1893, d. 14 Nov. 1955.
iii.   Edward Swabric, b. Ashwood, Wednesday, 9
        Jan. 1867, d. Vicksburg, Miss., Jan.
        1869, bur. Lower Merion.
iv.   Annie Maud Mixsell, b. Vicksburg, Miss.,
        Jan. 1869, d. Holly Springs, Miss., 14
        Feb. 1869, bur. Lower Merion.
   by second wife
v.   William Penn-Gaskell, b. San Antonio, Tex-
        as, 15 Jan. 1873, d. 27 July 1927, bur.
        Lower Merion; he was of Williston Town-
        ship, Chester Co., Pa.; m. at St. Luke's,
        8 Oct. 1904, Caroline Hare Davis, b. at
        Cape May, N.J., 20 July 1876, d. in the
        Pennsylvania Hospital, 2 Sept. 1942, the
        daughter of Sussex Delaware and Mary

Fleming (Hare) Davis.
Issue: surname Hall
1. Mary Fleming Penn-Gaskell, b. 1118 Spruce
   St. Philadelphia, 30 Dec. 1905; m. in
   the garden of Leventhorpe, 8 June 1927,
   Cortlandt Yardley White, III, b. Philadelphia, 2 July 1902, d. Philadelphia,
   25 Jan. 1950, marr. dissolved 1946,
   son of Cortlandt Yardley White, Jr.,
   M.D., and his wife Emily Heroy Sher-
   wood.
   Issue: surname White
   a. Cortland Yardley, IV, b. Philadelphia,
      15 April 1928; m. Episcopal Cathed-
      ral Church of St. Mark, Minneapolis,
      Minn. 7 Sept. 1957, Susan Swain Op-
      stad, b. Minneapolis, 24 Feb. 1936,
      daughter of Raymond Eugene and Helen
      Evelyn (Swain) Opstad.
      Issue: surname White
      α Cortlandt Yardley, V, b. Minneapolis,
        2. March 1964.
   b. Gulielma Penn-Gaskell, b. Philadel-
      phia, 16 April 1930; m. there, 4
      May 1956, Dr Max Krook, b. Stand-
      arton, S. Africa.
2. William Leventhorpe Penn-Gaskell, of
   Rebel Fox Farm (M.I.T. '32), b. Atlantic City, N.J., 9 Oct. 1908; m. (1)
   Christ Church, Philadelphia, 19 Sept.
   1936, Anna Colket McKaig, b. Radnor,
   26 March 1917, daughter of Edgar Stanley McKaig and Annah Colket French,
   of Alderbrook, Radnor, Pa., marr. dissolved 1958, and she m. (2) 7 July
   1959 Dr John D. Gadd of Cockeyville,
   Md., and William m. (2) at the Nesham-
   iny-Warwick Presbyterian Church, 2
   May 1959, Elizabeth Thomas, b. Warren,
   Pa., daughter of Clair Stanley Thomas.
   Issue: surname Hall *by first wife*
   a. Joannah Colket, b. Bryn Mawr, Pa.,
      23 Sept. 1941, bapt. St. David's
      P.E. Church, Radnor; m. old St.
      David's P.E. Church, Radnor, 16
      Feb. 1963, Charles Marshall Glass,
      son of Sydney W. Glass of Grange
      Farms, West Chester, Pa.

b. Miriam Penn-Gaskell.
by second wife
c. Christiana Elizabeth Penn-Gaskell, b.
Bryn Mawr, Pa., 2 Nov. 1960.
d. Peter Thomas Penn-Gaskell, b. Bryn
Mawr, 9 Jan. 1965.
vi. Peter Penn-Gaskell, b. N. Y. City, 14 March
1875, d. unm., Philadelphia, 26 April
1962.
vii. Amelia Penn-Gaskell, b. N. Y. City, 8 Jan.
1877, d. 26 April 1947, bur. 30 April
1947; m. Philadelphia, Cathedral Church
of SS Peter and Paul, by Archbishop Re-
gan, 10 Dec. 1902, Richard Philip Mac-
Grann, of Philadelphia and Killashandra
Farm, Lancaster, Pa., b. Grandview, Mann-
heim Township, Lancaster Co., 13 Oct.
1875, son of Bernard J. and Mary Frances
McGrann. He died 24 July 1935, was a
a member of the Class of 1891, Princeton
University.
Issue: surname MacGrann
1. Bernard Penn-Gaskell, lawyer, b. Grandview, Lancaster Co., 20 Nov. 1903;
Princeton A.B. 1924, U. of Pa. Law
School 1928; m., as 2nd husband, at
Holy Trinity P.E. Church, 24 March
1960, Sarah Henderson Keown, widow of
Edward W. Stevenson, she b. 7 Dec.
1896, daughter of William John and
Martha Foster (Kelder) Keown.
viii. Philip Penn-Gaskell, b. Ashwood, 24 Sept.
1878, d. 15 Nov. 1961; m. Wlmington,
21 Dec. 1901, Mary Eloise Fulton, b.
2108 Fitzwater St., Philadelphia, d. 21
June 1954, daughter of John Clifton and
Mary Elizabeth (Allison) Fulton.
Issue: surname Hall
1. Miriam Eloise, b. 4 Oct. 1902, m. at
Hagerstown, Md., 31 Dec. 1925, Harold
Searles Savidge, of Danville, Pa., b.
20 Dec. 1894, d. 23 Aug. 1960.
Issue: surname Savidge
a. Robert Fulton, b. Philadelphia, 21
March 1927, m. Church of Immaculate
Conception, Philadelphia, 11 April
1953, Mary Carol Hoffer, b. Phila-

delphia, 30 Dec. 1929, daughter of
Norman E. and Winifred M. Hoffer.
Issue: surname Savidge
α Mary Beth, b. Chestnut Hill, 27
   May 1954.
β Kathleen Allison, b. Chestnut
   Hill, 21 March 1957.
γ Mark, b. Chestnut Hill, 30 June
   1959, d. 2 July 1959.
δ Amy Courtney, b. Philadelphia,1
   Nov. 1962.
ε Robin Carol, b. Chestnut Hill, 6
   March 1968.
2. Amy Penn-Gaskell, b. 3916 Pine St.,
   Philadelphia, 27 Nov. 1905; m. Elkton,
   Md., 3 Jan. 1923, Francis Pelzer Lynah, b. Charleston, S.C., 6 Feb. 1899,
   son of Arthur A. and Eliza DeSaussure
   (Pelzer) Lynah.
   Issue: surname Lynah
a. Francis Pelzer, Jr., b. Charleston,
   S.C., 7 April 1924, m. Swarthmore,
   Pa., 23 Aug. 1947, Elmina Alden
   Kite, b. Ridley Park, Pa., 5 Feb.
   1927, daughter of William Stanley
   and Miriam Lovett (Eggleston) Kite.
   Issue: surname Lynah
α Francis Pelzer III, b. Bryn Mawr,
   Pa., 3 Dec. 1951.
β Stephen Kite, b. Milwaukee, Wisc.,
   26 Aug. 1955.
b. Philip Hall, b. New London, Chester
   Co., Pa., 20 Sept. 1912, m. 10 Nov.
   1935, Hortensia Luisa Medrano, b.
   Philadelphia, daughter of Higinio
   Julio Medrano, Cuban Consul at Phil-
   adelphia, by his wife Amelia Luis
   Iraola.
   Issue: surname Hall
α Amy Penn-Gaskell, b. Ridley Park,
   Pa. 24 Oct. 1941; was on 14 Dec.
   1967 engaged to m. Christopher
   Paul Schrode, b. Philadelphia, 23
   June 1940, son of Dr. Paul F.
   Schrode of Wynnewood, Pa., and
   the late Mrs. Claude Rains of
   Sandwich, N.H. Wedding to be 15
   June 1968.

β Miriam Penn-Gaskell, b. Philadelphia, 18 April 1949.

NOTES

[1] PGSP 1:10.

[2] Howard M. Jenkins, *The Family of William Penn,
Founder of Pennsylvania: Ancestry and Descendants*
(Philadelphia 1899). This had appeared earlier in
PMHB 20 (1896) 1-29, 158-175, 370-390, 435-455; 21
(1897) 1-19, 137-160, 324-326, 421-444; 22 (1898)
71-97, 171-195, 326-349, and it seems certain that
the bound volume of 1899 used the type originally
set for serial publication. A warehouse fire, however, burned all the stock of the volume, and so the
book was completely reset from new type, and reissued
with a title-page still dated in 1899, though the
reprint contains additional material which was from
Lea's article in the *New England Historical and Genealogical Register*, vol. 54 (July 1900). The reprint
also contains additional material in a chapter at
the end, and at certain places in the text, though
it was of the same format and binding as the first
printing. Those who have a copy of the book may
determine which printing they have by seeing if a
note appears on the back of the title-page, telling
of the fire; if there are on the pages running titles which indicate the contents of the page; if a
chapter follows page 252, where the original printing ended. Nothing in the volume shows that the
two printings are not identical except comparison
of the two face to face. What the true date of the
second printing was is not certain, as it is entirely possible that Mr. Lea had communicated his information to Mr. Jenkins before it appeared in print,
since Mr. Lea may well have known when it would be
published.

We should here present a select bibliography on
Penn, James Coleman, *A Pedigree & Genealogical Notes
from Wills, Registers, and Deeds, of the Highly Distinguished Family of Penn, of England and America,
designed as a tribute to the memory of the great and
good William Penn, the Founder of Pennsylvania* (London 1871); *Coleman's Reprint of William Penn's Original Proposal and Plan for the Founding & Building
of Philadelphia in Pennsylvania* (London 1881); John
J. Smith, *The Penn Family* (1867), 40 pages, reprinted in *Lippincott's Magazine*, Feb. 1870, 149-162 [be-
gins with the Admiral]; John W. Jordan, *Colonial and*

Revolutionary Families of Pennsylvania (New York 1911) 1:1-22; William I. Hull, *Eight First Biographies of William Penn in Seven Languages and Seven Lands* (Swarthmore College Monographs on Quaker History, #3, 1936); Thomas Clarkson, *Memoirs of the Private and Public Life of William Penn* (Philadelphia, 1st ed., 1813; London, Manchester, New York and Philadelphia, 2nd ed., 1849); William Hepburn Dixon, *William Penn, An Historical Biography from New Sources* (Philadelphia, 1st ed., 1852); Samuel E. Janney, *The Life of William Penn with selections from his correspondence and autobiography* (Philadelphia, 2nd ed., 1853); William J. Buck, *William Penn in America* (Philadelphia 1888); Mrs. Colquhoun Grant, *Quaker and Courtier, Life and Work of William Penn* (London 1907); John W. Graham, *William Penn of Pennsylvania* (London 1917): Mabel Richmond Brailsford, *The Making of William Penn* (New York 1930); Arthur Pound, *The Penns of Pennsylvania and England* (New York 1932); William I. Hull, *William Penn, a Topical Biography* (London, New York, Toronto 1937); Albert Cook Myers, *William Penn's Early Life in Brief 1644-1674* (privately printed 1937); Catherine Owens Peare, *William Penn, a Biography* (Philadelphia, 1st ed. 1957; 2nd ed. Ann Arbor 1966).   See also the following: Charles Knowles Bolton: *The Founders: Portraits of Persons Born Abroad who came to the Colonies in North America Before the Year 1701* (Boston 1919), 285-292; Eli K. Price, "The Proprietary Title of the Penns," reprinted from *The American Law Reporter*, August 1871, 8 pages; William Brooks Rawle, "The General Title of the Penn Family to Pennsylvania" (PMHB 23:60-60, 22 224-240, 329-355, 464-482); Nicholas B. Wainwright, "The Penn Collection" (PMHB 87:393-419).

Oliver Huckel, *A Dreamer of Dreams, Being a New and Intimate Telling of the Love-Story and Life-Work of "Will Penn the Quaker"* (New York, Crowell, copyright 1916), is a work of fiction based on the facts and fancies Mr. Huckel found in other works on Penn. On the title-page appear these words: "An authentic narrative freely arranged from the supposed journal of the fair Guli Springett, as found in an old oaken chest at Worminghurst, England. Also somewhat added by Letitia Penn." The word "authentic" is a pretense introduced by Mr. Huckel who gives himself away by the word "supposed." Pages 146-155 describe the voyage of the *Welcome* and it is claimed that "Thomas Pearson" kept a log on the voyage which was sent to

Guli Penn and was used by her in composing her "supposed" account. It proves to have contained some
sentences actually written by the genuine *Welcome*
passenger, Richard Townsend, in his old age and not
until many years after Guli Penn was dead. A mutiny
is threatened during the voyage! The number of the
passengers is said to be 116 and all are Quakers
except three Huguenots. Enough has been said to show
the worthlessness of this book as history, a copy
of which was discovered two days before that on
which this page is being typed.

[3]Lea's article appeared in NEHGR 54:324-339 and
was, of course, not available to Jenkins until after the first printing. It was used by him for the
second printing. Brigadier O. F. G. Hogg, *Further
Light on the Ancestry of William Penn* (London 1964),
48 pages. In this title the descendants are not discussed. Lea's earlier work was published as "Genealogical Gleanings in England" (PMHB 14:281-296;
16:328-342; 17:55-75), and contains much that does
not pertain to the Penn family under discussion.

[4]PGM 25, no. 2, pp. 69-129; no. 3, pp. 151-182.
The first issue did not reach me until 27 Nov. 1967
and the second on 1 May 1968, when the final draft
of the Penn section of the present volume was about
to be typed.

[5]Pound, *op. cit.* 202.
[6]Peare, *op. cit. 364.*
[7]Penn-Logan Correspondence, 4 Jan. 1701/2.
[8]Peare, *op. cit.* 364.
[9]MQA 21 f.
[10]HEAQG 620. The only other appearances of the
Penns in this source are when: (a) Elizabeth Simms
was received on certificate from Kensington Meeting
dated 2 6th mo. 1685, signed by William Penn and
Gulielma Penn, for an old servant; (b) Thomas Penn
received from London Two Weeks Meeting on certificate dated 8 3rd mo. 1732, received 25 6th mo. 1732.
[11]See Note 3.
[12]Public Record Office, London: Subsidy Roll
E/179/113/213, 1522-24.
[13]PRO E/179/247/1, 1550.
[14]PGM 25:120.
[15]NEHGR 54:326.
[16]Hogg, *op. cit.* 17.
[17]Subsidy Roll E/179/114/325, 1548-1550.
[18]PRO E/179/115/351, 1560.
[19]PRO E/179/115/431, 1594.

[20]Abstracted by H. F. Waters, *Genealogical Gleanings in England* (Boston 1901), 1:434; by Lea (PMHB 14:58; NEHGR 54:333), printed *in extenso* in Hogg, *op. cit.* 37-39, and in Coleman, *op. cit.* 2 f.

[21]On this man see PGM 25:120 f.

[22]Mrs. Roach (PGM 25:71 f.) accepts this Ann Greene as a daughter of William on the strength of this reference in the will. It must be admitted that this would be, *prima facie,* a just conclusion from the wording in the will as it stands in the abstract but there is grave doubt that this woman was William's daughter. Note that though she is "my daughter" her bequest is of the sort given to non-relatives and, indeed, Richard Bidle and his daughter are mentioned before her. Both Brigadier Hogg and I have suspected that "my" is an error for "his" and that Ann was a Bidle, not a Penn. The brigadier has personally examined the document and verified that it has "my" but this document is not the original paper signed by William but the PCC docket copy. The Greene to whom Anne was married was probably Marmaduke Greene of Ballincham, co. Cest., known from the apprentice papers of his son Robert who was apprenticed to Egidius [Giles] Penn, draper, 13 April 1602. Ann certainly had the daughter Elizabeth mentioned in William Penn's will, and probably also a Marmaduke Greene who died abroad, administration granted 3 Oct. 1623 to his sister Ann Sympson, which gives us the name of another probable child (NEHGR 54:325).

[23]On Ann George's ancestry, see Major Thomas George, *Pedigrees and History of the Families of George and Gorges* (Folkestone, Kent, 1903), where her ancestry is traced with certainty as far back as 1310 when the family acquired the Gloucestershire Manor of Baunton, which they held until 1707.

[24]NEHGR 54:334.

[25]PRO E/179/198/287, 1570-1; E/179/198/286, 1580-1.

[26]PMHB 14:291.

[27]PRO E/179/259/20, 1586-7.

[28]PRO E/179/116/451, 1597-8; E/179/116/445, 1599-1600; E/179/269/10, 1603-4.

[29]PRO E/179/116/445, 1599-1600.

[30]PRO E/179/116/504, 1621-2.

[31]NEHGR 54:334.

[32]Brailsford, *op. cit.* 354.

[33]NEHGR 54:330.

[34]NEHGR 54:328.

[35]NEHGR 54:334.

[36]NEHGR 54:330.

[37]NEHGR 54:328.

[38]NEHGR 54:326.

[39]NEHGR 54:327. Date wrongly copied in PGM 25:74 as 3 April.

[40]NEHGR 54:326f. *Calendar of State Papers Domestic,* James I 1611-1618, p. 543.

[41]*Acts of Privy Council 1617-1620,* p. 184.

[42]*Cal. State Papers Dom.,* Car. I 1629-1631, p. 365.

[43]*Ibid.* 57.

[44]*Ibid.* 241.

[45]*Ibid.* 199.

[46]State Papers 71, Barbary States, p. 33.

[47]*Cal. State Papers Dom.,* Car. I, 1637-8, p. 42.

[48]*Ibid.* 1656-7, p. 302; State Papers 71, Barbary States, p. 130 f.

[49]NEHGR 54:328.

[50]NEHGR 54:328, 334. As fourth child Mrs. Roach adds, but with doubt, an Elizabeth Penn, said to have been sister to the Admiral, born perhaps ca. 1605, died at Boston, Mass., 1640, who married in London before 1621, William Hammond, born in London and died there by 1634. The widow and four children arrived in Boston on the *Griffin,* 16 Sept. 1634, in the company of the Rev. Mr. Lothrop. The eldest of the children was Benjamin, born in London 1621, died at Rochester, Mass., 1703 aged 82; married at Sandwich, Mass., 1650, Mary Vincent, born in England, 1633. The other Hammond children were Elizabeth, Martha and Rachel. These Hammonds are, of course, attested (NEHGR 30:29; Jenkins, p. 253), but I know no evidence to prove that Elizabeth was sister of the Admiral as claimed, and I think it highly doubtful as to whether she was of this family.

[51]NEHGR 54:328.

[52]NEHGR 54:326 f.

[53]NEHGR 54:327.

[54]NEHGR 54:328.

[55]NEHGR 54:327.

[56]PGM 25:122, note 9.

[57]KPC 282; PMHB 53:295 note.

[58]PGM 14:296 shows the date from the Register of St. Mary Redcliffe as against the usual date of 30 Sept. 1670. See Granville Penn, *Memorials of the Profession and Life and Times of Sir William Penn, Knt., etc.* (London, 2 vols., 1833); DNB 15:753-56.

[59]Mrs.Roach (PGM 25:76, corrected p. 190) gives the year as 1642/3 but Mr.Dallett (*ibid.* 123) has 1643/4, and, according to him, the actual register has the month as June. This entry was, however, not made at the time of the wedding, as is obvious from the fact that Mr.Roche entered it from memory at a later time, and he was doubtless mistaken as to the month. If 1643/4 is right, then there was time for the birth of the Founder in that year.

[60]*Journal of the Friends Historical Society* (London), 5 (1908) 118.

[61]E.g. Brailsford 11 f.; Graham 14; Peare 11.

[62]The reference to the Penns of Penn, co. Bucks, was inadvertently left out of Mr.Lea's earliest transcription of the inscription which thus caused a small controversy as to whether the words actually appeared in the text. It was settled by Mr.Lea's explanation that the omission was inadvertent.

[63]See Hogg 33 f.; NEHGR 54:328; PMHB 14:172; 16: 246; PGM 25:123.

[64]Hogg 39-41; abstracted in PMHB 14:171f., also in part in Coleman; in PGM 25:76 the date of execution is given as 4 April 1669 and the date of probation as 6 Oct. 1670. The source of these incorrect dates has not been found. It is worthy of note that the Admiral makes no allusion to the place of burial of his father, lending confirmation to the conclusion reached above that Capt. Giles Penn died in foreign parts.

[65]On Sir William Coventry see DNB 4:1287-89.

[66]Probably the nephew unless this is the only place where the like-named brother-in-law recorded himself.

[67]Pepys' Diary gives the date.

[68]Besides the works listed in Note 2, see DNB 15:756-763.

[69]On the attempt to translate Penn's remains to America, see George L. Harrison, *The Remains of William Penn, Pennsylvania's Plea, The Mission to England, Visit to the Grave, Letters,* etc. (Philadelphia 1881).

[70]See DNB 14:1318-1322.

[71]Isaac Penington was born 1616, died 8 Oct. 1679, eldest son of Alderman and Lord Mayor of London, Sir Isaac Penington (1587?-1660) by his first wife Abigail Allen. Isaac and Mary Proude were married at St. Margaret's, Westminster, 13 May 1654. Of Isaac it was said that he was of station "the

most considerable of any that had closed with this
way," that is, became Quakers. Pepys comments on
Mary Penington: "most excellent witty discourse
with this very fine witty lady, and one of the best
I ever heard speak, and indifferent handsome." In
the period 1669-1673 she bought and rebuilt the property called Woodside near Amersham which is mentioned in her will. With the religious independence
shown by Isaac in becoming a Quaker, his brother Arthur chose to become, instead, a Catholic priest.
The Penington children were as follows:

i.   Mary, d. 1726, m. Daniel Wharely of Chal-
      font St. Giles, co. Bucks, a Friend and
      one of the trustees holding Letitia
      Penn's property in America.
ii.   John, eldest son, b. 1665, d. unm., 8 May
      1710, bur. Jordans.
iii. Isaac, drowned at sea, 1670.
iv.   William, b. 1665, d. 1703, an apothecary
      in London.
v.   Edward, b. 3 Sept. 1667, d. 11 Nov. 1701
      [not 1711, as in DNB 15:745, a misprint].
      DAB 14:428 f. says he came to America
      on Penn's second trip, arriving 30 Nov.
      1698, which is a year and a day too early
      if he came on the *Canterbury.* The DNB
      article says he m. at Burlington, 16 Nov.
      1699, Sarah Jennings, eldest daughter of
      Samuel Jennings, formerly of Colehill,
      co. Bucks, and deputy-governor of New
      Jersey 1681-1684, whose will dated 24 Ju-
      ly 1708, probated 18 Oct. 1709 (NJW 1:
      259) alludes to three daughters Sarah,
      Anne and Mercy, as wives of Thomas, Wil-
      liam and John Stevenson, and also to a
      grandson Isaac, son of Edward Penington
      dec'd. It would seem rather probable that
      Edward came in 1698 and not with Penn, as
      he needed time to court and marry Sarah
      Jennings; if he did come with Penn, then
      the date for the marriage must be wrong.
      Edward also is said to have become sur-
      veyor-general on 21 April 1698, but this
      may be the date of the commission, not of
      entering office. The son Isaac married
      Ann Biles and had a son Edward (1726-96).
[72]The certificate is in Jenkins (p. 53). On Gulielma's lease to a tenant, dated 22 July 1669, see

Journal of the Friends Historical Society (London)
2:20.

[73]See Waters, *op. cit.* 576; PMHB 57:97-116; Maria
Webb, *The Penns and Peningtons in the Seventeenth
Century* (1867), and her *Experiences in the Life of
Mary Penington* (Philadelphia 1881); L. Violet Hodg-
kin (Mrs. John Holdsworth), *Gulielma, Wife of William Penn* (London-New York-Toronto 1947); *Blackmansbury* [a periodical], vol. 1, no. 2 (June 1964), 21-
24; Evelyn Abraham Benson, ed., *Penn Family Recipes,
Cooking Recipes of William Penn's Wife Gulielma,
with an Account of the Life of Gulielma Maria Springett Penn* (York, Pa., 1966).

[74]On the date of death and location of the grave,
see PMHB 76:326-329.

[75]A son William, who had a son Herbert, was mentioned in the will of his brother in 1617.

[76]Knighted 22 June 1621 and died 17 Sept. 1639
aged 51; bur. at Ringmer; of Broyle Place, Ringmer,
Sussex, he m. Mary, daughter of John Bellingham of
Erringham. His issue is shown in *Blackmansbury* 1:23
f.

[77]PMHB 57:103.

[78]Marion Balderston, ed., *James Claypoole's Letter Book, London and Philadelphia 1681-1684* (San
Marino, Cal. 1967), 152.

[79]PMHB 17:64-66; Waters, *op. cit.* 575 f.

[80]She did m. Daniel Whearly or Wharely.

[81]This shows how the name was pronounced.

[82]Brigadier Hogg has kindly searched for the Lady Oxenden, and permits us to identify her. The
Heralds' *Visitation of Kent* and Phillpott's *Visitation of Kent*, both dated 1619, are the source. Anne,
daughter of Richard Theobald of Stonepitt, Kent,
married, first, Thomas Nevison of Estrey, Kent;
second, Edward Fagge of Ewell near Faversham, Kent.
By her first husband she had Margaret, sister to
Sir Robert Nevison, Knt., and the said Margaret married, 27 Sept. 1605, Sir John Oxenden, Knt., of
Dene, Kent, who was baptized at Wingham, 28 Aug.
1586, knighted at Whitehall, 17 Nov. 1608, died at
Dene, 27 Sept. 1657. By the second husband Edward
Fagge, Anne Theobald was the mother of Anne Fagge
who married Sir John Proude, Knt., and they became
the parents of Mary, wife, in succession, of Sir
William Springett and Isaac Penington.

[83]When she died, Penn was en route to America on
the *Welcome*.

[84]PMHB 76:79-82; in PGM 25:80 the year is given as 1670/1. On Hannah Callowhill Penn, see Sophia Hutchinson Drinker, *Hannah Penn and the Proprietorship of Pennsylvania* (Philadelphia 1958).

[85]PMHB 81:76-82 where Dr. Cadbury shows that Thomas and Hannah (Hollister) Callowhill had nine children, including two Hannahs, one born 18 April 1664, the other born 11 Feb. 1671, no death record for either. We conclude that it was the second who married William Penn. Six of the nine died young. Deaths of the two Hannahs and of Thomas are not recorded, but Hannah Penn was the only heir. See Pound for a similar conclusion.

[86]Waters, *op. cit.* 692; PMHB 17:66-70.

[87]Obviously in the sense of unthrifty.

[88]PMHB 17:70-72; Waters, 696. On 4 Oct. 1712 Thomas and Hannah Callowhill were both described as recently dead.

[89]The text is based on photostats supplied by the Pierpont Morgan Library.

[90]Letter of James Logan to Hannah Penn, Philadelphia, 11 3rd mo. 1721, printed in MHSP 1 (1864) 222-225, also in PMHB 14:174; Jenkins 120 f.

[91]Waters, *op. cit.* 435-37; PMHB 14:174-76; Jenkins 120 f.

[92]She was, of course, in England and never saw Pennsylvania.

[94]The first digit is not absolutely certain.

[95]The signatures of the witnesses are finely made but that of William Penn has been nearly all torn off. With the will is a sheet, obviously the last of a letter, of which the rest is gone:

> Inter est, & know this, yt h
> for thy childrens good thou
> comest, & by thy Sweet,
> grave & upright carriage
> & life among y[m] thou intro
> ducest the children befor
> they departure, with those cap[a]
> citys they are to h[ave]
> in the land; else am[bition]
> & avarice in Some in a
> their Just interest. I l[eave]
> all wth the Lord, & thee
> his will, to whom b[e]
> wth eternall praise
> thee & them life &

                        both here & fo[rever?]
                        again
                              Thy n in
                              will of Go[d]
                                 WP

[The right hand side of this sheet has been torn
off after the sixth line. Part of the signature is
showing: a large P with a smaller W under it but
whether "Penn" was spelled out cannot be determined.]

[95]MHSP 1 (1864) 222-225 note.

[96]For him see page 353.

[97]The remainder is missing.

[98]The Earl of Oxford and Earle Mortimer were one
man. See *Encyclopaedia Britannica*, 1967 ed., 16:
1179.

[99]No such Earl Poulet is known but Penn probably
meant John, 1st Earl Poulet, who died 1743. See
BPBK, 1967 ed., p. 2028.

[100]Was this really a stroke?

[101]No such phrases are in this will but perhaps
Penn was recalling the fourth will.

[102]This Thomas Penn was probably the Negro servant
mentioned under John Penn (No. 16) and who was also
probably the Thomas Penn who witnessed the wedding of
William Penn Jr. (No. 15).

[103]He was husband of Mary Hollister (daughter of
Dennis and sister of Hannah Callowhill, Hannah Penn's
mother. He was a merchant of Bristol (see Jenkins
pp. 68 and 89, where this identification is accepted,
though on p. 85 he makes Clement brother-in-law of
Hannah Penn and husband of her sister Mary. Clement
was adviser to his niece.

[104]Some imperfections in Waters' transcript of the
Latin have been silently amended by me but there are
still some places where what he has cannot be con-
strued.

[105]Waters, *op. cit.* 438; PMHB 17:62 f.

[106]The Penn descendants are listed by A. D. Chid-
sey, Jr., "The Penn Patents in the Forks of the Delaware" (*Pubs. of the Northampton Co. Hist. and Geneal. Soc.* 2 [1937] 41-47). E. M. Woodrow, *History of
Burlington and Mercer Counties, New Jersey* (1882),
p. 450: "It is said that William Penn, the founder
of Philadelphia, had an adopted son, and from him
descend the Penns of Cumberland, Burlington and O-
cean Counties." No evidence has been found for this
son and I doubt his existence. In the Genealogical

Society of Pennsylvania is an anonymous manuscript
entitled "Penn Family of New Jersey," a poor affair,
merely naming a good many Penns of different periods
without showing their relationship, not even con-
necting sons with fathers. In this work we read:
"There has been mentioned an alleged liaison of William Penn Jr. with a young lady of Bucks County,
when here 1703. Of this James Logan writes, 'Tis a
pity his wife came not with him, for her presence
would have confined him within bounds he was not too
regular in observing.' [MHSP 9:346, Logan to Penn,
22 9th mo. 1704]." Davis's *History of Bucks County*
is cited. The passage is on p. 190 of the 1st edition, vol. 1, pp. 152 f., of the 2nd edition, both
identical, with a frank statement of the weaknesses
of young William's character but not even innuendo
suggesting that he left an illegitimate child.

[107]NEHGR 54:330.
[108]NEHGR 54:331. PGM 25:79 wrongly puts the birth
of the twins in January.
[109]NEHGR 54:331.
[110]PMHB 74:110-112.
[111]HEAQG 405.
[112]NEHGR 54:332.
[113]2 PA 16:443.
[114]NEHGR 54:333; 2 PA 16:440.
[115]NEHGR 54:335.
[116]PGM 25:78.
[117]PGM 25:77 f.
[118]PGM 25:124.
[119]Jenkins, p. 116.
[120]PMHB 70:349-372.
[121]3 PA 1:34.
[122]On the Awbreys see *Journal of the Friends
Historical Society* (London), 1:129 f.; PMHB 13:292-
297, 488 f.; JCRFP 1:139 f.
[123]Pound, *op. cit.* 248.
[124]Jenkins, p. 117; MHSP 9:351, Penn to Logan,
16 11th mo. 1704/5.
[125]See Note 106.
[126]NEHGR 54:327.
[127]PMHB 17:63 f.; Waters, *op. cit.* 438 f.
[128]These two were also in Richard's will but they
died first.
[129]He was probably a Negro servant. See Note 102.
[130]At this date Thomas had no children and was
as yet unmarried.
[131]See DAB 14:432 f.; DNB 15:752 f., which last
reference says wrongly that Thomas was born during

the parents' visit to England; he was born in England but not on a visit. This writer also puts the port of Chester in New Jersey.

[132]Her sepulchral inscription is in Coleman, p. 9.

[133]Her sister Anne was first wife of Thomas, 1st Viscount Cremorne, married 15 July 1754, whose second wife was Philadelphia Hannah Freame, born in Philadelphia, 1740.

[134]Waters, *op. cit.* 439 f.; PMHB 17:64; also DNB 44:307 f.; DAB 14:432 f.

[135]James Hamilton (1710-1783), Governor of Pennsylvania under the Penns; the Rev. Richard Peters was Secretary of the Province.

[136]NEHGR 54:332.

[137]DNB 44:305.

[138]DNB 15:750.

[139]Letter of Thomas Penn to brother John.

[140]PGM 25:82.

[141]Mrs Roach calls her Alice (PGM 25:82).

[142]PMHB 34:191.

[143]PMHB 27:423.

[144]PMHB 34:119.

[145]DNB 44:306 f.; DAB 14:431 f.

[146]On Lynford Lardner, see KPC 316-324. Lardner was born 18 July 1715, died in 1774; m. (1) 27 Oct. 1749 at Christ Church, Elizabeth Branson, daughter of William and Elizabeth (Flower) Branson; (2) also at Christ Church, 29 May 1766, Catherine Lawrence. His will is in PhW Q:56, #52 of 1774, dated 30 Sept. 1774, probated 25 Oct. 1774, and makes no mention of his connection with the Penn family. The name Lynford, at times even Lynford L., was bestowed for several generations on members of the Van Buskirk family in Northampton County, but there can have been no relationship with Lardner. It is probable that the Van Buskirks knew Lardner personally, as he had a hunting lodge in Northampton County, or the association may have been through a sometime clerk in the Land Office, Robert Levers, two of whose daughters married Joseph Van Buskirk and his son William.

[147]Richard Penn's will is in NJW 5:387-389 where information in the codicils is given more fully but the date of one of the codicils is dittoed.

[148]In the will just cited the name Gardner appears in error for Lardner.

[149]Jenkins, p. 116; see also 3 PA 1:34.

[150]For their issue see PGM 25:173.

[151]BPBK 1413; new *Complete-Peerage* 3:132 f.

[152]PMHB 13:292-297, 488; GM 309 f.

[153]On the Fells, including Margaret (Askew) Fell, afterwards wife of George Fox, see DNB 6:1161-1164.

[154]DNB 1:1087-1090.

[155]Mr. Donald Lines Jacobus has kindly assisted me on this paragraph.

[156]For a Vaux pedigree showing ten George Vauxes (not quite all in a single line), see *Journal of the Friends Historical Society* (London), 6:186.

[157]Jenkins, p. 268.

[158]On the Durdins I owe much to John Insley Coddington, F.A.S.G., whose researches into this family's history have yet to be published.

[159]Testimony of Miss Winifred Penn-Gaskell of Scobitor, Widecombe-in-the-Moor, co. Devon, to John Insley Coddington, July 1922.

[160]Jenkins, p. 236.

[161]See DNB 15:748f.

[162]PGM 25:87.

[163]See Nicholas B. Wainwright, "The Penn Collection" (PMHB 87:393-419).

[164]See PGM 25:128 f.; *ibid.* p. 87, where it is wrongly stated that the grant was *signed* by Queen Victoria. The grant was in her name but does not bear her own signature, at least not in the printed form.

[165]On a dinner given to him at Philadelphia, 31 Jan. 1852, see PMHB 24:231.

[166]On the Stuarts' ancestry, see BPBK, 1967 ed. p. 397 under BUTE; also DNB 19:109 and Hogg (PGM 25:152-177).

[167]Mrs. Roach (PGM 25:96) cites Penn-Logan Correspondence for a death date of 20 Dec. 1823.

[168]This death date is from Mrs. Roach (*ibid.*).

[169]DNB 15:749 f.; DAB 14:430; KPC 305-315, 425-429.

[170]The name of the wife accepted in the text is shown in Jenkins, second printing, p. 208 note--the information is ot in the first printing. In the copy of the first printing in the Iowa Historical Library, Des Moines, is a clipping from the *Waynesburg Republican* of 11 May 1955. This attributes to the Pennsylvania folklorist, Henry W. Shoemaker, a fantastic account of the first wife. According to him, the first marriage took place at Gretna Green, and after the separation made necessary by the Penn

family, John Penn brought his first wife, Maria Cox,
to Pennsylvania and placed her in the home of a
friend, Peter Allen, at Harrisburg. The woman, however, ran off with a German serving boy and was later taken to Canada by two Indians who had abducted
her. After she had been pronounced legally dead because of twenty years absence, Mary Cox escaped from
the Indians and walked a thousand miles, ending up
at the Peter Fisher home at Fisher's Ferry below Sunbury on the Susquehanna River. There, by chance,
Governor John Penn came and was reunited with her
but only on her deathbed. This whole tale is without any historical foundation, though the marriage
at Gretna Green is likely enough.

[171]PMHB 29:93.

[172]DNB 15:751 f.; DAB 14:431 f.

[173]Jenkins says it was St. John's College, Cambridge; Mrs. Roach, St. John's College, Oxford.

[174]The account of this woman's descendants owes
much to that in PGM 25:97-119.

[175]See PhD D-17:351.

[176]PCC Admin. Acct Book, Nov. 1803.

[177]The date of his death is given wrongly in PGM
25:94 as 26 April 1840, which is, rather, the date
of his accession at his father's death, as is clearly shown in BPBK, 1967 ed., 2076, and doubtless in
all earlier editions later than 1840. The error appears to be the result of too quickly accepting an
account in the *London Illustrated News* [sic: the
title is really the *Illustrated London News*] of
July 1866, but cited secondhand from the *Penn-Logan
Correspondence* 1:xxxiv. [This was corrected in the
next issue, p. 153.]

[178]PGM 25:95 and 154 substitutes for the name
"Stuart" the name "John."

[179]Burke gives her the name Louise between Henriette and Hortense.

[180]PGM 25:101-104 presents a highly interesting
account of this man.

[181]This section leans heavily on data collected
by John Insley Coddington.

[182]PMHB 24:231.

[183]BPBK, 1967 ed., pp. 1081 and 1078 f.

[184]*Ibid.* 813.

[185]For an account of Jonathan Rashleigh's ancestry, see *Burke's Landed Gentry*, 1939 ed., p. 1890.

[186]For the children, four or five, see PGM 25:112.

[187]BPBK, 1967 ed., p. 492.

[188]*Ibid.* p. 597.
[189]*Ibid.* pp. 2074-2077.
[190]PGM 25:96.
[191]BPBK p. 1532.
[192]*Ibid.*p. 712.
[193]*Ibid.*p. 2080 f.

*PORTIFF/PORTEOUS/PROTEUS/PROTES, JAMES *proved*

The name of this man is spelled variously in the records and what spelling is correct is not clear. That he was a *Welcome* passenger was discovered by Albert Cook Myers who put him on List Q but this has been followed since only by List V.

As in the case of Ellinor Pain, the proof is found in the Minutes of the Board of Property, session of 26 4th mo. 1704,[1] when James Proteus and Ellinor Sykes (formerly Tain [sic: the name was really Pain]), both servants to Wm Wade, who had been on the *Welcome* and left a will mentioning his maids and men servants, asked for their head land and got it.

Portiff was also called servant to John Songhurst in the latter's will, as we shall see, and Songhurst had been executor of Wade's will. On Portiff's properties see Logan Papers 3:9. According to Abraham Ritter, *History of the Moravian Church in Philadelphia* (Philadelphia 1857), p. 46, the tombstone read: "Here lays the body of James Porteus, who departed this life, the 19th of January, 1733, aged seventy-two years." This date seems to be in error as James Porteus left a will dated 30 Nov. 1736, probated 22 Jan. 1736/7,[2] in which everything is left to friends, no wife or child being mentioned.

A sketch on James Proteus appears in Joseph Jackson's *Encyclopaedia of Philadelphia* (Harrisburg 1933), 4:1015. He gives the dates as 1665-1737 with some probability that these are correct. Porteus, he says, was thought to be a native of Dumfries, Scotland, was an architect and builder, built the Slate Roof House in 1699, probably had a lot of influence on the architecture of Christ Church. Jackson seems skeptical that this was Wade's servant who had a warrant in Chester County dated 10 5th mo. 1704. Porteus later lived, he says, in a house at the rear of the present 36 North Third Street, and was buried in the yard of that property. Jackson prints an illustration of the site in 1933 which shows trash on the grave.

NOTES

[1]2 PA 19:434, 438.   [2]PhW F:24, 1736.

POWNALL, GEORGE[1]	*disproved*
POWNALL, ELEONOR, his wife	*disproved*
POWNALL, REUBEN, his son	*disproved*
POWNALL, ELIZABETH, his daughter	*disproved*
POWNALL, SARAH, his daughter	*disproved*
POWNALL, RACHEL, his daughter	*disproved*
POWNALL, ABIGAIL, his daughter	*disproved*

These names appear on List X only, and the name of
the wife is there given wrongly as Mary. The truth
is that this family came on the *Friends' Adventure*,
arriving 28 7th mo. 1682, together with three servants, John Brearele, Thomas Leister[2] and Martha
Worrall. George Pownall registered himself as from
Lostock, Cheshire, also called Lostock Gralam[3] in
the deed of 21 1st mo. 1681[/2] whereby Pownall became a First Purchaser of 1000 acres in Group 41.[4]
Eastburn Reeder[5] in one place wrongly spells the
name "Hostock Grathan," in another as "Laylock."

George Powell or Pownall[6] loaded, 3 June 1682, on
the *Friends' Adventure* 2 chests, 1 coffer, 3 boxes,
1 bag, 2 bundles qty 40 lbs new shoes, 1½ pieces
English linen, 3 doz. woolen stockings for me, 2 cwt
wrought iron, 2 cwt nails, ½ cwt cast lead, ¼ cwt
gunpowder, ½ chest window panes, 3½ doz. felts.

An account of the English ancestry prepared by the
late Alfred R. Justice[7] shows the immigrant George
Pownall as baptized 26 Feb. 1633/4, son of George
and Elizabeth (Hewitt) Pownall, grandson of Humphrey
and Joan (Tue) Pownall, and great-grandson of Ralph
and Anne (Ryley) Pownall and of Thomas Tue. These
names have not been verified but there seems to be
no reason to doubt them.

An early Bucks County document[8] says that George
Pownall died from the fall of a tree on 30 8th mo.
1682 and that his son George was born 11 9th mo.
1682. Davis[9] rightly computes this date as one month
and two days after the arrival but Reeder says it was
within thirty days, and puts the birth of the son on
11 11th mo. 1682/3, on which day Justice dates the
father's death.

The marriage to Eleonor must have occurred in England and her maiden name has been discovered by no
one. She married, second, under the care of Philadelphia Monthly Meeting, 20 10th mo. 1693, Joshua Hoopes,
and she was disowned for disunity by Falls Monthly

Meeting on 7 5th mo. 1697.[10] The date of her death
has not been discovered.

Joshua Hoopes was from Cleveland, Yorkshire, and
came on the *Providence* of Scarborough, Robert Hop-
per, M[r], a husbandman, with his wife Isabell and
children Daniel, Margaret and Christian, date said
to be 9th mo. 1683, though it is not entered so in
Philadelphia Arrivals. His certificate was from
a Gainsborough Monthly Meeting held at Rowsby 4 3rd
mo. 1684, which shows that the arrival could not
have been in 1683. Isabell is stated by Mr. Edwards
to have died in the spring of 1684, which seems a
bit early in view of the date of the certificate.[11]
Falls Monthly Meeting recorded the death of Joshua
Hoopes an elder in the middle of the year 1723, but
when Eleonor died is unknown. Mr. Edwards makes
Eleonor marry, third, at Falls, intention 8 2nd mo.
1723, John Neal Jr. The marriage is authentic but
this must be another Eleonor, for if it were this
one, she would have been recorded as Eleonor Hoopes.
The date of the marriage of Elioner Pownall is shown
as 4 10th mo. 1723, but this is a report of the
marriage.[12]

George Pownall died without probate though it has
been stated that he died intestate, a term usually
meaning that administration was granted. On 22 8th
mo. 1705, the Minutes of the Board of Property[13]
show that George Pownall by lease and release dated
21-22 March 1681 purchased 1000 acres for which the
liberty land was not yet taken up and his son Rowland Pownall [sic: error for Reuben], eldest son,
desired a warrant for his brother George, their
father having died intestate.

Issue: surname Pownall
i. Reuben, b. ca. 1668, m. Crosswicks, New
    Jersey, 16 6th mo. 1699, Mary Stacy, b.
    2 4th mo. 1677, daughter of Mahlon Stacy
    by his wife Rebecca. The will of Mahlon
    Stacy dated 11 Jan. 1703/4, probated
    24 April 1704, mentions among others the
    daughter Mary but not her husband Reuben
    Pownall. He had been dismissed for dis-
    unity at Falls Meeting on 3 10th mo.
    1701. She was granted a certificate to
    go to England with her husband 4 4th
    mo. 1712. She was granted a certificate
    to Haddonfield, 1 10th mo. 1742, and she
    made her will 24 Sept. 1755, probated

10 May 1763[14], in which she calls herself
of Chester, Burlington County, widow, and
bequeaths only to one living sister and
the daughters of deceased sisters, and
mentions no children of her own. On 14
Feb. 1710 Reuben sold to his brother
George. On 18 1st mo. 1717/18 he applied
to the Board of Property for a grant of
a small island or two in the Delaware
over against his land in Makefield for a
cattle range. The note says that these
islands lie before Charles Read's land
and he ought to have them.[15] The last
reference to this Reuben found is as an
abutter of land mortgaged by Thomas Yardley, 11 Nov. 1729, but this does not
prove he was still living.[16] It appears
that he was the father of one daughter,
though accounts of this man usually show
no issue.

Issue: surname Pownall

1. Eleonor, m. Falls, int. 8 2nd 1723,
   marriage reported 4 10th mo. 1723,
   John Neal Jr. She is not mentioned in
   her mother's will in 1755.

ii. Elizabeth, had leave to m. from Falls, 6
    5th mo. 1692, Joseph Clows.[17] He was b.
    in Cheshire, 8 1st mo. 1661/2, son of
    John and Margery (-----) Clowes of ffur-
    nu Pool, Parish of Gosworth, Cheshire,
    and he arrived on the *Friends' Adventure*
    28 7th mo. 1682, with his brother John
    and sister Sarah. See TAG 32:24-26. The
    will of Joseph Clewes of Macclesfield,
    Bucks County, yeoman, was dated 3 12th
    mo. 1709/10, probated 27 Nov. 1711[18] and
    names wife Elizabeth and brother Reuben
    Powner or Pownall executors; children:
    Elizabeth, Rachel, John, Joseph, Thomas,
    George and an unborn child; witnesses:
    Mary Pownall, Richard Hough, Edward Kempe.

iii. Sarah, said by Dr. Arthur Edwin Bye, *History
     of the Bye Family and Some Allied Fami-
     lies* (Easton, Pa., 1956), p. 422, to
     have been b. 25 Dec. 1672, d. 1 Dec. 1694,
     m. probably Burling. I do not know what
     evidence he had.

iv. Rachel, had leave to m., 3 9th mo. 1697[19],

Thomas Janney, b. Pownall Fee, Cheshire,
5 12th mo. 1667/8, death date unknown,
son of Thomas and Margery (Heath) Janney,
late of Horton, Staffordshire, who had
been m. at James Harrison's house in Pownall Fee, 24 9th mo. 1660. Margery Heath
was sister of Anne Heath who m. 1 5th
mo. 1655 James Harrison, then of Kendall,
Northumberland, afterwards *Submission*
passengers and residents of Bucks County,
and a third sister, Jane Heath, was wife
of William Yardley of Ransclough, Staffordshire, to whom a sketch is devoted
hereafter. Rachel (Pownall) Janney d.
after 5 3rd mo. 1742. On the Janney
family see Miles White Jr., "Thomas Janney, Provincial Councillor" (PMHB 27:212-
237) and his "The Quaker Janneys" (*Pubs.
of the Southern Historical Association*
8:119-128; 196-211, 274-286).

Issue:surname Janney, perhaps others
1. Henry, b. 20 4th mo. 1699.
2. Sarah, b. 26 8th mo. 1700; m. 1722 with
   leave to m. 7 1st mo. 1722 Thomas Pugh.
3. Mary, leave to m. 2 4th mo. 1725 Thomas
   Routledge, b. 14 2nd mo. 1712, son of
   John and Margaret (Dalton) Routledge.
4. Abel, d. 1748; m. by N. J. lic. dated
   5 June 1740, Elizabeth Biles, he of
   Maidenhead, she of Bucks County. They
   went to Virginia. See also the Biles
   Excursus in the Brearly sketch above,
   and PMHB 26:358.
v.   Abigail, had leave to m. 5 12th mo. 1695,
   m. 20 12th mo. 1695, William Paxson, b.
   probably in 1665 [Reeder says 1765 which
   is, of course, impossible], d. 1719, 2nd
   son of James and Jane (Gurden) Paxson who
   m. at Marsh Gibbon, co. Bucks, England,
   6 8th mo. 1670. Clarence Vernon Roberts
   (*Roberts-Walton Ancestry* 209) shows that
   said James Paxson is supposedly a son of
   Henry and Joan (Clarke) Paxson of Marsh
   Gibbon who m. there 16 Aug. 1640. Jane
   (Gurden) Paxson d. in Bucks County 7 2nd
   mo. 1710, and James d. 29 7th mo. 1722.
   James Paxson brought a certificate dated
   at Thomas Elwood's, 3 2nd mo. 1682. See

Reeder, *op. cit.*, p. 9.
  Issue: surname Paxson
1. James, b. 5 9th mo, 1702, m. (1) 1723
    Mary Horsman; (2) 1730 Margaret Hodge.
2. Thomas, b. 20 9th mo. 1712, m. 1732 Jane
    Canby, daughter of Thomas Canby.
      Issue: surname Paxson.
    a. Joseph.
    b. Benjamin.
    c. Oliver.
    d. Isaiah.
    e. Jacob.
    f. Jonathan.
    g. Rachel.
    h. One who d. young.

vi.   George, b. Bucks County, 11 9th mo. 1682;
       had leave to m. 6 6th mo. 1707 [Reeder's
       date is 2 5th mo. 1707], Hannah Hutchin-
       son. He mortgaged 316 acres in Solebury
       17 March 1729.[20]
         Issue: surname Pownall
1. John, b. 1708, to North Carolina.
2. Rachel, b. 1714, d. 1788 aet. 74, unm.
3. Reuben, b. 1719; m. Effie Burd of New
    Jersey.
      Issue: surname Pownall
    a. Jane, b. 1747.
    b. Sarah, b. 1749.
    c. Reuben, b. 1750; m. Christ Church,
        Philadelphia, 9 Oct. 1782, Mary Lee.
        Their daughter Mary, b. 20 10th mo.
        1783, m. 1 1st mo. 1817 Richard
        Mattison; a second daughter Eliza-
        beth m. John H. Ely of Solebury
        and their eldest, Reuben Pownall,
        was living at Lambertville, N.J.,
        in 1900, aet. 83.
    d. George, b. 1752.
    e. John, b. 1755, probably the John of
        Bristol whose son Reuben was m. by
        I. Hicks, 19 Feb. 1807, to Maria
        Hoppel; hardly the John of Bucks
        County who d. intestate, admin.
        granted in New Jersey, 24 Oct.
        1771[21], to Elizabeth Pownall of
        Bucks, fellow-bondsman Joseph Hig-
        bee of Trenton.
    f. Rachel, b. 1756.

  g. Elisha, b. 1759, twin.
  h. Hannah, b. 1759, twin.
  i. Grace, b. 1761.
  j. Mary, b. 1766.
  k. Benjamin, b. 1768.
4. Simeon, b. 1721, m. Katherine Housel.
    Issue: surname Pownall
  a. Simeon, b. 1753, d.s.p. 1834; m.
     Sarah Williams.
  b. Levi, b. 1755; m. Wrightstown, 12
     6th mo. 1782, Elizabeth Buckman,
     b. 12 9th mo. 1756, daughter of
     Joseph and Martha (Carr) Buckman,
     on whom see p. 101. On this fami-
     ly see Alex. Harris, *A Biographi-
     cal History of Lancaster County,
     Pennsylvania* (Lancaster 1872), pp.
     450-452, where it is shown that
     Levi d. 1840 in his 85th year,
     leaving
       Issue: surname Pownall
     α Joseph, m. Phoebe Dickinson, daugh-
       ter of Joseph Dickinson.
     β Levi, b. 23 June 1783, d. 25 Jan.
       1863. For his marriage see Ja-
       netta Wright Schoonover, *The
       Brinton Genealogy*, p. 234.
     γ Simeon, m. Maria -----.
     δ Elizabeth.
     ε Catharine.
  c. Ann, m. Buckingham, 12 12th mo. 1781
     Joseph Ballance.
  d. Moses, d.s.p. 22 3rd mo. 1834 aet.
     74; m. Susan Webster.
  e. Mary.
  f. Hannah.
  g. Margaret, m. Buckingham 10 5th mo.
     1786 Benjamin Hamton.
  h. Katharine.
  i. Rachel.

NOTES

[1] On the Pownalls see Sterling W. Edwards, *The Descendants of George and Eleanor Pownall, Quakers who
settled in Bucks County, Pennsylvania, near the
Falls of Delaware, 1682* (Washington, D.C. 1945),
typescript, copy in the Genealogical Society of Pennsylvania; also Eastburn Reeder, *Early Settlers of
Solesbury Township, Bucks County, Pennsylvania*

(Doylestown 1900), Tract 1; Arthur Edwin Bye, *History of the Bye Family and Some Allied Families* (Easton 1956), pp. 412-423.
[2]This is the name which List X has as Robert Saylor.
[3]Frank Smith, *Genealogical Gazetteer of England* (Baltimore 1968), p. 335.
[4]1 PA 1:44. The deed is in Edwards, *op. cit.*, 10.
[5]See Note 1.   [6]PGM 23:48, Note 76.
[7]Genealogical Society of Pennsylvania, JU 19, pp. 3,5,7.
[8]Copy in Genealogical Society of Pennsylvania, GEN Z 27, pp. 25 f.
[9]DHBC 58.   [10]HEAQG 1022.
[11]Edwards, p. 27.   [12]HEAQG 1022.
[13]2 PA 19:467.   [14]NJW 4:337.
[15]2 PA 19: 634 and 685, substantially the same.
[16]PGSP 6:278.   [17]HEAQG 1022.
[18]PhW C:281, #226.   [19]HEAQG 1022.
[20]PGSP 6:283.   [21]NJW 5:403.

REEVES, JOHN   *disproved*

This name appears on List X only as John Reevas. The truth is that he came as servant to Robert Turner on the *Lion* of Liverpool, 14 8th mo. 1683, to serve four years and get £6/10 and the usual fifty acres, loose on 14 8th mo. 1687. He took up a lot on rent early in 1685 "on the Governor's Land."[1] John Reaves of Cape May, yeoman, made his will 29 Dec. 1714, probated 22 April 1715,[2] naming wife Sarah as executrix, and mentioning daughter Sary and John Ingrum "when his term is up." The witnesses were Daniel Wells, Henry Leonard (56 years old) and Hannah Lenord. Inventory came to £156/1/3 and was made by Daniel Wells and John Taylor, 10 Jan. 1714/5. Final account was filed 7 Aug. 1731 by John Ingram and his wife Sarah, the executrix named in the will, so it was the widow and not the daughter who married the erstwhile servant. Though the Reeve family is found in Burlington County, no connection with this man has been discovered.

NOTES
[1]PGM 24:92, note 88; W&S 3:250.   [2]NJW 1:378.

ROBERTSON, WILLIAM   *disproved*

This name is on List X only. The truth is that he came on the *Lion* of Liverpool arriving 14 8th mo.

1683, as servant of Joseph Fisher, to serve four
years, get fifty acres, loose on 14 8th mo. 1687.
No success has been had in tracing this man further.
Such William Robertsons as were found can be shown
to be hardly this one, and the problem is further
complicated by the fact that Robertson is provided
with variants like Robinson, Robeson, etc., making
identification doubly difficult.

ROCHFORD, DENNIS	*proved*
ROCHFORD, MARY HERIOTT, his second wife	*proved*
*+ROCHFORD, GRACE, daughter by first wife	*proved*
*+ROCHFORD, MARY, daughter by second wife	*proved*

Dennis Rochford is, of course, on all lists; his
wife Mary, on Lists A, B, C, D, E, F, G, I, M, O,
Q, U, V, X, Y and Z, and the two daughters are on
the same lists with the exception of List M where
they are indicated but not named.

The proof of this family's presence on the *Welcome*
is to be found in Rochford's own statement included
in Philadelphia Arrivals, the longest entry in either set of Arrivals, here transcribed from the original:[1]

> Dennis Rochford son of William Rochford, who
> was Born in Enisscorfey [Enniscorthy] in the |
> County of Waxford in Ireland aboute the year
> [16]47; And through the goodness and | Mercy of
> the Lord was Convinced of gods blessed truth Aboute
> the year [16]62: Went | into England & Landed in
> Whitehaven in Cumberland the 30th of 3^d mo. 1675.
> | Dwelt in Brighthelmston in Sussex 3 yeares &
> kept a grocers shop, And came into | this Pro-
> vince of Pennsilvania with Mary his wife [(]Daugh-
> ter of John Heriott of | the Parish of Hestper
> poynt in Sussex in old England she was Born on the
> 14th | of the 3^d month [16]52) in the ship Called
> the Welcom Robert Greenaway Comander | with two
> servants Tho: Jones & Jeane Mathewes. the said
> Dennis two Daughters | Grace & Mary Rochford dyed
> upon the Sea in the said ship Grace being | aboue
> 3 years old & Mary being 6 Months old the said
> Dennis Rochford Landed |wth his family in Pennsil-
> vania aboute the 24th day of the 8th Month 1682. |

> Mary Rochford the second Daughter of Dennis & Mary
> Rochford was | born in the Province of Pennsilvan-
> ia at Egely poynt in the County of | Philadelphia
> the 22th [sic] of the 8th Mo. 1683 betweene 10:

& 11th at night she | being their second Daughter
of that name.

Note that the text always spells the name Rochford
but the printed version[1] has Rutheford once, Roth-
ford twice, Rutherford thrice.

As will have been noted, Dennis stated that he was
son of William Rochford and was born in Enisscorfey
in the County of Waxford, Ireland, a place really
called Enniscorthy, co. Wexford. It has been stated
to me that Dennis's ancestry can be traced in Ireland but such works as are available for consultation, while they show Rochfords in Ireland, do not
reveal Dennis.[2] Dennis's statement omits all references to the first wife but identifies the second
wife Mary as daughter of John Heriott of the Parish
of Hestper poynt [Hurstpierpont], Sussex, and there
is evidence to show that she was sister to Thomas
Heriott, also a *Welcome* passenger, whose sketch
should be read in this connection.

At the Men's Meeting at New Garden, Ireland, 25
10th mo. 1670, there was discussion of whether Dennis Rochford and Grace Edmundson should marry. At
the General Meeting at Arthy, Ireland, 16 6th mo.
1673, their marriage was still a matter for discussion and their disengagement was approved. It appears that Grace Edmundson has said that a man had
died for love of her, and Friends thought this flip-
pant and required her to retract, which she did.
Yet Dennis appeared to have carried a torch for his
first love, for he named his first child for her.

Dennis was present in London as a witness to a
wedding, 22 9th mo. 1677. At Gatton, Sussex, 4 7th
1678, he declared his intention to marry Patience
Life, second intention and approved, 2 8th mo.
1678, and the marriage took place at Blackman's
Street, Southwark. The daughter Grace was born 19
5th mo. 1679 and her mother Patience was buried at
Rottingdean, 26 5th mo. 1679.[3]

Dennis next declared his first intention to marry
Mary Heriott on 17 1st mo. 1679/80, consent given
21 2nd mo. 1680. At Lewes Monthly Meeting in Sussex, on 21 4th mo. 1682, Dennis Rochford of Brighthelmston [Brighton] applied for a certificate to go
to Pennsylvania. The certificate was recorded on
20 7th mo. 1682 but was not copied into the minutes
and it has not been discovered in America. As will
be seen, Dennis Rochford loaded on the *Welcome*, 19
July 1682, the following dutiable merchandise: 14

cwt wrought iron; 1½ cwt haberdashery; 2 bushels pease; 3 flitches bacon; 1 chest window glass; 6 lbs shoes; 1 great saddle; cwt wrought pewter [duty 16s. 1½ d. From the free list: 7 parcels of apparel.][4] As these items are entered in the London Port Book, it is clear that the Rochfords had made the long journey to the Thames instead of boarding the *Welcome* at a stop which the ship might have made at Brighthelmston as it passed through the English Channel.

Before sailing Dennis Rochford subscribed £25 (the minimum accepted) to the Society of Free Traders[5] and later subscribed a like sum, this time marked "P.F." which probably means that Philip Ford had received his payment.

Minshall Painter[6] says that Rochford settled in Concord, Chester County, and I have seen his name in a Chester County deed as an abutter. In a return of part of Philadelphia County, 1684, a list of men from age 16 to 60, living between Peter Cox's Island to Andros Boon's, etc., has Dennis Rotchford above 16 "a hundred & 60 acker of Land and one Acker improved." Dennis was then aged 37 years.

The Lewes Monthly Meeting of 20 1st mo. 1694/5[7] shows that Ann Scrase was sister to Mary, widow of Dionis Rochford. He had died in Philadelphia County, 7 2nd mo. 1693,[8] so that there was plenty of time for the news to have reached Sussex. His widow Mary Rochford died by 28 10th mo. 1694, really buried at Philadelphia, 25 10th mo. 1694. Administration was granted 22 Dec. 5 William and Mary 1693 on the estate of Dennis Rochford to his widow Mercy, obviously an error for Mary, since when William Carter took administration on her estate, 8 12th mo. 1694/5,[9] she was called Mary Rotchford.

The minutes of Philadelphia Monthly Meeting[10] state that five small children were left on the death of their parents, and as the estate was heavily in debt, a committee was appointed to see what might be saved for the children and how they might be apprenticed or otherwise provided for.

Heriott's purchase from Penn in 1681 was inherited by Rochford and surveyed to him in 1685, 1200 acres in one plot, 3000 in another, which were found to straddle the Philadelphia-Bucks County line. But the 3000 acres were included in a 5000 acre tract also surveyed to William Biles and later owned by Thomas Hudson, then finally sold to a group of Long

Island Quakers of the Stevenson and Field families. Then commenced a fight over the property which lasted for many years, ending in support for the owners under the Heriott-Rochford claim. The first item is Board of Property Minutes, 7 1st mo. 1689/90[11] and the final entry 27 11th mo. 1719/20.[12] All of the Rochford items in any part of the volume just cited concern the property inherited from his brother-in-law Thomas Heriott. Rochford was himself a very unsuccessful business man and his property was all lost to his family.[13] He was among debtors to the estate of John Clarke, 17 Nov. 1691, listed in the inventory. John Clarke was murdered by Thomas Leatherland.[14]

Two other items may indicate something of his character. He had a warrant for 100 acres for his liberty lot of 5000 acres. When he applied for this lot, Thomas Holme told him that he had been ordered to allow no more than 80 acres to any whatsoever. Rochford, however, was unwilling to accept less than 100 acres.[15] Chester Court Records 52 f., show a suit of Rochford against John Sumption his servant, and he was awarded £4/10.

In the A. C. Myers Welcome Papers at the Chester County Historical Society in West Chester there is, under Rochford, an allusion to Gibson MSS on the Third Floor of the Historical Society of Pennsylvania. An attempt to locate these papers failed but the following is what Myers derived from them.

A complaint was filed 20 March 1724/5 by Joseph England who said that Dennis Rochford had by wife Mary three sons, Herriott, Solomon, Dennis; that Richard Scrase had by wife Ann Herriott, Richard, Ann, Elizabeth and Susanna Scrase, the three girls having married, respectively, John Older, Jonas Revet and James Larford [this surname highly doubtful]; that the three girls on 7/8 Jan. 1719/20 deeded their interest in the property to the said Joseph England. He further claimed that Rochford had wrongfully claimed the Heriott property under the will of Heriott and that the Scrases were also heirs. Further, the younger Richard Scrase had come to America and made a nuncupative will in Pennsylvania, date not given, date of arrival in America 1715 or thereabouts. Two Rochford sons were living "in low estate" in 1715.[16]

As for the "low estate" of the two Rochfords, one had married a daughter of Mayor William Hudson

who was a man of some importance in Philadelphia
even then; the other, a daughter of Edward James of
whom I know little. The will of Richard Scrase,
late of the County of Sussex, Great Britain, now of
Pennsylvania, was dated 1 Sept. 1715, probated 17
Sept. 1715, James Steele, executor; residuary lega-
tees; Uncle Walter Scrase and Charles Scrase of
Blackington, Sussex [i.e. Blechington].[17] There is
no sign that the will is nuncupative, as England
claimed; 1/- each to sisters Ann Scrase (wife of
John Houlder), Elizabeth (wife of Jonas Revett),
Susanna (wife of James Lurford, but the name of this
man is again highly doubtful); kinsmen: Dennis Roch-
ford, Solomon Rochford; witnesses: Thomas Shute,
Thomas Hood. Attached are depositions of Matthias
Breckner, Tayler, of Burlington, aged ca. 22, and of
Thomas Hood, which show that two days after he
made the will, Richard Scrase was regarded as mad
and had to be tied up. "They were all rogues and
cheated me out of my will," he said, while in Thomas
Shields' house.
   Further information on the Scrase family appears
in the sketch on Thomas Heriott.
   Solomon Rochford, potter [he had been apprenticed to a weaver], and Dennis Rochford, potter, two
of the sons of Dennis Rochford, late of Pennsylvania,
yeoman, and Mary, both deceased, one of the sisters
of Thomas Heriott, conveyed to Richard Hall, property on the east side of Second Street from the Delaware.[18] In the Blackwell Rent Roll of 1689[19] Dennis
is shown with a 20 foot lot, by purchase, 1/- for
five years, on the west side of Front Street, north
of Chestnut; also two 132 old purchase lots for 5/-
for five years, on the north side of High Street between Fourth and Fifth; also on the right of Tho:
Heriott by purchase, 1/6 for five years and on the
west side of Front Street, north of Chestnut. Rochford sold it to John Test.[20]

   Issue: surname Rochford
      by first wife Patience Life
   i.   Grace, b. England, 19 5th mo. 1679, d. at
        sea, 1682.
      by second wife Mary Heriott
   ii. Mary, b. England, ca. 1682, d. at sea, 1682,
        aged 6 mos.
   iii. Mary, b. Egely Point, Pa., late evening of
        22 8th mo. 1683; d. Philadelphia, unm.,
        9 3rd mo. 1702/3, eldest of the five

surviving children.

iv. Herriott, no birth or death record found; not living 1715; known only from Joseph England's complaint; presumably second of the five surviving children.

v. Solomon, no birth record found, b. ca. 1689, aged four when apprenticed 29 1st mo. 1695 to Thomas Hood, weaver; d. Philadelphia, 7 6th mo. 1765, aged 76; m. (1) Alice James, d. Philadelphia, 6 9th mo. 1744, daughter of Edward James; (2) Philadelphia Meeting House, 11 4th mo. 1747, Rebecca Bolton, b. Cheltenham, Pa., 29 1st mo. 1701, d. 20 Sept. 1759, 10th child of Everard Bolton. No probate has been seen and only one child, by first wife:

1. Patience, d. Philadelphia, 9 11th mo. 1739, evidently unm.

vi. Dennis, no birth record found; d. 10 11th mo. 1739, of drowning. An obituary in *The American Mercury* of 15 Jan. 1739/40 says that he "had the misfortune in the night to fall off of our Wharfs into the River and was drown'd." He was apprenticed ca. 21 11th mo. 1698/9 to Joshua Tittery, potter; m. 10 12th mo. 1714, Elizabeth Hudson, b. 19 4th mo. 1693, d. 28 11th mo. 1738, said to be daughter of Mayor William Hudson in whose will (see p. 45), she is not mentioned. Administration was granted 18 June 1741[21] to Duncan Murray, principal creditor, the daughter Mary having renounced.

Issue:

1. Elizabeth, d. Philadelphia, 16 7th mo. 1720.

2. Elizabeth, d. Philadelphia, 12 12th mo. 1730/1.

3. Mary, d. Philadelphia, 2 2nd mo. 1767, as "Mary Bell, daughter of Dennis Rochford." If any descendants of Dennis and Mary (Heriott) Rochford are now living, they must descend from her. She was almost certainly the Mary Rochford recorded in Christ Church registers as marrying, 1 Feb. 1759, John Logan. No probate has been found for either, and this John Logan was

not a son or grandson of James and Sarah (Read) Logan.

NOTES

[1]PMHB 8:334.

[2]See John O'Hart, *Irish Pedigrees* (Dublin 1892), 2:375 f.: Rochford of Kilbride, co. Meath, where neither Dennis nor co. Wexford appear; John Lodge, ed. by Merwyn Archdall, *Peerage of Ireland* (Dublin 1789), 3:13-30, on Rochfort, Earl of Belvedere; and two items not seen: *Journal of the Cork Hist. Soc.*, 2nd ser., 21:112; *The Irish Builder* 29:289; 35:78.

[3]Thanks are due Mrs. Marion Balderston for most of the items from English and Irish Friends records cited in this sketch.

[4]PGM 23:57, and Note 110.   [5]PMHB 11:175 f.
[6]PGSP 4:299   [7]PGSP 13:273 f.
[8]HEAQG 415.   [9]PhA A:178.
[10]PGSP 4:172 f.   [11]2 PA 19:22.
[12]2 PA 19:697.
[13]See 3 PA 3:4, 8, 10 f., 381; MIQ 278f.
[14]NJW 1:94.   [15]3 PA 3:313, 1684.
[16]Note that originally there had been five Scrase children--see PGSP 13:273 f.
[17]PhW D:45.   [18]PhD H-9, p. 359.
[19]PGM 23:76, 81.
[20]PhD E-1, p.5, 7 10th mo. 1685.
[21]PhA D:172.

RODNEY, WILLIAM   *disproved*

This claim, discovered and disproved by Walter Lee Sheppard, was first made by J. Henry Lea[1] who said of a William Rodney, born, as he supposed, ca. 1652, that Rodney had come to America with William Penn in 1682. He identified this man as son of another William born 1610, who married Alice, daughter of Sir Thomas Caesar knt., Baron of the Exchequer. He also identified the father as fourth and youngest surviving son of Sir John Rodney knt., of Rodney Stoke, Somerset, by wife Jane, daughter of Sir Henry Seymour knt., brother of Edward, Duke of Somerset, and of Queen Jane Seymour, third queen of Henry VIII. This information was introduced by Lea into his account of the apprenticeship papers dated 15 Aug. 1657 of one Caesar Rodney, son of William Rodney of Catcott, co. Somerset, to William Typpett of Bristol, haberdasher, and his wife not named.

Part of this information was later picked up by

Frederick L. Weis, *Magna Carta Sureties 1215* (1955),
Line 38: "William Rodney came to Pennsylvania with
William Penn in 1682."

The disproof is to be found in the fact that at
a Court for St. Jones County on Delaware Bay, 20 Dec.
1681, in the case of Sarah Bartlett vs Nicholas
Bartlett, William Rodney was foreman of the jury.[2]
In addition, William Rodney wrote to William Penn
from London on 14 Oct. 1690 a letter in which he
says he had been in Pennsylvania about ten years.[3]
Had he come with Penn in 1682, Penn would not have
needed to be told this. Therefore, George H. Ryder
is about right when he says[4] that William Rodney
emigrated to America ca. 1681.

William Rodney the immigrant is incontroverti-
bly to be placed in the family of Rodney of Stoke
Rodney, co. Somerset, which is discussed in Burke's
Peerage, Baronetage and Knightage, 104th edition
(1967), 2136-2138, apropos of the present 8th Baron
Rodney, but Lea, Weis and Burke are all mistaken in
the position which they select for him, having o-
mitted one generation.[5] He was therefore the only
Welcome claimant who had connections with both the
peerage and the royal family.[6]

There is now preserved a most interesting early
genealogy of the Rodneys compiled by Sir Edward Rodney (1590-1657), which was printed in *The Genealogist,* new series, 16:207-214, 17:6-12, 100-106, with
discussion by W. H. B. Bird in 26:1-7 [this mostly
on the pre-Rodney history of Stoke, a criticism of
Collinson's *History of Somerset* 3:602] and 26:93-
101 (a criticism of the earlier part of Sir Edward's
genealogy). The manuscript was formerly in the
possession of the late Hon. William Powell Rodney
(1794-1878), son of the 2nd Baron Rodney. I do not
know where it is now. Sir Edward had a fine sense
of the value of historical evidence; was careful
about drawing conclusions, and cited primary records
precisely. If Mr. Bird has exploded some of the account of the earliest Rodneys, it is from a part of
the narrative in which Sir Edward has himself suggested caution. The work was dedicated in 1655 to
daughters Elizabeth, Penelope [then wife of Peter
Gleane], Anne, Jane and Katherine Rodeney, as Sir
Edward normally spelled the name. There is internal
evidence that some of it was written as early as
1622. Mention is frequently made of a Pedigree which
the compiler evidently had before him but which was

not printed with the text, if extant with it.[7]

THE RODNEY FAMILY

Sir Edward begins with a tradition in the family
that the Rodeneys came to England with the Empress
Mathilda but he had found no evidence to prove this.
In 1601, at the time of the death of Sir George Rodney, of whom later, a piece of brass about two feet
square, which had been in the family, "miscarried."
On this brass were incised the names of the lands
granted to a Rodeney, presumably named Walter, by
the Empress Mathilda. This had been seen many times
by Sir Edward's mother, Jane Seymour, and its loss
had been greatly regretted by his father, but apparently had never been seen by Sir Edward himself
who was eleven when Sir George died, and he had no
copy of the list. In any case, the heir of the said
Walter Rodeney was Sir Henry. A Dr. Barlow, late
Dean of Wells and godfather of Sir Edward's son
George, is credited with the statement that he had
seen in "the White Book" of the Dean and Chapter of
Wells, the statement that this Sir Henry had served
as arbitrator of a dispute between the Dean and
Chapter of Wells and others. The Pedigree stated
that Sir Henry was steward to the young King Henry
II who was crowned in his father's lifetime [on 15
July 1170].

On 4 May 1638 Sir Edward was told by a Dr. Pierce
that the latter had seen in an ancient book of the
Cathedral Church of Wells the name Rodeney, which he
asserted to be as old as the foundation of Wells itself, i.e. it went back three hundred years before
the Conquest. On this Sir Edward was properly non-
committal.

One Mr. Rice Davies, who, as we shall see, had
married a daughter of Mr. Maurice Rodeney, reported
to Sir Edward that there was in Wales a river called
Aebba Rodeney, because Rodeneys has been slain there.
The Pedigree identified these men as Sir Richard
Rodeney, who, with his elder son Richard, was slain
at Hereford in 1234 by Leolin, Prince of Wales, obviously Llewellyn ap Iorwerth. The Sir Richard slain
at Hereford had married Jane, daughter of Sir John
Eastley, Knt., and his son Richard, also slain, had
married Margaret Burnell, and left a daughter Jane
who married Sir Thomas Patishall Knt. The Pedigree
also had a Sir Richard Rodeney slain at Acres [Acre]
in 4 Richard I, and a William Rodeney who died on

his way to Rome as ambassador of King John to the
Pope, and was buried at Viterbo.

Thus it was Thomas, the second son, who succeeded
in 1234 and he married Margaret, daughter of Sir
Arnold Mountney. They were parents, according to Sir
Edward, of the Sir Richard Rodeney who is the earliest scion of the family included in Burke. Thus
far we have been following Sir Edward. The six
generations shown are all accepted in a pedigree
chart made in 1909 or thereabouts by W. Nelson Mayhew and deposited in the Genealogical Society of
Pennsylvania.[8] They were convincingly attacked by
Mr. Bird in the reference cited and they are omitted
entirely in Burke, where it is not made quite clear
that they are rejected.

Sir Edward, however, did not know of a confirmation by the Dean and Chapter of Wells of a grant of
the village of Marh near Markham and Rodney to Sir
Richard de Rodeney and wife Lucy, a grant previously
held by a William de Rodeney, this confirmation cited
in Burke from the opening of the reign of Edward II.
This raises doubt as to the parentage of the said
Sir Richard, for the William from whom they inherited
is not found in Sir Edward's account.[9]

With the Sir Richard whose wife was Lucy, however,
we are on firmer ground. Sir Edward placed his birth
about 1250, though Burke favors a date of about 1270,
since he is first found in the Somerset Feet of Fines
in 1297, and his first wife was identified in the
Pedigree as Maud, daughter of Sir Osbert Gifford;
the second, the said Lucy, mother of the three sons;
and a third, unknown. Burke tells us that he was in
the king's service from 1307; in 1314-1316 commissioner of sea walls and dykes, first at Hambury Salt
Marsh in Gloucestershire and afterwards on the Somerset coast; was knighted at Keynsham Abbey in 1316;
in 1322 was constable of Bristol Castle. A descrip-
tion of his knighting appears in the 1631 edition of
John Selden's *Titles of Honour*.

According to Sir Edward, Sir Richard held the
following manors (names starred are still on the
map):

*Stoke Gifford since Stoke Rodney	£40	p.a.
*Backwell	70	
Tilleyscourt	6	
*Tiverton	27	
*Salford	15	
Windford	18	

Hallowtrow	12
*Lamyatt	30
Livington	9
*Dinder	13
*Over-Badgeworth	24
*Congresbury-Rodeney	16
*In Bristoll [not a manor]	50
	£330

Sir Edward alludes to the inflationary trend by remarking that in his time Rodeney-Stoke produced £300
and Backwell £200. From these holdings Maurice Rodeney sold land in Bristol worth £50 old rent and
Sir Edward's great-grandfather, Sir John, settled the
manors of Congresbury and Over-Badgeworth on his two
younger sons, but, as we shall presently see, these
two manors did not leave the family.

The eldest son and heir of Sir Richard was Sir
Walter but, we are told, the Pedigree called him Sir
William, and this is the name given in the Mayhew
pedigree cited above. Sir Edward cites his two wives
as, first, Katherine, daughter of Fulke Warren Knt.;
second, Alice, daughter of Sir John Clifford Knt. of
Somersetshire. The Mayhew pedigree reverses the order of the two marriages and calls the first Cicilie,
daughter of Sir John Clifford, and gives her a son
John; the second, according to this source, was Katherine Fitz Warren, daughter of Foulk Fitz Warren,
and she had sons William and Thomas. The son William
died *vita patris*, leaving a daughter who married Sir
Henry Lorly [Lorty?] Knt., and so the heir was the
second son Thomas who married Elizabeth Blewet, the
daughter of Sir John Blewet Knt. of Wiltshire, though
this identification, which doubtless came from the
Pedigree, was questioned by Sir Edward who knew of
no such family in Wiltshire. The Mayhew pedigree
spells the name Bluet.

Thomas was succeeded by his son of the same name
who married into the Cresse family. Mayhew here
again supplies the name of the wife, Jane Cresse, the
daughter of Hugh Cresse, and he calls her husband
Sir Thomas. He had, besides his heir, a daughter
Katherine and a son Thomas. The heir was Sir John
who married Alice of the Chedder family. Mayhew
calls her Catherine, daughter of Sir Robert Chedder,
and gives this couple Thomas, John, William and Jane
besides the heir, Sir Walter, who, in 3 Henry IV,
entered into an agreement with Sir William Bonvile
for the dowry of Alice, wife to Sir John Rodeney de-

ceased. Evidently, Sir Edward is right as to her
name. The last-named Sir Walter married a St. John,
and Sir Edward says she was of a family raised to
the peerage by Charles I with the title of Earl of
Bolingbroke. Mayhew says the wife's name was Doro-
thee and that she was a daughter of Sir Roger St.
John. There is now a Viscountcy Bolingbroke held
by a St. John descendant, but in the lineage printed
in Burke,[10] there is shown no Roger St. John and no
Earl of Bolingbroke. The first Earl of Bolingbroke
was, however, Oliver St. John, 4th Baron St. John of
Bletsho, created Earl of Bolingbroke 28 Dec. 1624,
died in 1646,[11] this earldom being extinct since
1711.

Next came Sir John Rodeney whose daughter Margaret was second wife to Thomas Burdet of Arrow, be-
headed in 17 Edward IV for some remarks made about
a white buck shot by the king in his park. From this
Burdet descended, so Sir Edward says, Sir Thomas
Burdet, Bart., of Bremeot, co. Warwick, living "now
1622." Having perhaps been concentrating too much on
the Burdet story, Sir Edward says nothing of Sir
John Rodeney's wife who was, according to Mayhew,
Jane, daughter of Richard Bridgemanston. Sir John's
heir was his son Sir Walter who married Margaret,
daughter of Lord Hungerford, and died 6 Edward IV,
leaving as heir a son Thomas, aet. 30. Thomas's
marriage was omitted in the Pedigree but Sir Edward's
father had written "Powlett" in the margin, and from
an *inquisitio post mortem* dated 18 Edward IV, Sir
Edward learned that her name was Isabel; that she
married, second, William Powlett Esq.; that she was
herself a second wife to Sir Thomas in succession
to Ione Moore, daughter of Thomas Moore. Sir Thomas
Rodeney died 16 Feb. 17 Edward IV, leaving a son
John then aet. 10. All that Mayhew has to offer on
this Sir Thomas is the statement that his wife was
Isabel.

The last-named Sir John married Ann, daughter of
Sir James Croft Knt., as Sir Edward says, but a note
by the editor says she was really daughter of Richard Crofte, guardian of the boy, and that his will
is in PCC 14 Blamyr. Sir John Rodeney and wife Ann
Crofte were the great-grandparents of Sir Edward
Rodeney, the compiler of the genealogy.

1. Sir John Rodeney, aet. 19 in 17 Edward IV, married, as stated, Ann, daughter of Richard Crofte,
and he died 18 Henry VIII 1527, she in 38 Henry VIII.

Mayhew gives the birth of Sir John as ca. 1 Edward IV which is inconsistent with the age of ten in 17 Edward IV. He also is more specific as to the death date, 20 Aug. 1527; Sir Edward also gives the date variously as 18 Henry VIII 1527 or 20 Henry VIII. As Henry VIII succeeded to the throne on 22 April 1509, his 20th year ended in 1529. Mayhew's date and Sir Edward's first date are both possibly the truth.

In any case, they had three sons, Walter, George and Francis. Of them a pretty story is told: the three boys were playing at some sport in the court-yard of the castle, and the two elder boys were competing and a dispute arose between them as to which had won. They agreed to allow the youngest brother Francis to decide. He chose his second brother George and this caused Walter to get angry and to threaten to get even with his younger brothers when he came into the property. Unknown to the boys, the father had heard the remark and now announced that he would make the younger brothers independent of Walter, and this he did by settling upon each of them one of the two manors, Congresbury and Over-Badgeworth, with the provision that if either died, the survivor would inherit his share. This happened, and both manors came to George.

Issue: surname Rodney
2 i.   Walter, d.v.p. 13 17 Henry VIII.
3 ii. George, b. ca. 1500, d. 1586?
  iii. Francis, d.s.p. and v.p.
  iv. Grace, d. 1558, m. Christopher Lyatt; not mentioned by Sir Edward, shown as third child by Mayhew.
  v.   Elizabeth, not mentioned by Sir Edward, shown as 4th child by Mayhew.

2. Sir Walter Rodeney, the eldest son, was knighted but died *vita patris* in 13 Henry VIII, buried at Backwell. He thus never inherited his father's property and could not have treated his brothers meanly, as he had threatened. He married Elizabeth, sister to Sir Walter Compton Knt., the Comptons said by Sir Edward to have been ennobled twice: first by Queen Elizabeth I as Baron Compton, probably the Henry who died 1589, son of Peter who died 1538/9 and grandson of William who died 1528; second by James I as Earl of Northampton in 1618, that is, William Compton, a son of the 1st Baron Compton.[13] Elizabeth married

second Sir John Chaworth and died 4 July 29 Henry
III.

>   Issue: surname Rodney
> 4 i.   John, aet. 8 in 13 Henry VIII.

3. George Rodeney, second son of his parents, by
the early death of his brother Francis inherited
both of the manors which his father had settled on
his two younger sons. He was an excellent business-
man. He married Elizabeth Kyrton of Chedder. He
died in 1580 aet. ca. 80, leaving one son and either four or six daughters--Sir Edward makes both
statements.

>   Issue: surname Rodney, order unknown
> 5 i.   John, b. at Stoke, ca. 1549.
>   ii.   Barbara, m. Walter Buckland Esq. of Stan-
>   lich, Wilts.
>   iii.   Agatha, m. Thomas Hodges, gent. of Somer-
>   set.
>   iv.   Honor.
>   v.   Lucretia.

4. John Rodeney, Esq., was aet. 8 in 13 Henry
VIII and aet. 13 when his grandfather died in 1527,
and he himself died 25 Dec. 2 Edward VI 1547. This
date is defective as the regnal year should be 1 or
the Anno Domini year 1548. His wife was Elizabeth,
daughter of Lord Mordaunt, "since Earl of Peterborough." Identification of the wife has been difficult. John Burke's *Extinct, Dormant and Abeyant
Peerages* (London 1840), p. 366 [a not very trustworthy book], says that Sir John Mordaunt (died
1562) had by wife Elizabeth Vere an eldest daughter
who married, first, James [sic] Rodney, Esq., and
second, John, son and heir of Sir Michael Fisher.
That the wife of John Rodeney Esq. would again marry is highly probable, and perhaps Burke is right
in all but the first name.[14]

>   Issue: surname Rodney
>   i. Maurice. He was taken "north" (whatever that
>   means precisely) by his guardian and raised
>   "carelessly," as Sir Edward thought. He
>   married, first, in his nonage, a smith's
>   daughter who is not thought worthy of being
>   given a name by Sir Edward, and was after-
>   wards divorced; second, Ione, daughter of
>   Sir Thomas Dyer, Knt., and she died 1591.

He was a "great housekeeper," i.e. an ex-
travagant man; sold the Bristol property
but d. in debt, 9 Aug. 1588.
   Issue: surname Rodney
1. Henry, d. of smallpox while an Oxford
   scholar.
2. Thomas, d. of smallpox while an Oxford
   scholar.
3. Sir George, minor when his father d. in
   1588; aet. 21 on 2 Feb. 1589; m. at
   his father's deathbed, ca. Aug. 1588,
   Anna, daughter of Matthew Smith Esq.,
   of Long Ashton, Somerset. She d. before him and he d.s.p., apparently by
   his own hand, 1 July 1601. At his
   death there was litigation between the
   two sisters, who claimed as heirs general, and Sir John Rodeney (#5) who,
   though heir male, claimed under the
   will in which he was named heir. A
   compromise was reached and the property was sold but Sir John bought it.
4. Dorothy, m. Rice Davies, lawyer of the
   Middle Temple, cited above.
5. Ione, m. ----- Trenchard.

   5. Sir John Rodeney, only son of George Rodeney
by his wife Elizabeth Kyrton, was born at Stoke, ca.
1549. He was the heir male of Sir George Rodeney
(#4,i,3), and also the heir named in the will, and
when the property was sold in order to end litigation, he bought it. He died 6 Aug. 1612, aet. 61
or 62. He married Jane Seymour, daughter of Sir
Henry Seymour, who, though he took no part in poli-
tics, was brother to Jane Seymour, Henry VIII's
third queen and mother of Edward VI, and to Edward
Seymour, Duke of Somerset, the Protector in Edward
VI's reign. According to Sir Edward, who was their
eldest son, Sir John Rodeney and Jane Seymour had
sixteen or seventeen children of whom only seven
survived their father. Jane died February 1634.

   Issue: surname Rodney
6 i.   Sir Edward, the compiler.
  ii. Henry, apprenticed to one Greene of Walbrooke
       in London; sent as factor to Barbary where
       he was drowned off the coast of Africa.
7 iii.George.
8 iv. William.

> v. Elizabeth, m. James Kirton of the Middle Temple.
> vi. Penelope, m. Sir Theodore Newton of Gloucestershire.
> vii.Jane, m. John Trenchard, younger son of Sir George Trenchard of Dorsetshire.

6. Sir Edward Rodeney, Knt., eldest son of Sir John Rodeney by his wife Jane Seymour, was born at Pilton, Monday, St. Peter's Day, a half hour after 2 P.M., 29 June 1590, and died 30 Nov. 1657. The death year in *The Genealogist* 17:106 is clearly a misprint. He compiled the genealogy which we have been following and in it gave a frank and moving account of his life. He was a student at Magdalen College, Oxford, where he must have acquired the learning which the genealogy displays, including the ability to write a good grade of 17th-century Latin. Afterwards he was at the Middle Temple, where "hee saluted only the Law afarre of[f], & mispent his time," as he himself confesses. He married on 29 May 1614, in the presence chamber of Somerset House and in the presence of Queen Anne [James I's queen], Mrs Frances Southwell, daughter of Sir Robert Southwell of Wood Rising in Norfolk by Lady Elizabeth Howard, eldest daughter of Charles Howard, Earl of Nottingham and Lord High Admiral. In a sketch of her father it is said[15] that it was his daughter Frances who married Sir Robert Southwell, and that his daughter Elizabeth married Henry Fitzgerald, the Earl of Kildare, but it would seem probable that Sir Edward would know what the first name of his mother-in-law was. The same sketch tells us, as Sir Edward does not, that Sir Robert Southwell commanded the *Elizabeth Jonas* against the Armada in 1588. Queen Anne invited James I to attend the wedding and when he came through the passageway, he knighted Edward Rodney on his wedding day. Sir Edward was a royalist during the Civil Wars and as he was writing the genealogy during the Commonwealth, was rather reserved in his comments on the troubles. His later life was much saddened by the death of his only son.

> Issue: surname Rodney
> i.   John, d. inf.
> ii. John, d. inf.
> iii. Edward, d.y.
> iv. William, d. aet. 2+.
> v.   George, d.v.p. aet. 22 by 1655. It should

be noted that he was kin to both Edward
VI through the Seymours and to Elizabeth
I through the Howards on his mother's
side.
vi. Elizabeth, living 1655.
vii. Frances, d. adult.
viii. Penelope, living 1655, m. Sir Peter Gleane,
Bart., of Norfolk.
ix. Anna, living 1655, m. Sir Thomas Bridges
Knt. of Kainsham, Somerset.
x. Jane, living 1655.
xi. Margaret, d.y.
xii. Mary, d.y.

7. George Rodeney or Rodney, second son of Sir
John Rodeney by his wife Jane Seymour, was born in
1608, died in 1630, and was of Lyndhurst, co. Hants.
He married Anne, daughter of Sir Thomas Lake and
widow of the 17th Lord de Ros. George and his brother William are shown as younger sons in the Visitation of Somerset in 1623,[16] but without additional
information about them, though their brother Edward
was correctly shown as already married. George had
two sons but it seems probable that the three daughters with which he is also credited are an error,
since he died at the age of 22 years.

Issue: surname Rodney
i. Anthony, an Army colonel, killed in Barce-
lona in a duel, 1705; m. Constantia, the
daughter and coheiress of Ralph Clarke.
Issue: surname Rodney
1. Henry, of Walton-on-Surrey, b. 1681, d.
1737, a cornet of horse, afterwards
captain of marines; m. Mary, eldest
daughter and coheiress of Henry Newton, Knt., Envoy Extraordinary to
Genoa, Tuscany, etc., LL.D., Judge of
Admiralty[17].
Issue: surname Rodney
a. Henry, matriculated 7 Dec. 1733 aet.
17, Balliol College, Oxford.
b. George Brydges, naval commander, 1st
Baron Rodney, K.B., created 12 April 1782, b. 19 Feb. 1718, d. 21
May 1792, on whom see Burke, *loc.
cit.*; DNB 17:81-87; also *Complete
Peerage* 11:66-70.
c. Another son?

           d. A daughter?
  ii.   George, captain of marines under William
         III; d. 1700.

  8. William Rodeney or Rodney, third son of Sir
John Rodeney by his wife Jane Seymour, was born in
1610 and died in 1669. He married Alice Caesar, one
of the five daughters of Sir Thomas Caesar by his
third wife, Susanna Ryder or Ryther, daughter of
Sir William Ryder or Ryther, who was born ca. 1544,
the son of Thomas Ryther or Ryder of Mucklestone,
Staffordshire, by his wife ----- Poole of Staffordshire, and grandson of Thomas Ryther of Lynstead,
Kent. Sir William was a haberdasher, was knighted
by Queen Elizabeth I as the result of conspicuous
services shown the Queen at the time of the Essex
rebellion, and died at Leyton, Essex, 30 Aug. 1611.
He married Elizabeth, daughter of Richard Stone of
Holme, Norfolk.[18]
  Sir Thomas Caesar[19] was the grandson of Pietro
Maria Adelmare of Treviso near Venice, but descended
from a family belonging to Fréjus in Provence. This
Pietro married Paola, daughter of Giovanni Pietro
Cesarini (perhaps of the same family as Giuliano
Cesarini, Cardinal of Sant' Angelo, president of the
Council of Basle 1431-8). One of the sons of Pietro
and Paola was Cesare Adelmare graduated in arts and
medicine at the University of Padua, and about 1550
migrated to England where he afterwards had a distinguished career in medicine, being elected Fellow
of the College of Physicians in 1554 and its censor
in 1555. He was naturalized in 1558 with immunity
from taxation, and was the medical adviser to both
Queen Mary and Queen Elizabeth I who on one occasion
paid him a fee of £100 for a single consultation.
He died in 1569 and was buried in the chancel of
St. Helen's Bishopsgate. As the queens usually addressed their physician as "Caesar," this name was
adopted by his children as a surname.
  Sir Thomas Caesar, the second son of the physician, was born at Great St. Helen's Bishopsgate in
1561 and was educated at the Merchant Taylors'
School which he left in 1578. He became a member
of the Inner Temple in October 1580 and M.P. for
Appleby in 1601, but his career at the bar was un-
distinguished. He was, however, on 26 May 1610
created cursitor baron of the Exchequer, and was
knighted in Whitehall the next month, but a letter

from his spiritual adviser, D. Crashaw, endorsed by
Sir Thomas's elder brother, 18 July 1610, reports
his death, so that he enjoyed his knighthood and his
office for a very short time. He married, first,
----- ----- who died in 1590, leaving three children,
all of whom died in infancy; second, Anne Lynn, daughter of George Lynn of Southwick, Northamptonshire and
relict of Nicholas Beeston of Lincolnshire, who had
no issue; third, 18 Jan. 1592/3, Susan, daughter of
Sir William Ryder by his wife Elizabeth Stone, as
stated above, and she bore him three sons and five
daughters, all of whom survived their father.

Sir Thomas Caesar had an elder brother, Sir Julius
Caesar, born at Tottenham, 1557/8, baptized in February 1557/8 at St. Dunstan's in the East, died 18 April 1636 aet. 79, buried in the Church of Great St.
Helen's where there is said to be a monumental inscription. He married, first, in 1582, Dorcas Martin,
relict of Richard Lusher of the Middle Temple and
daughter of Sir Richard Martin, alderman of London
and Master of the Mint; second, in 1595, Alice Green,
daughter of Christopher Green of Manchester and widow
of John Dent of London; third, at the Rolls Chapel,
19 April 1615, Anne, widow of William Hungate of East
Bradenham, Norfolk; sister of Lady Killegrew, and
granddaughter of Sir Nicholas Bacon. At her marriage
she was given away by her uncle, Sir Francis Bacon,
then attorney-general. Sir Julius had by his first
wife one daughter and four sons, of whom only the
youngest, afterwards Sir Charles Caesar (1590-1642),
Master of the Mint in 1639,[20] survived. By the second
wife he had three sons "who attained some slight distinction" but not enough to get them further mention
in the *Dictionary of National Biography*. There were
no children by the third wife. He had a very busy
career, holding numerous legal offices, including the
Master of the Rolls, but his reputation for legal a-
cumen is not high. He was a man said to be above
corruption, served for many years in positions with
little or no remuneration, and was charitable to the
needy persons who appeared before him.

Sir Thomas had also a younger brother, Henry Caesar, the fifth son of the physician. He entered the
English church, served finally as Dean of Ely and
died in Ely, 27 June 1636, buried in Ely Cathedral.
He had at times to undergo suspicion of Catholicism
and seems not to have married.

The William Rodney whom we have been discussing

was of both Moorlinch and Catcott which are near each
other in southern Somersetshire. This man has been
wrongly identified as the father of the immigrant.
We have not seen probate for this William. He is given
by Lea a son Anthony but the history of said Anthony
appears to be the same as that of his supposed first
cousin as shown on p. 449, so we think it probable
that William had no son Anthony.

Issue: surname Rodney, perhaps others, order un-
        certain
i.   Caesar, apprenticed 15 Aug. 1657 to a Bris-
        tol haberdasher named William Typpett,
        his father then said to be of Catcott,
        co. Somerset.[21]
ii.   John, not found in English records, but he
        came to America and d. at Philadelphia,
        leaving a will which calls him gent.,
        dated 15 Sept. 1694, probated in New Jer-
        sey 12 Dec. 1694,[22] recorded also at Phil-
        delphia.[23] He names wife Anne, sole
        heiress and executrix; son Caesar Rodney
        a minor [who has not been found later];
        daughter Penelopy Roach [of whom nothing
        more has been found], 20s for mourning;
        nephew William Rodney of Jones Co.;
        friend Thomas Boleman; nephew William
        Rodney and friends Philip Richards and
        John Jones of Philadelphia, merchants, to
        assist executrix; witnesses: John Wilkin-
        son, Alexander Deverex, Esther Wilkinson.
        The inventory of Capt. John Rodney came
        to £33/15/11, taken 28 Feb. 1694/5 by
        Jeremiah Basse and Isaac Marriott; bond
        of widow Anne Rodney of Burlington, Jere-
        miah Basse, fellow-bondsman, dated 2
        March 1694/5. The will alludes to the
        Indies and leaves to son Caesar four
        slaves if eight are living. The widow
        was probably the Hannah Rodney who, at
        Salem Monthly Meeting, 30 5th mo. 1699,
        had leave to m. William Thompson. This
        couple had issue: Jane (b. 29 7th mo.
        1700); Susannah (b. 28 8th mo. 1704);
        Samuel (b. 6 9th mo. 1707, perhaps m.
        31 11th mo. 1731 Edith Tyler); Mary (b.
        21 11th mo. 1710); Rebeckah(b. 19 12th
        mo. 1714/5, perhaps m. 17 2nd mo. 1738
        Erasmus Fetters); Benjamin (b. 11 8th

1719, perhaps m. Elizabeth Ware at Al-
loways Meeting House, 4 2nd mo. 1745,
both of Salem County).
9 iii. William.

9. William Rodney, one of the sons of William
Rodney by his wife Alice Caesar, is recorded in
England at the baptisms of two of his children and
in no other record thus far found. His wife's name
is given as Rachel in the baptismal record of her
son William and is alluded to in his will dated 1
May 1708. Otherwise, nothing is known of this pair.

Issue: surname Rodney, perhaps others
10 i.   William, b. 1660, d. 1708.
   ii. Rachel, mentioned in the will of her bro-
        ther William in 1708. Mayhew says she was
        bapt. at St. John's, Bristol, 20 Sept.
        1664, m. (?) Robert Curtis who d. 1695,
        and had a daughter Elizabeth Curtis who
        m. (1) by 11 Nov. 1699 William Brinckle
        (d. 1722); (2) between 1722 and 1725
        John Hamant.
   iii. Elizabeth, mentioned as living in 1708 in
        the will of her brother William.

10. William Rodney, the immigrant, was clearly a
son of William Rodney and wife Rachel -----, as his
will in 1708 alludes to his mother Rachel as living.
This fact makes it very improbable, if not altogeth-
er impossible, for the said Rachel to have been a
second wife to the William Rodney who married Alice
Caesar. Had William married, first, Alice Caesar,
and, second, Rachel -----, then the immigrant would
have had no Caesar blood, yet the name Caesar continued to be borne by many of the immigrant's descendants. The immigrant is generally said to have
been born in 1652, on what evidence I do not know.
Lea discovered the baptism of a William, son of William and Rachel Rodney, at Christ Church, Bristol,
14 March 1660, and having previously decided that
the immigrant's mother was Alice Caesar, he did not
know what to do with this baptism. Fortunately, he
printed the record, for it must be the baptism of
the immigrant William Rodney.
   In his letter to William Penn dated at London,
14 Oct. 1690, William Rodney stated that he had been
in Pennsylvania about ten years, so he must have arrived about 1680, probably in the company of his
uncle, Captain John Rodney. Though in his 22nd year

he served as foreman of a jury on 20 Dec. 1681.[2] In
pioneer conditions such as obtained on the Delaware
in 1681, a young man of gentle family and doubtless
superior education was likely to win recognition of
this kind. He has usually been thought to have married twice but it may be that he married, first, in
what is now the state of Delaware, a daughter of
John Richardson Sr. who left a will dated 12 Oct.
1703, probated in Kent County, 3 Jan. 1703,[25] in
which he mentions two grandsons, William and Thomas
Rodney. These were the names of the two eldest sons
of William Rodney, but dates of birth are supplied
for them which are after the marriage to Mary Hollyman, as we shall see. If they were Mary Hollyman's
sons, then it is hard to see how they could have
been grandsons of John Richardson Sr. Thomas Hollyman, presumed father of Mary Hollyman, was buried
at Philadelphia, 12 11th mo. 1694/5. If he left a
widow, unknown to us, who married, second, John
Richardson Sr., it would be unusual at this period
for John Richardson to describe his wife's grandsons
as his.

In any case, William Rodney of Talbot County,
Maryland, was received on certificate 18 10th mo.
1688 at Philadelphia Monthly Meeting, and on 25 11th
mo. 1688, he had leave to marry Mary Hollyman. As
stated, she was probably a daughter of the Thomas
Hollyman who was buried at Philadelphia, 12 11th mo.
1694/5, and sister of Sarah Hollyman who had leave
to marry John Densey. The death of Mary Hollyman
Rodney is given by Mayhew as 20 Dec. 1692, after
which William Rodney married, second, 20 Feb. 1693,
Sarah Jones, daughter of Daniel Jones. William Rodeney was witness to the will of William Dyre of the
County of Sussex, Esq., dated 20 Feb. 1687/8, probated at the Prerogative Court of Canterbury, 5 4th
mo. called June 1688.[26] The certificates brought by
Rodney from Talbot County before his marriage to
Mary Hollyman were signed by Sarah Edmondson and
William Pavatt, and one from the Quarterly Meeting
was signed by William Dixon.[27]

The will of William Rodney was dated 1 May 1708,
probated 4 Oct. 1708,[28] and names wife Sarah, mother
Rachel, sisters Rachel and Elizabeth, and all of
the children shown below except Rachel who was already dead. William Rodney is shown as son-in-law
of Daniel Jones in his will dated 21 Aug. 1694,
probated 21 March 1694/5,[29] and Sarah Rodney was

appointed administratrix of John Shepherd, 4 Oct.
1708,[30] the very day on which William Rodney's will
was probated. I do not know what connection there
may have been with Shepherd.[31]

Issue: surname Rodney
   by first wife Mary Hollyman
11 i.   William, b. 27 Oct. 1689, d. 1731/2.
  ii. Rachel, b. 18 Nov. 1690, d. 7 Sept. 1695,
       so recorded by Mayhew.
 iii. Thomas, b. according to Mayhew, 11 Aug.
       1692, bur. at Philadelphia, 7 9th mo.
       1709 (Mayhew), but 6 Nov. 1709 (so Hin-
       shaw[32]) among non-Quakers.
     by second wife Sarah Jones
  iv. Daniel, b. 13 Feb. 1694/5, d. 19 Dec. 1744,
       admin. to wife Margaret, 25 Jan. 1744,[33]
       and she, a widow, made her will 20 Oct.
       1773, probated 23 March 1781, naming
       grandson Nathaniel Luff.[34]
   v. John, b. 13 April 1696, d. unm., 1708, ac-
       cording to Mayhew.
  vi. Anthony, b. 20 March 1698/9, d. 5 May 1720,
       according to Mayhew; admin. granted to
       brother Daniel, 7 May 1720[35] His wife
       was probably the Sarah, wife of George
       Nowell, who made her will, 25 Dec. 1729,
       probated 11 Feb. 1729,[36] heir and execu-
       tor being Daniel Rodney.
12 vii. Caesar, b., according to Mayhew, 12 Oct.
       1701, d. 3 May 1745. The birthdate con-
       flicts with that given for George, one
       of the two dates being wrong.
viii. George, b., according to Mayhew, 8 Feb.
       1701/2, which is too soon after Caesar's
       birth; bur. 12 April 1725.
  ix. Sarah, b. 5 Aug. 1704, d. 10 April 1720,
       according to Mayhew; obviously d. unm.[37]

    11. William Rodney, eldest son of William Rodney
by his first wife Mary Hollyman, was born according
to Mayhew on 27 Oct. 1689 and died in 1731/2. He
married Ruth Curtis to whom administration was granted 19 Oct. 1732,[38] and they were both witnesses to
the will of William Coe, 12 Sept. 1720.[39] This one
is probably the William Rodney in William Cramer's
will, 20 Dec. 1726, probated 31 Dec. 1726.[40] The
following list of children is taken from Mayhew.

Issue: surname Rodney
i.   Penelope, b. 1712, m. 7 May 1733 James Ga-
        rid; called granddaughter in the will of
        Priscilla Gilbert, widow, 22 Jan. 1719/20,
        probated 10 May 1721.[41]
ii.   Thomas, b. 14 Sept. 1716, bur. 18 Sept. 1716.
iii.   William, b. 18 Feb. 1719, d., according to
        Mayhew, 6 Jan. 1735. If Mayhew is wrong,
        it is possible that this was the William
        Rodney of Worcester Co., Md., planter,
        whose will dated 3 Dec. 1767 was probated
        in Sussex Co., Del., 19 Oct. 1770, and
        mentions wife Mary and son-in-law Thomas
        Prettyman, as well as the children shown
        below.[42]
                Issue: surname Rodney
        1. William, mentioned in father's will, per-
           haps the William who by 15 April 1794
           had m. Mary or Polly, widow of William
           Sharp whose will was dated 21 Dec.
           1789.
        2. Lydia.
        3. Leah, m. Simpler.
        4. Susanna, m. Marvil.
        5. Comfort, m. Marvil.
        6. Magdaline, m. Jones.
iv.   Mary, b. 25 Jan. 1721, d. 20 Aug. 1724.
v.   John, b. 7 Sept. 1722, d. 25 Nov. 1792; m.
        (1) 4 Oct. 1748 Sarah Paynter; left will
        in which he names second wife Ruth [who
        was a Hunn], dated 14 May 1791, probated
        14 Jan. 1793,[44] also the following
                Issue: surname Rodney
        1. Daniel b. 10 Sept. 1764, d. 2 Sept. 1846,
           m. 5 March 1788, Sarah, daughter of
           Major Henry Fisher; served in the Re-
           volution; was judge of common pleas,
           presidential elector, governor of
           Delaware 1814-1817, and congressman.
           See the article under his name in the
           *Twentieth Century Biographical Diction-
           ary of Notable Americans*.
        2. Caleb, b. 29 April 1767, d. 29 April
           1840; merchant of Lewes, speaker of
           Delaware Senate, acting governor of
           Delaware. See sketch of him *ibid*.
        3. John.
        4. Thomas.

        5. Penelope, m. ---- Kollock and had Jacob,
           John, Myra, Hester, Hannah.
        6. Daughter who m. Isaac Turner and had
           Hannah and Mary Turner.

12 Caesar Rodney, seventh or eighth son of William Rodney by his second wife Sarah Jones, depending on solution of the conflict in birthdates between his and that of his brother George, was born, according to Mayhew, 12 Oct. 1701, and died 3 May 1745. He married Elizabeth Crawford, born 8 June 1700, died Nov. 1763, daughter of the Rev. Thomas Crawford and she appears to have married, second, ----- Wilson, since the will of Caesar Rodney the Signer and that of his brother William allude to their half-sister, Sarah Wilson, and her son Caesar Rodney, surname not clear; William's will also mentions half-sister Sarah's children Elizabeth and Thomas. The following list of the children is in part based on Mayhew.

Issue: surname Rodney
i.   Caesar, b. 7 Oct. 1728. d. unm., testate. will dated 20 Jan. 1784, codicil dated 27 March 1784, probated 14 Aug. 1784,[45] d. 26 June 1784 (Mayhew says 29 June). He was a Signer of the Declaration of Independence, a major general of militia in the Revolution. He was buried at Poplar Grove but in 1888 the remains were removed to Christ Episcopal Churchyard in Dover, Del. See DAB 16:81 f.; also *Appleton's Cyclopaedia of American Biography* 5:300; also *Twentieth Century Biographical Dictionary of Notable Americans* under his name. John Adams wrote of him: "the oddest looking man in the world; he is tall, thin and slender as a reed, pale; his face is not bigger than a large apple, yet there is sense and fire, spirit, wit, and humor in his countenance."
ii.   Elizabeth, b. 16 Sept. 1730, d.s.p. 1765.
iii.   George, b. 2 March 1731/2, d. 1750.
iv.   Sarah, b. March 1733/4, d. 1734.
v.   Mary, b. 30 Oct. 1735, d. 1782. She m. and in 1784 her daughter Elizabeth Gordon and other children are alluded to in the Signer's will.
vi.   William, b. 19 July 1738, d. 10 Sept. 1787;

m. 19 March 1762 Lydia Paradee, daughter
of John and Lydia (Edingfield) Paradee.
His will was dated 6 Sept. 1781, probated
in St. Jones Co., 13 Sept. 1787.[46]
      Issue: surname Rodney
1. Letitia, mentioned in father's will and
   in the Signer's.
2. Daughter, m. ----- Frazer and had daughter Elizabeth living 1781.

vii.   Daniel, b. 22 July 1741, d. 1764; probably
       m. Meriam who was administratrix 18 Jan.
       1764.
          Issue: surname Rodney
   1. Sarah, mentioned in Signer's will, 1784.

viii. Thomas, b. 4 June 1744, d. at Rodney, Jef-
       ferson Co., Miss., 2 Jan. 1811. He m. 8
       April 1771 Elizabeth Fisher, daughter of
       Jabez Maude Fisher. He had an active
       career during the Revolution in various
       capacities including colonel of militia.
       He was also a judge of various courts
       ending as Federal judge for Mississippi.
       See DAB 16:83 f.; and *Twentieth Century
       Biographical Dictionary* under his name,
       and *Appleton's Cyclopaedia, loc. cit.*
          Issue: surname Rodney
   1. Lavinia, mentioned in Signer's will,
      1784.
   2. Caesar Augustus, b. 4 Jan. 1772, d. at
      Buenos Aires, where he was ambassador
      to the United Provinces of La Plata,
      10 June 1824. He had as distinguished
      career in public life as any of the
      Rodneys, was attorney-general under
      Jefferson and Madison 1807-1811. In
      1793 he married Susan Hunn, daughter
      of Capt. John Hunn by his wife Mary
      Silsbee, on whom see Edwin Jaquett
      Sellers, *Genealogy of the Jaquett Fam-
      ily* (Philadelphia, rev. ed., 1907),
      pp. 152-4. See also the three ency-
      clopaedias cited above.
         Issue: surname Rodney
      a. Mary, b. 20 March 1795, m. Rev. Dr.
         Theophilus Parvin.
             Issue: surname Parvin
         α Theophilus, A.M., M.D., LL.D., b.
           Buenos Aires, 9 Jan. 1829, d. 29

Jan. 1898. For issue see Sellers.
b. Elizabeth, b. 17 March 1796, m. John
Eschenberg; six ch. in Sellers.
c. Caesar, b. April 1797, d. 1810.
d. John Hunn, b. April 1799.
e. Thomas McKeen, b. 11 Sept. 1800, d.
24 April 1874; m. Susan Fromberger;
4 ch. in Sellers.
f. Lavinia, b. 1802, d. 15 Aug. 1840.
g. Joseph, b. 1804.
h. Susan Augusta, b. 1806, m. James Wallace; 4 ch. in Sellers.
i. Sarah Ann, b. 21 Sept. 1808, d. 13
Dec. 1886.
j. Louisa Victoria, b. 4 June 1810, d. 1
May 1888, m. Dr. Edward Worrell.
k. Matilda Caroline, b. 24 June 1812, d.
1814.
l. George Clinton, b. 10 March 1814.
m. Caroline Matilda, b. 29 Sept. 1816, d.
2 Oct. 1876, m. William L. May.
n. Hannah Caesaria, b. 29 Aug. 1819, d.
23 Oct. 1888, m. William H. W. Cush-
man.
o. Ellen, b. 22 July 1822.

NOTES

[1]NEHGR 55:335.
[2]*Court Records of Kent County Delaware 1680-1705*
(American Historical Society 1959), p. 49.
[3]PMHB 4:197-199.
[4]DAB 16:31, sketch of the Signer, Caesar Rodney.
[5]See also *Complete Peerage* 11:66-70.
[6]I have not overlooked certain descendants of
William Penn but in their case the connection with
the peerage and royalty was after the migration.
[7]George Gatfield's *Guide to Printed Books and Manuscripts relating to English and Foreign Heraldry
and Genealogy* (Detroit reprint 1966), p. 389, mentions some long pedigrees of the Harley and Rodney
families in the possession of the Earl of Egmont in
St. James Place, but whether this is what Sir Edward
had or not is not clear.
[8]It is dated 1909 but shows some information from
sources published in 1910.
[9]The William who died at Viterbo, if historical,
was a much earlier man.

[10]BPBK p. 278.   [11]DNB 17:639 f.

[12]We have not been able to identify this Lord Hungerford certainly.

[13]On the Comptons Walter Lee Sheppard has been of help.

[14]The first Earl of Peterborough was John Mordaunt, not created until 1627/8, a fact which could have been known to Sir Edward.

[15]DNB 10:5.

[16]Harleian Soc. 11:93 f.

[17]DNB 14:370.   [18]DNB 17:539-41.

[19]DNB 3:654-660 contains several articles on the Caesar family in England.

[20]DNB 3:654.   [21]See Note 1.

[22]NJW 1:392.   [23]PhW A:279.

[24]HEAQG 95, 104.   [25]KC 26

[26]Waters, *Genealogical Gleanings in England* 844.

[27]MQA 15.   [28]KC 29.

[29]KC 7.   [30]KC 33.

[31]It is surprising that no full account of the Rodneys has heretofore appeared in print, in view of the historical eminence of Caesar Rodney. Brief references to the family appear in the Hart Collection in the Genealogical Society of Pennsylvania (HA 204 p. 91), and in the May Atherton Leach Collection (vol. 182) and W. Nelson Mayhew's chart (F* 91, vol. 4).

[32]HEAQG 447.   [33]KC 106.

[34]KC 320.   [35]KC 38.

[36]KC 59.

[37]William Rodney's will makes allusion to the orphans of Richard Wilson but I have come to the conclusion that they could not have been grandchildren of William.

[38]KC 65.   [39]KC 39.

[40]KC 50.   [41]KC 42.

[42]KC 86.   [43]KC 211.

[44]KC 339.   [45]KC 361.

*ROWLAND, JOHN   *proved*
*ROWLAND, PRISCILLA SHEPHERD, his wife   *proved*
*ROWLAND, THOMAS, his brother   *proved*

John Rowland is on all lists, as should be his wife Priscilla and his brother Thomas, but Priscilla is only on Lists A, B, C, D, E, F, G, H, I, M, Q, U, V, W, X, Y and Z, and Thomas only on Lists A, B, C, D, E, F, G, H, K, M, N, O, P, Q, R, S, T, U,

V, W, X, Y and Z.   Thomas Rowland was buried at Middletown, Bucks County, 17 3rd no. 1690; Priscilla
Rowland died between 12 1st mo. 1704/5 and 3 Dec.
1715, and John Rowland died between 3 Dec. 1715 and
3 March 1715/16, all three without issue.

   The proof of their presence on the *Welcome* is to
be found in their own statement in Bucks Arrivals[1]
where their origin is given as Billingshurst, Sussex.   As Billingshurst was also the home of the
Buckman family, also *Welcome* passengers, the question naturally arises as to whether the Rowlands
were related to the Buckmans.   Dr. Arthur Edwin Bye,
in an article on the Widow Buckman,[2] ventures to
suggest that the Widow Joan Buckman was sister of
John and Thomas Rowland, but he advances no proof
of this conjecture and ignores evidence already in
print when he wrote that the widow had been Joan
Bagham when she married Edward Buckman.   In the
next column, however, he goes on to accept his own
conjecture as proved, and speaks of the Rowlands'
nephews, the brothers William, Edward and Thomas
Buckman.   There may have been a connection between
the Buckmans and Rowlands but there is no evidence
to show it and it should be pointed out that the
only persons named heirs in John Rowland's will were
not Buckmans, of whom many were then living in the
neighborhood, but Mary Tomlinson and Thomas Rogers
the younger whose mother had been a servant to the
Rowlands at the time of the crossing.

   John Rowland was a First Purchaser of 1250 acres
in Group 49,[3] and his brother Thomas was a First
Purchaser in Group 19 of 2500 acres,[4] while Priscilla Shepherd, then of Warminghurst, was a First Purchaser of 500 acres in Group 20.[5] There was another
First Purchase by a Thomas Rowland of 1000 acres in
Group 40,[6] but this was probably that of another
Thomas Rowland, later of Chester County, to be mentioned below.

   John Rowland married Priscilla Shepherd, while
still in England, 1st intentions, 12 2nd mo. 1682,
2nd intentions, 10 3rd mo. 1682, and their marriage
is also confirmed by deed of John Rowland of Bristol,
yeoman, and wife Priscilla, to William Buckman of
Newtown, property conveyed by William Penn, 19 6th
mo. 1681, when Priscilla was called by the name of
Priscilla Shepherd, date of deed 12 1st mo. 1704/5,
recorded 3 10th mo. 1705,[7] the last date on which
Priscilla is still shown as living.

That Thomas and John were brothers is proved by
Bucks Deeds 1:10 f., 117, 323, 354; 2:169; 3:113 f.
Thomas is shown as alive and joins with John in 1:
117 (1 4th mo. 1684), 1:10 f. (1 10th mo. 1685) but
is dead by 9 7th mo. 1690 (1:323) when John is called
his only heir. At Middletown Monthly Meeting 2 6th
mo. 1688, Tho Rowland is directed to draw a certificate, and he is living also 7 9th mo. 1689, 6 1st
mo. 1690, but on 5 4th mo. 1690 is spoken of as dead,
and he was buried on 17 3rd mo. 1690.
      Bucks Deeds 3:113 f. (10 1st mo. 1702/3, recorded
5 3rd mo. 1703), show John Rowland selling for £12
to George Hayworth of Bristol Township, and the recital states that Penn had granted to Thomas Rowland,
13-14 July 1681, 2500 acres, and that Thomas died intestate [no administration found in either Bucks or
Philadelphia counties] and John now sells from this
right. Deeds 3:27 (11 4th mo. 1700, recorded 24 8th
1700), John Rowland of Bucks County, yeoman, and
wife Priscilla, convey to John Hiatt land granted
by Penn 22 3rd mo. 1686. Deeds 2:149 f. (10 1st mo.
1694, recorded 12 8th mo. 1697), John Rowland and
wife Priscilla sell for £20 to Arthur Cook, property called Little Money Hill, inherited by Priscilla
from Ralph Smith in his will dated 9 2nd mo. 1685.
[See at the end of this sketch the excursus on this
Ralph Smith.]
      Priscilla Rowland was the first woman to sign
the marriage certificate of John Town to Deborah
Bottle,[8] and Jno Rowland was also a signer. The
marriage certificate of Shadrach Walley to Mary
Sharpe, 12 1st mo. 1688, was signed by, among others,
Jo Rowland, Tho Rowland, Willm Buckman, Tho Rogers,
Priscilla Rowland, Hannah X Rogers.
      The minutes of the same Middletown Monthly Meeting
(19th century copy at the Genealogical Society of
Pennsylvania) contain a character reference dated
Philadelphia 1682, signed by John Songhurst, Mary
Songhurst, Elizabeth B[arber], for John and Thomas
Rowland, stating that Thomas Rowland was clear in
respect of marriage. The day on which this certificate was signed must have been between the arrival
of the *Welcome* and the end of the year 1682 Old Style,
that is to say, between 28 8th mo. 1682 and 24 1st
mo. 1682/3, and in view of the nature of the certificate, rather earlier in this period than late.
      The will of John Rowland[9] dated 3 Dec. 1715, pro-
bated 3 March 1715/16, with inventory dated 30 May

1716, £604/10, a large sum, taken by Jeffrey Pollard
and William Brelesford, contains an undated codicil
above the signature which manumits slave girl Lica.
Mention is made of dwelling house at Bristol, bol-
ting house and lot; a church, unidentified; to Mary,
wife of Henry Tomlinson, £50; to Thomas Rogers Ju-
ner, who is named executor; trustees: Anthony Burton
on behalfe of the Church, Robert Cobert; signed Jn°
Rowland; witnesses: John Large, Jn Hall, Timothy
Towne. The connection with Thomas Rogers Jr. was
that he was a son of Hannah Mogeriàge who had come
on the *Welcome* as a servant to the Rowlands.

The Blackwell Rent Roll of 1689[10] shows Priscilla
Shepherd as owner of an old purchase 49½ foot lot
on Walnut Street, 1/- for five years; Tho Rowland
owner of an old purchase lot on High Street 66 feet,
2/6 for five years[11]; John Rowland owner of an old
purchase lot of 33 feet at High and Third from the
Schuylkill, a year term, rent not stated.[12]

As we have seen that Priscilla Rowland was still
living in 1705, we are surprised to find Mrs. Jane
W. T. Brey, *A Quaker Saga* (Philadelphia 1967), p.
143, alluding to a will of Priscilla Rowland dated
9 2nd mo. 1696, probated 26 3rd mo. 1696, where,
not stated. Inquiry of Mrs. Brey brought forth the
reply that the dates given for execution and the probate of this will should have been, rather, 1685
and 1686, respectively. As this did not help the
problem but actually made it worse, in view of all
the evidence already presented to show that Priscilla did not die in 1686, Mrs. Brey consulted her
source which proved to be a secondary source at the
Genealogical Society of Pennsylvania. It was now
discovered that there was really no will of Priscilla Rowland, but a reference to Priscilla Rowland
in the will of Ralph Smith, as shown above, and the
date of probation should really be 20 4th mo. 1686.

A. Excursus on Ralph Smith

The will of Ralph Smith dated 9 2nd mo. 1685,
probated in Bucks County, 20 4th mo. 1686[13] is here
described from personal inspection of the original.
It is stated[14] that Ralph Smith, the governor's
gardiner, was buried att the burying place in the
point, 5 3rd mo. 1685, a cemetery probably the one
from which many of the Pemberton graves were removed
to another site within the bounds of the restored
Pennsbury Manor; if not, one quite near that spot.

The will directs that after the house is built, money remaining after payment goes to two sisters, Jane Lloyd and Susana pikes of sharles towne in New England [printed as Shaules Town, really Charles-town, Mass.], and they also get money from the sale of 110 acres. A horse goes to James Harison [Penn's steward at Pennsbury] and he and James Atkinson are named executors. Sister Susana gets all linen and wollen and tools, etc. And 193 acres above and backwards of the Governors manor pensbury called Little money Hill with a new house now to be built as by agreement with Charles Brigham, to pSlla the wife of John Rowland, and after her decease to her owne natuaral relations before marrig as she shall be minded to give it vnto. The witnesses were John Martin, Richard Willson, Jo^n Clark. This suggests that there was a blood relationship between Priscilla (Shepherd) Rowland and Ralph Smith. That she should die childless, as she did, Ralph Smith could hardly have foreseen, since she had been married only about four years when he died. She did not, however, pass the property on to any of her natuaral relations before marrig, but instead she and John Rowland sold the property in 1694 to Arthur Cook. Perhaps by then all her natuaral relations before marrig were dead. We know nothing of them.

T. B. Wyman's *Charlestown Estates* shows that a Joseph Pike married, first, Susanna Smith, 10 Nov. 1680, she admitted to the church 3 June 1683 and died 27 Oct. 1688, mother only of

    i. Susanna, b. 7 Aug. 1681, d. 18 Aug. 1681.
   ii. Anna, b. 15 12th mo. 1682/3, d. 24 March 1683.
  iii. Mary, b. 27 7th mo. 1684, d. 29 Sept. 1684.

All of her issue was dead when Ralph Smith made his will though the probability that she might have other children still existed. There were Lloyds in Charlestown but no Jane is shown, and it is possible that only Susanna was to be understood to be living there, and that we should look for Jane Lloyd elsewhere.

B. Excursus on Unrelated Rowlands

In the study of the Rowlands from Billingshurst, Sussex, other Rowlands with similar names were discovered in early Pennsylvania. Philadelphia Wills C:143, 3 3rd mo. 1708, probated 16 Nov. 1708, is the will of Thomas Rowland living on the Westharn [wes-

tern] side of Brandewine Creek, Chester County, yeoman; dearly beloved wife Mary, land purchased from
Mary Moore in Aston Township; daughter Mary, other
children too; executors: wife and trusty friend John
Dutton of Aston; trustees: George Harland, John
Baldwin; to John Robeson, if he proves a good lad,
£5; to Elizabeth Idings £30; witnesses: Michael m h
Harland, John R Renfro. This man has sometimes been
confused with his namesake from Billingshurst.

He seems to have had no connection with a John
Rowland of the Township of Charlestown, Chester
County, yeoman, whose will was dated 8 April 1745,
probated 8 May 1745.[15] He names wife Martha; mother
Persilla "half the Sallery at new Providenc due me
during her lifetime"; son Elijah and daughter Rachel,
minors; sister Ellinor; "Obadiah shall have 5/- when
demanded"; administration to widow Martha and Corn[s]
Anderson, 8 May 1745, as no executor has been appointed. This John Rowland was a New Side Presbyterian parson, born in Wales, educated at the Log
College in Bucks County; licensed 7 Sept. 1728; or-
dained evangelist, Reaville, N.J., 11 Oct. 1739;
settled at Amwell, N.J., church at Reaville, N.J.,
1738-1742; Maidenhead church 1738-1742; Hopewell
church at Pennington 1738-1742; Norriton 1741-1745;
Charlestown 1742-1747.[16]

He was probably the son of Samuel Rowland of New
Britain, Bucks County, whose will is dated 4 Jan.
1737, probated 30 Jan. 1737.[17] He mentions well-beloved son John Rowland; well-beloved wife Prisilla
Rowland; married daughter Ellinor; other daughters
Margaret and Mary, if they come or send. The widow
renounced by mark, 25 Jan. 1737/8.

NOTES
[1]PMHB 9:225; BHBC 673.   [2]*The Historian* 3:66.
[3]1 PA 1:45; also 3 PA 2:6, three pieces, under
Old Rights.
[4]1 PA 1:42; 3 PA 3:392.
[5]*Ibid.*; also 3 PA 3:381.   [6]1 PA 1:44.
[7]BD 3:242.
[8]Middletown Monthly Meeting, p. 18 of marriages.
[9]BW file 166.   [10]PGM 23:71
[11]*Ibid.* 81.   [12]*Ibid.* 89.
[13]BW file 111, abstracted PGSP 1:209 f.
[14]BHBC 681.   [15]PGSP 3:188 f.
[16]F. L. Weis, *Colonial Clergy of the Middle States*
says he was of Lower Providence 1742-47 but he had
died in 1745.   [17]BW file 404.

SAYLOR, ROBERT   *disproved*

This name appears on List X only. As we have not
found such a man, we are inclined to think that it
is a misreading of the name Thomas Leister which we
discuss elsewhere.

?SCOTT, MARGARET?   *possible*

With some trepidation we introduce this name as
that of a possible *Welcome* passenger. We feel reasonably sure that there was on the ship a certain unmarried woman, old enough to be called an "old maid",
who lived before and perhaps during and even after
the year 1685 in the home of John Day. There is a
slight possibility that this "old maid" was named
Margaret Scott. Thus, it will be understood that
the question marks surrounding the name are intended
to express doubt about the name, rather than about
the validity of the claim.

The evidence, such as it is, begins with a letter
of William Penn to Thomas Lloyd, 18 5th mo. 1685,
in which Penn asks Lloyd to prod John Songhurst into
making a report on the estate of John Snashfold who
had died on the *Welcome*, and whose possessions were
in the custody of Songhurst without the latter having
been formally granted administration on the estate.
Among the persons who, says Penn, could help Songhurst in rendering an account of the estate, was
"Tucker's wife," to be identified with Jane Batchelor, a *Welcome* passenger, and "an old maid yt lived
with J. Day." That is to say, Penn recalls in 1685
that there was such an old maid on the *Welcome* in
1682 but has forgotten her name, remembering only
that she lived with J. Day, presumably while Penn
was still in America.

When this passage in Penn's letter was discovered
by Walter Lee Sheppard, the question at once arose
as to whether "J. Day" had also been a passenger,
but we have now come to the conclusion that he was
not, though we believe the evidence about him ought
to be presented in an effort to lead to the identity of "an old maid yt lived with J. Day."

John Day was a First Purchaser of 1250 acres in
Group 9[1] and Mrs. Balderston believes that he came
on the *Elizabeth, Anne & Catherine*, on which ship
he loaded, 17 July 1682, possibly also on the next
day, though here the record says Thomas Day.[2] He
subscribed £50 to the Society of Free Traders,[3] and

was received at Philadelphia from Ashwell Monthly
Meeting on a certificate dated 12 3rd mo. 1682. On
25 3rd mo. 1688 he was again granted a certificate
to England where he was when he and William Penn on
31 Dec. 1689 witnessed the Webb power of attorney
which we have cited above on page 44.

Mrs. Balderston informs me that she had found
John Day in New Jersey but this was probably another
man of the same name. Our man had a wife Hannah
and the following children, order of births unknown:

i. Hannah, b. Nicholas Collaby Parish, London,
    20 12th mo. 1680, d. 27 Jan. 1698.
ii. Sarah, b. 16 Jan. 1691/2, d.. 24 9th mo.
    1715; m. 12 8th mo. 1710, John Durborow,
    son of Hugh, and he m. (2) Rebecca Hay-
    wood who d. 9 10th mo. 1777 aged 80.
       Issue: surname Durborow
       by Sarah Day
    1. John, bur. 5 3rd mo. 1714.
    2. Sarah, b. 19 9th mo. 1715.
       by Rebecca Haywood
    3. John, d. 11 11th mo. 1722.
iii. Grace, d. 10 8th mo. 1721; m. 12 8th mo.
    1710 Edward Pleadwell who m. (2) Ann
    ----- who was reported to have m. out of
    unity 31 10th mo. 1736, and he was con-
    demned for marrying contrary to discipline
    27 4th mo. 1735.
       Issue: surname Pleadwell
    1. Hannah, d. 31 5th mo. 1711.
    2. Sarah, b. 23 2nd mo. 1720; as Sarah
       Priest late Pladwell reported to have
       m. out of unity, 27 6th mo. 1751.
iv. John, b. England, d. by 1692, *vita patris*.

John Day's will, dated 15 8th mo. 1692, probated
15 April 1696,[4] calls him merchant of Philadelphia,
going to sea; to wife Hannah the brick house on Delaware Front Street; to eldest daughter Hannah, the
house and lot in Germantown and lot on High Street
between 6-7th Street from Delaware, another 3-4th
Street; daughter Grace and youngest daughter Sarah;
sister Margaret Cock or Cook and her daughter Mary,
both in England; Cousin Hannah Gardiner's daughter
Hannah; land to Quarterly Meeting for a meeting
house or school; land on Taconi Creek; executors:
John Parsons and wife Hannah Day; witnesses: Richard
Sutton, Margaret Scott (she by mark).

The cousin Hannah Gardiner with a daughter Hannah was almost certainly the wife of Thomas Gardiner (son of Thomas) of Burlington, treasurer of West Jersey. The papers in the treasurer's estate[5] show that he had a wife Hannah and a daughter Hannah, who was living in 1692, and afterwards married Isaac Pierson.

It is possible also that the Margaret Scott who witnessed this will by mark was "the old maid yt lived with J. Day." This Margaret Scott may be the sister of John Scott of Wellinborough, whose will was dated 6 April 1702, probated 3 Nov. 1702.[6] Among others he mentions brother Martin Scott and sisters Margaret, Bridget [whose daughter was named Mary Lucas] and Elizabeth. Martin Scott's will dated 19 June 1702,[7] omits Margaret from among the sisters and shows Edward Lucas as brother-in-law. The sister Margaret may thus have died between 6 April and 19 June 1702, and she may be the Margaret Scott who witnessed John Day's will. She may thus also have been the *Welcome* passenger.

A John Day was of London, carpenter.[8] In a reference shortly to be cited, we learn that William Penn sold to John Day, 18-19 6th mo. 1681, 1250 acres surveyed 7 8th mo. 1682 [while the *Welcome* was at sea] but the actual survey covered only 210 acres. Day's will [date not stated but it was 15 8th mo. 1692] devised this to wife Han'ah making said Ha'ah & John Parsons joint executors. They sold 4 5th mo. 1696 to David Haverd [now] dec. who died intestate leaving son John as heir. David's widow Mary and said Hannah, now wife of James Atkinson, request a patent from the Board of Property, session of 3 10th mo. 1701,[9] but Hannah had not yet married when she conveyed 5 7th mo. 1698.[10]

Two years later, at the session of 3 3rd mo. 1703, the Board recorded that[11] William Penn had deeded on [date left blank] to Edw'd Jefferson of Ashwell, co. Hertford, mal[t]ster, & wife Mercy, who married, second, Tho. Phitty. Said Tho & Mercy sold 7 10ber 1685 to John Day of Ashwell, co. Hertford, 200 acres, & said John Day when of the county of Burlington, yeoman, deeded 100 acres, 9 11th mo. 1690, to Henry Paxson of Neshamineh [Bucks Co., Pa.]. Was the John Day just mentioned the same or different from the John Day whose certificate from Ashwell was received in 1682, as stated above? There may have been two John Days, both from Ashwell.

There is a deed dated 30 Oct. 1682, immediately
following the arrival of the *Welcome* when a passenger thereon could hardly have gotten used to walking
on land again, which mentions John Day's 100 acres
in Springfield, northlie of West Branch of Assis-
cunk Creek.[12] A little later, on 18-19 Dec. 1682,
John Day bought from Thomas Budd.[13] These transac-
tions must concern a John Day who was certainly in
America before the *Welcome* arrived but we still do
not know whether he was the man who came from Ashwell in 1682.

We now approach a will, that of John Day of New
Hanover, Burlington County, yeoman, dated 10 12th
mo. (Feb.) 1723/4, probated 6 June 1724,[14] which
mentions daughter Elizabeth and her husband Thomas
Branson; grandson Thomas Barton [i.e. the testator
was not young], and names as executors the daughter,
John Hervey and John Wright. Furthermore, John Day
is mentioned many times in *New Jersey Wills*, vol. 1,
in incidental circumstances[15] and in one instance,
John Day, his wife Elizabeth and daughters Elizabeth,
Mary, Sarah, are heirs of Thomasin Towle.[16] We have
now sufficient evidence to show that a John Day was
living in New Jersey, probably from 1691 to his death
in 1724, and that he came from Ashwell in Hertfordshire, whether he had ever been of Philadelphia or
not. Certainly, there must have been two John Days,
one who died by 1696, the other who died 1724, both
testate, and they were not father and son, if at all
related. The Philadelphia man, indeed, had New Jersey kinsmen, but he does not mention his namesake in
his will. I am inclined to think that the New Jersey John Day came from Ashwell in 1682, deposited
his certificate and then moved on to New Jersey, and
that the John Day who died by 1696 was the carpenter
from London. He must also have arrived in America
by 1684, for Penn remembers that he was there before
Penn made his first return to England.

What happened after the Philadelphian died is to
be found in the Minutes of the Philadelphia Monthly
Meeting.[17] On 28 4th mo. 1695 Richard Sutton, who
had witnessed John Day's will with Margaret Scott,
was told to hold off courting widow Hannah Day and
the same again on 30 6th mo. 1695[18]; on 27 10th mo.
1695 Hannah Day was told not to entertain Richard
Sutton or William Rakestraw[19]; on 28 2nd mo. 1699
James Atkinson and Hannah Day declared 1st intentions, and he was told to bring a certificate from

his meeting at Newton [Newtown, Bucks County][20] and
again on 30 4th mo. 1699, they were again warned a-
gainst marriage, "it not appearing that her husband
John Day is certainly dead"[21] but the deed cited
above shows that they ultimately did marry. It is
strange that the Philadelphia Friends were as late
as 1699 still unwilling to accept the fact of death
of a man whose will had been duly probated in 1696.

Blackwell's Rent Roll of 1689 has John Day as
owner of an old purchase lot of 20 feet on Front
Street, 1/- for 5 years,[22] and another old purchase
lot of 26 feet, 1/- for 5 years, on High Street.[23]

NOTES

[1] 1 PA 1:41.   [2] PGM 23:50 f., also 99.
[3] PMHB 11:171.
[4] PhW #139 for 1696, A:334, abstracted PGSP 2:28.
[5] NJW 1:178.   [6] NJW 1:409.   [7] NJW 1:410.
[8] 3 PA 3:331.   [9] 2 PA 19:205.   [10] 2 PA 19:203.
[11] 2 PA 19:374. [12] 1 NJA 21:353. [13] *Ibid.* 399.
[14] NJW 1:130.
[15] NJW 1:29 (1694), 78 (1693), 151 (1715), 155
(1696), 183 (1693), 216 (1694), 318 (1704), 334
(1691), 346 (1692), 417 (1704), 468 (1695), 517
(1698).
[16] NJW 1:468.   [17] PGSP vol. 4, several references.
[18] PGSP 4: 191-194.   [19] PGSP 4:199.
[20] PGSP 4:247. [21] PGSP 4:249.   [22] PGM 23:71.
[23] PGM 23:81.

SELFORD, ROBERT   *disproved*

This name appears on List X only. The truth is
that Selford came as the second of Robert Turner's
seventeen servants on the *Lion* of Liverpool, arriving 14 8th mo. 1683, loose on 14 8ths mo. 1687,
to get £6 and the usual fifty acres. He was a brickmaker in Philadelphia County, who died intestate,
administration on 18 5th mo. 1688 to four creditors
(PhA A:45 #102 of 1688; see also PGM 24:92, Note 87).

SHARPLES, JOHN	*disproved*
SHARPLES, JANE, his wife	*disproved*
SHARPLES, PHEBE, his daughter	*disproved*
SHARPLES, JOHN, his son	*disproved*
SHARPLES, JAMES, his son	*disproved*
SHARPLES, CALEB, his son	*disproved*
SHARPLES, JANE, his daughter	*disproved*
SHARPLES, JOSEPH, his son	*disproved*

†SHARPLES, THOMAS   *disproved*

John Sharples and all of the family listed above
are named on Lists A, B and H; on Lists J, L and W,
John is curiously called Jan, as if he were a Dutch-
man; John and family are on List Y, but they are not
mentioned at all on Lists C, D, E, F, K, M, N, P, Q,
R, S, T, X, Z. On Lists G and O they are mentioned
only to be denied, and on List U they are all named
but put on the *Friendship*. List B alleges as proof
papers in the possession of Benjamin Ferris of Delaware.

The Sharpless family is, to my knowledge, the only family formerly considered qualifying for membership in the Welcome Society who were later taken off
the list. As the result of the recent expansion of
the list of qualifying ships, they would presumably
now be back on the list, but they were definitely
not *Welcome* passengers.

The son John, aged 16 in 1682, stated that his
brother Thomas died at sea on 17 5th mo. 1682, a day
on which the *Welcome* had not yet sailed from Deal.

A letter of Benjamin Ferris to Edward Armstrong
dated 29 12th mo. 1851, says: "They [the Sharples
family] had seven children . . . with whom they embarked for America, with William Penn, they being
some of the first settlers of his new province of
Pennsylvania." Gilbert Cope, *Genealogy of the Sharpless Family Descended from John and Jane Sharples*
(Philadelphia 1887), p. 74, states that the family
arrived on 14 6th mo. 1682, on the testimony of the
son John, and that the ship *Lion* arrived 13 6th mo.
1682. Mrs. Balderston reports, however, that John
Sharples loaded on the *Friendship* of Liverpool,
Robert Crossman, master: 1 chest 20 lbs pewter,
4 lbs haberdashery, 76 ells English linen, 20 lbs
Norwich stuffs, 2 casks qty 4 cwt cheese.[1]

Sharples was a First Purchaser of 1000 acres in
Group 40.[2] The Blackwell Rent Roll of 1689[3] shows
for him an old purchase lot of twenty feet, 1/- for
five years, on Front Street.

Besides the excellent genealogy by Gilbert Cope,
already cited, there is another by Bart Anderson,
also impressive, *The Sharples-Sharpless Family* (West
Chester, two vols., 1966), and there is an article
on the family in Jordan.[4]

According to this last authority, the grandfather
of the immigrant was Richard Sharples, born 1555,

died 1641, who by his first wife Cicely ----- was
father of Jeffry or Geoffrey Sharples of Wyburnbury,
Cheshire, who died 15 Dec. 1661, having married 27
April 1611 Margaret Ashby. This last couple are
claimed by both Bart Anderson and Jordan as parents
of the immigrant, John Sharples, baptized at Wyburnbury, Cheshire, 15 Aug. 1624, died in Ridley Township, Chester County, Pennsylvania, 11 4th mo. 1685,
having married 27 2nd mo. 1662, Jane Moor, who died
1 9th mo. 1722. The following list of their children is based on Anderson, with some additions from
Jordan.

Issue: surname Sharples
i.   Phebe, b. Mearemoore, Cheshire, 20 10th mo.
       1663, d. Ridley, 2 4th mo. 1685, unm.
ii.   John, b. Blakenhall, Cheshire, 16 11th mo.
       1666, d. Ridley, 9 7th mo. 1747; m. 23
       9th mo. 1692, Hannah Pennell, b. 23 7th
       mo. 1673, d. 31 10th mo. 1721, daughter
       of Robert and Hannah (Hyandson) Pennell,
       9 children.
iii.   Thomas, b. Hatherton, Cheshire, 2 11th mo.
       1668, d. at sea 17 5th mo. 1682.
iv.   James, b. Hatherton, Cheshire, 5 1st mo.
       1670/1, d. Nether Providence ca. 1746;
       m. (1) 3 1st mo. 1697/8 Mary Edge, d.17
       2nd mo. 1698; (2) Mary Lewis, b. 10 5th
       mo. 1674, d. ca. 1753 in Nether Provi-
       dence; 9 children by second wife.
v.   Caleb, b. Hatherton, Cheshire, 22 2nd mo.
       1673, d. Ridley, 17 7th mo. 1686.
vi.   Jane, b. Hatherton, Cheshire, 13 6th mo.
       1676, d. Ridley, 28 3rd mo. 1685.
vii.   Joseph, b. Hatherton, Cheshire, 28 9th mo.
       1678, d. Middletown Township, Chester
       Co., spring of 1757; m. at Haverford
       Monthly Meeting, 31 3rd mo. 1704, Lydia
       Lewis, b. Glamorganshire, 8 3rd mo. 1683,
       d. 1763, daughter of Ralph and Mary Lewis
       of Teverig, Wales, and Upper Darby, Pa.;
       10 children.

NOTES

[1]PGM 23:40.   [2]1 PA 1:49
[3]PGM 23:71.   [4]JCRFP 3:1356.

SHORT, MIRIAM the elder   *possible*
SHORT, MIRIAM, her daughter   *highly probable*
SHORT, ADAM, her son   *highly probable*

SHORT, ANN, her daughter   *highly probable*

The three children appear on Lists S, T and V, and Ann Short is also on List Q. The mother has appeared on no previous list. The discovery that Ann Short was a passenger has been attributed to the late Dr. John G. Herndon.

The proof is circumstantial: all three children are later found recorded in Pennsylvania or Delaware, and they were the beneficiaries of the will of their uncle, Isaac Ingram, executed on the *Welcome*. It would be difficult to see how these two nieces and one nephew could be expected to profit from the goods Ingram had on the ship unless they were also present with him when he died. Moreover, the younger Miriam Short is recorded in Chester County almost immediately after the arrival of the *Welcome*, then married to the well-known passenger, George Thompson.

The reason for thinking that Miriam Short the elder, mother of the other three Shorts, was on the vessel is found in Ingram's will where she is described as "late deceased," a phrase peculiarly appropriate if she had started the voyage and then succumbed to the smallpox. She may well have been the Miriam Short, Quaker, of Kingsbury, Warwickshire, who in 1663 was presented in the Episcopal Visitation for not attending church.[1]

Though it appears probable that the order of the births was Miriam, Ann and then Adam, we shall discuss Adam first, since we can say much less about him than about his sisters.

ADAM SHORT

Adam Short later lived in New Castle County, now Delaware, and was probably first married to a woman of whom we know nothing, evidently the mother of all his children. He married ca. 1712, when he could not have been less than thirty, even if an infant on the *Welcome*, Martha Metcalf, widow of Thomas Metcalf whose will was dated 26 Aug. 1708; and a Miriam Short, probably Adam's daughter by the first wife, married at Swedes' Church, Wilmington, 6 Jan. 1728, John Bush. This information is to be found in Gilbert Cope's *Genealogy of the Baily Family of Bromham, Wiltshire, England* (Lancaster, Pa., 1912), pp. 12-14. The will of Adam Short Sr. of New Castle Hundred, dated 29 March 1748, probated 6 Nov. 1748, mentions wife Martha, sons Adam, Henry, Abram;

daughter Miriam Daly; grandsons Abraham and Isaac
Bush; John Daley.[2] The will of Martha Short, widow
of Adam, of New Castle, dated 19 Dec. 1748, probated 20 July 1751,[3] mentions two grandchildren, Hester and Mary Buss [Bush?], and names Miriam Daley
executrix.

In 1693 Adam Short had brought suit against Thomas Wynne who died during the proceedings.[4] On 31
Oct. 1719 Adam Short had a survey of 86 acres near
Christiana Creek and assigned this right to John
Hore. When the Maryland boundary question was in
the courts, Adam Short was a witness for Lord Baltimore, then aged 78.[5] He was then living and had
lived for 49 years in New Castle County, and was
able to recall events in 1682, 1684 and 1685. If
we could be sure of the precise date on which this
testimony was given, we should get Adam's birth
year, but in any case the data in this paragraph
make it seem very unlikely that Adam was only a
small child in 1682. In any case, he was one of
the last *Welcome* passengers to die.

Issue: surname Short, order unknown
i.   Adam, living 1748 when mentioned in his
        father's will.
ii.   Henry, living 1748 when mentioned in his
        father's will.
iii.   Abram, living 1748 when mentioned in his
        father's will; d. 1781, then had daugh-
        ter Priscilla.
iv.   Miriam, m. (1) Swedes' Church, Wilmington,
        6 Jan. 1728, John Bush, who had d. by
        1748; (2) ----- Daily
            Issue:
            by first husband John Bush
        1. Abraham}{both living 1748 when
        2. Isaac   }{when mentioned in Adam's will.
        3. ?Hester}{both mentioned in Martha
        4. ?Mary   }{Short's will in 1751.
            by second husband Daily
        5. John, mentioned in Adam's will 1748.

MIRIAM SHORT

As has been intimated above, not long after the
arrival of the *Welcome,* Miriam Short the younger was
married to the *Welcome* passenger, George Thompson,
by a Lutheran clergyman named Lawrence Carolus Lockenius, and both the young husband and the clergyman
were charged with violation of the laws of the pro-

vince. Thompson was before the court on 14 Feb.
1682/3, and as no one appeared against him, the
charges were dropped. A fuller discussion of these
events and of Thompson's subsequent history will be
found in the sketch devoted to him. It should be
said here, however, that by 6 11th mo. 1684 Miriam
(Short) Thompson had borne a child and was in need
of public maintenance for herself and the child.
It is not certain that George Thompson had died--he
may have deserted her.

Whatever the truth about Thompson, Miriam married,
second, at an unknown time and place, William White
of New Castle County, wheelwright, whose will dated
22 Dec. 1702, probated 14 Sept. 1703,[6] names wife
Miriam as executrix; children: Samuel, John, Elizabeth, son-in-law [stepson] Ralph Tomson [sic: not
Semson, as it has been read]; witnesses: John Grubb,
Frances Grubb, Hugh Bawdon, overseer: John Bailey.

Following the death of William White, Miriam married, third, at Chichester, 30 9th mo. 1704, Aaron
Coppock of Aston Township, who moved to Nottingham
in 1713. Aaron was born 25 10th mo. 1662, died 10
10th mo. 1726, leaving a will dated 3 10th mo. 1726,
probated 17 Dec. 1726,[7] naming minor son John; unnamed wife; daughters Lydia Coppock, Meriam Coppock,
both unmarried; Sarah Frayser, Martha Robinson (wife
of John, who had John, Aaron, Mary, Ruth, Martha,
Miriam), Mary Sinclair; sons-in-law Ralph Thomson,
John White, Samuel White; daughter-in-law [step-
daughter] Elizabeth White; executrix: beloved wife
Miriam assisted by Jonas King; signed Aron Copock;
witnesses: James Wright, Samuel Lightler. Mr. Colket
remarks that Sarah Frayser, Martha Robinson and
Mary Sinclair, were daughters of an earlier wife of
Aaron Coppock.

Issue of Miriam Short:
> *by first husband George Thompson*

i.   Ralph, b. ca. 1683, taxed in Marlborough
           Township 1719-1726, East Fallowfield
           Township 1735-1740. No record of marriage
           or probate in Chester County or in such
           Lancaster County sources as have been ex-
           amined.

> *by second husband William White*

ii.   Samuel, m. 21 2nd mo. 1726 Hannah Pigott
           of Cecil County, Maryland.[8] It is not
           absolutely certain that he, his brother
           John White and sister Elizabeth White

were children of Miriam Short as well as
of William White, but the will of Aaron
Coppock calls the boys sons-in-law and
Elizabeth daughter-in-law which he would
probably not have done, had they been
merely step-children of his second wife.

iii.   John, m. 31 Oct. 1717 Mary Job, daughter
       of Andrew and Elizabeth Job of Notting-
       ham.
iv.   Elizabeth, unm. 1726.
   by third husband Aaron Coppock
v.   John, minor 3 10th mo. 1726; m. 16 1st mo.
       1731, Margaret Couson; said to have had
       two descendants present with John Brown
       in the affair at Harper's Ferry in 1859,
       a point not investigated.
vi.   Miriam, m. 12 8th mo. 1727, Richard Jones.
vii.   Lydia, unm. 1726.

ANN SHORT

Ann Short married, 1st intentions, Chichester
and Concord Monthly Meeting, 2nd intentions, Bir-
mingham, 11 2nd mo. 1687,[9] Joel Baily, baptized at
Bromhill, Wiltshire, 29 Jan. 1658, died between
9 12th mo. 1731/2 and 8 April 1732. The following
account of their descendants is based on Gilbert
Cope's *Genealogy of the Baily Family of Bromham,
Wiltshire, England* (Lancaster, Pa., 1912).

Issue: surname Baily
1 i.   Mary, b. 19 9th mo. 1688, d. 1741.
2 ii.   Ann, b. 10 10th mo. 1691, d. 12 8th mo.
        1774.
3 iii. Daniel, b. 3 10th mo. 1693, d. ca. 1783.
4 iv.   Isaac, b. 24 10th mo. 1695, d. 1732.
5 v.   Joel, b. 17 12th mo. 1697, d. 1775.
6 vi.   Thomas, d. ca. 1764.
7 vii. John, d. ca. 1793.
8 viii. Josiah, d. 14 3rd mo. 1791.

1. **Mary Baily**, eldest child of Ann Short by her
husband Joel Baily, was born 10 9th mo. 1688 and
died in September or October 1741. She married,
first, ca. 1708, Alexander Stuart, who died 5 11th
mo. 1714/5; second, in 12th mo. 1715/16, George
Harlan, born 4 10th mo. 1690, died 1732, son of Michael Harland (James, William) by his wife Dinah
Shore.[10]

Issue:
  by first husband Alexander Stuart
i.   Jane, b. June 1709, m. 14 3rd mo. 1730
     Josiah Taylor.
ii. Robert, b. 25 11th mo. 1710, m. ca. 1732
     Martha Richardson.
iii. Ann, b. 4 6th mo. 1712.
iv. Mary, b. 8 3rd mo. 1714.
  by second husband George Harlan
v.   John, b. 1716, m. 5 4th mo. 1740 Sarah
     Wickersham.
vi. Rebecca, b. 1718, m. by 19 9th mo. 1741
     Stephen White.
vii. Dinah, b. 1720, m. (1) by 31 3rd mo. 1740
     Robert Davis; (2) 1 July 1762 James Har-
     lan (James, George, James, William).[11]
viii. Hannah, b. 1720, m. by 17 4th mo. 1742
     Joseph Martin.
ix. Joel, b. 10 11th mo. 1724, d. 3 9th mo.
     1796, m.16 10th mo. 1746 Hannah Wickers-
     ham.
x.   Michael, b. 10 11th mo. 1724, d. 15 10th
     mo. 1806, m. 1 5th mo. 1766 Susan Carls-
     ton.
xi. George, b. 1726, d. 1813, m. 14 9th mo.
     1750 Susanna Harlan (Ezekiel, Ezekiel,
     George, James, William).

2. Ann Baily, second child of Ann Short by her
husband Joel Baily, was born 10 10th mo. 1691, died
12 8th mo. 1774; married in 1710 Jeremiah Cloud Jr.
who died in February 1747/8.

Issue: surname Cloud
i.   Elizabeth, b. 14 10th mo. 1711, m. 5 8th
     mo. 1738 Thomas Underwood who m. (2)
     Sarah Keeler.
ii. Joel, b. 7 4th mo. 1715, m. 4 7th mo. 1741
     Esther Stubbs who m. (2) John Carson.
iii. William, b. 11 1st. 1718, m. 24 8th mo.
     1739, Mary Pierce.
iv. Jeremiah, b. 20 11th mo. 1723, m. 9 May
     1750 Lydia Harlan.
v.   Benjamin, b. 26 1st mo. 1725, prob. d.y.
vi. Mordecai, b. 28 2nd mo. 1729, m. (1) 19 8th
     1753 Ann Harlan; (2) 1789 Agnes Morrison.
vii. Rachel, b. 10 8th mo, 1733, prob. d.y.

3. Daniel Baily, third child of Ann Short by her
husband Joel Baily, was born 3 10th mo. 1693, died

ca. 1783; married 16 1st mo. 1720/21, Olive Harry,
born ca. 1704, died 4 10th mo. 1766 in 63rd year.

Issue: surname Baily
i.   William, b. 9 10th mo. 1721, m. (1) 18 10th
      mo. 1745 Betty Cloud; (2) 16 12th mo.
      1762 Hannah (Johnson) Taylor, widow.
ii.   Ann, b. 6 3rd mo. 1723, m. 10 2nd mo. 1748
      Joshua Pierce.
iii. Elizabeth, b. 16 10th mo. 1725, d. unm.,
      5 4th mo. 1818.
iv.   Daniel, b. 21 1st mo. 1731, m. Ann -----.
v.   Lydia, b. 27 1st mo. 1734, m. 17 10th mo.
      1753 Jesse Miller.
vi.   Olive, b. 2 1st.mo. 1736, m. 13 2nd mo.
      1754 Benjamin Leonard.
vii. Caleb, b. 14 2nd mo. 1738, m. 28 9th mo.
      1763 Ann Dixon.
viii. Nathan, b. 1 10th mo. 1744, m. ----- -----.
ix.   Ruth, b. 16 4th mo. 1748, m. 5 11th mo.
      1767 Joshua Edwards.

4.   Isaac Baily, fourth child of Ann Short by
her husband Joel Baily, was born 24 10th mo. 1695,
died 1732; married, 1 1st mo. 1727/8, Abigail Johnson, widow of Thomas Wickersham Jr., and she married, third, Mordecai Cloud.

Issue: surname Baily
i.   Isaac, b. ca. 1728, m. (1) 8 9th mo. 1749
      Sarah Jackson; (2) 22 8th mo. 1699 Sarah
      Yarnall.
ii.   Joel, m. 14 11th mo. 1759 Lydia Pusey.
iii. Betty, b. 1732, perhaps m. April 1757 Owen
      Evans.

5.   Joel Baily, fifth child of Ann Short by
her husband Joel Baily, was born 17 12th mo. 1697,
died 1775; married 28 8th mo. 1724, Betty Caldwell,
born ca. 1705, died 15 12th mo. 1775.

Issue: surname Baily
i.   Betty, b. 8 1st mo. 1727/8, m. 18 3rd mo.
      1748 Francis Swayne.
ii.   Hannah, m. 22 3rd mo. 1750 John Webster
      who m. (2) Jane Brinton.
iii. Ann, m. 13 5th mo. 1752 David Hayes.
iv.   Joel, b. 16 12th mo. 1732, m. (1) 11 10th
      1759, Elizabeth Marshall; (2) 4 7th mo.
      1776 Margaret (Jackson) Evans, widow;
      (3) 28 11th mo. 1793 Mary Woodward.

v.   Mary, m. 12 10th mo. 1757 Thomas Harlan,
        widower.
vi.   Phebe, b. 15 10th mo. 1738, m. ca. 1770
        Benjamin Mendenhall.
vii.   Isaac Baily, b. 9 10th mo. 1743, m. 4 5th
        1768 Lydia Gilpin Painter.
viii. Joshua, b. 20 4th mo. 1747, m. 13 5th mo.
        1778 Ann Jackson.

6. Thomas Baily, sixth child of Ann Short by her husband Joel Baily, was born at an unknown date and died ca. 1764, having married ca. 1734 Sarah Bentley.

Issue: surname Baily
i.   Isaac, m. (1) 9 3rd mo. 1758 Mary Jones;
        (2) 17 4th mo. 1765 Hannah Scarlet.
ii.   Mary, m. 20 Nov. 1756 Caleb Hayes.
iii.   John, m. 8 5th mo. 1766 Hannah Pennock.
iv.   Jemima, m. William Leonard.
v.   Ann, m. James Powell.
vi.   Hannah, m. 3 Jan. 1771 Isaac Powell.
vii.   Thomas, d. by 24 Oct. 1828.
viii. Sarah, b. ca. 1755, m. 4 Nov. 1778 William
        McNeill.

7. John Baily, seventh child of Ann Short by her husband Joel Baily, was born at an unknown date and died ca. 1793. He married, first, 29 3rd mo. 1729, Lydia Pusey, born 16 6th mo. 1713; second, 8 4th mo. 1732, Mary Marsh.

Issue: surname Baily
  by first wife Lydia Pusey
i.   John, b. 29 7th mo. 1729, m. 22 11th mo.
        1753 Lydia Wickersham.
  by second wife Mary Marsh
ii.   William, b. 4 8th mo. 1733, m. 18 10th mo.
        1759 Mary Musgrove.
iii.   Susannah, b. 17 8th mo. 1735, m. 21 5th
        mo. 1755 Ellis Pusey.
iv.   Ann, b. 11 10th mo. 1737, m. by lic. dated
        31 Aug. 1761 Richard Jones.
v.   Betty, b. 18 6th mo. 1741, m. 18 9th mo.
        1765 John Ferree.
vi.   Mary, b. 24 10th mo. 1746, m. 11 10th mo.
        1780 William Farquhar.
vii.   Sarah, b. 28 1st mo. 1748, m. 9 6th mo.
        1779 Aaron Clayton.
viii. Elisha, b. 7 8th mo. 1751, m. 31 3rd mo.
        1785 Hannah Starr.

ix.   Hannah, b. 16 6th mo. 1754, m. 8 4th mo.
        1778 Caleb Pusey.

8. Josiah Baily, youngest child of Ann Short by
her husband Joel Baily, was born at an unknown date
and died 14 3rd mo. 1791. He married 9 3rd mo. 1734
Sarah Marsh who died 20 2nd mo. 1791.

Issue: surname Baily
i.   Joel, b. 14 12th mo. 1734/5, m. 24 11th mo.
        1757 Hannah Wickersham.
ii.   Josiah, d. apparently unm., 25 2nd mo. 1826.
iii.   Sarah, m. ca. 1770 John Pyle.
iv.   Lydia, m. 11 5th mo. 1774 Jesse Harlan.
v.   Henry, m. Rachel -----.

                          NOTES

[1]*Friends Historical Journal* (London) 4:147.
[2]*New Castle Wills 1682-1800*, p. 42.
[3]*Ibid*. p. 49.
[4]*Minutes of the Provincial Council* 1:394.
[5]2 PA 16:733, 743.
[6]PhW B:163.   [7]CW 1:205.
[8]See Gilbert Cope, *op. cit.*, p. 14, for the
marriages cited.
[9]*Ibid*.
[10]Alpheus H. Harlan, *History and Genealogy of the
Harlan Family* (n.d. or pl. but ca. 1914), p. 21.
[11]*Ibid*. p. 9. Other Harlans mentioned in this
sketch cannot be identified from this book.

SMITH, ROBERT   *probable*

This name appears only on List U which says he
loaded gunpowder on the *Welcome*. Duty had to be paid
on gunpowder whether for sale or not but the quantity in this case was too small to suggest he was a
merchant.
The *Minutes of the Board of Property of the Eastern Division of New Jersey from 1685 to 1705* (Perth
Amboy 1949), 1:87, show that in 1685 Robert Smith
applied for headland of 25 acres and for purchase of
75 more acres "for importing himself in the year
1682." At a meeting of the Council on 6 June 1701
(*ibid*. 243) Robert Smith, with others, petitioned
for lots in Perth Amboy.
Administration of the estate of Robert Smith of
Burlington County was granted to Sarah Smith on 10
May 1705, and Daniel Leeds and George Wills had
signed the bond with her as fellow-bondsmen on 10

March 1705. Inventory of personal estate came to
£185/8/6 including the sloop *Primrose* £40 and £38
due from Henry Jacobs, and was made by Daniel Leeds
and Mordeca Andrews, 27 March 1705.[1]

The widow Sarah Smith had previously been the
wife of Leonard Headley or Hedley of Elizabeth Town,
on whose estate inventory was dated 8 Feb. 1683/4
and administration granted to the widow Sarah, now
wife of Robert Smith of the same place, 5 Feb.
1684/5.[2] Sarah Smith paid a debt to the estate of
Thomas Carhart of Woodbridge, 20 April 1697.[3] A
plantation had been leased to Robert Smith by Alice
Rowse of Rawey [Rahway] in Elizabeth Town, in her
inventory of £232/1/9, 9 July 1690.[4] A patent was
issued to Robert Smith of Elizabeth Town for a lot
of one acre in Perth Amboy bounded south by Smith
St., east William Hodgson, west by William Young,
north by a street, 7 June 1701, and Robert Smith
was an abutter in a similar deed of same date to
William Young.[5] It seems probable that all the
items cited pertain to the same Robert Smith and
that after living more than twenty years in East
Jersey he removed to Burlington in West Jersey not
long before his death. No issue is seen but there
may have been some not discovered.

It is worth noting that there was another Robert
Smith of Elsenburgh, Salem County, Laborer, who made
his will 3 9th mo. 1721 and in it leaves all his
worldly estate to brothers Thomas and Richard Smith
and sisters Elizabeth and Mary Smith, appointing
brother Thomas as executor; witnesses: Andrew Thompson, Jno Pledger and Nathan Smart. The inventory
dated 5 4th mo. (June) 1721 came to £39/15/8, made
by Andrew Thompson and Joseph Morris.[6]

NOTES

[1]NJW 1:431.   [2]NJW 1:218; 1 NJA 21:63.
[3]NJW 1:81.   [4]NJW 1:396.
[5]1 NJA 21:325.   [6]NJW 1:431.

SMITH, WILLIAM   *proved*

The name of William Smith appears on all lists
except List I from which it may have been inadvertently omitted. The proof is to be found in Philadelphia Arrivals, which shows that Richard Townsend
brought with him three servants, the first named
William Smith, all of whom were to serve seven years,
hence loose in 1689.

Now the name William Smith is, as would be expected, frequent in the records of early Pennsylvania, and perhaps as many as ten different men of these same names can be distinguished, though in some instances fuller information might permit reduction of this number. It seems clear, however, that the *Welcome* passenger was the one mentioned in the following passage discovered by Walter Lee Sheppard in the minutes of Abington Monthly Meeting under date of 28 7th mo. 1702. At this meeting a certificate was granted Richard Townsend to go to Maryland to visit Friends there, and

> Some discourse hath been this day Concerning ye Lameness of William Smith and in order to seek for Some remeady have appointed William Jenkins, William Howel & Evan Thomas to be assistant in that Case & what Money may be wanting this meeting do allow it out of ye Stock and ye said Friends are desired to bring a report to ye next Monthly Meeting, which Said person was taken Care of by ffrds unto his dying day, &c.

No such report was made, however, at the next meeting, and it may be deduced from the peculiar wording of this minute that the said William Smith probably died between the time of the meeting and the time the clerk wrote up his minute thereof. The connection with Richard Townsend serves to identify the lame man as Townsend's erstwhile servant, and it appears that the *Welcome* William Smith died in September 1702, then lame and doubtless unmarried and childless, else we should have heard otherwise in this connection.

At this time we do not propose to enter into a discussion of the other men named William Smith except to say that of the three who were servants, the William Smith who was servant of Phineas Pemberton was most likely the man who married a daughter of Thomas Croasdale, as described above on pages 150 f.

†*SNASHFOLD, SNASHOLD or SNATHALL, JOHN   *proved*

This name appears on List Q at the end, as if recently discovered, and also on List V. The proof is in a letter of William Penn to Thomas Lloyd dated 18 5th mo. 1685:

> . . . . desire that J. Songhurst be called to account for ye estate of honest Jon Snashold yt

died in ye same ship, Tuckers wife, & an old maid
yt lived with J. Day, & his own pocket book with
J. Song has shown me will help besides J. Song
owed him money.[1]

At the Quarterly Meeting of Sussex held at Ifield,
22 4th mo. 1685, there was discussed the business
depending on our friend William Penn re the goods
of John Snashall deceased, and meeting desired that
William Garton write again to John Songhurst about
giving a speedy account of John Snashal's estate to
England as he can. An undated letter of William
Penn ca. 1686: "love to J. Songhurst & tell him
Richd Snashold about not hearing concerning his brother's estate in his hands." Again, William Penn
to J. H., 30 9th mo. 1686: "remember me to J. Song
& tell him R. Snashold much complains for an account
of his Bro's estate & so does Jo Burchall's kindred
& others." The Warminghurst Quarterly Meeting wrote
to Pennsylvania Quarterly Meeting at Philadelphia
about this matter on 23 7th mo. 1689 and 16 10th
mo. 1689--the Philadelphia entries 1 7th mo. 1690
and 1 10th mo. 1690. The Shipley Quarterly Meeting
on 28 7th mo. 1691 reported that it had received
the list of the goods sent to Philadelphia by John
Snashall.

The Board of Property on 23 6th mo. 1728 recorded
as follows in regard to J. Snashall who died intestate. His nearest kinswoman was Joan Beach of Hove,
Sussex, only daughter of Richard Snashfold of Hackham, brother and heir of John, who by her attorney
granted the 500 acres in Pennsylvania to James Steel
who desires a warrant. Granted 22 Dec. 1727 Warrant
89 in right of John Snathold. See Warrants and Surveys 7:213, survey return of land of James Steel,
who had obtained a number of warrants for Liberty
land, total 60 acres, one warrant. John Snashold's
500 acres, 8 acres of Liberty Land, 22 Dec. 1727.
The above James Steel was probably the one who married at Lewes, Sussex, 15 7th mo. 1697, Martha Hammond. John Snashold was a First Purchaser of 500
acres in Group 57.[2]

John Snashfold was a very active Quaker from a-
bout 1657-1659, making trouble for the Church of
England, often in jails. He was a blacksmith of
Chiltington West, Sussex. On 14 2nd mo. 1669 he
declared for the first time intentions to marry
Elizabeth Shaw of Thakeham. The marriage was approved by his brother Richard and her Shaw rela-

tives, but they did not marry until 1 2nd mo. 1673
and at his house, on which occasion among witnesses
were Ambrose Riggs, John Songhurst, Edward and Thomas Buckman, John Barnes and Jane Batchelor, Judith
Buckman, Joan Buckman. Most monthly meetings were
at his house but on 25 and 26 3rd mo. 1682 he bought
the 500 acres from Penn, and sold his house 12 5th
mo. 1682 to go to Pennsylvania with Penn, and so
monthly meetings had to be elsewhere, i.e. alter-
nately at Penn's and at John Shaw's house until a
central location could be found. This John was not
afterwards seen as living in any English record,
offering confirmation to the belief that he was a
Welcome passenger who died during the crossing.
    Richard Snashfold (John's brother) was of Shipley
Meeting in 1657 but of Thakeham, buried at Steyning,
10 3rd mo. 1702. His wife Joan, also of Thakeham,
was buried at Steyning, 3 8th mo. 1689. They had
two daughters: Sarah, born 24 12th mo. 1657, married
6 2nd mo. 1680, Richard Verill; and Joan, who married, first, 21 9th mo. 1682, John Ridley; second,
by 1728, ----- Beach.
    Another John Snashall of Sussex, also a black-
smith, of Hurstpierpont, was born 9 2nd mo. 1656,
married at Pain's Place, Cuckfield, 25 4th mo. 1681,
Elizabeth Hammond of the parish of Crecklefield,
died 21 10th mo. 1701, buried at Twiniham. They had
Elizabeth, born 2 1st mo. 1683, and Mary, born 1685,
died 22 2nd mo. 1708, buried 1 3rd mo. 1708 at Twiniham, aged 23. This man was probably the John Sr. of
Hurstpierpont who married at Lewes, 27 2nd mo. 1706,
Elizabeth Bradford, under the care of Lewes and Chichester Meeting.
    Warrants and Surveys 1:882 contain a warrant by
Penn for Snashold's city lot to John Songhurst, at
his request, 10 6th mo. 1683, S[nas]hold purchaser
of 500 acres.
    The line is, of course, extinct.

NOTES

[1]For "Tuckers wife" see Jane Batchelor; for "an
old maid yt lived with J. Day" see Margaret Scott.
The English records cited in this sketch were all
kindly furnished me by Mrs. Marion Balderston.
    [2]1 PA 1:46.

SONGHURST, JOHN the elder   *proved*
SONGHURST, MARY, his wife   *highly probable*

SONGHURST, SARAH, his daughter   *highly probable*
SONGHURST, JOHN, his son   *highly probable*

Except for List I, where the name is spelled as
Longhurst, the name of the elder John Songhurst appears on all lists. The wife, daughter and son, appear only on Lists O and V, though List U regards
them as probable passengers. John Songhurst had an
elder daughter, Elizabeth, wife of John Barber, who
is discussed in the sketch devoted to him (pp. 39-
48).

The proof for John the elder is that he was named
executor in the wills of William Wade and Isaac Ingram, both executed aboard the *Welcome*, and was a
beneficiary of the latter will. He also took care
of the estates of John Snashfold, a *Welcome* passenger who died during the crossing, and of John Burchall, who was probably in the same category, though
formal administration was not granted to Songhurst
on either estate. Songhurst was a First Purchaser
of 1250 acres in Group 19 with John Barnes,[1] and a-
gain of 250 acres in Group 57, this time alone.[2]

The proof for his wife Mary is that she can be
shown to have been in Philadelphia in the year 1682
Old Style, that is, before 25 March 1682/3, as sometime in 1682 she signed a character reference for
John and Thomas Rowland which was afterwards presented at Middletown Monthly Meeting. Such a re-
commendation was more probably written out soon after the *Welcome* arrived, but in any case before 25
March 1683. Also, on 1 11th mo. 1683/4 Mary Songhurst, with Elizabeth Wynne, presented Richard
Tucker and Jane Batchelor for marriage on behalf of
the Philadelphia Women's Meeting. The proof for the
daughter Sarah is merely the fact that she would
naturally have accompanied her parents, and the same
is true also for the son John who in 1682 was only
fourteen. In the 1687 will of his father he is
shown to be in England, but *if he return,* then he
is to inherit. This proviso is more probably due
to the possibility of death rather than to induce a
return. It is improbable that he would not be taken
along in 1682, but clear that he had gone back to
England, and was there, aged nineteen, when his
father made his will.

John Songhurst was said by Armstrong to be of
Chillington[3] [i.e. Chiltington], and Whiting says he
was of Conehurst, while Besse[4] says he was from
Hitchfield [Itchingfield on Cary's 1801 map], and

was sent to goal [sic] for tithes; fined 1673 £10
for preaching, £20 for the house the meeting was in.
All these places are close together in Sussex.

John Songhurst the elder died 25 11th mo. 1688/9,
leaving a will dated 26 7th mo. 1687, probated in
Pennsylvania on 5 Nov. 1 William and Mary 1689[5] and
in Gloucester County, New Jersey, on 2 Dec. 1689[6]:
£200 to son John Songhurst "if it shall please God
he shall live to return from Old England to Pennsylvania" [as it did]; friends Thomas Budd, John
Goodson, Benjamin Chambers, to assist him as executor; £100 each to daughters Elizabeth and Sarah;
servants James Portis [in New Jersey copy John Po-
ris] and William Gaskin; Joseph Lugwell 20s; Thomas
Clark £20 if he serves out his time; witnesses: Benjamin Chambers, John Goodson. Letters testamentary
were granted 2 Dec. 1689 to John Songhurst of Philadelphia, yeoman, son and executor, who filed bond
the same day, Zechariah Whitpaine of the same, merchant, fellow bondsman.

On 22 Xber 1720 John Songhurst [the younger] appeared before the Board of Property[7] and produced
original deeds of Penn to his father for 250 acres,
23-24 May 1682, and of Penn to Jno Burchall for 500
acres, 15-16 May 1682, whose brother Thomas Burchall
sold to John Songhurst (the elder) on 24-25 July
1688. He asked for a patent but the Board of Property was reluctant to grant one.

Warrants and Surveys 1:864 contain Warrant No.
2130:

> William Penn, Proprietor & Governor, at the re-
> quest of Jno Songhurst that I would grant him to
> take up within the Liberties of the City for the
> proposition of purchase the land of his own 500
> acres, ten acres; for his daughter the widow Bar-
> ber 2500 acres, fifty acres; for John Burchall
> 500 acres, ten acres; for Humphrey Killingbeck
> 1000 acres, twenty acres; for Jno Snashold 500
> acres. These are to will and require thee forth-
> with to survey or cause to be surveyed for him
> the Land of the said persons within the Liber-
> ties of the City in all one hundred and twenty
> acres where not taken up according to the method
> of townships by me appointed and make return
> thereof unto my Secretary's office. Given at
> Philadelphia the 10th of 6th mo. 1683 for Thomas
> Holme Surveyor General. Wm. Penn.

Blackwell's Rent Roll of 1689 shows Songhurst as
owner of an old purchase lot of 51 feet, 2/- for five
years, on Mulberry Street.[8]

John Songhurst was a Quaker preacher, author of
two pamphlets on the need of love and gentleness:
(1) *A Testimony of Love and Good Will*, etc. (1680);
(2) *An Epistle of Love and tender Good will* (1681).
Mr. Colket cites a letter of James Harrison from
London, 15 2nd mo. 1682, for the statement that John
Songhurst was then organizing a company to go to
America. Mr. Colket also appears to have seen evidence that Songhurst's death took place in New Jersey, though he was buried in Philadelphia, 25 11th
mo. 1688. The maiden name of his wife Mary has not
been discovered.

Issue: surname Songhurst
i.   Edmund, b. 3 11th mo. 1661, d. 9 9th mo.
       1669, never came to America.
ii.   Elizabeth, eldest daughter, perhaps also
       eldest child, as her birthdate has not
       been found; d. Philadelphia, 8 11th mo.
       1726; m. (1) in England, 1st int., 8
       12th mo. 1681/2, 2nd int., 12 2nd mo.
       1682, John Barber, a *Welcome* passenger;
       (2) in England, date unknown, Robert
       Webb; (3) in Philadelphia, 28 5th mo.
       1704, Samuel Richardson. Issue by Webb
       only. For a full account see the sketch
       devoted to John Barber, above, pp. 39-48.
iii.   Sarah, b. 20 9th mo. 1664, d. Philadelphia,
       4 6th mo. 1733; m. (1) 7 10th mo. 1686,
       Zachariah Whitpaine, a *Welcome* passenger;
       (2) 14 10th mo. 1697, Charles Sanders;
       (3) 13 9th mo. 1704, as second wife, Dr.
       Griffith Owen. For a fuller account see
       the sketches devoted to Zachariah Whit-
       paine and Griffith Owen.
iv.   John, b. 9 10th mo. 1668, d. Philadelphia,
       November 1735, without issue, testate,
       bur , according to Hinshaw,[9] 3 9th mo.
       1735, but the day must be wrong as five
       day later he made a codicil to his will
       which was dated 27 6th mo. 1735, witnes-
       es: Joshua Johnson, Jno Kearsley, Henry
       Drinker, Nicholas Rogers; codicil dated
       8 9th mo. 1735, witnessed by Joshua John-
       son, Henry Drinker and Anthony Peel; pro-

bated 8 Nov. 1735 by Johnson, Drinker and
Rogers.[10] The will does not mention his
wife Olive, name unknown, who was bur.
at Philadelphia, 6 4th mo. 1735. John
Songhurst of the City of Philadelphia,
carpenter, leaves £20 each to cousins
Sarah Currey, Joyce Merritt, Stephen Armitt, Zachariah Whitbin [all identified
in the Whitpaine sketch]; £10 and the
residue of the real estate to Mary Wol-
vin; to 4 children of cousin Isaac Williams: Isaac, Zachariah, Lydia, Mary, of
whom some, at least, are minors [all i-
dentified in the Whitpaine sketch]; residue of personal estate to cousin Mary
Williams, wife of aforesaid Isaac Williams the father, he named executor; the
codicil leaves the bequest of Armitt to
his two minor children now living.

NOTES

[1] 1 PA 1:42.
[2] 1 PA 1:46; 3 PA 3:386, 391 for surveys; pp. 13
f. for six properties.
[3] List B; also 3 PA 3:341.
[4] Besse's *Sufferings* 1:715, 719.
[5] PhW A:155, No. 66, abstracted in PGSP 1:78 but
described from a photograph of the original.
[6] NJW 1:434.   [7] 2 PA 19:707.
[8] PGM 23:76.   [9] HEAQG 422.
[10] PhW E, No. 349.

*STACKHOUSE, THOMAS   *disproved*
*STACKHOUSE, MARGERY, his wife   *disproved*
 STACKHOUSE, JOHN, his nephew   *disproved*
 STACKHOUSE, THOMAS, his nephew   *disproved*
 STACKHOUSE, JOHN, error for Thomas   *mythical*

Thomas Stackhouse appears under his right name
on Lists F, O [here denied], Q, U [here probably on
the *Lamb*], V [here on the *Lamb*], but masquerades as
John Stackhouse, hence mythical, on Lists A, B, C,
D, E, G, H, I, J, K, L, M, N, P, R, S, T, W, X, Y
and Z. His wife is called Margery on Lists A, B,
C, D, E, F, G, H, I, M, U [here probably on the
Lamb], V [on the *Lamb*], X, Y and Z, and is the unnamed wife on Lists J, K, L, N, P, S, T and W. The
two nephews, John Stackhouse and Thomas Stackhouse,
are claimed to have been probably on the *Welcome* by

Dr. Arthur Edwin Bye.[1] These nephews were, of course,
present in Bucks County in close proximity and association with their uncle but no evidence has been
found to show on what ship they came, and if they
did accompany their uncle and aunt, as Dr. Bye wishes
to maintain, then the ship was the *Lamb*.

In the Settle certificate in the Middletown Minutes the two Stackhouses, Thomas and Margery, appear
between the Croasdales and the Cowgills; they were
omitted by design in the Roberts version and inadvertently in the Buckman-Potts.[2] Like the others in
the Settle group, they were long suspected of having
come on the *Friends' Adventure*, but are now believed
to have come on the *Lamb*, though Stackhouse is not
listed in the English Port Books as having loaded
anything on that ship. Mr. Myers never collected
any data on the Stackhouses in his Welcome Papers
but left them on the list.[3]

Thomas Stackhouse married Margery Hayhurst probably in 4th mo. 1682, they having declared their
intentions in 2nd mo. and 3rd mo. 1682. There is a
possibility that Stackhouse was in some way related
to Thomas Croasdale, the only householder mentioned
in the Settle certificate not otherwise known to
have been related to some of the others. In Bucks
Deeds 3:103 William Crosdell of Buckingham, yeoman,
son and heir of Thomas Crosdell late of New Hey in
Co. of York, England, yeoman, and John Crossdell
of Bucks, yeoman, the other son, recite that Penn
granted by lease and release dated 21 and 22 April
1682, 1000 acres to Thomas Crosdell, 250 acres
whereof were purchased with money of Thomas Stackhouse and included to save charge. This tract was
sold but not conveyed by Stackhouse to Nicholas
Walne who sold his interest to Robert Heaton of
Bucks, yeoman. Now the Crosdells at the request of
Thomas Stackhouse and Nicholas Walne convey to Robert Heaton, and the deed is signed by both Crossdells, Thomas Stackhouse and Nicholas Walne, witnessed by Samuel Hough and John Stackhouse, acknowledged 10 4th mo. 1702, recorded 18 11th mo. 1702.
This is not, of course, definite proof of a relationship between Thomas Stackhouse and Thomas Croasdale but it seems probable that such existed.

Margery Stackhouse was buried 5 11th mo. 1682/3.
Thomas Stackhouse made an inventory of the estate
of Cuthbert Hayhurst 11 11th mo. 1683/4. The 1687
memorial on selling liquor to the Indians was signed
by Thomas Stackhouse in his own hand and by Thomas

Stackhouse Jr. by mark.

The will of Thomas Stackhouse of Belmount in Bensalem Township, Bucks County, yeoman, dated 26 9th mo. 1705, probated 31 Aug. 1706,[4] names loving wife Margaret sole executrix; nephew Thomas Stackhouse £1; nephew John Stackhouse £3; brother John Stackhouse, sister Jennit, sister Ellin, 1s each[5]; witnesses: Jeremiah Scaife, John Romford, Jonathan Scaife, probated by the Scaifes, 31 6th mo. 1706. Jordan suggests that the sister Ellin was identical with Ellen Cowgill, the widow in the Settle certificate, who had a daughter Jennet. Middletown Monthly Meeting minutes show that Thomas Stackhouse Sr. was still living there on 7 10th mo. 1699. Powell Stackhouse and William R. Stackhouse, *The Book of John Stackhouse and Elizabeth Buckingham, his wife* (Moorestown, N.J., 1906), say that Thomas and Margery Stackhouse "came in the time of William Penn" [which is true enough] but had no issue; had, instead, nephews Thomas and John, supposed to have been brothers. Jordan, in his Cowgill sketch, says that in 1701 Thomas Stackhouse went to live with Margaret Atkinson, widow of Christopher, and afterwards married her. An account of the Bucks County Atkinsons[6] shows Margaret Fell, widow of Christopher Atkinson, having Thomas Stackhouse Sr. living at her house and the Meeting was, of course, scandalized by this, and dealt with them, after which they declared intentions 4 12th mo. 1702/3, and were married in 1st mo. 1702/3, that is, before 25 March. She married, third, in 1st mo. 1708/9, John Frost, and died 1714, being buried 19 March 1714/15.[7] Appended to this is Note B on Thomas Stackhouse Sr.[8] in which passage on the *Welcome* is claimed, and it is stated that Margery was a Hayhurst and that she died 5 11th mo. 1682, that is, 1682/3, the date given above for her burial. Ellen Cowgill is here also identified as the sister Ellin of Stackhouse's will.

On the nephew, Thomas Stackhouse Jr., we may point out that Middletown Monthly Meeting minutes show that he married Grace Heaton on 27 7th mo. 1688, 1st intentions 5 5th mo. 1688, passed 2 6th mo. 1688. He is also mentioned on 7 5th mo. 1687, 4 6th mo. 1687, and he signed by mark the memorial on selling liquor to the Indians. On 5 11th mo. 1687 his difference with Thomas Atkinson is noted, which was ended by the latter's death, but the widow is

to pay Thomas Stackhouse Jr., so it is his difference, not his uncle's. The nephew John Stackhouse
was in Bucks County by 1685, died 9 2nd mo. 1757;
married at Middletown, 7th mo. 1702, Elizabeth Pearson, died 21 6th mo. 1743, daughter of Thomas and
Grace (Vipon) Pearson. They had nine children:

   i.   Thomas, b. 29 1st mo. 1706.
   ii.   John, b. 11 3rd mo. 1708, d. 23 7th mo.
           1743, m. Elizabeth Buckingham.
   iii.   Samuel.
   iv.   Margaret, b. 6 8th mo. 1711, d. 2 5th 1774.
   v.   Samuel, b. 6 10th mo. 1716, d. 20 7th 1742.
   vi.   James, b. 10 1st mo. 1718.
   vii.   Grace, b. 27 7th mo. 1720.
   viii. Elizabeth.
   ix.   Sarah, b. 21 7th mo. 1726.[9]

NOTES

[1]*The Historian* 3:67; also his *Friendly Heritage*
(New York 1959), pp. 195-199.
[2]See Introduction, Section E. [3]PGM 23:52.
[4]PhW C:40, abstr. PMHB 15:195.
[5]The small sum left to these three suggests that
the heirs were present in Bucks, since to send so
small a sum as a shilling to England would be ex-
pensive, but we have seen no evidence of them in
Bucks County records. In any case, the mythical
John was not this one.
[6]PMHB 31:168 f. [7]PMHB 31:442. [8]PMHB 31:440 f.
[9]Powell Stackhouse and William R Stackhouse,
*The Book of Descendants of John Stackhouse and Eli-
zabeth Buckingham, his wife* (Moorestown, N.J., 1906),
provides accounts of some of the descendants.

STRAWN, LANCELOT   *disproved*

   This man was the second husband of the *Welcome*
passenger, Mary Buckman, widow of Henry Cooper, and
a full account of him appears in the Buckman sketch
(pages 80-82). He had but one child, Jacob Strawn,
but Jacob had nine sons and three daughters, all of
whom lived to have issue, and when the count was
complete, Jacob Strawn had 128 grandchildren, so by
now there is a numerous posterity.
   In the year 1848, Lancelot's great-grandson, John
Straughan, as he spelled the name in his later years,
prepared an account of his own life which was shown
me by the late J. Donald Strawn (1888-1966) of Char-

don, Ohio, with whom I long collaborated on a Strawn genealogy as yet unpublished. This John Straughan, born 1776, died in Columbiana County, Ohio, in 1856, was one of the 18 children of Jacob's son Daniel. He was about twenty-five when his grandfather died in 1800. In this document John Straughan made the claim that Lancelot Strawn was a *Welcome* passenger, crossing the Atlantic on the same ship as his future wife, and this claim has been repeated by certain descendants.

No evidence has been found to support the claim and Lancelot Strawn is first recorded in William Buckman's will when his wife is merely called Mary Strawhen, her husband's first name not given, and in Friends' records shortly after the marriage when she was disowned for marrying out. Lancelot died in 1720, intestate, this being the only occasion when his first name is recorded in a contemporary document except for his presence at a Buckman wedding as witness.

It seems quite clear that the claim is false and results from misunderstanding the true Buckman tradition that Mary crossed on the same ship as William Penn.

*TEAREWOOD, THOMAS   *disproved*

This name appears on List X only and then incorrectly as Theo Tearewood. The truth is that he came as servant to Joseph Fisher on the *Lion* of Liverpool, arriving 14 8th mo. 1683, to serve four years and get the usual fifty acres, loose on 14 8th mo. 1687.

He left a will dated 13 Dec. 1696, probated 12 Jan. 1696/7 (PhW A:349, #146; see PGSP 2:30), in which he calls himself of Philadelphia County, yeoman, mentions neither wife nor child, and leaves legacies to William Beavan and wife, John Barns and wife, Joseph Wright, John Sankless, John Lewis, Joseph Fisher Sr.; residue ½ to Joseph Fisher Jr., ½ to Mary and Martha Fisher; Friend Joseph Fisher Sr. to be sole executor; witnesses: Joseph Wright, George X Fisher, Edward Farmer. Two hundred acres in Dublin Township are mentioned.

THOMPSON, GEORGE   *proved*

This name appears in this spelling on all lists except that in the case of Lists K, N, P, S and T, the spelling is Thomson. Though the latter spelling is sometimes found in primary records, all four sig-

natures of this man which appear one on each of the
four wills executed aboard the *Welcome*, namely,
those of John Barber, Thomas Heriott, Isaac Ingram
and William Wade, the longer spelling is used. On
the will of Heriott, Thompson signs as grocer.   We
therefore think it probable that Thompson was English and not Scandinavian, as the spelling Thomson
or Thomasen would suggest.

He apparently first settled in Chester County.
Chester County Deeds A, pt. 2, p. 332, 4 4th mo.
684, shows George Thomson of Concord selling land
in Concord to John Bezer of Chichester, yeoman, and
this is the only George Thompson deed found thus
far in Chester County or elsewhere.   Dr. George Smith[1]
claims Thompson was not a Friend, and the absence of
references to him in any Friends record thus far examined seems to confirm this.

Late in Old Style 1682 George Thompson married
Miriam Short, a *Welcome* passenger, and this marriage
was performed by Lawrence Carolus Lockenius, a Swe-
dish Lutheran clergyman.   The *Record of the Courts
of Chester County, Pennsylvania, 1681-1697* (1910)
contains the following items:[2]

p. 23   Court held at Chester 14 Feb. 1682 [1682/3]
        George Thompson appeared at ye Co[r]t & none
        appearing against him was Cleared by Pclam-
        ation.   Lawrence Carolus [Lockenius], for
        marrying ye aboves[d] Geo: Thompson & one
        Merriam Short, Contrary to the Lawes of ye
        Province . . .

p. 49   Court held at Chester 6 11th 1684 [1684/5]
        Ordered that y[e] Inhabitance of Concord
        Bethell and Chichester doe meet on the 3[d]
        of the next weeke att Henry Renolds to
        Conferre together how to Provide a main-
        tenance of Miriam Thomson and her child.

This evidence shows that George Thompson and Miriam
Short were married by Lockenius in some way not valid under the existing laws of the province of Pennsylvania; that for lack of witnesses Thompson was
cleared of the charge; that a little more than two
years later Thompson sold his land in Concord to
Bezer; that early in the next year, Miriam Thompson
and her child were in need of public assistance.
This suggests that George Thompson had either died
or deserted his family.   That he died is the conclusion to be reached from the fact that his wife mar-

ried, second, at unknown date and place, William
White, of whom more later.

The matter may, however, not be so simple. The
Lutheran pastor Rudman made a list of Lutherans ca.
1698[3] and on this list is a George Thompson and not
among the single men. By deed dated 29 9th mo. 1692,
acknowledged 6 Dec. 1692, recorded 3 Aug. 1693,[4]
Arthur Cooke of the town and county of Philadelphia,
merchant, conveyed a lot on the Delaware bank originally patented to him by William Penn, 28 10th mo.
1689, to George Thompson and Andries Derickson of
the same, value £300; and by deed dated 1 July 5
William and Mary 1693, George Thompson conveyed his
moiety of this lot to Andr's Derickson for £130.
Furthermore, the will of Ann Cox, widow, signed by
mark, 3 Aug. 1699, probated 18 Sept. 1699,[5] shows
among other things that she was not a Friend; names
two "clerks" of Philadelphia, Thomas Clayton and
John Arrow Smith; mentions son William Trotter;
daughter Ann, wife of George Thompson; daughter E-
lizabeth Shepperd, widow, who, at probation of the
will, was in the Island of Barbadoes. Among non-
Quaker burials is that of Elizabeth, daughter of
George and Ann Thompson, 11 6th mo. 1695. At the
First Presbyterian Church, Philadelphia, 3 March
1707/8, George Thompson married Elizabeth Morris-
field, and henceforth there are no baptisms of any
children of this couple in this church's register.

If all these items set forth in the preceding
paragraph pertain to a single man, and they seem to
do so, it is barely possible that Miriam Short's
husband was that man. He had used a Lutheran pastor for his marriage to Miriam Short. It seems
possible that in some way unknown the marriage of
George Thompson to Miriam Short was dissolved, so
that she was free to marry again. This is, of course,
far from proved.

Whatever the truth about the fate of George
Thompson after 1684, Miriam appears certainly to
have married at an unknown date William White of
New Castle County, wheelwright, whose will dated
22 Dec. 1702, probated 14 Sept. 1703,[6] names wife
Miriam as executrix; children Samuel, John, Elizabeth; son-in-law Ralph Tomson [sic: not Semson, as
it has been read]; witnesses: John Grubb, Frances
Grubb, Hugh Bawdon, overseer: John Bailey. Whether
the three White children were by Miriam is unknown.
This many children would not be large for the peri-

od 1684-1702, but we do not know when the White-Thompson marriage took place. In any case, Miriam married, third, at Chichester, 30 9th mo. 1704, Aaron Coppock of Aston Township who moved to Nottingham in 1713. He was born 25 10th mo. 1662, died 10 10th mo. 1726, leaving a will dated 3 10th mo. 1726, probated 17 Dec. 1726,[7] naming son John, a minor; unnamed wife; daughters Lydia Coppock, Meriam Coppock, both unmarried; Sarah Frayser, Martha Robinson [wife of John, who had John, Aaron, Mary, Ruth, Martha, Miriam], Mary Sinclair; sons-in-law Ralph Thomson, John White, Samuel White; daughter-in-law Elizabeth White; executrix: beloved wife Miriam assisted by Jonas King; signed Aron Copock; witnesses: James Wright, Samuel Lightler.

This will by its wording tends to support the view that the three White children were Miriam's as well as William's, for had they been only step-children of Miriam and not her own, Aaron Coppock would not have called them his sons-in-law and his daughter-in-law.

It is clear that George Thompson had by his wife Miriam Short only one child, namely, Ralph Thompson. Cope says that Ralph was taxed in Marlborough Township 1719-1726 and in East Fallowfield Township in 1735-1740.[8] In 1740 he would have been about 57 years old. No probate or land records of Ralph Thompson have been found in Chester County, and a search for him in Lancaster County, so far as it went, turned up nothing.

Thomas Maxwell Potts[9] has an account of this family which contains some of the information given above but he errs in thinking Ralph Thompson had married a daughter of Aaron Coppock.

A fuller account of Miriam Short's ancestry and descendants appears in the Short sketch.[10]

NOTES

[1]*History of Delaware County, Pennsylvania* (Philadelphia 1862), p. 508.

[2]Also in Cope and Futhey's history of the same county, p. 24.

[3]PMHB 2:227. [4]2 PA 19:130-134.

[5]PhW No. 215 (PGSP 3:27). [6]PhW B:163.

[7]CW 1:205.

[8]Gilbert Cope, *Genealogy of the Baily Family* (Lancaster 1913), p. 14.

[9]*Our Family Ancestors* (Canonsburg Pa. 1895), 370.

[10]For our earlier account of this family see TAG
38:159-162. See also 3 PA 24:101, survey in 1742.

THREWECKS, ROBERT   *disproved*

This name appears only on List X. The truth is
that this man came as servant to Robert Turner on
the *Lion* of Liverpool, arriving 14 8th mo. 1683, to
serve four years, receive £8 and fifty acres, loose
on 14 8th mo. 1687.

There was also another Robert Threwecks, servant
of Robert Turner, who was to serve thirteen years,
loose on 14 8th mo. 1695. Mrs. Balderston (PGM 24:
92, Note 88) deduces that he was son of the preceding Robert Threwecks and was aged eight at the
crossing.

No further trace of either has been found.

TOOLE, MARY   *disproved*

This name appears on List X only. The truth is
that she came as servant to Joseph Fisher on the
Lion of Liverpool, arriving 14 8th mo. 1683, to
serve four years, get £3 and fifty acres, loose on
14 8th mo. 1687. No success has been had in tracing her further. In the case of women servants,
it is particularly difficult to find them afterwards
unless we are fortunate enough to find a marriage
record or an application for head rights, or some
other record.

TOWNSEND, RICHARD		*proved*
TOWNSEND, ANN HUTCHINS, his wife		*proved*
TOWNSEND, HANNAH, his daughter		*proved*
TOWNSEND, JAMES, his son		*proved*
TOWNSEND, ANN, his supposed daughter		*mythical*
TOWNSEND, WILLIAM, his brother		*disproved*

Richard Townsend is on all lists but on List E
the name is spelled Townshend. His wife Ann and the
children Hannah and James are on Lists A, B, C, E,
G, H, I, M, O, Q, U, V, X, Y and Z. Another daughter Ann, who never existed, is also shown on List
X. The brother William appears on no lists whatever, but the claim that he came with his brother
Richard on the *Welcome*, which is here said to have
carried 160 passengers of whom all but 63 died on
the way, is made by Mrs. John Sass in a 1964 document deposited in the Iowa Historical Library in
Des Moines. No evidence has been found to support
this claim for William, and his son Joseph is known

to have come to America in 1712. Jordan,[1] however,
shows William as buried at Bucklebury, England, 19
July 1692, having married, for the second time, at
Faringdon Magna, Berks., 1 April 1863 [sic], Mary
Lawrence. Though the marriage cannot have taken
place in 1863, there is no reason to doubt Jordan's
burial date, so this disposes of the claim.

The other Townsends are, however, among the best
attested *Welcome* passengers. First, Philadelphia
Arrivals show Richard, his wife Ann and the daughter
Hannah, though not the son James, together with the
three servants, William Smith, Natha[niel] Harrison
and Bartholomew Green, who were to serve for seven
years. In this entry, Richard Townsend is called
"carpenter, servant to ye Society for 5 years, to
have £50 p. ann." Second, Abington Friends Records
of Births and Deaths, the original of which is now
at the Friends Historical Library, Swarthmore, Pa.,
has as the first entry: "James Townshend Son of
Rich^d & Anne Townshend was Born on board ye Ship
called ye Welcome in Delaware River ye 2 of 9th mo.
1682." It is quibbling to say that James was not a
Welcome passenger, for he crossed the Atlantic on
that ship *in posse*, if not *in esse*. Third, in his
84th year Richard Townsend wrote a memoir of his
life which is printed in Proud's *History of Pennsylvania* 1:228-232; in Hazard's *Register* 6:198 f.;
in James Bowden's *History of the Society of Friends
in America* (London 1850), 2:17-19, and in the various editions of Watson's *Annals of Philadelphia*.
We have not succeeded in locating the original document which is not in either Swarthmore cr at the Department of Records in Arch Street. Proud's version
is a bit longer than the others and runs as follows:

> Whereas King Charles the Second, in the year
> 1681, was pleased to grant this province to
> William Penn . . . . which act seemed to be an
> act of Providence to many religious, good, people;
> and the Proprietor, William Penn, being one of
> the people called Quakers, and in good esteem,
> among them and others, many were inclined to em-
> bark along with him, for the settlement of this
> place. To that end, in the year 1682 several
> ships being provided for Pennsylvania, I found a
> concern on my mind to embark with them, with my
> wife and child; and about the latter end of the
> Sixth-month, having settled my affairs in London,

where I dwelt, I went, on board the Ship Welcome,
Robert Greenaway, Commander, in company with my
worthy friend, William Penn; whose good conversation was very advantageous to all the company.
His singular care was manifested, in contributing
to the necessities of many, who were sick of the
small-pox, then on board; out of which company
about thirty died. After a prosperous passage
of about two months, having had, in that time
many good meetings, on board, we arrived here.
At our arrival we found it a wilderness; the
chief inhabitants were Indians, and some Swedes,
who received us in a friendly manner, and though
there was a great number of us, the good hand of
Providence was seen in a particular manner; in
that provisions were found for us by the Swedes
and Indians, at very reasonable rates as well as
brought from divers other parts, that were inhabited before. Our first concern was to keep
up and maintain our religious worship, and in
order thereunto, we had several meetings in the
houses of the inhabitants; and one boarded meeting house was set up, where the city was to be,
near Delaware, and where we had very comfortable
meetings; and after our meetings were over, we
assisted each other in building little houses
for our shelter. After some time I set up a mill
on Chester creek; which I brought ready framed
from London; which served for grinding of corn,
and sawing of boards, and was of great use to us.
Besides, I, with Joshua Tittery made a net, and
caught great quantities of fish; which supplied
ourselves and many others; so that not withstan-
ding it was thought near three thousand persons
came in the first year, we had no lack. We were
so providentially provided for, that we could
buy a deer for about two shillings, and a large
turkey for about one shilling, and Indian corn
for about two shillings and six pence per bushel.
The Indians were to us very civil. As soon as
Germantown was laid out, I settled my tract of
land, which was about a mile from thence, where
I set up a barn and a corn mill, which was very
useful to the country round. But there being few
horses, people generally brought their corn upon
their backs, many miles. I remember, one man
had a bull so gentle, that he used to bring the
corn on his back. In this location, separated

from any provision market, we found flesh meat
very scarce, and on one occasion we were supplied by a very particular providence, to wit:
As I was in my meadow, mowing grass, a young
deer came and looked on me while I continued
mowing. Finding him to continue looking on, I
laid down my scythe and went towards him, when
he went off a little way--I returned again to
the mowing, and the deer again to its observa-
tion. So that I several times left my work to
go towards him, and he as often quietly retrea-
ted. At last when going towards him, and he
not regarding his steps, whilst keeping his eye
on me, he struck forcibly against the trunk of a
tree, and stunned himself so much as to fall,
when I sprang upon him and fettered his legs.
From thence I carried him home to my house, a
quarter of a mile, where he was killed, to the
great benefit of my family. I could relate several other acts of providence, of this kind. Being now in the eighty-fourth year of my age, and
the forty-sixth of my residence in this country,
I can do no less than return praises to the Al-
mighty for the great increase and abundance
which I have witnessed. My spirit is engaged
to supplicate the continuance thereof; and as
the parents have been blessed, may the same mer-
cies continue on their offspring, to the end of
time.

                     Richard Townsend.

Richard Townsend declared his first intentions
20 2nd mo. 1677, second intentions 18 3rd mo. 1677,
at Newberry Meeting, and married at Buckleberry,
Berkshire, 25 3rd mo. 1677, Ann Hutchins, daughter
of Richard Hutchins of Newberry.[2] In 1677 he was
also of Black Friars, London, a carpenter. He was a
First Purchaser of 250 acres in Group 3.[3] On 31 8th
mo. 1701 it was recorded[4] that contributions were
taken because he had "lost a great part of what he
had, lately by a great Flood." He rented a house
left by John Martin.[5] In 1719 he was one of 46 persons to sign the memorial to William Penn. He and
wife Anne were received at Philadelphia Meeting,
31 5th mo. 1713, on certificate from Abington Meeting dated 26 5th mo. 1713. He was buried 30 1st
mo. 1731/2, and his wife was buried, as his widow,
15 1st mo. 1732/3. An obituary appeared in *The
Pennsylvania Gazette*, 30 March 1731/2: "This day

was decently interred here, Mr. Richard Townsend, a
very ancient preacher among Friends, and a man of
exemplary innocence and piety." Another obituary
in *A Collection of Memorials* (1787) dates the death
on 30 3rd mo. 1737, five years and two months late.

Richard Townsend's will was dated 11 Jan. 1727/8,
probated 14 April 1733.[6] It names wife Ann Townsend
executrix; children: James, Joseph, Hannah, Mary,
Sarah; witnesses: John Warder, Chas Brockden, Sarah
Dillwyn.

He appears in Warrants and Surveys several times,
as follows:

3:588	1682	Bristol Township
1:382	1683	Liberties
2:114	1684	Bristol Township
1:383	1690	Liberties
6:84	1702	Wissahickon Mill
3:197	1690	Liberties
6:85	1702	Bristol

According to Jordan,[1] the *Welcome* passenger was
probably son of another Richard Townsend imprisoned
at Cirencester 1660-1662, 1675. It has been suggested to me by Mr. F. J. Dallett that Richard Townsend
may have been a relative of that Theophile Townend
of Cirencester who married Philip Theodore Lehnmann,
the *Welcome* passenger, in the sketch on whom details
are given more fully. There is a brief sketch of
Richard Townsend in Jane W. T. Brey, *A Quaker Saga*
(Philadelphia 1967), 102 f.

The dates of the children are from a Bible record
found in the F. W. Leach Collection in the Genealogical Society of Pennsylvania.

Issue: surname Townsend
  i.   Joseph, b. 2 10th mo. 1678, d. 20 3rd mo.
         1681, bur. Chequer Alley, London.
1 ii.   Hannah, b. 3 8th mo. or 13 8th mo. 1680.
2 iii. James, b. 2 9th mo. 1682 on the *Welcome*.
3 iv.   Mary, b. Brattleboro Mills, 22 or 23 3rd
         mo. 1685.
4 v.   Joseph, b.there, 16 5th mo. 1687.
5 vi.   Sarah, b. Philadelphia, 5 9th mo. 1689.

1. Hannah Townsend, second child and eldest daughter of Richard and Ann (Hutchins) Townsend, was born
in London, 3 or 13 8th mo. 1680, and came to America with her parents on the *Welcome* in 1682. She died
18 2nd mo. 1763 aged 80 [actually 83]. By 28 8th

mo. 1706 she had married at Abington Monthly Meeting, Isaac Cook of Germantown, born 1676, son of William and Jane (-----) Cook, late of Roxbury Township. The will of Isaac Cook dated 2 9th mo. 1767, probated 28 April 1773, mentions Hannah Davis, Mary, Richard, Jacob, and son-in-law Thomas Davis.

Issue: surname Cook
i.   Richard, certificate from Abington to Philadelphia, 26 3rd mo. 1753.
ii. Jacob, m. out by 24 2nd mo. 1755, declined to appeal; marriage not found.
iii. Hannah, m. int. Abington, 27 8th mo. 1735, Thomas Davis, later of Roxborough; his will probated 27 Dec. 1791.
iv. Isaac, b. 22 8th mo. 1714, d. by 1 July 1767; m. after 27 6th mo. 1739 Eleanor Tunis [not Dennis], b. 8 7th mo. 1719, d. 12 9th mo. 1747; (2) by 29 10th mo. 1753, out, Susannah Supplee, she accepted into meeting, 29 8th mo. 1774.
v.   Mary, b. 3 2nd mo. 1717, living 1767.

2. James Townsend, third child of Richard and Ann (Hutchins) Townsend, was born on the ship *Welcome*, while it was in the Delaware River, 2 9th mo. 1682, a few days after arrival. He was a carpenter of Bristol Township, living 22 9th mo. 1732, but was dead by 30 3rd mo. 1736, date of his widow's decease. He declared intentions at Abington, 31 4th mo. 1703, to marry Elizabeth Tomlinson, who died as his widow, 30 3rd mo. 1736. On 12 7th mo. 1713,[7] James Townsend of Bristol Township, carpenter, sold 60 acres to Joseph Townsend, millwright, both called sons of Richard Townsend. He probably then removed to Talbot County, Maryland, for on 4 Sept. 1722, James Townsend, late of Talbot County, Maryland, but now of Philadelphia, and wife Elizabeth, conveyed land in Maryland.

Issue: surname Townsend
i. Elizabeth, m. (1) ----- Whaley; (2) Richard Dickinson Sr., sawyer.
ii. Mary, m. Abraham Bernard or Barnet, bricklayer.

3. Mary Townsend, fourth child of Richard and Ann (Hutchins) Townsend, was born at Brattleboro Mills, near Philadelphia, 22 or 23 3rd mo. 1685, and died in 2nd mo. 1751 aged 66 years, death re-

corded at Third Haven Monthly Meeting in Maryland.
She married at Abington Monthly Meeting, 25 1st mo.
1706, John Bartlett, born 14 12th mo. 1675, died 1
or 2 9th mo. 1748, a blacksmith, son of Thomas Bartlett. They resided at Ratcliffe Manor, Talbot County, Maryland.

Issue: surname Bartlett

i.   John, b. 15 7th mo. 1706, d.y.
ii.   Joseph, b. 28 11th mo. 1707/8, d. 1 1st
        mo. 1772; m. 11 10th mo. 1735 Martha
        Milton, b. 9 1st mo. 1716/17, d. 7 11th
        mo. 1771.
iii.   Richard, d.y.
iv.   Thomas, d.y.
v.   Mary, d.y.
vi.   Esther, d.y.
vii.   Hannah, m. (1) Isaac Turner, (2) 30 1st
        mo. 1776 Samuel Rowland of Caroline Coun-
        ty.
viii.   Sarah, m. 29 9th mo. 1729, Joseph George
        of Kent County.

   4. Joseph Townsend, fifth child of Richard and
Ann (Hutchins) Townsend, was born at Brattleboro
Mills near Philadelphia, 16 5th mo. 1687, and died
14 3rd mo. 1725. He married at Abington, 11 9th
mo. 1712, Elizabeth Harmer, born 26 8th mo. 1687,
died 21 7th mo. 1754, daughter of William and Ruth
(-----) Harmer. He should not be confused with his
first cousin of the same name, born, according to
Mrs. Sass's manuscript, at Buckleberry, Berkshire,
18 Nov. 1684, died 9 April 1766, son of William
Townsend (born 1652) by his second wife Mary Lawrence (died 1692). This Joseph, Richard Townsend's
nephew, married in England, 27 Sept. 1710, Martha
Wooderson, who died 2 March 1767. Joseph and Martha
came to America with her sister Joan in 1712, and
their children were William, Mary, Joseph (born
8 April 1715, m. Lydia Reynolds), John, Hannah,
Martha, Richard, Esther. Mrs. Sass also states
that this Joseph had a brother William who was of
Reading, England. It was at the house of this Joseph in East Bradford Township, Chester County,
that his uncle, Richard Townsend, died.

Issue: surname Townsend, perhaps others

i.   Anne, b. 20 12th mo. 1713/14; m. at Christ
        Church, Philadelphia, 15 Dec. 1735, Tho-
        mas Sugar, carpenter, who m. (2) 23 Aug.

1744 at the same church, Elizabeth Collins. They removed to East Marlborough,
Chester County, Pa.

5. Sarah Townsend, sixth and youngest child
of Richard and Ann (Hutchins) Townsend, was born in
Philadelphia, 5 9th mo. 1689, recorded at Abington,
and died 13 2nd mo. 1732, recorded at Third Haven
Monthly Meeting in Maryland. She married at Abington, 26 9th mo. 1711, James Bartlett of Talbot County, Maryland, brother of John Bartlett who married
her sister Mary, and he was born ca. 1677, died 7
2nd mo. 1765.

Issue: surname Bartlett
i.   James, b. 13 6th mo. 1713, d. 9 12th mo.
       1779; m. Deborah -----.
ii.   Josiah, b. 12 3rd mo. 1715, apparently d.
       y.
iii.   Child, b. 13 4th mo. 1719, d.y.
iv.   Jonathan, b. 2 5th mo. 1721.
v.   Daniel, b. 1723, twin, m. Rebecca -----
       who m. (2) Thomas Sheriff.
vi.   Ann, b. 1723, twin, m. (1) 5 2nd mo. 1739
       Isaac Milton; (2) ----- Delahunte.

                         NOTES

[1]JCRFP 3:1353; 5:632-637.   [2]PGSP 3:232 f.
[3]1 PA 1:40; 3 PA 3:32 f., 2 bank lots and 2 city
lots.
[4]PGSP 6:81.   [5]PGSP 7:76.
[6]PhW E:232.   [7]PhD E-9, p. 101.

TURNER, ROBERT   *disproved*
TURNER, MARTHA, his daughter   *disproved*

These names appear on List X only as *Welcome* passengers. The truth is that they came on the *Lion*
of Liverpool, as free passengers, arriving 14 8th
1683. The compiler of List X compounds his error
by giving also a passenger list of the *Lion* on
which he puts Martha, wife of Robert Turner, but
she had already died in Ireland, as we shall see!
With the Turners there came also on the *Lion* the
following seventeen servants:

Name	Service	Money	Land
Rob[t] Threwecks	4	8	50
Henry furnace	4	3/8	50
Rob[t] Selford	4	6:p	50
Ben: Acton	4	3/8	50

John Reeves	4	6/10	50
Row: Hambidge	4		50
Richard Curtis	4	3	50
John Furnace	4	3	50
Dan Furnace	9		50
Robt Threwecks	13		50
Lemuel Bradshaw	4	27?	50
Robt Lloyd	4	4	50
Wm Long	4	3	50
Hen: Hollingsworth	2		50
Aiolce Cales	4	3	50
Rach: Furnace	6		50
Jos: Furnace	4	3	50

The first column indicates the number of years of
service required. To the right of the columns, not
copied because of space difficulties, is the date of
freedom for each servant which in every case is the
day on which the number of years would be up begin-
ing with 14 8th mo. 1683. The middle column shows
the amount due each servant at the end of term. It
appears that in most cases the amount is in pounds,
but some may be in shillings. The third column is
the number of acres to be expected. Each of these
servants is discussed in his alphabetical position.

The heading in Philadelphia Arrivals shows that
this Robert Turner is late of Dublin in Ireland,
Merch^t. It appears probable that he was not the
only Robert Turner present in America at the same
time and that he was older than his namesake. The
other man appears without designation of older or
younger, or other differentation, as the first
servant listed in an undated document which shows
the names of ten servants who came with the Fenwick family on the *Griffin*.[1] The only other record
of this man may be the Philadelphia will of John
Fuller dated 25 3rd mo. 1690, probated 5 10th mo.
1692,[2] which mentions Robert Turner the younger
and Robert Turner the elder [our man?], and says
that testator's mother was Elizabeth Cuppage then
living in Lemstone, Kingdom of Ireland. Fuller may
thus have known our Robert Turner in Ireland.[3] There
was a Robert Turner and also a Richard Turner in the
list of debtors in the estate of one John Clarke
who was murdered in New Jersey, date of account
17 Nov. 1691.[4]

Our Robert Turner was a First Purchaser of 5,000
acres in Group 45,[5] the only other person in this
group being Joseph Fisher, also 5,000 acres, who

also came on the *Lion* with his family and servants,
and was almost certainly a brother-in-law of Robert
Turner.
    Blackwell's Rent Roll of 1689 shows Robert Turner
as owner of an old purchase 102-foot lot on Mulberry
(now Arch) Street, 5/- for 5 years,[6] and of another
old purchase 204-foot lot on the southeast corner of
Front and Mulberry,[7] as well as of still another lot
on the south side of High Street between 6th and 7th
Streets, 396 feet, 15/- for 5 years.[8] In February
1689/90 he had a warrant for a bank lot above Sassafras (now Race) Street, having purchased from Robert
Taylor and Richard Crosby their lots on the front
from Delaware,[9] and in 1693 he was rated at £900. He
had land at Sweadland in the Northern Liberties and
was described as of there when on 21 July 1691 he
sold 100 acres to Thomas Chaunders of Sealsgreen in
Gloucester County, New Jersey.[10] He had other interests in New Jersey. As early as 12 April 1677 he had
been one of several, including Penn, to whom one-
ninetieth share of the Province was leased.[11] On a
patent for East Jersey dated 15 March 1682/3 Robert
Turner was one of the patentees.[12] On 14 Aug. 1689
Robert Turner of Philadelphia, merchant, sold 100
acres to Peter Long of Burlington County, carpenter.[13] It is probable that a more thorough search
of the land records of both Pennsylvania and New
Jersey would turn up more of his holdings but would
not materially alter the general picture.
    Mr. Myers found in Irish Friends records the fol-
lowing information. Robert Turner was born in October 1635 at Cambridge, England, son of Robert and
Mary Turner of Royston, co. Hertford, and his mother
died in Dublin, Ireland, in 1670.   He married, first,
in Dublin, 27 1st mo. 1662, Elizabeth Ruddock of
Dover who died in 1663; second, at Rosenallis, Queens
County, Ireland, 7 10th mo. 1665, Martha Fisher of
Cheshire who died in 3rd mo. 1682 and was almost
certainly a sister of the Joseph Fisher already mentioned who likewise came from Cheshire. He married,
third, under the care of Newark Monthly Meeting in
12th mo. 1686, Susanna Welch, daughter of William
and Sarah (-----) Welch. A New Jersey deed[14] of 27
Feb. 1700/1 proves this marriage and shows that her
father and husband were then both dead.
    Robert Turner was buried at Philadelphia, 24 Aug.
1700, listed among the non-Quaker burials,[15] so he
may have become a Keithian before his death. Letters

of administration were granted on 28 April 1701 to
Francis Rawle, John Guest Esq. having declined.¹⁶

While he was still in Dublin he was addressed by
James Claypoole, still in London.¹⁷

Issue: surname Turner
  by first wife Elizabeth Ruddock
i.   Elizabeth, b. 12 1st mo. 1663, d. 1678.
  by second wife Martha Fisher
ii.   Martha, b. 24 7th mo. 1668, d. Philadel-
      phia, 18 July 1745; m. Philadelphia
      Monthly Meeting, 27 7th mo. 1689, Fran-
      cis Rawle the younger, b. ca. 1663 at
      Plymouth, England, 5 March 1726/7. Fran-
      cis Rawle, the elder, son of William
      Rawle of St. Juliot, Cornwall, and his
      son of the same name, came to America on
      the *Desire* from Plymouth, arriving 23
      4th mo. 1686, with servants Thomas Jan-
      veiries alias January, ffrancis Jervins,
      John Marshall, Samuel Rennell, Isaac Gar-
      nier, Elizabeth Saries. On the Rawles,
      see Edwin John Rawle, *Records of the Rawle
      Family* (Taunton [Somerset] 1898), 172-202
      being on the Philadelphia Rawles. The
      marriage certificate of Francis Rawle and
      Martha Turner appears on pp. 178-180 and
      is dated 19 8th mo. 1689 and has, among
      others, the names of the following wit-
      nesses: Joseph Fisher, Thomas Fitzwater,
      William Markham, John Whitpaine, William
      Hudson, Joanna Markham, Isabel Fisher,
      Sarah Whitpaine, Elizabeth Fitzwater and
      Mary Hudson. See also JCRFP 1:151   and
      Thomas A. Glenn, *Some Colonial Mansions*
      (Philadelphia 1899) 2:184-197. Francis
      Rawle the younger was a baker, was rated
      in 1693 at £105.¹⁸
        Issue: surname Rawle
      1. Robert, d.s.p. 1730.
      2. Francis, merchant at Paramaibo, d. 14
         May 1779; m. 26 April 1733 Margaret
         Fisher.
      3. William, d. Philadelphia, 26 Dec. 1741;
         m. Margaret Hodge.
      4. Joseph, removed to Somerset County, Ma-
         ryland where he d. unm. 1762.
      5. John, d. unm. 1759.
      6. Benjamin, m. Hannah Hudson, d. 1784; is-

                    sue.
            7. Mary, m. William Cooper of Camden and
                Philadelphia.
            8. Rebecca, d. unm., 2 Oct. 1759.
            9. Elizabeth, d. unm. 1758.
           10. Jane, m. Philadelphia Monthly Meeting,
                31 3rd mo. 1728, Abraham England of
                New Castle.
    iii.   Robert, b. 25 6th mo. 1672, d. same year.
    iv.   Abraham, b. 28 7th mo. 1673, d. 1675.
    v.   Mary, b. 7 12th mo. 1674, m. Joseph Pidgeon
            but remained in England and d. *vita pat-
            ris.*
        by third wife Susanna Welch
    vi.   Robert, bur. 18 10th mo. 1692.

                            NOTES

[1] 1 NJA 21:590.   [2] PhW A:188.
[3] MIQ 257-262 is a good account of the Turners;
Turner's certificate dated 3 5th mo. 1683 is in
MQA 10. A magazine called *American Genealogist* in
its issue of February 1900 has been cited but has
not been seen.
[4] NJW 1:94.   [5] 1 PA 1:45.
[6] PGM 23:72.   [7] PGM 23:73.
[8] PGM 23:82.
[9] PGM 23:97; 2 PA 19:23; PhD E-1-5:176.
[10] 1 NJA 21:659.   [11] 1 NJA 21:405.
[12] 1 NJA 21:56.   [13] 1 NJA 21:439.
[14] 1 NJA 21:678. [15] HEAQG 448. [16] PhA A;341.
[18] Marion Balderston, *James Claypoole's Letter Book
London and Philadelphia 1681-1684* (San Marino 1967),
pp. 178 f., 189 f. The dates of the two letters
are 9 11th mo. 1682/3 and 6 12th mo. 1682/3.
[18] PGM 23:104.

    WADE, ROBERT   *disproved*
    This claim is made only in a note in *Publications
of the Genealogical Society of Pennsylvania* 1:49
and is doubtless merely an error based on confusion
with the genuine *Welcome* passenger, William Wade.
As a matter of fact, Robert Wade arrived on the
Griffin in late 1675. He and his wife Lydia were
on hand to greet William Penn at Upland when he arrived.[1] Robert Wade's will was dated 9 5th mo.
1698,[2] and he calls himself Robert Wade of Essex
House, Chester County, and names brother Thomas Wade
in England; brother John Wade; children of brother

Thomas Wade excepting Robert and Ledia, these two
to come to America and inherit the property; sister
Rachell's two daughters in old England; dear, loving
and tender wife Ledia Wade, sole executrix; overseers: John Jones of Philadelphia, merchant, Jacob
Chandler.
There can be no connection with William Wade.

NOTES

[1]See the article by Walter Lee Sheppard which is
to appear in Welcome Society Publications, vol. 1,
in which a list of *Griffin* passengers includes Robert
Wade. See also PGSP 4:302; George Smith, M.D., *History of Delaware County, Pennsylvania* (Philadelphia
1862), p. 510; Lydia Sharpless Hawkins, "Lydia Wade,
the first American Hostess of William Penn" (*Bulletin of the Friends Historical Association* 21:63-65).
[2]PhW A:412.

†*WADE, WILLIAM   *proved*

This name is on all lists but as Wade left no
wife or child, the line has been extinct since 1682.
According to the first of two wills which he duly
executed, both of them recorded, he was of Westham,
co. Sussex, yeoman, but the second will says he was
late of the Parish of Hankton, Sussex, yeoman. He
has also been said to be from Watham,[1] and Mrs. Balderston informs me that she has seen evidence that
he was of Cold Waltham. Watham is clearly a corruption of the last name, and there is a parish of
Westham but Smith's *Genealogical Gazetteer of England* (1968) has no parish of Hankton, and no parish
of slightly different name, which might have been
corrupted to Hankton, anywhere in Sussex. Cold
Waltham is about five miles north of Arundel in the
western part of Sussex.
Wade was a First Purchaser of 1250 acres in Group
19,[2] and subscribed £100 to the Society of Free Traders.[3] Though he died in 1682, he was in 1689 listed
on the Blackwell Rent Roll[4] as owner of a 25-foot lot
on Sassafras (now Race) Street, an old purchase, 1/3
for three years.
As stated above, he made two wills, not an unusual
thing in itself, but in this case both of them were
duly recorded and probated, which is unusual. The
first, dated 24 Aug. 1682, calls him late of Westham,
Sussex, yeoman, executed on the eve of departure of

the *Welcome*, and it was probated at the Prerogative
Court of Canterbury (124 Cottle) on 28 Oct. 1682.
As this was the day of arrival of the vessel in A-
merica, we have here a problem. How, without modern
telegraphy or radio, the news of his death could have
been communicated to London from Philadephia is not
easy to see. It may be that the will was signed and
left with Philip Ford and that when news of his death
finally reached London, Ford or some other person
offered it for probate, and the date of the *Welcome's*
arrival somehow got written down as date of probate
through error. This suggestion limps badly and the
same is true of another. It may be that Wade died
somewhere in mid-Atlantic after 20 Sept. 1682, and
that by chance the *Welcome* encountered some east-
bound ship on which Penn was able to send letters.
If so, this circumstance would seem so remarkable
that we should have heard of it. In any case, this
first will was transcribed by Henry Fitzgilbert Waters, *Genealogical Gleanings in England* (Boston
1901), 1:663 f., which text is followed herein, and
also elsewhere[5]:

> William Wade, late of Westham, Sussex, yeoman,
> bound to Pennsylvania in America, 24 August 1682,
> proved 28 Oct. 1682. I do order and appoint
> Philip Ford living in London, in Bow Lane, mer-
> chant, to be my executor and do give him ten
> pounds and do allow him reasonable charges. I do
> give unto my brother Edmund Wade five pounds. To
> my brother Thomas Wade five pounds. To my brother
> Edmund's eldest son Edmund Wade one hundred pounds.
> To his younger son Thomas Wade all my estate in
> in goods in Pennsylvania, paying every servant
> both men and maids five pounds apiece when they
> have served their times out. To the meeting at
> Asen five pounds, at Mascall Picknols and Moses
> French and Samuel Web's disposing, and what re-
> mains over in England to be equally divided be-
> tween my two brothers Edmund and Thomas Wade, ex-
> cept the hundred pounds I have in Sosiet[y]s
> stock, my will is that it should be divided be-
> tween my brother Edmund Wade's two sons, Edmund
> and Thomas.

Waters chose to omit the names of the witnesses but
they appear in the other abstract as Daniel Martin,
John Epley, Thomas Hollyman.[6]
The second will, executed aboard the *Welcome*, is

now transcribed from a photograph of the original:

    The Last will and testament of William Wade
Late of ye p[ar]ish of hankto^m in ye County of
Sussex, | made ye twentieth day of September in
ye foure & thirtieth yeare of ye Raine of Charls
ye Second | King of England &c: and in ye yeare
according to ye account now used in England one |
thousand six hundered Eighty & two: To the Intent
y^t my goods & Chattels Lands & tennemets | may
heare after Com unto such persons and Remain &
bee unto such vses as by mee the said | William
Wade hearein doe and shall Limit and appoint in
this my Last will & testament; | I doe therfore
will order giue and deuise as ffolloweth; Imprimas
I giue deuize and bequeath | unto my Brother Ed-
mond Wade the some of twenty pound which hee doeth
owe unto me | by bill or bond to be paid unto mee
or my asines one demand which debt soe due unto
mee | I doe herby Remitt & discharge; Item I giue
unto my Brother Thomas Wade the some | of ffifty
pound which he doeth owe unto mee by bill or bond;
to be remitted & discharged | unto him. If I die
before I ariue att pensilvania; Item moreover I
giue unto my | Brother Thomas Wade the some of
twenty pound: being parte of a bonde of ffifty
po[und] | due to mee ffrom my said Brother: to be
paide att ye time Called michalmas in ye year |
one thousand six hundered Eighty & fower of which
said bonde of ffifty pound | [he] shall only bee
accountable to pay unto my Executors (hearafter
named) the some of | Thirty pound parte of ye said
some of ffifty pound aforesaid; Item I giue unto |
[the] two sonns of my said Brother Edmond Wade,
namely Edmond & Thomas Wade, | to each of them two
hundered & ffifty pound of Lawfull English mony to
bee paid | unto them when they shall ataine to y^e
age of one & twenty yeares; Item I giue | vnto my
ffriends Samuell Webb: Mosses ffrench: & Maskcoll
Picknoll the some [of] | ffiue pound to bee dis-
posed of by them for the use of poore ffriends be-
longing | to ye meeting of | all furstone in the
aforesaid County of Sussex^7; Item I giue ffiue
pounds toward ye building of a meeting house in
pensiluania; Item [as] | many seruants being my
aprentises as shall ariue in pensilluania and |
Liue to serue out there times with my Executors:
I giue unto Each of them | the some of fiue pounds
in mony or goods to ye uallu therof; Item I giue

unto my | trusty friends John Songhurst & Beniamin
Chambers to Each of them ye some of | ffiue pounds
beside all resonable Charges defrayed for there
seruis, whom I | alsoe heareby make Autherize & a-
point Executors & ouerseers of this my Last | Will:
and to see mee buried; And I doe Allso apoint
phillip fford of London | marchant to bee ouerseer
of this my Concerns in England & to bee accountable
to | my Executors aforesaid; And as for my Estate
in pensiluania & the Improuement there[of] | I will
& bequeath the same to my next of kinn: And lastly
I do hearby Reuoke & Call | back all former wills;
Executors and bequeaths; and doe Apoint theas pres-
ents only [to] | stande in force for and as my Last
will & testament. In wittnes whereof I ha[ue] | to
this my Last will & testament sett to my hand and
seale ye day and yeare first | aboue written. |
Sealed Published & declared by ye said   william wade
| William Wade for & as his Last will   [seal]
| and testament in ye presence of us
Memorandom before ye Insealing & deliuering of thease
presence | it is desired by mee William Wade that
if ther shall arise any | disagreement (in ye full-
filling of this my will) between my Relations | &
my Executors: I doe hearby order & apoint that my
Executors shall Chuse one man and my relations
shall Chus | another man & there award shall fully
determine ye difference.
George Thompson
Richard Ingelo   Witnesses
William Lushington

It will have been noted that William Wade had at
least several servants, both men and maids, on the
Welcome, but of these the names of only Elinor Pain
and John Porteous have come to light.

See also the following paragraph from a letter of
William Penn to Thomas Lloyd, 18 5th mo. 1685:

Also there is ye estate of Wm Wade, | a[l]most
300£ in Money, J Song & B | Cham bers were exect^{ers}
So see they | dont embezzell[8] it, for they write
not | to his heirs, wch opens | their mouths, nor
B chambers as | he should do to his employers, w^{ch}
| they take ill, my words help a little | to

stop great chargs only the so | ciety is agreived
here, nor accompt | came wth me tho I stayed
mett & | Labourd for one Lot they know not | w^t
to make of it.[9]

NOTES

[1]3 PA 3:343.
[2]1 PA 1:42; 3 PA 3:388, purchase with John Brooks,
7 1st mo. 1686.
[3]PMHB 11:178.   [4]PGM 23:71.
[5]PMHB 29:317.
[6]This man may be the father-in-law of William
Rodney; see above p. 454.
[7]Alfriston is a Sussex parish about 14 miles east
of Brighton. The spelling "Asen" which appears in
the London will, is probably an abbreviation for
the same parish.
[8]This word then connoted wasting and not theft.
[9]Joseph Jackson, *Encyclopaedia of Philadelphia*
(Harrisburg 1933), 4:1184, also 1015, is sure that
William Wade was in Pennsylvania before Penn came,
but he is probably merely confusing William with
Robert.

WALMSLEY, THOMAS	*disproved*
WALMSLEY, ELIZABETH RUDD, his wife	*disproved*
†*WALMSLEY, MARGARET, his daughter	*disproved*
†*WALMSLEY, MARY, his daughter	*disproved*
WALMSLEY, HENRY, his son	*disproved*
WALMSLEY, THOMAS, his son	*disproved*
WALMSLEY, ELIZABETH, his daughter	*disproved*
†*WALMSLEY, ROSAMOND, his daughter	*disproved*

Thomas Walmsley appears on all lists but List O
denies the *Welcome* claim and Lists U and V put the
the entire family on the *Lamb*. The wife Elizabeth
is named on Lists A, B, C, D, E, F, G, H, I, M, Q,
U, V, Y and Z, but U and V, of course, put her on
the *Lamb*. She and the children are lumped together
in "and family" on Lists J, K, L, N, P, S, T, W and
X. The daughters Margaret, Mary and Rosamond are
included in the "six children" of Lists A, C, E, F,
H, I, M and U (here on the *Lamb*) and on Lists B, D,
G and Q, they are probably included in the three
others whose sex is unspecified, and they are named
only in List V as on the *Lamb*. The same is true of
their sister Elizabeth except that she is actually
named, with the two sons, on Lists B, D, G, Q and
V, but elsewhere they are included in the "family"
except for Lists Y and Z who say nothing whatever

This Last will and testament of William Wade late of ye parish of Hankin in ye County of Sussex
yeaman made ye ____ of September in ye ____ thirtieth yeare of ye Rame of Charles ye second
King of England &c: and in ye yeare according to ye ancient now used in England ____
thousand six hundred eighty & two, To the intent ye my goods & chattells lands & tenements
may beare after dem unto such persons and remain & bee unto such uses as by mee the said
William Wade hearein doe and shall Limit and appoint in this my Last will & testament;
I doe therfore will order giue and douise as followeth; Imprimus I giue douise and bequea
unto my Brother Edmond wade the some of twenty pound which hee doeth ow unto me
by bill or bond to be paid unto mee or my asines and demand which debt I doe ow unto no ____
I Doe hereby acquitt & discharge, Item, I giue unto my Brother Thomas Wade the some
of fifty pound wch hee doeth ow unto me by bill or bond to be remitted & discharge
unto him If I die before I ____ all paid ____, Item, moreouer I giue unto ____
Brother Thomas Wade the some of twenty pound being parte of a bond of fifty
due to mee ffrom my said Brother to be paide all ye time called mihalmas in ____
one thousand six hundred eighty & foure of which said bonds of fifty pound
shall only bee accountable to pay unto my Executors (hearafter named) the some of
Thirty pound parte of ye said some of fifty pound aforesaid; Item, I giue unto ____
two sonns of my said Brother Edmond wade; Namsly Edmond & Thomas Wade;
Each of them two hundred & fifty pound of Lawfull english meny to bee ____
unto them when they shall atain to ye age of one & twenty yeares, Item, I gi____
unto my ffreinds Samuell Hobb. Messes ffrench & Maskell Puknoll me some____
fiue pound to bee disposed of by them for the use of poor freinds belonging
to ye meeting of all furstone in the afore said County of Sussex; Item, I giue
fiue pounds toward ye building of a meeting house in pensiluania; Item,
many servants being my aprentisos as shall arius in pensiluania and
Liue to serue out their times with my Executors I giue unto Each of them the
some of fiue pounds in mony or goods to ye ualu therof, Item, I giue unto my
trusty freinds, John Songhurst & Bemamin Chambers to Each of them ye some ____
fiue pound beside all resonable charges defrayed for Issue Iemis, whome I
allsoe heareby make Clutierize & apoint Executors & ouerseers of this my Last
will and to see mee buried, And I doe Allso apoint phillip ffford of London
marchant to bee ouerseer of ____ my Concerns in England & to bee accountable to
my Executors aforesaid, ____ as for my estate in pensiluania & the Improuement therof
I will & bequeath the same to my next of kinn; And Lastly I doe heareby Reuoke ye
bath all former wills, Executors and bequeaths, and doe Except these presents only
stande in force for and as my Last will & testament In wittnes wherof I have
to this my Last will & testament sett to my hand and seale ye day and yeare first
about written;

Sealed Published & Deliuered by ye said
William Wade for & as his Last will
and testament in ye presents of us

William Wade

Memorandum before ye Insealing & Deliuering of these presents
it is desired by mee William Wade that if ther shall arise any
disagreement (in ye fulfilling of this my will) betwen my ____
Relations & my Executors. & I doe heareby order & apoint that
my Executors shall Chuse one man & my relations shall chuse
another man & their awards shall fully determin ye differenc____

George Prous ____

Richard ____
William Cushingbon ____

of the daughters, though they name the two sons.

The Walmsley family is shown in the Middletown Monthly Meeting minutes as one of the families covered by the Settle certificate of 7 4th mo. 1682, on which see the Introduction, Section E, as "Thom walmsley Elizabeth his wife and [six] children." The missing number of the children has been supplied from the Comly and the Roberts versions of this certificate--the Potts and Jordan versions omit the children--but that there really were six children at the start of the voyage is shown by the records of the six in the Yorkshire Friends records, as given below.

In common with all the Friends shown in this remarkable certificate, this family undoubtedly came on the *Lamb* of Liverpool. Clarence Vernon Roberts, *Roberts-Walton Ancestry* (privately printed 1940), pages 282-284, contains a generally excellent account of the Walmsleys but accepts the *Welcome* claim. The error was not made, however, in Joseph C. Martindale's *History of the Townships of Byberry and Moreland* (Philadelphia, rev. ed. by Albert W. Dudley, n.d.), pp. 353-363, which claims that the family "came about the time of Penn's first visit," which is true, and landed at Burlington, which may be true, for ought I know.

Thomas Walmsley of Wadington Eaves, Yorkshire, married on 13 9th mo. 1665, at the house of Jane Walne at Slaine Merow, Yorkshire, Elizabeth Rudd of Smelfats, daughter of Giles Rudd of Mouldhole, and he died or was buried in Pennsylvania on 11 11th mo. 1682/3. Comly says that he died of dysentery within a fortnight of landing. This statement contains one false assumption and one error: the assumption is that Walmsley arrived on the *Welcome*, the error, that the 11th month was November. If Walmsley had come on the *Welcome*, he survived the crossing about ten weeks, but as the *Lamb* arrived somewhat earlier than the *Welcome*, he had been in America the better part of three months when he died.

The widow Elizabeth declared first intentions on 3 10th mo. 1684, second intentions, 1 11th mo. 1684, at Middletown, and married John Pursley or Purslow who had arrived in the Delaware in 6th mo. 1677, a husbandman from Dublin, Ireland.[1] There was no issue by him and no connection can be found between him and any other Pursley, Purslow or Pursell family in Bucks County.

Administration was granted on the estate of Thomas Walmsley to Elizabeth Walmsley of Neshamineh,
10 10th mo. 1684, registered 12 11th mo. 1684; inventory of £27/10 taken by James Dilworth and David
Davis.²

Issue: surname Walmsley
i.   Margaret, b. 11 6th mo. 1666, Wadington
      leanehead, Yorkshire; probably d. at sea.
ii.   Mary, b. 9 2nd mo. 1669, Wadington lane-
      head, Yorkshire; probably d. at sea in
      1682.
iii. Henry, b. 25 5th mo. 1671, Wadington lane
      head, Yorkshire, and therefore aged 11,
      not 7, as Comly makes him, when he came
      over the Atlantic. There is a manuscript
      genealogy of the Walmsleys compiled by
      William F. Corbett (1834-1881) in the
      Genealogical Society of Pennsylvania, and
      a sketch of the family in the Comly Gene-
      alogy, pp. 1018-1026. Henry married 5
      8th mo. 1699, at Middletown, Mary Searle,
      and she d. 7 8th mo. 1747, he ca. 3rd
      mo. 1759. In the estate of Henry Walms-
      ley (Bucks file 997) there is administra-
      tion bond dated 10 May 1759, calling him
      of Bensalem, yeoman, and signed by ffran-
      cis Walmsley her mark and Thomas Walms-
      ley his mark, Thomas Tomlinson; inventory
      of parsonal estate, 14 May 1759, filed 6
      June 1759 by Peter Praul, John Bennet,
      not totalled. In the letter written ca.
      1790 by Benjamin and Abraham Sands,³
      the statement is made that some of Hen-
      ry's children were still living.
      Issue: surname Walmsley
      1. Thomas, b. 1706, d., according to Cor-
         bett, 14 8th mo. 1786 which must be
         wrong as his will is dated 14 2nd mo.
         called February 1788 (BW file 2113),
         and admin. was granted 20 Sept. 1788
         to Sarah Reed. Thomas Walmsley of
         Southampton, names eldest son Henry
         Walmsley (who was doubtless witness
         to his aunt's bond in 1760); daughter
         Margaret Parsons [who had m. 20 March
         1763 at Churchville, George Parson];
         son Ralph Walmsley his surviving is-
         sue not named; two granddaughters:

Esther Reed, Sarah Reed; daughter Mary
Reed.

2. Frances, d. unm., 26 1st mo. 1760; signed
father's admin. bond in 1759; her own
estate inventoried by Peter Praul, Arthur Searl, 25 Feb. 1760, not totalled
but very small; bond signed by Thomas
Walmsley, Henry Walmsley, both by mark,
Thomas Goheen., 25 Feb. 1760.

3. Elizabeth, d. 9 1st mo. 1772; m. 1719
William Carver.

4. Joan, d. 10 3rd mo. 1772; m. 1719 Thomas
Tomlinson.

5. Rebecca, d. 18 9th mo. 1775; m. 25 8th
mo. 1731 Abel Walton.

6. Sarah, d. 27 10th m. 1787, m. -----
Kinsey.

iv. Thomas, b. 24 10th mo. 1673, Wadington leane
head, Yorkshire, d. 17 11th mo. 1754; m.
3 5th mo. 1698 Mary Paxson, b. 19 12th
mo. 1678/9, d. 22 2nd mo. 1755, daughter,
according to Corbett, of John Paxson, but
Comly Genealogy says of William and Mary.
Issue:surname Walmsley

1. Elizabeth, b. 12 5th mo. 1699, d. 15
2nd mo. 1771; m. 30 1st mo. 1718 Jeremiah Walton.

2. Mary, b. 12 7th mo. 1701, d. 18 4th mo.
1764; m. 1720 John Worthington.

3. Thomas, b. 8 6th mo. 1706, d. 30 6th mo.
1728; m. 27 3rd mo. 1728 Hannah Walton.

4. William, b. 9 12th mo. 1708, d. 16 6th
mo. 1773; m. (1) 1735 Sarah Titus, (2)
6 6th mo. 1764 Susannah Comly, widow
of Walter. His will was dated 10 12th
1771 in Byberry, probated 28 June 1773
(PhW P:423), and names children Silas,
Thomas, William, Mary Knight, Sarah
Bolton, son-in-law Thomas Knight.
Issue: surname Walmsley, order un
known

a. Silas, living 1771.
b. Thomas, living 1771.
c. William, living 1771.
d. Mary, living 1771, m. Thomas Knight.
e. Sarah, m. Isaac Bolton, b. 27 April
1735, d. 6 Feb. 1783, 6th child of
Isaac Bolton (Everard) and Sarah

Jones (sometimes called Tones, probably wrongly).
Issue: surname Bolton

α William, b. 12 Sept. 1767, d. 19 Sept.
1823.
β Joseph, b. 28 Oct. 1769, d. 1852 at
Black River, N.Y.; m. 16 Oct. 1733
Jane Knight. Two ch.
γ Isaac, b. 7 Oct. 1771, d. 1853; m.
Elizabeth Townsend. Six ch.
δ Mary, b. 2 Sept. 1773, m. 1800 Nathan Marshall.
ε Margaret, b. 2 Sept. 1773, d. 1795,
m. 1794 James Hayton.
ζ Jesse, b. 30 June 1777, d. 1800.
η Thomas, m. ----- Comly, to Black
River, N.Y.
θ Sarah, m. William Woodward.
5. Agnes, m. 25 9th mo. 1728 Job Walton.
6. Abigail, b. 1715, d. 19 11th mo. 1789,
(1) 2nd mo. 1738 Isaac Comly, (2) 1753
Richard Walton.
7. Phebe, b. 1718, d. 27 7th mo. 1794, m.
26 2nd mo. 1742 Isaac Carver.
8. Esther, d. 12 2nd mo. 1791, m. 25 8th
mo. 1755 Stephen Parry.
9. Martha, d. 28 2nd mo. 1768, m. 25 5th
mo. 1761 [?] David Parry.

NOTES

[1]PMHB 9:225. In DHBC 66 he is wrongly called
Paisley.
[2]PGSP 1:202.   [3]See above, pp. 137 f.

WALN, NICHOLAS		*disproved*
WALN, JANE TURNER, his wife		*disproved*
WALN, JANE, his daughter		*disproved*
WALN, RICHARD, his son		*disproved*
*WALN, MARGARET, his daughter		*disproved*

Nicholas Waln appears on all lists but List O denies he was on the *Welcome*; on List O there is a
"no" in the margin, and Lists U and V state that he
came on the *Lamb*. W. J. Buck and W. M. Mervine both
say he was on the *Welcome*.[1] His wife is called Jane
only on Lists U and V, is called "wife" on Lists B,
D, F, G, Q, Y and Z, and is included in the family
on Lists J, K, L, N, P, S and T. The three unnamed
children are on Lists B, D, F, G and Q, and are in

the family on K, L, N, P, S, T, W, Y and Z. List U
wrongly calls them Elizabeth, Nicholas and William,
and they are incorrectly named on List V as Jane,
Nicholas, Richard and Anne.

Nicholas with his unnamed wife and three unnamed
children appear in the version of the Settle certificate[2] now in the minutes of the Middletown Monthly
Meeting in second position after Cuthbert Hayhurst,
and also in the Buckman-Potts and Jordan copies of
the certificate; in the Comly version, they are between the Stackhouses and the Cowgills, and are de-
signedly omitted from the Roberts version which ends
as soon as the names which Mr. Roberts was concerned
with are reached. The family was long suspected as
having come on the *Friends' Adventure*, and on List
Q, for reasons unknown, there is a "no" in the margin opposite their names. Whether Mr. Myers had
some specific reason for doubting their claim is not
clear. It is now certain, however, that they came,
rather, on the *Lamb* on which ship Nicholas Walne
loaded on 26 June 1682, 1 cask qty 7 cwt wrought
iron.[3]

Nicholas Waln was a First Purchaser of 1000 acres
in Group 44,[4] is listed in Old Rights[5] with his son
Richard, and in the Explanation of the Map of Philadelphia.[6]

The following account is based largely on John W.
Jordan, *Colonial and Revolutionary Families of Penn-
sylvania* (New York 1911), 1:200-225, with additions
and some corrections. See also William M. Mervine's
Genealogical Register (Philadelphia 1913), pp. 15-27;
F. A. Godcharles, ed., *Encyclopaedia of Pennsylvania
Biography* 21:134-144; Arthur Edwin Bye, *A Friendly
Heritage* (New York 1959), p. 212. We have not been
able to locate a copy of Oliver Hough and Warren S.
Ely's *Colonial Families of Philadelphia* (1911) which
is said to have a Waln sketch.

The Godcharles work cites a baptism dated 9 June
1583 of John Walne, son of Nicholas, and rightly expresses the belief that these men were probably ancestral to the family under discussion. The family
was originally from Burholme in Bolland, West Riding,
Yorkshire, and belonged as early as 1654 to Bolland
Meeting, a branch of Settle.

Richard Walne of Burholme in the district of Bolland, born ca. 1620, died 7 April 1659, buried at
Newton Friends Graveyard. He married Jane Rudd, the
daughter of Edward Rudd of Knowmeare, and sister of

Dorothy Rudd and Mary Rudd, the wives of William and
Cuthbert Hayhurst, respectively, who also came on
the Settle certificate, though Dorothy was then dead.
She was also the cousin of Elizabeth Rudd, daughter
of Giles Rudd, who also came on the same certificate
with her first husband Thomas Walmsley. Jane Waln,
widow, died on 6 8th mo. 1669, buried at Newton, a
burial missed by Jordan with the result that Jane
is confused with the daughter of the same name.

Issue: surname Waln, order probable

i.   Jane, m. 31 8th mo. 1667, William Birket
       of Newton, a marriage wrongly assigned
       by Jordan and Mervine to her mother.
       At their house, 1 8th mo. 1673, her bro-
       ther Nicholas was m. to Jane Turner of
       Windyeath, and at the house of Jane Bir-
       ket in Slainmerow, 9 April 1696, Richard
       Scott m. Jennet Stackhouse who may have
       been the Jennet mentioned as sister in
       Thomas Stackhouse's will.

ii.   Richard, came to America at unknown date
       and unknown ship. Jordan thinks he may
       have been the Richard Wall [sic] who
       brought a certificate from the Monthly
       Meeting held at Edward Edwards' house in
       Stock Orchard, co. Gloucester, dated 26
       4th mo. 1682. It seems to me highly im-
       probable that this was Richard Waln who
       d. 26 1st mo. 1698, bur. at Cheltenham,
       28 1st mo. 1698. His wife Joan d. 2 12th
       mo. 1701/2, bur. at Cheltenham, 4 12th
       mo. 1701/2. They brought with them a son
       Richard who d. 6 2nd mo. 1689, leaving a
       daughter Sarah who m. at Cheltenham, 14
       Feb. 1694/5, George Shoemaker, and was
       the heir of her grandfather's will dated
       15 1st mo. 1697/8, probated 9 12th mo.
       1701/2.

1 iii. Nicholas, b. ca. 1650, d. 4 12th mo. 1721/2.
2 iv. Anne, b. 15 6th mo. 1654, d. 1710.
  v.   Edward, b. 22 7th mo. 1657, no further
       trace.

1. Nicholas Waln, the immigrant, younger son of
Richard and Jane (Rudd) Waln, was born about 1650
and doubtless before the family became Friends. He
died in the Northern Liberties of Philadelphia, 4
12th mo. 1721/2, and not in 1744 as stated in List B.

His will is dated 30 11th mo. 1721/2, probated 19
March 1721/2, mentions wife Jane and son Richard as
executors; also sons Nicholas and William, daughters
Jane, Hannah, Mary, Sarah, Elizabeth. Nicholas Waln
married Jane Turner of Windyeath at William Birkett's
house, 1 8th mo. 1673.   There is a good signature of
Nicholas Waln in the minutes of the Middletown Monthly Meeting when on page 17 he signed the memorial on
selling liquor to the Indians. He was a prominent
citizen, and after the deaths of his two uncles,
Cuthbert and William Hayhurst, he was the leader of
the Settle group. See Jane W. T. Brey, *A Quaker
Saga* (Philadelphia 1967), pp. 372-374.

    Issue: surname Waln
    i.   Jane, b. Yorkshire, 16 5th mo. 1675; m. at
          Middletown, 27 3rd mo. 1691, Samuel Al-
          len Jr.
    ii.   Margaret, b. Yorkshire, 3 8th mo. 1677, d.
          28 1st mo. 1676, a death date in the
          Settle records which must be in error,
          perhaps for 1678.
    iii. Richard, b. Burholme, 6 4th mo. 1678, but
          Settle record dates it 6 1st mo. 1678/9;
          d. 1756; m. at Abington, by 31 7th mo.
          1706, Ann Heath, bur. Philadelphia 1724,
          daughter of Robert and Susanna (Woolner)
          Heath. His will is dated 1 Dec. 1753,
          probated 16 June 1756.
          Issue: surname Waln
          1. Nicholas, b. 25 6th mo. 1707, d. 3 7th
             mo. 1707.
          2. Nicholas, b. 19 1st mo. 1709/10, d. 6th
             mo. 1744; m. 23 3rd mo. 1734, Mary
             Shoemaker.
          3. Jane, b. 6 6th mo. 1711, d. 17 6th mo.
             1711.
          4. Jane, b. 20 12th mo. 1712/13, d. 4 8th
             mo. 1714.
          5. Anne, b. 16 12th mo. 1714/15, m. 5th mo.
             1753 Jonathan Maris.
          6. Richard, b. 5 4th mo. 1717, d. 8th mo.
             1764; m. Hannah -----.
          7. Susanna, b. 9 4th mo. 1719, m. 9th mo.
             1739 Joseph Levis.
          8. Robert, b. 21 1st mo. 1720/1; m. Rebec-
             ca Coffin.
          9. Joseph, b. 18 10th mo. 1727, d. 1760;
             m. 31 10th mo. 1747 Susanna Paul.

10. Mary, b. 15 6th mo. 1724; m. Joseph Brown.

iv. Margaret, b. Yorkshire, 10 11th mo. 1680/1, according to Middletown record; Settle record dates it 12 11th mo. 1682/3, but this is after both the *Lamb* and the *Welcome* had arrived in America. While in general it is better to accept the record made at the time, there is simply no way in which this record can be accepted. She d. *vita patris*, unm., date unknown, but after 1682.

v. Hannah, b. Bucks County, 21 7th mo. 1684; m. (1) 1st mo. 1704, Thomas Hodges, widower of her cousin Jane Dilworth (see below) and his will is dated 21 1st mo. 1707/8[7] and names wife Hannah, calls Nicholas Waln father-in-law; (2) 9th mo. 1712 Benjamin Simcock, son of Jacob and Alice (Maris) Simcock.

vi. Mary, b. Bucks County, 7 2nd mo. 1687, d. 19 5th mo. 1771 [not 1721, as Jordan has it], m. 1706 John Simcock, son of Jacob and Alice (Maris) Simcock.

vii. Ellen, b. 27 1st mo. 1690, d. unm., 4 11th mo. 1707/8.

viii. Sarah, b. 9 4th mo. 1692, m. (1) 1711 Jacob Simcock, b. 28 7th mo. 1686, d. 12th mo. 1716/17, also son of Jacob and Alice (Maris) Simcock; (2) 27 12th mo. 1721/2 Jonathan Palmer.

ix. John, b. 10 6th mo. 1694, d. 1720; m. 30 6th mo. 1717 Jane Mifflin, b. 1696, the daughter of John and Elizabeth (Hardy) Mifflin.

x. Elizabeth, b. 27 1st mo. 1697, m. Philadelphia Monthly Meeting, 24 2nd mo. 1719 James Duberry.

xi. Nicholas, b. 24 1st mo. 1698/9, d. unm., 11 12th mo. 1721/2.

xii. William, b. 15 1st mo. 1700/1, m. Ann Hall, daughter of William and Mary (-----) Hall of Springfield Township, Chester Co., Pa.

2. Anne Waln, younger daughter of Richard and Jane (Rudd) Waln, was born 15 6th mo. 1654, and died in 1710, leaving a will dated 27 6th mo. 1710, in which she names her children as James, William, Richard and Rebecca, all named Dilworth, appointing sons William and Richard as executors; overseers: Nicholas Waln and Edman Orbwood; witnesses: William,

Richard and John, all named Buzby. She married first
at the house of her brother Nicholas Waln at Chapel
Croft, co. Lancaster, 9 5th mo. 1680, James Dilworth
of Thornley in Lancashire, husbandman, when he came
to America but at the time of the marriage of Bradley Hall, Lancashire, flaxman. They came to America
with their son William on the *Lamb* of Liverpool, arriving 8th mo. 1682,[8] as was long known because Dilworth so registered them in Bucks Arrivals. Both
Anne and James were prominent Friends ministers, did
much travelling together, and she was away on a visit to Friends in England by way of Barbadoes, leaving at the end of 1st mo. 1699, when James Dilworth
died of yellow fever in Bristol Township, Philadelphia County, in 7th mo. 1699, buried 15 7th mo. 1699.
His will dated 8 7th mo. 1699, probated 10 Dec. 1700,
mentions children William, Richard, Jane, Hannah,
Jennitt, Rebecca, James, all minors; appoints as executors brother-in-law Nicholas Waln and Edmund Orp-
wood, if his wife Anne did not arrive; witnesses:
Richard Tomlinson, William Preston, Arthur Cooke,
Griffith Jones. She married, second, at Abington
Monthly Meeting, 29 6th mo. 1701, Christopher Sib-
thorp, who died testate between 25 10th mo. 1707
and 24 11th mo. 1707/8. All the children were by
the first husband Dilworth who loaded on the *Lamb*,
26 June 1682, 2 rashes, 1 cask, 1 bundle qty 150
lbs woolen cloth; 50 lbs Norwich stuffs; ¼ cwt haberdashery; 200 lbs new shoes; 8 doz. woolen stockings for men; 6 cwt cheese.[9]

Issue: surname Dilworth
i.   William, b. England, 15 4th mo. 1681 (or
        24 5th mo., as Lancashire records have
        it), came to America with his parents
        in 1682; was mentioned in the wills of
        both parents; m. Sarah Webb, daughter of
        Richard and Eliza (-----) Webb, and was
        still living in 1710.
ii.   Richard, b. 8 5th mo. 1683, d. Philadel-
        phia, 6 8th mo. 1749; m. (1) at Abington
        Monthly Meeting, 25 6th mo. 1707, Eliza-
        beth Worrell, daughter of John Worrell;
        (2) at Abington, 26 4th mo. 1721, Anne
        Marle. His will dated 7 1st mo. 1748/9,
        probated 14 10th mo. 1749, names wife
        Ann and son Jacob as executors; son James
        and daughter Sarah; brother James. His
        line is followed in F. A. Godcharles, ed.,

Encyclopaedia of Pennsylvania Biography
(New York 1934), 21:134-140.
Issue: surname Dilworth

1. Jacob, d. 12th mo. 1809; m. Gwynedd, 26
   12th mo. 1750/1 Elizabeth Nanna.
2. James, d. 1765; m. Abington, 2nd int.,
   29 7th mo. 1729, Sarah Potts, widow
   of Daniel Potts and daughter of Peter
   Shoemaker Jr. and wife Margaret, according to Godcharles, though I think
   the marriage may be a second one for
   his uncle James.
3. Sarah.

iii. Jane, b. 18 1st mo. 1685; m. 8 3rd mo. 1701
     at Dublin Meeting, Thomas Hodges who af-
     terward m. her cousin Hannah Waln (see
     p. 521). Jane was dead by 1704.
iv. Hannah, b. 25 12th mo. 1688; m. Oxford Mee-
     ting, 9 4th mo. 1709, John Worrell Jr.
v.   Jennet, b. 20 1st mo. 1690, m. 27 1st mo.
     1710, Samuel Bolton, b. 31 10th mo. 1689,
     5th child of Everard Bolton by his first
     wife Elizabeth, of Cheltenham. The death
     date given for Samuel (12 Sept. 1757)
     properly belongs to his nephew.
     Issue: surname Bolton, perhaps others
   1. Isaac, d. Philadelphia, 26 6th mo. 1727.
   2. Everard, d. Philadelphia, 9 10th mo.
      1744, father not identified in the
      record.
   3. Hannah, m. (1) John Coombs, (2) 1746,
      John Clark, for which marriage she
      was dismissed by Philadelphia Monthly
      Meeting, 31 6th mo. 1746.
vi. Ann, b. 9 12th mo. 1691, d. 24 12th mo.
     1691.
vii. James, b. 3 9th mo. 1695, m. 31 1st mo.
     1718, Sarah Worrell. He may have m. (2)
     29 7th mo. 1729, Sarah Potts, b. 22 5th
     mo. 1698, widow of Daniel Potts and the
     daughter of Peter Shoemaker Jr., by his
     wife Margaret, which marriage has been
     assigned to his nephew of the same name
     but fits much better here chronologically.
viii. Rebecca, m. 31 10th mo. 1711 George Shoe-
     maker, widower of Sarah Waln, her first
     cousin once removed, on whom see page
     519.

ADDENDUM

The Godcharles sketch already cited above cites from Yorkshire Friends Records the marriage of an Isabel Wallne, daughter of Nicholas Wallne of Hey Heade, to one Jonathan Scott. These marriages are entered under the names of both parties, and in one instance the marriage is said to have taken place on 6 11th mo. 1666 at Widow Walnes, Hey Head; in the other, on 6 11th mo. 1667 at Jane Wallne's at Slainmerowe. The difference in the year is probably nothing more than a calendar confusion, that is, the marriage took place on 6 11th mo. 1666/7. The cited sketch concludes that the two places are identical, and that the widow was the mother of the bride. I have a different view--at this time Jane Wallne, widow, must surely be the widow of Richard Waln of Burholme, and the bride Richard's sister, so we can state that the father of Richard Waln and the grandfather of the immigrants Nicholas Waln and Anne (Waln) Dilworth was also named Nicholas.

NOTES

[1]PMHB 7:67.   [2]See Introduction, Section E.
[3]PGM 23:54, Note 98, *Huntington Library Quarterly* 26:50.
[4]1 PA 1:45. [5]3 PA 3:40, nos. 14-41, p. 43, no. 164.
[6]3 PA 3:353. [7]PMHB 15:200.   [8]PMHB 9:233.
[9]PGM 23:53, Note 94; PMHB 9:233; BHBC 680.

WALTON, ROBERT   *mythical*

This name appears on no list but the claim is made in a sketch of the ancestry of Katherine de Valcourt Craig (b. 1874) which may be found in F. A. Virkus's *Abridged Compendium of American Genealogy* 6:167: 'Robert Walton, cavalier, from England in the "Welcome," 1682, settled at Philadelphia, Pa., m. Frances -----.' The name is missing, however, from the list of emigrants on page 814 of the same volume. That a cavalier would be on the *Welcome* is certainly unlikely, and no evidence has been found to show that the man was ever in Pennsylvania, particularly not in Norman Walton Swayne's *Byberry Waltons* (Philadelphia 1958), which says nothing about any Robert Walton. Unless evidence is adduced by some one, we conclude that the man is mythical.

WEST, JOHN   *highly probable*

This name appeared for the first time among *Welcome* passengers on List U, though Mrs. Balderston,
from whose article that list was compiled, seems to
have been afterwards inclined to delete it.[1] It was
not picked up when List V was put together, though
Walter Lee Sheppard, who had much to do with compiling that list, has published an able article,
"John West and the *Welcome*,"[2] in which he draws
the conclusion that, though there were other ships
on which John West might have come, the *Welcome* was
the most probable, and with that conclusion there
can be no quarrel.

The principal evidence for putting West on the
Welcome is the fact that on 11 Aug. 1682 he loaded
on that ship, not on another, 22 cwt of red and white
lead and tinware to the value of £24/10.[3] We know
also that he was a First Purchaser of 1250 acres in
Group 35,[4] and had made an investment of £50 in the
Society of Free Traders.[5] If we had no more information than this, and could prove his presence af-
terward in Pennsylvania, we should cheerfully have
accepted this as proof of his presence on board the
vessel without asking for more. However, John West's
first warrant was dated 29 6th mo. 1682,[6] a time
when the *Welcome* was about to sail for America, and
if John West had asked personally for it in Pennsylvania, he could not have been on the *Welcome* at all.

He might, however, have been represented by an
attorney in Philadelphia, but said agent could not
have been his daughter, Hannah, wife of Benjamin
East, for at this moment she was busy with other
duties, namely, bringing into the world her eldest
child, John East, whose birth is recorded as having
occurred at Brooks Wharf, 21 8th mo. 1682, parents
being of [St.] Mary Somerset, London,[7] on which day
the *Welcome* was at sea. Her husband Benjamin East
was also a First Purchaser of 1250 acres in Group
7.[8] His first survey was made 30 6th mo. 1685 for
585 acres "up Tacony Creek," in Oxford Township,
Philadelphia County.[9] With wife Hannah, Benjamin
East, "mar[chan]t," sold two lots of land; one, 28
1st mo. 1685, 200 acres in Oxford Township adjoining William East, for £20, to Thomas Graves, part
of a grant from William Penn dated 13 Oct. 1681. He
gave a power of attorney, 18 July 1685, to William
O'Rion of Philadelphia, blacksmith, to deliver the

property to Thomas Graves.[10]   The other property he
sold 16 Nov. 1685, for £5, two lots in the city of
Philadelphia totalling 25 acres, to Barnabas Wilcox,
obtained by warrant from William Penn, 16 5th mo.
1684, and the following day he gave power of attorney to Robert Longshore to make delivery.[11]   Meanwhile, he had returned to England where on 16 Aug.
1683 Benjamin East of Brooks Wharf, London, sugar
baker, made an agreement with John West of Exeter
and Richard West of London, fishmonger, to protect
the dowry of his wife Hannah East "in natural love
and affection" in case she should outlive him--as
she did--and mentions 700 acres and messuage in
Pennsylvania, part of his 1250 acres allotment as
the dower.   This was sealed "in the presence of
Charles Marshall, John West and George Shyets," undoubtedly in England but the place not shown.[12]

     To Benjamin East (purchaser of 1250 acres) there
was surveyed on 20 4th mo. 1683 by warrant dated 14
4th mo. 1683, a lot in Philadelphia on Schuylkill
side S 72, E by vacant land,396, S 18, W by 2nd
Street from Schuylkill Front Street 23½ feet, returned to office 9 5th mo. 1684.[13]   On the same day
as the preceding, 20 4th mo. 1683, there was surveyed
to John West (purchaser of 1250 acres) by virtue of
a warrant dated 15 4th mo. 1683, a lot on Schoolkill
side S 72 E by Benjamin East 396 feet, S 18 W by 2nd
Street from Schuylkill 23½, returned to office 9 5th
mo. 1684.[14]   Another record of this lot says it was
on Mulberry Street.[15]   These records prove that both
Benjamin East and John West were present in Philadelphia on 20 4th mo. 1683, because there is no indication that there was any agent involved.   Before
William Penn's arrival, his deputy William Markham
had not always been careful to indicate whether a
transaction was by principal or by agent, but Penn
changed this, and after his arrival always saw to
it that the presence of an agent was recorded.

     John West, however, had 200 acres in Oxford Town-
ship surveyed to him 25 9th mo. 1682, in the month
following the arrival of the *Welcome*,by warrant
dated 29 6th mo. 1682, recorded 5 8th mo. 1684,[16]
and in this case also no agent is involved, so this
puts John West in Philadelphia immediately after the
arrival of the *Welcome*.

     This pair of surveys are the sole proof that John
West was ever in America.   Mrs. Balderston is surely
mistaken in saying that John West operated the Penny

Pot Tavern on Front Street, for this was James West,
shipwright, who is mentioned in this connection on
8 1st mo. 1689/90[17] and shown to be dead by 18 12th
mo. 1721/2,[18] leaving a wife Prudence as administratrix who was herself dead by 20 8th mo. 1722,[19] and
a son Charles West. No connection has been found
between John West and James West.

At this point we should interpolate that Blackwell's Rent Roll of 1689 shows that Benjamin East
and William East were owners of Old Purchase lots
of 25 feet, for five years, on Front Street between
Mulberry and High, and similar lots of 39 feet on
High.[20]

In any case, after being present in Philadelphia
in both November 1682 and June 1683, Benjamin East
must soon have returned to England, for he was there
on 16 Aug. 1683 when he made the dower agreement
noted above. It is probable that his father-in-law
John West went with him then and remained in England
for the rest of his life, for no further proof of
his presence in Pennsylvania has been found. Benjamin East was, however, back in Pennsylvania when
additional surveys were made to him in 1684[21] and he
was of Philadelphia when he conveyed in 1685. He
must have died in America not long after, for his
widow remarried, as we shall see, in 1687.

Benjamin East probably came to America the first
time on the ship *Hester and Hannah*, of which his
brother William East was master. It loaded in March
1682[22] and arrived in the Delaware 8 Aug. 1682, in
time for Benjamin East, if he was aboard, to take
up his land later in the same month and to arrange
for John West's first survey. The West properties
in America were the subject of litigation in the
middle of the next century, since the Edward Cary
Gardner manuscript collection in the Historical
Society of Pennsylvania includes notes of a title
search in this period. A much fuller history of the
interlocking East and West properties is encompassed
in the "Norris of Fairhill Manuscripts" in the same
repository.[23] Besides several of the original warrants and surveys, there are lists of properties
laid out to each man, quoted by Mr. Sheppard, but
which add little to our knowledge of the documents
cited above.[24]

To recapitulate, Benjamin East was in Pennsylvania by August 1682, able to take out his first warrant on the 29th, to order his first survey on the

30th, to take out his father-in-law's first warrant,
and to hand it to him when the latter arrived on the
Welcome, if he did.   As it was on this ship that
West shipped trading goods, and no other, he probably came with his property, though I find Mr. Sheppard's belief that he would have accompanied this
merchandise to protect it a little strong. Rather
it seems to me that he would have decided to go to
America and availed himself of the opportunity to
make a little money on the trip by taking along the
goods.

THE WEST FAMILY

    1. Of the antecedents of John West little is
known save that he had a brother Thomas living in
1698, then in debt to John; a sister who had married
----- Axton and had a son Tom Axton, in 1698 late of
Risborn or Risborough, co. Bucks, likewise in debt
to his uncle whose will of that year forgave these
debts.   John West was born, probably in 1623, and
died at Wandsworth, Surrey, of an apoplexy or con-
vulsions, 18 4th mo. 1698 aet, 76, when of Snow Hill,
Sepulcres[25] Parish, and of Peel Street Monthly Meeting, buried in Chequer Alley.

    His occupation is variously given as citizen and
freeman, citizen and girdler,[26] tinman and innman.
To judge from the large sums bequeathed in his will,
he was well to do.   At his death he had leases on
two properties from the Worshipful Company of Sadd-
lers, the two messuages being in Snow Hill, Parish
of St. Sepulchres without Newgate, one by the Sign
of the Crown, in his own tenure, the other by the
Sign of the Bull, then in tenure of Rowland Steward.
He also had a copyhold in Wandsworth, Surrey, a
freehold in Banbury, co. Oxford, now in the hands
of Salathiel Gardner, and he also owned messuages
and lands and tenements distinct from these which
he bequeathed to his wife, though she died before
inheriting them.   We have already seen the evidence
for his holdings in America.

    He married, first, probably as early as 1653 or
even before, Mary -----, mother of all the children,
who died 8 10th mo. 1680, aet. 54, at Snow Hill, of
consumption, buried in Chequer Alley; second, after
his trip to America, 22 7th mo. 1685, at Devonshire
House Monthly Meeting, to which both belonged, Mary
-----, widow of ----- Marsh, and she died 30 11th
mo. 1698/9 aet. 58, of Sepulchers Parish. By her
former husband Marsh she had two daughters Ann Marsh

and Mary Sellwood, each of whom received fifty shillings from their stepfather's will. Their mother
would have received, had she survived her husband,
£5 and all lands, tenements and messuages, not o-
therwise bequeathed, but she died first.

The will of John West of the Parish of St. Sepulchre, London, citizen and girdler, was dated 20 3rd
mo. 1698, with a codicil dated 1 9th mo. 1698, probated in July [1699?] in the Prerogative Court of
Canterbury, which on 25 Jan. 1745 supplied a certified copy to the Court of Philadelphia, now in file
167 of 1747, recorded in Philadelphia Wills H:317.
This document is lengthy and complex. He leaves relatively large sums to a considerable number of minor grandchildren, but it is suspected that there
may well have been other grandchildren of age, and
it is certain that there was a grandson named James
Street, then aged six, who is completely ignored in
the will for reasons that do not appear, and thus
he never shared in his grandfather's property in A-
merica, as did a half-brother, half-sister and full
brother.

Burial is directed in Bonehill Fields, co. Middlesex, in the burial place of the Quakers, but he
was actually buried in Chequer Alley. He was careful to provide for the death of one or more or of
all the grandchildren in America, in which case the
survivors shared the inheritance of the deceased,
or if all died, then the grandchildren in England
were to inherit; likewise, the same arrangement was
made for the grandchildren in England, and if all
of them died, then the American grandchildren inherited. In the event that all of the grandchildren
died under age, then son Richard was to inherit.
Charitable bequests and bequest to friends are mentioned.

The order of birth of the children is uncertain.
There is also recorded the death by the plague of a
Mary West, 17 5th mo. 1665, buried in Bunhill Fields,
age at death and names of parents not stated. As
another Mary West was surely born before 1665, perhaps this one was not a child of our John West.

Issue: surname West, all by first wife
i.   Mary, b. at least by 1653, m. at Peel St.
     John St. Meeting, 17 5th mo. 1671, Simon
     Harris, upholsterer; both had d. by 1698
     and the language of the will suggests
     that there were other sons.

Issue: surname Harris, perhaps others
1. Thomas, to get £100 at age 21, so b. after 1678.
2. John, to get £80 at age 21, so b. after 1679.

ii.   John, probably the John of Exeter involved in Benjamin East's dower agreement 1683; probably an older child as the will says he was bound to his father for £600 on 18 May 1675 for property in Croudon, co. Bucks, and was in 1698 in default of £325. If the estate fell short of legal [legacy?] payments, then John was to pay £100 of what was in default, and was released from the balance, and also from a £50 bond to his stepmother. The codicil says that the Croudon property is now under bond to son Richard for £400, dated 7 Oct. 1698, and this property is to go equally to son Benjamin and grandson Thomas Harris. What had happened to son John is not stated; had he died, we should probably have been told so.

iii. James, b. ca. 1656, d. aet. 19 of a fever, 22 6th mo. 1675, Pulchers Parish, of Westminster Monthly Meeting, bur. Chequer Alley.

iv. Rebecca, b. 10 5th mo. 1663, Parish of St. Sepulchre, London; d. 25 7th mo. 1682 aet. ca. 19 at Snow Hill, of stoppage of the stomach; really only 17 at her death which must have occurred in her father's absence, if he were on the *Welcome*.

v.   Benjamin, b. 19 8th mo. 1664; living 1698, having already had his portion of £500; therefore he and his wife Sarah get only £5 each, though his wife and children also get annuities from the rent of the Bull.
Issue: surname West, perhaps others
1. John, to get £50 at age 21, so b. after 1677.

vi. Richard, m. Anne -----; gets the copyhold at Wandsworth and the freehold at Banbury and annuities from the Bull.
Issue: surname West
1. Mary, to get £40 at age 21.
2. Richard, to get £40 at age 21.

```
		3. Anne, to get £40 at age 21.
2 vii.	Hannah, probably youngest; m. (1) Benjamin
		East; (2) Daniel Street who gets £5 in
		her father's will.  The three children
		of Hannah shown below each get £50 at
		age 21 and all real estate in America
		as tenants in common.
			Issue:
				by Benjamin East
		1. John.
		2. Mary.
				by Daniel Street
		3. Benjamin.
		4. James, was not mentioned in his grand-
			father's will and did not share in the
			estate.
```

2. Hannah West was the only child of her parents
to come to America. Shortly after the death of her
mother, she married, first, as spinster, 25 1st mo.
1680, at the Bull and Mouth, Benjamin East of Brooks
Wharf, London, sugar baker, son of William East of
Tower Street, London, and brother, as we have seen,
of William East, master of the *Hester and Hannah* and
later of the *Gulielma,* William Penn's personal ship,
named for his first wife, Gulielma Maria Postuma
Springett. At the wedding John, Thomas, Richard,
William, Moses and another John West signed the certificate. Benjamin East[27] made at least two trips
to America but did not bring his wife on the first
one as she was then pregnant. Benjamin East died
in 1686 in Pennsylvania, administration being granted to his widow Hannah, 6 9th mo. 1686.[28] Hannah
married, second, at her own house in Pennsylvania,
16 11th mo. 1686/7, Daniel Street, a carpenter,
born in 1658, died Thursday, 20 July 1738 aged 80.[29]
Hannah is said to have died in August 1706, aged
71.[30] The date may be right but, if so, the age at
death is far too high, for if true, then she married
first at age 45, had a first child at age 47, was
born when her father was twelve, and was 23 years
older than her second husband!
	Issue:
		by Benjamin East
i.	John, b. Brooks Wharf, London, 21 8th mo.
		1682; a cordwainer; d. in or before 1707
		at sea, intestate, unm. and without is-
		sue, and his share descended to his sis-
		ter Mary. See Lewis D. Cook, "Isaiah At-

kins of Truro, Mass." (TAG 20:193-199);
also Walter Lee Sheppard, article cited
in Note 2.

ii. Mary, b. 23 Aug. 1685, Oxford Township
(Abington recs. say 22 6th mo. 1685), d.
by 17 July 1722, intestate; m. ca. 1706
Joseph Cook, cooper, b. Newport, R.I.,
son of Arthur and Margaret (Yoakley)
Cook, and he m. (2) by 17 July 1722, Margaret Widdowson, daughter of Robert Widdowson, late of London, taylor, when
Joseph and Margaret gave a power of attorney.[31] Joseph Cook died intestate in
or before 1747. See A. R. Justice, *Ancestry of Jeremy Clarke of Rhode Island
and Dungan Genealogy*, p. 528. Mr. Cook
assigns a son Benjamin to Joseph and Mary
Cook and says he d. intestate and s.p.
but Mr. Sheppard did not find said Benjamin in the Norris of Fairhill Papers.
Issue: surname Cook
1. John, did not d. intestate and s.p., as
Mr. Cook says, but the Norris of Fairhill Papers say he had son John and
daughter Mary "who lives at James Morgan's in Frankfort. "
2. Rebecca, at first put down as Mary in
the Norris Papers but later corrected;
m. at First Presbyterian Church, Philadelphia, 4 Oct. 1726, William Miller
whose will is dated 15 Nov. 1745, probated 14 Dec. 1745 in Kent County,
Delaware,[32] naming friend Joseph Miller executor. Rebecca gave a power
of attorney on 11 Oct. 1748 when of
Philadelphia, wife of William Miller
of Kent County, Delaware, to Isaac
Griffiths; still other powers of attorney dated 23 June 1763, 15 March
1765.
Issue: surname Miller
a. Joseph, bapt. First Presbyterian
Church, Philadelphia, 4 Sept. 1727.
b. Mary, bapt. *ibid.*, 7 Nov. 1728; m. a
sea captain, James Gibbons, master
of the *Ann* registered at Philadelphia, 22 April 1752. He d. 1772,
admin. to widow Mary, 13 Jan. 1772.

              Issue: surname Gibbons, per-
              haps others
      α Jane, m. Christ Church, 5 May 1795
         Gabriel Duvall.
      β James, captain in Revolutionary ar-
         my; m. 14 March 1782, Ann Phile,
         daughter of Dr. Frederick Phile,
         and had James, b. 24 Jan. 1783,
         d. Richmond, Va., 26 Dec. 1811,
         and Frederick Phile, b. 18 Jan.
         1784.[33]
    c. Eleanor, bapt. First Presbyterian
      Church, Philadelphia, 2 Dec. 1740.
3. Hannah, b. Philadelphia 1707, d. 21 March
   1783 in 77th year, bur. North Cemetery,
   Truro, Barnstable Co., Mass.; m. Truro,
   by the pastor, John Avery, Isaiah Atkins, d. 3 April 1782 in 79th year.
   Isaiah and Hannah were bapt. as adults,
   18 Dec. 1726, she admitted that day to
   Truro Church. *Mayflower Descendant*
   34:15 wrongly identifies Hannah as the
   daughter of William Cook (Jacob, Jacob,
   Francis) of Kingston, Mass. This was
   denied (*ibid.* 18:256) but she was again
   wrongly identified as daughter of Josiah
   Cook of Eastham though his will (*ibid.*
   5:185 f.) names no daughter Hannah.
   Lewis D. Cook quotes a letter of attorney[34] to Joseph Fox and John Lukens,
   both of Philadelphia, Pa., Esqs., by
   Henry Atkins Junior of Boston in the
   Province of Massachusetts Bay in New
   England, merchant; Isaiah Atkins of
   Truro in the County of Barnstable in
   said Province, Gent., and Hannah his
   wife; and Rebecca Miller of the city
   of Philadelphia, widow, (the said Hannah & Rebecca being daughters of
   Joseph Cook deceased by Mary his wife
   also deceased, which Mary Cook was one
   of the daughters of Benjamin East deceased by Hannah his wife, also deceased, which Hannah East was one of
   the daughters of John West deceased,
   and the aforesaid Mary Cook was one of
   the grandchildren & a devisee named in
   the last will & testament of the said

John West deceased). This document
was acknowledged in Pennsylvania by Rebecca Miller, 15 March 1765; by Isaiah
Atkins & wife Hannah in Barnstable Co.,
9 Jan. 1764; and by Henry Atkins Jr.
in Boston, 16 Jan. 1764. Henry Atkins'
involvement in the matter is explained
by the following deed, 23 March 1749,
acknowledged in Barnstable Co., rec.
28 June 1749:[35] Isaiah Atkins & wife
Hannah to Henry Atkins Jr. of Boston,
½ the John West-Benjamin East property
in Pennsylvania and Delaware. The Norris of Fairhill Papers contain earlier
powers of attorney for Isaiah Atkins
and wife Hannah, signed in Barnstable,
7 April 1749, and from Henry Atkins of
Boston, 21 April 1750, as well as the
one from Rebecca Miller already cited.
How Hannah Cook came to be living at
Truro when she married Isaiah Atkins
remains a mystery.

   Issue: surname Atkins (Truro recs.)
a. Benjamin, b. 20 Aug. 1726, bapt. 25
   Dec. 1726.
b. Hannah, b. 22 Feb. 1727/8, bapt. 26
   Feb. 1727/8.
c. John, b. 1 April 1730, bapt. 17 May
   1730.
d. Silas, b. 15 Jan. 1732/3, bapt. 4 Mar.
   1732/3.
e. Nathaniel, b. 6 July 1736, bapt. 15
   Aug. 1736.
f. Mary, b. 18 June 1738, bapt. 23 July
   1738.
g. Isaiah, b. 25 April 1740, bapt. 1 June
   1740.
h. Henry, b. 4 May 1743, bapt. 12 June
   1743.
i. Zaccheus, b. 3 April 1744.
   4. ?Joseph, bur. 15 7th mo. 1710, recorded
      among non-Quaker burials.
   by Daniel Street
iii.   Benjamin, b. 26 Feb. 1688 about 12:30 A.M.;
       d. intestate but not s.p. He sold 100
       acres to Jno Clayton; 210 acres in Mont-
       gomery Co. to Thomas, David and John Ed-
       wards.

Issue: surname Street, probably no other
1. Benjamin, the person whom the Norris of
   Fairhill Papers say his father *has*;
   obviously the Benjamin who gave a power of attorney as mariner of Boston,
   12 May 1746 (Norris Papers).
iv. James, b. 26 Aug. 1692 at 4:00 P.M. He was
     aged six when his grandfather West made
     his will without mentioning him, and he
     and his heirs never shared in his grand-
     father's estate, though he did in the
     estate of his father. This suggests that
     he may really not have been a child of
     Hannah (West)(East) Street but a child of
     Daniel Street by a later wife. If so, the
     the date of Hannah's death given in the
     Street Genealogy (1706) must be wrong.
     The genealogy says he d. 10 Nov. 1753 aet.
     42, which again is a bad age, this time
     too low, for in 1753 he would have been
     past his 61st birthday. He m. Mary Grif-
     fith, b. 24 April 1702, a Saturday night,
     second daughter of Robert and Alice Grif-
     fith.
     Issue: surname Street
1. Hannah, 3 Dec. 1720 about midnight, d.
   8 July 1740 aet. 20.
2. Joseph, b. 5 June 1722, a Tuesday, about
   3:00 P.M.
3. Benjamin, b. 4 March 1723, Wednesday at
   2:00 o'clock; m. Elizabeth Collins; a
   line continued in the genealogy.
4. James, b. Friday 17 Dec. 1725 about 8:00
   A.M., d. 1 Oct. 1744.
5. Mary, b. 10 Oct. 1727, about 6:30, a
   Tuesday.
6. Thomas, b. Saturday, 15 Nov. 1729 about
   sunset; m. Margaret -----; a line continued in the genealogy.
7. Daniel, b. 18 Feb. 1731, Friday night a-
   bout 8:00 P.M.; m. Mary Foster; a line
   continued in the genealogy.
8. Griffith, b. 6 March 1733, 8:30 A.M., a
   Friday, d. 9 June 1733 aet. 4 mos.
9. Alice, b. Friday 5 April 1734, d. 28
   Aug. 1742, aged 8.

NOTES
[1]*Huntington Library Quarterly* 26:55.

[2]NEHGR 117:274-279, to be reprinted in Welcome Society Publications, vol. 1.

[3]PGM 23:58, Note 112.   [4]1 PA 1:44.

[5]PMHB 11:179, John West In[n]man of Snow Hill; his wife Mary West invested £23 PF, i.e. paid to Philip Ford.

[6]W&S 3:590.

[7]Friends Records, London Quarterly Meeting, cited by Sheppard, p. 274.

[8]1 PA 1:40; 3 PA 3:331, 366.

[9]3 PA 2:585, 699. [10]PhD E-1, vol. 5, pp. 108, 11.

[11]PhD C-2, p. 159, rec. 3 4th mo. 1701.

[12]PhD pp. 458, 460.   [13]W&S 3:234.

[14]W&S 3:235; 3 PA 1:50 f.; 3 PA 2:699.

[15]W&S 2:130.   [16]W&S 6:122.

[17]2 PA 19:29.

[18]2 PA 19:273; PhA A:344, 1 Oct. 1701.

[19]2 PA 19:338. Mrs. Roach informs me that the widow from whom James West had bought was probably Jurian Hartsfield's (2 PA 19:57, 10 10th mo. 1690/1). Humphrey Edwards, who m. the widow of Jurian Hartsfield, sold to one Smith and some other.

[20]PGM 23:87, 90.

[21]3 PA 2:696, 640 acres, 26 4th mo. 1684; another city lot, 6 5th mo. 1684.

[22]PGM 23:38 f.

[23]Philadelphia County vols. 112-121; Chester and Montgomery Counties, vol. 36.

[24]See also 2 PA 7:194; 3 PA 2:696, 16 5th mo. 1684 for additional lot. The Norris Papers have the original of another warrant dated 5 8ber 1707, William Penn to Daniel Street, 500 acres in right of John West, purchaser of 1250 acres, who devised to his grandchildren, the children of daughter Hannah, wife of Daniel Street.

[25]There never was a saint named "Sepulchre." The phrase "Saint Sepulcher" derives from the Latin for "holy sepulchre."

[26]A girdler had nothing to do with what are now called "foundation garments." He made metal bands used to hold building construction together.

[27]See 3 PA 3:331.   [28]PhA A:22.

[29]Henry A. Street and Mary A. Street, *The Street Genealogy* (Exeter, N.H., 1893), pp. 364-374, on Daniel Street's family. The birth and death dates are said to have come from an old Bible.

[30]*Ibid.*

[31]See Power of Attorney, 17 July 1722, Joseph Cook

of Philadelphia, cooper, and wife Margaret, daughter
of Robert Widdowson, late of London, taylor (PhD F-3
p. 48). Other deeds of value on this couple are cited by Lewis D. Cook: tripartite deed, 9 7th mo.
1701 (PhD G-20, p. 413); Joseph Cook then resident
at New York, etc.; deed 18 Sept. 1706 (Philadelphia
Exemplification Record Book 8:317); deed 25 Nov.
1707 (*ibid.* p. 380); Joseph Cook and wife Mary, only
sister of John East late of the County of Philadelphia, cordwainer, dec.; deed 17 Feb. 1709 (PhD E-6,
vol. 7, p. 114); deeds 20 March 1711/12 (PhD E-7,
vol. 8, p. 151).

[32]KC 109.   [33]PGSP 9:69.

[34]Recorded Philadelphia County Exemplification
record book 6, p. 178, recorded 25 March 1765.

[35]PhD G-11, p. 280. See also *ibid.* D-16, p. 370,
23 June 1763, Isaiah Atkins and wife Hannah, Henry
Atkins Jr. and wife Elizabeth, Rebecca Miller; also
ibid., H-19, p. 81, 24 June 1763.

WHITPAINE, ZACHARIAH   *proved*
WHITPAINE, JOHN, his brother   *possible*
WHITPAINE, ANN, perhaps his sister   *possible*

Though proved as a *Welcome* passenger by his signature on the will of Isaac Ingram, executed aboard
the ship, the name of Zachariah Whitpaine appears
only on Lists N, O, P, S, T, U and V. The reason
for the late discovery of this claim is the fact
that, though the signature was actually on Ingram's
will, it was inadvertently omitted from the docket
copy thereof, and so was never discovered by those
content to read only the docket copy. Mrs. Balderston claims that he also witnessed William Wade's
will on the *Welcome* but this is not so. She also
thought (List U) that his brother John Whitpaine
may have been on the *Welcome*, and this is possible
though rather improbable, as John does not occur in
Philadelphia records before 27 7th mo. 1689 when
the death of John Patrick was recorded in Philadelphia and the deceased was then identified as the
uncle of both Zachariah and John Whitpaine. Nothing
more has been found concerning the said John Patrick
and we do not know how he was uncle to the Whitpaines. As Zachariah was not quite seventeen when
the *Welcome* arrived, it is rather less likely that
he was allowed to bring a younger brother with him.
They were, of course, not orphans when Zachariah
came.

The only evidence for Ann Whitpaine is the following passage in Clara A. Beck's "Men, Women and
Events in the Early History of Whitpaine Township"
(*Montgomery County Historical Sketches* 5 [1925]
202-209): "Near the site of the old Whitpaine properties is the tombstone of Ann Whitpaine, wife of
Thomas McCarty 1714 age 57." The location was on
the old William Funk farm "recently" purchased by
Jesse Cassel between Blue Bell and Broad Avenue.
If the age at death is correct, then this woman was
born in 1657 and if the sister of Zachariah and John,
she was older than they.

The name Whitpaine was sometimes spelled Whippen
in the 18th century and this probably indicates the
pronunciation then current. Whitpaine Township in
Montgomery County, lying northeast of Norristown
between North Wales, Ambler and Conshohocken, was
doubtless named for the father of our two Whitpaines.

He was Richard Whitpaine, citizen and butcher of
London, who died there, 9 3rd mo. 1689, leaving a
will dated 27 April 1689.[1] He had extensive properties in Pennsylvania though there is no record of
his ever crossing the ocean. According to the reference cited, he had 7,000 acres, and, again, 1550
acres bought 8-9 Jan. 1685 from Samuel Fox of Rochester, Kent, taylor.[2] Richard Whitpaine, dec., is
shown as an abutter, 13 Jan. 5 William and Mary
1693.[3] Richard Whitpaine, butcher, subscribed £50
to the Society of Free Traders.[4] On 14 Feb. 1785,[5]
one Thomas Forrest claimed for himself and others
city lots as heirs of John Whitpaine of the City of
Philadelphia dec., based on specified holdings of
Richard Whitpaine, and as John Whitpaine died without issue, the heirs must have been, as his will
states, children of his brother Zachariah and their
descendants. This Thomas Forrest was not himself a
Whitpaine descendant, but his wife Ann, whom he had
married at Christ Church, 28 April 1770, was a Whitpaine, as we shall see.

Richard Whitpaine's last wife, widow and executrix was named Mary, but he had an earlier wife
named Alice who was presumably the mother of the
sons. Alice may have been a Patrick, since the two
sons, as stated above, had an uncle John Patrick.
Despite the great land holdings in America, Richard
Whitpaine's widow was in severe financial distress.
A power of attorney dated 20 Jan. 1692/3 was granted by Richard Mathews of London, merchant, to Sam-

uel Stacy, also of London, merchant, and now bound
for Pennsilvania, to collect debts due by the estate
of Richard Whitpaine, late citizen and butcher of
London, dec'd, by John Whitpaine of Clift, Sussex
Co. [i.e. Cliffe, a suburb of Lewes], mercer, now
in Penna, and by Zachariah Whitpaine of Philadelphia, merchant.[6] A large house had been built for
Richard Whitpaine on Front Street, called "Whitpaine's Great House," but the construction was poor
and the structure did not last long.[7] This, then
called Sarah Whitpaine's house, was rented in 1695.[8]
The Pennsylvania Council was to meet in this house
on 26 July 1701, when in the tenure of Joseph Shippen.[9]

Though undoubtedly younger than Zachariah, John
may be discussed first as he left no issue. On 26
3rd mo. 1692 John asked leave of the Philadelphia
Monthly Meeting for marriage in Rhode Island, received it 24 4th mo. 1692, name of bride not stated.
Austin[10] shows that she was Content Gould, born 28
April 1671, died 3 Sept. 1720, ninth child of Daniel
Gould (Jeremiah) by his wife Wait Coggeshall. John
Whitpaine was buried 3 12th mo. 1696/7, leaving a
will dated 1 Feb. 1696/7, probated 15 Feb. 1696/7,[11]
which calls him of Philadelphia, names his wife Content, father Richard Whitpain dec., brother Zachariah Whitpain dec. and his three unnamed children;
trustees David Lloyd, John Budd, Thomas Mowrey. It
is clear that John had no issue and possible that
Content was content to return to Rhode Island after
his death, since Austin found the date of her death
in Rhode Island records.[12]

Zachariah Whitpaine, probably the elder brother,
was born in Little Eastcheap, London, 16 10th mo.
1665, recorded at Ratcliffe and Barking Meeting, and
was buried in Philadelphia, 20 11th mo. 1693/4. He
was a merchant and councilman of Philadelphia.[13]
Unlike his brother, he left issue, having married at
Philadelphia Monthly Meeting, 7 10th mo, 1686, Sarah Songhurst, daughter of John Songhurst by his
wife Mary, all three of the Songhursts being also
Welcome passengers. The marriage record identifies
the fathers of both parties.

Zachariah Whitpaine and wife Sarah made a journey
to England and were there at the accession of William
and Mary in what is called "the Glorious Revolution"
in 1688. They came away soon afterwards and were
apparently the first to bring the news of the Revo-

lution to Pennsylvania. The Provincial Council met
24 12th mo. 1688/9 at dead of night in Griffith
Jones's house to hear Zachariah Whitpaine who had
come out of London 10 or 12 Xber last (1688) on the
ship *Mary*, John Harris, master, arrived at midnight,
and reported to the Council on the events in London
at the time of the Revolution.[14]

Zechariah Whitpaine, late of the town and county
of Philadelphia, died intestate, administration being granted 7 2nd mo. 5 William and Mary 1693 to
Charles Sanders, principal creditor, to whom a *quietus est* was given on 1 March 1697/8.[16] Despite
this apparent closing of the accounts of the estate,
administration was again granted on 16 July 12 Anne
1713[17] to John Whitpaine, son and heir, and mention
is now made of Sarah Owen, formerly widow of Zechariah Whitpaine.

Before that, however, the widow Sarah Whitpaine
married, second, at Philadelphia Monthly Meeting,
14 10th mo. 1697, Charles Sanders, erstwhile principal creditor and administrator of her deceased
husband, and he died at Philadelphia, 21 7th mo.
1699, leaving a will dated 30 Sept. 1699, probated
15 Oct. 1699.[18] No child is mentioned but the wife
is pregnant; trustees and overseers: William Clark,
Patrick Robinson, Samuel Buckley; nephews Charles
and John, sons of brother William Sanders of London; witnesses: Robert Webb [by this time second
husband of Sarah Songhurst's sister Elizabeth],
Thomas Mowry.[19] Charles Sanders had been a witness
to the will of William Dyre of Sussex County, Esq.,
20 Feb. 1687/8, probated 5 4th mo. called June
1688.[20]

Sarah (Songhurst)(Whitpaine) Sanders married,
third, as second wife, at Philadelphia Monthly
Meeting, 13 9th mo. 1704, Dr. Griffith Owen, whose
children were all by his first wife Sarah Barnes
who had died 22 10th mo. 1702. For his history see
the sketch devoted to him.

Sarah Owen died at Philadelphia, 4 6th mo. 1733,
leaving a will dated 29 April 1733, probated 11
Aug. 1733[21]. She names son William, and his own
father is mentioned but not named; daughter Mary
Williams; son-in-law Isaac Williams Jr.; brother
John Songhurst; two granddaughters Sarah and Joyce
Marriott; Trusty Friend Samuel Powell for bequest
to Women's Meeting; Sarah Lee, single woman; grandson Stephen Armitt; grandchildren Sarah Marriott,

Stephen Armitt, Joyce Marriott, Sarah Armitt, Zachariah Whitpain, and Isaac, Lydia, Zachariah and Mary Williams, children of son-in-law Isaac Williams, to whom their shares go in trust; witnesses: Andrew Robeson, Sarah Tosomn [so it appears each time written but doubtless Tomson is intended], C. Brockden, first two of whom probated the will.

Issue of Sarah Songhurst
  by first husband Zachariah Whitpaine
  i.   Zachariah, b. London, 26 8th mo. 1687, bur.
        Philadelphia, 20 1st mo. 1701/2; listed
        as first child in the ante-nuptial agree-
        ment of Charles Sanders and Sarah Whit-
        paine, photostatic copy in the A. C. My-
        ers Welcome Papers at the Chester County
        Historical Society; a school boy at Penn
        Charter School when he signed, first among
        his fellows, an address to William Penn
        dated 29 11th mo. 1699/1700.[22]
  ii.   Mary, b. 28 6th mo. 1689, d. 29 7th mo.
        1748; m. (1) at Philadelphia Meeting
        House, 1 3rd mo. 1708/9, Samuel Marriott,
        b. 3 11th mo. 1684, d. 26 6th mo. 1717,
        son of Isaac and Joyce (Ollive) Marriott
        of Burlington, New Jersey, the bride er-
        roneously called in the printed record
        daughter of Jehu Whitpaine; as Mary Mar-
        riott, daughter of Sarah Owen, granted
        a certificate 27 3rd mo. 1709; m. (2) at
        Burlington Meeting House, 12 2nd mo. 1720,
        Isaac Williams of Burlington County. The
        will of Samuel Marriott dated 17 Aug.
        1717, probated 4 Sept. 1717,[23] names wife
        Mary, children Sarah, Joyce and Mary.
        Philadelphia Meeting received on certi-
        ficate 27 8th mo. 1727, Isaac Williams,
        wife and daughter. His will, dated 29
        Sept. 1768, probated 28 Nov. 1768,[24]
        calls him a Philadelphia tavern-keeper;
        names wife Mary [a second wife], Daniel
        Williams and Reuben Harris; children:
        Hannah and Mary (wife of Henry Wood);
        among others, cousin Sam (son of Wm Cor-
        rey); grandchildren Isaac, Henry, Zacha-
        riah, Mary, Elizabeth, Abigail and one
        other unknown. Isaac Williams d. 17 11th
        mo. 1768 aged 73.
        Issue:

by first husband Samuel Marriott

1. Joyce, b. 18 8th mo. 1710, d. aged 6 weeks.
2. Sarah, b. 4 8th mo. 1711, m. between 29 April 1733, when her grandmother's will shows her single, and 27 5th mo. 1733, when Sarah Currie formerly Mariott was condemned for marrying out of unity, William Currey; finally condemned for marrying contrary to discipline, 28 5th mo. 1738.
   Issue: surname Cùrrie
   a. Sarah, d. 14 8th mo. 1741, Philadelphia Monthly Meeting record.
   b. William, d. 3 6th mo. 1747 (*ibid.*).
   c. Samuel, called cousin in Isaac Williams' will.
3. Samuel, b. 3 12th mo. 1713, not in his father's will 1717, no further trace.
4. Mary, b. 31 10th mo. 1715, not in grandmother's will in 1733 or later traced. Mr. Colket's account of this family says she m. 24 11th mo. 1744/5 Joseph Saull of Gloucester County. There is, however, a Mary Williams who d. at Philadelphia, 19 3rd mo. 1727, and she might just possibly be Mary Marriott mistaken for a Williams, a daughter, rather than a step-daughter of Isaac Williams, dying at a time when this family had only just moved to Philadelphia.
5. Joyce, b. ca. 1716 or possibly earlier as she was executrix of her grandmother in 1733; d. without surviving issue, 8 7th mo. 1786, variously called aged 74 or in 72nd year; m. at Philadelphia Monthly Meeting, 13 3rd mo. 1736, the noted Quaker philanthropist, Anthony Benezet, b. St. Quentin in France, 31 Jan. 1713, d. Philadelphia, 3 5th mo. 1784, bur. 4 5th mo. 1784, son of Jean Etienne Benezet.[25] The Benezets lived in Wilmington, Abington, Burlington, as well as in Philadelphia. When Anthony died, he left "an ancient and feebel widow."
   Issue: surname Benezet

          a. Anthony, d. 23 4th mo. 1743.
          b. Mary, bur. 12 5th mo. 1738.
             by second husband Isaac Williams
     6. Isaac, b. 6 4th mo. 1725, Burlington;
       in grandmother's will 1733; had son
       Isaac d. Philadelphia, 19 12th mo.
       1762 aet. 2.
     7. Lydia, d. 11 10th mo. 1744, not recor-
       ded at Burlington or in father's will
       but living 1733 when in grandmother's
       will.
     8. Zachariah, d. 22 8th mo. 1744, not re-
       corded at Burlington or in father's
       will but living 1733 when in grand-
       mother's will.
     9. Mary, not recorded at Burlington; in
       wills of grandmother in 1733 and of
       father in 1768; m. 30 8th mo. 1746
       Henry Wood of Gloucester County, pro-
       bably mother of some or all of the
       grandchildren in her father's will.
   10. Hannah, in father's will in 1768; not
       in grandmother's in 1733, so either
       b. later than 1733 or a child of the
       second wife, even both.
iii. John, b. 26 Oct. 1691, father's heir in
     1713; his will dated 20 Sept. 1718, pro-
     bated 28 Oct. 1718, names wife Ann, mi-
     nor children Sarah and Zachariah; bur.
     23 7th mo. 1718[26] when he had a wife
     Ann who as widow released 26 May 1718.
     She was his stepsister, Ann Owen, b.
     Radnor, 11 12th mo. 1692, bur. 1 2nd mo.
     1735, daughter of Dr. Griffith Owen by
     his first wife Sarah Barnes, and as widow
     she was administratrix and sister and
     next of kin to her brother Griffith Owen,
     late of Philadelphia, surgeon, 8 March
     1731/2.[27]
     Issue: surname Whitpaine
    1. Sarah, b. ca. 1714, bur. 18 Feb. 1781
      aged 67; reported m. 24 9th mo. 1732,
      to Stephen Armitt, b. 17 4th mo. 1705,
      d. 29 10th mo. 1751, second son and
      child of Richard Armitt (son of John)
      by his wife Sophia Johnson who were m.
      26 7th mo. 1701. Richard Armitt was
      received on certificate from Leek
      Monthly Meeting, Staffordshire, dated

2 8th mo. 1701, and he had a sister
Sarah also received from Leek on certificate dated 21 11th mo. 1702/3, who
m. 9 10th mo. 1707 at Philadelphia Meeting House, William Powell Jr. Richard
and Sophia's eldest child John, b. 8
10th mo. 1702, d. 21 5th mo. 1762 aged
59 testate, m. 27 7th mo. 1728, Mary
Emlen, on whom see above, p. 182. The
will of Stephen Armitt, dated 1 Dec.
1751/2, probated 18 Jan. 1752, calls
him joyner, mentions wife Sarah, brother John, and children Sarah, Ann,
John, Richard, Samuel and Mary.
    Issue: surname Armitt
a. Sarah, b. 15 9th mo. 1733, m. Phila-
    delphia Monthly Meeting, 16 12th mo.
    1766, James Logan, b. Dec. 1728,
    d. 25 Sept. 1803, son of James and
    Sarah (Read) Logan. No issue.[28]
b. Ann, b. 29 4th mo. 1735.
c. John, b. 21 9th mo. 1737, m. 14 4th
    mo. 1763, Elizabeth Howell, daughter
    of Joseph Howell; granted certifi-
    cate as widow, 31 10th mo. 1794.
d. Richard, b. 13 12th mo. 1739.
e. Samuel, b. 12 8th mo. 1742, dismissed
    for m. out of unity, 29 8th mo. 1766.
f. Stephen, d. 7 2nd mo. 1743.
g. Stephen, d. 14 6th mo. 1747.
h. Mary, b. 6 6th mo. 1748, probably m.
    at Christ Church, Philadelphia, 19
    July 1779, Capt. Thomas Bell.
2. Zachariah, mariner, b. ca. 1716, aged
    19 in 1735, d. intestate by 7 March
    1753; in father's and grandmother's
    wills; admin. to his widow and relict
    Sarah, who was Sarah Hensey, m. at
    Christ Church, Philadelphia, 28 July
    1742, and she m. there (2) 28 June
    1755, Joseph Dodd.
    Probable issue: surname Whitpaine
a. John, b. 16 Jan. 1743, bapt. Christ
    Church, 16 June 1745; either he or
    his brother was probably father of
    Sarah Withpain who m. 2 June 1786
    at the German Reformed Church in
    Philadelphia, John LeTelier.

     b. William, d. 2 6th mo. 1747.

     c. Anne, b. 27 April 1748, bapt. Christ
Church, Philadelphia, 17 Aug. 1752,
m. there, 28 April 1770, Thomas Forrest, b. 16 June 1747, bapt. Christ
Church, 16 Aug. 1747, son of William
and Sarah (-----) Forrest. It was
this Thomas Forrest who in 1785
applied for city lots on Richard
Whitpaine's rights (see p. 537).

     d. William, b. 4 July 1751, bapt. Christ
Church, 17 Aug. 1752, perhaps the
father of Sarah (Whitepaine) LeTelier mentioned at the bottom of p.
543.

by second husband Charles Sanders

iv.   William, b. 17 Dec. 1698, not in father's
will, d.y.

v.   William, b. posthumously, mentioned as possible in father's will, d. testate between 13 March and 29 April 1734. His
will, executed 11 Sept. 1733, probated
29 April 1734[29], names cousin William
Sanders, son of uncle Charles Sanders,
5/-, if legally demanded [probably error
for cousin Charles, son of uncle William;
this testator cannot be a nephew of Sarah
Songhurst's second husband, for the bequest to Mrs. Minshall below prevents
that solution to this difficulty]; cousins [sic: William and] Isaac Sanders;
Sarah wife of Isaac Minshall a pocket-
watch [she was his stepsister Sarah Owen
and wife of Jacob Minshall; if Isaac's
wife were really meant, then her name
was Rebecca]; Stephen Armitt; his main
heir is nephew Zachariah Whitpaine, son
of [half-brother] John Whitpaine, dec.,
a minor; if he should die, then to his
sister Sarah Armitt. Residue to Zachariah
Whitpaine and Stephen Armitt, husband to
said Sarah; executors: Charles Brockden,
John Songhurst [testator's uncle], William
Moode and William Parsons. A codicil
dated 13 March 1734 names children of
brother-in-law Isaac Williams.[30]

NOTES

[1]2 PA 19:399.

[2]2 PA 19:397, date of record 30 6th mo. 1703.

[3]*Ibid.* 126.   [4]PMHB 11:178.

[5]*Colonial Records* 13:507.

[6]1 NJA 21:449; see also 4 PA 1:150, dated 1689.

[7]Watson's *Annals of Philadelphia* 1:428.

[8]8 PA 1:178.   [9]*Colonial Records* 2:26.

[10]*Genealogical Dictionary of Rhode Island,* p. 307.

[11]PGSP 2:23 No. 137.

[12]For John Whitpaine's surveys, see 3 PA 3:305, 387.

[13]PMHB 18:504.

[14]For surveys of Zachariah Whitpaine see 3 PA 3: 385, 387; 3 PA 2:47. Blackwell's Rent Roll of 1689 (PGM 23:73 f., 81) shows Zach Whitpaine as owner of lots of 20 and 40 feet on Walnut Street; another, Old Purchase, 61 feet, on Bank Street between Walnut and Spruce, and Zachary Whitpaine and Co. as possessors of an Old Purchase lot of 132 feet on the south side of High Street between Third and Fourth from the Delaware.

[15]PhA A:162.   [16]PhA A:249.

[17]PhA B:101.   [18]PGSP 3:32.

[19]At this period there was at least one and perhaps two other women named Sarah Sanders in Philadelphia. One of these declared 1st intentions, 29 1st mo. 1695, 2nd intentions, 26 2nd mo. 1695, to marry John Wood (PGSP 4:188). At the second appearance John Wood's certificate was unsatisfactory and the Friends at Newtown Meeting were to be written to. Perhaps this marriage never took place and this woman was the Sarah Sanders who declared 1st intentions, 24 12th mo. 1698/9, 2nd intentions, 31 1st mo. 1699, at Philadelphia Monthly Meeting, to marry Thomas Rich (PGSP 4:242, 244). Whatever the truth about these marriages, it is clear that in neither instance could the bride to be have been our Sarah.

[20]Henry F. Waters, *Genealogical Gleanings in England* (Boston 1901), 1:844. The will was proved in Sussex County, Delaware, 5 4th mo. 1688 by oaths of Charles Sanders and William Rodeney, and later proved in PCC (186 Dyke) 4 Sept. 1690. The testator was the son of the Quaker Mary Dyer hanged at Boston in 1660.

[21]PhW E No. 333, pp. 252 f.

[22]See Arthur Pound, *The Penns of England and America* (New York 1932), p. 235; *Journal of the Friends Historical Society* (London) 2:91.

[23]NJW 1:305.   [24]PhW O, o. 223.
[25]DAB 2:177 f.   [26]2 PA 19:644, 686.
[27]PhA C:191, No. 67.
[28]JCRFP 1:30; KPC 13 f.
[29]PhW E, No. 354, p. 275.
[30]Another William Sanders, buried at Philadelphia,
10 Feb. 1726, was reported to have m. Esther Skively
or Skinsley, 27 2nd mo. 1723, and she d. 5 10th mo.
1748. Their children were Elizabeth (b. 19 9th mo.
1723); John (b. 14 5th mo. 1725); Hannah (b. 18 9th
mo. 1726). There was no known connection with our
William Sanders.

*WIGGLESWORTH, THOMAS   *disproved*
*WIGGLESWORTH, ALICE HAYHURST   *disproved*

The surname of this couple appears in a number of
variant spellings but after long examination of all
occurrences it seems to me that the spelling adopted
above is most probably the "correct" one, even though
in the Middletown Monthly Meeting transcript of the
Settle certificate, which we have ordinarily accep-
ted as the most trustworthy text, the spelling is
Wriglesworth. The name is Thomas Wrightsworth on
Lists A, B, C, D, E, G, H, I, J, K, L, M, N, O [or
Wigglesworth but denied], R, T, U, W, Y and Z; it
is Wigglesworth on Lists F, S and V [here put on the
Lamb]; on List Q the name is Wrigglesworth, but, for
a wonder, List X does not have the couple at all.
The wife is included but not named on Lists D, E, F,
G, H, J, K, L, M, P, S, T, Y and Z; she is Alice on
List Q, and List U gives also the variant Wrightsworth but on the *Lamb*. [1]
Whatever their name, this pair made part of the
group of Friends who came on the Settle certificate
which has been thoroughly discussed in the Introduction, Section E, where the evidence that they came
on the *Lamb* is fully displayed.
The marriage of Thomas Wigglesworth to Alice Hayhurst was under the care of the Settle Monthly Meeting and took place on 2 7th mo. 1665 at John Driver's house. She was a sister of Cuthbert Hayhurst,
the leader of the Settle party, and the daughter of
Cuthbert Hayhurst of Essington by his wife whose
name was likewise Alice. Alice Wigglesworth was
buried at Middletown, Bucks County, 17 3rd mo. 1690.
Thomas Wigglesworth evidently died between 13
9th mo. 1682, the date of his will, and 11 1st mo.
1683, date of the inventory taken by Nicholas Waln,

James Dilworth, Thomas Stackhouse, John Eastburne,
registered 27 12th mo. 1685/6, recorded 24 3rd mo.
1686.[3] Whether the year of the inventory should be
read as 1682/3 or 1683/4 is uncertain but probably
the latter, so that Wigglesworth lived more than a
year after he made his will. It was signed by mark
and mentions the children of brothers and sisters
to whom 5/- are left to each, if demanded; wife
Alice, whole executrix and residuary legatee; witnesses: Nicholas Waln, Alexander Giles, probated
by the widow, 4 12th mo. 1685/6. Administration
[sic] was granted 24 3rd mo. 1686 to Alice Wigel-
stone [sic] of the County of Bucks, widow of Thomas Wigelsworth [sic].

It is obvious that there was no issue. Alice's
two brothers, Cuthbert and William Hayhurst, both
of whom died soon after their arrival, would be
doubtless included in the phrase "brothers and
sisters" in the will, and they had children present
in Bucks County, but it is not known that Thomas
had any of his own brothers and sisters in Bucks
County, and that they were elsewhere seems to be implied by the phrase "if demanded."

NOTES

[1]PGM 23:53 Note 97.   [2]PMHB 31:440 f.
[3]PGSP 1:210.

*WOODROOFFE, JOSEPH   *proved*

This name appears on all lists, the proof being
the fact that he witnessed the will of John Barber
executed aboard the *Welcome*.

He was probably the Joseph Woodroofe of Salem
County, who died intestate in 1709,[1] administration
being granted 10 June 1709 to Thomas Hayward, principal creditor. Inventory of £18/6/9, 15 Sept.
1709, was taken by Ben Knapton and Alex'r Grant;
additional inventory £5/10/10, 11 Oct. 1709, by
William Bustill and Obadiah Heuston; account, 11
Dec. 1709.

He was probably also the son of Thomas Woodroofe
of Salem County, whose will was dated 17 Aug. 1699,[1]
naming son Joseph, daughter deceased; son John Woodroofe; Wm Hall, Benjamin Knapton, Daniel Smith. A
codicil of 30 Oct. 1699 reduces John's share and
revokes the bequest to Daniel Smith.

Salem Monthly Meeting records[2] show that Thomas

Woodroofe, son of John, yeoman, was born in the Parish of Cowley "upon Costwould Hills," in Gloucestershire; married Edith Pitt, daughter of Joseph
Pitt of Dorsetshire, gent.; arrived April 1679 in
the ship *Surkress* [really *Surcease*] with his wife
and the following children:

Thomas [bur. Philadelphia, 9 11th mo. 1694]
Edith [not in father's will unless she is the
  unnamed deceased daughter]
John [living 1699, mentioned in father's will]
Isaac [not mentioned in father's will, 1699]
Mary, b. at sea on the ship *Surkress* [not in
  father's will unless she is the unnamed de-
  ceased daughter].

Joseph Woodrooffe was a surveyor.[3] As the *Welcome* passenger has not been found elsewhere, it is
almost certain that he was the New Jersey surveyor,
since the witness to Barber's will was not present
at its probation and his signature had to be attested.

NOTES

[1]NJW 1:522.   [2]HEAQG 48.
[3]1 NJA 21:629.

WORRALL, MARTHA   *disproved*

This name appears only on List X. The truth is
that Martha Worrall came as servant to George Pownall
on the *Friends' Adventure*, arriving 28 7th mo. 1682,
to serve four years, loose on 29 7th mo. 1686. She
married at Middletown, 6 12th mo. 1685, as his second
wife, Samuel Dark, whose first wife was Ann Knight.
Samuel Dark has already been discussed above on page
274. We have found no evidence that Samuel Dark had
issue by his second wife Martha Worrall.

She may have been a relative of Peter Worrall of
Northwich, co. Chester, who, with wife Mary but no
children, registered his arrival on 7 8th mo. 1687,
having crossed on the ship *Ann & Elizabeth*. The
name of the master of this vessel appears in one of
two forms of the entry as "---- Gotter," the paper
having otherwise faded, but the other instance shows
him as Thomas Gotter and Peter Worrall as wheelwright.

WYNNE, ELIZABETH CHORLEY   *highly probable*

The consensus has been that Elizabeth, second
wife of Dr. Thomas Wynne, did not accompany him on

the *Welcome*. The contrary view was expressed in 1888
by the compilers of List F, but they vitiated their
acuteness in this respect by including also her two
daughters by Joshua Maude, although there was evidence apparently unknown to them that these young
ladies crossed on the *Submission*. List H also includes Elizabeth Wynne as a passenger, and in 1940
Mr. Colket (List O) agreed with this judgment and
even suggested that some of the Wynne children,
those for whom evidence is lacking (Jonathan, Sidney
and Hannah), might have been also on the *Welcome*.
He appears to have been able to convince at that
time Henry Paul Busch, who was then the president
of the Welcome Society, that Elizabeth was, indeed,
on the *Welcome*, for in a list of names of "new" passengers, Elizabeth Wynne has been added in what was
probably Mr. Busch's handwriting. Usually, however,
the consensus has been that Elizabeth was not on the
Welcome and her name is missing from other lists.
      Moreover, in an able article on Elizabeth[1] Mr.
F. J. Dallett feels quite sure that she and her eldest daughter Elizabeth Rowden came on a ship arriving later than the *Welcome*. No evidence has been
found to prove this view right, and the mere absence
of Elizabeth Wynne's name from any of the hypothetical passenger lists has no probative value whatever.
      Mr. Dallett noted, however, that Elizabeth Row-
den was one of the witnesses to the will of Richard
ap Thomas, late of Whitford garden, fflintshire, on
18 9th mo. 1683,[2] and that Richard ap Thomas came
on the ship *Morning Star* of Chester which sailed in
7th mo. 1683,[3] arriving 14 9th mo. 1683. No place
called Whitford Garden has been found but there is
in Flintshire a Whitford, about five miles north of
Caerwys, where Thomas Wynne was born, and so it is
entirely possible that Richard and Elizabeth Rowden
had known each other in Wales. Mr. Dallett thinks
Elizabeth Rowden came also on the *Morning Star*, but
the reasoning behind this conclusion is faulty. If
right, then we should also conclude that the other
witness to the same will came on the *Morning Star*
but we know that Farcliff Hodges came on the *Submission*, as the log of that ship clearly shows.
      I am happy to note that Milton Rubincam, in a
splendid article on Elizabeth Rowden,[4] is willing
to concede that Dr. Wynne may have been accompanied
"possibly by his wife (who, however, may have come
on a later vessel)."

Now in the printed version of Bucks Arrivals[5] we find this passage:

> Jane Mode and Margery Mode, daughters of Thomas Winn of Walley.[6] His wife came and arrived at the time aforesaid. Harriet [sic][7] Hodges, servant to the said Thomas Winn.

The sentence beginning with "His wife" does not appear in the version of Bucks Arrivals now at the Historical Society of Pennsylvania but the Doylestown version has the sentence in a different form as I would read it:

> Jane Mode and Margery Mode daughters of Thomas Winn of Walles his wife came and arrived at the time aforesaid [i.e. on the *Submission*]. Farcliffe [sic] hodges, Servant to the said Thomas Winn.

The meaning is certain but perhaps not clear. The two Maude girls, as their name should be spelled, came on the *Submission* and they are here identified as daughters of Thomas Wynne's wife, and nothing is said to imply that their mother accompanied them on the same vessel. The *Submission* Log is in accord with this interpretation: it shows that the Maude girls were accompanied by their stepsister Rebecca Wynne, and Farcliffe Hodges came as a servant of "the owners" of the ship and his services were for sale. Apparently, Thomas Wynne ultimately acquired them. In printing the Log, L. Taylor Dickson[8] says that Hannah Logan Smith, the presumed transcriber of Bucks Arrivals in the 9th volume of the *Pennsylvania Magazine of History and Biography*, was in error in stating that Elizabeth Wynne came on the *Submission*, and that Elizabeth probably came on the *Welcome*. What Hannah Logan Smith's error was was that she did not realize that the subject of the verbs "came and arrived" was not the word "wife" but "Jane Mode and Margery Mode"; we should now render the next clause as "daughters of the wife of Thomas Winn of Wales," etc

In Dr. John W. Jordan's article on the Wynnes[9] occurs another erroneous passage:

> This third [so she was long thought] wife who survived Dr. Wynne and was named in his will as executrix, did not accompany him to Pennsylvania, but, accompanied by her first [sic] husband and daughters Jane and Margery Maude, sailed from

Liverpool, September 5, 1682, in the Ship "Submission."

It is clear, first, that the author of that passage,
Dr. Jordan or a collaborator, was following Hannah
Logan Smith's printing of the Doylestown version of
Bucks Arrivals, or, making the same error in interpretation, if the original was consulted; second,
that something was left out, since Joshua Maude, the
father of the two girls Jane and Margery Maude or
Mode, and the second, not the first, husband of
Elizabeth Wynne, had been dead at the least for ten
years in 1682, and no one has ever suggested that
his ghost came to America. Probably it was intended to say something like this: ". . . but, accompanied by her first husband's daughters Jane and
Margery Maude," etc. Dr. Jordan was, of course, un-
aware that Joshua Maude was Elizabeth's second husband of three or four. The absence of Elizabeth
Wynne and Elizabeth Rowden from the *Submission* Log
is the base for an exceptionally strong *argumentum
ex silentio*.

There is another silence that may be of no significance. The first record of the presence of Elizabeth Rowden in Pennsylvania is the witnessing of
the will already cited on 18 9th mo. 1683, a full
year after the arrival of the *Welcome*, but young
women of marriageable age are not likely to be recorded frequently as such. The first record of her
mother is still later, 1 11th mo. 1683/4, when she
joined Mary Songhurst, a highly probable *Welcome*
passenger, in presenting for marriage Richard Tucker
and Jane Batchelor, the latter also a *Welcome* passenger. This was, of course, the *Wiegenzeit* of the
infant Philadelphia, and to argue from the silence
that Elizabeth Wynne was not present in Philadelphia
when we hear nothing of her, is to imply that as soon
as a woman landed in Pennsylvania she must at once
have begun to sprinkle her signature about. We
might expect this with men like Penn and Wynne but
not with a woman.

We conclude, therefore, that there is a strong
probability that Elizabeth Wynne accompanied her
husband on the *Welcome*, but in view of the fact that
Rebecca Wynne and the Maudes came on the *Submission*,
and Mary (Wynne) Jones, her husband Dr. Edward Jones
and their children, on the *Lyon*, and that, though
there is no positive proof, Jonathan Wynne is supposed to have come with the Jones, and no informa-

tion at all on what ship Sidney and Hannah Wynne
came, we should hesitate to put Elizabeth Rowden on
the *Welcome*.
According to the long accepted view, now over-
thrown by Mr. Dallett's article, Thomas Wynne married for his third wife, 20 5th mo. 1676, Elizabeth
Parr of Rainhill, Lancashire, daughter of the Rev.
Thomas Parr, and widow of Joshua Maude of Wakefield,
Yorkshire, and it was she who was the wife mentioned
in Dr. Wynne's will. Mr. Dallett has convincingly
shown that the putative "second wife," supposedly
the first wife's sister, Elizabeth (Buttall)(Rowden
Wynne, never existed at all. No such Elizabeth is
found in the will of Martha Buttall's father, so she
had no sister Elizabeth who could have married Dr.
Wynne as his second wife.
The truth is that Dr. Thomas Wynne married, second, under the care of Hardshaw East Meeting, 20 5th
1676, Elizabeth Maud of Rainhill, Lancashire, a place
seven miles east of Liverpool, and Mr. Dallett is of
the opinion that she "followed him to Pennsylvania."
Joshua Maude (1627-1672) was of the Cliffs, Wakefield,
Yorkshire, son of John and Sarah Maude of Alverthorpe
Hall near Wakefield.[10] In 1667 Joshua Maude, gentleman, aged 38, of Wakefield, married Elizabeth Rawden,
widow, aged 34, of Drax. According to Mr. Dallett,
she was probably Elizabeth Chorley, daughter of John
Chorley, armiger, of Rainhill, by Elizabeth, daughter
of Hugh Ley of Liverpool, and she had married, first,
----- Rowden or Rawden, of whom nothing is known;
second, Joshua Maude, as stated; third, Dr. Thomas
Wynne, as stated, and she had one daughter by her
first husband (Elizabeth Rowden) and two by her second husband (Jane and Margery Maude), but no issue
by her third husband. Mr. Dallett's caution about
the maiden name of Elizabeth seems stronger than it
needs to be, and we are glad to find Mr. Rubincam
of the same opinion.
Elizabeth survived all three of these husbands,
and, we think, probably married a fourth, Thomas
Sharp of Newtown, co. Gloucester, West New Jersey,
at the house of John Wills, 17 7th mo. 1701, marriage
recorded in Burlington Monthly Meeting minutes.[11]
We think that the said Thomas Sharp was one who
died without probate and was not the Thomas Sharp
of Newton Township, Gloucester County, whose will
was dated 5 8th mo. 1724, probated 24 Oct. 1729,[12]
who then had a wife Judith and who shows no Wynne

connections. The reason for feeling rather sure
that the wife of Thomas Sharp, whom he married in
1701, was our Elizabeth Wynne, will be found in the
connection of her daughter, Elizabeth Rowden, with
New Jersey and with people named Wills. In any case,
Elizabeth (Chorley)(Rowden)(Wynne) Sharp, if this
was she, was dead by 7 Jan. 1706, for testimony was
given in Sussex County, now Delaware, that a certain
property in Sussex Court, had belonged at one time
"to Doct^r Thomas Wynne, And from ye Sd Thomas Wynne
After the Death of him & Elizabeth his Wife to ye
Sd Plt."[13] The source from which we draw this item
gives no specific information as to the other details
of the suit, but Elizabeth, whether she married a
fourth husband or not, must have been dead in 1706.
Mr. Raymond B. Clark has searched the land records
of Sussex County for me without discovering any deed
of Thomas or Elizabeth Sharp.

Elizabeth was not, however, dead when Elizabeth,
daughter of Norton and Rachell Claypoole, was born
at Lewis [Lewes], Delaware, 16 3rd mo. 1687 about 7
P.M., "in the presence of Thomas Wynne and Elizabeth
his wife, ye midwife, & Jane Maud, her daughter, Hannah Bailey" and several other women. This must be
assuredly one of the earliest American birth certificates of record.[14] The words "her daughter" apply,
of course, only to Jane Maude and not to Hannah Bailey. Was the latter really Ann Baily, formerly Ann
Short, and a *Welcome* passenger herself?

In any case, Charles Pickering appeared before
the Pennsylvania Provincial Council on 6 Oct. 1693[15]
on behalf of Widdow Wynne, whose husband Thomas
Wynne, late of Sussex Countie, dec., was summoned
to court at New Castle to answer complaint of Adam
Short and others, but had died three or four hours
before judgment. The name had been wrongly given as
Thomas Guin and the Council remanded the matter to
the Provincial court.

On 1 Feb. 1894 Elizabeth Wynne conveyed a 175-acre
island in the Delaware, subsequently known as Fisher's Island, to Thomas Fisher and his wife Elizabeth,
formerly Maude, her daughter.[16] The name of Thomas
Fisher's wife was not Elizabeth but Margery, as we
shall see.

The three daughters of Elizabeth Wynne were:

1. Elizabeth Rowden,[17] daughter by the first husband, ----- Rowden or Rawden, is first found recorded
in America on 18 9th mo. 1683 as witness to the will

of Richard ap Thomas, late of Whitford garden, in fflintshire,[18] and next recorded at Philadelphia Monthly Meeting, 1 8th mo. 1684,[19] when John Brock and Elizabeth Rowden declare first intentions of marriage, and Thomas Wynne, father-in-law [stepfather] of Elizabeth, being immediately to depart for England, together with his wife, proposed an early marriage. John and Elizabeth again appeared on 5 6th mo. 1684 and were passed.[20] John Brock was born at Bramhall, Cheshire, 12 8th mo. 1657, son of Richard and Mary (-----) Brock,[21] was received at Falls Monthly Meeting on certificate dated 2 6th mo. 1682 from Congleton Monthly Meeting, Cheshire, and had arrived on the *Friends' Adventure* with servants Job Houle, Eliza Eaton and William Morton (who came on the *Freeman*),[22] and he had loaded on the *Friends' Adventure*, 1 June 1682, 5 dozen woolen stockings.[23]

He was afterwards a Justice of the Peace in Bucks County. Letters of administration were granted in Philadelphia County on the estate of John Brock to his widow, 5 Oct. 1704,[24] and she had leave to marry, 1 9th mo. 1704, 2nd intentions at Philadelphia Monthly Meeting (Ellizabeth Brock and Richard Ayrs), Richard Eayres of Evesham, Burlington County, yeoman, whose will was made 9 8th mo. 1736, probated 20 May 1738.[25] He names wife Elizabeth, children: Richard [aged 4+ in 1704]; Thomas [nearly 7 in 1704] and Margaret Wills [aged 8 in 1704, afterwards wife of Daniel Wills, son of Daniel and Margaret (Newbold) Wills]; stepson [called son-in-law] Ralf Brock; son Richard sole executor; witnesses: William Garwood, Thomas Jennings, Gab. Blond (inventory 20 June 1738, £478/12/2, made by Philo Leeds and Edward Mullin, including Bible and other books, servant boy and £60 in the hands of Ralf Brock).

Elizabeth Eayre, widow of Richard Eayre, late of Evesham Township, Burlington County, gent., made her own will 14 Nov. 1747, probated 22 June 1753,[26] and mentions son Ralf Brock who is to have the rent due in Yorkshire, Great Britain, and her land in Wistow, Yorkshire, is to go to grandson Ralf Brock, son of Ralf Brock.[27] Granddaughters Jane (daughter of John and Jane Miers), of Lewis Town on Delaware; Tabitha Brock, Elizabeth Brock, Susanna Brock and Elizabeth [sic] Pierce, daughters of Richard Brock; Charity, wife of John Garwood. Richard Eayre was executor of her deceased husband. Daughter Margaret Wills [i.e. stepdaughter]; children of daughter Mary

Clarke (not named); granddaughter Elizabeth Wright;
grandchildren living in Pennsylvania; executors:
son-in-law [stepson] Thomas Eayre, grandson John
Garwood; witnesses: Richard Eayre, Sarah Eayre,
Gabriel Blond. Inventory of 22 June 1753 taken by
John Hiller and Henry Burr came to £106/3/6. (Where
Charity Garwood and Elizabeth Wright should appear
in the family is not clear.)

    Issue: surname Brock, all by first husband
i.   John, eldest son; by Dec. 1725 he had d.,
      obviously unm., and his property had by
      then descended to his brother Ralph who
      lost it by sheriff's sale in that month.[28]
ii.   Ralph, millwright, living 1747 after which
      he has not been found. Richard Eayre and
      Elizabeth Eayre late relict of John Brock
      late of Bucks dec., released to Ralph
      Brock, millwright, 3 Nov. 1713.[29] He was
      of Makefield Township, Bucks Co., 10 Dec.
      12 Anne 1713.[30] It may be cautiously sug-
      gested that he went to England.
iii. Jane, m. John Miers, according to her mo-
      ther's will of 1747. Whether or not Jane
      was living is not clear, but at one time
      this couple had lived in Lewes, Delaware,
      and it is possible that this was the John
      Miers who m., if so, a second marriage,
      Ann Cummings at Wilmington Monthly Mee-
      ting, 2 1st mo. 1748, the record as abs-
      tracted by C. H. B. Turner (papers in the
      Genealogical Society of Pennsylvania)
      calling him James Miers, but John Miers'
      will, 31 Nov. 1749, probated 28 Feb.
      1749/50[31] names wife Anne and, among
      others, daughter Jane Cord, shown below.
      Issue: surname Miers, probably all
    1. Jane, unm. when mentioned in grandmo-
      ther's will in 1747, as child of her
      parents. She m. Joseph Cord and was
      called Jane Cord in her father's will.
      Deeds of Joseph Cord and wife Jean
      dated 10 12th mo. 1753 and 30 7th mo.
      1784 were cited by Turner (*ibid.* 1:
      79c, 85).
iv.   Richard, b. Makefield, ca. 1695, d. Sole-
      bury by 1753 and probably before 1747
      as he appears not to be living when men-
      tioned in that year in his mother's will.

He m. 1718 Susanna Scarborough, daughter
of John.
> Issue: surname Brock

1. Tabitha
2. Elizabeth
3. Susanna
4. Elizabeth, m. by 1747 ----- Pierce. She
   and the three sisters listed above are
   named in their grandmother's will.
5. ?John, m. Abington Meeting, 4 5th mo.
   1753, Sarah Jenkins.
6. ?Hannah, m. Abington Presbyterian Church
   17 Sept. 1740, Nathaniel Davis. Neither she nor her brother John are in
   Elizabeth Eayre's will in 1747.

v.   Mary, m. by 1747 ----- Clarke and then had
     unnamed children. As Richard Eayre's will
     does not mention her, she cannot have
     been a stepdaughter of Elizabeth.

vi. Elizabeth, aged 14 in 1709, not living 1747.

2. **Jane Maude**, elder daughter by the second husband Joshua Maude, was aged 15/2/1 in 1682 when she
came on the *Submission* with her sister Margery and
her stepsister Rebecca Wynne.[32]   She married first,
at Lewes, Delaware, 15 7th mo. 1687, Isaac Bowde,
whose estate[33] calls him Isaac Bonde [Bowde, Baro-
de] and shows administration to his former wife Jane
Scott, 6 Sept. 1692[34]; second, by 6 Sept. 1692, -----
Scott, who may have been the Thomas Scott mentioned
in the will of John Fisher the elder; third, -----
Lucas, not identified, but probably a widower with
small children for whose provision the Court ordered
Cornelius Wiltbanck to take steps; fourth, Cornelius
Wiltbanck, eldest son of Helmanus Wiltbanck by his
wife Jane -----.[35]   This fourth marriage probably
took place by February 1703, the date of the court
order cited above. Jane Maude had no issue by any
of her four husbands and died between 21 Jan. 1717/8,
when she was mentioned in the will of James Seatton,
and 1720, when Cornelius Wiltbanck married, second,
Hannah (Kollock) White. Cornelius Wiltbanck's will,
dated 10 March 1723/4,[36] calls him gent., names
wife Hannah, son Isaac, brother Abraham Wiltbanck
and cousins [probably children of Hannah] Ambrose
and Jacob White; daughters-in-law Mary and Comfort
White. It was probated 1 April 1724. The Lucas
stepchildren probably included Peter Lucas whose
will[37] is dated 7 March 1720/1, probated 27 March

1721, mentions sister Sarah Lucas who gets 200 acres
and she is named residuary legatee and executrix;
witnesses: William Stuart and William Darter. A note
says that Peter Lucas and John Lucas were brought up
by Cornelius Wiltbanck, and that Peter was aged 16
on 16 May 1705 [b. 1689] and John aged 14 in January
1706 [b. 1692].[38]

3. Margery Maude, younger daughter by the second
husband Joshua Maude, was aged 11½ when she came on
the *Submission* with her sister Jane and stepsister
Rebecca Wynne. In 1692 she married at Lewes, Delaware, Thomas Fisher, son of John Fisher, and he died
between 17 Nov. 1713, date of his will, probate date
not recorded, and 8 2nd mo. 1717 when his widow had
married, second, ----- Green.[39] For Margery Maude's
issue, see the sketch devoted to John Fisher.

T. B. Deem[40] rejects a claim that Thomas Wynne
had by Margery Maude a daughter who was ancestress
to the Fisher and Gilpin families. He is justified
in rejecting the statement but all that is the matter with it is that it calls Thomas Wynne's wife
Margery when her name was really Elizabeth. Otherwise, the statement is correct.

EXCURSUS ON THOMAS WYNNE'S SERVANT

With the three girls, Rebecca Wynne, Jane Maude
and Margery Maude, there came also on the *Submission*
a person whose name, sex and status have all been
previously doubtful.

The Philadelphia copy of Bucks Arrivals calls this
person "ffarclif Hedges, apprentice to Thomas Winn,"
and the Doylestown copy, "ffarcliffe hodges, Servant to the said Thomas Winn," but the first name
was printed as "Harriet," raising doubt as to the
sex. The *Submission* Log says at the end: "hed the
owners servants for sale Farclife Hodges & Ellen
Holland" but this was printed as "hed the owners
servants for sale Janeclif Hodges & Ellen Holland."

As the name "Harriet" is found to exist only in
a secondary transcript of the primary document, we
can abandon it, and we can be sure that the first
name was Farcliff and the second Hodges, and this
is confirmed by the fact that Faircliff Hodges was
a witness to the will of Richard ap Thomas on 18
9th mo. 1683, already cited above.

Thus, Farcliff Hodges or, perhaps, Faircliff

Hodges, came as a servant on the *Submission,* and his
services were subsequently acquired by Dr. Thomas
Wynne who appears to have attempted to make him a
chirurgeon and practitioner of physick. If so, he
disappears from the record. We find no such physician later practicing in Pennsylvania or Delaware.

NOTES

[1]"Mrs. Thomas Wynne of Philadelphia and her Family: Corrections to the Pedigrees of Wynne and
Maude (PGM 22:222-225), which is to be reprinted in
Welcome Society Publications, vol. 1.
[2]PGSP 3:165; see Dallett, p. 223, note 3; also
PhA A:217, abstracted PGM 19:265.
[3]PMHB 4:319; 9:233.
[4]*National Genealogical Society Quarterly* 54:214.
[5]PMHB 9:231.
[6]Certainly a misreading of a rather obscurely
written word but I shall affirm, *more amicorum,*
that "Walles" was intended, not "Walley."
[7]Harriet is not found so early as this and the
manuscript really has ffarcliffe.
[8]PGSP 1, the first article in the series.
[9]JCRFP 3:1189-1197.
[10]See Joseph Foster, *Pedigrees of Yorkshire,* vol.
1 under Maude.
[11]HEAQG 275.   [12]NJW 1:412.
[13]C. H. B. Turner, *Records of Sussex County,* pp.
129 f.
[14]*Ibid.* p. 137.   [15]*Colonial Recs.* 1:394.
[16]2 PA 19:490.
[17]*National Genealogical Society Quarterly* 54:214-
216.
[18]PGSP 3:165.   [19]PGSP 1:268.
[20]HEAQG 981 has a different date, 30 5th mo. 1684.
[21]JCRFP 5:857, 331.
[22]PMHB 9:224; BHBC 672.   [23]PGM 23:447.
[24]PGM 20:42; PhA B: [25]NJW 2:160.
[26]NJW 3:102 f.
[27]Should any descendant wish to investigate the
name of Elizabeth Rowden's father, this statement
offers a good clue for research at Wistow, Yorkshire.
[28]BD 6:39 f. [29]BD 5:18.   [30]BD 5:21.
[31]SC 56. [32]PMHB 9:231.   [33]SC 13.
[34]Hist.Soc. Pa. AM 2013, p. 136.   [35]PGM 17:27.
[36]SC 22. [37]PGSP 12:195; SC 29.
[38]Court Doc. Feb. 1705.   [39]2 PA 19:678.
[40]His Wynne Genealogy, p. 260.

WYNNE, JOHN   *highly improbable*

The person now to be discussed is presumed to be
a brother of Dr. Thomas Wynne, the subject of the
next sketch to which the reader is referred for the
background of the problem. It is not certain that
Dr. Thomas Wynne actually had a brother John, but
if the pedigree of Dr. Wynne presented hereafter is
correct, he was baptized at Yskeiviog, Flintshire,
North Wales, on 20 July 1627, and he had an older
brother John baptized there on 12 April 1625, both
of them sons of another Thomas Wynne by wife unknown.
As yet, I do not see that it has been proved that
the well-known immigrant to Pennsylvania was the
person baptized at Yskeiviog on 20 July 1627 but
neither has it been disproved.

The late Thomas Allen Glenn, who was in his day
the leading authority on the Welsh immigrants to
Pennsylvania, says in his book, *Merion in the Welsh
Tract* (Norristown 1896), p. 275, that with Dr. Thomas Wynne came his brother John. For this statement
he cites no specific document but alludes to John
F. Watson's *Annals of Philadelphia*, volume and page
not given. I have been unable to locate the reference in Watson whose book was first published in the
early 19th century and has gone into several editions. While frequently entertaining, the book is
without the normal documentation we now expect and
retails much that must have been untrustworthy oral
tradition circulating in the Philadelphia of Watson's day. Mr. Glenn, however, goes on to wonder
whether this brother John was the John Wynne on a
jury in Sussex County, Delaware, in the year 1687,
again with no fuller reference given. Once more I
have been unsuccessful in finding the corroborating
document.

In the sketch of the Wynnes in Dr. John W. Jordan's *Colonial and Revolutionary Families of Pennsylvania* (New York 1911), 3:1190, we find the juror
promoted to the bar and called a practitioner at
law in the same county, and here the learned coun-
sellor is equated with the person baptized at Yskeiviog on 12 April 1625.

We are therefore faced with a strange phenomenon.
We are asked to believe that an older brother of a
man of the prominence of Dr. Wynne could come to
America with him and thereafter escape recording except once as either a juryman or a lawyer. This is,
however, the best I have been able to do in support

of Glenn's statement. The source of "John Wynne"
seems likely to be what I take to be an error in
the printed list of First Purchasers in 1 *Pennsylvania Archives* 1:42, where in Group 25 there is a
record of 5,000 acres purchased by John ap John and
John Wynne in partnership.

The trouble with using this reference as proof
of the existence of a John Wynne is the fact that
there is no record of a purchase by Dr. Thomas Wynne
in the same lists, whereas there are later documents
which show that Dr. Wynne purchased land in partnership with John ap John, claimed land under this right
which was afterwards sold by the Thomas Wynne descendants. The reference given must be in error in
stating the first name of the Wynne partner, doubtless caused by the duplication of John in John ap
John.

T. B. Deem, whose book *A Genealogical Summary of
the Ancestry of the Welsh Wynnes, who Emigrated to
Pennsylvania with William Penn* (Knightstown, Indiana, 1907), occasionally says something that is true,
says on page 231 that John ap John who purchased
land with Dr. Thomas Wynne, is alleged to have been
his brother. This seems to display ignorance of the
Welsh system of patronymics, and if the pedigree of
Dr. Wynne which is presented a bit later on page 566
is to be accepted, then Deem's allegation must be
rejected, for the pedigree shows that Dr. Wynne's
father was a Thomas Wynne, not a John Wynne. Moreover, I can hardly believe that if John ap John were
a Wynne, that he would be recorded with a patronymic
in the same context in which his brother is recorded
with a surname.

The result of all this may be recapitulated as
follows: it is alleged by 19th century writers that
Dr. Thomas Wynne brought with him a brother John,
but as yet no document has been located to support
the allegation. Until such a document is produced·
and stands up under skeptical assault, I refuse to
believe in the existence of this John Wynne as present in early Pennsylvania or Delaware.

WYNNE, THOMAS   *proved*

Thomas Wynne, usually called by modern writers
Dr. Thomas Wynne, though in his day chirurgeons and
practitioners of physick normally did not use the
title, appears, of course, on all lists. The proof
of his presence on the *Welcome* is the fact that he

was one of the witnesses to Thomas Heriott's will
executed aboard the vessel, and was named executor
and a beneficiary (£5) of the will of Isaac Ingram,
also executed aboard the *Welcome*. After William
Penn, Wynne was the most important passenger.

The question of whether his wife Elizabeth was
also a passenger has been thoroughly discussed in
a special sketch under her name. By his first wife
he had five daughters and one son, but one of the
daughters seems not to have come to America or at
least was not here when he died. The eldest of the
daughters was already married to Dr. Edward Jones
and with him and their two eldest children and,
possibly, her brother Jonathan, crossed the Atlantic on the *Lyon* in 1682; the daughter Rebecca and
the stepdaughters Jane and Margery Maude, crossed
on the *Submission*. On what ship the other step-
daughter Elizabeth Rowden and the daughters Sidney
and Hannah crossed is unknown, and it would not be
impossible that some or all of them, including the
son Jonathan, who was only thirteen in 1682, came
also on the *Welcome*.

THE WYNNE FAMILY

The following account of the Wynne family is
based, as will be seen, on many sources, but for
the ancestry principally on the work of Thomas Allen Glenn in his book, *The Welsh Founders of Pennsylvania* (Oxford 1911), in a volume called vol. 1--
though no more was published--pages 90-107. The
account there given is largely identical with that
found in Richard Yerkes Cook, *The Ancestry of Thomas Wynne* (Philadelphia 1904). It appears that the
research underlying Mr. Cook's book was done by Mr.
Glenn. The Cook book has a frontispiece purporting
to be a portrait of Dr. Wynne, though it is not so
stated, and I should say without much hesitancy that
it seems likely to be the work of a 19th century
artist.

Mr. Glenn sharply denies the validity of a pedigree printed in the *Magazine of American History*
but does not identify the author, give the reference
more precisely, though he says he advised against
its publication. This is undoubtedly by Wharton
Dickinson and appears in the *Magazine of American
History* 8:662-665. Since Mr. Glenn does not describe the rejected pedigree or say why he rejected
it, the Dickinson pedigree has been examined.

Dickinson says that the father of Dr. Thomas Wynne was Peter Wynne of Lee wood and the Tower, who had a residence at Caerwys, and was the fifth of eleven sons of Sir John Wynne of Gwydir, born 1563, eldest son of Maurice or Morris Wynne by his first wife Jane Bulkeley of Beaumaris, Maurice being son of John ap Meredith ap Ieuan. Gwydir is on the eastern border of Carnarvonshire which is separated from Flintshire, where Caerwys is, by Denbighshire. In other words Caerwys and Gwydir are not in the same neighborhood. In attempting to verify this I have, of course, found much material on Sir John Wynne of Gwydir but this is the only reference to a son named Peter.

Sir John Wynne of Gwydir is a well-known figure, the author of a history of his family which was printed in 1770, 1781, 1827, 1859, 1878, and, lastly, at Cardiff in 1927. The last printing has been examined. It is edited by John Balburgh, C.B.E., with the title, *The History of the Gwydir Family written by Sir John Wynn of Gwydir, Knight and Baronet, Faithfully printed from his autograph manuscript.* With the contents of this work we have no concern, since it cannot help any problem among Sir John's descendants. As to them we have amassed information from the following:

John Balburgh's Introduction to the *History*
Richard Williams, ed., *Royal Tribes of Wales by Philip Yorke Esq.* [Liverpool 1887], pp. 7-9.
Thomas Nichols, *Annals and Antiquities of the Counties and County Families of Wales* (London 1872), pp. 367 and 418 f.
J. Y. W. Lloyd, *History of the Princes, the Lords Marcher and the Ancient Nobility of Powys Fadog* (London, 6 vols., 1881-1887), 3:358 on Sir John Wynn; 4:269-274 on Sir John and Gwydir.
Thomas Allen Glenn, *Merion in the Welsh Tract* (Norristown 1896), p. 387.
Dictionary of National Biography 21:1172-1175, articles on Sir John Wynn and a descendant.
Burke's Peerage, Baronetage and Knightage, 104th ed. (1967), pp. 2715 f. on the family of Wynn.

From these sources we put together the following:

Sir John Wynn of Gwydir, whose ancestry is shown in Burke, was born in 1553, succeeded to Gwydir on 10 Aug. 1580, was knighted 14 May 1606, and made a baronet on 29 June 1611 when this rank was created.

He married Sidney, daughter of Sir William Gerard or
Gerrard, Chancellor of Ireland, and she died 8 June
1632, buried at Llanrwst beside her husband who had
died 1 March 1626/7.   They are said to have had ele-
ven--one source says ten--sons and two daughters.
The sons were:

i.   (Sir) John, knt., d.s.p. and *vita patris*,
            at Lucca.
ii.   (Sir) Richard, 2nd Baronet, d.s.p. 19 July
            1649 aet. 61, having m. Anne, daughter of
            Sir Francis D'Arcie of Isleworth.
iii.   Thomas, d. inf., according to Glenn.
iv.   (Sir) Owen, 3rd Baronet, b. 1592?, d. 13
            Aug. 1660 aet. 60; m. Grace, daughter of
            Hugh Williams of Weeg.
            Issue:
        1. (Sir) Richard, 4th Baronet; m. Sarah,
               daughter of Sir Thomas Myddelton, Ba-
               ronet, of Chirk Castle.
               Only issue:
            a. Mary, m. 30 July 1678 Robert, 16th
               [Burke says 13th] Baron Willoughby
               of Eresby, afterwards Marquis of
               Lindsay and Duke of Ancaster. She
               inherited Gwydir.
v.   Robert, in holy orders, d. 1657 aet. 24.
vi.   William, Prothonotary of Wales, must have
            d. before the death of the 4th Baronet,
            and without surviving male issue.   He
            purchased Branas in Eidernion, co. Meri-
            oneth, and m. Katherine (bur. 5 Sept.
            1706 aet. 69), daughter of Thomas, Vis-
            count Bulkeley.
            Issue:
        1. Richard, d. before 1706 when his widow
               was buried; had two sons and one daugh-
               ter, all d. inf.
        2. Sidney, m. Edward Thelwall of Plas-y-
               ward, Denbighshire.
               Issue: surname Thelwall
            a. Jane, b. 25 Dec. 1665; m. 1689 Sir
               William Williams, Baronet.
            b. Sidney, m. Calwallader Wynn of Foelas.
            c. Mary, m. Edward Vaughan.
vii.   Maurice, purchased Crogan, Merionethshire,
            d.s.p. 1670/1.
viii.   Ellis, d. 20 Nov. 1619, unm.
ix.   Henry or Harri, d. 27 July 1671; held vari-

ous offices including Judge of the Mar-
shallsea and Prothonotary; m. Catherine
Lloyd. Both Yorke and Nichols make him
the tenth son.
  Issue (all known):
1. (Sir) John, 5th and last Baronet; d.s.p.
   7 or 11 Jan. 1718/19, after which the
   baronetcy was extinct. He m. Jane,
   daughter and heiress of Eyton Evans of
   Watstay by his wife Ann Powel, and Jane
   inherited Watstay before 1678. Sir John
   changed the name of Watstay to Wynnstay, and it passed at his death to
   Watkin Williams, son of Sir William
   Williams, 2nd Baronet, by his wife
   Jane Thelwall, as shown on p. 563. He
   afterwards became Sir Watkin Williams-
   Wynn (1692-1749), on which see BPBK,
   104th ed. (1967), pp. 2716-2718. Wynnstay was destroyed by fire, 5 March
   1858, afterwards rebuilt. See [Askew
   Roberts], *Wynnstay & the Wynns, A Volume of Varieties put together by the
   author of "The Gossiping Guide to Wales"*
   (Oswestry 1876). Nichols (*op. cit.*,
   p. 367) has views of Wynnstay; Williams,
   (*op. cit.*, opp. p. 10) has a portrait
   of the 5th Baronet.
x.   Roger, d. inf.
xi. Roger, d. inf.

Nothing has been found on the alleged two daughters
and Balburgh, who speaks of only ten sons, goes out
of his way to call the ten sons and two daughters
legitimate. Perhaps he knew of others not legitimate. In any case, no Peter appears. Had Peter been
both the fifth son of Sir John, 1st Baronet, and the
father of Dr. Thomas Wynne, the 5th Baronet would not
have been the son of Henry, but either Dr. Thomas
Wynne or his son Jonathan, depending on the date of
demise of the 4th Baronet, which is unknown. Had Dr.
Thomas Wynne been the son of any other of the sons
of old Sir John Wynn, then the baronetcy would not
have become extinct but Jonathan Wynne, of Wynnstay,
Blockley Township, Philadelphia County, Pennsylvania,
would have become the 6th Baronet at the very latest
and since the male line from him has not failed to
this day, there would have been Wynne baronets in
Philadelphia at least to the Revolution!

Having shown that the Dickinson pedigree is impossible, we are ready to approach the one compiled by Mr. Glenn and published by him and by Mr. Cook. We have not been able to subject it to as searching an analysis as in the case of the Dickinson offering, but shall set it down for what it is worth. The greatest weakness in it is, we think, in the final generation, for we do not know just how Mr. Glenn came to be so sure that he had found the right baptism. He did not succeed in locating the will of the physician's father, or any land records the devolution of which might prove the line. As a result we must caution the reader that the verdict is "not yet proved."

I. Ednowain, Lord *per Baroniam* of Tegainl, lived at Llas-y-Coed, Parish of Bodfari.[1]

II. Madog ap Ednowain of Bodfari, Lord of Tegainl, m. Arddun or Arddyn, daughter of Bradwen, descendant of Ysbws and Ysbwch (who were father and son), sister of Ednovain ap Bradwen, Merionethshire.

III. Iorwerth ap Madog of Bodfari and Yskeiviog in Tegainl, m. Arddyn, daughter of Lewellyn ap Owen ap Edwin.[2]

IV. Ririd ap Iorwerth, m. Tibot, daughter of Robert de Pulford, of Cheshire.

V. Iorwerth ap Ririd, died by 1339, m. Nest, a daughter of Iorwerth ap Grono (who m. Middufis, daughter of Owain Cyfeilsioc, Lord of Powys) ap Einion ap Seissylet.

VI. Rotpert ap Iorwerth of Bodfari and Yskewiog, 1313, m. Adles, daughter of Ithel Vychan of Mostyn (d. 1300) ap Ithel Garn ap Meredith ap Uchtred ap Edwin of Tegainl, by his wife Adles, daughter of Richard ap Cadwallader, Lord of Ceredigion (d. 1172).[3]

VII. Cynric ap Rotpert of Bodfari and Yskewiog (descended from Emma Plantagenet), m. Angharad, daughter of Madoc Lloyd of Brynecunallt ap Iorwerth Voel (descended from Tudor Trevor).[3]

VIII. Ithel Vaughan[4] of Holt Denbigh and Northrop, m. the heiress of Robin, brother of Robed, ancestor of the Gwydir family, and descended from Owen Gwynedd, Prince of North Wales.

IX. Cynric ap Ithel Vychan of Bodfari and Yskewiof living after 1420, m. Tanglwystl, daughter of Gruffyd Lloyd ap David ap Meredith ap Gruffyd.

X. Harri ap Cynruc of Yskeiviog, born ca. 1485,
m. Alice Thelwall, daughter of Simon Thelwall Esq. of Plas y Ward (son of David Thelwall of Plas y Ward by his wife Tibot or
Tabitha) by his wife Janet Langford (daughter of Edward Langford Esq. of Ruthin, Denbighshire [d. 16 Henry VII] by his wife ?
Eleanor Dutton [d. 5 Edward IV], daughter
of John of Dutton).

XI. John Wynne ap Harry of Yskeiviog, d, by 1572,[5]
m. Katherine, daughter and heiress of Ithel
ap Jenkin ap David ap Howell.[6] They are said
to have had 13 children, the eldest vicar
of Caerwys.

XII. Rees ap John Wynne, b. Yskeiviog ca. 1538. It
is said that there are six baptisms of his
seven children in Yskeiviog parish church.

XIII. John ap Rees Wynne of Yskeiviog, b. ca. 1570,
d. by 1640, m. at Bodfari Church, 29 Oct.
1588, Grace Morgan.

XIV. Thomas ap John Wynne of Yskeiviog or of Bron
Vadog, b. 1589, bapt. 20 Dec. 1589, d.
1638/9.[7]
Issue:

i. Harri, bapt. 6 Nov. 1619.
ii. Edward, bapt. 9 April 1622.
iii. John, bapt. 12 April 1625.
iv. Thomas, bapt. 20 July 1627.
v. Peter, bapt. 30 Jan. 1630.

The fullest account of the Wynnes, by no means
complete, is by T. B. Deem, *A Genealogical Summary
of the Ancestry of the Welsh Wynnes, who Emigrated
to Pennsylvania with William Penn* (Knightstown, Indiana, 1907), a work not to be used without the
greatest caution. The first 178 pages are devoted
to Wynne's ancestry, mostly on lines outside of
Wales and this has not been scrutinized. A fair
part of the book consists of sketches of prominent
Wynnes, many of whom are not connected into lines of
descent. A shorter account appears in John W. Jordan's *Colonial and Revolutionary Families of Pennsylvania* (New York 1911), 3:1189-1197, which is more
reliable, so far as it has been tested. Brief accounts are by Wharton Dickinson in the *Magazine of
American History* 8:662-665, already mentioned above;
by Howard W. Lloyd in Glenn's *Merion in the Welsh*

Tract (Norristown 1896), 261-275 (on Wynnewood and the Wynnes); another by the same author in his *Lloyd Manuscripts* (Lancaster, Pa., 1912), p. 347; by James J. Levick, "John AP Thomas and his friends" (PMHB 3:301-328), a short paragraph (p. 325) on Thomas Wynne.

William MacLean Jr. published an interesting article entitled "Dr. Thomas Wynne's Account of his Early Life" (PMHB 25:104-108). See also Francis J. Dallett, "Mrs. Thomas Wynne of Philadelphia and her Family: Corrections to the Pedigrees of Wynne and Maude" (PGM 22:222-225); my own article (TAG 39:4-7) and Mr. Dallett's (TAG 41:218-220). No connection can be found with the Virginia Wynnes discussed *ibid.* 37:234-240; 38:13-19.

Dr. Thomas Wynne was a Welshman able to speak and write in both Welsh and English. He was born, according to his own statement, near Caerwys, Wales, a place name sometimes spelled Cajerwit, and in Flintshire.[8] This does not conflict with the baptism mentioned on page 566 as having been recorded in the church at Yskeiviog, for the two places are near each other, and it would be natural for Dr. Wynne to locate his birthplace by alluding to the larger community. Shortly before coming to America, he was living in Bronvadog, for one John Thomas in his will dated 8 Feb. 1682 alluded to Wynne as late of Bronvadog near Caerwys.

In an autobiographical tract published in 1679, he says:

I was baptized and brought up a Protestant, and having learned the Articles of their Faith, and the Prayer of the Church, I thought all was well until I was about fifteen years old.

About 1655 he first became energetically engaged in Quaker activities which was about the time he married, first, Martha Buttall, of Wrexham, daughter of Randle Buttall of Wrexhàm, whose will dated 15 June 1680, probated at St. Asaph in 1684,[9] describes himself as "oulde and weake," mentions daughter Abigail; Samuel Buttall, eldest son of Nathaniel, eldest son of testator; sons Nathaniell, Samuel, Jonathan, 1/-, daughter Rebecca, 1/-, son-in-law Thomas Winne, 1/-, as well as Charles, 1/-, probably a grandson. The will of Jonathan Buttall of Battersea, Surrey, dated 26 Aug. 1695,[10] mentions

sister Martha Wynn's children. The mother of all
Thomas Wynne's children, she must have died about
1675, for Thomas Wynne married, second, under the
care of Hardshaw East Meeting, 20 5th mo. 1676, E-
lizabeth Maud of Rainhill, Lancashire, seven miles
east of Liverpool. She was then the widow of Joshua
Maude of the Cliffs, Wakefield, Yorkshire, son of
John and Sarah Maude of Alverthorpe Hall near Wakefield, and he was born 21 April 1627. In 1667 Joshua
Maude, gentleman, aged 38, of Wakefield, married
Elizabeth Rawden, widow, aged 34, of Drax. She was
very probably the daughter of John Chorley, armiger,
of Rainhill, by Elizabeth, daughter of Hugh Ley of
Liverpool, and she married, first, ----- Rowden or
Rawden, of whom nothing more is known; second, Joshua Maude, as stated; third, Thomas Wynne, as stated, and perhaps, fourth, Thomas Sharp. For fuller
details concerning her history and her three daughters, see the sketch devoted to Elizabeth Wynne herself.

On 1 Dec. 1661 Thomas Wynne was arrested at Wrexham in company with his brother-in-law Nathaniel
Buttal and others, and charged with unlawful assembly. Besse[11] reports that "being met together in
their own hired house at Wrexham, [they] were pulled
out by Soldiers, and carried before some Justice of
the Peace, who sent them with a Mittimus from Constable to Constable, to the Common Goal [sic] at
Writhan, several of them being very poor men with
large families who suffered much by their confine-
ment." Whether then or later, Thomas Wynne remained
at Denbigh a "prisoner near six Years for the Testimony of Jesus," and was released about the time Penn
was imprisoned in the Tower where he wrote *No Cross,*
No Crown.

Wynne was a pamphleteer but his first book was
put out in 1677, *The Antiquity of the Quakers, proved*
out of the Scriptures of Truth, of which a small
part was in Welsh. In answer to this, one William
Jones, an opponent of the Quakers, published an anonymous book called *Work for a Cooper, Being an An-*
swer to a Libel Written by Thomas Wynne, the Cooper,
the Ale-Man, the Quack and the Speaking Quaker (1679),
and it contained what purports to be a portrait of
Thomas Wynne, reproduced by Glenn (p. 266). To this
Wynne replied with *An Anti-Christian Conspiracy DE-*
TECTED and Satans Champion DEFEATED. Being a Reply
to an envious & Scurrilous Libel, without any Name

to it, *CALLED WORK FOR A COOPER. Being also a vindication of my Book, entitled, The Antiquity of the
Quakers* (1679). At the end is a signed testimony
of a London Friend, William Gibson, who died of a
fever, 20 Nov. 1684, aged 55. He was of the Parish
of St. Edmund the King, and his funeral was from a
meeting in White Hart Court, burial in Bunhill
Fields. At least a thousand Friends attended the
funeral, among whom was most probably Thomas Wynne
who had by then returned to England from Pennsylvania.[12]

When he wrote the *Reply*, Wynne was living near
the place where he was born and where he says his
father died before he was eleven. He had early
wished to become a physician but as his mother was
without the means to set him to "Chyrurgery," he
became for a time a cooper, but Richard Moore of
Salop brought him to "Desections" in Salop. The
anatomists, Dr. [Walter] Needham[13] and Dr. Hollins,
furthered his profession. He carved out a wooden
skeleton and was ultimately licensed, and had been
for twenty years, when he wrote this tract which
was dated at Caerwis, 1 11th mo. 1678, that is, 1
Jan. 1678/9. His work in medicine won for him a
brief mention in James Thacher, M.D.'s early *American Medical Biography* (Boston 1828), 1:28, where it
is said that he "and his brother" practiced in Philadelphia.

In 1681 Thomas Wynne was present at an interview
between Richard Davies, a Welsh Friend, and Dr. William Lloyd, newly appointed Anglican bishop of St.
Asaph, who, though not a Friend, treated all dis-
senters in an irenic spirit. The story is told in
*An Account of the Convincement, Exercizes, Service
and Travels of that Ancient Servant of the Lord,
Richard Davies* (6th ed., 1825, pp. 112-118). In
1682 Thomas Wynne was selected by Friends as one of
three from the country to treat with the authorities
for the release of 139 Quakers imprisoned at Bristol. George Whitehead had an audience with Charles
II on 17 Feb. 1682.[14] Wynne and Davies interviewed
Sir Lionel Jenkins, Secretary of State, and King's
Secretary, Henry Hyde, 2nd Earl of Clarendon (1638-
1709). Jenkins treated them scornfully but Hyde
was more kind.

On 14-15 7br 1681, in partnership with John ap
John, Thomas Wynne bought 5,000 acres in Pennsylvania.[15]

Mr. Colket says that at London with Wynne, as the
time of the sailing neared, "was his wife and probably some children," but I do not know what evidence
he had for this statement. In any case, Wynne embarked on the *Welcome*, and must have had his hands
full during the voyage, caring for those stricken
with smallpox. He remained in America only two years
at the first visit. On 9 11th mo. 1682/3 he was one
of four to plan building the first Philadelphia Meeting House.[16] On 10 March 1683 he was elected Speaker
of the first Provincial Assembly.[17] On 11 April 1683
he was a commissioner in the New Jersey boundary
dispute. He probably returned to England with Penn
on the *Endeavour*. He was in London in December 1684
when he was arrested with 23 others while on his way
to the meeting at White-Hart Court, and on 8 Dec.
1684 was indicted for riotous assembly, sent to Newgate Prison, and fined 4 nobles with the others. As
stated above he probably attended the funeral of William Gibson on 29 Nov. 1684.

Just when he returned to Pennsylvania is unknown
but he erected a mansion near Lewes, now in Delaware,
appraised at his death at £80. On 13 April 1687 he
was named Justice in Sussex County by Thomas Lloyd,
and this "comition" was read in Open Court on 3 3rd
mo. 1687.[18] In 1688 he represented Sussex County in
the Assembly, the name being printed in the lists as
Thomas Wayne. He was a Justice of the Peace on 2
Jan. 1689[/90?][19] and was a puisne judge from 5 Sept.
1690 to his death in 1692.[20]

He died in March 1692 and was buried in the Arch
Street Friends graveyard on 17 March 1691/2. His
will was dated 15 1st mo. 1691/2, probated 20 2nd
mo. 1692,[21] by the wife Elizabeth Wynne. He names
her, son Jonathan Wynne; children in America: Jonathan, Mary, Rebeckah, Sidney, Hannah; daughter Tibatha [Tabitha] in England. A bond of £50, half
paid, to brother-in-law Sam[l] Buttall; overseers:
with wife, Thomas Lloyd Dep[t] Gov[r], Griffith Owen;
witnesses: Arthur Cooke, Phineas Pemberton, Richard
Thomas, Theo[r] Roberts, Mary Holme. The estate came
to £430/1/3, and included one servant, three slaves
(one a baby), 24 cows, 9 with calves, bulls, steers,
coalts, pigs and 15 books, with a feather bed and
boulsters 661 pounds [weight or value?]; inventory
taken by Nehemiah Field and Albertus Jacobs, who
did not total the inventory because they could not
appraise the medicines and other pertinences of a

physician.

A **memorial** appears in *Persecution Exposed, In Some Memoirs Relating to the Sufferings of John Whiting, and many others of the People called Quakers* (1715), page 219:

> Thomas Winne, an Antient eminent Public Friend of North-Wales about Caerwis in Flintshire, who writ a Book called, The Antiquity of the Quakers, in 1677. And another, entituled, An Antichristian Conspiracy detected, in vindication of it, against a perverse Adversary who writ against it, 1679. He afterwards went to Pennsylvania, in the Year 1682, and was Surveyor there, where he died, and was buried at Philadelphia, the 17th of the 1st Month, 1691/2.

When he died, he was being sued by Adam Short and others but we know no details.[22] He and his wife Elizabeth had bought on 3 3rd mo. 1688 from Henry Stretcher and John Millington the island afterwards called Fisher's in Broadkill Marshes. After his death, she granted this island, 1 12th mo. 1693, to Thomas Fisher and his wife Margery, her daughter. The record has the following note[23]: "This was Certainly Granted Away by the Govern't of New York."

The dispersal of the children of Thomas Wynne is interesting: The only son Jonathan remained in Blockley Township; two daughters settled in the Welsh tract, now called "the Main Line," and two others married Maryland men. Two stepdaughters married in Sussex County and their half-sister married first a Bucks County man and then one from Burlington County.

Issue: all by first wife, surname Wynne

1 i.   Mary, b. ca. 1659, d. 29 7th mo. 1726.
  ii.   Tibatha [Tabitha], known only from reference to her in her father's will which says she is in England; probably m. but Wharton Dickinson says the opposite. He says the the same of Sidney who certainly married.[24]
2 iii. Rebecca, b. 1662, still living *8 5th mo. 1725.*
3 iv.   Sidney, probably d. not long after 1690.
4 v.   Hannah, d. 22 7th mo. 1750.
5 vi.   Jonathan, b. 1669, bur. 28 12th mo. 1720/1.

1. **Mary Wynne**, eldest daughter of Dr. Thomas Wynne by his first wife Martha Buttall, was born ca. 1659, died 29 7th mo. 1726, though this date has been

thought doubtful, since her husband left a widow
Mary when he died in 1737. She married Dr. Edward
Jones, chirurgeon, born at Bala, Merionethshire,
Wales, ca. 1645, son of John Lloyd, so the name
Jones is a patronymic and not a surname in this case.
Dr. Jones was buried at Merion Meeting House, 26 12th
mo. 1737, aged, according to one source, 80, but 92,
according to Thomas Chalkley's *Journal*.[25] Dr. Jones
was recorded as Jonathan Wynne's brother-in-law in
1705.[26] Edward and Mary (Wynne) Jones and their
two eldest children came on the *Lyon* in August 1682,
arriving on the 13th of that month in the Schuylkill, John Compton, master, as is shown by a letter
dated at School Kill River, 26 6th mo. 1682 and
signed Ed[d] Jones.[27] The will of Edward Jones is dated 27 3rd mo. 1732, probated 2 Aug. 1738, and names
sons Jonathan, Edward, Evan, son John to support son
Thomas; wife Mary; son-in-law John Cadwallader;
daughters Martha, Elizabeth, Mary; granddaughter
Martha Roberts. Edward Jones's property shows on
the Explanation of the Map of Philadelphia.[28]

Issue: surname Jones
i.   Martha, b. 10 3rd mo. 1678, d. 16 2nd mo.
1747; m. Merion Meeting House, 26 10th
mo. 1699, John Cadwallader, b. ca. 1677,
d. 23 5th mo. 1734,[29] bur. 24 5th mo.
1734. Among their children was Mary who
m. Samuel Dickinson and their son John
was drafter of the Articles of Confede-
ration[30] and the founder of Dickinson
College.
ii.   Jonathan, b. 3 11th mo. 1680, d. 30 7th
mo. 1770 aged 90; m. Merion, 4 8th mo.
1706, Gainor Owen, b. 26 8th mo. 1688,
bur. 15 4th mo. 1742, daughter of Robert
and Rebecca (-----) Owen.
iii. Edward, b. 17 8th mo. 1683, bur. 1 7th mo.
1732; m. (1) Hannah -----, bur. 7 1st
mo. 1724/5; (2) Mary -----, bur. 29 7th
mo. 1732. One of his wives was daughter
of William Palmer; resided in Blockley
Township.
iv.   Thomas, b. 30 4th mo. 1686, living 3 Feb.
1743/4, when his brother John bequeathed
to his wife £10 "to enable her to keep
and maintain my loving brother Thomas
Jones." John had been directed to do this
in their father's will. Thomas probably

had some disability and never married.

v.   Evan, b. 25 1st mo. 1689, will dated 22
May 1753, probated 24 May 1755 in Ulster
Co., N.Y.:[31] Evan Jones of Hermitage, co.
Ulster, practitioner of physick; wife
Bridgett and five sons, John, Thomas,
Evan, James and Edward, daughter Mary.
Son John has received £432 for education
and expenses while studying physick a-
broad, and will get the library and shop
interests and only so much money as will
make him equal, including the advance.
Evan Jones m. (1) by 7 Feb. 1727 Mary
Stevenson of Flushing and Burlington,
daughter of Thomas Stevenson, and she d.
19 6th mo. 174- in 70th year; (2) Bridget
Matthews, daughter of Col. Vincent Matthews of Fort Albany, N.Y.

vi.   John, b. 15 3rd mo. 1691, d. between 3 Feb.
1743/4 and 17 April 1744/5; m. Crosswicks,
N.J., 12 9th mo. 1717, Mary Doughty, b.
17 2nd mo. 1699, daughter of Jacob Doughty.[32]

vii.   Elizabeth, b. 22 11th mo. 1693, bur. 6 12th
mo. 1759; m. 2 8th mo. 1724, Rees Thomas
Jr., b. 22 2nd mo. 1693, d. Aug. 1738.

viii. Mary, b. 28 7th mo. 1696, m. 28 9th mo.
1723, John Roberts, b. 12 8th mo. 1701.

2. Rebecca Wynne, third daughter of Dr. Thomas
Wynne by his first wife Martha Buttall, was born in
1662, came on the *Submission* with her two stepsis-
ters, Jane and Margery Maude, and was still living
on 8 5th mo. 1725. She married, first, in 3rd mo.
1685 at Third Haven Meeting, now Easton, Talbot County, Maryland, Solomon Thomas, who died without issue; second, 23 7th mo. 1692 at the home of the
bridegroom, John Dickinson of Talbot County, planter.
He was the son of Charles Dickinson of London by his
wife Ellen, according to Richard Henry Spooner[33] who
also says that John first settled in Virginia, then
in 1660 in Talbot County, and gave his age when de-
posing in 1713 as 80 years. Another source maintains
that John's father was Walter Dickinson of Crosia
Doré whom Spooner regards as John's brother. The
will of John Dickinson is dated 7 Oct. 1714 [or
1717?], probated 29 April 1718[34]: wife Rebecca gets
dwelling plantation "Ridle" for life, at her death
this to son John; son Charles 150 acres, part of

tract bought of William Edmundson in Dorchester County, he to choose half; remainder of said tract to
son John and daughter Sedney; daughter Mary Kersey
silver marked M.D. [she not identified by anything
in the *Maryland Calendar of Wills*]; wife Rebecca ad-
minstratrix and residuary legatee; witnesses: William
Thomas, Silvester Abbot, Anne Thomas, Peter Sharp.

Issue: surname Dickinson, all by second husband

i. John, m. (1) Third Haven, 11 4th mo. 1724,
    Rebecca Powel, d. 1728 aged 30; (2) 9 3rd
    1730 Elizabeth Harrison.

ii. Charles, m. Third Haven, his mother sign-
    ing certificate, 8 5th mo. 1725, Sophia
    Richardson, who, among others, is men-
    tioned in the will of her father David
    Richardson of Talbot County, 7 April 1722,
    probated 17 July 1722,[35] with wife Ruth
    whose own will also of Talbot County, 6
    Oct. 1727, probated 3 July 1728,[36] has,
    among others, a daughter Sophia, wife of
    Charles Dickinson.

iii. Sidney, m. 3 11th mo. 1720 Edmundson Ste-
     vens.

iv. Mary, m. by 1714 ----- Kersey, not identi-
    fied.

3. Sidney Wynne, fourth daughter of Dr. Thomas
Wynne by his first wife Martha Buttall, was married
at West River, Maryland, 20 Dec. 1690, to William
Chew, and died not many years after, to judge from
the fact that she had only two children. He was the
son of Samuel Chew (John) who married ca. 1658 Anne
Ayres, only daughter and heiress of William Ayres
of Nansemond County, Virginia, and of Maryland, and
William inherited from his father a lot in the town
of Herrington, and died 28 Feb. 1709/10 in Ann Arundel County, Maryland, without probate. See Francis
B. Culver, "Chew Family" (*Maryland Historical Magazine* 30:157-175); also Lawrence Buckley Thomas, *The
Thomas Book* (New York 1896), pp. 268 f.; also Walter
W. Spooner, *Historic Families of America* (New York
n.d.), 2:185-195 on Chew, especially page 188, where
the birth of William is put on 12 April 1671. Both
Thomas and Spooner give him only a son, ignoring
the daughter. William is mentioned in the will of
his father, 26 July 1676, probated 12 June 1677,[37]
and in the will of his mother, 20 Feb. 1694, probated 5 May 1695,[38] and as father of a nephew in

the will of his brother Samuel, 16 July 1718.[39]

Issue: surname Chew

i.   Benjamin, b. ca. 1700, m. Jan. 1726/7 Sarah
      Bond, d. 1762; removed to Cecil County,
      Maryland, Dec. 1752; a Justice of the
      Peace; disowned by Nottingham Friends in
      Oct. 1755; made his will 10 Jan. 1761,
      probated 4 Jan. 1763, and the widow's will
      was probated 21 April 1769.
         Only Issue: surname Chew
      1. Benjamin, perhaps the captain of this
         name of the Baltimore privateer *Chase*,
         30 April 1777; m. 1 May 1750, Cassan-
         dra Johns, daughter of Richard and Ann
         (-----) Johns. They certainly had the
         first son, probably also the second.
            Issue: surname Chew
         a. Nathaniel, midshipman, later captain
            and prisoner of the British; m.
            1792 Margaret Rodgers, daughter of
            Commodore John Rodgers, U.S.N., and
            his wife Minerva Denison.
               Issue: surname Chew
            α John.
            β Benjamin Franklin.
            γ Washington Pinkney, d. 7 April 1850,
               m. 24 Jan. 1831 Mary Hall, d. 20
               Oct. 1837.
            δ Emeline R[odgers?].
            ε Henrietta Mary, m. Cyrus Huntington,
               D.D.
            ζ Elizabeth Ann.
         b. Sarah, m. ----- Johns.
         c. Phinehas, living 1768.
         d. Mary, m. ----- Elliott and had Sarah
            who m. John O'Donnell.
         e. Ann, m. Capt. Isaac Van Bibber.
         f. Henrietta, m. (1) ca. 1778 Hugh Davy,
               d. ca. 1783; (2) John James of Cu-
               raçao.
ii.   Sidney, m. Charles Pierpoint, on whom see
      A. B. Stickney, "The Pierpoints of Hert-
      fordshire, England, and Ann Arundel Coun-
      ty, Maryland" (TAG 33:237). Charles Pier-
      point's will dated 1748 (Will Book 25:
      390) is said to name fourteen children.

4. Hannah Wynne, sixth daughter of Dr. Thomas
Wynne by his first wife Martha Buttall, was born in
England or Wales at an unknown date but before 1675
and died 22 7th mo. 1750, buried at Old Haverford
Burying Ground. She married at Merion Monthly Meeting, on either 11 or 25 8th mo. 1695, Daniel Humphrey, bachelor, of Haverford West, then in Chester,
now Delaware County, Pennsylvania, yeoman, born at
Llangelynin, Merionethshire, 6th mo. 1660, died probably at Haverford shortly before 7 April 1735, date
of probation of his will dated 26 9th mo. 1734/5,
son of Samuel Humphrey or Humphreys of Portheven,
parish of Llanegrin or Llanglyning. An article by
Hampton L. Carson, "The Humphreys Family" (PGSP 8:
121-138) has little concern with the first generations; an unsatisfactory account of this Humphrey
family appears in Frederick Humphreys, *The Humphreys
Family in America* (New York 1883), pp. 989-991, and
was based on papers of the late Major General Andrew
Atkinson Humphrey (1810-1883). See also T. B. Deem's
Wynne Genealogy 255-260. When Hannah (Wynne) Humphrey died, there was this memorial to her: "Our
friend, Hannah Humphrey, widow, received a gift in
the ministry, about the year 1700, which she exer-
cized in humility and lowliness of mind, to the comfort and edification of the hearers in general and
lived in love and unity with Friends."

Issue: surname Humphrey

i.   Samuel, b. 3 6th mo. 1696, d.s.p. 24 2nd
        mo. 1784 aged ca. 88. He left a legacy
        to his brother Charles.

ii.   Thomas, b. 20 4th mo. 1697, prob. d. minor.

iii.   Jonathan, b. 9 7th mo. 1698, bur. Merion,
        27 8th mo. 1771; m. 9 8th mo. 1724 Sarah
        Doughty, b. 19 11th mo. 1704, bur. Merion,
        23 7th mo. 1744, daughter of Jacob Dough-
        ty.

iv.   Hannah, b. 29 11th mo. 1699, d. 1 8th mo.
        1785; m. Haverford Meeting House, 27 4th
        mo. 1758, Abraham Dawes of Whitpain Town-
        ship, widower, b. 1 9th mo. 1704, d. 1
        Feb. 1776, his obituary in *Pennsylvania
        Gazette* of 7 Feb. 1776. No issue by Han-
        nah.

v.   Benjamin, b. 7 11th mo. 1701/2, d. by 1735;
        m. Merion Meeting House, 24 12th mo.
        1725/6, Esther Warner, bur. 26 11th mo.
        1775, daughter of Isaac and Ann (Craven)

Warner, and she m. (2) 19 10th mo. 1740, Richard George of Blockley Township, b. 10th mo. 1699, bur. 2 12th mo. 1771. Jordan (1:245) says that her issue will be found under the Tunis Family but no such sketch can be found in the three volumes (JCRFP).

vi. Elizabeth, b. 16 8th mo. 1703, d. spinster, 31 1st mo. 1790 in 87th year, obituary in *Pennsylvania Gazette* of 10 Feb. 1790.

vii. Mary, b. 10 12th mo. 1704/5, d. before 27 Sept. 1735 when her husband remarried; m. Christ Church, Philadelphia, 24 July 1724, David Parry, whose death is recorded at that church 14 April 1741. His second wife, married as stated, was Elizabeth Davis.

Issue: surname Parry (Christ Church records)
1. Catherine, bapt. 8 March 1728 age 4 mos. and no death record; m. at Christ Church, 10 June 1751, Edward Duffield on whom see above, p. 177.
2. Rowland, bapt. 24 June 1730, aged 7 wks, 1 day, d. 16 April 1735.
3. John, d. 27 Jan. 1730/1.
4. John, bapt. 18 Oct. 1732 aged 10 wks, d. 25 Aug. 1733.
5. Margaret, bapt. 28 Nov. 1734, d. 24 Aug. 1740.

viii. Solomon, b. 16 10th mo. 1706, d. 19 9th mo. 1758; m. Mary Parker, b. 19 5th mo. 1714, d. 19 10th mo. 1765, daughter of Richard Parker; moved from Haverford to Darby ca. 1738. Of Mary: "loving and faithful as a wife, careful in the education of her children, and very useful in the neighbourhood where she resided, visiting, assisting, and consoling the sick and those in affliction."

ix. Joshua, b. 10 1st mo. 1707/8, d. 13 11th mo. 1793; m. Merion Meeting House, Sarah Williams, b. 13 4th mo. 1720, d. 2nd mo. 1777; (2) 9 12th mo. 1777, Ann Webber, d. 24 3rd mo. 1802; to Darby 1790. What is stated below about their descendants comes chiefly from the unsatisfactory account in *The Humphreys Family in Ameri-*

      ca.
       Possible issue: surname Humphrey
1. Clement.
2. Daniel: three daughters and a son Edward, alleged to have been b. 1 June 1726, a quite impossible date for this Daniel. He had an uncle Edward whose father was, of course, also a Daniel, but the date will not fit the uncle any better.
3. Joshua, b. 17 June 1751; m. Mary Davids, and he d. 1838, said to have designed the U. S. *Constitution*. The sketch of Major General Andrew Atkinson Humphrey in *The Twentieth Century Biographical Dictionary of Notable Americans*, vol. 5, not paged, identifies the general as grandson of this Joshua by his son Samuel (1776-1846) whose wife was Letitia Atkinson. The fact that the two works cited are in agreement as to this Joshua's dates does not increase their credibility as they both might derive from the same error.
4. Jane, d. unm. at advanced age.
x. Edward, b. 28 12th mo. 1709/10, d. 1 Jan. 1776 in 66th year; no issue; obituary in *Pennsylvania Gazette* of 10 Jan. 1776.
xi. Martha, b. 9 9th mo. 1711, d. 12 April 1774, aged 62/5/3; m. First Presbyterian Church, Philadelphia, 24 2nd mo. 1738, Stephen Pascall, b. 2 8th mo. 1714, d. 5 12th mo. 1800 aged 87. See above, p. 316. They were Friends at their deaths.
xii. Charles, b. 19 7th mo. 1714, d. 18 1st mo. 1786, bur. Haverford "not a member of Haverford meeting." His will dated 8 Nov. 1785, probated 27 Jan. 1786, shows no wife or child; probably m. Margaret Parry.
xiii. Rebecca, b. 2 10th mo. 1714, bur. 23 5th 1780, spinster.

5. Jonathan Wynne, youngest child and only son of Dr. Thomas Wynne by his first wife Martha Buttall, was born supposedly in 1669, buried at Merion Meeting House burial ground, 28 12th mo. 1720/1, leaving a will dated 29 Jan. 1719, probated 17 May 1721,[40] naming dear and beloved wife Sarah executrix; trustees: Edward Jones, Daniel Humphrey, or John Cadwallader and Jonathan Jones, that is, two brothers-in-

law, or a nephew-in-law and a nephew; witnesses:
Rowland Ellis, Thomas Jones and Edward Jones Jr.,
the latter two probably nephews. He married, probably ca. 1694, Sarah -----, buried 27 2nd mo. 1744.
She is regularly called Sarah Graves or Greave, and
is presumed to have been a sister of Thomas Graves
of Christiana Hundred, Newcastle County. The sole
evidence adduced for this is a Quaker record seen
by Mr. Colket which says that Jonathan's daughter
Sidney married her first cousin Samuel Graves. The
said Samuel could have been her first cousin in one
of three ways: (a) if Jonathan Wynne married Sarah
Graves, as supposed; (b) if Samuel Graves's mother
had been a Wynne, possibly only if she were Tabitha,
of whom nothing more is known than her name; (c) if
Jonathan Wynne and Thomas Graves had married sisters, in which case we should have no clue at all.

Jonathan may have come to America with his eldest
sister Mary and her husband, Dr. Edward Jones, on
the *Lyon*, arriving 17 Aug. 1682, but no evidence has
been found to prove it. He built a house called
"Wynnestay" about 1701,[41] but the giving of this
name to the house does not prove that our Wynnes
were closely related to the English family of Wynnes
who gave the same name to their house.[42]

The following passage is taken from the Minutes
of the Board of Property on 26 4th mo. 1704:[42]

> John'n Wynne haveing A Right to the Remainder
> untaken of his Father's purchase of 200 [should
> be 2500] acres, it appears upon the best Inquiry
> that Can be made at Present that there is no more
> than 1,850 a's of it laid out, he therefore re-
> q'sts a Warrant for the remaining 600 a's and
> 40 a's of Land to Compleat his purchase, his
> Brother-in-Law, Edw'd Jones Sen'r, haveing taken
> vp 10 acres, see the Welsh Min's.

Also on the same 26 4th mo. 1704[44] Jonathan Wynne
conveyed 150 acres which his father had sold to
Richard Orme of Radnor. To James Steel a tract of
200 acres was conveyed in the right of John ap John
and Thomas Wynne by Jonathan Wynne, only son of Thomas Wynne, date of patent 14 7ber 1736.[45]

There is a Chester County deed[46] of 19 Dec. 8
Anne, proved by Randall Speakman and Matthew Robinson, grantor Jonathan Wynne of merrion, co. Philadelphia, yeoman, son and heir of Thomas Wynne, formerly of Philadelphia, cirurgon & Practitioner of

Physick, dec.; grantee: David Powell of the City of Philadelphia, yeoman, 13 3rd mo. called May 1708.

Philadelphia Deeds D-23, p. 381, 28 Oct. 1738, acknowledged that day, recorded 23 April 1790: Noah Abraham of Nantmell Township, Chester County, yeoman, and wife Mary, convey to John Petty of City and County of Philadelphia, merchant, a city lot, land granted for life to John Wynne and wife Mary, with a life interest to Mary, as shown in Book E-7, vol. 8, p. 17. The lot was 66 by 306 feet on the south side of High Street. Jonathan's will of 29 Jan. 1719 had left the land to his two eldest daughters, the latter the wife of Noah Abraham, and now Jonathan and John and Mary are all dead.

The deed referred to in Book E-7 is dated 22 Feb. 1709 and shows that Jonathan Wynne gave the said life interest *to his nephew* John and Mary his wife for natural love and affection. This was witnessed by Richd Moore, Francis Knowles and Joshua Lawrence.

The strange thing about this deed is the allusion to a nephew John Wynne. There is abundant evidence to prove that Jonathan Wynne had no brother, being constantly referred to as the only son of his father. All his nephews known to us were sons of sisters and bore other surnames. This leads me to the conclusion that the John Wynne in question was the illegitimate child of one of the children of Dr. Thomas Wynne; if, of one of the daughters, he would have borne as surname his mother's maiden name, as often happened in such cases; if child of Jonathan himself, then he would have borne his real surname but have been styled his father's "nephew" to conceal the truth.

In any case, there is another deed[47] of Noah Abraham of Nantmel in the County of Chester, yeoman, and wife Mary; Jonathan Wynne of Nantmel aforesaid cooper; Samuel Greaves of County of Newcastle upon Delaware, weaver; and wife Sidney; Martha Wynne, Elizabeth Wynne, John Wynne, the said Mary Abraham, Jonathan Wynne, Sidney Greaves, Martha Wynne, Elizabeth Wynne and John Wynne, children of Jonathan Wynne, late of Blockley in the County of Philadelphia, yeoman, deceased, to Thomas Wynne of Blockley aforesaid, another of the children of Jonathan Wynne, deceased; Sidney and Elizabeth signing by mark, proved 14 Sept. 1761, recorded 16 Oct. 1761.[48]

Issue: surname Wynne
6 i.   Thomas, bur. 27 11th mo. 1757.
  ii. Hannah, in her father's will left certain
       property in partnership with her sister
       Mary, which property was sold in 1738 by
       Mary and her husband Noah Abraham without
       Hannah being mentioned, so she must have
       died before that year. I do not think
       she was the Hannah Gwin bapt. as adult
       at Abington Presbyterian Church, 16 Dec.
       1736 who seems to have already m. at that
       church on 6 Aug. 1735, Joshua Jones.
  iii. Mary, m. First Presbyterian Church, Phila-
       delphia, 28 9th mo. 1729, with license,
       Noah Abraham, later of Nantmel Township,
       Chester County, where he d. intestate,
       admin.. 29 May 1759 to James Abraham who
       may have been the man of that name of
       East Nantmel Township who also d. intes-
       tate, admin. 1 Nov. 1770 to another Noah
       Abraham. In 1738 Mary joined with her
       husband in the deeds cited above. Whether
       she had issue is not certain.
  iv. James, bur. Merion, 24 8th mo. 1714.
7 v.   Jonathan, d. 1788.
8 vi. John, d. 19 April 1787.
9 vii. Sidney, under age in 1719.
10 viii. Martha, d. 29 12th mo. 1774.
  ix. Elizabeth, under age in 1719; m. First Pres-
       byterian Church, Philadelphia, 22 7th mo.
       1737, Ralph Lewis. They are alleged by
       Jordan[49] and others to have had issue. A
       thorough search of all the records which
       might conceivably show their issue has
       been unsuccessful but the record may ex-
       ist and I hope some day to find it.

   6. Thomas Wynne, eldest child of Jonathan Wynne
(Thomas) by his wife Sarah -----, was buried 27 11th
mo. 1757. He married at Philadelphia Monthly Meeting,
28 10th mo. 1722, Mary Warner, born 22 6th mo. 1703,
daughter of Isaac Warner and his wife Anne Craven,
and she married, second, at Merion, 7 4th mo. 1762,
James Jones of Blockley Township, widower, buried
30 4th mo. 1791 aged 90.

   Issue: surname Wynne
   i.   Ann, b. 2 12th mo. 1724/5, d. 5 July 1807,
        bur. Lower Merion. She m. at First Pres-

byterian Church, Philadelphia, 27 4th mo.
1743, with license, Phineas Roberts of
Merion.

    Issue: surname Roberts
1. Esther, m. 26 10th mo. 1770 Jonathan
   Palmer.
2. Sidney, b, 6 Sept. 1756, d. 7 Sept.
   1812, m. John Jones.
3. Isaac, d. *vita patris,* left issue.
4. Hannah, d. *vita patris*, m. ----- Stree-
   per and left issue.
5. Titus.

ii.   Lydia, m. Jonathan Edwards.
iii. Sarah, m. Michael Stattleman.
iv. Thomas, d. inf.
v.   Thomas, lieutenant, b. 21 Jan. 1733/4; m.
    Gloria Dei Church, 27 Jan. 1757, Marga-
    ret Coulton, and she m. (2) Samuel Clap-
    hamson.
       Issue: surname Wynne
    1. Thomas, b. 1762, d. 10 Oct. 1810, m. ca.
       1786, Elizabeth Rees, b. 1762, d. 1
       Nov. 1840.
         Issue: surname Wynne
      a. Margaret, m. John Dungan.
      b. Thomas, m. Hannah Sharp.
      c. Phoebe, m. Leonard Knight.
      d. Samuel C., b. 1795.
      e. Elizabeth, m. William Rose.
      f. Anne, m. William Davy.
      g. Susanna, b. 28 March 1804, d. 23 Ju-
        ly 1844; m. 1822 Jacob Duffield.
      h. Polly, d. unm., aged 18.
    2. Phebe, m. John Adams, snuffmaker.
vi.   Jonathan, d.y.
vii. Isaac, d.y.
viii. Deborah, d.y.
ix.   Mary, m. Samuel Pearson.

    7. Jonathan Wynne, fifth child of Jonathan Wynne
(Thomas) by his wife Sarah -----, died in 1788, testate. He married 16 6th mo. 1730, Ann Warner, died
in the spring of 1788, daughter of Isaac and Ann
(Craven) Warner. Jonathan was a cooper of Nantmel
Township, Chester County, in 1738 when he joined
in the deeds selling his father's property. He was
of East Nantmel Township when he made his will[50]
on 9 April 1788, probated 19 April 1788: aged and
signed by mark; beloved son Jonathan and beloved

wife Ann were named administrators but she died and
the son served alone; two-thirds of the property go
to the three children Wardner [sic], Thomas and E-
lizabeth; one-third among the other six children
Samuel, Mary, James, Hester, Isaac and Hannah; witnesses: Jacob Vance, Rachel Gordin (she proved as
Rachel Rogers).

Issue: surname Wynne
i.   Jonathan, probably eldest son, served as
      father's administrator in 1788; probably
      the Jonathan Wynne Esq. on whose estate
      administration bond was signed 27 June
      1817, John Wynne, adm.[51]
ii.   Samuel.
iii. Mary, prob. m. Christ Church, 23 March
      1752, Henry Iddings.
iv.   James.
v.   Hester.
vi.   Isaac.
vii. Hannah.
viii. Warner or Wardner.
ix.   Thomas.
x.   Elizabeth.

8. John Wynne, sixth child of Jonathan Wynne
(Thomas) by his wife Sarah -----, died 19 April
1787. He married ca. 1750, Ann Pastorius, born 5
Nov. 1729, died 1 Sept. 1790, daughter of Heinrich
Pastorius (Franciscus Daniel), on whom see Marion
Dexter Learned, *Life of Francis Daniel Pastorius*
(Philadelphia 1908), page 307.

Issue: surname Wynne (after Learned)
i.   Pastorius, d. unm., 25 April 1787.
ii.   Sarah, m. Christ Church, 11 Feb. 1772, James
      Hall.
iii. Isaac, b. 29 March 1759, d. 16 Feb. 1798;
      m. 8 July 1784, Mary Eastburn, b. 3 Aug.
      1769, d. 26 Aug. 1813, daughter of Robert
      and Esther (Franks) Eastburn.
iv.   Mary.
v.   Ann, b. 1 Aug. 1765, d. 5 Aug. 1857; m.
      15 May 1789, Thomas Hooton Jr., b., ac-
      cording to Learned, 20 July 1866, but
      probably 1766, d. 11 June 1806, son of
      Thomas and Bathsheba Hooton of Evesham
      Township, Burlington County, New Jersey.

9. Sidney Wynne, seventh child of Jonathan Wynne

(Thomas) by his wife Sarah -----, was under age when her father made his will in 1719. She married at First Presbyterian Church, Philadelphia, 1 4th mo. 1732, Samuel Grave, born 10 2nd mo. 1710, died 6 7th mo. 1741, probably the Samuel Greave, yeoman, whose will is dated in Christiana Hundred, Newcastle County, Delaware, 21 7th mo. 1741, probated 3 Nov. 1741, and mentions wife Sarah and the children shown below.[52]

Issue: surname Grave, Greave or Graves
i.   John, will[53] dated 25 12th mo. 1772, pro-
      bated 8 Jan. 1773, mentions deceased
      father Samuel, wife Jane; children
      Thomas, William, Ann Hayes, Sarah Allen,
      Mary Dowd, Jane Hicklin, Hannah Greave;
      executor: son Samuel Greave.
ii.   Samuel.
iii. Jonathan, whose will[54] dated 7 5th mo.
      1774, probated 11 June 1774, mentions son
      Joseph, father Samuel, and sons Jonathan
      and David.
iv.   Martha, m. Jacob Chandler.

10. Martha Wynne, eighth child of Jonathan Wynne (Thomas) by his wife Sarah -----, was under age in 1719 when her father made his will. She died 29 12th mo. 1774. She married at Merion Monthly Meeting House, 30 8th mo. 1741, James Kite, who was not the cooper of this name buried 31 5th mo. 1745. Virginia A. Kite of Marksville, Va., published sometime after 1905 *The Kite Family: A Fragmentary Sketch of the Family from the Origin in the 9th Century to the Present Day*. This feeble booklet shows James Kite marrying Martha Wynne (1708-1774) in 1741, and then shows James as son of Abraham Kite who was born in either 1685 [p. 38] or 1865 [p. 371] by his wife Mary Peters. The parents, at any rate, really were married under the care of Philadelphia Monthly Meeting, 27 6th mo. 1708. Miss Kite further states that Abraham was the son of another James Kite who died in 1713, having married in 1680, Mary Warner (1660-1686), daughter of William Warner. Finally, she attempts to maintain that the last-named James was the son of a Sir George Kite. This much is certainly true: James and Martha Kite received a certificate from Merion Monthly Meeting dated 15 8th mo. 1767 which they did not deposit at Philadel-phia Monthly Meeting until 28 12th mo. 1770.

Issue: surname Kite
i.   Mary, b. 1742, included in the 1767 certi-
      ficate.
ii.   Abraham, b. 1743, included in the certifi-
      cate.
iii. Sarah, b. 1744, included in the certificate.
iv.   Jonathan, b. 1748, not in the certificate
      but probably bur. from Philadelphia
      Monthly Meeting, 28 2nd mo. 1793 age 46.
v.   William, m. 1785 Margaretta Kyl; not in
      the certificate.
vi.   James, b. 1753, included in certificate.

NOTES

[1]No sketch on him in DNB.
[2]This generation is omitted by Jordan.
[3]This generation is omitted by Jordan but VIII
is called eighth from Ednowain.
[4]Jordan: Ithel Vychan.   [5]Jordan: 1582.
[6]Jordan calls XI the twelfth from Ednowain Ben-
dew.
[7]I do not know whether there was a document found
by Glenn which gives this date or whether he counts
from the baptism to the age of Dr. Wynne at the
time he says his father died.
[8]3 PA 3:343.   [9]PMHB 40:240 f.
[10]PMHB 40:239 f.
[11]*Sufferings* 1:748.
[12]On William Gibson, a First Purchaser of 500, not
5000 acres in Group 34 (1 PA 1:43), see Walter Lee
Sheppard (TAG 40:39-42).
[13]DNB 14:164 f.
[14]See Samuel Take, *Memoirs of George Whitehead*
(1830), 2:131.
[15]2 PA 19:279; 1 PA 1:42 in Group 25 (calling him
John Winn); 3 PA 3:388, two properties dated 15 11th
mo. 1683, also p. 393; Old Rights in 3 PA 3:40,
twelve properties of Jonathan and Thomas Wynne; also Blackwell Rent Roll of 1689 (PGM 23:721) old
purchase lot of 51 feet, 2/6, five years paid, on
High Street.
[16]PGSP 1:252.   [17]2 PA 9:636.
[18]C. H. B. Turner, *Sussex County Records* 113, 118;
GM 271.
[19]2 PA 9:664.   [20]2 PA 9:630.
[21]PGSP 1:84.   [22]See Adam Short.
[23]2 PA 19:490.
[24]*Magazine of American History* 8:662-665.

[25]Edition of 1751, p. 301.
[26]2 PA 19:491; GM 314; GWF 1:81.
[27]PMHB 4:314-317.   [28]3 PA 3:371.
[29]KPC 371.   [30]PMHB 60:1-14.
[31]NYW 5:67.   [32]NYGBR 30:254.
[33]*Thomas Family of Talbot County, Maryland* (Baltimore 1914), p. 86.
[34]*Maryland Calendar of Wills* 4:156.
[35]*Ibid.* 5:102.   [36]*Ibid.*6:105.
[37]*Ibid.* 1:102.   [38]*Ibid.*2:87.
[39]*Ibid.* 4:177.
[41]See Askew Roberts, *op. cit. supra*, p. 564.
[42]GM 277.   [43]2 PA 19:491.
[44]2 PA 19:431 f.   [45]3 PA 1:79.
[46]CD A, pt. 2, p. 308.
[47]PhD H-14, p. 284, dated 4 Nov. 1735.
[48]On Jonathan Wynne and family, see Deem 235-243.
[49]JCRFP 3:1194.   [50]CW 8:202, file 3925.
[51]CW file 6442.   [52]NC 33.
[53]NC 71.   [54]NC 75.

*YARDLEY, WILLIAM[1]	*disproved*
*YARDLEY, JANE HEATH, his wife	*disproved*
*YARDLEY, ENOCH, his son	*disproved*
*YARDLEY, THOMAS, his son	*disproved*
*YARDLEY, WILLIAM, his son	*disproved*

These names appear on List X only. The truth is
that the Yardleys came on the *Friends' Adventure*,
arriving on 28 7th mo. 1682. William Yardley had
loaded on this vessel on 31 May 1682, the following:
3 bundles, 2 tubbs, 3 chests, 1 pack, 2 boxes qty
2 cwt wrought iron, ½ cwt pewter, 30 lbs woolen cloth,
100 ells English linen, 40 lbs new shoes, 2 cwt nails,
½ chest window glass, ½ cwt haberdashery wares.[2]
    William Yardley registered himself and his fami-
ly as coming on this ship from Ransclough near Leek,
Staffordshire, and with them one servant, Andrew
Heath, to receive meat, drink, apparel and the accustomed land, loose on 28 7th mo. 1686 after a term
of four years. Andrew Heath was probably a nephew
of Jane Heath Yardley. For his subsequent history
see *supra*, pages 237-239.
    Leek is in northern Staffordshire but Ransclough
is missing from the standard genealogical atlas and
gazetteer. It is barely possible that it was the
name of Yardley's property rather than of a locali-
ty. When, on 20-21 1st mo. 1681, William Yardley

became a First Purchaser of 500 acres in Group 43,[3]
his residence was stated as Rushton Spencer, co.
Stafford, a place which lies about ten miles northwest of Leek, on the Cheshire border, about a mile
east of Congleton, Cheshire, where there was a meeting of Friends of which the Yardleys were members.
They brought a certificate from Congleton Meeting
dated 2 6th mo. 1682 and deposited it at Falls Monthly Meeting on 6 1st mo. 1683.[4]

Having landed in Pennsylvania, a warrant was obtained on 6 8th mo. 1682 from Deputy Governor William
Markham, as William Penn had not yet arrived on the
Welcome, and the survey was completed and the patent
issued on 20 10th mo. 1682. The original 1681 deed
and the receipt for £10 were in 1881 in the possession of A. S. Cadwallader of Yardley, Pa., the borough of which the name commemorates the family.
The land thus described was known as "Prospect Farm"
and the name survived at least to 1881, when the
farm was owned and occupied by Thomas S. Cadwallader. If the Cadwalladers were descendants, they were
only collateral descendants of the original William,
for, as will be seen, his descendants died out completely by 1703. We are told in Thomas W. Yardley's
Genealogy of the Yardley Family 1402-1881 (Philadel-
lia 1881), that the city lot corresponding to this
farm was No. 8, north of Chestnut Street, extending
from Second to Third Streets, and was sold by the
sons on 21 8th mo. 1696[5] but was not recorded until
28 7th mo. 1768. The Blackwell Rent Roll, however,
in 1689 shows an Old Purchase lot on Spruce Street,
51 feet, 2/5.[6]

Jane Yardley is known to have been a Heath of
Staffordshire, perhaps of Horton in that county, but
of her parents nothing is known. She was, however,
sister to Margaret Heath, wife of Thomas Janney, and
to Ann Heath, wife of James Harrison, on both of whom
see the excursus at the end of this sketch. Jane
is said in the Genealogy to have died 28 6th mo.
1691 but whether this date is Old Style or New Style
I cannot say.

William Yardley led an active life in the community, county and province, serving in the Assembly
in 1682-1683; on the Provincial Council 1688-1689,
was a Justice of the Peace and Judge of Common Pleas
1685-1689 and Sheriff 1690-1693. He died 6 5th mo.
1693 aged 61. At his death he left half of Prospect Farm to his son Enoch, the other half to the

younger sons who, however, sold their share to Enoch.
The latter two also sold on 9 Dec. 1695, to Matthew
Grange of Burlington County, yeoman, 100 acres which
their father had bought of Percival Tole [Towle] 26
8th mo. 1691.[7]

It has been claimed that William Yardley was a
grandson of a Sir John Drake and grand-nephew of Sir
George Yeardley (ca. 1587-1627), Governor of Virginia.[8] While I have had no opportunity to investigate this matter thoroughly, I am exceedingly skeptical of any connection between the Yeardleys of
London and the Yardleys of Staffordshire; even more
so of any connection with a Sir John Drake of whom
I can say nothing.

    Issue: surname Yardley
i.   Enoch, eldest son, came with parents in
       1682; served in the Assembly in 1699;
       had certificate from Falls Monthly Meeting
       dated 1 10th mo. 1697 to m. Mary Fletcher,
       daughter of Robert Fletcher of Abington.
       Enoch d. 23 11th mo. 1702/3, the same day
       his brother Thomas died, after which Ma-
       ry m. at Falls Meeting House, 17 11th
       mo. 1704, as third wife, Joseph Kirkbride
       on whom see *supra*, pages 268-272. It is
       clear that an epidemic, probably of small-
       pox, raged in southern Bucks in the win-
       ter of 1702/3, and wiped out the entire
       Yardley family except for the two widows
       who survived to remarry.
       Issue: surname Yardley
    1. Jane, b. 14 9th mo. 1698, d. 23 9th mo.
       1698.
    2. Mary, b. 19 12th mo. 1699/1700, d. 19
       12th mo. 1702/3, her third birthday.
    3. Sarah, b. and d. 20 12th mo. 1702/3, the
       day after sister Mary's death. With
       her, the descendants of William Yard-
       ley were all dead.
ii.   Thomas, came with parents in 1682; m. 6 9th
       mo. 1700 Hester Baker (so Falls record)
       or Blaker (so Davis), and he d. 23 11th
       mo. 1702/3, the day on which his brother
       Enoch died. She had leave to m. (2) at
       Falls Monthly Meeting, 4 8th mo. 1704,
       William Browne of Chichester.
       Issue: surname Yardley
    1. William, b. 14 6th mo. 1701, d. 14 1st

mo. 1702/3, exactly 19 mos. old.
2. Hester, b. 18 7th mo. 1702, d. 9 11th
   mo. 1702/3.
iii. William, came with parents in 1682; d. unm.
     12 12th mo. 1702/3, not 1792/3, as Davis,
     has it.

The property then descended, upon the extinction
of William Yardley's line, to his brother, Thomas
Yardley, of The Beeches, Rushton, Staffordshire, who
had a son Thomas. The latter, supplied with powers
of attorney from his father and his brother Samuel
Yardley, arrived in America in 1704, but he did not
sell the property until 25 5th mo. 1710, and then to
Joseph Janney who was not his cousin, of course, being nephew to Jane Heath Yardley. Joseph Janney was
a "straw man," for he sold the property to Thomas
Yardley Jr. on 14 6th mo. 1710.
Having thus acquired title to the property in
his own right, he lived there until his death in
1756, having had a distinguished career as judge in
Bucks County 1725-1741 and having served in the Assembly in 1715 and 1722. He married, as Davis dates
it, in 12th mo. 1706/7, Ann Biles, born 14 2nd mo.
1685, daughter of William and Johannah (-----) Biles
and on her see *supra*, pp. 57 f. This marriage was
reported at Falls Monthly Meeting as contrary to
discipline but not until 3 10th mo. 1707, which is
sufficient to raise doubt that it had taken place
as early as the preceding February. Not quite all
Yardleys of Bucks County were descended from this
couple.

Issue: surname Yardley or Yeardley
i.   Mary, b. 4 8th mo. 1707, d. 1767; m. 30
      12th mo., probably 1727/8 rather than
      1728/9, reported to have m., at Falls,
      6 1st mo. of that year, Amos Janney, b.
      15 11th mo. 1701/2, of Loudoun Co., Va.,
      but d. Fairfax Co., Va., 1747, eldest
      son of Abel and Elizabeth (Stacy) Janney,
      on whom see p. 594.
ii.   Jane, b. 20 11th mo. 1709, m. 2 5th mo.
      1729, Francis Hague of Loudoun County,
      Virginia.
iii. Rebecca, b. 27 7th mo. 1710, d. unm.
iv.   Sarah, b. 30 7th mo. 1712 or perhaps 1720,
      as sometimes said, but in view of her

marriage date, 1712 is better; m. (1) 6
9th mo. 1731, Benjamin Canby, (2) David
Kinsey.
v.   Joyce, b. 3 10th mo. 1714, d. unm.
vi.   William, b. 25 3rd mo. 1716 [so Davis] or
      24 1st mo. 1717 [so HEAQG 1041]; m. (1)
      20 4th mo. 1748, Ann Budd of New Jersey,
      d. 1753; (2) 31 3rd mo. 1756, Sarah Kirk-
      bride, d. 21 1st mo. 1783, daughter of
      Mahlon and Mary (Sotcher) Kirkbride, on
      whom see *supra* , p. 271.
          Issue: surname Yardley
              by first wife Ann Budd
      1. Ann, b. 10 4th mo. 1749, d. 25 2nd mo.
         1815; m. Upper Makefield Meeting House
         26 1st mo. 1769 Abraham Warner, son of
         Joseph Warner.
      2. Sarah, b. 17 2nd mo. 1751, d. 9 1st mo.
         1786, m. 19 11th mo/ 1772, Timothy Tay-
         lor, son of Benjamin Taylor.
      3. Margaretta, b. 6 12th mo. 1752, m. 15
         4th mo. 1773 Stacy Potts of Trenton.
              by second wife Sarah Kirkbride
      4. Mary, b. 27 1st mo. 1757, m. 16 9th mo.
         1779, Jonathan Woolston.
      5. Hannah, b. 19 3rd mo. 1758, m. 21 10th
         mo. 1779 John Stapler.
      6. Achsah, b. 17 2nd mo. 1760, m. 24 4th
         mo. 1794, Thomas Stapler.
      7. Letitia, b. 12 7th mo. 1762, m. 12 9th
         mo. 1782 Jonathan Wills Jr. of Phila-
         delphia.
      8. Thomas, b. 2 10th mo. 1763, m. 19 10th
         mo. 1786 Susanna Brown.
      9. Mahlon, b. 17 7th mo. 1765, m. 1787
         Elizabeth Brown.
      10. Samuel, b. 28 2nd mo. 1767, d. 27 3rd
          mo. 1778.
      11. William, b. 8 6th mo. 1769, m. 1793
          Elizabeth Field.
      12. Joseph, b. 19 3rd mo. 1771, m. 1798
          Sarah Field.
vii. Hannah, b. 13 11th mo. 1718/9, d. unm.
viii. Thomas, b. 1 11th mo. 1720/1, d.s.p. 12
      3rd mo. 1803; had leave to m., Falls,
      2 8th mo. 1751, Mary Field, b. 21 Feb.
      1730/1 rec. at Falls 7 11th mo. 1753,
      d. by 1758, daughter of Robert Field

(Benjamin, Robert, Robert) by his wife Mary
Taylor. His will calls him of Newtown (BW
File 2879). It may be that some of the items
assigned below to the son of Richard Yardley belong to him. Indeed, he may have been
the husband of Elizabeth Poole who married
her at Middletown Meeting, 13 4th mo. 1758.

ix. Samuel, b. 16 4th mo. 1723, d. 12 8th mo. 1726.
x.   Samuel, b. 13 7th mo. 1729, d., according to
     Davis, in 1759 with a wife named Jane. He
     was dismissed 7 11th mo. 1753 for disunity,
     the very day his sister-in-law, Mary (Field)
     Yardley, was received at Falls Meeting. It
     is probable he was the man who m. at Christ
     Church, 28 Nov. 1759, Jane Logan. If he did
     die in 1759, he had a short marriage.

UNPLACED YARDLEYS

Though not the son of Thomas and Ann (Biles) Yardley, a Richard Yardley, miller, of Solesberry, who
made his will 7 Jan. 1761, probated 4 March 1761
(BW File 1061), probably was a relative, perhaps even
a younger brother. The will mentions sons Thomas,
Samuel, Richard, daughter Mary, wife of Joseph Harvey, and appoints as executors wife Mary and sons
Enoch, William and Benjamin. The son Enoch, who m.
at Christ Church, 4 April 1768, Mary Lambwood, d.
testate, leaving a will dated 21 Oct. 1773, probated
17 Nov. 1773 (BW File 1416), calling him of Newtown,
mentions wife Mary, perhaps pregnant; esteemed brother Samuel and Richard Yardley, executors. His brother Richard was probably the man who m. at Christ
Church, 16 Nov. 1759, Lucy Stackhouse. Either his
brother Thomas or the man mentioned at the top of
this page, had leave to m. at Middletown, 5 4th mo.
1758, Elizabeth Poole, and did m. her on 13 4th mo.
1758. Some Thomas Yardley was dismissed, 2 6th mo.
1758, from Falls Meeting for military association.
A Thomas Yardley, the same or another, was likewise
dismissed for disunity, 6 5th mo. 1767.

EXCURSUS ON HEATH

As has been intimated above, the wives of William
Yardley, Thomas Janney and James Harrison, were all
named Heath, undoubtedly sisters, and Janney's wife
was late of Horton, a parish not quite three miles
northwest of Leek in northern Staffordshire. The
Yardleys have been treated above. As the Janneys
and the Harrisons have been discussed adequately in

print, no full scale account of them is necessary
but it would be well to present an abstract of what
is known for reference purposes.
 The three sisters probably had at least one brother who was the father of Andrew Heath, the erstwhile servant of William Yardley who is treated as
a *Welcome* claimant, *supra*, pages 236 f.

A. JANNEY

 The Janney family is the subject of two good
articles by Miles White Jr., one, "The Quaker Janneys" (*Publications of the Southern Historical Association* 8:119-128, 196-211, 274-286); the other,
"Thomas Janney, Provincial Councillor" (PMHB 27:
212-237), from which articles the following has been
abstracted.
 I. Randle or Randall Janney, mentioned in son's
will.
 II. Thomas Janney of Stiall, Cheshire, will dated 23 Sept. 1602.
 III. Randle or Randall Janney, buried 30 Oct.
1613, married Ellen Alrodd.
 IV. Thomas Janney, baptized 27 June 1605, died
17 12th mo. 1677; married 3 Sept. 1625 Elizabeth
Worthington, died 19 12th mo. 1681/2, both buried
in Mobberley Friends graveyard, Cheshire.
 V. Thomas Janney, baptized 11 Jan. 1634, came
to America with wife Margery on the *Endeavour* of
London from Stiall, Cheshire, arriving 29 7th mo.
1683, bringing also the children: Jacob, Thomas,
Abel, Joseph, and servants: John Neild for 5 years,
Hannah Falkner for 4 years. Thomas Janney married
24 9th mo. 1660 at James Harrison's in Pownal Fee,
Margery Heath, late of Horton, co. Stafford, and
she died between 1697 and 1700. He was a distinguished minister among Friends, travelled widely
for religious purposes, and while on such a trip
died in Cheshire, 12 12th mo. 1696/7, buried in
the Mobberley Friends graveyard in Cheshire, aged
63.
 Issue: surname Janney
 i. Jacob, b. Pownall Fee, Cheshire, 18 3rd mo.
    1662, bur. Bucks Co., 6 8th mo. 1708; he
    m. at Falls Monthly Meeting, 26 10th mo.
    1705, Mary Hough, b. Bucks, 6 7th mo. 1684,
    d. 21 11th mo. 1711/2, daughter of John
    and Hannah (-----) Hough, and she m. (2)
    2 3rd mo. 1710, at Falls, John Fisher.

Issue: surname Janney
1. Thomas, b. 27 12th mo. 1707/8, d. 8 4th
   mo. 1788; m. Wrightstown, 28 10th mo.
   1732, Martha Mitchell. This marriage
   is shown by White but is not in the
   printed Wrightstown marriages.
ii. Martha, b. Cheadle, 17 5th mo. 1665, d. at
   Cheadle Holme, 4 12th mo. 1665/6, bur. at
   Mobberley.
iii. Elizabeth, b. Pownall Fee, 15 11th mo. 1666/7,
   d. 17 11th mo. 1666/7, bur. Mobberley.
iv. Thomas, b. Pownall Fee, 5 12th mo. 1667/8, m.
   in Bucks Co., Rachell Pownall, on whom see
   supra, p. 428.
v. Abel, b. Mobberley, 29 10th mo. 1671, m. New
   Jersey, 1700, Elizabeth Stacy, b. Dorehouse,
   Yorkshire, 17 8th mo. 1673, daughter of
   Mahlon and Rebecca (Ely) Stacy.
   Issue: surname Janney
   1. Amos, b. 15 11th mo. 1701/2, d. Fairfax
      Co., Va., 1747; m. 1727/8 Mary Yardley.
      b. 4 8th mo.1707, d. 1767, daughter of
      Thomas and Ann (Biles) Yardley, on whom
      see pp. 590 f.
   2. Rebeckah, b. 9 9th mo. 1706, d. Wilmington,
      Del.; m. Joseph Poole, b. 1704, d. 1762.
   3. Mahlon, b. 18 2nd mo. 1706.
   4. Thomas, m. 1735 Hannah Biles, daughter of
      William and Sarah (Langhorn) Biles, on
      whom see p. 57.
   5. Jacob, b. 10 4th mo. 1710, d. Delaware,
      14 11th mo. 1782; m. at Kennet, 13 6th
      mo. 1740, Elizabeth Levis.
   6. Abel, m. (1) by 7 5th mo. 1742 Elizabeth
      Biles?; "to Pertomock"; (2) at Swede's
      Church, Philadelphia, 31 March 1755,
      Elizabeth Meredith, and he d. Loudoun
      Co., Va., 12th mo. 1797.
   7. Elizabeth, m. (1) 22 10th mo. 1737, John
      Stackhouse; (2) Christ Church, 21 Jan.
      1745, David Wilson.
vi. Joseph, b. Pownall Fee, 26 1st mo. 1675/6,
   d. ca. 1729; m. Falls, 18 6th mo. 1703,
   Rebeckah Biles, b. 27 10th mo. 1680, the
   daughter of William and Johannah (-----)
   Biles, on whom see p. 57.
   Issue: surname Janney
   1. Martha, m. N.J., Nov. 1732, Nicholas Par-
      ker.

2. Ann, d. by 1729.
3. Abel, d. Loudoun Co., Va., 1774; m. Falls,
   2 8th mo. 1733, Sarah Baker.
4. William, d. Loudoun Co., Va., 1791; m. at
   Falls, 26 7th mo. 1739, Elizabeth Moon,
   b. 16 10th mo. 1719, daughter of Roger
   and Ann (Nutt) Moon.
5. Jacob, d. Loudoun Co., Va., 3 8th mo. 1786;
   m. 20 3rd mo. 1742, Hannah Inglesden.
6. Sarah, d. Loudoun Co., Va., after 1797,
   m. before 3 9th mo. 1742, John Hough.

B. HARRISON-PEMBERTON

Some information on the Harrisons appears in the articles on the Janneys cited above, but many primary records of the family are contained in the *Submission* Log and in Bucks Arrivals. There is a lengthy article on the Pembertons, with their Harrison connections, in John W. Jordan, *Colonial and Revolutionary Families of Pennsylvania* (New York 1911), 1:276-315. See also J. H. Battle, *History of Bucks County, Pennsylvania* 912-914. Some material bearing on the Pennsylvania Pembertons is in Walter K. Watkins, "The Pemberton Family" (NEHGR 46:393-398), and also in Sarah Elizabeth Titcomb, *Early New England People: Some Account of the Ellis, Pemberton, etc., and Allied Families* (Boston 1882), pp. 52-56 on the Pennsylvania Pembertons. There is nothing on the Pennsylvania family in John R. Totten, "The Genealogical Record of the Rev. Ebenezer[3] Pemberton (1704/5-1777)" (NYGBR 54:2000-226).

The apposite entries in the Log of the *Submission* are as follows:

James Harrison	54	Ann Harrison	58
Agness Harrison	80	Richd Radclife	21
Robt Bond	14	Joseph Steward	14½[9]
phinehas pemberton	32½	phebe pemberton	22½
Abigal pemberton	02½	Ralph pemberton	70
Joseph mather	18	Joseph pemberton	16 weeks
Lydia Wharmby		Elizabeth Breadbury	16
Allis Dickenson		Jane Lyon	16½

The following appears in Bucks Arrivals:

James Harrison of Bolton in the County of Lancaster Shoomaker aged about 54 yeares & Ann his wife aged about 61 yeares sailed away from Liuerpoole towne side the 5th day of the 7th month

1682 in the Ship Submission of liuerpoole the master James Settle arriued att Chaptank in maryland
the 2nd day of the 9th month 1682 & at Apoquimene
in this Province the 15th day of the 11th month.
[Children] Phebe his Daughter & wife to Phinehas
Pemberton [Free person] Agness Harrison ye mother
of the s^d James Harrison aged about 81 yeares Came
at the aforesd time & arriued in maryland at the
aforesd time & in this province the 9th of the
[faded] 1682. [Servants] Joseph Steward his servant or apprentice to serue according to agreemt
with his parents. Allis Dickerson & Jane Lyon to
serue each of them 4 years wages is passage meate
drink apparel & land accustomed free from the time
of theire arriual after the expiration of foure
yeares. [elsewhere free persons] Lydia Wharmby of
Bolton [and] Robt Bond son of Thomas Bond of Wad-
dicar hall [Woodacre Hall] near Garstang aged a-
bout 15 or 16 yeares being left by his father to
the tuition of the sd James Harrison.

Immanuel Harrison, of whom little is known but
his name, married a woman named Agnes who, as his
widow, came on the *Submission* in 1682 and died in
Bucks County, 6 6th mo. 1687.   As her age is given
in both the *Submission* Log and in Bucks Arrivals as
about 81, she was born ca. 1601.   Besides their
second child James, shown below, they had also an
eldest child Anne, a third child Robert, and a fourth
Mary who married Joseph Endon and had two daughters:
Mary, wife of John Clark, and Margaret, wife of John
Walker.

Their son James Harrison, born ca. 1628, came also
on the *Submission* in 1682, aged about 54, then a
shoemaker though he was afterwards employed by William
Penn as steward of Pennsbury Manor.   As stated, he
brought with him his widowed mother, his wife Ann
Heath, born 13 12th mo. 1624, died 5 1st mo. 1690,
whom he had married 1 5th mo. 1655, when he was of
Kendall, Westmoreland.   Note that if the birth date
reported is right, Ann Heath Pemberton's age in 1682
was 58, as stated in the *Submission* Log, and not 61,
as her son-in-law, Phineas Pemberton set down in the
Bucks Arrivals.   The Harrisons' son Joseph, born 20
4th mo. 1662, was already dead by 1665, and so were
any other children the couple might have had, so
that the only child who accompanied the parents to
Pennsylvania was the daughter Phebe, born 7 2nd mo.
1660, already married to Phineas Pemberton.

Some of the Pemberton data given in the *Submission* Log appear on pages 595 f. The following is the apposite passage in Bucks Arrivals:

Phinehas Pemberton of Bolton aforesaid grocer aged about 33 yeares & his wife Phebe aged about 23 yeares both Came in the ship [one line cancelled and illegible] Submission & arriued in maryland the 2nd day of ye 9th month 1682 as afforesaid. Ralph Pemberton father of the said Phinehas Pemberton aged 72 yeares arriued in maryland in the Ship & at the time aforesaid. Ralph Pemberton, Phebe Pemberton, Joseph & Abigall Pemberton arriued in this Riuer from maryland the 9th day of the 3 month 1683. [From Children's column] Abigal about 3 years of age Joseph not one year of age. [From Servants' column] William Smith seruant to the sd Phinehas Pemberton came in the Ship friends adventure ariued the 28 day of the 7th month 1682 to serue 4 yeares wages is passage meat drink apparrel dureing the term & land accustomed free ye 28 of the 7th month 1686. [The following appears immediately after the foregoing but with a line pointing to Ralph Pemberton's name] Joseph Mather & Elizabeth Bradbury servants to Phines [sic] Pemberton to serue each 4 yeares wages is pas meat drink apparel dureing the term & land accustomed free at the expiration of 4 yeares from the time of theire arrival.

The Pemberton pedigree would therefore appear to be as follows:

I. William Pemberton,[10] who died at Aspull, Lancashire, 26 Nov. 1642, married 10 Dec. 1602, Ann ----- who died 23 Dec. 1642.
Issue: surname Pemberton
i. Alice, d. at Aspull, 29 11th mo. 1675.
ii. Margery, d. 1670.
iii. Ralph, on whom see further.
iv. Ellen, m. before 4 Dec. 1674 and doubtless long before that, John Allred, and d. in England 22? Dec. 1684, having had six children:

1. Alice.
2. Phineas.
3. John, who m. and had issue.
4. Owen, b. 1674.
5. Theophilus, b. 1686.

6. Solomon, b. 1689. If the date of
   the mother's death be right, then
   the birthdates of the last two
   children must be wrong or they were
   not her children.

II. **Ralph Pemberton**, born at Aspull, parish of
Wigan, Lancashire, 3 Jan. 1611, died in Bucks County, Pennsylvania, 17 5th mo. 1687, having come to
America on the *Submission* in 1682 with the
Harrison-Pemberton party. His age was then 71 but
the *Submission* Log gives it as 70 and Bucks Arrivals as 72. This is one of the few instances where
averaging two errors will reach the truth! He married on 2 Sept. 1648, Margaret Seddon, who died on
2 Sept. 1655, daughter of Thomas Seddon of Warrington. Besides the son Phineas shown below, they had
a son Joseph born 12 2nd mo. 1652, died 3 6th mo.
1655, and perhaps one or two more not recorded.

III. **Phineas or Phinehas Pemberton** was born in
the parish of Wigan, Lancashire, 30 11th mo. 1650,
died at a plantation called Bolton in Bucks County,
Pennsylvania, 1 1st mo. 1702. He married, first,
on 1 11th mo. 1676/7, at the house of John Haydock
in Coppull near Standish (Hardshaw Monthly Meeting),
Phebe Harrison, born 7 2nd mo. 1660, died in Bucks
County, 30 8th mo. 1696, daughter of James and Ann
(Heath) Harrison who were of Stiall-Green at the
time of her marriage; second, under the care of
Falls Monthly Meeting, 18 3rd mo. 1699, Alice
Hodgson, died 28 6th mo. 1711, daughter of Robert
Hodgson, late of Rhode Island, deceased, and she had
married, second, as second wife, in 1704, Thomas
Bradford.

Issue: surname Pemberton, all by first wife
i.   Ann, b. 22 8th mo. 1677, d. 3 5th mo.
     1682, bur. at Langtree, 11 miles south-
     west of Bolton, Lancashire. She narrowly
     missed coming to America.
ii. Abigail, b. 14 4th mo. 1680, s. 2 9th mo.
     1750, bur. 4 9th mo. 1750 at Abington,
     m. 14 9th mo. 1704, Stephen Jenkins of
     Abington, b. Tenby, Pembrokeshire, Wales,
     d. 14 9th mo. 1761, bur. at Abington,
     son of William and Elizabeth (Griffith)
     Jenkins.
iii. Joseph, b. 11 3rd mo. 1682, d. 9th mo.
     1702; came to America on the *Submission*
     "not one year old," as his father wrote.

iv. Israel, b. 20 12th mo. 1684/5, d. 18 or 19
    Jan. 1753 in 69th year; m. 12 2nd mo. 1710
    Rachel Read, b. 1691, d. 24 2nd mo. 1765,
    daughter of Charles Read by his wife Amy
    Child. From this couple descend all of
    the later persons named Pemberton.
v. Samuel, b. 3 12th mo. 1686, d. 23 11th mo.
    1691/2.
vi. Phoebe, b. 26 12th mo. 1689, d. 30 3rd mo.
    1699.
vii.Priscilla, b. 23 2nd mo. 1692, d. 29 2nd mo.
    1771; m. 1709 Isaac Waterman, d. 16 11th
    mo. 1748/9, aet. 67/8/-.
viii. Ralph, b. 20 7th mo. 1694, d. 18 9th mo.
    1694.
ix. Phineas Jennings, b. 17 2nd mo. 1696, d., it
    is said, in 1701.

NOTES

[1]On the Yardleys see Thomas W. Yardley, *Genealogy of the Yardley Family* (Philadelphia 1881): DHBC, 2nd ed., 3:122-126; Arthur Edwin Bye, *A Friendly Heritage along the Delaware* (New York 1959), 156-162.

[2]PGM 23:46.

[3]1 PA 1:45.

[4]HEAQG 1041; PGM 23:46.

[5]Old Style or New Style? The purchaser was Edward Shippen.

[6]PGM 23:75.

[7]1 NJA 21:486.

[8]Sir George Yeardley originated in London. See DAB 20:605 f.; DNB 21:1223 f., *Appleton's Cyclopaedia of American Biography* 6:640.

[9]On him see *supra*, p. 73.

[10]Walter K. Watkins (NEHGR 46:392-398) thought (p. 392) that Phineas Pemberton's father Ralph was a second son of Ralph and Frances Pemberton of St. Albans, but H. F. Waters, *Genealogical Gleanings in England* (Boston 1901), 1:772, who prints (330 f., 334, 771 f.) abstracts of the St. Albans Pemberton wills, says that Watkins had changed his mind and thought that Ralph was a son of William.

ADDENDA

No sooner had the preceding page been typed in its final form than there arrived in a single mail communications bringing to my attention the names of six additional *Welcome* claimants hitherto not considered, and in the subsequent research concerning them still another was turned up. Unfortunately, it has been impossible to devote as much time to these claimants as in the case of the others, and their respective accounts cannot be inserted at the proper place into the alphabetical sequence. They are, however, taken into consideration in the Recapitulation in the Introduction and the names on these pages have been included in the Index.

HOWELL, WILLIAM   *improbable*

This claim was first called to my attention by Mr. Larry F. Mikesell of Mapleton, Iowa, who referred me also to Mr. Jefferson Hayes-Davis of Colorado Springs. Their assistance is gratefully acknowledged.

Who first made the claim I do not know but I have found it in the *Twentieth Century Biographical Dictionary of Notable Americans* (Vol. 5, unpaged, under "Richard Howell"). The father of the New Jersey Governor Richard Howell (1754-1803) is correctly identified as Ebenezer Howell, and then the governor is said to be "a descendant of William Howell, who came over with William Penn on the *Welcome*." Both Mr. Mikesell and Mr. Hayes-Davis assure me that the claim is also made by the late Morgan Howell's *Howell Genealogy* (1942), a work I have not seen. Therein William Howell is described as father to Ebenezer Howell (1727-1790) who was, surely, the father of the governor, and the latter was, in turn, grandfather of Varina Howell, second wife of the Confederate President Jefferson Davis. Mr. Hayes-Davis is a grandson of President and Mrs. Davis.

At first sight it seems improbable that a man old enough to have been a *Welcome* passenger, even one only a child at the crossing in 1682, could have been father to a son born as late as 1727. There are, to be sure, instances of men fathering sons at an advanced age, but this is probably not one of them. In Josiah Granville Leach's *Genealogical and Biographical Memorials of the Reading, Howell, Yerkes, Watts, Latham and Elkins Families* (Philadelphia

1898), already cited above on p.258 in connection
with the Thomas Howell family which is unrelated to
this William Howell, there is (p. 139) allusion to
William Howell of Castlebight, Wales, who, according
to Mr. Leach, is said by others to have come with
William Penn and "is claimed by at least one authority," not identified by Mr. Leach, to have been
ancestor of Major Richard Howell, the Governor of
New Jersey. "Such claim would seem to be an error."
Mr. Leach then alludes to William Howell's will
but without stating its date or location, and says
it makes no mention of a son. He then goes on to
identify the governor's parents as Ebenezer Howell
and Sarah Bond, his grandparents as Reynold and
Mary Howell. Whether the grandparents were as he
states I do not know, but the parents were certainly
Ebenezer and Sarah, and Sarah was probably a Bond.
    Mr. Walter Lee Sheppard has found for me the will
of William Howell of Cheltenham Township, Philadelphia County, Pennsylvania, yeoman, dated 20 12th mo.
called Feb. 1709[/10], probated 21 April 1710
(PhW C:202, but a photograph of the original will
was examined). Specific bequests of household
goods are made to daughters Margaret Howell, Eales
[doubtless Alice is meant] Howell, Mary Howell [and
overwritten is Edward], Hannah Howell, Deborah Howell, son-in-law John Edwards; wife Mary Howell, the
plantation in Cheltenham of 400 acres more or less,
with all goods and chattels and cattle not specifically willed to the others. After wife's death to
be divided among daughters above named; if any die
without marriage or children, her share to be divided among the other daughters. Wife Mary is named
executrix with assistance of Daniel Thomas; overseers: Samuel Carr [this has been read as Cart but
there is an ink smudge], John Edwards, Daniel Thomas and Thomas Canby, all of Philadelphia. The will
is clearly signed in a good hand but the will itself was written by another. Inventory dated 7 April 1710 was made by Daniel Potts and Isaac Knight
and totalled £116/1/2. The witnesses to the will
were David Potts, Thomas Potts, Thomas Edward [by
mark], William Hugh [by mark] and Daniel Thomas.
    This testator was certainly incapable of being
the father or the grandfather of Ebenezer Howell
born in 1727, so that it is clear that, whoever
was the father of Ebenezer Howell, it was not this
William, and this William was therefore certainly

not an ancestor of Governor Richard Howell.

On this matter we should cite the will of the governor's brother: Lewis Howell of the Town of Newark [Delaware], practitioner of physick, dated 8 March 1776, probated 25 Aug. 1778 (NC 89), which names brother Richard, mother Sarah, father Ebenezer, sister Susannah, and makes uncle Elnathar [sic] Davis an executor. Gilbert Cope's Sharpless Genealogy prints a sketch of the governor (pp. 324-6) and says (p. 204) that his father Ebenezer was born at sea ca. 1727 and died at Shiloh [Delaware] in 1790. Ebenezer "is thought to have been" a son of Thomas Howell of Wales, and a Reynold Howell of Newcastle County, Delaware, was a relative. We may state that if the father was a Thomas Howell, he was at least not the Thomas Howell discussed above (pp. 258 f.) as a *Welcome* claimant.

The governor's dates as given above come from the encyclopaedia cited. *Appleton's Cyclopaedia of American Biography* 3:285 says he was born in 1753 and died 28 April 1802. The *Dictionary of American Biography* 9:304 agrees with the latter death date but has the same birth date as the former. It ought to be relatively easy to settle the death date by consulting a newspaper obituary but we have had no opportunity to do so. There is an article by Daniel Agnew on the governor in *Pennsylvania Magazine of History and Biography* 22:221-230, but nothing is said there concerning the ancestry beyond the fact that the father was Ebenezer.

We have found no record of the ship on which William Howell came to America but in the *Pennsylvania Genealogical Magazine* 23:116, Mrs. Roach incidentally remarks of Micah Thomas that he had come as a servant to William Howell. The date there given, 24 3rd mo. 1688, is not that of arrival but of the granting of administration to Micah Thomas on his father's estate. The proof that Micah Thomas had come as William Howell's servant is in the Board of Property minutes dated 23 6th mo. 1703 (2 PA 19:396) which again offers nothing on the date of arrival or the vessel. William Howell had been a purchaser under Lewis David's grant, date of record rather than of purchase, 5 8th mo. 1702 (*ibid.* 328). William Howell is shown as a member of Abington Monthly Meeting in a passage of its minutes quoted above on p. 482 in connection with William Smith.

PUSEY, CALEB   *possible*
PUSEY, ANN (STONE) (WORLEY), his wife   *possible*
PUSEY, ANN, his daughter   *possible*
WORLEY, HENRY, his stepson   *possible*
WORLEY, FRANCIS, his stepson   *possible*

My attention was first called to this claim by Mr.
George Ely Russell who had noticed it in *Kentucky
Ancestors*, Vol. 2, No. 1 (July 1966), p. 13, where
Mrs. C. R. Davis of Lansing, Illinois, is concerned
primarily with the Worley family of Kentucky which
she traces back to a Francis Worley of Chester County, Pennsylvania. She says that Francis Worley came
to America with his brother Henry Worley, their
mother Ann (Stone)(Worley) Pusey and their stepfather Caleb Pusey, on the *Welcome* which she describes
as the nineteenth ship sent by Penn in 1682. Correspondence has been had with Mrs. Davis and led ultimately to Mrs. Mary S. Patterson of Swarthmore, Pa.,
who answered my letter of inquiry addressed to the
Caleb Pusey House, Inc., an organization which has
obtained title to and restored the house of Caleb
Pusey. Mrs. Patterson kindly supplied a printed
sheet giving the results of her own research on the
Pusey-Worley family, including a fac-simile of the
marriage certificate of Caleb and Ann. The statements made on this sheet are in every case supported
by allusion to primary evidence of a documentary nature. For this reason the remainder of this sketch
rests heavily on the sheet.

The earliest record of Caleb Pusey in America appears to be the death record of his daughter Ann in
12th mo. 1682/3, not more than three months after
the *Welcome* arrived, but we have not located a
ship record or any document that proves his presence
in America before the *Welcome* arrived. It may be
pointed out that though I have myself not made any
detailed search for such a document, Mrs. Patterson,
whose competence is unquestioned, has obviously done
so and thus far found nothing. It therefore seems
entirely possible that the Pusey-Worley party did
come on the *Welcome*, and for reasons that will presently appear, there is reason to think that the verdict might well have been "probable" rather than
"possible" but I prefer to be cautious.

For many years Caleb Pusey was the manager of the
well-known Chester Mills. The basic mill of this
establishment was brought, framed, on the *Welcome* by

Richard Townsend, whose testimony on this point is
quoted *in extenso*, above on p. 498--see also *Historical Papers and Addresses of the Lancaster County
Historical Society* 2:17. Though the mill was brought
framed on the *Welcome* and "after some time" set up
on Chester Creek by Townsend, this does not really
prove that Pusey came on the same ship. Townsend
may not have begun work on the erection of the mill
until he knew that the prospective manager was on
hand, but it is also possible that "after some time"
means that Townsend was busy with his own concerns
in the early weeks after the arrival.

On the other hand there is further confirmation
of the presence of Pusey in Pennsylvania in 1682
in a document not mentioned by Mrs. Patterson. This
is a record of the Board of Property not made until
20 7th mo. 1716 (2 PA 19:610 and 674), where it is
recorded that Isaac Taylor of the County of Chester,
Surveyor, produces certificates of Caleb Pusey and
Henry Worley [both then still living], declaring
that William Berkingham and John Berkingham came as
servants in or about 1682 and served their time to
Joseph Richards. This does not necessarily have
any significance as to the ship on which Pusey,
Worley or the two Berkinghams, came, one ship or
more than one, but it does seem to show that Pusey
and Worley had arrived in or about 1682.

In any case, Caleb Pusey was the son of William
Bartholomew *alias* Pusie, as the latter signed his
will in 1657. The reason for the double name has
not been discovered, but William's wife was Margaret and they were of Upper Lambourn, a hamlet west
of Oxford and Wantage in Berkshire, close to the
Wiltshire border. They had five sons and four
daughters; of the sons, Caleb and John were First
Purchasers, having each bought 250 acres on 10-11
8br 1681 (2 PA 19: 285 f.). John Pusey was described as of London, Dyer, and his widow Frances
Pusey gave a power-of-attorney on 2 Feb. 1692
[probably 1692/3] to convey John's 250 acres to
Caleb (2 PA 19:285 f.). Of the five sons of
William and Margaret, only Caleb crossed the sea
but it is generally assumed that John was the
father of Caleb's two nephews who afterwards came
to Pennsylvania and joined their uncle, being the
progenitors of all the later Puseys of the third
generation in Pennsylvania, since Caleb lacked
sons.

Caleb was born in 1651 and was a lastmaker by trade, and an early writer of religious papers published by the Friends. At Devonshire House Monthly Meeting on 27 3rd mo. 1681, "Caleb Pizey of Buttolph without Bishopsgate, London," married Anne Worley, widow, and she signed the certificate with her first husband's surname and not, as was usual with Friends, her new married name. Of the sixteen witnesses to the certificate, only John Pizey and Henry Stone had names showing obvious relationship to the parties. John was doubtless the brother of Caleb, and Henry Stone may have been Anne's father, or at least that was her father's name. She was then the widow of Henry Worley of Bedlam [Bethlehem], Parish of Bishopsgate, London, who had died in 1674.

The first child was the daughter Ann who must have come to America as an infant and died in Pennsylvania in 12th mo. 1682/3. Another Ann was born 12 1st mo. 1684/5 and she married on 5 1st mo. 1706/7 John Smith, and moved to London Grove, Chester County. They had a daughter Lydia Smith, who is mentioned in her grandfather's will. In 1738 she married Thomas Jackson and they had at least Ann who married Mordecai Cloud in 1757; Mary who married William Windle in 1761, and Caleb who married Hannah Bennett in 1765, all having issue.

Caleb Pusey's third daughter was Lydia, born 4 7th mo. 1689, married on the same day as her sister's marriage, that is, 5 1st mo. 1706/7, George Painter of Philadelphia.

Henry Worley, one of the stepsons, married Mary Vernon in 1699, and after close association with Caleb Pusey in the mill, of which he became a partner and chief miller, moved to Philadelphia where his administration papers were filed 25 Aug. 1727. A 1736 deed shows his surviving children in that year were Henry Worley, millwright of Potomack, Virginia; Nathan Worley of Chester, joyner; Ann Worley (Howell) Reynolds, wife of Henry Reynolds of West Nottingham, yeoman; and Mary Worley Gatchell, wife of Elisha Gatchell Jr., cordwainer of East Nottingham.

The other stepson, Francis Worley, married in 1693 Mary Brassey, daughter of Thomas Brassey, a First Purchaser of 5000 acres. A record in the minutes of the Board of Property dated 23 5th mo. 1705 (2 PA 19:458) shows that Thomas Brassey had two daughters: (a) Rebecca, wife of Thomas Thomson of Salem; (b) Mary, wife of Francis Worley. Francis Worley was a prominent surveyor who moved from the Conestoga area which became Lancaster County to what is now York County. Francis and Mary had at least sons Caleb and Daniel who are mentioned in Caleb Pusey's will; a daughter Rebeckah who came back to Chester Meeting from Conestoga in 1718 to marry John Hendricks. The wedding certificate shows signatures of Francis and Mary Worley, of their son Bracey [Brassey] and also Caleb and Susannah. About 1722 Susannah moved to the area of Plymouth Meeting where the trail is lost. Caleb Worley made his will in 1750, probated 1751 in Lancaster County.

As we have seen, Caleb Pusey had no son and the name would have died out with him but for the fact that his nephews Caleb Pusey Jr. and William Pusey came to America about 1700 and joined their uncle in the milling business, after which they moved to London Grove. William married Elizabeth Bowater on 5 9th mo. 1707, and they had John, born 1708, married Katherine Maris; William, born 1710/11, married Mary Passmore; Lydia, born 1713, married John Bailey; Joshua, born 1714, married Mary Lewis; Elizabeth, born 1716, married John Baldwin; Jane, born 1719, married Nathaniel Pennock; Mary, married 1742 Joseph Dixson; and Hannah, married 1750 George Carson.

Caleb Pusey Jr. married 5 9th mo. 1712 Prudence Carter, and had Caleb, born 1713, married Margaret -----; Robert, born 1715; Thomas, born 1718, married Mary Swayne; Margaret, born 1721, married John Perry; Ann, born 1723, married William Swayne; David, born 1726, married Sarah Dixson.

The will of Caleb Pusey Sr. of the Township of Marlboro, County of Chester, Pennsylvania, was signed on 2 1st mo. called March 1725/6, in the presence of Swaine, Wm Lowdon and Joseph Skeen. It leaves to the two stepsons Francis and Henry Worly £50 each; to dear granddaughter Susanna Parrish £10 when 20 or 21 or at marriage; the same to granddaughter Lydia Smith; to cousin [nephew] Caleb Pusey largest dictionary and 200 acres. Loving kinsmen William and Caleb Pusey are to be trustees; son-in-law John Smith to be sole executor. The exact date of Caleb Pusey's death seems to be in doubt. Robert Proud is cited for the date 14 1st mo. 1726/7, but the New Garden Meeting memorial says he died 25 12th mo. 1726/7. Mrs. Patterson merely says his wife

died in London Grove in 1725 and her husband about
a year later.

Caleb Pusey's house at 15 Race Street, Upland,
Delaware County, Pennsylvania, is said to have been
erected in 1683 and to be the only house still standing known to have been visited by William Penn.

WHARELY, DANIEL   *highly improbable*

Mrs. Patterson also informs me that members of
the Worley family whose ancestors are described in
the preceding sketch have sometimes claimed as a
Welcome passenger Daniel Wharely who spelled his
name in a variety of ways. He married on 4 9th mo.
1686 Mary Penington, younger half-sister of Gulielma Maria Springett, first wife of William Penn. On
the marriage certificate he is said to be described
as son of Henry and Ann Worley, late of Hunsden, co.
Hertford, and it has been concluded by Mrs. Patterson
with excellent reason that if this Daniel had been
a son of Caleb Pusey's wife, she would have been described in a different way. In 1686 Ann Stone was
Ann Pusey and was in America. It therefore becomes
probable that Daniel Wharely was a brother of Ann
Stone's first husband, Henry Worley of London, and
not his son.

In a Philadelphia deed dated 2 March 1714/15 [PhD
G-2, p. 252] the grantors are a group of persons de-
scribed as trustees of Letitia Penn Aubrey's real
estate holdings: William Aubrey, of London, merchant;
Daniel Wharely, Chalfont St. Gyles, co. Bucks, gent.;
Henry Gouldney of London, linen draper, and James
Logan, County of Philadelphia, gent.; grantee:
John Church. Daniel Wharley and wife Mary sold
land which Mary had purchased on 17-18 3rd mo. 1681
[2 PA 19:443]. On 19 3rd mo. 1725 the Board of
Property noted that Daniel Wharely of London, woolen
draper, had a grant from Penn of 3000 acres on 3-4
April 1695 [*ibid.* 730 f.], and it was noted that
Daniel Wharely Jr. had been eldest son and sold the
land but that there were other children, names not
given.

No record, however, has been found which shows
the presence of Daniel in America. It seems extremely improbable that a man who became Penn's
brother-in-law, though not so early as the time of
the *Welcome*'s crossing, could have been in Pennsylvania without leaving any trace of his presence
which has thus far come to light.

ADDENDUM ON ROBERT TURNER

Mr. Henry Hollingsworth, who possesses a copy of the records of the Friends Meeting at Lurgan, co. Armagh, Northern Ireland, has kindly supplied me with the following record of a Turner family of that meeting which may or may not pertain to that Robert Turner who came to America on the *Griffin*, as described above on p. 504.

Thomas Turner sonn of Robart Turner, of Turners towne in Northumberland [sic] in England and of Deborah his wife, was borne at Turnerstown aforesaid in the yeare, 1618 and about the second month ANNO DOMINI, 1652 he tooke to Wife, Ann the daughter of James Greer (of ye rock near Annick) in Cumberland [sic], aforesaid and of mary his wife who was borne at Annick aforesaid in the yeare, 1633, and had by her Children borne as followeth,

Deborah Turner first daughter of Thomas Turner and of Ann his wife was borne about Eighteenth day of the eleauenth month Anno Dom 1653:

Robart Turner first sonn of Thomas Turner, and of Ann his Wife was borne in England, about ye Eighteenth day of the Eleauenth month Anno Domini, 1655, [Was he on the *Griffin*?]

Mabell Turner, . . . 1st month A.D. 1657 in England.

And about ye beginning of the first month in the yeare 1658, the said Thomas Turner with his wife and children (yt were liuing) came to ireland.

John Turner . . . born at Tougherraine in the County of Downe 4 1st mo. 1660. [P. 226 has the place of birth as in Parish of Magherlin, co. Downe.]

Thomas Turner . . . borne Drummonically Parish of Sego Co Ardmagh 25 5th mo. 1662.

James . . . ditto 2 mo 1664.

Jacob . . . do. 26 2 mo. 1665.

Bethiah . . . borne at tearsoye or tearsoge [Torsoghe] Par of Shankell Co Ardmagh 20 12 mo 1667.

Mary . . . borne Lurgan Co Armagh, beginning of ye second month A.D. 1669.

Nathanniell Turner . . . Lurgan 18 11th mo. A.D. 1673.

Mr. Hollingsworth also has a copy of the 1664 Hearth

Tax for Shankill and Seagoe Parishes and finds Thomas Turner had a hearth and paid 2 shillings at Drumnescally.

ADDENDUM ON LEMUEL BRADSHAW

The same Lurgan Quaker minutes show that Lemuel Bradshaw, mentioned above on pp. 53 f., as a servant to the other Robert Turner, was the son of James and Ann Patterson Bradshaw of Drumoneycally.

ADDENDUM ON HAYHURST

The following information pertaining to the Hayhurst family as shown on p. 233 has been kindly furnished by Mr. Paul Hayhurst of Fairmont, West Virginia.

Mary Wiggins, the wife of John Hayhurst shown on this page, was first cousin once removed of her husband, being daughter of Bezaleel and Rachel Hayhurst Wiggins, as shown on p. 231. Mr. Hayhurst says they had seven children of whom two were sons Bezaleel and Benajah.

Ruth Hayhurst and Joseph Warner removed about 1770 to Harford County, Maryland where they became wealthy farmers, were members of Deer Creek Meeting and are buried in the Friends Burying Ground at Darlington, Maryland.

James Hayhurst born in 1732 died in 1783. He removed to Maryland near Bel Air. Mr. Hayhurst credits him with six children named James, Hannah, Elizabeth, Sarah, Ruth and David, of whom four are mentioned in their mother's will quoted on p. 233. The younger James married Mary Warner and moved to Uniontown, Pa., then to Ohio. Elizabeth married Thomas Lacey and remained in Bucks County. Sarah married ----- Newberry as shown by the mother's will. David married Sarah Warner, sister of the Mary Warner who married his brother James, and they removed to what is now Fairmont, West Virginia, and had eight sons and two daughters.

ADDENDUM ON WILLIAM GIBSON

William Gibson, the eminent Quaker preacher and London haberdasher, was not a passenger on the *Welcome* but only lately have I discovered that anyone thought otherwise.

Born at Caton in Lancashire about 1629 to parents as yet unidentified, he married on 22 6th mo. 1662

Elizabeth, daughter of William Thompson of Crossmoor in Lancashire, and she survived him to die in Lombard Street, London, 29 5th mo. 1688 aged 58.   He died 20 Nov. 1684 aged 55, and his funeral has already been described above on p. 571 in connection with Thomas Wynne. William and Elizabeth (Thompson) Gibson had the following children:

i.   Rebecca, b. Sankey (Hardshaw Monthly Meeting rec.), 20 3rd mo. 1663.

ii.   John, b. there, 30 1st mo. 1665.

iii. William, b. ca. 1667-9; m. at Brewer's Hall 2 12th mo. 1698/9, Jane, daughter of Evan Thomas late of Awswestry, co. Salop, living in Castle Alley, Burchin Lane, London.

iv.   Hannah, b. ca. 1671, d. 21 11th mo. 1674/5 aged 3, of smallpox, bur. in Chequer Alley.

v.   Patience, b. 29 3rd mo. 1673 at Bull and Mouth St. within Aldersgate; d. Chester, Pa. 15 Nov. 1722 aged 48 years, 5 months, 15 days; m. at Penketh, Lancs., 27 11th mo. 1692, John Wright, bodice maker, b. at Warrington, Lancs., 15 2nd mo. 1667, d. in Hempfield Township, Lancaster Co., Pa., 1 Oct. 1749 aged 82 years, 5 months, 15 days, son of James and Susannah (Croudson) Wright. An account of this family was published by Walter Lee Sheppard in *The American Genealogist* 40 [1964] 35-42, who cites a work we have not seen, William and Thomas Evans, *Piety Promoted* (Philadelphia, new ed., 1854) 1:245. Mr. Sheppard's article is the source for all the biographical data on William Gibson. There is also an article on him in DNB 7:1166 f.

vi.   Elizabeth, b. 26 7th mo. 1676 in George Yard, Lombard Street, London, d. at the same place, 19 5th mo. 1677, aged 9 mos.

In the article just cited Mr. Sheppard pointed out that William Gibson was a First Purchaser of 500 acres (not 5,000 as stated in 1 PA 1:45) in Group 34, and then goes on to say: 'We conclude that he actually visited Pennsylvania either late in 1682 or early in 1683, for we find a warrant dated 12th of 4th month 1683 [W&S 1:387] of William

Penn's, "at the request of William Gibson, purchaser
of 500 acres, that I would grant him to take up his
lott in the City proportional to his purchase."'
Having read this at the time it was published, I
should have been alerted to the thought that there
lay in Mr. Sheppard's mind at least a suspicion
that Gibson had crossed on the *Welcome* and later I
was puzzled by Mr. Sheppard's concern with Gibson
as a possible passenger. Not understanding this, I
passed over him at the proper place in the alphabetical sequence and must now treat him in this adden-
dum.

Following the publication of Mr. Sheppard's article, Mr. F. J. Dallett in a series of notes on early
Pennsylvanians (TAG 41:218-220) expressed the opinion
that Gibson had not come to America. He cited Penn's
letter to Jasper Yeates dated 5 12th mo. 1682/3
[PMHB 6:471], which refers to William Gibson as if
he were in London, mentioning him between two others
who certainly were there. In the next month, on 15
March 1682/3, the Duke of York granted the East Jersey patent to 24 men of whom William Gibson of London,
haberdasher was one (1 NJA 21:56), but this does not
mean, of course, that Gibson was necessarily present
in London on the date of the patent. Such business
was doubtless the result of considerable negotiation
on the part of a few for all, and as a matter of fact
one of the twenty-four was certainly in America at
that time, namely, William Penn himself. The next
record cited by Mr. Dallett is Gibson's will which
describes him as of the Parish of St. Edmund the King
and is dated last of July [i.e. the 31st] 1683.
Seemingly, Gibson had not come to America at all.

At this point Mrs. Marion Balderston published
*James Claypoole's Letter Book London and Philadel-
phia 1681-1684* (San Marino 1967), on page 204 of
which is a letter to William Penn dated 1 2nd mo.
1683 in London and including these words: "But I
shall say the less because William Gibson goes in
this vessel (F. Richardson, master) and can give
thee a more full account." [See Mr. Sheppard's
comments on this passage in his review of the
book (PGM 25:145 f.).] Accordingly, William Gibson
was still in London on 1 April 1683, then intending
to sail on the *Endeavour*, Francis Richardson, master, which Mrs. Balderston has found in the Port
Books, loading only for New York and New Jersey.
Thus, we have evidence that Gibson left on the

Endeavour early in April 1683 and with a lucky passage could have landed Gibson somewhere in the New
York area soon enough for him to reach Philadelphia
overland by the 12th of June. Next Gibson approached
Penn in person for the city lot--the warrant does
not note the intermediacy of an attorney--and have
started back on the same or another ship which, a-
gain with a speedy passage, could have gotten him
to London by the last day in July. There was just
time enough for these two voyages and no more. If
it be suggested that the will was executed elsewhere
than in London, it should be pointed out that among
the witnesses was "Harbt Springett," a relative of
Penn's first wife Guli, and he was presumably in
London. Why anyone would make such a trip is very
puzzling. In those days ocean voyages were not undertaken for recreational purposes. Perhaps Gibson
was already ill with the disease which caused his
death the next year at the early age of fifty-five,
and have decided to return to die in the bosom of
his family.

Mrs. Balderston tries to cure the difficulty by
suggesting that the *Endeavour* man was son William
Gibson Jr., but this will not do. It is unnecessary
to rely on the assertion that Claypoole, if he meant
William Gibson Jr., would have said so, for said
William Jr. was in 1683 between fourteen and sixteen years of age, too young to entrust with any
such business.

The 500 acres were not taken out by William
Gibson but by his son William on 7 4th mo. 1701
[W&S 1:390] and returned 24 4th mo. 1701 [W&S 4:33].

After William Gibson's death a power of attorney
was issued in 1685 by John Osgood, linendraper,
Francis Camfeild, merchant, John Dew, joiner, and
John Vaughan, joiner, all of London and "owners of
the share of William Gibson, late of London, decd,
haberdasher," to Thomas Boell, late of Edmonton,
Middlesex, gardiner, "now about to sail in the ship
Francis and Dorothie, Richard Bridgeman, master,
for Pennsilvania or East New Jersey, to survey
10,000 acres of their land and act as agent. Elizabeth, widow of said William Gibson, gives her consent" [1 NJA 21:71 f.]. Elizabeth Gibson is shown
as abutter of land in Amboy, 25 June 1687 [*ibid.*
105]; as an abutter of land in the Town of Wickatunck [Monmouth Co.], 25 March 1687 [*ibid.* 112];
as Widowe Gibson, again land in Wickatunck, 1 April

1688 [*ibid.* 119]; again the same, 3 April 1696, long
after her death [*ibid.* 240] and, finally, 3 Dec. 1695
[*ibid.* 247]. On 6 April 1687 Elizabeth, widow of
William Gibsone of London, haberdasher; John Gibson
of London, haberdasher, son of said William; Jane
Barnes of London, widow, administratrix of said
William Gibson, gave a deed to Thomas Cox for 1/24
share in East Jersey [*ibid.* 120]. On 22 Jan. 1689/90
there was a confirmation to Robert West of London,
one of the proprietors, in the right of Widow Gibson,
for 1500 acres in Monmouth County [*ibid.* 171]. What
property of Gibson, Osgood, Camfeild, Dew and Vaughan
had acquired does not appear, but certainly it was
not the proprietary right of 1683.

Mr. Sheppard also informs me that he has examined
the minutes of Philadelphia Monthly Meeting to see
whether he could find mention of William Gibson's
being moved by the Spirit to preach in Philadelphia,
but found nothing. Obviously, it was a quick trip
and perhaps he was not even in Philadelphia for one
First Day Meeting!

ADDENDUM ON DAVID BREARLEY

The David Brearley (p. 56) who was kept a prisoner
for treason was the later Chief Justice of New Jersey
and not his father. On him see *Appleton's Cyclopaedia
of American Biography* 1:363, also *The Twenieth Century
Biographical Dictionary of Notable Americans* s.v. David Brearley. He was born near Trenton, 11 June 1745,
and died at Trenton, 16 Aug. 1790. In the Revolution
he was at first lieutenant colonel of the 4th Battalion of the 2nd Establishment, later in the 1st New
Jersey Regiment. He was elected Chief Justice on 10
June 1779, resigned in 1789 to become the first U. S.
District Judge from this district. He was a member of
the Constitutional Convention of 1787, signed the
Constitution itself and presided over the New Jersey
Convention which ratified it. He was a presidential
elector in 1788 and in 1785 was a compiler of the
Protestant Episcopal prayer-book. His brother Joseph
was a soldier in the Revolution, became a major in
1777, and served as aide to General George Washington.

ADDENDUM ON ANN WHITPAINE MCCARTHY

The Ann Whitpaine mentioned (p. 538) as wife of
Thomas McCarthy was doubtless wife of Thomas McCarty
of Hanover Township, Philadelphia County, yeoman,
whose will was dated 18 March 1725/6, probated 10

April 1730 (PhW E:129, #149), and mentions wife Hannah (undoubtedly the same as Ann) and daughters Mary and Hannah; friend Charles McCarty, executor, and trustees John Ball, Barnabas Roads; witnesses: Edward McVeagh, James McVeagh and John Roades. Thomas McCarty and Ann McCarty (she by mark) were among witnesses to the will of Samuel Taylor of Whitpaine Township, Philadelphia County, carpenter, dated 22 10th mo. 1708, probated 24 Aug. 1709 (PhW C:171 #134).

Her putative brother John was older than his brother Zachariah, as we learn from the recital in a much later deed (Montgomery County Deeds 43:416-419, recorded 6 Feb. 1828), which gives a history of the property from Richard Whitpaine to the grantors, Rees Thomas of Merion, gent., and Anthony Morris of the City of Philadelphia, brewer, and wife Phebe; grantee: George Kastner of Whitpaine Township. See p. 539 above.

ADDENDUM ON THOMAS WYNNE

Replace Note 1, p. 586, with the following: This man apparently is identical with the Owain ap Edwin who is discussed in DNB 14:1284. A discussion of this man will appear in an article by Dr. David H. Kelley in 1970 in TAG.

ADDENDUM ON EDWARD BEESON

The previous paragraph was already typed when there arrived a copy of *The Treesearcher*, organ of the Kansas Genealogical Society, Vol. 11, No. 1, April 1969. In this (p. 72) is a review of Steve Beason's book, *A History of the Beason-Beeson Family* (2nd ed., 1968). In this review we read:

> The immigrant ancestor of the Beeson family in America was Edward Beeson (Beason) who was born in Lancaster, England c 1660. He married Rachel Pennington and it is believed that they came with William Penn on the ship *Welcome* which landed at New Castle, Delaware in October 1682. From Irishtown in New Castle County they moved to Berkeley County, Virginia, where there was a settlement of Quakers. . . . The children of Edward and Rachel Beeson were: Edward, Richard, Ann and William. Edward married second Elizabeth -----. Their children were Elizabeth and Rachel.

No opportunity has been had to check this claim but I regard it as extremely improbable.

INDEX

Minor variants in spelling are listed under the standard spelling. More than one occurrence of the name may appear on the page listed. When a surname appears on only one page, the various individuals bearing that name are not itemized. Individuals who bear the same name are not distinguished except in the case of the William Penns. Casual references to William Penn the Founder and to the *Welcome* are ignored: only when something significant is said about these topics are they included. When both maiden name and married name of a woman are known, they are entered in both places even if only one of the names appears on the page. In a few instances anonymous allusions to a person are listed under his name.

Flora 381 Florence 386
Georgiana 386 Granville
381 Harriet 386f Hermione
395 Hilda 395 Juliana 381
Louisa 380 384 397f 400
Mary 380 384 Sophia 380
Thomas 380 386 395 Violet
386 William 381 386
KNUT/NUTT 31
KOLKANS 280
KOLLOCK Hannah 457 557 Hes-
ter 457 Jacob 457 John
457 Myra 457 Penelope 457
KROOK 408
KYRTON Elizabeth 446f
KYL 586
LABOUCHERE 388
LACEY 609
LADD 169
LAKE 449
LAKIN 259
Lamb the 7 24f 134 140 143f
146 148 150f 186 225-228
238f 489 512 514 517f 521f
547
LAMBE 159
LAMBERT Ann 89 Elizabeth 58
Mary 58 99 Thomas 58 237
LAMBWOOD 592
LANCASTER Ann 98 Edward 28
188 275f Harry F 98 Israel
96 Martha 98 Phebe 98 Sarah
98 Thomas 98
LANE Anne 45f Bernard 139
Christian 46 Edward 45f
Eleanor 45f Elin 139 Eliz-
abeth 45f James 45f Jennet
139 Mrs Julian C 264f Mary
27 108f 140 Samuel 45f
Sarah 140 William 45f
LANGFORD 567
LANGHORN George 244 Grace 57
R 341 Sarah 57 594
LANGTON 260
LANTZ 249
LARDNER Catherine 422 Elizabeth
422 Frances 369 Hannah 369
377f John 369 Lynford 369 422
Robert 369

LARFORD James 247 436f Su-
sanna 247 436f
LARGE Ebenezer 205 John 463
Sarah 205
LASSELL Thomas 37f
LAUSIN 254
LAWRENCE Catherine 422 Edward
292 Joshua 581 Mary 378 497
502 Richard 324 William
123
LAWSON-SMITH 403
LAYCOCK 297
LAYLOR 28
LEA J H 320 366 413-416 439f
452f
LEACH/LEECH Eleonor 278 Es-
there 28 35 276f Frank W
35 53 180 500 Isaac 277
Isabel 278 Jacob 277 John
277 Josiah G 35 258 276
600f May Atherton 10 460
Mary 277 Thomas 277 Tobias
28 35 276-278
LEAHY 400
LEARNED M D 280 584
LEATHERLAND 436
LEE Charles 186 Daniel 100
Hannah 151 Jane 284 Mar-
garet 99f Mary 176 430
Michael 360 Sarah 540 Wil-
liam 151
LEEDHAM/LEEDOM Benjamin 101
Hannah 101 John 90 233 Mary
233 Richard 88 Susanna 99
LEEDS Daniel 480f Philo 555
Thomas 142
LEES 295
LEGH 336
LEHNMANN Johann Georg 278
Philip Theodor 26 62 278-
280 319 332 500 Theophila
278f 500
LEISTER Thomas 280f 426 466
LEONARD Ann 85 Benjamin 478
Hannah 432 Henry 432 Jemima
479 Olive 478 William 479
LETELIER John 544 Sarah 544f
LEVERS Mary 97 Robert 422
LEVICK 568